THE REMAINS

OF

ARCHBISHOP GRINDAL.

The Parker Society.

Instituted A.D. M.DCCC.XL.

For the Publication of the Works of the Fathers and Early Writers of the Reformed English Church.

THE REMAINS

OF

EDMUND GRINDAL, D.D.

SUCCESSIVELY BISHOP OF LONDON,
AND ARCHBISHOP OF YORK AND CANTERBURY.

EDITED FOR

The Parker Society,

BY THE

REV. WILLIAM NICHOLSON, A.M.

RECTOR OF ST MAURICE WITH ST MARY KALENDAR, WINCHESTER.

WIPF & STOCK · Eugene, Oregon

Wipf and Stock Publishers
199 W 8th Ave, Suite 3
Eugene, OR 97401

The Remains of Edmund Grindal, D.D.
Successively Bishop of London, and Archbishop of York and Canterbury
By Nicholson, William
ISBN 13: 978-1-60608-061-0
Publication date 12/8/2009
Previously published by Cambridge University Press, 1843

CONTENTS.

		PAGE
I.	BIOGRAPHICAL Notice	vii
II.	Sermon at the Funeral Solemnity of the Emperor Ferdinand	1
III.	Dialogue between Custom and Verity	35
IV.	Occasional Services for the Plague	75
	1. Form of Prayer and Public Fast	84
	2. Homily concerning the Justice of God	95
	3. Thanksgiving for the Abatement of the Plague	111
	4. Thanksgiving for the Cessation of the Plague	115
V.	Injunctions and Articles of Inquiry.	
	I. For the Province of York:	
	1. Injunctions for the Clergy	122
	2. Injunctions for the Laity	132
	3. Injunctions to the Dean and Chapter of York	145
	4. Order for the removal of Rood-lofts	154
	II. For the Province of Canterbury:	
	1. General Articles of Inquiry for the Metropolitical Visitation	156
	2. Articles of Inquiry for Cathedral Churches	178
	3. Injunctions to the Dean and Chapter of Bangor	183
	4. Articles agreed upon in the Synod of 1575-6	185
	5. Mandate for the publication of the above Articles	191
VI.	Disputation at Cambridge A.D. 1549	193
VII.	Examination of certain Londoners before the Ecclesiastical Commissioners, A.D. 1567	199
VIII.	Letters of Archbishop Grindal	217

To John Foxe, 219—237.
To Bishop Ridley, 238.
To his Archdeacons, 240, 246, 415.
To the Suffragan Bishops, 241.
Miscellaneous, 242, 261, 286, 293, 362.
To Sir William Cecil (Lord Burleigh), 244, 253—261, 264—266, 267—275, 280—286, 287—290, 291—292, 295—298, 299—315, 320—326, 329—333, 342—346, 348—352, 355—361, 363, 365, 391, 397—400, 401—403.

CONTENTS.

PAGE

To the Magistrates of Frankfort, 247.
To Archbishop Parker, 252, 267, 290, 294, 299, 326, 347, 353.
To the Lord Robert Dudley, (Earl of Leicester) 261.
To Hierome Zanchius, 276—280, 333—342.
To the Privy Council, 316—320, 392, 396.
To his Officers, 361, 408—414, 417—420, 423—429.
To Queen Elizabeth, 364, 376.
Letters and Documents relating to the Archbishop's Sequestration, 372—403.
To Bishop Whitgift, 370.
To Dr Matthew Hutton, Dean of York, 394—396.
To the Bishop of London, 404—408, 421.
To the Bishops, 429.

IX. Miscellaneous Pieces:
  1. Animadversions on Justus Velsius' Norma, Latin and English 436
  2. Form of Revocation offered to Hadrian Hamsted, Latin and English 441
  3. Account of the Archbishop's Court of Faculties 446
  4. Opinions and Directions concerning Ecclesiastical Discipline 451

X. The Archbishop's Last Will and Testament 458

XI. Appendix 465
  1. The Queen's Letter to the Bishops 467
  2. Lord Burleigh's Message to the Archbishop 469
  3. Speech to the Archbishop in Council 471
  4. Christiani Hominis Norma, auctore Justo Velsio 474
  5. A Form of Meditation 477

XII. Index 485

BIOGRAPHICAL NOTICE

OF

ARCHBISHOP GRINDAL.

EDMUND GRINDAL was born in the year 1519, in the parish of St Bees in Cumberland. Of his family and early history little is known. One remarkable incident, however, is on record connected with his boyhood, which shews his diligence in learning. His book was the companion of his walks, and thereby on one occasion became the preserver of his life. While he was walking in the fields, an arrow lighted upon his breast, and, had not the book intercepted it, would probably have been fatal[1].

He was the intimate friend and companion of Edwin Sandys, who was a native of the same place, and who afterwards succeeded him in the sees of London and York. At the usual age he was sent to Magdalen College, Cambridge, whence he afterwards removed successively to Christ's College and Pembroke Hall. Of this last-named society he became fellow, president, and master. He seems to have taken the degree of B.A. about A.D. 1538, in which year he was admitted to a fellowship; upon which, as a title, he was ordained, July 4, 1544, by John Bird, bishop of Winchester. In 1541 he proceeded to M.A., and in the year 1548, served the office of senior proctor.

His academical career gave promise of future eminence. "Before he came to be taken notice of in the church (ob-

---

[1] Sæpenumero mihi in mentem venit, honoratissime Antistes, illius sagittæ, quæ de cœlo delapsa, ruri cum puer ambulares, pectus tuum ita feriit, ut nisi liber, quem pro præcordiis tum forte gerebas, vim teli intercepisset, actum fuisset de vita tua. Conrad. Hubert. Epist. dedicatoria in Buceri Scripta Anglicana.

serves Strype), he made a figure in the university, as one of the ripest wits and learnedest men in Cambridge[1]." In proof of which we find him, in June, A.D. 1549, selected out of the whole university, as one of the four disputants against the doctrine of transubstantiation, at a public disputation held before king Edward's visitors[2]. In the same year he was appointed Lady Margaret's preacher, and also president, or vice-master, of his college. In the following year, 1550, bishop Ridley appointed him one of his chaplains, together with Bradford and Rogers, both afterwards martyrs in queen Mary's reign. It is not improbable that Ridley, besides knowing Grindal as a member of his college, had also been impressed with a favourable opinion of his learning and abilities during the recent disputation at which he had presided. The high estimation in which the bishop held him is apparent in the following extract from a letter which he wrote to Sir John Cheke[3]: "Now the man master Grindal, unto whom I would give this prebend [that of Cantrells or Kentish Town], doth move me much; for he is a man known to be both of virtue, honesty, discretion, wisdom, and learning." Shortly after this, August 24, 1551, he was preferred to the office of precentor of St Paul's. While thus connected with bishop Ridley, he was constantly employed in preaching throughout the diocese; a satisfactory evidence of the reputation in which he was held, when the choicest men were selected for the pulpits, in order to impress the popular mind in favour of the reformed religion.

In the same year we find him engaged in two private conferences on the eucharistic controversy; the question being the true meaning of the words, "This is my body," whether to be understood figuratively or literally. The disputants were, on the protestant side, Grindal, Horn, Cheke, and Whitehead; and on the other, Fecknam, Young, and Watson. In December of this same year he was appointed chaplain to king

---

[1] Grind. p. 6.   [2] See p. 194.
[3] See bishop Ridley's Works, Parker Soc. p. 331.

Edward, with a salary of £40.; and in July 1552, he obtained a prebend in Westminster.

In the month of November a project was under consideration for dividing the diocese of Durham, then vacant by the deprivation of bishop Tonstall[4]; and it seems that Grindal was nominated for one of these bishoprics. Newcastle-upon-Tyne was to have been the newly-erected see; but the design was frustrated through some influence at court.

On July 6, 1553, king Edward died, and with him the hopes of those who looked favourably upon the advancing work of the Reformation. Foreseeing the storm which was gathering over the church, Grindal, in company with many others of great piety and learning, of whom several afterwards attained to places of eminence under queen Elizabeth, took refuge on the continent. His first place of exile was Strasburgh; and so little hope did he entertain of a change in the aspect of ecclesiastical affairs in England, that he applied himself diligently to learn the German language, that he might be able to exercise his ministry in those parts[5]. From Strasburgh he occasionally visited other places, and spent some time at Wasselheim, Spires, and Frankfort.

One of Grindal's chief employments during his exile was to collect "the writings and stories of the learned and pious sufferers in England, and to publish them; for which purpose he had a great correspondence here." The results of his inquiries he communicated to John Foxe, who incorporated them into his laborious work, the "Acts and Monuments." How much Foxe was indebted to Grindal, will appear from the correspondence given in this volume, to which the reader is referred. (pp. 219—238.)

The unhappy dissensions amongst the English exiles at Frankfort, in 1554, are too well known to require explanation

[4] See bishop Burnet's account of this matter, ii. 442, Oxford, 1829.

[5] Desperans de patriæ salute, Wasselheimii linguæ Germanicæ operam dederis, quod eam ita adeptus sis, ut vox tua etiam in Germanicis ecclesiis audiri potuisset. Conrad. Hubert. Epist. Dedic. in Buceri Script. Anglic.

here. It is sufficient to observe that there were two parties, one desirous of maintaining the exclusive use, in public worship, of king Edward's second book; the other, headed by Knox and Whittingham, endeavouring to approximate the services to those then in use at Geneva. These dissensions and heart-burnings were matters of deep concern to the brethren at Strasburgh and elsewhere, who saw in them, not only a scandal to the reformed English church, but the elements of danger to the cause of the Reformation in general. With the hope of allaying them, Grindal and Chambers were deputed to visit Frankfort, carrying a letter signed by themselves and others, in which they pressed with much earnestness the dangers of the present controversy. This mediation does not seem to have been successful; but in the following year another deputation, consisting of Grindal, Cox, Chambers, and some others, met with better success: and at length, after much controversy, the differences were quieted[1].

Upon the death of queen Mary, Nov. 17, 1558, those who had fled at the commencement of her reign, for the most part returned. Amongst the earliest of these was Grindal, who in the end of December was on his way to England.

All the piety and wisdom of the returning exiles were now called into requisition for the restitution and settlement of the church. The work of reformation, which had advanced under king Edward, had been entirely defaced and obliterated by his successor. Grindal was a man of too much reputation to be left without employment in this important crisis. He was therefore soon called upon to take a share in settling several weighty ecclesiastical matters, which were immediately brought under consideration. The first thing to which the attention of the authorities was directed

---

[1] For an account of this painful controversy see Collier's Eccl. Hist. VI. 144—152. See also "A brief Discourse of the Troubles at Frankfort, &c." first printed about A.D. 1575.

was the revision of the Book of Common Prayer, in order to its being submitted to queen Elizabeth's first parliament. For this purpose a committee of divines met at the house of Sir Thomas Smith, in Canon Row, Westminster, consisting of Cox, Sandys, Whitehead, Grindal, and Pilkington, who had all been exiles, with Parker, May, Bell, and Sir T. Smith. Grindal was probably selected for this important work, not only on account of his reputation for learning and piety, but also from the circumstance that he had been the chaplain and intimate friend of bishop Ridley, and therefore "well acquainted with the reasons and methods used under king Edward in the composing the Common Prayers, wherein that bishop, with archbishop Cranmer, had the chief hand[2]." Various questions of discipline and ritual came under his judgment in this assembly. The original papers laid before the divines are extant among the Petyt MSS. in the Inner Temple Library, in which are several comments and suggestions in Grindal's own hand-writing.

In the following March a solemn conference was held at Westminster, before the Lord Keeper Sir Nicholas Bacon, and many of the nobility and gentry, between eight divines on the Romish side, and eight on the protestant, of which latter Grindal was one[3].

On Sunday, May 12, 1559, the new Book of Common Prayer was used for the first time in the Queen's chapel, and on the Wednesday following at St Paul's, on which occasion Grindal preached before an august assembly of the court, the privy council, the lord mayor, and the aldermen of the city. He was also employed in the summer as one of the commissioners for the royal visitation in the north of England, "to require the oath of supremacy, to inspect cathedrals, and the manners of the clergy, and the like."

[2] Strype, Grind. p. 33.

[3] For an account of this conference see Strype, Annals, I. i. 128, 137. Burnet, Reform. II. 776, et seq. and Cardwell's History of Conferences, &c. 56—92.

About this time also, Dr John Young being removed by the royal visitors from the mastership of Pembroke College, Cambridge, for refusing the oath of supremacy, Grindal was appointed to succeed him. This honourable post he resigned in May 1562. In July of the same year, 1559, the deposition of Bonner from the see of London, made under Edward VI., but which had been set aside during queen Mary's reign, was confirmed; and Grindal, who had been well known in the diocese as chaplain to bishop Ridley, was nominated to succeed to the vacancy. He was consecrated in the chapel of Lambeth palace, 21 December, 1559, by archbishop Parker[1], assisted by bishops Barlow, Scory, and Hodgson[2]; on which occasion a sermon was preached by Alexander Nowel, afterwards dean of St Paul's, from Acts xx. 28.

Shortly after his elevation we find him preaching at various times before the Queen, and at St Paul's cross. On one of these occasions, March 3rd, 1560, "there was a mighty audience; for the people were greedy to hear the gospel." He was also appointed, by the Queen's special letters, one of the commissioners for revising the Calendar, and altering certain of the lessons[3], as well as for reforma-

---

[1] Grindal was present at archbishop Parker's consecration. See extract from Regist. Parker, Wilkin's Concil. iv. 199, and Cardwell, Doc. Ann. i.

[2] It may be well in reference to this subject to correct, at the desire of the editor of the Zurich Letters, a verbal inaccuracy in p. 63, notes 1 and 2, of that volume, where Scory, bishop of Hereford, and Barlow, bishop of Chichester, are said to have been *consecrated* to their respective sees, whereas they were only *confirmed* to them, on Dec. 20, 1559, at Bow Church, in the presence of archbishop Parker, at whose consecration they had assisted three days before; having themselves received episcopal consecration, bishop Barlow in 1536, and Scory in 1551, as it had been stated with respect to the latter in an earlier note. In some cases indeed *confirmation* and *consecration* are confounded together. The register of the services at Bow Church at what is familiarly spoken of as the *consecration* of bishops, more correctly designates it as *confirmation*. "1779, May 29. Early Prayers, Service of the day. No Sermon. Bishop of Lincoln confirmed at xi. o'cl. The Litany." "1813, Oct. 1. Confirmation of Dr Howley, bishop of London."

[3] Wilkins, Concil. iv. p. 223.

tion in other ecclesisatical matters. The other commissioners were archbishop Parker, Dr Bill, and Dr Haddon.

In this year the bishop held his primary visitation of his diocese and cathedral. In the following year, 1562, he was engaged in that "famous synod, wherein divers weighty matters of religion were to be discussed, and the orders and usages of the church corrected and purged, and a worship settled according to the prescript of the gospel, and an uniformity in all prescribed. In this our bishop was much employed, for the giving notice thereof to all the bishops of the province, and for the summoning of all that had a right to sit there, to meet at St Paul's for that purpose on the 12th day of January. But this was the least matter he had to do in relation to this synod; for he was one of those select learned men, appointed to prepare and adjust matters for to lay before the synod, against the time they should sit. I have seen his hand in many of the papers drawn up to be debated in that notable convocation; he being, together with archbishop Parker, bishop Sandys, bishop Cox, and some few more, all along from the Queen's first access to the crown hitherto, employed in consultation for the reformation of religion[4]."

About the middle of the following year, 1563, the plague broke out with great violence in Kent, and soon extended to London, and other places of the realm. This severe visitation originated with the army, just returned from New-haven, or Havre-de-grace, which, after an unsuccessful defence, had been surrendered to the French. The bishop drew up and put forth a Form of Prayer and Fasting[5], meet for this time; and afterwards, upon the abatement and ultimate removal of the plague, he prepared suitable forms of Thanksgiving. These forms will be found in this volume; and the circumstances attending their preparation will be best learned from the

---

[4] Strype, Grindal, p. 99.

[5] This form was the basis upon which other forms of prayer, in times of public danger, were afterwards drawn up during the Queen's reign.

bishop's letters to Sir W. Cecil, to which the reader is referred[1].

In April 10, 1564, he proceeded to the degree of doctor in divinity. On the 3rd of October following he preached a sermon at St Paul's, at the funeral solemnity of the emperor Ferdinand II. This is the only sermon of his which is now extant; and as he was reputed a preacher of some eminence, it is therefore interesting as a specimen of his style.

It does not seem necessary to notice in this brief memoir various matters, of more or less importance, which were transacted by bishop Grindal during the remainder of his continuance in the see of London. Most of these matters will be found either detailed at length, or cursorily alluded to, in the collection of letters contained in this volume. Those letters indeed are, for the most part, the only source from which the details of his life have been collected by his biographer Strype. One circumstance, however, is of too great importance to be passed over without special notice. In the year 1568, the first edition of the great Bible, commonly called the Bishops' Bible, was published. Archbishop Parker was the chief promoter of this undertaking, in the execution of which he secured the assistance of the best qualified men, both for learning and character. Amongst these were several bishops, from which circumstance this edition derived its name. Bishop Grindal appears to have executed the minor prophets, that portion of the work bearing his initials E. L[2].

In April, 1570, Grindal was nominated to the archbishopric of York, which had been vacant, by the death of archbishop Young, since June, 1568. His register dates

---

[1] Pp. 258, et seq.

[2] "The tenth allotment contained Hosea, Joel, Amos, to Malachi inclusive; and had the letters E. L. for Edmundus London." Strype, Parker. II. 222; where see an account of this edition of the holy scriptures. See also Collier's Eccl. Hist. vi. 530.

his translation from London on May the 1st, and his instalment by proxy on June the 9th. He was confirmed at Canterbury, on the Monday after Trinity Sunday, by archbishop Parker, and was succeeded in the diocese of London by Edwin Sandys, his early friend and companion. The state of his new diocese and province, upon his arrival, was far from encouraging. He found the greater part of the gentry in the north opposed to the reformation, and the common people sunk in ignorance and superstition[3]. So great indeed was the contrast between this part of the country and the southern parts, that the archbishop observed to Sir W. Cecil, "This seems to be, as it were, another church, rather than a member of the rest[4]." To remedy these evils the archbishop, with as little delay as possible, instituted a metropolitical visitation, beginning on the 15th of May, 1571, prorogued from time to time, until October 10, 1572. The Articles of Inquiry and the Injunctions, given forth for this visitation, are contained in this volume, and will sufficiently explain the most obvious evils to which the archbishop found it necessary to apply remedies. It was not so much against the efforts of innovators in discipline that he had now to contend, as against the popular superstitions, and popish practices, which still had a powerful hold upon the vulgar mind. By the prudent management of the archbishop, and especially by his diligence in providing men of piety and learning for the ministry, he succeeded in greatly improving the condition of this province. "By the care and diligence of the archbishop (observes Strype[5]) the number of papists daily diminished, especially in his diocese, who were a few years ago so many and prevalent in the north parts. He shewed his faithfulness in his inspection over his church, by taking what care he could that none but men of some ability and learning might be admitted to the cure of souls. And for this purpose he provided that such as came for

[3] See Letters, p. 325. [4] P. 326. [5] Grindal, p. 273.

institution to any living should be first well examined; and such as he found unlearned he rejected, notwithstanding their presentation." An instance of such rejection is related by Strype[1], which sufficiently indicates the necessity that existed for such vigilance. On more than one occasion, indeed, we find the archbishop interposing his authority, for the protection of parishes from unlearned and unfit ministers, presented by corrupt or careless patrons[2]. His care also for the due administration of religious and charitable foundations was manifested by visitation, and reformation of the abuses which he found in them. While in the see of London, he had been the means of reforming, and indeed of saving from absolute ruin, the Savoy Hospital, in the Strand[3], a charitable foundation for the entertainment and relief of poor travellers, which, by the gross injustice and fraudulent management of the master, one Thurland, had been brought almost to destruction. He rendered a similar service, in the year 1574, to Sherburn Hospital, near Durham, by procuring certain unreasonable and injurious leases, granted by the late master, to be annulled.

Upon the death of archbishop Parker, in May, 1575, the see of Canterbury remained vacant for nearly six months. In November Grindal was nominated as his successor. On the 10th of January following his election took place in the Chapter House, at Canterbury; and on the 15th of February he was confirmed by bishops Sandys of London, Horn of Winchester, Cox of Ely, Davies of St David's, and Gest of Sarum. In the year 1576, he instituted a metropolitical visitation, which was continued from time to time, for several successive years, interrupted probably by the troubles into which the archbishop shortly after fell. The general Articles of Inquiry for this Visitation are contained in this

[1] Ibid. pp. 273, 274.   [2] See Letters, pp. 330, 346.
[3] See Strype, Grind. pp. 234—239, and Letters in this Vol. p. 302, and 349.
[4] See Strype, Grind. p. 274, and Letter, dated Feb. 3, 1574, p. 352.

volume; and as they seem to have escaped the notice of the collectors of such documents, they will be read with additional interest.

We now arrive at a period in the archbishop's life, from which, to its close, his course was one of sorrow and humiliation. He had risen successively to the places of highest eminence in the church; but this his last and highest advancement was the commencement of his troubles. He had scarcely completed a year from the time of his nomination to the primacy, when he had the misfortune to fall under the Queen's displeasure, from which, although he occasionally afterwards received some tokens of her friendly regard, he never entirely emerged.

The causes of this displeasure can be but briefly stated in this memoir. They will appear with more distinctness and force from the documents themselves, contained in this volume[5]. It may suffice in this place to observe, that the archbishop looked with a favourable eye upon the exercises, called *prophesyings*[6], considering that they might, notwithstanding certain incidental inconveniences, be made, in the main, subservient to the cause of true religion. "The archbishop (says Collier) believed this mismanagement accidental to the meetings: he thought the design was serviceable for the improvement of the people and clergy; and therefore endeavoured to make it answer upon experiment, and bring the practice up to the plan[7]…. Thus the archbishop endeavoured to guard against the abuse, and continue the exercise[8]. But the Queen was of a different sentiment. She thought these meetings gave encouragement to novelty, made people

---

[5] See pp. 376—403, and Appendix I—III.

[6] For an account of these prophesyings, see p. 372.

[7] See the "Orders for reformation," &c., pp. 373, 374 of this volume.

[8] Fuller observes, that Sir Francis Bacon, "in his *Worthy Considerations about Church Government* (tendered to King James), conceiveth, that such prophesying, which Grindal did favour, might be so discreetly cautioned and moderated, as to make them, without fear of faction, profitable for advancing of learning and religion." Fuller, Church Hist. Book IX. sect. iv. c. 4.

ramble in their fancy, and neglect their affairs; that their curiosity was too much indulged, and their heads overcharged with notions by these discourses; and that, by raising disputes and forming parties, things might possibly grow up to a public disturbance. She told the archbishop, the kingdom was overfurnished with instructions of this nature; that she would have the exercise of prophesying suppressed, the preachers reduced to a smaller number, and homilies read instead of sermons. She conceived three or four preachers in a county might be sufficient, and that therefore licenses for the pulpit should be granted with more reserve. The Queen delivered herself upon this subject with something of vehemence and disgust; and gave her pleasure in charge to the archbishop. Grindal, to give him his due, was a prelate of more conscience and courage, than to be dazzled with the lustre of a court, to resign against his judgment, and be overruled into insignificancy. He wrote a long letter to the Queen, to excuse his incompliance. It is penned with a mixture of freedom and regard. He writes like a subject in the state, and a governor in the church; and takes care neither to forget her Majesty nor himself[1]."

"Whether Grindal was right or not, in pleading for the prophesying meetings, I shall not pretend to determine; though it must be said, he has offered a great deal in defence of these exercises. And it is most likely, could they have been kept within the compass of his regulations, they would have proved serviceable to the church. But this consideration apart, it is certain he writes with the spirit of a primitive bishop: his application is religiously brave, and has not the least appearance of interest or fear. And besides the piety of the address, it is managed with great force and advantage. To which we may add, the advice is admirable and well directed. Nothing could be more serviceable than to disengage the Queen from the flattery of her court, and bring

---

[1] Collier's Eccles. Hist. vi. p. 565—567.

her off from some lofty mistakes her favourites seem to have led her into[2]."

Upon the merits of this letter of Grindal's Fuller observes, " What could be written with more spirit or less animosity? more humility and less dejection? I see a lamb in his own can be a lion in God and his church's cause[3]."

The issue of this painful matter (says Strype[4]) was, "that all the archbishop could say or write moved not the Queen from her resolution, but she seemed much offended with him, and resolved to have him suspended and sequestered; and seeing he would not be instrumental in it, sent her own commandment, by her letters, to the rest of the bishops, wholly to put down the exercises[5]." In June 1577, the archbishop was, by order of the privy council, confined to his house, and sequestered for six months. In the latter end of November, the Lord Treasurer Burleigh sent a kind message to the archbishop, directing him how to proceed in making a formal submission to the Queen; but he " thought not fit to comply so far as was advised; but still esteeming himself not to have done amiss, he would not ask pardon which supposed a fault[6]." In January following there was some talk of depriving him, but the proposal was so ill received, that it was immediately dropped. Still however he continued under sequestration; nor does it appear certain, that he was ever after fully reconciled to the Queen[7].

In the year 1580 a convocation was held, at which, the

---

[2] Ibid. p. 575.   [3] Ch. Hist. Book ix. sect. iv. c. 5.
[4] Grindal, p. 336.   [5] See Append. i.   [6] Grindal, pp. 348—350.
[7] The poet Spenser frequently quotes Grindal's sayings, as though current at the time, and alludes to his troubles. The name Algrind is merely a transposition of the syllables of his name. Thus in the Shepherd's Calendar for May, speaking of pastors:

"But shepheards (as Algrind used to say)
"Mought not live ylike men of the laye."

Again, in the Shepherd's Calendar for July:

"Such one he was (as I have heard
"Old Algrind often sayne)
"That whilome was the first shepheard,
"And lived with little gayne."

And

archbishop still continuing under sequestration, Aylmer, bishop of London, presided. Some of the clergy at first were for refusing to proceed to business without their primate; but it was at last agreed that Dr Toby Matthew, dean of Christchurch, should draw up in Latin a petition to the Queen for the restitution of the archbishop[1]. A letter was also written to the Queen, and signed by twelve bishops, to the same effect[2]. But neither of these addresses, though written with much earnestness and respect, had any success.

There was one matter of great importance, which our archbishop earnestly recommended to the consideration of this convocation, viz. the reformation of church discipline; and he drew up a form of public penance, intended to be used at the restoration of penitents, who had been excommunicated for scandalous offences, to the communion of the church[3]. It does not however appear that any thing was definitely arranged.

And shortly after:

"Sike one (sayd Algrind) Moses was,
"That saw his Maker's face."

In this latter eclogue, which is a pastoral dialogue, allegorically commending meek and lowly pastors, Grindal's elevation and misfortunes are described. One of the shepherds makes the inquiry, the other replies:

"But say mee, what is Algrind, hee
"That is so oft benempt?"
"Hee is a shepheard great in 'gree,
"But hath been long ypent.
"One day hee sat upon a hill,
"As now thou wouldest mee:
"But I am taught by Algrind's ill
"To love the lowe degree.
"For sitting so with bared scalp,
"An eagle sored hye,
"That, weening his white head was chalke,
"A shell-fish down let flye:
"She ween'd the shell-fish to have broke,
"But therewith bruz'd his brayne:
"So now astonied with the stroke,
"Hee lyes in ling'ring payne."
"Ah! good Algrind!" &c. &c.

The eagle is probably queen Elizabeth. These passages shew the high estimation in which Grindal was held by his contemporaries.

[1] See the petition in Fuller's Church Hist. Book ix. sect. iv. c. i. p. 120.
[2] See Cardwell, Doc. Ann. ii. p. 386.
[3] See pp. 455—457 of this volume. In connexion with this paper is inserted also the Argument on the use of Excommunication, though it is

In the year 1582 it would appear that the archbishop was, to a certain extent at least, restored to the exercise of his ecclesiastical jurisdiction. This may be inferred from the circumstance, that the customary writs and instruments from this date run in the archbishop's own name, without the names of his officials. The archbishop had been now for some time afflicted with blindness; and in the latter part of this year, all hope of recovery seeming to have vanished, he tendered to the Queen his resignation, which she now seemed disposed to accept, assigning to him an honourable pension during the remainder of his life. This matter remained in hand for some months; for we find that in April 1583 it was still unsettled[4].

Whitgift was nominated as his successor; but he, it seems, declined to enter upon the see as long as Grindal was alive[5]. Fuller quaintly remarks: " Being really blind, more with grief than age, he was willing to put off his clothes before he went to bed, and in his life-time to resign his place to Dr Whitgift; who refused such acceptance thereof. And the Queen, commiserating his condition, was graciously pleased to say, that as she had made him, so he should die an archbishop; as he did, July 6th, 1583. Worldly wealth he cared not for, desiring only to make both ends meet; and as for that little that lapped over, he gave it to pious uses in both universities, and the founding of a fair free-school at St Bees, the place of his nativity[6]." The same author, in his Church History, observes: " Whoso beholds the large revenues conferred on Grindal, the long time he enjoyed them, the little charge encumbering him, dying a single man, will admire at the mean estate he left behind him[7]."

" He was buried, according to his desire, in the chancel of

by no means certain that Grindal was the author of it. See p. 451, and the note from Strype.

[4] See pp. 402, 403.
[5] See Fuller's Church Hist. Book. ix. sect. v. c. 10.
[6] Fuller's Worthies, p. 219.   [7] Book ix. sect. v. c. 11.

Croydon church. And on the south side of the communion table against the wall is his effigies in stone, lying at length, raised a pretty height from the ground; his hands in the posture of praying: his eyes have a kind of white in the pupil to denote his blindness; a comely face; a long black beard somewhat forked, and somewhat curling; vested in his doctor's robes[1]."

The following are the inscriptions upon his tomb.

Edmundus Grindallus

Cumbriensis, Theologiæ Doctor, eruditione, prudentia, et gravitate clarus, constantia, justitia, et pietate insignis, civibus et peregrinis charus: ab exilio (quod Evangelii causa subiit) reversus ad summum dignitatis fastigium (quasi decursu honorum) sub R. Elizabetha evectus, ecclesiam Londinen. primum, deinde Eborac. demum Cantuarien. rexit. Et cum hic nihil restaret, quo altius ascenderet, e corporis vinculis liber ac beatus ad cœlum evolavit 6°. Julii, anno Dom. 1583 ætat. suæ 63. Hic, præter multa pietatis officia, quæ vivus præstitit, moribundus maximam bonorum suorum partem piis usibus consecravit. In parœcia divæ Beghæ (ubi natus est) scholam grammaticam splendide extrui, et opimo censu ditari curavit. Magdalenensi cœtui Cantabr. (in quo puer primum academiæ ubera suxit) discipulum adjecit. Collegio Christi, (ubi adultus literis incubuit) gratum $M\nu\eta\mu\acute{o}\sigma\nu\nu o\nu$ reliquit. Aulæ Pembrochianæ (cujus olim Socius, postea Præfectus extitit) ærarium et bibliothecam auxit, Græcoque prælectori, uni Socio, ac duobus Discipulis, ampla stipendia assignavit. Collegium Reginæ Oxon. (in quod Cumbrienses potissimum cooptantur) nummis, libris, et magnis proventibus locupletavit. Civitati Cantuar. (cui moriens præfuit) centum libras, in hoc, ut pauperes honestis artificiis exercerentur, perpetuo servandas atque impendendas, dedit. Residuum bonorum pietatis operibus dicavit. Sic vivens moriensque, ecclesiæ, patriæ, et bonis literis profuit.

[1] Strype, Grind. 430.

GRINDALLUS doctus, prudens, gravitate verendus,
  Justus, munificus, sub cruce fortis erat.
Post crucis ærumnas Christi gregis Anglia fecit
  Signiferum, Christus cœlica regna dedit.

Præsulis eximii ter postquam est auctus honore,
  Pervigilique greges rexit moderamine sacros;
Confectum senio durisque laboribus, ecce,
  Transtulit in placidam mors exoptata quietem.

Mortua marmoreo conduntur membra sepulchro;
  Sed mens sancta viget, fama perennis erit.
Nam studia et musæ, quas magnis censibus auxit,
  GRINDALLI nomen tempus in omne ferent.

The necessary brevity of this memoir, as well as other considerations[2], preclude any general remarks upon the character and public conduct of this eminent prelate. He lived in arduous and trying times; and we, perhaps, are scarcely in a capacity for forming a very accurate judgment upon many points then in controversy, the importance of which may to us seem exaggerated or the reverse. We should endeavour as much as possible to throw ourselves into the position of those distinguished men, to whom we stand so deeply indebted, and view their dangers and their labours with the eye and the feelings of a contemporary.

It does not appear that archbishop Grindal left much behind him in print. The following is the list of his remains, given by Bishop Tanner[3] in his *Bibliotheca:*

[2] The design of the Parker Society being simply the publication of the works of the eminent writers of our church in the 16th century, *without further comment* than may be necessary for illustration, it is deemed essential to the carrying out of this design, to abstain from observations, which under ordinary circumstances a biographer might be expected to introduce.

[3] The following is Tanner's account of Archbishop Grindal:

Grindall [Edmundus] filius Gulielmi, patria Cumbrius, in oppido cœnobio S. Beghs (Beccæ) virginis claro natus, A. D. MDXIX. Primo in collegio Magdalenensi, dein in collegio Christi, tandem in aula Pembrochiana Cantabrigiæ literis academicis institutus, ubi A. MDXXXVIII. socius,

Scripsit Anglice, I. *Concionem habitam apud crucem Paulinam ad exequias Ferdinandi imperatoris Octob.* 3. MDLXIV. in Matth. xxiv. 44. Pr. "Emonge many evyll and naught." Lond. MDLXIV. 4to.

II. *A dialogue between Custom and Truth.* Extat in secunda et seqq. edit. Foxii. Strype in *Vita Grindal.* 313.

III. *Disputationem Cantabr.* 24 Junii. MDXLIX. *cum doctore Glynn.* Fox, p. 1383.

IV. *Epistolam apologeticam ad Reginam, in defensione prophetiæ et jurisdictionis eccles.* Pr. "With most humble remembrance." Extat apud Th. Fuller, Hist. Eccl. ix. p. 123.

V. *Epistolam I. M. Parkero* 9 Dec. MDLXXIII. Strype in *Vita Parker*, 455.

VI. *Epistolas IV. M. Parkero*, MS. Coll. Corp. Chr. Cantab. Miscell. i. 431.

VII. *Epistolas XXX.* plus minus, in Strype in *Vita Grindal.* l. c.

VIII. *Articles agreed upon in Convocation*, A. MDLXXV. in vol. 4 Concil. M. Brit. et Hib. p. 284. seq.

IX. *Mandatum Archiepiscopi Cantuar. ad publicandum articulos in convocatione* A. MDLXXV. *stabilitos.* Ibid. p. 285.

et A. MDXLVIII. academiæ procurator, postea collegii Pembroch. præses electus, et Ridleio episcopo Londinensi a sacris domesticis, et præbenda S. Pauli donatus fuit. Regnum ineunte Maria, solum vertit, et primo Argentorati, dein Francofurti sedem fixit: illa vero extincta in patriam rediit. A. MDXLIX. fuit concionator dominæ Margaretæ apud Cantabrigienses. A. MDLI. 12 Martii pensio annua XL. librarum Edmundo Grindal, S. T. baccalaureo, capellano regio data est, durante beneplacito. MS. Cotton Julius, B. 9. A. MDLI. 24 Augusti E. G. sacr. th. baccalaureus collatus est ad præcent. S. Pauli. Reg. Rydley. vac. per ejus resignationem MDLIV, April 24. Bonner. A. MDLII. mense Julii præbendarius Westmonasteriensis factus. A. MDLIX. unus disputantium ex partibus protestantium fuit. Et eodem anno ab Elizabetha regina ad episcopatum Londinensem, A. MDLXX. ad archiepiscopatum Eboracensem, et A. MDLXXV. ad Cantuariensem evectus est........ Vitam ejus descripsit Johannes Strype, M.A. London MDCCX. fol. Anglice. Eodem anno prodierunt in 8vo. *Memorials concerning his suspension and disgrace, with his letter to Q. Elizabeth in vindication of prophesying.* Obiit apud Croidon 6 Julii, MDLXXXIII. ætatis LXIV. Epitaphium ejus describitur ex Godwin inter MSS. Ant. Wood c. ii.

X. *Articles to be inquired of in his Metropolitical Visitation.* p. 286.

XI. *Orders for reformation of abuses about the learned exercises and conferences among the ministers of the church.* p. 287.

XII. *Episcoporum epistola ad Reginam Elizabetham pro restauratione Archiep. Cantuar. Edmundi Grindal.* p. 293.

XIII. *Synodi libellus supplex Reginæ porrectus, de eadem materia.* p. 295.

XIV. *A Form of Penance laid before the synod by the Archbishop of Canterbury, with his directions for it.* p. 298.

XV. Sub finem Malachiæ prophetæ in Bibliis episcopalibus (the Bishops' Bible) dantur literæ E. L. forsan legendæ Edmundus Londinensis, qui translator *Minorum prophetarum* fuit.

Of the above writings the following are contained in this volume: I. II. III. IV. V. VI. VII. VIII. IX. X. XI. XIV.

Strype has incorporated the substance of many of the archbishop's epistolary remains into his account of his life. Most of the letters contained in this volume have never before been printed entire. They have been collected by the editor from the various MSS. in the British Museum, the Library at Lambeth Palace, the State Paper Office, the Inner Temple Library, and the Library of Corpus Christi College, Cambridge. It is right also to state, that in all cases where it has been in his power, the editor has carefully collated the documents given by Strype with the originals. The Articles and Injunctions for the province of York, fragments of which only are given in Strype's Life, have been extracted entire from the Register at York.

The editor thankfully acknowledges his obligations to the officers in charge of the several libraries and MSS., from which he derived many of the articles contained in this volume, for the facilities which they kindly afforded him. His thanks are especially due to the lord bishop of London, to the Cathedral authorities at York, and to the Rev. S. R. Maitland, librarian to his grace the archbishop of Canterbury, for the privilege of examining archbishop Grindal's registers. His thanks are also due to the very reverend the Master of Corpus Christi College, Cambridge, the Rev. the Master of Pembroke College, the Rev. Samuel Carr, of Colchester, as well as to other friends, who have kindly favoured him with communications. He is also bound to acknowledge the liberality of Mr Stewart, bookseller, London, in allowing him a copy of the document on p. 313, from a very rare tract in his possession.

CORRIGENDA.

In p. 169, note 2, *instead* of the sentence beginning in the fifth line of that note, *read* John Marshall was the author of a book called "A Treatise of the Cross."

p. 243. The translation of one clause in the Latin was inadvertently omitted. Supply, in line 5 of the translation, the words: "I have not yet replied, for I know not to whom to direct my reply."

p. 395, note 2, *for* Appendix III. p. 408, *read* p. 471.

A SERMON

PREACHED IN THE

CATHEDRAL CHURCH OF ST PAUL

AT THE

FUNERAL SOLEMNITY

OF

THE EMPEROR FERDINAND,

OCTOBER 3, 1564.

[GRINDAL.]

A Sermon, at the
Funeral solemnitie of the most high
and mighty Prince Ferdinandus, the late Emperour of most famous memorye, holden in the Cathedrall Churche of saint Paule in London, the third of October, 1564. Made by the reuerend father in God, Edmund Grindall, bishop of London.

℃ Imprinted at London by John Day, dwelling ouer Aldersgate, beneath saint Martins.

Cum gratia & priuilegio Regiæ
Maiestatis.

℃ These bookes are to be sold at hys shop under the Gate.

A SERMON

AT THE FUNERAL SOLEMNITY[1] OF THE MOST HIGH AND MIGHTY PRINCE FERDINANDUS[2], THE LATE EMPEROR OF MOST FAMOUS MEMORY, HOLDEN IN THE CATHEDRAL CHURCH OF ST PAUL IN LONDON, THE THIRD OF OCTOBER, 1564. MADE BY THE REVEREND FATHER IN GOD EDMUND GRINDAL, BISHOP OF LONDON.

The Prayer for the universal Church, the Church of England and Ireland, the Queen's Majesty, the States of the realm, &c., as is ordinarily accustomed, were first made.

MATTH. XXIV.

Ideo et vos estote parati, quia qua hora non putatis, ea filius hominis venturus est.

Therefore be ye also ready, for the Lord will come at the hour which ye think not on.

AMONG many evil and naughty affections, which follow the nature of man corrupted by sin, right honourable and beloved in Christ, few or none bring greater inconveniences with them, than doth the inordinate hope and expectation of long life. And this affection is so much the more hurtful and perilous, for that it is grounded so deeply, and sticketh so firmly in our nature, that it cannot easily be remedied or removed: which thing, beside common experience, hath of old time been noted

[1 "The funerals of the Emperor Ferdinand, lately deceased, were appointed by the Queen to be celebrated in St Paul's Church, as was customarily done in those days, out of honour to the neighbouring crowned heads, which was done accordingly October 3. There was erected for the solemnity, in the choir, an hearse richly garnished, and all the choir hung in black, with the escutcheons of his arms of sundry sorts."—Strype, Grindal, p. 146.]

[2 Ferdinand I., brother of Charles V., was born A.D. 1503. He married Anne, sister of Louis, king of Bohemia, A.D. 1521; was elected king of the Romans, A.D. 1531; and upon the abdication of his brother succeeded to the empire, A.D. 1558. He died at Vienna, July 26, 1564, and was buried at Prague. See Modern Universal History, Vol. XI.]

by divers and sundry proverbs, as this for one: *Nemo est tam senex, qui non putet annum se posse vivere*[1]: "There is no man so old, but that he thinketh he may live yet one year longer;" and when that is done, yet another, and another yet after that, and so *in infinitum*, until all years and days be clean past and expired. The like hope of long life is expressed by this proverb, *Ægroto anima dum est, spes est*[2]: "The sick man, as long as he hath life and breath, so long hath he hope:" signifying that, even in the greatest and most dangerous diseases, the sick parties ever hope to live and to escape; so that neither old age, which by natural course foresheweth death at hand, neither yet extremity of sickness, be it never so grievous, can remove from us this inordinate expectation and vain hope of long life, so long as this body hath any breath abiding, or life left in it.

Out of this evil root spring many branches of great inconveniences: for when men be in expectation of long life, and promise unto themselves continuance of many years, they fall by little and little into carnal security, they grow remiss in all godly exercises, delight altogether in pleasures of this world, little or nothing thinking of the world to come, or of any amendment or correction of life, but deferring it to a longer time; and so oftentimes prevented with unlooked-for death, and found asleep in their wicked security, they tumble headlong, or they be ware[3], into the pit of damnation. For the curing therefore of this dangerous disease in our sick nature, the Holy Ghost hath provided in the scriptures two special remedies. The one is the setting forth before our eyes the severity of God's terrible judgment at the last day, when the Lord himself shall come with the voice and summoning of the archangel, with the sound of the trumpet from heaven, in judgment, to render to every man according to that he hath done in the flesh, be it good or evil; and therewith also the suddenness of the same judgment, which shall "come as a thief in the night," without giving any forewarning, as a snare that catcheth the bird, and as the lightning which most suddenly in one moment flasheth from east to the west over all heaven. The other remedy is the often warning which the scriptures do give us, to put us

Thess. iv.

Cor. v.

Luke xxi.
Matt. xxiv.

[1 Cicero De senect. cap. vii. ad fin.]
[2 Cic. ad Atticum. Lib. ix. Ep. 10.]
[3 Before they are aware.]

in remembrance of our forgetfulness of the frailty of our nature, continually subject unto death, who will not suffer us long to continue here upon this earth, but shortly, and very often suddenly also, bringeth us most certainly to an end of this uncertain life. The text which I have chosen ministereth just occasion to think of both these matters, being a parcel and the very conclusion of a sermon, made by Christ himself sitting on mount Olivet, upon occasion that his disciples asked him of the signs of his coming and of the end of the world. The words are these: *Ideo et vos, &c.* "Therefore be ye also ready, Matt. xxiv. for the Lord will come at the hour which you think not on." Which sentence, as most notable and worthy to be regarded, our Saviour in that sermon doth sundry times repeat, *Vigilate ergo, &c.* "Therefore." Wherefore? It is the conclusion of a similitude going before, which is this: "If the good man of the house had known what hour the thief would have come, he would surely have watched, and not have suffered his house to have been broken up. And therefore be you ready." As if he should say: The good man of an house would be diligent to save and preserve his house and worldly goods, being things corruptible: how much more ought you to be continually vigilant, lest the day of judgment, which cometh suddenly, as a thief in the night, find you sleeping in sin and wickedness, and so you lose a far more excellent treasure, redeemed not with gold and silver, but with the precious blood of the immaculate 1 Pet. i. Lamb Christ our Saviour!

Although therefore this text most properly pertaineth to put us in remembrance of making preparation against the general judgment; yet notwithstanding I intend presently to apply it to the preparation towards death, partly by reason of this present occasion, and partly for that both tend to one effect. For St Augustine saith, "Look in what state the last August. ad day of our life doth find us, in the same state will the last day Epist. 80. of the world judge us[4]." I purpose therefore, by occasion of this text, to put you in remembrance of three things:

First, of the exhortation in the scripture, moving us to prepare to die.

[[4] In quo enim quemque invenerit suus novissimus dies, in hoc eum comprehendet mundi novissimus dies: quoniam qualis in die isto quisque moritur, talis in die illo judicabitur. August. ad Hesych. Epist. 80, ad init. Ed. Basil. 1569. Tom. II. col. 350.]

Secondarily, of the causes that ought to move us to this preparation.

And thirdly, of the true ways and means how to prepare to die.

And by the way I intend somewhat to speak of the cause of this solemn assembly.

I. For the first. As it is said here, "Be in readiness, &c." so are there very many places in the scriptures, tending to the same effect. In Luke xii. Christ saith thus: *Sint lumbi vestri præcincti, et lucernæ ardentes in manibus vestris.* "Let your loins be girded, and your candles burning in your hands." By girding of the loins is signified the bridling, or rather mortifying, of our carnal and corrupt affections; and by burning candles is signified the light of faith, and christian conversation, the very fruit of true faith, and so, in sum, that we should be altogether in a readiness. Saint Peter also, when he maketh mention of the end of all things to be at hand, useth much like exhortation: "Be ye sober (saith he) and vigilant in prayer;" signifying thereby, that temperance in meats and drinks, sobriety of conversation in all the parts of our life, vigilancy and continuance in prayer and other godly exercises, are sure signs that we make preparation for death and for the coming of Christ. Of such like exhortation to prepare against death the scriptures are most full, and so plain, that this part needeth no long prosecution.

<small>1 Pet. iv.</small>

II. Now for the second part. There be two causes that ought (if we be not altogether insensible) to move us to prepare for death. The one is the necessity of death: the other is the uncertainty thereof. The inevitable necessity of death is very well expressed by Saint Paul in these words: *Statutum est omnibus hominibus semel mori, et post hoc judicium.* "It is ordained," or it is a statute, concluded and enacted in the high court of the heavenly parliament, and such a statute as never shall be repealed, "that all men," of what estate or condition soever they be, "shall once die, and after that followeth the judgment." The wise man saith: *Moritur doctus simul et indoctus.* "The learned and unlearned both die." The ethnicks[1] also did very well express this necessity of death. For Horace saith thus:

<small>Heb. ix.</small>

<small>Eccles. ii.</small>

[1 Ethnicks: heathen.]

Pallida mors æquo pulsat pede pauperum tabernas,
Regumque turres[2].

"Pale death, or death that maketh the most beautiful and best coloured faces pale, doth knock as indifferently at princes' palaces, as at poor men's cottages." Another poet hath these words: *Mors sceptra ligonibus æquat.* "Death maketh sceptres and mattocks equal, and as soon arresteth he the prince that carrieth the sceptre, as the poor man that diggeth with the mattock." David calleth death *Viam universæ carnis,* 1 Kings ii. "the way of all flesh." But what needeth many testimonies in so plain a matter, so universally known by daily experience in all places and times?

Now, as concerning the uncertainty of death, (which is the second and greatest cause to move us to be in readiness,) this may be truly affirmed, that as nothing is more certain than that death will come, so is there nothing more uncertain than the hour when it will come. And therefore is our life in the scriptures compared to things that upon light and sudden causes are alterable, as grass, a flower, shadow, smoke, vapour; and death resembled to the stealing in of a thief, to a snare entangling the bird, and the hook catching the fish unawares. This uncertainty is also touched in my text: *Quia qua hora non putatis, &c.* "For the Lord will come at the hour which ye think not." But both these things shall appear more clearly by examples. Isai. xl. Job viii. James iv. Luke xxi.

And to begin first with the examples of the latter part. Nothing doth more evidently declare the uncertainty of death, than the sudden deaths of persons of all ages and degrees, of which we find plenty both in profane histories and in the scriptures. Pliny, in the seventh book of his Natural History, hath a whole chapter entitled *De mortibus repentinis*[3]: and the like chapter hath Valerius Maximus[4]; where they write, that many upon most light causes suddenly have died. One at Rome, as he went forth at his chamber-door, did but strike Plin. Nat. Hist. lib. 7. cap. 53.

[[2] Hor. Carm. Lib. I. Od. IV. 13.]

[[3] Q. Æmilius Lepidus jam egrediens incusso pollice limini cubiculi. C. Aufidius, cum egressus in Senatum iret, offenso pede in comitio. Legatus quoque, qui Rhodiorum causam in Senatu magnà cum admiratione oraverat, in limine curiæ protinus expiravit progredi volens. Plin. Nat. Hist. Lib. VII. cap. 53.]

[[4] Valerius Maximus, Lib. IX. cap. 12. De mortibus non vulgaribus.]

his finger a little on the door-cheek, and immediately fell down dead. Another did but stumble as he went forth, and died forthwith. An ambassador of the Rhodians, after he had declared his message to the senate, departing forth of the council-chamber, fell down by the way suddenly, and there died. Æschylus the poet lying on sleep bareheaded near the sea, a great sea-fowl, thinking his head to be a stone whereon he might break the shell-fish which he carried, let it fall on his head, wherewith he was killed out of hand. Lucian, a man indeed learned and eloquent, but a derider of all religion, and namely[1] a blasphemer of christian religion, travelling by the way, was suddenly set upon and worried with dogs; a death worthy such a blasphemer, and a terrible example to all contemners and deriders of religion and piety. The scriptures also want not like examples. The churlish rich man Nabal, who at his sheep-shearing held a feast in his house like a king, but denied to relieve David, then persecuted and in distress, within ten days after was smitten of the Lord, and so died. Ananias and Sapphira, pretending that they gave their whole patrimony to the relief of the poor in the primitive church, but indeed reserving a portion to themselves, and so lying to the Holy Ghost, were immediately stricken of God, and so ended their lives, to the fearful example of all hypocrites and dissemblers, namely in matters pertaining to God's religion. Herod Agrippa, being in his most glorious magnificency contented to hear himself magnified and extolled as a God and not a man, was suddenly smitten by the angel of the Lord, and died a most miserable death. The rich man, of whom mention is made in the 12th of Luke, that intended to pull down his barns and granaries, and to build larger, said to his soul: "Soul, thou hast provision laid up in store for many years, and therefore take thine ease, eat, drink, and be merry." But what became of him? God said unto him: "Thou fool, even this very night shall thy soul be taken from thee; and then who shall have that thou hast provided?" The example of Nabuchodonosor is very terrible, who, walking in his palace, and glorying in his strong and stately city Babylon, whiles the words were yet in his mouth, was suddenly stricken with a plague worse than death; for

[1 Namely: especially.]

the use of reason was taken from him, and he himself, turned forth among beasts, became as a beast, eating hay like an ox; to teach all posterities ensuing, not to glory in things of this world which are but vain, but that "he which glorieth should glory in the Lord." It shall not be amiss if I add one example of mine own knowledge: for God's judgments exercised in our days are also to be observed and marked. I knew a priest who had rapped together four or five benefices, but was resident upon never a one of them. All this sufficed him not; and therefore he longed for a prebend also, there to spend at ease the milk and the fleece of the flocks which he had never fed. At length by mediation of money he obtained a prebend: and when his man brought him home the seal thereof, cast into a marvellous joy, he burst forth into these words of the psalm, taken out of his portesse[2], which was all his study: *Hæc requies mea.* "This is my rest, (saith the priest) this is my place of quiet; here intend I to make merry so long as I live." What followed hereof? Assuredly, *nulla requies*, "no rest"; but within a few days after he was stricken with a palsy, that he could not stir himself, and besides bereft of all his wits and understanding, that where before he was accounted a worldly wise man, afterwards he was altogether foolish, and not long after died. And who is there that hath lived any number of years, but they have known or heard of many that have died suddenly? Some sitting in their chairs, some sleeping in their beds; some have fallen down dead going in the streets; some have fallen off from their horses; besides many other like cases, coming by fraud, force, or violence, wrought by one man against another, whereof be infinite and too many examples. Wherefore, to conclude this part, let all those whom God hath blessed with prosperity in this world, learn further out of these examples, that when they are in the highest and best state of wealth, favour, honour, and dignity, then have they most cause to be vigilant and in a readiness; for then most commonly God's stroke is nearest at hand, and sudden destruction lighteth upon such as in the midst of worldly prosperity have not God before their eyes, but cast him clean out of their remembrance.

[Psal.cxxxii. 14.]

[[2] Portesse, portass, or portus: a breviary.]

Now to come to necessity, a few examples in that shall suffice. Daily experience sheweth that all are subject to death. Some note that it is not without an emphasis, and to be marked, that in the 5th of Genesis, where mention is made of the old fathers that lived some seven, some eight, some nine hundred years, ever in the end Moses addeth these words, *Et mortuus est*, "and he died;" to give us to understand, that live we never so long, yet at length cometh death, and maketh an end of all. If strength could have preserved from death, Sampson had yet lived; if wisdom, Solomon; if valiancy, David; if beauty, Absolom; if riches, Crœsus; if largeness of dominion, Alexander the Great had yet remained alive. But what need we to seek far examples? Behold, this present assembly and solemnity most lively expresseth to all our senses the brittleness of our nature, and the necessity of death. For if the most noble and mighty prince Ferdinandus, the Roman emperor, for whose funeral this preparation and concourse is here made, hath entered the way of all flesh, and though he were the greatest and honourablest of all earthly kings, hath as a subject obeyed the irrevocable statute of the heavenly emperor spoken of before; let us, in respect far inferior persons, assure ourselves we shall follow, and that how soon we cannot tell. And because it is commonly used that something should be spoken at the funerals of great and notable personages in their praise and commendation, agreeable to their conditions, I will also, agreeably to the said custom, speak something in commendation of the virtues of this most noble prince. In which doing I shall do no new thing, but therein follow the steps of the most godly, ancient, and best learned fathers of the church. Gregory Nazianzen, who for his excellent knowledge was called Theologus, that is, the divine, wrote divers and sundry funeral orations or sermons, and in them highly commended the parties discessed[1]; as Basilius Magnus, Cyprian, Athanasius, his own father, (for his father was a married bishop,) and divers other[2]. St Ambrose in like sermons highly commended Va-

[1 Discessed: departed, deceased.]

[2 In Cypr. Orat. 18. Tom. I. p. 274. In patrem Orat. 19. p. 286. In Basil. Orat. 20. p. 316. In Athanas. Orat. 21. p. 373. Edit. Paris. 1630.]

lentinianus and Theodosius the emperors[3]. Which was not done of these learned fathers, either for vain ostentation of eloquence, or for flattery of their friends remaining alive; but partly to continue a reverent and honourable memory of the parties deceased, and partly to excite and stir up others by rehearsal of their virtues to the imitation of the same.

And here I must crave pardon, if I shall not so largely and particularly speak in the commendation of this noble emperor, as did Ambrose of Valentinian and Theodosius. For this prince was to me personally unknown: Ambrose was much conversant with both the other. And therefore of this prince I can report only those things which either are credibly written of him in the histories of our time, or that are notorious by common fame, or that I myself have heard by very certain report of men of good credit. And here I will briefly pass over those things which orators could prosecute with much eloquence at great length; as, first of all, his high parentage and nobility of birth, being indeed very notable, descending in direct line from sundry emperors. Frederick the emperor, of that name the third, was his great grandfather: Maximilian the emperor, son to the said Frederick, was his grandfather: Philip, king of Spain, father to Charles the last emperor, and to him: his mother was the daughter and heir of the king of Spain: his father's mother was the only daughter and heir to Carolus Audax, Charles the Bold, duke of Burgundy, and lord of all the Low Countries; indeed a duke by style, but, when he lived, terrible to the mightiest kings of his time; he himself also descending lineally from the kings of France. So that there was compacted in this prince's person, as it were, a bundle of the principal nobility of the christian world; out of the compass of the which world there is no true nobility, but all barbarie. I will likewise pass over the dignity and honour of his estate, which was the highest type of all worldly preeminency, to the which he ascended by all steps and degrees of honour. As first of all, after the death of Maximilian the emperor, his grandfather, besides other his titles and styles, he was created, not a duke, which is a place of great honour, and namely in those

[3 Ambrosii Orat. funebr. de obitu Valent. Imp. Tom. III. p. 3. de obitu Theodos. Imp. Tom. III. p. 47. Ed. Basil. 1567.]

countries, but an archduke, I mean archduke of Austria, and (that more is) the only archduke of the world, so far as I have read or heard. Other there were archdukes in style, but he only, so long as he lived, was archduke in possession. Soon after he was crowned king of Boheme, then elected king of Romans, after that king of Hungary, and last of all emperor of Rome; which is the highest step and degree of honour that any man in christianity can attain unto. When I say the highest, I do not here except the pretenced supereminency of the pope's holiness: for I take his holiness, in challenging to be above the emperor, to be an usurper; and in this point I have Tertullian to make with me, who writeth plainly thus: *Imperator omnibus hominibus major, solo Deo minor.* "The emperor (saith he) is greater than all men, and yet less than God alone[1]."

Thus much concerning the royal progeny and imperial state of Ferdinandus; which things I have briefly passed over, as matters more meet for them that write panegyrical orations, than for the pulpit. For although they be the gifts of God, and therefore to be esteemed in their kind, yet be they the things that rather make a great man, than a good and a christian man. For the like hath often happened, as well to evil men and to heathen men, as to good and christian men.

I will therefore commend unto you the gifts of the mind, and the godly virtues, which were in this noble emperor: in the which, for the causes afore alleged, I must be more brief than otherwise the matter requireth. For surely, I have heard that he abounded in all kinds of virtue; that he was a lover of justice, a lover of truth, and a hater of the contraries; that he was full of clemency, full of humbleness of mind, no proud man, no haughty man, but humble, mild, and full of affability. He was also not unlearned; and both in Latin and all other vulgar tongues so skilful, that he was well able to treat in the same with the most part of the nations of christendom.

[1 Colimus ergo et imperatorem sic, quomodo et nobis licet et ipsi expedit, ut hominem a Deo secundum; et quicquid est, a Deo consecutum, et solo Deo minorem. Hoc et ipse volet. Sic enim omnibus major est, dum solo vero Deo minor est. Tertull. ad Scap. p. 86. Ed. Paris. 1641.]

But out of all his virtues, I will at this time especially commend unto you three, whereof two are notoriously known throughout all christendom; the third I myself have heard by report of them that were of good credit and excellent learning. And the first is his fortitude, travails, and continuance in wars against infidels and sworn enemies of the christian name and religion, I mean the Turks. The principal office required of a christian prince, over and above the duty of another christian, is the right use of the sword, put by God into his hand, for the defence of the godly and innocent, and for the repressing and punishing of the wicked. This sword is never so well occupied, as when it is drawn in wars to defend christians against infidels and enemies of christian religion. For these wars have a privilege or prerogative above all other kind of wars; for they are called in the scriptures *bella Domini*, "the Lord's wars." [Numb. xxi. 14.] In these kind of wars against Turks and Mahumetists[2] this noble prince spent a great piece of his young and middle age, not sparing therein neither his treasure, or his travail even in his own person; and therefore, in that point, may very well be compared to the most godly and valiant prince king David, of whom, for his valiancy against the Philistines and other infidels, it is written, that he fought the Lord's battles. 1 Sam. xxv.

But here methinketh I hear some man making unto me this objection, and saying: "Sir, ye commend this man highly for his wars against the Turks; but I beseech you, what success had his wars? Had not the Turk the upper hand? Have we not lost, for all his wars, the better part of the kingdom of Hungary? How then is he worthy commendation, that loseth and not winneth by his wars?" To that I answer, that counsels, wars, and other actions are not to be judged by the success, but by the purpose, intent, and prudent disposition towards the same. One poet wisheth that he should never have good success, which measureth doings by success: Ovid.

"Careat successibus, opto,
Quisquis ab eventu facta notanda putat[3]."

To direct wars and other actions to some good end, and

[2 Mahometans.]   [3 Ovid. Heroides. Ep. II. 85.]

to prosecute the same by prudent advice, industry, and activity, pertaineth (as God's gift) to the praise of a man; but the success of things is reserved to God alone, who disposeth them according to his divine wisdom.

And therefore, if God had determined at that time (as appeareth manifestly he had) to plague christendom by the Turk, as he did the Jews by Nabuchodonosor, (for God can use both evil men and wicked spirits for his executioners,) and that for the sins of the christian princes and people, and namely for contemning and persecuting the doctrine of the gospel, then offered unto them; what could all the kings of christendom have done to the contrary? But if we will judge this matter after the manner of men, and by common reason, the fault of the losses in Hungary is rather, yea, justly, to be imputed to other christian princes, (who at that time, for old, rusty, private titles, were at mortal and deadly war one against another, and so opened the way to the Turk,) than to king Ferdinand, who continually laboured for aid against the Turk, but could obtain none, and was left alone to match with a most mighty tyranne[1], who hath alone a dominion in greatness equal almost to all christendom, besides the conspiracy of divers Hungarian princes (for[2]

[1 Tyranne: *tyrannus*, tyrant.]
[2 i. e. on account or in favour of the Vaivode's quarrel.—His populis, Vavoidæ titulo, præerat Joannes Zapolia, cum Ludovicus Ladislai filius, Hungariæ rex, infelici prælio ad Mugacium cum Solymano conflixit, sicuti libro primo diximus; et ex regis morte occasionem augendæ potentiæ captans, Hungariæ procerum favore rex electus est, et Albæ regalis loco et more majorum regia ornamenta ac coronam sumpsit. Sed cum postea Ferdinandus Cæsaris frater, qui Annam Ludovici ultimi regis sororem uxorem duxerat, contrario procerum favore in regem assumptus esset, hinc Joannes Turcico robore fretus, illinc Ferdinandus suis fraternisque viribus, et uterque regulorum inter se dissidentium opibus subnixi, magno reipublicæ christianæ detrimento, de regno diu certarunt. Thuani Hist. Lib. ix. 2. Vol. i. p. 311. Edit. Lond. 1733.

"His brother-in-law, Lewis the Young, being slain in the battle of Mohais, he, by virtue of his wife's title (Anne of Hungary), was crowned king of Bohemia at Prague; and after having defeated John de Zapolles, count of Scepus, *Vaivode* of Transylvania, who was his competitor for Hungary, he entered into quiet possession of that kingdom, and was crowned at Belgrade." Modern Univ. Hist. Vol. xi. p. 169.

"The feudal institutions however subsisted both in Hungary and Bohemia in such vigour, and the nobles possessed such extensive power,

Vavoida his quarrel) with the Turk against him, which troubled him more than all the Turk's force. And I beseech you, in this case who could hope to have good success?

And yet his wars against the Turk did not always lack success. For proof whereof, I shall desire you to call to remembrance, how nobly and valiantly the city of Vienna in Austria was defended against the Turk, chiefly by his means[3]. They that write the histories of our time make report, that the city of Vienna, then being a weak town and not fortified, the great Turk[4] having passed through Hungary with an huge army, shewing by the way infinite examples of barbarous tyranny and cruelty, sparing neither age nor sex, no, not forbearing to rip the bodies of christian women great with child, was by him besieged round about with five great camps, the multitude of the enemies being so great, that a man, standing in the tower of the great church there, should for eight miles compass round about the town see nothing but tents and pavilions. The Turk so approached the town, that he procured the walls to be undermined, and great breaches being made in three several places, three terrible assaults were given three sundry days; and yet, through God's good protection, the town, of itself weak and newly fortified, was defended by a wall of christian men's bodies, and the Turkish tyranne repelled with shame and loss of great numbers of his soldiers, to the notable benefit of all christendom. For if the Turk had then surprised Vienna, not only all Germany, but all Italy, France, yea, and England also, would have before this time trembled and quaked. And surely, I

---

that the crowns were still elective; and Ferdinand's rights, if they had not been powerfully supported, would have met with little regard. But his own personal merit, the respect due to the brother of the greatest monarch in christendom, the necessity of choosing a prince able to afford his subjects some additional protection against the Turkish arms, (which, as they had recently felt their power, they greatly dreaded) together with the intrigues of his sister, who had been married to the late king, overcame the prejudices which the Hungarians had conceived against the archduke, as a foreigner; and though a considerable party voted for the *Vaywode* of Transylvania, at length secured Ferdinand the throne of that kingdom." Robertson's Hist. of Charles the Vth, Book IV. Vol. II. p. 374. Edit. 1812.]

[3 A.D. 1529.]   [4 Soliman I.]

think, we of England, that think ourselves in most safety, as we have a proverb of " the pope to come to our own doors," so should we have had the Turk, or[1] this day, to have come to our own doors, if Vienna had not been so stoutly and valiantly defended, and that chiefly by the good means of this noble emperor Ferdinandus. For although the emperor Ferdinand, then king of the Romans, was not there in person, yet is his commendation never the less. For the war was his, the town was his, the army was collected by his providence, and, as they use to speak in the Latin phrase, *Ferdinandi auspiciis totum bellum gerebatur.* So that I conclude, if the emperor Ferdinand had never done any other notable act in all his life (as he hath done many) besides the defence of Vienna, yet were he, for that alone, worthy of perpetual memory and of eternal fame and renown.

The second thing worthy high commendation in this prince, in my judgment, was his peaceable government, after he attained the imperial crown[2]. And although to some it may seem strange to commend in one man two contrary things, war and peace, yet indeed, the varieties of times and other circumstances considered, it is no strange thing at all. His wars were against God's enemies; his peace was with God's people. Ever sithence he was created emperor, (his wars with the Turks once compounded,) he hath only studied to maintain public peace: he hath not attempted (as other men have) to enlarge his dominion with the effusion of christian blood: he hath not stirred up any civil wars, under colour and pretence of religion, or for any other titles; but rather peaceably governed, nourishing concord and amity among all the states of the empire: so that by means thereof Germany, before afflicted both by civil

[[1] Or: ere.]

[[2] Princeps prudentia, justitia, liberalitate, mansuetudine, assiduitate, vigilantia nulli secundus; sed supra eas omnes virtutes pietatis in illo et pacis in domo Dei constituendæ præcipuum studium fuit. Nam ut in impetu Turcorum, cui impar viribus erat, sustinendo ac frangendo mora et arte uti optimum factu experientia didicerat; sic et in religionis negotio non igne et ferro grassari, ad quod ipsum et Galliæ regem plerique hortabantur, sed colloquiis, disputationibus, amicis collationibus, conciliis denique, sive nationalibus sive œcumenicis, rem gerere tutius judicabat. Thuani Hist. lib. xxxvi. 15. Tom. II. 396. See also Modern Universal History, Vol. XI. 171.]

and foreign wars, is at this present, by many men's judgment, more flourishing both for men and wealth, than it was at any one time this hundred years; that this man might well have used like words with Augustus the emperor, when he died: *Germaniam lateritiam accepi, marmoream relinquo.* I received a Germany of brick, I leave it of marble[3].

Therefore, as in his wars I compared him to valiant king David, so in this latter time, for his peaceable government, he may be very well compared to Salomon, who is termed, by the interpretation of his name, *pacificus,* "peaceable," or a prince of peace. And so he alone hath matched two most worthy princes in two several and most princely qualities.

The third thing that I commend specially in this prince, which I must speak, not of knowledge, but of most credible report, is his chastity: he was a chaste prince, a prince that did truly and (as they say) precisely, keep his wedlock[4]:—a notable virtue in any man, but more notable in a prince, and most notable in so great a prince, specially in this loose and licentious age. For in these days it is to be feared that not only princes, but others of far meaner estate, think unchaste life and the breach of matrimony a thing not only in themselves worthy of no reprehension, but also account others, of like state in power and authority, very fools and dastards, if they of conscience forbear to do the same. Like in that to the ethnicks, of whom St Peter writeth these words: *Atque hoc absurdum* 1 Pet. iv. *illis videtur, quod non accurratis una cum illis in eandem luxus refusionem.* "And it seemeth to them a strange or fond thing, that ye run not with them into the same excess of riot, or looseness." But let these men assure themselves of that which followeth in the same place: "These men (saith St Peter) shall 1 Pet. iv. give account to him that is prepared to judge the quick and the dead." God hath not given a particular, but a general law: neither hath he given his commandments to poor men only, or to men of mean estate, but to all men and to all estates, high and low, emperors, kings, queens, lords, ladies, rich, poor. Yea,

[3 Urbem excoluit adeo, ut jure sit gloriatus, marmoream se relinquere, quam lateritiam accepisset. Suetonius in August. c. 28.]

[4 He was interred by the body of queen Anne his wife, with whom he had lived in the utmost harmony of conjugal affection. Mod. Univ. Hist. Vol. xi. p. 171.]

the greatest prince of the world shall as well tremble at the judgment-seat of Jesus Christ, and pass as hard an account, as the poorest man of the earth, and an harder too, for that he hath a greater charge committed unto him, according as it is written : *Cui multum creditum, multum requiretur ab eo ;* and, *Potentes potenter tormenta patientur.* "To whom much is committed, of him much shall be required ;" and, "The mighty shall suffer mighty torments." Let no man think, therefore, that high estate in this world giveth him a license to live wickedly and unchastely ; but rather follow this prince, who virtuously, godly, and christianly lived in honourable matrimony ; and may therefore herein justly be compared to the virtuous emperor Gratianus, one of his predecessors, to whom St Ambrose giveth this laudable testimony : *Fuit Gratianus castus corpore, ut præter conjugium nescierit alterius fœminæ consuetudinem*[1]. 'Gratianus was a chaste man of his body, who out of wedlock, or besides his wife, knew not the company of any other woman.'

<small>Luke xii. Wisd. vi.</small>

<small>In orat. de obit. Valentinia.</small>

And behold, I beseech you, how wonderfully God blessed him for his chaste observation of matrimony. For where other princes, living heretofore incontinently, have been plagued of God with sterility and want of royal issue of their bodies, and so the direct line of succession hath been cut off after them, God hath not only given unto this prince plenty of honourable children, both sons and daughters, but also, according to the verse of the psalm, caused him see *filios filiorum,* his children's children, to a very great number.

<small>[Psal. cxxviii. 6.]</small>

The honourable marriages of his daughters in sundry places of christendom I omit : but one thing I cannot but note unto you, that he received at God's hand the same blessing which God granted unto David, whereof he himself maketh mention in the third[2] book of the kings, the first chapter, in these words: *Benedictus Dominus Deus Israel, qui dedit hodie sedentem in solio meo, videntibus oculis meis.* "Praised be God (saith David, when Salomon his son was proclaimed king before his death,) which hath given me one of mine own

<small>1 Kings i.</small>

[1 Ambros. Orat. funebr. de obit. Valent. ad fin. Basil. 1567. Tom. III., p. 12.]

[2 "The *first* book of the Kings, commonly called the *third* book of the Kings." Title in the authorised version.]

to sit this day on my seat, mine eyes looking on." Like occasion to praise God had Ferdinandus the emperor, of whom we speak; for he, afore he died, saw the most excellent and noble prince Maximilian[3], his eldest son (now emperor), crowned king of Romans, and thereby in most sure certainty (if he lived) to succeed him. A great blessing to a prince, and a great blessing to a country, where the case standeth so. God, for his mercies' sake, at his good appointed time send such a blessing in England! Amen, Amen[4].

Thus much I have thought good to speak in the commendation of this noble emperor, both to continue an honourable memory of the virtues that were in him, as the occasion of this time and place justly requireth, and also to stir up those that be present, of all estates, to follow these good things that were commendable in him. And here I might cease to speak any more of him, were it not that there remaineth yet one scruple to be removed. For it will be objected, peradventure, that this prince, thus commended, dissented from us in religion; and an answer therein required. I answer, that the matter of religion is a matter of great weight indeed, and such a matter as we must commend unto God only. Let us, whom God in his mercy hath lightened with the bright beams of his gospel, render unto Him most hearty thanks for the same. Let us thankfully embrace it, and christianly use it, to the glory of God and our own health. And let us pray instantly to God, the giver of all good gifts, that he will, in his good appointed time, so lighten the eyes and direct the hearts of all christian princes, [James i.]

[3 "Nulla re felicior fuit quam successore Maximiliano, qui vestigiis paternis insistens rara prudentiæ et æquitatis laude imperium post ejus obitum administravit." Thuani Hist. lib. xxxvi. 15. Tom. II. p. 397.]

[4 The protestant succession was a matter of deep anxiety to the bishops of the reformed church. In the year 1560 Archbishop Parker, Grindal, and Cox, bishop of Ely, "took upon them the courage and the honesty to write a secret letter to the queen, to persuade her to marry, shewing her how the safety and welfare of the church and kingdom depended upon issue of her royal body:" concluding, "that till they should see that fortunate day, they should never repose themselves to minister in their offices comfortably, in perfect joy and quiet of heart." Strype, Grindal, p. 61.]

that they may see the light of the truth, and walk thereafter in the right way, to the extirpation of all superstition and error, and to the true setting forth and maintenance of sincere religion, and to the glory of God, who is to be blessed for ever. And yet, something to answer them as concerning this prince, divers matters may be alleged, whereof I will rehearse some, which argue that he was not so much addicted to the Romish religion as some men would have the world to believe. And herein I will not deal subtlely or craftily, as to affirm before this auditory, for a more strength to our cause, that the emperor afore his death thought in all points of religion as we do, (for I do not think so myself of him:) only I will allege a few things which, either by the evidence of the matter, or else by good record, are manifest to all the world. And first of all, it cannot be denied, but that he was contented to be crowned emperor without a mass, which no emperor did before him a great many of years. And if any man would deny this, there be divers persons here present that were then at Frankfort, and saw the whole solemnity of his coronation, which was done for more surety in this case at afternoon, not aforenoon, as was accustomed. Now if the emperor had so much esteemed the mass, as other have done before him, he would not have suffered it to have been left off at his coronation. And if any, for excuse hereof, should affirm that he was contented at that time to dissemble the matter till he had obtained the imperial crown, those, under colour of friendship, should be his enemies, as diffaming[1] him, that for ambition' sake he would do a thing contrary to his conscience; which whosoever doth affirm thinketh not honourably, nor as he ought to think, of so good and so worthy a prince. Furthermore, I have heard for a truth, that afore his coronation he faithfully promised the princes-electors, that he would never be crowned of the pope; and the sequel declared the same very manifestly to be true; for he was never crowned of him indeed, remaining so long in the empire without the pope's approbation, which before time was used[2]. Let it then be in-

[1 Diffaming: defaming.]
[2 Pope Paul the Fourth would not admit the validity of the renunciation of Charles, or the election of his brother, because in neither

differently[3] considered, whether this was not much derogatory to the holy see, and whether St Peter's prerogative was not much touched herein? What a schismatical matter would this have been made, and what stirs would have ensued, if the emperor Ferdinand had lived in the days of pope Gregory the Seventh, who procured the deposing, yea and death also, of the emperor Henry the Fourth[4]; or in the days of pope Alexander, who set his foot in the neck of the emperor Fredericus Barbarossa[5]! But the pope is a wise man; for although he retain the same mind that the other his predecessors had, yet, because the times do not serve his purpose, he dissembleth the matter, and is contented rather

case the consent of the holy see had been obtained. He even refused audience to Don Martin de Gusman, whom Ferdinand had sent to take the usual oath in his name......The emperor ordered his ambassador to make the necessary protest, and take his leave, if in three days after this intimation he should not be favoured with an audience; for he considered that ancient custom of procuring the confirmation of the pope, and going to receive the imperial crown at Rome, as a superfluous ceremony, after having obtained the consent of the electors; an opinion which hath been adopted by all his successors in the empire. The ambassador punctually executed the orders of his master; and though almost all the princes of christendom condemned the conduct of the pope, yet he persisted in his refusal even after the death of Charles; but he himself dying soon after, Pius IV., who succeeded him, confirmed the imperial dignity to Ferdinand.—Mod. Univ. Hist. Vol. xi. 169. Ed. 1762. See also Thuan. Hist. lib. xxi. 2. Tom. i. p. 707-8.]

[3 Indifferently: impartially.]

[4 Hildebrand died A.D. 1085: Henry IV. A.D. 1106, during the pontificate of Pascal II. But the contests between the ecclesiastical and secular powers, stirred up by Hildebrand, may fairly be assigned as the cause of the melancholy termination of Henry's life. Pope Pascal II., following up the ambitious policy of his predecessor, encouraged and supported the unnatural rebellion of his son, by which Henry was deprived of his throne, and died in misery.]

[5 In the year 1177 he (Frederic I.) concluded a treaty of peace at Venice with Alexander, and a truce with the rest of his enemies. Some writers affirm, that upon this occasion the haughty pontiff trod upon the neck of the suppliant emperor, while he kissed his foot, repeating at the same time those words of the royal psalmist: "Thou shalt tread upon the lion and adder: the young lion and the dragon shalt thou trample under feet." The greatest part, however, of modern authors have called this event in question, and consider it as utterly destitute of authority and unworthy of credit. Mosheim, Eccl. Hist. Cent. xii. part ii. ch. 2. Vol. iii. p. 49. Ed. 1826.]

to take a piece than lose all. And surely this one act is a plain demonstration, that this emperor did not think himself bound in conscience so much to tender the pope's supremacy, as the canonists would have it esteemed, who make it a matter *De necessitate salutis*[1], "Of necessity to salvation;" for otherwise he would not have done as he did, to have gained ten empires. Besides all this, there is extant abroad in print an oration, pronounced in the late Tridentine Council by the emperor Ferdinand's ambassador, in which oration there is request made by the emperor, that liberty may be granted to have the communion administered in both kinds[2]. Whereupon may very well be gathered, that the emperor was not ignorant of the sacrilege of the Romish church, in depriving the people of God of the one half of the sacrament, where Christ himself instituted both: or else, if he had thought the one to be as sufficient as both, which is the popish doctrine, what needeth to make any further suit? And for further declaration of his earnestness in this point, I will add that which I saw written in August last past by a man of good credit and estimation, that Ferdinandus the emperor, not long before his death, gave license to all his own countries to have the use of the sacrament in both kinds. I do not affirm this but of report; but surely, if it be true, I do not doubt but that

Margin: Extra. de major. et obed. cap. i. 'unam sanctam.'

[1 Porro subesse Romano Pontifici omni humanæ creaturæ declaramus, dicimus, definimus, et pronunciamus omnino esse de necessitate salutis. Extravag. Commun. Lib. i. tit. viii. de majoritate et obedientiâ, cap. i. "Unam Sanctam" ad fin. Corpus Juris Canonici. Tom. iii. p. 211. Edit. Ludg. 1671.]

[2 Addebat Pontifex Ferdinandum Cesarem a se petiisse, ut Maximiliano filio, Bohemiæ regi, integræ cœnæ usus gratia fieret: nam, quominus aliter quam a Christo institutum fuisset sacramentum illud perciperet, religione ipsum attineri: eandem postea gratiam omnium suorum subditorum nomine Cesarem a se petiisse: quod hactenus illi cardinales denegaverint.—Thuan. Hist. lib. xxxii. Tom. ii. 251.

The Council of Trent evaded the settlement of this question by referring it entirely to the decision of the pope: Nunc eorum, pro quibus petitur, saluti optime consultum volens, decrevit (synodus) integrum negotium ad sanctissimum Dominum nostrum esse referendum, prout præsenti decreto refert, qui pro sua singulari prudentia id efficiat, quod utile reipublicæ Christianæ et salutare petentibus usum calicis fore judicaverit. Canones Concil. Trid. Sessio xxii. Decretum super petitione concessionis calicis.]

God revealed unto him other parts of religion also, which we have not yet heard of.

But, as I have said, we will commend that matter unto God; and whatsoever his religion was, this solemn action for memorial of him may very well be used notwithstanding. And being fallen into the mention of this public action and solemnity, it shall not be amiss somewhat to say of the true use, meaning, and purpose of the same, for the better satisfaction of doubtful minds. For there is no doubt but there will be two contrary judgments concerning the same. The one part will say, there is too little done; the other will say, there is too much. The first part will allege that, although they cannot but confess the action to be done very honourably and with much magnificency, yet the principal matter of all is wanting (will they say): for here is an honourable memorial of the emperor Ferdinandus, but here is (say they) no prayer for the soul of Ferdinandus. To those I answer, that the holy scriptures, the word of God, is the candle and the lantern for our steps. By it we ought to direct our steps, if we will please God; without it we walk in darkness, and know not whither we go. But first of all, in the scriptures we find no commandment to pray for the souls departed, unless they will cite the place of the book of Machabees. And then St Jerome shall make them answer, who permitteth indeed these books of Machabees to be read; but because they be not of the canon of the scriptures, they be not (saith St Jerome[3]) sufficient of themselves to establish any doctrines in the church of God. Secondarily, we have no example in the canonical scriptures of any invocation for the dead: for we read in the old testament that the fathers, as Jacob and others, were buried with mourning and with much honour, for a testimony of the resurrection, which is here also meant; but that any prayer was used for them we read not. Likewise we read in the new testament of Stephen and other, but of no prayer for them or any others,

Psal. cxix.

2 Macc. xii. Hieron. in prefat. in lib. Solomo.

[3 Sicut ergo Judith et Tobiæ et Machabæorum libros legit quidem ecclesia, sed eos inter canonicas scripturas non recipit; sic et hæc duo volumina legat ad edificationem plebis, non ad auctoritatem ecclesiasticorum dogmatum confirmandam.—S. Hieron. In prov. Solom. Prefat. Tom. III. p. 25. Edit. Basil. 1565.]

after their death, read we any where in the old testament or in the new. Thirdly, where in the old testament be sacrifices and expiations appointed for many and sundry things, whereof some seemed small offences; yet was there never any sacrifice appointed for any purgation or expiation of the dead. And therefore, if Judas Machabeus offered a sacrifice for the dead, seeing none such is prescribed in the law of Moses, in that doing he added to the law, and so offended God; and is no more in this point to be followed than Lot and David, being otherwise godly men, are to be followed in their evil acts: nor the author of that book more to be credited in this sentence without the scripture, than in his commending of one in the same story who did kill himself, contrary to the scriptures[1]. Besides that, divers of the oldest written copies of the story of the Machabees in Greek have no mention at all of the praying for the dead: so that that place is suspected to have been corrupted of purpose by some addition, put to many years after. For most certain it is, if prayer for the dead had been so necessary, as many now-a-days would have it seem, it had not lacked all authority and example of the canonical scriptures, as it doth.

<small>2 Macc. xiv.</small>

<small>Vide Aug. cont. Gaudent.</small>

Now, if they shall allege that the ancient doctors make for them, (for scripture, other than afore is alleged, they have none that maketh any thing for the purpose,) first, it is to be said that men's writings alone are not sufficient in matters of faith and religion. It cannot be denied, but from Gregory's time, when the corruption of religion increased very much, the doctrine of purgatory and praying for the dead hath gone with full sail, being maintained principally by feigned apparitions, visions of spirits, and other like fables, contrary to the scriptures. But the eldest writers and doctors of the Church, (for Dionysius, even by the judgment of Erasmus, is not so old as they make him,) speak not at all of praying for the dead. And although in Chrysostom and Saint Ambrose sometime there is mention of praying for the dead, yet it is in a far other meaning with them, than the schoolmen and other

[1 S. August. contra Secund. Gaudentii Epist. Lib. II. cap. xxiii. Tom. VII. col. 351-4. Edit. Basil. 1569. Non plane sapientiæ sed insipientiæ dedit exemplum, non Christi martyribus sed Donati circumcellionibus imitandum. Ibid. col. 352.]

of the latter time, being men ignorant in the tongues and other good learnings, have collected and gathered of them. For it is manifest, that those holy fathers meant nothing less than, by praying for those that were departed, to establish purgatory or third place; without the which, neither the pope himself nor any of his clergy would any thing at all contend for praying for the dead. For the terror of purgatory being taken away, their gain would cease; and withal their prayer for the dead, invented for filthy lucre, were at an end. For it is confessed of all men, that, if there be no third place, prayer for the dead is in vain; for those that be in heaven need it not; those that be in hell cannot be holpen by it: so that it needeth not or booteth not, as the old proverb goeth. If the ancient fathers therefore, when they pray for the dead, mean of the dead which are already in heaven, and not elsewhere; then must we needs by their prayer understand either thanksgiving, or else take such petitions for the dead, (as they be indeed in some places,) for figures of eloquence and exornation of their style and oration, rather than necessary grounds of reason of any doctrine. But I will make this matter more plain by an example or twain, not intending at this time to make any longer discourse or disputation concerning this matter. S. Ambrose, in his funeral oration or sermon concerning the death of Theodosius the emperor, doth much commend his virtues, and especially he commendeth him for his great lowliness and humbleness of spirit; for that he, being an emperor, submitted himself to the discipline of the church, and did public penance for the murder committed at Thessalonica by his commandment, lamenting his oversight therein with abundance of tears; which few private men in these days would be contented to do. In the process of this oration, Saint Ambrose laboureth to persuade all men that Theodosius, who had lived so godly, was undoubtedly saved; and at length pronounceth thereof plainly, using these words[2]: *Fruitur nunc augustæ memoriæ Theodosius luce perpetua,* In Orat. de *tranquillitate diuturna, et pro iis quæ in hoc gessit corpore* obit. Theod. *munerationis divinæ fructibus gratulatur;* that is, " The emperor Theodosius, of most honourable memory, now enjoyeth perpetual light and continual quietness: and for those

[[2] Ambros. Opera. Tom. III. p. 51. Basil. 1577.]

things which he did in this body he doth rejoice in the fruition of God's reward." How could S. Ambrose have more plainly expressed his certain persuasion concerning the blessed state of Theodosius? And yet within a few lines after he hath these words: *Domine, da requiem perfecto servo tuo Theodosio, requiem quam parasti sanctis tuis*[1]. "Lord, give rest to thy perfect servant Theodosius, the rest, I mean, which thou hast prepared for thy saints." First, he calleth Theodosius the perfect servant of God: but purgatory, by the confession of the patrons thereof, is not for the perfect, but for the imperfect. And moreover, what needeth S. Ambrose to pray to God to give Theodosius rest, seeing he hath pronounced afore that Theodosius was already in possession of that rest, and therefore not in purgatory, where is pain (as they teach), contrary to rest? It is evident therefore that S. Ambrose in this, and like places, meant not to establish the doctrine of purgatory, or praying for the dead, but useth only a figure of eloquence and vehemency of affection. Likewise in the Greek liturgy entitled[2] to Chrysostom are contained these words following: *Præterea offerimus tibi rationalem hunc cultum pro omnibus in fide quiescentibus majoribus, patribus, patriarchis, prophetis, et apostolis, præconibus, et evangelistis, martyribus, confessoribus, continentibus, et omni spiritu in fide initiato; præcipue pro sanctissima, immaculata, super omnes benedicta, Domina nostra, deipara et semper virgine Maria*[3]. "Moreover we offer unto thee this reasonable worship for all the forefathers resting in faith; for the fathers, patriarchs, prophets, apostles, preachers, and evangelists, for martyrs, confessors, continent persons, and every spirit endued with faith; but chiefly for the most holy, immaculate, and blessed above all other, our Lady the Mother of God, and evermore a virgin, Mary."

[1 Ibid. p. 52.] [2 Entitled: attributed.]

[3 Ἔτι προσφέρομέν σοι τὴν λογικὴν ταύτην λατρείαν ὑπὲρ τῶν ἐν πίστει ἀναπαυομένων, προπατέρων, πατέρων, πατριαρχῶν, προφητῶν, ἀποστόλων, κηρύκων, εὐαγγελιστῶν, μαρτύρων, ὁμολογητῶν, ἐγκρατευτῶν, καὶ παντὸς πνεύματος ἐν πίστει τετελειωμένου. (Ἐκφώνως) Ἐξαιρέτως τῆς παναγίας, ἀχράντου, ὑπερευλογημένης, ἐνδόξου δεσποίνης ἡμῶν, θεοτόκου, καὶ ἀειπαρθένου Μαρίας. Chrys. Liturg. Goar. Rituale Græc. p. 78. Paris. 1647.]

These are Chrysostom's words: shall we now gather hereof, because Chrysostom affirmeth the reasonable worshipping at the holy communion to be offered for the patriarchs, for the apostles, yea, and for the blessed virgin, therefore the patriarchs, apostles, and the blessed virgin are in purgatory? It is too great an absurdity. This oblation therefore is only a thanksgiving to God for the saints of God departed, with the remembrance of them by name, who did in true faith depart out of this world. These places, well weighed, are sufficient to declare the true meaning of many other like places, alleged out of the fathers for praying for the dead, and for purgatory.

But to answer to the second sort, who think this too much, and to come too near to the superstitious rites abrogated: I would those men would follow the example of the Israelites, in a time of variance between them and some of their brethren. The story is contained the twenty-second of Joshua: the effect is this. When the tribes of Reuben and Gad, and the half tribe of Manasseh, had received their portion beyond Jordan, at their return home they builded a piece of work like a great altar; which when the rest of the Israelites heard of, they intended war against the two tribes and the half, and sent messengers unto them, burdening them with apostasy and revolting from God's religion, for that they had builded another altar besides the altar in the tabernacle, which was the only altar appointed by God. The two tribes and the half answered, and that with calling of God to witness, that they meant no such thing, nor never intended to offer any sacrifice upon it; but only builded it for a bounder and for a testimony, both for them and their children, that the bounds of their possessions reached so far. The rest of the Israelites were with this answer very well satisfied and contented, and abstained from any war-making against them. So I do not doubt, but those who think this action to have any affinity with the superstitious abrogated ceremonies, (if any such men be,) when they shall understand that there is no such thing neither done nor meant, they will be likewise satisfied. First of all, here is no invocation or massing for the dead; nothing else done, but that is godly: first, singing of the psalms; afterwards, reading of the scriptures, which put us in

Josh. xxii.

remembrance of our mortality and of the general resurrection, with doctrine and exhortation. All which things tend to edifying of the living, not benefiting of the dead. The rest of things tend to the honourable memorial of this great prince, as hath been used in all ages, even among God's people. Herein also we declare, that we reverence and honour the authority of magistrates, as those in whom the image of God here on earth is represented unto us. Purgatory gaineth nothing by this day's action or such like, but rather receiveth a blow; for at such times there is always just occasion ministered to speak against that foolish fable. And as for this magnificence and costs, the Queen's majesty's act therein deserveth great commendation, shewing herself therein a prince of honour, by doing the office of a prince to the greatest prince that reigned, thereby exercising the amity that ought to be betwixt christian princes. And that such acts for princes dead are with such circumstances lawful and commendable, may appear by the scriptures. The prophet Jeremiah, rebuking king Joachim[1], saith thus: *Pater tuus nonne comedit et bibit, et fecit judicium et justitiam, et bene erat ei? &c.* "Did not thy father (saith he, meaning good king Josias) eat and drink, and did judgment and justice, and it went well with him?" What meaneth the prophet by eating and drinking? No man can live without meat and drink. He meaneth that Josiah did not only eat and drink for necessity, but also upon just occasions made great and royal feasts, and was sumptuous in other matters meet for his estate; but he joined withal judgment and justice, he destroyed the monuments of idolatry, he ministered judgment to the idolatrous priests, he ministered justice to the oppressed, to the widow and fatherless; and God was well pleased with him, saith the prophet. And so, if the example of Josias be followed in the rest, God will not be offended with this. And (which is more special) it is threatened to wicked kings by the same prophet, "They shall not mourn for him, Alas that noble prince! &c. but as asses shall they be cast abroad," &c. So that this our doing is an honour due, even by the scriptures, to this worthy and most noble prince.

Let no man here object diversity of religion. Joseph did

[1 Jehoiakim.]

Jer. xxii.

Jer. xxii.

Gen. l.

not refuse to take the Egyptians, being of a divers religion, in his company to solemnize the burial of his father. And David sent a princely embassage to Hanun, king of the Ammonites, to comfort him upon the death of his father Nahash. I am of St Augustine's mind: "Whatsoever," saith he, "tendeth to the edifying or increase either of faith or of charity is commendable." These kinds of actions, besides the intents before alleged, tend to the increase of charity, to the continuance and confirmation of unity, concord, and amity with a most noble and mighty prince our neighbour; and therefore cannot but be commended of all those that be lovers of peace and unity. But let this suffice of that matter.

2 Sam. x.

III. Now resteth something to speak of the third part, which is, how a man should prepare himself to die. Wherein I intend to be very short, because I have spent much time in the former matters. A very necessary matter it is for a man to prepare himself to die well and christianly; for in that resteth all: and therefore they are pronounced happy "that die in the Lord." But this preparation must be made according to the direction of God's word, not according to the device of man's phantasy. In times past men made preparations afore death, but (God knoweth) far out of square. Some redeemed for money great plenty of indulgences from Rome; and he that had the greatest plenty of them, to be cast with him into his grave when he was buried[2], (which I myself have seen done,) was counted the best prepared for death. Others made provisions or foundations to have great number of masses said for them after death, thereby to be the sooner delivered out of purgatory. Other there were that thought it a more reason-

Rev. xiv.

[2 "He (the Protector Somerset) pulled down in Paul's church-yard, and other places, many churches and religious fabrics for the building of Somerset House. And not only were the tombs of the dead rased, but their bones carried away in cartloads, and buried in Blomesbury. Yet this notice of former superstitions was gained by this barbarity, used by him and others under the reigns of king Henry and king Edward, that among a great number of rotten carcases were found caskets full of pardons, safely folded and lapped together in the bottom of their graves: which Dr Haddon himself had observed, when they digged dead men out of their graves, and carried away their bones, occasioned by pulling down many churches and convents, as he wrote in his answer to Osorius." Strype, Memorials, Vol. II. part i. p. 283.]

able and speedy way, to quench the fire of purgatory afore they fell into it; and therefore they procured a great number of masses and trentals[1] to be said for them afore death. Some of those that have been learned (the more was the pity!) have died in an observant or grey friar's cowl, and afterward been buried in the same, and so thought themselves well prepared. But, alas! all these preparations were preposterous. Parchment and lead[2], masses and trentals, were they before death or after, the grey or black colour of the friar's cowl, were very slender matters of defence before God's judgment-seat. These things therefore, being not only not commanded of God, but also tending to the diminishing of the efficacy and virtue of Christ's cross, were more apt to kindle the unquenchable fire of hell, than to quench the phantastical fire of purgatory, which is nowhere.

It is not to be denied but our forefathers were wise men, and in very many things highly to be commended; and yet lamentable it is to hear, into what gross errors and superstitions they were carried by those that made a merchandise of religion, "teaching things not convenient for filthy lucre's sake," as St Paul foreshewed. To be brief therefore, as the time overspent requireth, the true preparation to die well is to live well. A few words, but a long lesson. St Augustine hath a like saying: *Non potest male mori, qui bene vixit; et vix potest bene mori, qui male vixit*[3]. "He cannot die evil that hath lived well; and hardly (hardly, saith he) can he die well that hath lived evil. He saith, *hardly*, for that no man can limit the measure of God's mercies. He may, when his merciful will is, call at the eleventh hour, as Christ our Saviour, in the parable of the workmen sent into the vineyard, declareth. He may call at the last end of our life, as he did the thief on the cross. But that is not his ordinary way: let no man presume upon that, but let every man obey the voice of God, when he calleth him, who by his holy word calleth all men at all times, when they read or hear it.

Tit. i.

Matt. xx.

Luke xxiii.

[[1] Trental. A service of thirty masses for the dead.]
[[2] The indulgences were written on parchment, with a leaden seal.]
[[3] Mori male times, et male vivere non times. Corrige male vivere; time male mori. Sed noli timere: non potest male mori qui bene vixerit.—August. de Discipl. Christ. ad fin. Tom. IX. 917. Ed. Bas. 1569.]

When I say, that to live well is the very best preparation to die well, let no man think that I herein go about to extol the dignity or merit of man's works; but that I understand by living well all those qualities and virtues which pertain to a true christian man, amongst which those that be of the first table of the commandments of God are most principal: as namely christian belief, the true knowledge of God, assured faith in the mercies of God for the merits of Christ only; out of which, as out of a most plentiful fountain, springeth true invocation of God, true mortification of the old man, and contempt of the world, with all the works of charity and mercy. Of which I will cease to speak any further at this present, both for that I am excluded by time now overpast, and also, for that the particular tractation of these is the principal matter of all our other sermons. Of the which, as ye have oftentimes heard heretofore, so shall you also hereafter hear often of me and other my brethren, by the grace and aid of Almighty God: who grant unto every one of us, that, when the uncertain hour of death shall come, we may be found vigilant and well prepared; that, departing from hence with a joyful conscience, we may be partakers of that blessedness and felicity, which in the scriptures our Saviour promiseth to those servants, whom the Lord, at his coming, shall find watching and ready. Which blessedness God grant us all, and that through the merits and death of the same our Saviour Jesus Christ: to whom, with the Father and the Holy Ghost, be all honour, glory, and empire, now and for ever. Amen.

THE PRINCIPAL MOURNERS AND ASSI-
STANTES AT THE FUNERALS OF FERDINANDE, THE LATE
EMPEROUR, &c. CELEBRATED AT THE CATHEDRAL
CHURCH OF S. PAULES IN LONDON, THE
THIRD OF OCTOBER,
1564.

¶ Ecclesiastical persons.

The Archbishop of Canterbury, Primate of England.
The Bishop of London.
The Bishop of Rochester, chiefe Almoygnor to the Quenes Maiestie.
The Dean of Paules, with the whole Colledge ther.

¶ The Lordes, Counsellors, and Knights.

William Marques of Winchester, Lord treasorer of England, chief mournor.
Thomas Earle of Sussex, Lord Lieutenaunt of Ireland, and Captain of the Pensioners. 2. mournor.
Henry Earle of Huntington. 3. mournor.
Henry Lord Straunge, eldest sonne to the Earle of Darby. 4. mournor.
Henry Lord Harbert, eldest sonne to the Earle of Pembroke. 5. mournor.
Henry Lord Darly, eldest sonne to the Earle of Lenex. 6. mournor.
John Lord Lumley, sonne in law to the Earle of Arundell. 7. mournor.
Henry Lord of Hunsdon. 8. mournor.
Syr Edwarde Rogers, Knighte, comptroller of her Maiesties householde. 9. mournor.
Syr Fraunces Knolles, Knight, Vice-chamberlayne. 10. mournor.

Syr William Cecil, Knight, principal Secretary to her Maiestie. 11. mournor.

Syr Richard Sackeuile, Knight, undertreasorer of the Eschequer. 12. mournor.

Syr Nicholas Throkmerton, Knight, Chamberlayne of the Eschequer. 13. mournor.

Syr George Howard, Knight, Maister of the Armorie.

[GRINDAL.]

A

FRUITFUL DIALOGUE

BETWEEN

CUSTOM AND VERITY,

DECLARING

THESE WORDS OF CHRIST:

"THIS IS MY BODY."

REPRINTED FROM FOXE'S ACTS AND MONUMENTS.

THE FOLLOWING ARE FOXE'S INTRODUCTORY
OBSERVATIONS.

"BECAUSE great controversy hath been and is yet amongst the learned, and much effusion of christian blood about the words and meaning of the sacrament; to the intent that the verity thereof more openly may be explained, and all doubtful scruples discussed, it shall not be out of place to adjoin to the former discourses of Peter Martyr, and of Doctor Ridley above mentioned, another certain learned treatise in form of a dialogue, as appertaining to the same argument, compiled (as it seemeth) out of the tractations of Peter Martyr, and other authors, by a certain learned and reverend person of this realm; who, under the persons of Custom and Verity, manifestly layeth before our eyes, and teacheth all men, not to measure religion by custom, but to try custom by truth and the word of God: for else custom may soon deceive, but the word of God abideth for ever." [Foxe. fo. 1328. Edit. 1576.]

PREFACE.

The following account of this Dialogue is from Strype, Life of Grindal, p. 464.

"I do not find our Archbishop left much in print behind him: yet one tract (whereof, as we are informed by the foresaid MS. history[1], he was author) may be worth mentioning to such who have any mind to see a specimen of his learning, viz. *a Dialogue between Custom and Truth*, which is still to be seen in John Fox's Acts and Monuments; written in a clear method, and with much rational evidence, against the *real*, that is, the gross and corporal, presence in the sacrament. Fox indeed concealeth his name, (forbid, I suppose, by the author to disclose it,) only signifying, 'that it was writ by a certain learned and reverend person of this realm.'

"This discourse was writ by him soon after his coming back into England, for the better service of the church, that was then to be purged of popish doctrines and superstitions; as appears from those words, wherein *Custom* is brought in thus speaking: 'Are you so great a stranger in these quarters? Hear you not how men do daily speak against the sacrament of the altar, denying it to be the *real* body of Christ?' *Verity* answereth, 'In sooth, I have been a great while abroad, and returned but of late into this country: wherefore you must pardon me, if my answers be to seek in such questions. But you have been longer here, &c.' In this tract, after he had excellently explained the sense of those words of Christ, *This is my body*, he proceeded to produce divers sentences out of the ancient bishops

[1 "Dialogum illum scripsit apud Foxium de Consuetudine et Veritate." Bishop Wrenn's MS. History of the Masters of Pembroke College, Cambridge, in the library of that college.]

and doctors of the church to confirm his interpretation; because *Custom* had boasted of doctors and old writers, and men inspired with the Holy Ghost, that were against the doctrine of the protestants; and that in these days the wisest and best learned called them *heretics*. And at length in the conclusion of his discourse he tells *Custom*, 'That as shortly, and in as few words as he could, he had declared unto him what Christ meant by those words, *This is my body;* what the apostles thought therein, and in what sort they delivered them to their successors; and in what sense and meaning the holy fathers, and old writers, and the universal and catholic church had evermore taken them.'"

A FRUITFUL DIALOGUE[1]

DECLARING

THESE WORDS OF CHRIST:

"THIS IS MY BODY."

CUSTOM AND VERITY.

Custom:—I marvel much what madness is cropen[2] into those men's hearts, which now-a-days are not ashamed so violently to tread down the lively word of God, yea, and impudently to deny God himself.

Verity:—God forbid there should be any such! Indeed I remember that the Romish bishop was wont to have the bible for his footstool, and so to tread down God's word evermore, when he stood at his mass. But, thanks be to God! he is now detected, and his abominations be opened and blown throughout all the world: and I hear of no more that oppresseth God's word.

Custom:—No more! say you? Yes, doubtless, there are an hundred thousand more; and your part it is, Verity, to withstand them.

Verity:—As touching my part, you know it agreeth not with my nature to stand with falsehood. But what are they? Disclose them, if you will have them reproved.

Custom:—What! are you so great a stranger in these quarters? Hear you not, how that men do daily speak against the sacrament of the altar, denying it to be the real body of Christ?

Verity:—In good sooth, I have been a great while abroad, and returned but of late into this country: wherefore you must pardon me, if my answer be to seek in such questions. But go forth in your tale. You have been longer here, and are better acquainted than I. What say they more than this?

[1 The text is that of the edition of 1576.]
[2 Cropen: crept.]

Custom:—Than this? Why, what can they possibly say more?

Verity:—Yes, there are many things worse than this: for this seemeth in some part to be tolerable.

Custom:—What! methinketh you dally with me. Seemeth it tolerable to deny the sacrament?

Verity:—They deny it not, so much as I can gather by your words.

Custom:—Nay, then, fare you well: I perceive you will take their part.

Verity:—I am not partial, but indifferent to all parties: for I never go further than the truth.

Custom:—I can scarcely believe you. But what is more true than Christ, which is truth itself? or who ever was so hardy, before this time, to charge Christ with a lie for saying these words: "This is my body?" The words are evident and plain: there is in them not so much as one obscure or dark letter; there is no cause for any man to cavil. And yet, that notwithstanding, whereas Christ himself affirmed it to be his body, men now-a-days are not abashed to say, Christ lied, it is not his body. The evangelists agree all in one; the old writers stand of our side; the universal and catholic church hath been in this mind these fifteen hundred year and more. And shall we think that Christ himself, his evangelists, all the whole catholic church, have been so long deceived, and the truth now at length begotten and born in these days?

<small>Matt. xxvi. Christ's words.</small>

<small>The evangelists. The old writers. The catholic church.</small>

Verity:—You have moved a matter of great force and weight, and whereto without many words I can make no full answer. Notwithstanding, because you provoke me thereto, if you will give me license, I will take part with them of whom you have made false report; for none of them ever reproved Christ of any lie: but contrariwise they say, that many men of late days, not understanding Christ's words, have builded and set up many fond lies upon his name. Wherefore first I will declare the meaning of these words, "This is my body;" and next, in what sense the church and the old fathers have evermore taken them. First, therefore, you shall understand, that scripture is not so to be taken always as the letter soundeth, but as the intent and purpose of the Holy Ghost was, by whom the scripture was uttered. For if you follow the bare

<small>The doctrine of the papists commonly standeth upon false reports.</small>

<small>The sense of 'Hoc est corpus meum' expounded.</small>

words, you will soon shake down and overthrow the greatest
part of the christian faith. What is plainer than these words,
Pater major me est, "My father is greater than I am?" Of [John xiv.]
those plain words sprang up the heresy of the Arians, which
denied Christ to be equal with his Father. What is more evident than this saying, "I and my Father are both one?" There- [John x.]
of arose the heresy of them that denied three distinct persons.
"They all had one soul and one heart," was spoken by[1] the [Acts iv.]
apostles: yet had each of them a soul and heart peculiar to
himself. "They are now not two, but one flesh," is spoken by [Gen. ii. 24.]
the man and his wife: yet hath both the man and the wife his
several body. "He is our very flesh," said Reuben by Joseph [Gen. xxxvii.]
his brother; which, notwithstanding was not their real flesh.
"I am bread," said Christ; yet was he flesh, and no bread. [John vi. 35.]
"Christ was the stone," saith Paul; and was indeed no material [1 Cor. x.]
stone. "Melchizedek had neither father nor mother;" and yet [Heb. vii. 3.]
indeed he had both. "Behold the Lamb of God," saith John
Baptist by Christ: notwithstanding Christ was a man, and not
a lamb. Circumcision was called the covenant, whereas it was [Gen. xvii. 13.]
but a token of the covenant. The lamb was named the pass-
over; and yet was it eaten in remembrance only of the passover. Jacob raised up an altar, and called it, being made but
of lime and stone, "The mighty God of Israel." Moses, when [Gen. xxxiii. 20.]
he had conquered the Amalekites, set up an altar, and called it
by the names of God, "Jehovah" and Tetragrammatum[2]. [Exod. xvii. 15.]
"We are all one loaf of bread," saith Paul; yet were they not [1 Cor. x.]
thereby turned into a loaf of bread. Christ, hanging upon the
cross, appointed St John to his mother, saying, "Lo! there is
thy son:" and yet was he not her son. "So many as be baptized into Christ," saith Paul, "have put on Christ;" and "so [Gal. iii.]
many as are baptized into Christ, are washed with the blood of [Rom. vi.]
Christ:" notwithstanding no man took the font-water to be the
natural blood of Christ. "The cup is the new testament," [1 Cor. xi. 25.]
saith Paul; and yet is not the cup indeed the very new testament. You see, therefore, that it is not strange, nor a thing

[[1] i.e. about, concerning. And so in the following sentences.]

[[2] The sacred name יְהֹוָה, so called from its consisting of four letters.
"Et nomen Domini *tetragrammaton* in quibusdam Græcis voluminibus
usque hodie antiquis expressum literis invenimus." S. Hieronym. Præ-
fat. in lib. Regum, Tom. III. p. 16. Basil. 1565.]

unwont in the scriptures, to call one thing by another's name. So that you can no more, of necessity, enforce the changing of the bread into Christ's body in the sacrament, because the words be plain, "This is my body;" than the wife's flesh to be the natural and real body and flesh of the husband, because it is written, "They are not two, but one flesh;" or the altar of stone to be very God, because Moses with evident and plain words pronounced it to be "The mighty God of Israel." Notwithstanding, if you will needs cleave to the letter, you make for me, and hinder your own cause: for thus I will reason, and use your own weapon against you. The scripture calleth it bread. The evangelists agree in the same. Paul nameth it so five times in one place. The Holy Ghost may not be set to school to learn to speak. Wherefore I conclude by your own argument, that we ought not only to say, but also to believe, that in the sacrament there remaineth bread.

Custom:—Methinketh your answer is reasonable, yet can I not be satisfied. Declare you, therefore, more at large, what moveth you to think this of the sacrament. For I think you would not withstand a doctrine so long holden and taught, unless you were enforced by some strong and likely reasons.

Verity:—First, in examining the words of Christ, I get me to the meaning and purpose for which they were spoken. And in this behalf I see that Christ meant to have his death and passion kept in remembrance. For men of themselves be, and evermore were, forgetful of the benefits of God. And therefore it was behoveful, that they should be admonished and stirred up with some visible and outward tokens; as with the passover lamb, the brazen serpent, and other like. For the brazen serpent was a token that, when the Jews were stinged and wounded with serpents, God restored them and made them whole. The passover lamb was a memory of the great benefit of God, which, when he destroyed the Egyptians, saved the Jews, whose doors were sprinkled with the blood of a lamb. So likewise Christ left us a memorial and remembrance of his death and passion in outward tokens, that when the child should demand of his father, what the breaking of the bread and drinking of the cup meaneth, he might answer him, that like as the bread is broken, so Christ was broken and rent upon the cross for to redeem the soul of man; and like as wine fostereth and comforteth the body, so doth the blood of Christ cherish and relieve the soul. And this do I gather by the words of Christ, and by the institution and order of the sacrament: for Christ charged the apostles to do this in the remembrance of him. Whereupon thus I conclude:

Fes-[1] Nothing is done in remembrance of itself:
ti- But the sacrament is used in the remembrance of Christ:
no. Therefore the sacrament is not Christ.

Fe- Christ never devoured himself:
ri- Christ did eat the sacrament with his apostles:
son. Ergo, the sacrament is not Christ himself.

Beside this, I see that Christ ordained not his body, but a sacrament of his body. A sacrament (as St Augustine declareth) is an outward sign of an invisible grace. His words are, *Sacramentum est invisibilis gratiæ visibile signum*[2]. Out of which words I gather two arguments. The first is this: the token of the body of Christ is not the thing tokened; wherefore they are not one. The second is this:

Fe- One thing cannot be both visible and invisible:
ri- But the sacrament is visible, and the body of Christ invisible:
son. Therefore they are not one.

Which thing St Augustine openeth very well by these words[3], *Aliud est sacramentum, aliud res sacramenti. Sacramentum est quod in corpus vadit: res autem sacramenti est*

[1 For the meaning and design of these logical formulæ, see Abp. Whately's Logic, p. 92. Ed. 1834. The figures and moods of reasoning according to the rules of logic are contained in the following mnemonic hexameters:

Fig. 1. Barbara, Celarent, Darii, Ferioque, prioris.
Fig. 2. Cesare, Camestres, Festino, Baroco, secundæ.
Fig. 3. { Tertia, Darapti, Disamis, Datisi, Felapton.
         { Bokardo, Ferison habet: quarta insuper addit
Fig. 4. Bramantip, Camenes, Dimaris, Fesapo, Fresison.]

[2 The substance of this definition is of frequent occurrence in St Augustine. De sacramento sane quod accepit, cum ei bene commendatum fuerit, signacula quidem rerum divinarum esse visibilia, sed res ipsas invisibiles in eis honorari. S. August. de catechizandis rudibus, cap. 26. Ed. Basil. 1569. Tom. IV. col. 923.]

[3 S. August. in Joan. tract. 26. Tom. IX. col. 227.]

corpus Domini nostri Jesu Christi[1]. Moreover, I remember that Christ ministered this sacrament not to great and deep philosophers, but to a sort of ignorant and unlearned fishers; which notwithstanding understood Christ's meaning right well, and delivered it, even as they took it at Christ's hand, to the vulgar and lay people, and fully declared unto them the meaning thereof. But [neither] the lay people, nor scarcely the apostles themselves, could understand what is meant by *transubstantiation, impanation, dimensions, qualitates, quantitates, accidens sine subjecto, terminus a quo, et terminus ad quem, per modum quanti*[2]. This is no learning for the unlearned and rude people; wherefore it is likely that Christ meant some other thing than hath been taught of late days. Furthermore, Christ's body is food, not for the body but for the soul; and therefore it must be received with the instrument of the soul, which is faith. For as ye receive sustenance for your body by your bodily mouth, so the food of your soul must be received by faith, which is the mouth of the soul. And for that St Augustine[3] sharply rebuketh them that think to eat Christ with their mouth, saying, *Quid paras dentem et ventrem? Crede, et manducasti:* "Why makest thou ready thy tooth and thy belly? Believe, and thou hast eaten Christ." Likewise, speaking of eating the selfsame body, he saith to the Capernaites, which took him grossly, as men do now-a-days: "The words that I speak are spirit and life. It is the spirit that quickeneth; the flesh profiteth nothing." And St Augustine upon these words of Christ saith[4], *Non hoc corpus quod videtis manducaturi estis,*

Christ is no food for the body, but for the soul.

August. in Joan. tract. 25.

John vi.

August. Quinquagint. 2. Ps. xcviii.

[1 "The sacrament is one thing, the matter of the sacrament is another. The sacrament is that which goeth into the body: but the matter of the sacrament is the body of our Lord Jesus Christ."]

[2 These are logical and scholastic expressions, of frequent occurrence in the writings of Romish controversialists on the doctrine of transubstantiation.]

[3 Respondit Jesus et dixit eis, 'Hoc est opus Dei, ut credatis in eum quem misit ille.' Hoc est ergo manducare cibum, non qui perit, sed qui permanet in vitam æternam. Ut quid paras dentes et ventrem? crede, et manducasti. S. August. in Joan. tract. 25. cap. 6. Basil. 1569. Tom. IX. col. 218.]

[4 Spiritus est qui vivificat, caro autem nihil prodest. Verba, quæ locutus sum vobis, spiritus est et vita. Spiritaliter intelligite quod locutus sum. Non hoc corpus, quod videtis, manducaturi estis, et bibituri

neque bibituri sanguinem, quem effusuri sunt qui me crucifigent. Sacramentum aliquod vobis trado. Id spiritualiter acceptum vivificat: caro autem non prodest quicquam. That is to say: " You shall not eat the body which you see, and drink that blood which they shall shed that shall crucify me. I have commended to you a sacrament. Understand it spiritually, and it shall give you life: the flesh profiteth nothing."

Custom:—What mean you by this spirit, and by spiritual eating? I pray you, utter your mind more plainly. For I know well that Christ hath a body, and therefore must be eaten (as I think) with the mouth of the body. For the spirit and the soul, as it hath no body and flesh, so it hath no mouth.

Verity:—You must understand, that a man is shaped of two parts, of the body and of the soul; and each of them hath his life and his death, his mouth, his teeth, his food, and abstinence. For like as the body is nourished and fostered with bodily meats, or else cannot endure; so must the soul have his cherishing, otherwise will it decay and pine away. And therefore we do and may justly say, that the Turks, Jews, and heathen be dead, because they lack the lively food of the soul. But how then, or by what mean, will you feed the soul? Doubtless, not by the instrument of the body, but of the soul; for that which is received into the body, hath no passage from thence into the soul. For Christ saith, "That whatso entereth into the belly, is conveyed into the draught." And whereas you say that the spirit hath no mouth, like as it hath no body or bones, you are deceived; for the spirit hath a mouth, in his kind; or else how could a man eat and drink justice? For undoubtedly his bodily mouth is no fit instrument for it. Yet Christ saith, that he is blessed that "hungereth and thirsteth for justice." If he hunger and thirst for justice, belike he both eateth and drinketh it; or otherwise he neither abateth his hunger, nor quencheth his thirst. Now, if a man may eat and drink righteousness with his spirit, no doubt his spirit hath a mouth. Whereof I will reason thus: Matt. xv.

What is to hunger and eat righteousness. Matt. v.

illum sanguinem, quem fusuri sunt qui me crucifigent. Sacramentum aliquod vobis commendavi; spiritaliter intellectum vivificabit vos. S. August. in Psalmum xcviii. Tom. VIII. col. 1105.]

Argument.	*Da-*	Of whatsoever sort the mouth is, such is his food:
	ti-	But the mouth of the spirit is spiritual, not bodily:
	si.	Therefore it receiveth Christ's body spiritually, not bodily.

<small>How Christ's body is taken by faith. John vi.</small>

And in like manner Christ, speaking of the eating of his body, nameth himself the bread, not for the body, but of life, for the soul; and saith, "He that cometh to me shall not hunger; and he that believeth in me shall never thirst." Wherefore, whoso will be relieved by the body of Christ, must receive him as he will be received, with the instrument of faith appointed thereunto, not with his teeth or mouth. And whereas I say that Christ's body must be received and taken with faith, I mean not that you shall pluck down Christ from heaven, and put him in your faith, as in a visible place; but that you must with your faith rise and spring up to him, and, leaving this world, dwell above in heaven; putting all your trust, comfort, and consolation in him, which suffered grievous bondage to set you at liberty and to make you free; creeping into his wounds, which were so cruelly pierced and dented for your sake. So shall you feed on the body of Christ; so shall you suck the blood that was poured out and shed for you. This is the spiritual, the very true, the only

<small>Gregory.</small>

eating of Christ's body: and therefore St Gregory calleth it, *Cibum mentis non ventris;* "The food of the mind, and not

<small>Cyprian.</small>

of the belly." And St Cyprian saith likewise, *Non acuimus dentem, nec ventrem paramus*[1]: that is, "We sharpen not our tooth, nor prepare our belly."

Now, to return to our former purpose: seeing it is plain that Christ's body is meat for our spirit, and hath nothing to do with our body, I will gather thereof this reason. The sacrament is bodily food, and increaseth the body: ergo, the sacrament is not the very body of Christ. That it nourisheth the body, it is evident; for Christ calleth it the fruit of the vine, whose duty is to nourish. And for a proof, if you consecrate a whole loaf, it will feed you so well as your table-bread: and if a little mouse get an host, he will crave no more meat to his dinner.

[[1] Hæc quotiens agimus, non dentes ad mordendum acuimus, sed fide sincera panem sanctum frangimus et partimur. De Cœna Domini, ad calcem Cypriani Oper. Oxon. 1682. p. 44. This treatise is one of those falsely attributed to Cyprian.]

But you will say, these are worldly reasons. What then if the old fathers record the same? Irenæus saith, *Quando mixtus calix et fractus panis percipit verbum Dei, fit eucharistia corporis et sanguinis Domini, ex quibus augetur et consistit carnis nostræ substantia*[2]. Bede witnesseth the same by these words: *Quia panis carnem confirmat, et vinum sanguinem operatur in carne, hic ad corpus Christi mystice, illud ad sanguinem refertur*[3]. Wherefore, as I said before, seeing that Christ's body is spiritual meat, and the bread of the sacrament bodily, I may conclude that the sacrament is not Christ's body. Beside this, whereas it was forbidden in the old law, that any man should eat or drink blood, the apostles notwithstanding took the cup at Christ's hands, and drank of it; and never staggered, or shrank at the matter: whereby it may be gathered, that they took it for a mystery, for a token and a remembrance, far otherwise than it hath of late been taken.

Irenæus, lib. v. contra Valentinum.

Beda super Lucam.

Christ's body is spiritual meat.

Drinking man's blood against the law.

Again, when the sacrament was dealt, none of them all crouched down, and took it for his God, forgetting him that sat there present before their eyes; but took it, and ate it, knowing that it was a sacrament and remembrance of Christ's body. Yea, the old councils commanded that no man should kneel down at the time of the communion, fearing that it should be an occasion of idolatry. And long after the apostles' time, as Tertullian writeth[4], women were suffered to take it

Kneeling to the sacrament forbidden in old councils.

The sacrament carried home in napkins.

[2 Ὁπότε οὖν καὶ τὸ κεκραμένον ποτήριον καὶ ὁ γεγονὼς ἄρτος ἐπιδέχεται τὸν λόγον τοῦ Θεοῦ, καὶ γίνεται ἡ εὐχαριστία σῶμα Χριστοῦ, ἐκ τούτων δὲ αὔξει καὶ συνίσταται ἡ τῆς σαρκὸς ἡμῶν ὑπόστασις. Irenæus advers. Hæres. Lib. v. cap. 2. Oxon. 1702. p. 397.

"When the mixed cup and the broken bread receive the word of God, there is made the eucharist of the body and blood of the Lord, from which the substance of our flesh derives increase and consistence."

Fractus is the reading in several editions of Irenæus, but it is obvious that the Greek γεγονὼς requires *factus*. The passage was often cited as in the text by writers of the 16th century. See Grabe's note, *ad locum*.]

[3 Beda in Lucam, cap. 22. Colon. 1612. Tom. v. col. 424. "Because bread confirms the flesh, and wine produces blood in the flesh, the former is mystically referred to the body, the latter to the blood of Christ."]

[4 Speaking of a Christian woman married to a heathen husband, Tertullian asks, how it was possible for her to conceal from him her

home with them, and to lap it up in their chests. And the priests many times sent it to sick persons by a child[1]; which, no doubt, would have given more reverence thereto, if they had taken it for their God. But a great while after, about three hundred years agone, Honorius the Third[2], the bishop of Rome, took him and hanged him up, and caused men to kneel and crouch down and all-to[3] be-god him.

Pope Honorius III. first author of worshipping the sacrament. An. 1220.

participation of the eucharistic bread before her ordinary meals. He says: "Non sciet maritus quid secreto ante omnem cibum gustes? Et si sciverit panem, non illum credit esse qui dicitur." Tertull. ad Uxorem. Lib. II. c. 5. Paris. 1641. p. 190.

The following passages also refer to the same custom:

Cum quædam arcam suam, in qua Domini sanctum fuit, manibus indignis tentasset aperire, igne inde surgente deterrita est, ne auderet attingere. Et alius, qui et ipse maculatus, sacrificio a sacerdote celebrato, partem cum ceteris ausus est latenter accipere; sanctum Domini edere et contrectare non potuit; cinerem ferre se apertis manibus invenit. Cyprian. de lapsis. Oxon. 1682, p. 132.

Ἐν Ἀλεξανδρείᾳ δέ, καὶ ἐν Αἰγύπτῳ, ἕκαστος καὶ τῶν ἐν λαῷ τελούντων, ὡς ἐπὶ πλεῖστον, ἔχει κοινωνίαν ἐν τῷ οἴκῳ αὑτοῦ, κ.τ.λ. S. Basil. Epist. 289. Paris. 1638. Tom. III. p. 279.

See also Gregor. Nazian. Orat. XI. In which he gives an account of the miraculous cure of his sister Gorgonia by application to the reserved sacramental elements. Εἴ που τι τῶν ἀντιτύπων τοῦ τιμίου σώματος ἢ τοῦ αἵματος ἡ χεὶρ ἐθησαύρισεν, τοῦτο καταμίγνυσα τοῖς δάκρυσιν, ὢ τοῦ θαύματος! ἀπῆλθεν, εὐθὺς αἰσθομένη τῆς σωτηρίας. Greg. Naz. Op. Paris. 1630, Tom. I. p. 187.]

[1 Serapion, an aged Christian, who had before borne an unblemished character, lapsed during a persecution and sacrificed. He had consequently been excluded from communion with the church; but afterwards, lying at the point of death, he sent for a presbyter. Ἔδραμεν ὁ παῖς ἐπὶ τὸν πρεσβύτερον· νὺξ δὲ ἦν· κἀκεῖνος ἠσθένει· ἀφικέσθαι μὲν οὖν οὐκ ἐδυνήθη. ...... Βραχύ τι εὐχαριστίας ἐπέδωκεν τῷ παιδαρίῳ, κ.τ.λ. Euseb. Hist. Eccl. Lib. VI. c. 44. Paris. 1675. p. 246.]

[2 Ne propter incuriam sacerdotum divina indignatio gravius exardescat, districte præcipiendo mandamus, quatenus a sacerdotibus eucharistia, in loco singulari, mundo, et signato semper honorifice collocata, devote ac fideliter conservetur. Sacerdos vero quilibet frequenter doceat plebem suam, ut cum in celebratione missarum elevatur hostia salutaris, se reverenter inclinet, idem faciens cum eam defert presbyter ad infirmum. Decret. Gregor. IX. Lib. III. tit. 41. cap. 10. Corp. Jur. Can. Lugd. 1671. Tom. II. col. 3178.]

[3 all-to: altogether, entirely: see Nares's Glossary.]

Furthermore, if the bread be turned and altered into the body of Christ, doubtless it is the greatest miracle that ever God wrought. But the apostles saw no miracle in it. Nazianzenus, an old writer, and St Augustine, entreating of all the miracles that are in the scripture, number the sacrament for none. As for the apostles, it appeareth well that they had it for no marvel, for they never mused at it, neither demanded how it might be; whereas, in other things, they evermore were full of questions. As touching St Augustine, he not only overtrippeth it, as no wonder, but by plain and express words testifieth that there is no marvel in it. For speaking of the Lord's supper, and of the other sacraments, he saith these words: *Hic sacramenta honorem ut religiosa habere possunt, stuporem autem ut mira non possunt*[4]: that is to say, "Sacraments here may have their honour as things religious, but they are not to be wondered at as miracles." Moreover, a little before the institution of the sacrament Christ spake of his ascension, saying, "I leave the world: I tarry but a little while with you. Let not your hearts be troubled, because I go from you: I tell you truth, it is for your profit that I go from you; for if I go not, the Spirit of comfort cannot come to you;" with many other like warnings of his departure. St Stephen saw him sitting at the right hand of his Father, and thought it a special revelation of God: but he never said, that he saw him at the communion, or that he made him every day himself. And in the Acts of the Apostles St Peter saith, that Christ must needs keep the heaven till all be ended. Esay, Solomon, and St Stephen say, that God dwelleth not in temples made with man's hand. St Paul wisheth that he were dissolved and dead, and were with Christ: not in the altar, doubtless, where he might be daily; but in heaven. And, to be brief, it is in our "Credo," and we do constantly believe, that "Christ is ascended into heaven, and sitteth at his Father's right hand;" and no promise have we, that he will come jumping down at every priest's calling. Hereof I gather this reason:

Apostles and old doctors make no miracle nor marvel at the sacrament.

John xiv.

[John xvi. 7.]

[Acts vii. 56.]

Acts iii. [Isai. lxvi. 1. 1 Kings viii. 27; Acts vii. 48.] [Phil. i. 23.]

[4 Honorem tanquam religiosa possunt habere, stuporem tanquam mira non possunt. S. August. de Trinitate, Lib. III. cap. 10. Basil. 1569. Tom. III. col. 289.]

Christ's body cannot both be gone, and be here:
But he is gone, and hath left the world:
Therefore it is folly to seek him in the world.

<small>If Christ were both gone and tarried, then he should seem to have left himself behind him.</small>

Custom:—Fie! you be far deceived, I cannot in no wise brook these words. You shut up Christ too straitly, and imprison him in one corner of heaven, not suffering him to go at large. No, doubtless, he hath deserved more gentleness at your hand, than to be tied up so short.

Verity:—I do neither lock up neither imprison Christ in heaven, but according to the scriptures declare that he hath chosen a blessed place, and most worthy to receive his majesty; in which place whoso is inclosed, thinketh not himself (as I suppose) to be a prisoner. But if you take it for so heinous a thing, that Christ should sit resident in heaven in the glory of his Father, what think you of them that imprison him in a little box; yea, and keep him in captivity so long, until he be mouldy and over-grown with vermin; and when he is past men's meat, be not contented to hang him till he stink, but will have him to a new execution, and burn him too? This is wonderful and extreme cruel imprisoning. But to return to the matter: we are certainly persuaded by the word of God, that Christ, the very Son of God, vouchsafed to take upon him the body and shape of man; and that he walked and was conversant amongst men in that same one, and not in many bodies; and that he suffered death, arose again, and ascended to heaven in the selfsame body; and that he sitteth at his Father's right hand in his manhood, in the nature and substance of the said one body. This is our belief, this is the very word of God. Wherefore they are far deceived, which, leaving heaven, will grope for Christ's body upon the earth.

<small>The body of Christ imprisoned by the papists in a box, and afterward burned when he is mouldy.</small>

Custom:—Nay, sir, but I see now you are far out of the way. For Christ hath not so gross and fleshly, as you think, but a spiritual and a ghostly body; and therefore, without repugnance, it may be in many places at once.

<small>Christ's body is spiritual in the sacrament, say the papists.</small>

Verity:—You say right well, and do grant that Christ's body is spiritual. But, I pray you, answer me by the way, can any other body than that which is spiritual be at one time in sundry places?

Custom:—No, truly.

Verity:—Have we that selfsame sacrament, that Christ gave to his disciples at his maundy[1], or no?

Custom:—Doubtless we have the same.

Verity:—When became Christ's body spiritual? Was it so even from his birth?

Custom:—No: for doubtless, before he arose from death, his body was earthly, as other men's bodies are.

Verity:—Well, but when gave Christ the sacrament to his disciples? before he rose from death, or after?

Custom:—You know yourself, he gave it before his resurrection, the night before he suffered his passion.

Verity:—Why then, methinketh he gave the sacrament at that time when his body was not spiritual.

Custom:—Even so.

Verity:—And was every portion of the sacrament, dealt to the apostles and received into their mouths, the very real and substantial body of Christ?

Custom:—Yea, doubtless.

Verity:—Mark well what ye have said, for you have granted me great repugnance. First, you say, that no body, being not spiritual, can be in sundry places at once. Then say you, that at the maundy Christ's body was not spiritual: and yet hold you, that he was there present visible before the apostles' eyes, and in each of their hands and mouths all at one time: which grants of yours are not agreeable[2]. But I will gather a better and a more formal reason of your own words, in this sort:

The pope's doctrine repugnant to itself.

Fe-   No body, being real, natural, and organical, and not spiritual, can be in many places at once:

ri-   Christ's body in the sacrament was in the apostles' hands and mouths at one time, which were many places:

son.   Ergo, Christ's body in the sacrament was not a real, natural, and organical body, but spiritual.

[¹ Maundy: a supper, or feast; so called from the maunds, or baskets (the *sportulæ* of the Romans), in which food was carried for distribution to the poor. The last supper is so called, because Christ doled or dealt out the bread and wine to the Apostles; or, as others hold, from the last charge (*mandatum*) which Christ then gave them. The Thursday before Easter is still called Maundy Thursday, in allusion to Christ's Maundy.]

[² i.e. consistent.]

Custom:—Indeed you have driven me into the straits, before I was ware of you; and I know not how I may escape your hands honestly. But the best refuge that I have is this; I will not believe you.

<small>The papists, though they be convicted, yet they will not believe.</small>

Verity:—I desire you not to give credence to me. Believe the word of God; yea, believe your own belief: for they both witness against you, that Christ's body is taken up into heaven, and there shall remain until he come to judge.

Custom:—Tush, what speak you of the word of God? There be many dark sayings therein, which every man cannot attain to.

<small>Custom meddleth but little with scripture.</small>

Verity:—I grant you, there be certain obscure places in the scripture; yet not so obscure, but that a man with the grace of God may perceive: for it was written not for angels, but for men. But, as I understand, Custom meddleth but little with scripture. How say you by[1] St Augustine, St Jerome, St Ambrose? What, if they stand on our side?

Custom:—No, no; I know them well enough.

Verity:—So well as you know them, for[2] all old acquaintance, if they be called to witness, they will give evidence against you. For St Augustine commonly, in every of his books, but chiefly in an epistle to his friend Dardanus, declareth that Christ's body is placed in one room. I marvel you be not nearer of his counsel. His words are these:

<small>August. ad Dardanum.</small>

Noli dubitare ibi nunc esse hominem Christum Jesum, unde venturus est: memoriterque recole et fideliter crede christianam confessionem; 'quoniam resurrexit, ascendit in cœlum, sedet a dextris Dei Patris, nec aliunde quam inde venturus est ad vivos mortuosque judicandos.' Et venturus est in eadem corporis substantia, cui immortalitatem dedit, naturam non abstulit. Secundum hanc formam non est putandus ubique diffusus: cavendum enim est, ne ita divinitatem astruamus hominis, ut humanitatem amittamus Dei[3]. "Do not doubt the man Jesus Christ to be there, from whence he shall come. And remember well, and faithfully believe, the christian confession, that 'he is risen, ascended into heaven, sitteth at the right

[[1] i.e. about, or with regard to.]
[[2] i.e. notwithstanding.]
[[3] S. August. Epist. lvii. ad Dardanum, Basil. 1569. Tom. II. col. 272.]

hand of God the Father, and from thence shall come, and from no other place, to judge the quick and dead:' and shall come in the same substance of body, to which he gave immortality, and took not the nature from it. After this form he is to be thought not to be dispersed in all places; for we must beware so to defend his divinity, that we destroy not his humanity." And in another place of the same epistle: *Una persona Deus et homo; et utrumque est unus Christus. Ubique per id quod Deus, in cœlo autem per id quod homo*[4]. Likewise upon the xivth Psalm: *Donec seculum finiatur, sursum est Dominus: sed etiam hic nobiscum est veritas Domini. Corpus enim in quo resurrexit in uno loco esse oportet; veritas autem ejus ubique diffusa est*[5]. "While the world shall last, the Lord is above, and also the verity of the Lord is with us. For the body wherein he rose again must be in one place; but the verity of him is everywhere dispersed." In like manner writeth Damasus, an old bishop of Rome, in his Credo[6]: *Devictis mortis imperiis, cum ea carne in qua natus et passus est et resurrexit, ascendit in cœlum, manente eadem natura carnis in qua natus et passus est.* St Ambrose, writing

August. ibid.

August.

Damasus.

[4 Ibid. col. 273. "One person is God and Man; and both together are one Christ. As God, he is every where; but as Man, he is in heaven."

[5 This passage is not found in St Augustine's Commentary on the 14th Psalm, but upon St John's Gospel: Propter nos scriptum est, et nobis servatum, et propter nos recitatum; et recitabitur etiam propter posteros nostros, et donec seculum finiatur. Sursum est Dominus, sed etiam hic est veritas Domini. Corpus enim Domini, in quo resurrexit, uno loco esse potest; veritas ejus ubique diffusa est. S. August. in Joan. Tract. xxx. Tom. ix. col. 247.]

[6 Damasus was bishop of Rome from A.D. 367 to A.D. 384. The passage referred to is found in a synodical epistle addressed to Paulinus bishop of Antioch. Vid. Baronius, Ann. Eccles. Tom. iv. p. 429. Antwerp. 1601. The epistle is given at length by Theodoret, under the title, "Confessio fidei quam Papa Damasus," &c. &c.

Εἴ τις μὴ εἴπῃ, τὸν τοῦ Θεοῦ Λόγον παθόντα σαρκὶ, καὶ ἐσταυρωμένον σαρκὶ, καὶ θανάτου γευσάμενον σαρκὶ, γεγονότα τε πρωτότοκον ἐκ τῶν νεκρῶν, καθὸ ζωή ἐστὶ καὶ ζωοποιὸς ὡς Θεὸς, ἀνάθεμα ἔστω. Εἴ τις μὴ εἴπῃ, ὅτι ἐν σαρκὶ, ἥνπερ ἀνέλαβε, καθέζεται ἐν τῇ δεξιᾷ τοῦ Πατρὸς, ἐν ᾗ καὶ ἐλεύσεται κρῖναι ζῶντας καὶ νεκροὺς, ἀνάθεμα ἔστω. Theodoreti Eccles. Hist. Lib. v. cap. 11. Paris. 1673. p. 214. See also, Concilia Omnia, Colon. 1538, Tom. i. p. 229, where the epistle is given in Latin.]

upon the xxivth chapter of Luke, recordeth the same: *Ergo nec supra terram, nec in terra, nec secundum terram, quærere debemus Dominum, si volumus invenire. Non enim supra terram quæsivit, qui stantem ad Dei dextram vidit. Maria quærebat in terra tangere Christum, et non potuit; Stephanus tetigit, quia quærebat in cœlo*[1]. "Wherefore neither above the earth, nor upon the earth, nor according to the earth, we ought to seek the Lord, if we will find him; for he did not seek him above the earth, which did see him sitting at the right hand of God. And Mary sought upon the earth to touch Christ and could not: Stephen touched him, because he sought him in heaven." St Jerome, in an epistle to Marcella, proveth that the body of Christ must needs be contained in some place; for he saith: *Veri Dei est ubique esse; veri hominis alicubi esse.* "The property of God is to be everywhere; the property of man is to be in one place." The same Jerome, in another place, calleth it a foolish thing to seek for him in a narrow place, or in a corner, which is the light of all the world: *Stultum est eum parvo in loco vel abscondito quærere, qui totius mundi est lumen.* "Foolishness it is, in a small place or in a hid corner to seek him which is the light of the whole world[2]." Origen saith likewise: *Audiendi non sunt, qui Christum demonstrant in ædibus.* "They are not to be heard, which shew Christ in houses[3]." The same also recordeth Bede, writing upon these words of Christ: "Now a little while shall you see me[4]." He speaketh

[1 S. Ambros. in Luc. cap. xxiv. Basil. 1567. Tom. v. p. 166.]

[2 The passage alluded to seems to be the following. After applying to Christ several texts of scripture which speak of the omnipresence of God, the author observes: Profecto non ambiges, etiam ante resurrectionem sic in Dominico corpore habitasse Deum Verbum, ut in Patre esset, et cœli circulum clauderet, atque in omnibus infusus esset et circumfusus; id est, ut cuncta penetraret interior, et contineret exterior. Stultum est igitur illius potentiam unius corpusculi parvitate finiri, quem non capit cœlum. Hieron. ad Marcellam, Basil. 1565, Tom. III. p. 138.]

[3 Sed prædicente nobis omnia Salvatore, neque in solitudinem exeamus, neque qui profitentur Christum in domibus esse credamus. Orig. in Matth. cap. xxiv. Tract. xxx. Tom. II. p. 145. Basil. 1571.]

[4 The passage cited in the text occurs in a homily on St John xvi. 16. Propterea me resuscitatum a mortuis modico tempore videbitis, quia non semper in terra corporaliter mansurus, sed per huma-

in Christ's person. "Therefore," saith he, "shall you see me but a little while after my resurrection, because I will not still abide in the earth bodily; but in the manhood which I have taken will ascend up to heaven." What needeth more words? All the old fathers witness the same. You may by these soon judge the rest. Now to return to the matter: Seeing that the word of God in many and sundry places, the "Credo," and the Abridgement of the Faith; seeing all the old fathers do constantly agree in one, that the body of Christ is ascended into heaven, and there remaineth at the right hand of the Father, and cannot be in more than one place; I do conclude, that the sacrament is not the body of Christ; first, because it is not in heaven, neither sitteth at the Father's right hand; moreover, because it is in a hundred thousand boxes, whereas Christ's body filleth but one place: furthermore, if the bread were turned into the body of Christ, then would it necessarily follow, that sinners and unpenitent persons receive the body of Christ. *[The sacrament is not the real body of Christ, and why.]*

Custom:—Marry, and so they do. For Paul saith plainly, that they receive the body of Christ to their own confusion.

Verity:—No, not so. These are not Paul's words, but he saith, "Whoso eateth of this bread, and drinketh of this cup unworthily, eateth and drinketh his own condemnation, not judging the body of the Lord." Here he calleth it, in plain words, bread. And although the sacrament be very bread, yet doth the injury redound to the body of Christ. As if a man break the king's mace, or tread the broad seal under his foot, although he have broken and defaced nothing but silver and wax, yet is the injury the king's, and the doer shall be taken as a traitor. St Ambrose declareth the meaning of St Paul by these words, *Reus est corporis Domini, qui pœnas dabit mortis Christi, quoniam irritam fecit mortem Domini*[5]. The cause of the ordinance thereof was the remembrance of the death of Christ, which whoso forgetteth, receiveth the sacrament to their condemnation. That same witnesseth St Augustine: "For the sacrament," saith he, "is an outward token of love *[The wicked receive not the body of Christ. 1 Cor. xi. 29.]* *[Ambrosius.]* *[Augustinus.]*

nitatem quam assumpsi jam sum ascensurus in cœlum. Beda, Homiliæ Æstivales, Dominic. Jubilate. Colon. 1612. Tom. VII. col. 17.]

[5 Quid est autem reos esse, nisi pœnas dare mortis Domini? Occisus est enim pro iis, qui beneficium ejus irritum ducunt. S. Ambros. in 1 Cor. xi. Basil. 1567. Tom. v. p. 276.]

and charity. For like as many grains of corn are become one piece of bread, even so they that receive it ought to be one." Then saith he, *Mysterium pacis ac unitatis nobis Christus in mensa sua consecravit. Qui accepit mysterium unitatis, et non servat unitatem, non mysterium accepit pro se, sed testimonium contra se*[1]. He that readeth the gospel, wherein is declared the passion and death of Christ, and liveth contrary to the gospel, shall doubtless be the more guilty of the death of Christ, because he heareth and readeth the word of God, and regardeth it not.

The place of St Paul of receiving unworthily expounded. In a certain country the manner is, that when the gospel is read, the king shall stand up with a naked sword in his hand, declaring thereby that he beareth his sword in defence of the gospel[2]. But if he himself oppresseth the gospel, he beareth the sword against himself; for the gospel shall turn to his judgment and condemnation. So will Christ so much more extremely punish a man, which, knowing himself to be wicked and without repentance, and therefore none of the flock of Christ, yet notwithstanding will impudently creep into the company of christian men, and receive the sacraments with them, as though he were one of the number. And this meant St Paul by the unworthy receiving of a sacrament of Christ's body. Wherefore a man may unworthily take the sacrament, and be guilty of the death of Christ, although he receive not Christ's body into his mouth, and chaw it with his teeth. But what, if I prove that every massing priest is guilty of the body and blood of Christ?

[1 In Sermone ad Infantes, apud Fulgentium, p. 612. Paris. 1671. Cf. Cyprian. Epist. ad Magnum:

Denique unanimitatem Christianam, firma sibi atque inseparabili caritate connexam, etiam ipsa Dominica sacrificia declarant. Nam quando Dominus corpus suum panem vocat, de multorum granorum adunatione congestum, populum nostrum quem portabat indicat adunatum: et quando sanguinem suum vinum appellat, de botris atque acinis plurimis expressum, atque in unum coactum, gregem item nostrum significat commixtione adunatæ multitudinis copulatum. Ep. 69. Oxon. 1682. p. 182.]

[2 The country intended is Poland. "Expugnata itaque ab idolis Polonia, Mieczslaus princeps ad evidentius signum Christianitatis instituit, ut infra officium missæ, dum evangelium prælegeretur, singuli virorum ad medium gladii e vaginis depromerent; quo se testarentur propter evangelium Christi ad mortem usque decertare paratos esse." Guagninus, Sarmatiæ Europeæ descriptio, Spiræ, 1581, p. 10.]

Custom:—I dare say you cannot prove it.

Verity:—But if I do prove it, will you believe me?

Custom:—I may well enough, for it is impossible to do it: for priests commonly are confessed before they go to mass; and how can they then take the sacrament unworthily?

Verity:—Indeed confession, if it be discreetly used, is a laudable custom, and to the unlearned man and feeble conscience so good as a sermon: but notwithstanding, because it was never neither commanded of Christ, nor received of the apostles, nor much spoken of the old doctors, it cannot make much for the due receiving of the sacrament. But how like ye these words of St Ambrose? *Is indigne sumit, qui aliter sumit quam Christus instituit*[3]. "He taketh it unworthily, that taketh it otherwise than Christ ordained it."

Custom:—This liketh me very well. But what gather you of it?

Verity:—This will I gather. The massing priest taketh the sacrament otherwise than Christ either commanded or taught: ergo, he taketh it unworthily, and so consequently to his condemnation.

Custom:—That is not so; for he doth altogether as Christ commanded him.

Verity:—That shall appear; for Christ commanded it to be done in his remembrance: the priest doth it in remembrance of dead men. Christ took bread, and left it bread: the priest taketh bread and conjureth it away. Christ took bread and gave thanks: the priest taketh bread and breatheth upon it. Christ took bread and brake it: the priest taketh bread and hangeth it up. Christ took bread and dealt to his apostles: the priest, because he is an apostle himself, taketh bread and eateth it every whit alone. Christ in a sacrament gave his own body to be eaten in faith: the priest, for lack of faith, receiveth accidents and dimensions. Christ gave a sacrament to strengthen men's faith: the priest giveth a sacrifice to redeem men's souls. Christ gave it to be eaten: the priest giveth it to be worshipped. And to conclude, Christ gave bread: the priest saith he giveth a God. Here is difference

Marginalia: Confession. Ambrosius. The priest taketh the sacrament not as Christ ordained it: ergo, the priest taketh it unworthily. Difference between Christ's ordinance and the priest's receiving.

[3] Indignum dicit esse Domino, qui aliter mysterium celebrat, quam ab eo traditum est. S. Ambr. in 1 Cor. xi. Tom. v. p. 276.]

enough between Christ and the priest. Yet moreover, Christ at his supper spake his words out, and in a plain tongue: the priest speaketh nothing but Latin or Greek, which tongues he oft-times perceiveth not; and much he whispereth, lest any other poor man should perhaps perceive him. So it cometh to pass, that the priest knoweth no more what he himself saith, than what he doth. Thus you may see, that the massing priest receiveth the sacrament of Christ's body far otherwise than ever Christ minded; and so therefore unworthily, and to his condemnation.

Now, if you think yourself satisfied, I will return to my former question, and prove more at large, that Christ's body cannot be eaten of the wicked; which thing must necessarily ensue, if the bread were turned into the body of Christ. Christ, in the 6th of John, speaking of the eating of his body, saith, "He that eateth of this bread shall live for ever." Whereof I gather thus: But sinful men take the sacrament to their condemnation, and live not for ever; Ergo, in the sacrament they receive not the body of Christ. Again, Christ saith, "He that eateth me shall live for my sake[1]." Hereof I conclude thus: But impenitent persons cannot live for Christ's sake. Moreover, Christ's body must be received with faith, and not with the mouth, as Gregory recordeth, saying, that it is eaten with the teeth of the soul, not of the body; as I have above more largely declared: but wicked and impenitent persons lack faith: wherefore they cannot eat the body of Christ. Again, Christ's body cannot be divided from his spirit: but wicked men have not the spirit of God: ergo, they have not Christ's body. Hereunto agree all the old writers, affirming constantly, that the unfaithful be no meet vessels to receive the body of Christ. St Augustine saith: *Qui non manet in Christo, et in quo non manet Christus, procul dubio non manducat carnem Christi, nec bibit ejus sanguinem, quamvis tantæ rei mysterium ad judicium suum manducet ac bibat*[2]. And in

Gregorius.

Augustinus.

[1] Ὁ τρώγων με, κἀκεῖνος ζήσεται δι' ἐμέ—propter me. Joh. vi. 57.]

[2 Hoc est ergo manducare illam escam, et illum bibere potum, in Christo manere, et illum manentem in se habere. Ac per hoc, qui non manet in Christo, et in quo non manet Christus, procul dubio nec manducat spiritaliter carnem ejus, nec bibit ejus sanguinem, licet carnaliter et visibiliter premat dentibus sacramentum corporis et sanguinis Christi; sed magis tantæ rei sacramentum ad judicium sibi

the person of Christ, he saith likewise: *Qui non manet in me, et in quo ego non maneo, ne se dicat aut existimet manducare corpus meum, aut sanguinem meum bibere.* Ambrose avoweth the Ambrosius. same by these words: *Qui discordat a Christo non manducat carnem ejus, nec bibit sanguinem, etsi tantæ rei sacramentum accipiat.* In like manner writeth Prosper[3]: *Qui discordat a* Prosperus. *Christo, nec carnem Christi edit, nec sanguinem bibit, etsi tantæ rei sacramentum ad judicium suæ præsumptionis quotidie accipiat.* And therefore St Augustine saith: *Mali sacramentum* Augustinus. *habent, rem autem sacramenti non habent*[4]. Thus by the word of God, by reason, and by the old fathers it is plain, that sinful men eat not the body of Christ, receive they the sacrament never so oft: which thing could not be, if in the sacrament there remained nothing but the body of Christ.

The sacrament in the scriptures is named *fractio panis*, "the breaking of bread;" which, to say the truth, were but a cold breaking, if there remained no bread to break, but certain fantasies of white and round. Yet whereas they, with words, crossings, blessings, breathings, leapings, and much ado, can scarcely make one god, they have such virtue in their fingers, that at one cross they be able to make twenty gods; for if they break the sacrament, every portion, yea, every mite, must needs be a god. After the apostles' time there arose up heretics[5], which said that Christ, walking here amongst men bodily upon the earth, had no very body, but a thing like a body, and so therewith dimmed men's sight. Against whom the old fathers used these arguments. Christ increased in growing, fasted, hungered, eat, wept, sweat, was weary, and in conclusion died, and had all other properties of a very body: wherefore he had a body. I will use the same kind of reasoning: It feedeth, it tasteth like bread, it looketh like bread, the

The sacrament called breaking of bread.

Against transubstantiation.

manducat et bibit. S. August. in Joan. Tract. xxvi. Tom. ix. col. 230. Basil. 1569.]

[3 Prosper. Sentent. ex operib. D. Aug. 341. Ed. Paris. 1671. p. 128.]

[4 Vide August. de Civit. Dei, Lib. xxi. c. 25. Tom. v. col. 1311. et in Joan. Tract. xxvi. Tom. ix. col. 227.]

[5 The Gnostics or Docetæ; so called from asserting that Christ lived and suffered only ἐν δοκήσει, 'in appearance,' and not in reality. The founder of this heresy was Simon Magus; and it was espoused in later times by Basilides, Valentinus, Marcion, Saturninus, Marcus, Cerdon, and the Manichees.]

little sely[1] mouse taketh it for bread, and (to be short) it hath all the properties and tokens of bread: ergo, it is bread. The old fathers, when there remained any part of the sacrament more than was spent at the communion, they used to burn it[2], and of it there came ashes. But there is nothing in the sacrament that can turn to ashes but only bread, (for I think they burned not Christ's body to ashes:) ergo, in the sacrament there remaineth bread. Henry the emperor, the sixth of that name, was poisoned in the host[3], and Victor the bishop of Rome in the chalice[4]. But poison cannot hang in God's body and blood: wherefore there remaineth bread and wine. What needeth many words in a matter so evident? If you demand either God's word, or the doctors and the ancient writers, or your reason, or your eyes, or nose, or tongue, or fingers, or the cat, or the ape, or the mouse, all these agree in one, and answer together, "There is bread." Wherefore, if you reject so many and so constant witnesses, and so well agreeing in their tale, specially being such as will lie for no man's pleasure, I will appeal from you, and take you as no indifferent judge. If all these witnesses suffice you not, I will call the sacrament itself to record. It crieth unto you, and plainly doth advertise you, what you should think of it. "I am," it saith, "grated

Reasons proving bread in the sacrament.

The sacrament giveth witness that it is bread.

[1 Sely: poor, simple, inoffensive.]

[2 Sed hoc quod reliquum est de carnibus et panibus in igne incendi præcepit. Quod nunc videmus etiam sensibiliter in ecclesia fieri, ignique tradi quæcunque remanere contigerit inconsumpta, non omnino ea quæ una die vel duabus aut multis servata sunt. Hesych. in Levit. Lib. II. p. 178. apud Albertin. Euchar. p. 851.]

[3 Henry VII. (not VI.) is said, by some authors, to have been poisoned by a Dominican, named Bernard Politian, in administering the Eucharist. The fact however has been disputed by others. See Modern Univ. Hist. Vol. XI. p. 28. The reader who wishes to examine the authorities for the fact, may consult the references in Albertinus de Eucharistia, p. 124. With regard to the denial of the fact, that writer observes: Bellarminus timide [ait], "Neque enim desunt, qui has historias falsas esse contendunt." Gardinerus audacissime, "Mendacium esse aut fabulam." Unde manifesto patet, quam vere dictum sit, "Desperationem audaces facere:" alioquin adversarii nunquam eo devenirent, ut rem, tot testimoniis suorum fultam et confirmatam, sublestæ fidei esse adeo inverecunde dicere sustinerent.]

[4 He (Victor III.) died on the 16th of September, A.D. 1088, not without suspicion of poison having been given him in the chalice, while he was celebrating mass. Modern Univ. Hist. Vol. IX. p. 573.]

with the tooth; I am conveyed into the belly; I perish; I can endure no space; I canker; I suffer green mould, blue mould, red mould; I breed worms; I am kept in a box for fear of bats. If you leave me out all night, I shall be devoured before morning; for if the mouse get me, I am gone. I am bread; I am no God: believe them not." This crieth the sacrament daily, and beareth witness itself.

Custom:—The devil on such-like reasons; and therefore I will never trouble my brains to make you answer: but if it be true that you have said, why is the sacrament so well of Christ himself, as of his apostles and the old fathers, called the body of Christ?

Verity:—Because it is no strange thing in scripture so to speak; as I have declared before. But will you stand to St Augustine's arbitrement in the matter?

Custom:—To no man sooner.

Verity:—St Augustine, in an epistle to his friend Boni- facius, giveth a good cause why the sacrament, although it be not the body of Christ, is notwithstanding called the body of Christ. His words be these: *Si sacramenta quandam simili-tudinem earum rerum quarum sacramenta sunt non haberent, omnino sacramenta non essent. Ex hac autem similitudine plerumque earum rerum nomina accipiunt. Ergo, secundum quendam modum, sacramentum corporis Christi corpus Christi est, sacramentum sanguinis Christi sanguis Christi est*[5]. " If sacraments had not a certain similitude of those things whereof they be sacraments, then were they no sacraments; of the which similitude many times they take their name. Wherefore, after a certain manner, the sacrament of the body of Christ is the body of Christ; and the sacrament of the blood of Christ is the blood of Christ," &c. And upon psalm xxxiii he writeth likewise: *Christus quodammodo se ferebat in manibus suis, cum diceret, Hoc est corpus meum*[6]. "Christ, after a certain manner and fashion, as it were, did bear himself

<small>The cause why the scripture calleth the sacrament the body of Christ. Augustinus ad Bonifacium, Epist. 23.</small>

<small>August. in Ps. xxxiii.</small>

[5 S. August. Ep. ad Bonifac. 23. Basil. 1569. Tom. II. col. 93.]

[6 Quomodo ferebatur in manibus suis? Quia, cum commendaret ipsum corpus suum et sanguinem suum, accepit in manus suas quod norunt fideles; et ipse se portabat quodammodo cum diceret, 'Hoc est corpus meum.' S. August. in Psalm. xxxiii, concio secunda. Tom. VIII. col. 234.]

in his own hands, when he said, This is my body." "In [a] manner," he saith, "and after a fashion;" not in very deed. Again, when faithful men receive the sacrament, they think not of the bread, nor mark the wine, but they look further, and behold the very body of Christ spread upon the cross, and his very blood poured down for their sakes. So in baptism men regard not greatly the water, but account themselves washed with the blood of Christ. So saith St Paul: "Whatsoever we be that are baptized, we are washed in the blood of Christ." Wherefore to the faithful receivers you may say, that the water of baptism is the blood of Christ, and the bread and wine the body and blood of Christ: for to them it is no less than if the natures were altered and changed. Which thing you may very well learn of Chrysostom, whose words are these: *Mysteria omnia interioribus oculis consideranda sunt, hoc est, spiritualiter. Interiores autem oculi, postquam panem vident, creaturas transvolant, neque de illo pane a pistore cocto cogitant, sed de eo qui se dixit panem esse æternæ vitæ.* "All mysteries must be considered with inward eyes, that is to say, spiritually. As [but] the inward eyes, when they see the bread, they pass over the creatures, neither do they think of that bread which is baked of the baker, but of him which called himself the bread of eternal life[1]." For these two causes the bread and wine are called the body and blood of Christ. Now I think you are satisfied concerning the meaning of these words, "This is my body."

Custom:—Yet one thing moveth me very much.

Verity:—What is that?

Custom:—The doctors and old writers, men inspired with the Holy Ghost, have evermore been against your doctrine; yea, and in these days the wisest men and best learned call you heretics, and your learning heresy.

Verity:—As touching the old writers, I remember well they speak reverently of the sacraments, like as every man ought to do; but whereas they deliver their mind with their right hand, you, Custom, receive it with the left. For whereas they say, that it is the body of Christ, and that it must be verily eaten, meaning that it doth effectually lay before the eyes Christ's body, and that it is to the faithful man no

[1 Vide note 1, p. 64.]

less than if it were Christ himself, and that Christ must be eaten in faith, not torn nor rent with the teeth; you say that, howsoever it be taken, it is Christ's body, and that there is none other eating but with the mouth.

And that the fathers meant no other thing than I have said, it shall appear by their words. But as touching the learned and wise men of these days, I cannot blame them if they call my doctrine heresy; for they would condemn all ancient writers of heresy, if they were now alive. But I will answer you to them anon. In the mean while mark you how well their learning agreeth. They say, "You must follow the letter; you must stick to the letter." But Origenes saith: *Si secundum literam sequaris id quod scriptum est, Nisi manducaveritis carnem Filii hominis, non erit vita in vobis, ea litera occidit*[2]. "If ye follow, after the letter, that which is written, Unless ye shall eat the flesh of the Son of man, there shall be no life in you; this letter killeth."

Augustine in the third book, "De Doctrina Christiana:" *Principio cavendum est [ne] figuratam dictionem secundum literam accipias. Ad hoc enim pertinet id quod ait apostolus, "Litera occidit." Cum enim figurate dictum sic accipitur tanquam proprie dictum sit, carnaliter sapitur; neque ulla animæ mors congruentius appellatur*[3]. "First, thou must beware that thou take not a figurative speech after the letter. For thereto pertaineth that the apostle saith, 'The letter killeth.' For when a thing is spiritually meant, and the same is taken literally as properly spoken, that is a carnal taking: neither can any other be called the killing of the soul, rather than that." And in the same book he teacheth a man to know the plain sense from a figure, saying thus: *Si præceptiva locutio est flagitium jubens, aut beneficentiam vetans, figurata est: Nisi manducaveritis carnem Filii hominis, et biberitis ejus sanguinem, non erit vita in vobis. Flagitium videtur jubere: ergo figura est præcipiens passioni Domini esse communicandum, et suaviter in memoria recondendum, quod pro nobis caro ejus crucifixa sit*[4]. "If the commanding speech be such as commandeth a thing

The doctors, how they call the sacrament the body of Christ, and why.

The words of the doctors against the pope's doctrine.
Orig. in Levit. Hom. xvii.

[John vi. 53.]

August. de Doctrina Christiana, lib. iii. cap. 5.
2 Cor. iii.

A rule to know a figurative speech from the literal.
Aug. de Doct. Christ. lib. iii. c. 16.

[2 Origen. sup. Levit. cap. x. Hom. vii. Basil. 1571. Tom. I. p. 141.]
[3 S. August. de Doctr. Christ. lib. iii. cap. 5. Tom. III. col. 48. Basil. 1569.]
[4 Ibid. c. 16. Tom. III. col. 53.]

wicked and horrible to be done, or a charitable thing to be undone, then this is a figurative speech: 'Unless ye shall eat the flesh of the Son of man, and shall drink his blood, there shall be no life in you.' Because in this speech he seemeth to command a wicked thing, it is therefore a figurative speech, commanding that we should communicate with the passion of our Lord, and sweetly to retain it in our remembrance."

In like manner Chrysostom plucketh you from the plain

Chrysost. in Joan. Hom. 47.

letter and the bare words by this saying: *Caro non prodest; hoc est, secundum spiritum verba mea intelligenda sunt; quia qui secundum carnem audit, nihil lucratur. Quid est autem carnaliter intelligere? Simpliciter, ut res dicuntur, neque aliud quippiam cogitare. Non enim ita judicanda sunt quæ videntur; sed mysteria omnia interioribus oculis videnda sunt, hoc est, spiritualiter*[1]. "'The flesh profiteth not;' that is to say, My words must be taken and expounded after the Spirit: for he that heareth after the flesh, gaineth nothing. Now what is it to understand carnally? To take things simply as they be spoken, and not to consider any meaning further therein. For things must not be judged as they are seen; but all mysteries must be seen with inward eyes, that is to say, spiritually."

What is so heinous in these days, as to call the sacrament the token or the remembrance of Christ's body? Yet did the old writers in manner never call it other. Tertul-

Tertullianus contra Marcion. lib. iv.

lian in the fourth book against the Marcionists: *Christus accepit panem, et corpus suum illum fecit, 'Hoc est corpus meum'*

[[1] Τὸ πνεῦμά ἐστι τὸ ζωοποιοῦν· ἡ σὰρξ οὐκ ὠφελεῖ οὐδέν. Ὃ δὲ λέγει τοιοῦτόν ἐστι· πνευματικῶς δεῖ τὰ περὶ ἐμοῦ ἀκούειν· ὁ γὰρ σαρκικῶς ἀκούσας οὐδὲν ἀπώνατο, οὔτε χρηστόν τι ἀπέλαυσε. Σαρκικὸν δὲ ἦν τὸ ἀμφισβητεῖν πῶς ἐκ τοῦ οὐρανοῦ καταβέβηκε, καὶ τὸ νομίζειν ὅτι υἱός ἐστι τοῦ Ἰωσὴφ, καὶ τὸ, πῶς δύναται ἡμῖν τὴν σάρκα δοῦναι φαγεῖν; ταῦτα πάντα σαρκικά. ἅπερ ἔδει μυστικῶς νοεῖν καὶ πνευματικῶς. S. Chrysost. Hom. in Joan. cap. vi. Hom. μζ. Ed. Eton. 1612. Tom. II. p. 750.

Τί δέ ἐστι τὸ σαρκικῶς νοῆσαι; Τὸ ἁπλῶς εἰς τὰ προκείμενα ὁρᾷν, καὶ μὴ πλέον τι φαντάζεσθαι· τοῦτο γὰρ ἐστὶ σαρκικῶς. Χρὴ δὲ μὴ οὕτω κρίνειν τοῖς ὁρωμένοις, ἀλλὰ πάντα τὰ μυστήρια τοῖς ἔνδον ὀφθαλμοῖς κατοπτεύειν· τοῦτο γὰρ ἐστὶ πνευματικῶς. Ibid.]

dicendo, id est, figura corporis mei[2]. "Christ took bread and made it his body, saying, 'This is my body,' that is to say, a figure of my body." Ambrose, upon the eleventh to the Corinthians: *Quia morte Domini liberati sumus, hujus rei memores, in edendo et potando carnem et sanguinem, quæ pro nobis oblata sunt, significamus*[3]. "Because we are delivered by the Lord's death, in the remembrance of the same by eating and drinking we signify the body and blood which were offered up for us." Chrysostom, in the eighty-third Homily upon the gospel of Matthew: *Quando dicunt, Unde patet Christum immolatum fuisse? hæc adferentes eorum ora consuimus. Si enim mortuus Christus non est, cujus symbolum ac signum hoc sacrificium est*[4]? "When they object unto us, and ask, How know you that Christ was offered up? then, alleging these things, we stop their mouths. For if Christ died not, then whose sign or token is this sacrifice?" Augustine to Adimantus: *Non dubitavit Christus dicere, Hoc est corpus meum, cum daret signum corporis sui*[5]. "Christ doubted not to say, This is my body, when he gave but a sign of his body." Augustine upon the third psalm: *Christus adhibuit Judam ad convivium, in quo corporis et sanguinis sui figuram discipulis suis commendavit et tradidit*[6]. "Christ received Judas to the supper, in which he commended and delivered a figure of his body and blood unto his disciples." Rabanus: *Quia panis corpus confirmat, ideo ille corpus Christi congruenter nuncupatur. Vinum autem, quia sanguinem operatur in carne, ideo ad sanguinem Christi refertur*[7]. "Because the bread strengtheneth the body, therefore it is aptly called

margin notes: S. Ambros. in 1 Cor. xi. — Chrysost. in Matth. Hom. 83. [82.] — August. ad Adimantum. — Rabanus de Institut. Clericorum.

[2 Tertull. advers. Marcion. lib. iv. c. 40. p. 571. Paris. 1641.]

[3 S. Ambros. Oper. Tom. v. p. 275. Basil. 1567.]

[4 Ὅταν γὰρ λέγωσι, Πόθεν δῆλον ὅτι ἐτύθη ὁ Χριστός; μετὰ τῶν ἄλλων καὶ ἀπὸ τῶν μυστηρίων αὐτοὺς ἐπιστομίζομεν. Εἰ γὰρ μὴ ἀπέθανεν ὁ Ἰησοῦς, τίνος σύμβολα τὰ τελούμενα; Chrysost. in Matth. cap. xxvi. 28. Hom. πβ. Eton. 1612. Tom. II. p. 510.]

[5 S. August. contra Adimant. c. 12. Basil. 1569. Tom. VI. col. 187.]

[6 S. August. in Psal. iii. ad initium. Tom. VIII. col. 16.]

[7 Rabanus Maurus, de Institutione Clericorum, lib. i. cap. 31. in Bibliotheca Patr. Paris. 1654. Tom. x. col. 581.

Rabanus Maurus was Abbot of Fulda, of the order of St Benedict, and afterwards Archbishop of Mentz. He flourished in the early part of the 9th century.]

Christ's body. And likewise the wine, because it increaseth blood in the flesh, it doth resemble the blood of Christ." Druthmarus Monachus in Matthæum: *Vinum lætificat et sanguinem auget, et ideo non inconvenienter per hoc sanguis Christi figuratur*[1]. "Wine maketh glad the heart, and increaseth blood; and therefore the blood of Christ is not unaptly signified thereby." Irenæus witnesseth plainly, that in the sacrament remaineth bread and wine, by these words: *Quemadmodum terrenus panis, percipiens vocationem Dei, jam non communis panis est, sed eucharistia, ex duabus rebus constans, terrena et cœlesti*[2]. "As the earthly bread, receiving the vocation of God, is now no common bread, but the eucharist, consisting of two things, the one earthly and the other heavenly." Here he recordeth, that there remaineth in the sacrament an earthly nature, which is either bread, or nothing. Gelasius, writing against Nestorius, avoweth the same, saying: *In eucharistia non esse desinit substantia panis, et natura vini. Etenim imago et similitudo corporis et sanguinis Domini in actione mysteriorum celebratur*[3]. "In the eucharist the substance of the bread and nature of the wine cease not to be. For the image and similitude of the body and blood of the Lord is celebrated in the action of the mysteries." Chrysostom, in his twentieth homily upon the second epistle to the Corinthians, preferreth a poor man before the sacrament, and calleth him the body of Christ, rather than the other. Whereof I may gather this reason:

Marginal notes: Druthmarus in Matth. — Irenæus contra Valentin. lib. iv. — Gelasius. — Chrysost. Hom. xx. in Epist. 2. ad Corinth.

[1] Druthmari Monachi, Expos. in Matth. in Biblioth. Patr. Paris. 1654. Tom. xvi. p. 361.

Christianus Druthmarus, called Grammaticus, was a monk of Corbey, and flourished about the middle of the ninth century.]

[2] Ὡς γὰρ ἀπὸ γῆς ἄρτος, προσλαμβανόμενος τὴν ἔκκλησιν τοῦ Θεοῦ, οὐκέτι κοινὸς ἄρτος ἐστὶν, ἀλλ' εὐχαριστία, ἐκ δύο πραγμάτων συνεστηκυῖα, ἐπιγείου τε καὶ οὐρανίου· οὕτως καὶ τὰ σώματα ἡμῶν μεταλαμβάνοντα τῆς εὐχαριστίας, μηκέτι εἶναι φθαρτὰ, τὴν ἐλπίδα τῆς εἰς αἰῶνας ἀναστάσεως ἔχοντα. Irenæus advers. Hæres. Lib. iv. c. 34. Oxon. 1702. p. 327.]

[3] Certe sacramenta quæ sumimus corporis et sanguinis Domini divina res est, propter quod et per eadem divinæ efficimur consortes naturæ; et tamen esse non desinit, etc. Gelasius de duabus natur. advers. Eutych. et Nestor. in Biblioth. Patr. Tom. iv. par. 1. col. 422. Paris. 1654.]

Bo- The poor man is not the natural and real body of Christ:
car- Every poor member of Christ is the body of Christ, rather than the sacrament:
do. Ergo, the sacrament is not the natural and real body of Christ.

His words are: *Hoc altare veneraris, quoniam in eo proponitur corpus Christi; eum autem, qui re ipsa corpus est Christi, afficis contumelia, et negligis pereuntem*[4]. "This altar thou dost reverence, because the body of Christ therein is set before thee: but him that is the body of Christ indeed, thou dost spitefully entreat, and dost neglect him ready to perish." Chrysostom in the eleventh homily upon Matthew: *Quod si hæc vasa sanctificata ad privatos usus est transferre periculosum, in quibus non verum corpus Christi, sed mysterium corporis Christi continetur, quanto magis vasa corporis nostri?*[5] "If it be so perilous a matter to translate these sanctified vessels unto private uses, in the which not the true body of Christ, but a mystery of the body of Christ is contained, how much more then these vessels of our body?" Athanasius upon these words, "Whosoever shall speak a word against the Son of man," saith: *Ea quæ Christus dicit non sunt carnalia, sed spiritualia. Quod enim comedentibus suffecisset corpus, ut totius mundi fieret alimonia? Sed idcirco meminit ascensionis Filii hominis in cœlum, ut eos a corporali cogitatione avelleret*[6]. "The words that Christ here speaketh,

Chrysost. Hom. xi. super Matt.

Athanas. in verba Evang. "Qui dixerit verbum in Filium hominis." [Luke xii. 10.]

[4] Σὺ δὲ τὸ μὲν θυσιαστήριον τοῦτο τιμᾷς, ὅτι δέχεται τοῦ Χριστοῦ σῶμα· τὸν δὲ αὐτὸ τὸ σῶμα τοῦ Χριστοῦ ὄντα καθυβρίζεις, καὶ περιορᾷς ἀπολλύμενον. S. Chrysost. Hom. xx. in Epist. sec. ad Corin. ad fin. Eton. 1612. Tom. III. p. 656.]

[5] S. Chrysost. Opus Imperf. in Matth. Hom. xi. Ed. Paris. 1724. Tom. VI. ad finem. p. 63.]

[6] Ἐνταῦθα γὰρ ἀμφότερα περὶ αὑτοῦ εἴρηκε, σάρκα καὶ πνεῦμα· καὶ τὸ πνεῦμα πρὸς τὸ κατὰ σάρκα διέστειλεν, ἵνα μὴ μόνον τὸ φαινόμενον, ἀλλὰ καὶ τὸ ἀόρατον αὐτοῦ πιστεύσαντες μάθωσιν, ὅτι καὶ ἃ λέγει οὐκ ἔστι σαρκικὰ, ἀλλὰ πνευματικά. Πόσοις γὰρ ἤρκει τὸ σῶμα πρὸς βρῶσιν, ἵνα καὶ τοῦ κόσμου παντὸς τοῦτο τροφὴ γενήται; Ἀλλὰ διὰ τοῦτο τῆς εἰς οὐρανοὺς ἀναβάσεως ἐμνημόνευσε τοῦ υἱοῦ τοῦ ἀνθρώπου, ἵνα τῆς σωματικῆς ἐννοίας αὐτοὺς ἀφελκύσῃ, καὶ λοιπὸν τὴν εἰρημένην σάρκα βρῶσιν ἄνωθεν οὐράνιον, καὶ πνευ-

be not carnal, but spiritual. For what body might have sufficed for all that should eat, to be a nourishment of the whole world? But therefore he maketh mention of the ascension of the Son of man into heaven, to the intent to pluck them away from that corporal cogitation." Augustine to Marcellinus: *In illis carnalibus victimis figuratio fuit carnis Christi, quam pro peccatis nostris erat oblaturus, et sanguinis quem erat effusurus: in isto autem sacrificio gratiarum actio atque commemoratio est carnis Christi quam pro nobis obtulit, et sanguinis quem pro nobis effudit. In illo ergo sacrificio quid nobis sit donandum figurate significatur; in hoc autem sacrificio quid nobis donatum sit evidenter ostenditur. In illis sacrificiis prænunciabatur Filius Dei occidendus: in hoc pro impiis annunciatur occisus*[1]. "In those carnal oblations the flesh of Christ was figured which he should offer for our sins, and the blood which he should bestow for us; but in this sacrifice is the giving of thanks and memorial of the flesh of Christ which he hath offered for us, and of the blood which he hath shed for us. In that sacrifice, therefore, is signified figuratively what should be given for us; in this sacrifice what is given to us is evidently declared. In those sacrifices the Son of God was before preached to be slain; in this sacrifice he is shewed to be slain already for the wicked." Origenes, upon Matthew, expounding these words, "This is my body," saith: *Panis iste, quem Christus corpus suum fatetur esse, verbum est nutritorium animarum*[2]. "The bread, which Christ confesseth to be his body, is a nutritive word of our souls." Augustinus: *Nulli aliquatenus dubitandum, unumquemque fidelium corporis et sanguinis Domini tunc esse participem, quando in baptismate membrum efficitur Christi.*

ματικὴν τροφὴν παρ' αὐτοῦ διδομένην μάθωσιν. S. Athanas. in verba Evangelii, "Quicunque dixerit, &c." Op. Paris. 1627. Tom. I. p. 979.]

[1 The passage in the text is not from Augustine, but from a work of Fulgentius: In illis enim carnalibus victimis figuratio fuit carnis Christi quam pro peccatis nostris ipse sine peccato fuerat oblaturus, et sanguinis quem erat effusurus in remissionem peccatorum nostrorum; in isto autem sacrificio gratiarum actio atque commemoratio est carnis Christi quam pro nobis obtulit, et sanguinis quem pro nobis idem Deus effudit, etc. Fulgentius, Liber ad Petrum de fide, cap. 19. Ed. Raynaudi. Paris. 1671. pp. 494, 495.]

[2 Origen, in Matth. cap. xxvi. tract. 35. Basil. 1571. Tom. II. p. 176.]

Sacramenti quippe illius participatione ac beneficio non privabitur, quando in se hoc invenit quod sacramentum significat.
"No man ought in any wise to doubt but that every faithful man is then partaker of the body and blood of the Lord, when in baptism he is made a member of Christ. For he shall not be deprived of the participation and benefit of that sacrament, when he findeth in himself that thing which the sacrament doth signify." Ambrosius: *Tanta est vis verbi, ut panis et vinum maneant quæ sunt, et mutentur in aliud*[3]. "Such is the force and strength of the word, that the bread and wine remain the same as they were, and yet are changed into another thing." For it is not any longer common bread, but it is turned into a sacrament; yet notwithstanding there remaineth bread and wine. Tertullian writing against an heretic named Marcion, which taught that the creatures of God, as flesh, bread, and wine, and such like, were naught and uncleanly: *Non abjecit Deus creaturam suam, sed ea repræsentavit corpus suum*[4]. "God hath not cast away his creature, but by it he hath represented his body." Origenes upon Leviticus, speaking of the drinking of Christ's blood, saith: *Non sanguinem carnis expetimus, sed sanguinem verbi*[5]. "We do not desire the blood of the flesh, but the blood of the word." Ambrose called the sacrament, *typum corporis Christi*, and Basilius *antitypum*; which is as much as to say, as a token, a figure, a remembrance, and example of Christ's body. Origenes upon Matthew xv.: *In isto pane quod est materiale ejicitur in secessum; id autem quod fit per verbum*

<small>Ambrosius.</small>

<small>Tertullianus contra Marcion.</small>

<small>Origenes in Levit.</small>

<small>Origen. super Matth. cap. 15.</small>

[3 Si ergo tanta vis est in sermone Domini Jesu, ut inciperent esse quæ non erant, quanto magis operatorius est, ut sint quæ erant, et in aliud commutentur! S. Ambros. de Sacramentis, lib. iv. cap. 4. Basil. 1567. Tom. iv. p. 439. It should be observed that the genuineness of this treatise has been strongly disputed. See Albertinus de Euch. pp. 507, 508.]

[4 Sed ille quidem usque nunc nec aquam reprobavit Creatoris quâ suos abluit, nec oleum quo suos unguit, nec mellis et lactis societatem qua suos infantat, nec panem quo ipsum corpus suum repræsentat. Tertull. contra Marcion, Lib. i. c. 14. Paris. 1641. pp. 439, 440.]

[5 Sed tu qui ad Christum venisti, Pontificem verum, qui sanguine suo Deum tibi propitium fecit, et reconciliavit te Patri, non hæreas in sanguine carnis, sed disce potius sanguinem verbi. Origen. in Levit. xvi. Hom. 9. Basil. 1571. Tom. i. p. 157.]

Dei pro fidei ratione prodest[1]. "In this bread that thing which is material passeth through man's body: but that which is made by the word of God by means of faith doth profit." And lest perhaps you think that he spake those words of our common table-bread, he concludeth the matter himself with these words: *Hæc diximus de pane symbolico.* "These things we have spoken of the mystical bread." Augustinus declareth, that it must needs be a figure and a re-

<small>Augustinus, contra adversarium Legis et Prophetarum.</small>

membrance of the body of Christ: *Ista secundum sanæ fidei regulam figurate intelliguntur. Nam alioqui horribilius videtur esse humanam carnem vorare quam perimere, et humanum sanguinem potare quam fundere*[2]. "These things are understanded figuratively, according to the rule of sound and true faith. For otherwise it seemeth to be more horrible to eat man's flesh, than to kill a man; and more horrible to drink man's blood, than to shed it."

<small>August. in Ps. xcviii.</small>

And therefore he saith upon psalm xcviii.: *Non hoc corpus quod videtis estis manducaturi, nec bibituri sanguinem quem fundent qui me crucifigent. Sacramentum aliquod vobis trado*[3]. "Ye shall not eat this body which you see, and drink that blood which they shall shed that shall crucify me. I com-

[1 Πᾶν τὸ εἰσπορευόμενον εἰς τὸ στόμα εἰς κοιλίαν χωρεῖ, καὶ εἰς ἀφεδρῶνα ἐκβάλλεται· καὶ τὸ ἁγιαζόμενον βρῶμα διὰ λόγου Θεοῦ καὶ ἐντεύξεως, κατ' αὐτὸ μὲν τὸ ὑλικὸν, εἰς τὴν κοιλίαν χωρεῖ καὶ εἰς ἀφεδρῶνα ἐκβάλλεται· κατὰ δὲ τὴν ἐπιγινομένην αὐτῷ εὐχὴν, κατὰ τὴν ἀναλογίαν τῆς πίστεως ὠφέλιμον γίνεται, καὶ τῆς τοῦ νοῦ αἴτιον διαβλέψεως, ὁρῶντος ἐπὶ τὸ ὠφελοῦν· καὶ οὐχ ἡ ὕλη τοῦ ἄρτου, ἀλλ' ὁ ἐπ' αὐτῷ εἰρημένος λόγος ἐστὶν ὁ ὠφελῶν τὸν μὴ ἀναξίως τοῦ Κυρίου ἐσθίοντα αὐτόν. Καὶ ταῦτα μὲν περὶ τοῦ τυπικοῦ καὶ συμβολικοῦ σώματος. Orig. in Matth. cap. xv. Ed. Rothomag. 1668. Huetii. Tom. I. p. 254. The passage in the text is cited from the Latin. Basil. 1571. Tom. II. p. 27.]

[2 Hominem Christum Jesum, carnem suam nobis manducandam bibendumque sanguinem dantem, fideli corde atque ore suscipimus; quamvis horribilius videatur humanam carnem manducare quam perimere, et humanum sanguinem potare quam fundere. Atque in omnibus sanctis scripturis, secundum sanæ fidei regulam figurate dictum vel factum si quid exponitur, de quibuslibet rebus et verbis quæ sacris paginis continentur expositio illa ducatur, non aspernanter sed sapienter audiamus. S. August. contra advers. legis et proph. Lib. ii. c. 9. Basil. 1569. Tom. VI. col. 634, 635.]

[3 Vide supra, page 44, note 2.]

mend unto you a sacrament." Tertullian: *Aliud a pane* Tertullianus. *corpus Jesus habet; nec pro nobis panis traditus, sed ipsum Christi verum corpus traditum est in crucem, quod panis figura in cœna exhibitum est*[4]. "Jesus hath another body than bread; for bread was not given for us, but the very true body of Christ was given upon the cross; which body was exhibited in the supper under the figure of bread." This recordeth Theodoret, an ancient writer, and avoweth that Theodoretus. there is no turning or altering of the bread in the sacrament. His words are these: *Symbola visibilia corporis et sanguinis sui appellatione honoravit, non mutans naturam, sed naturæ addens gratiam*[5]. "He hath honoured and dignified the visible signs with the name of his body and of his blood, not changing the nature, but adding grace to nature." And in another place, where he maketh a true christian man to reason with an heretic, he giveth to the heretic this part, to hold with the turning of bread and wine into the natural body and blood of Christ. The heretic's words are these: *Sacramenta Dominici corporis et sanguinis alia sunt ante sacram invocationem; post invocationem vero mutantur, et alia fiunt.* "The sacraments of the Lord's body and blood before the holy invocation are one thing; but after invocation they are changed and made another." This maketh Theodoret to be the heretic's part. Then bringeth he forth the true christian man, which reproveth the heretic for so saying: *Incidisti in laqueos quos ipse struxeras: neque enim sancta illa symbola post consecrationem discedunt a natura sua: manent enim in priori et substantia et figura; etenim et oculis videri et digitis palpari, ut ante, possunt*[6]. "Thou art fallen

[4 Tertull. adv. Marcion. Lib. iv. cap. 40. Paris. 1641. p. 571.]

[5 Ὁ γὰρ δὴ τὸ φύσει σῶμα σῖτον καὶ ἄρτον προσαγορεύσας, καὶ αὖ πάλιν ἑαυτὸν ἄμπελον ὀνομάσας, οὗτος τὰ ὁρώμενα σύμβολα τῇ τοῦ σώματος καὶ αἵματος προσηγορίᾳ τετίμηκεν, οὐ τὴν φύσιν μεταβαλών, ἀλλὰ τὴν χάριν τῇ φύσει προστεθεικώς. Theodoreti, Dial. i. Paris. 1642. Tom. iv. p. 18.]

[6 ΕΡΑΝΙΣΤΗΣ. Ὥσπερ τοίνυν τὰ σύμβολα τοῦ δεσποτικοῦ σώματός τε καὶ αἵματος ἄλλα μέν εἰσι πρὸ τῆς ἱερατικῆς ἐπικλήσεως, μετὰ δέ γε τὴν ἐπίκλησιν μεταβάλλεται, καὶ ἕτερα γίνεται· οὕτω τὸ δεσποτικὸν σῶμα μετὰ τὴν ἀνάληψιν εἰς τὴν οὐσίαν μετεβλήθη τὴν θείαν.

into the snares which thou thyself hast laid. For those self-same holy signs, after the consecration, do not go from their nature; for they abide still both in their former substance and figure, and may be both with eyes seen, and felt with hands, as before." To the same agreeth well Chrysostom, saying: *Postquam sanctificatur panis, non amplius appellatur panis, tametsi maneat natura panis*[1]. "After the bread is sanctified, it is called bread no more, although the nature of bread still remain." Hereby you may understand, how and in what sort the old fathers, how the primitive and beginning church, how the apostles, how Christ himself, took these words, "This is my body."

Chrysostomus.

Now, to withstand and stoutly to go against, not only ancient writers, or the congregation of christian people, which at that time was not overgrown, no, neither spotted with covetousness and worldly honour, but the apostles also, and God himself, no doubt it is great fondness. But what speak I of the old fathers? It is not long since the sacrament grew out of his right understanding. For this word *transubstantiatio*, whereby they signify turning of the bread into the body of Christ, was never neither spoken, neither heard, neither thought of among the ancient fathers or in the old church.

Transubstantiation a new invention.

ΟΡΘΟΔΟΞΟΣ. Ἑάλως αἷς ὕφηνες ἄρκυσιν· οὐδὲ γὰρ μετὰ τὸν ἁγιασμὸν τὰ μυστικὰ σύμβολα τῆς οἰκείας ἐξίσταται φύσεως· μένει γὰρ ἐπὶ τῆς προτέρας οὐσίας καὶ τοῦ σχήματος καὶ τοῦ εἴδους, καὶ ὁρατά ἐστι καὶ ἁπτά, οἷα καὶ πρότερον ἦν. Theodoreti, Dial. II. Paris. 1642. Tom. IV. p. 85.]

[[1] Sicut enim, antequam sanctificetur panis, panem nominamus, divina autem illum sanctificante gratia, mediante sacerdote, liberatus est quidem appellatione panis, dignus autem habitus est Dominici corporis appellatione, etiamsi natura panis in eo permansit. S. Chrysost. ad Cæsarium Monachum*. Paris. 1717. Tom. III. 744.]

* "When this passage was first produced by Peter Martyr, it was looked upon as so unanswerable, that they of the Romish Church had no other way to avoid the force of it but to cry out it was a forgery. Peter Martyr left it in the Lambeth Library, but it was ravished thence in the reign of Queen Mary. Bigotius, a learned French Papist, published the original, but the whole edition was suppressed. Yet Le Moyne published it again in Latin among his *Varia Sacra:* and a learned prelate, who now so deservedly holds the primacy in our own church, and whose indefatigable industry against popery will never be forgotten, having procured the sheets, which the Sorbon doctors caused to be suppressed in Bigotius' edition of Palladius, published it in our own tongue with such of the Greek fragments as are now remaining, &c." Bingham, Origines Eccl. Lib. xv. cap. 5, sect. 4. The Benedictine editors, apparently upon insufficient grounds, have not received the epistle as a genuine work of St Chrysostom.

But about five hundred years past, pope Nicholas II., in a council holden at Lateranum in Rome[2], confirmed that opinion of the changing of bread, and would have made an article of the faith, and placed it in the "Credo." After which time ensued Corpus Christi day, masses of Corpus Christi[3], reservation of the sacrament with honour, with canopies, with censing, with kneeling, with worshipping and adoration, and with so much as any man could devise. For they thought they could not do too much to him, after that the bishop of Rome had allowed him for a God.

But not fully two hundred year before that time, when this doctrine first began to bud (and yet notwithstanding had not so prevailed, but that a great number of learned and good men could know the sacrament to be a sacrament, and not [Christ] himself), Charles the great, king of France and emperor of Rome, demanded of a great learned man, whose name was Bertramus, what he thought by that strange kind of calling down Christ from heaven, and turning a little gobbet of bread into his natural body. To whom Bertramus made answer in this wise: *Dicimus quod multa differentia separantur corpus in quo passus est Christus et sanguis quem in cruce pendens fudit, et hoc corpus quod in mysterio passionis Christi quotidie a fidelibus celebratur......Etenim hoc corpus pignus et species est, illud autem ipsa veritas......Apparet ergo quod tam multa differentia separentur, quantum est inter pignus et eam rem pro qua pignus traditur, et quantum inter imaginem et rem eam cujus imago est, et quantum inter speciem et veritatem*[4]. "This we say, That there is a great difference

_{Carolus Magnus.}

_{Bertramus.}

[2 A.D. 1059. At this, the second council of Lateran, the opinions of Berengarius were condemned, and he himself signed a recantation. Vid. Baronius, Annal. Tom. XI. p. 257. Antw. 1608. Also, Concilia, Tom. IX. col. 1011. Paris. 1671.]

[3 Transubstantiation was made an article of faith at the fourth Lateran council, held A.D. 1215, under Innocent III. See Art. I. De fide catholica. Concilia, tom XI. col. 143.

The festival of Corpus Christi was instituted A.D. 1264, by Urban IV. See Concilia, tom. XI. col. 817—820.]

[4 The Book of Bertramus or Ratramnus was written at the request of Charles the Bald, not of Charlemagne. The passages referred to are the following: Hujus doctissimi viri [S^{ti} Ambrosii] auctoritate perdocemur, quod multa differentia separantur corpus in quo passus est Christus, et sanguis quem pendens in cruce de latere suo profudit, et

and separation betwixt the body in the which Christ suffered, and the blood which he shed upon the cross, and this body which every day is celebrated in the mystery of the passion of Christ. For this body is a pledge and a similitude, but the other is the very truth itself. Ergo, it appeareth that these two are separated asunder by no less difference than is between a pledge, and the thing whereof the pledge is given; or than is between an image of a thing, and the thing itself whereof the image is; or than is between the form of a thing, and the verity itself." This wrote Bertramus, Druthmarus, and many others; and yet were never in all their time once reproved of heresy. This wrote Johannes Scotus also, in whose lifetime men had not eyes to espy his heresies: but about two hundred years after his death he was judged and condemned for an heretic, and his books burned, in a council holden at Vercelli in Lombardy, in the year of our Lord God 1050[1]. Since which time even until this day, although idolatry had great increase, yet there never wanted some good men, which boldly would profess and set forth the truth; although they were well assured that their worldly reward should be spite, malice, imprisoning, sword, fire, and all kinds of torments.

Thus, so shortly and in so few words as I could, I have declared to you what Christ meant by these words, " This is my body;" what the apostles thought therein, and in what sort they delivered them to their successors; in what sense and meaning the holy fathers and old writers, and the universal and catholic church, hath evermore taken them.

Bertramus, Druthmarus. Joan Scotus condemned for a heretic 200 years after his death.

hoc corpus quod in mysterio passionis Christi quotidie a fidelibus celebratur. p. 46. * * * * Et hoc corpus pignus est et species; illud vero ipsa veritas. p. 58. * * * * Apparet itaque quod multa inter se differentia separantur, quantum est inter pignus et eam rem pro qua pignus traditur, et quantum inter imaginem et rem cujus est imago, et quantum inter speciem et veritatem. p. 58. Bertram. de corp. et sang. Christi. Genev. 1541.]

[1 Vid. Baronius, Annal. xi. p. 182. Antw. 1608; and Concilia, Tom. ix. col. 1055. Paris. 1671.]

OCCASIONAL SERVICES

FOR

THE PLAGUE.

A.D. 1563.

A Fourme

to be vsed in Common prayer twyse aweke, and also an order of publique fast, to be vsed euery Wednesday in the weeke, duryng this time of mortalitie, and other afflictions, wherwith the Realme at this present is visited.

Set forth by the Quenes Maiesties speciall commaundement, expressed in her letters hereafter folowyng in the next page.
xxx Julii 1563.

HISTORICAL NOTICE.

[From Strype's Life of Grindal, pp. 104—107.]

The English nation, being in war with France, had, by means of the French Protestants, gotten into their hands New-Haven, an important seaport town in France, lying near Boulogne; which place might have been to England instead of Calais, lost in the last reign. And the English were resolved to maintain it against all the strength of France. But it pleased God that the plague got in among the English army there, and prevailed very much, to the great weakening of the queen's forces; so that she was fain to make terms with France, and to surrender the place. Her soldiers being transported hither, brought the plague into England; first spreading itself in Kent, where they landed, and proceeded as far as the metropolitical city, where it raged this year, and in other places of the realm. These unsuccesses were justly looked upon to proceed from the punishing hand of heaven; and therefore, as the archbishop for the city of Canterbury, so our bishop for London, framed certain suitable prayers to be used on certain days of the week, besides Sundays and festivals. The bishop of London sent his precept to his archdeacon, that the people of every parish should be exhorted not only to meet on those days, religiously to pray, and implore God's compassion and pardon; but also at home in their own houses with their families to use fasting and abstinence[1]. And this he ordered prudentially as well as piously; that so in those resorts to the parochial churches the assemblies might not be crowded, nor too numerous; which might occasion the contagion to spread the more. But this was prevented by the frequency of these assemblies, and the liberty and

[1 For several letters relating to these forms of Prayer and Thanksgiving, see "Letters," infra, date 1563.]

counsel of serving God at home as well as in public. And for the making this the more known to all, the bishop wrote to his archdeacon Molins in this tenor:

<small>Grind. Regist. Lond. fol. 35.</small>

"*Salutem in Christo.* Forasmuch as it hath pleased God to visit divers parts of the city of London with the sickness of the plague; considering the frequent and great assemblies of people for public prayer and preaching, (which in common calamities and afflictions have been most commendably used) in this contagious time might be occasion to spread the infection of the disease: these are therefore to require you to give order to all pastors, curates, and ministers within the city and suburbs of London, being under your jurisdiction, that they on Sunday next earnestly exhort their parochians diligently to frequent the common prayer in their several parish churches, during this time of God's visitation; and that not only on Sundays and holidays, but also on Wednesdays and Fridays: and further to exhort them in their private houses and families to use private prayer, fasting and abstinence, with other the fruits of faith and true repentance; most earnestly praying to Almighty God, that it may please him to remember us in his mercy, and to turn away from us, if it be his blessed will, this his plague and punishment, most justly poured upon us for our sins and unthankfulness. I commend you to God. From Fulham the 22nd day of July, 1563.

Yours in Christ,

EDM. LONDON."

To Mr Mullins, archdeacon
of London, give these.

A Form of Notification to be given to the Curates of London.

<small>The archdeacon's notification.</small>

"For avoiding peril of infection, which might grow, if in this time great assemblies of people should be made at

Christ's church for general prayer, as hath been accustomed in time of unseasonable weather, &c. and yet for the exciting of people to repentance and godly prayer in this time of God's visitation; it is ordered by the bishop of London, that all curates, &c. shall on Sunday next monish and exhort their parochians diligently to frequent common prayer in their parish churches on all Sundays and holidays, and also on Wednesdays and Fridays; and beside, to be diligent in private prayer in their private houses, joined with fasting and abstinence; praying most instantly to Almighty God for the ceasing of this infection: which God grant, if it be his holy will. Amen."

In this very juncture came a letter from Sir Will. Cecil, the secretary, to our bishop, for this very thing, viz. to consult concerning a fast for the judgment of the plague then lying upon the nation: to whom he answered, that it was in his thoughts to provide some common prayer for that occasion, before his letter came; and that he had sent to the dean of Paul's, [Alexander Nowel,] to compose an homily meet for the time; which the said dean had accordingly done: yet the bishop signified, that he meant it but for his own cure. But upon the secretary's letter, wherein he admonishes him to get a form of prayer to be used throughout England, he proceeded further by the help of Mr Dean, and soon sent the secretary a copy of what he had done, desiring, after he had perused it, to convey it to the archbishop then at Canterbury; and so to return it after his review to the print. Then he propounded these things to be considered by the secretary: 1. In what form the fast was to be authorised, whether by proclamation, or by way of injunction, or otherwise; because it must needs pass from the queen. 2. Whether any penalty is to be prescribed to the violators thereof, or no. 3. Whether to have it general throughout the realm, or but in this province. 4. To add, diminish, or amend the form and circumstances of the fast, as they are there devised.

He signified moreover to the said secretary, that because it was not safe for great assemblies now to meet, lest it might spread the infection, therefore he had ordered the fast to be on certain days of the week, when the parishioners should assemble in their respective parishes: and that he had sent orders to London to the ministers, to exhort their people to come diligently to their parish churches on these days; and also for private prayer and abstinence. Some, he found, were offended, that he had not appointed general assemblies, as were used, it seems, in the late time of unseasonable weather; which he thought not meet, for fear of spreading the infection: and therefore he put it to the secretary, in the drawing up the queen's order for the fast, that an admonition should be annexed, that in towns and places infected general concourses be forborne; and moderate assemblies, as of those that be of one parish, to meet at their parish churches, to be more commendable. And whereas by this fasting, which was to be enjoined on the appointed prayer-days, viz. Mondays and Wednesdays, there would be considerable quantities of provision spared, he advised that a good portion thereof should be weekly bestowed in the back lanes and alleys of London, and among the poor strangers, who were the sorest visited.

The form being finished, and some suitable sentences of scripture, or a psalm, added by the secretary's advice, and passed the review of the archbishop, it was soon printed by Jugg, the queen's printer. It began in August to be used in London on Wednesday, and so continued Mondays and Wednesdays, till some abatement of the plague, and till by God's goodness it ended in a thanksgiving for peace and health. And the same day it began at London, the bishop provided it to begin at Fulham also, where he now was.

BY THE QUEEN.

Most reverend father in God, right trusty and right well-beloved, we greet you well. Like as Almighty God hath of his mere grace committed to us, next under him, the chief government of this realm and the people therein, so hath He, of his like goodness, ordered under us sundry principal ministers to serve and assist us in this burden. And therefore, considering the state of this present time, wherein it hath pleased the Most Highest, for the amendment of us and our people, to visit certain places of our realm with more contagious sickness than lately hath been, for remedy and mitigation thereof we think it both necessary and our bounden duty, that universal prayer and fasting be more effectually used in this our realm. And understanding that you have thought and considered upon some good order to be prescribed therein, for the which ye require the application of our authority for the better observation thereof amongst our people, we do not only commend and allow your good zeal therein, but do also command all manner our ministers ecclesiastical or civil, and all other our subjects, to execute, follow, and obey such godly and wholesome orders, as you, being primate of all England, and metropolitan of this province of Canterbury, upon godly advice and consideration shall uniformly devise, prescribe, and publish, for the universal usage of prayer, fasting, and other good deeds, during the time of this visitation by sickness and other troubles.

> Given under our signet, at our manor of Richmond, the first day of August, the fifth year of our reign.

To the most reverend father in
God, our right trusty and right
well-beloved the archbishop of
Canterbury, and primate of all
England.

[GRINDAL.]

THE PREFACE.

We be taught by many and sundry examples of holy scriptures, that upon occasion of particular punishments, afflictions, and perils, which God, of his most just judgment, hath sometimes sent among his people to shew his wrath against sin, and to call his people to repentance and to the redress of their lives, the godly have been provoked and stirred up to more fervency and diligence in prayer, fasting, and alms-deeds, to a more deep consideration of their consciences, to ponder their unthankfulness and forgetfulness of God's merciful benefits towards them, with craving of pardon for the time past, and to ask his assistance for the time to come, to live more godly, and so to be defended and delivered from all further perils and dangers. So king David in the time of plague and pestilence, which ensued upon his vain numbering of the people, prayed unto God with wonderful fervency, confessing his fault, desiring God to spare the people, and rather to turn his ire to himward, who had chiefly offended in that transgression. The like was done by the virtuous kings Josaphat and Ezechias in their distress of wars and foreign invasions. So did Judith and Hester fall to humble prayers in like perils of their people. So did Daniel in his captivity, and many other more in their troubles.

Now therefore calling to mind, that God hath been provoked by us to visit us at this present with the plague and other grievous diseases, and partly also with trouble of wars, it hath been thought meet to set forth by public order some occasion to excite and stir up all godly people within this realm, to pray earnestly and heartily to God to turn away his deserved wrath from us, and to restore us as well to the health of our bodies by the wholesomeness of the air, as also to godly and profitable peace and quietness. And although it is every Christian man's duty of his own devotion to pray at all times, yet, for that the corrupt nature of man is so slothful and negligent in this his duty, he hath need by often and sundry means to be stirred up and put in remembrance of his duty; for the effectual accomplishment whereof, it is ordered and appointed as followeth:

First, that all curates and pastors shall exhort their parishioners to endeavour themselves to come unto the church, with so many of their families as may be spared from their necessary business, (having yet a prudent respect in such assemblies to keep the sick from the whole in places where the plague reigneth,) and they to resort, not only on Sundays and holy-days, but also on Wednesdays and Fridays during the time of these present afflictions, exhorting them there reverently and godly to behave themselves, and with penitent hearts to pray unto God to turn these plagues from us, which we through our unthankfulness and sinful life have deserved.

Secondly, that the said curates shall then distinctly and plainly read the general confession appointed in the book of service, with the residue of the morning prayer, using for both the lessons the chapters hereafter following. That is to say:

For the first lesson, one of these chapters out of the old testament.

The 2 Kings xxiv. Leviticus xxvi. Deuteronom. xxviii. Hieremy xviii. unto these words: "Let us, &c." and xxii. 2. Para. xxxiv.; Esay i.; Ezechiel xviii. and xix.; Joel ii.; 2 Esdras ix.; Jonas the ii. and iii. chapters together. Which chapters would be read orderly on Sundays, Wednesdays and Fridays.

And for the second lesson, one of these chapters out of the new testament.

Matthew iii. vi. vii. xxiv. xxv.; Luke xiii.; Acts ii. beginning at these words: "Ye men of Israel, hear these words," to the end of the chapter; Rom. ii. vi. xii. xiii.; Galat. v.; Ephesians iv. v.; 1 Tim. ii.; Apoca. ii.

A FORM

OF

COMMON PRAYER.

THE ORDER FOR THE WEDNESDAYS.

¶ On Wednesdays (which be the days appointed for general fast, in such form as shall hereafter be declared) after the morning prayer ended, as is aforesaid, the said curates and ministers shall exhort the people assembled to give themselves to their private prayers and meditations. For which purpose a pause shall be made of one quarter of an hour and more, by the discretion of the said curate; during which time as good silence shall be kept as may be.

That done, the litany is to be read in the midst of the people, with the additions of prayer hereafter mentioned.

Then shall follow the ministration of the communion, so oft as a just number of communicants shall be thereto disposed, with a sermon, if it can be, to be made by such as be authorised by the metropolitan or bishop of the diocese, and they to entreat of such matters especially as be meet for this cause of public prayer; or else, for want of such preacher, to read one of the homilies hereafter appointed, after the reading of the gospel, as hath been accustomed. And so the minister, commending the people to God with the accustomed benediction, shall dismiss them.

If there be no communion, then on every of the said Wednesdays after the litany, the ten commandments, the epistle, gospel, the sermon or homily done, the general usual prayer for the state of the whole church shall be read, as is set forth in the Book of Common Prayer. After which shall follow these two prayers:

"Almighty God, the fountain of all wisdom, &c." And "Almighty God, which hast promised, &c." with the accustomed benediction.

THE ORDER FOR FRIDAYS.

¶ On Fridays shall be only the morning prayer, and the litany, with the prayers now appointed to be annexed to the same.

¶ HOMILIES TO BE READ IN ORDER ON WEDNESDAYS.

1. First, an Homily entituled, "An Homily concerning the Justice of God in punishing of impenitent sinners, &c." newly now set forth for that purpose.
2. The viii. Homily of the first tome of Homilies, entituled, "Of the Declining from God."
3. The ix. Homily of the same tome, entituled, "An Exhortation against the Fear of Death."
4. The Homily of Fasting, in the second tome of Homilies.
5. The Homily of Prayer, in the same tome.
6. The Homily of Almsdeeds, in the same tome.
7. The Homily of Repentance, in the same tome also.

When these homilies are once read over, then to begin again, and so to continue them in order.

After the end of the collect in the litany, which beginneth with these words, "We humbly beseech thee, O Father, &c." shall follow this Psalm, to be said of the minister, with the answer of the people.

¶ THE PSALM TO BE SAID IN THE LITANY,
before one of the prayers newly appointed. Whereof one verse to be said of the minister, and another by the people, clerk, or clerks.

1. O COME, let us humble ourselves, and fall down before the Lord, with reverence and fear. *Psal. xcv.*
2. For he is the Lord our God: and we are the people of his pasture, and the sheep of his hands.
3. Come therefore, let us turn again unto our Lord; for he hath smitten us, and he shall heal us. *Hos. vi.*
4. Let us repent, and turn from our wickedness: and our sins shall be forgiven us. *Acts iii.*

Jonah iii.	5. Let us turn, and the Lord will turn from his heavy wrath, and will pardon us, and we shall not perish.
Psal. li.	6. For we knowledge our faults: and our sins be ever before us.
Lam. iii.	7. We have sore provoked thine anger, O Lord; thy wrath is waxed hot, and thy heavy displeasure is sore kindled against us.
	8. Thou hast made us hear of the noise of wars, and hast troubled us by the vexation of enemies.
Isai. lxiv.	9. Thou hast in thine indignation stricken us with grievous sickness, and by and by we have fallen as leaves beaten down with a vehement wind.
Judith viii. Job xi. Wisd. xi.	10. Indeed we acknowledge that all punishments are less than our deservings: but yet of thy mercy, Lord, correct us to amendment, and plague us not to our destruction.
	11. For thy hand is not shortened, that thou canst not help: neither is thy goodness abated, that thou wilt not hear.
Isai. lxv.	12. Thou hast promised, O Lord, that afore we cry thou wilt hear us: whilst we yet speak, thou wilt have mercy upon us.
	13. For none that trust in thee shall be confounded: neither any that call upon thee shall be despised.
Tob. iii. Job v. Hos. vi.	14. For thou art the only Lord, who woundest and dost heal again, who killest, and revivest, bringest even to hell, and bringest back again.
Psal. xxii.	15. Our fathers hoped in thee; they trusted in thee, and thou didst deliver them.
	16. They called upon thee, and were helped: they put their trust in thee, and were not confounded.
Psal. vi.	17. O Lord, rebuke not us in thine indignation: neither chasten us in thy heavy displeasure.
Psal. xxv.	18. O remember not the sins and offences of our youth: but according to thy mercy think thou upon us, O Lord, for thy goodness.
	19. Have mercy upon us, O Lord, for we are weak: O Lord, heal us, for our bones are vexed.
Baruch iii. Jonah ii.	20. And now in the vexation of our spirits and the anguish of our souls we remember thee, and we cry unto thee: hear, Lord, and have mercy.
Dan. ix.	21. For thine own sake, and for thy holy name's sake, incline thine ear, and hear, O merciful Lord.
	22. For we do not pour out our prayers before thy face, trusting in our own righteousness: but in thy great and manifold mercies.

23. Wash us throughly from our wickedness, and cleanse us from our sins.

24. Turn thy face from our sins, and put out all our misdeeds.

25. Make us clean hearts, O God: and renew a right spirit within us.

26. Help us, O God of our salvation, for the glory of thy name: O deliver us, and be merciful unto our sins for thy name's sake. Psal. lxxix.

27. So we that be thy people and sheep of thy pasture shall give thee thanks for ever, and will always be shewing forth thy praise from generation to generation.

Glory be to the Father, &c.

¶. After this Psalm, shall be said by the curate or minister, openly and with an high voice, one of these three prayers following. And after that orderly the rest of the collects appointed in the litany. At which time the people shall devoutly give ear, and shall both with mind and speech to themselves assent to the same prayers.

¶ A PRAYER, CONTAINING ALSO A CONFES-
sion of sins, which is to be said after the
litany, as well upon Sundays, as
Wednesdays and Fridays.

O ALMIGHTY, most just and merciful God, we here acknowledge ourselves most unworthy to lift up our eyes unto heaven; for our conscience doth accuse us, and our sins do reprove us. We know also that thou, Lord, being a just judge, must needs punish the sins of them which transgress thy law. And when we consider and examine all our whole life, we find nothing in ourselves that deserveth any other thing but eternal damnation. But because thou, O Lord, of thy unspeakable mercy, hast commanded us in all our necessities to call only upon thee, and hast also promised that thou wilt hear our prayers, not for any our desert, (which is none,) but for the merits of thy Son our only Saviour Jesus Christ, whom thou hast ordained to be our only Mediator and Intercessor; we lay away all confidence in man, and do flee to the throne of thy only mercy, by the intercession of thy only Son our Saviour Jesu Christ. And first of all, we do most lament and bewail, from the bottom of our hearts, our unkindness and unthankfulness towards thee our

Lord, considering that, besides those thy benefits which we enjoy as thy creatures, common with all mankind, thou hast bestowed many and singular special benefits upon us, which we are not able in heart to conceive, much less in words worthily to express. Thou hast called us to the knowledge of thy gospel. Thou hast released us from the hard servitude of Satan. Thou hast delivered us from all horrible and execrable idolatry, wherein we were utterly drowned, and hast brought us into the most clear and comfortable light of thy blessed word, by the which we are taught how to serve and honour thee, and how to live orderly with our neighbours in truth and verity. But we, most unmindful in times of prosperity of these thy great benefits, have neglected thy commandments, have abused the knowledge of thy gospel, and have followed our carnal liberty, and served our own lusts, and through our sinful life have not worshipped and honoured thee as we ought to have done. And now, O Lord, being even compelled with thy correction, we do most humbly confess that we have sinned, and have most grievously offended thee by many and sundry ways. And if thou, O Lord, wouldest now, being provoked with our disobedience, so deal with us as thou might, and as we have deserved, there remaineth nothing else to be looked for, but universal and continual plagues in this world, and hereafter eternal death and damnation, both of our bodies and of our souls. For if we should excuse ourselves, our own consciences would accuse us before thee, and our own disobedience and wickedness would bear witness against us. Yea, even thy plagues and punishments, which thou dost now lay upon us in sundry places, do teach us to acknowledge our sins. For seeing, O Lord, that thou art just, yea, even justice itself, thou punishest no people without desert. Yea, even at this present, O Lord, we see thy hand terribly stretched out to plague us and punish us. But although thou shouldest punish us more grievously than thou hast done, and for one plague send an hundred; if thou shouldest pour upon us all those the testimonies of thy most just wrath, which in times passed thou pouredst on thy own chosen people of Israel, yet shouldest thou do us no wrong; neither could we deny but we had justly deserved the same. But yet, O merciful Lord, thou art our God, and we nothing but dust and ashes. Thou art our Creator, and we the work of thy hands. Thou art our Pastor, we are thy flock. Thou art our Redeemer, and we thy people redeemed. Thou art our heavenly Father, we are thy children. Wherefore punish us not, O Lord, in thine anger, but chasten us in thy mercy. Regard not the horror of our sins, but the repentance thereof. Perfect that work which thou hast begun in us, that the whole world may know, that thou art our God and merciful deliverer. Thy people of Israel oftentimes offended thee, and thou most justly afflictedst them: but as oft as they returned to thee, thou didst receive them to mercy. And though their sins were never so great, yet thou always turnedst away thy wrath from them, and the punishment prepared for them, and that for thy covenant's sake, which thou madest with thy servants, Abraham, Isaac, and Jacob. Thou hast made the same covenant with us, O heavenly Father, or rather a covenant of more excellency and efficacy; and that namely through the mediation of thy dear Son Jesus Christ our Saviour, with whose most precious blood it pleased thee that this covenant should be, as it were, written, sealed, and confirmed. Wherefore, O heavenly Father, we now casting away all confidence in ourselves or any other creature, do flee to this most holy covenant and testament, wherein our Lord and Saviour Jesus Christ, once offering himself a sacrifice for us on the cross, hath reconciled us to thee for ever. Look therefore, O merciful God, not upon the sins which we continually commit, but upon our Mediator and Peace-maker, Jesus Christ; that by his intercession thy wrath may be pacified, and we again by thy fatherly countenance relieved and comforted. Receive us also into thy heavenly defence, and govern us by thy Holy Spirit, to frame in us a newness of life, therein to laud and magnify thy blessed name for ever, and to live every of us according to the several state of life, whereunto thou, Lord, hast ordained us. And although we are unworthy, O heavenly Father, by means of our former foul life, to crave anything of thee; yet, because thou hast commanded us to pray for all men, we most humbly here upon our knees beseech thee, save and defend thy holy church. Be merciful, O Lord, to all commonweals, countries, princes, and magistrates, and especially to this our realm, and to our most gracious queen and governor, Queen Elizabeth. Increase the number of godly ministers; endue them with thy grace, to be found faithful and prudent in their office. Defend the Queen's majesty's council, and all that be in authority under her, or that serve in any place by her commandment for this realm. We commend also to thy fatherly mercy all those that be in poverty, exile, imprisonment, sickness, or any other kind of adversity, and namely those whom thy hand now hath touched with any contagious and dangerous sickness; which we beseech thee, O Lord, of thy mercy, (when thy blessed will is,) to remove from us; and in the mean time grant us grace and true repentance, stedfast faith, and constant patience, that whether we live or die, we may always continue thine, and ever praise thy holy name, and be brought to the fruition of thy Godhead. Grant us these, and all other our humble petitions, O merciful Father, for thy dear Son's sake Jesus Christ our Lord. Amen.

¶ Or else, in the stead of the other, this Prayer may be used; and so to use the one one day, the other another.

O ETERNAL and ever-living God, most merciful Father, which of thy great long-suffering and patience hast hitherto suffered and borne with us most miserable offenders, who have so long strayed out of thy way, and broken all thy laws and commandments, and have neither by thy manifold benefits bestowed upon us unworthy and unthankful sinners, nor by the voice of thy servants and preachers, by continual threatenings out of thy holy word, hitherto been moved, either, as thy children, of love to return unto thee our most gracious Father; either for fear of thy judgments, as humble and lowly servants, to turn from our wickedness. And therefore, most righteous Judge, thy patience being (as it were) overcome at the last, with our obstinate unrepentance, thou hast most justly executed those thy terrible threats, now partly upon us, by plaguing us so (*with most dreadful and deadly sickness*) (*with troubles of wars*) (*with penury and scarceness of food and victual*), whereby great multitudes of us are daily afflicted and consumed. We beseech thee, O most merciful Father, that in thy wrath thou wilt remember thy old great mercies, and to correct us

¶ Note to pray against any of these plagues, as they shall touch us.

in thy judgments, and not in thy just anger, lest we be all consumed and brought to nought. Look not so much upon us and upon our deservings, O most righteous Judge, to take just vengeance on our sins; but rather remember thy infinite mercies, O most merciful Father, promised to us by thy dearly beloved Son, our Saviour Jesus Christ, for whose sake, and in whose name, we do earnestly and humbly crave mercy and forgiveness of our sins, and deliverance from this horrible sickness, being thy just punishment and plague for the same. And as thy holy word doth testify, that thy people of all ages, being justly plagued for their sins, and yet in their distress unfeignedly turning unto thee and suing for thy mercy, obtained the same: so likewise we, most worthily now afflicted with grievous and dreadful plagues for our iniquities, pray thee, O most merciful Father, to grant us thy heavenly grace, that we may likewise both truly and unfeignedly repent, and obtain thy mercy and deliverance from the same; which we beseech thee, O Father of all mercies, and God of all consolation, to grant us, for the same Jesus Christ's sake, our only Saviour, Mediator, and Advocate. Amen.

¶ THIS PRAYER may be said every third day.

It had been the best for us, O most righteous Judge, and our most merciful Father, that in our wealths and quietness, and in the midst of thy manifold benefits, continually bestowed upon us most unworthy sinners, we had of love hearkened to thy voice, and turned unto thee our most loving and gracious Father; for in so doing we had done the parts of good and obedient loving children. It had also been well, if at thy dreadful threats out of thy holy word, continually pronounced unto us by thy servants our preachers, we had of fear, as corrigible servants, turned from our wickedness. But, alas! we have shewed hitherto ourselves towards thee neither as loving children, O most merciful Father, neither as tolerable servants, O Lord most mighty. Wherefore now we feel thy heavy wrath, O most righteous Judge, justly punishing us with grievous and deadly sickness and plagues; we do now confess and acknowledge, and to our most just punishment do find indeed that to be most true, which we have so often heard threatened to us out of thy holy scriptures, the word of thy eternal verity, that thou art the same unchangeable God; of the same justice that thou wilt, and of the same power that thou canst, punish the like wickedness and obstinacy of us impenitent sinners in these days, as thou hast done in all ages heretofore. But the same thy holy scriptures, the word of thy truth, do also testify that thy strength is not shortened but that thou canst, neither thy goodness abated but that thou wilt, help those that in their distress do flee unto thy mercies; and that thou art the same God of all, rich in mercy towards all that call upon thy name; and that thou dost not intend to destroy us utterly, but fatherly to correct us, who hast pity upon us, even when thou dost scourge us; as by thy said holy word, thy gracious promises, and the examples of thy saints in thy holy scriptures, expressed for our comfort, thou hast assured us. Grant us, O most merciful Father, that we fall not into the uttermost of all mischiefs, to become worse under thy scourge; but that this thy rod may by thy heavenly grace speedily work in us the fruit and effect of true repentance, unfeigned turning and converting unto thee, and perfect amendment of our whole lives; that, as we through our impenitency do now most worthily feel thy justice punishing us, so by this thy correction we may also feel the sweet comfort of thy mercies, graciously pardoning our sins, and pitifully releasing these grievous punishments and dreadful plagues. This we crave at thy hand, O most merciful Father, for thy dear Son our Saviour Jesus Christ's sake. Amen.

¶ *A short meditation to be said of such as be touched in affliction.*

Jer. xiv.   O FATHER, doubtless our own wickedness do reward us: but do thou, O Lord, according to thy name. Our oft transgressions and sins be many. Against thee have we sinned; yet art thou the comforter and helper of thy humble subjects in the time of their trouble. For thou, O Lord, art in the midst of us, and thy name is called upon us. Forsake us not, O God, forsake us not, for the merits of thy only Son our Saviour Jesus Christ; to whom with thee and the Holy Ghost be all honour and glory. Amen.

¶ Psalms which may be sung or said before the beginning or after the ending of public prayer.

1, 2, 3, 4, 5, 6, 13, 15, 25, 26, 30, 32, 46, 51, 67, 79, 84, 91, 102, 103, 107, 123, 130, 143, 147.

THE ORDER FOR THE GENERAL FAST.

¶ It is most evident to them that read the scriptures, that both in the old church under the law, and in the primitive church under the gospel, the people of God hath always used general fasting, both in times of common calamities, as war, famine, pestilence, &c., and also when any weighty matter, touching the estate of the church or the commonwealth, was begun or intended. And it cannot be denied, but that in this our time, wherein many things have been reformed according to the doctrine and examples of God's word and the primitive church, this part for fasting and abstinence, being always in the scripture, as a necessary companion, joined to fervent prayer, hath been too much neglected [1].

Wherefore, for some beginning of redress herein, it hath been thought meet to the queen's majesty, that in this contagious time of sickness and other troubles and unquietness, according to the examples of the godly king Josaphat, and the king of Ninive, with others, a general fast should be joined with general prayer throughout her whole realm, and to be observed of all her godly subjects in manner and form following: 2 Chron. xx. Jonah iii.

1. First, it is ordained that the Wednesday of every week shall be the day appointed for this general fast.

2. Secondly, all persons between the age of sixteen years and sixty (sick folks and labourers in harvest, or other great

[1 Grindal pressed much the religious exercise of fasting, the great neglect whereof he blamed protestants for; and that it might be matter wherewith the adversaries the papists might reproach us; saying, "Surely my opinion hath been long, that in no one thing the adversary hath more advantage against us, than in the matter of fast; which we utterly neglect: they have the shadow." This caused him to put in those words into the said office, " For some beginning of order herein, a command was now issued," &c. &c. Strype, Grindal, p. 107.]

labours, only excepted) shall eat but one only competent and moderate meal upon every Wednesday. In which said meal shall be used very sober and spare diet, without variety of kinds of meat, dishes, spices, confections, or wines, but only such as may serve for necessity, comeliness, and health.

3. Item, in that meal it shall be indifferent to eat flesh or fish, so that the quantity be small, and no variety or delicacy be sought. Wherein every man hath to answer to God, if he in such godly exercises either contemn public order, or dissemble with God, pretending abstinence and doing nothing less.

4. Item, those that be of wealth and ability ought that day to abate and diminish the costliness and variety of their fare, and increase therewith their liberality and alms towards the poor; that the same poor, which either in deed lack food, or else that which they have is unseasonable and cause of sickness, may thereby be relieved and charitably succoured, to be maintained in health.

5. Last of all, this day, being in this manner appointed for a day of general prayer and fasting, ought to be bestowed, by them which may forbear from bodily labour, in prayer, study, reading or hearing of the scriptures, or good exhortations, &c. And when any dulness or weariness shall arise, then to be occupied in other godly exercises; but no part thereof to be spent in plays, pastime, or idleness, much less in lewd, wicked, or wanton behaviour.

When there is a sermon, or other just occasion, one of the lessons may be omitted, and the shortest of the three prayers appointed in the litany by this order may be said, and the longest left off.

Forasmuch as divers homilies, appointed before to be read in this form of common prayer, are contained in the second tome of homilies, now lately set forth by the queen's majesty's authority; therefore it is ordered, that the churchwardens of every parish shall provide the same second tome or book of homilies with all speed, at the charges of the parish.

¶ An Homyly concernyng the Justice of God in punyshyng of impenitent sinners, and of his mercies towardes all such as in theyr afflictions unfaynedly turne unto hym.

Appoynted to be read in the tyme of sicknes.

AN HOMILY CONCERNING THE JUSTICE OF GOD[1].

THE most righteous God, and the same our most merciful Father, abhorring all wickedness and impiety, and delighting in all righteousness and innocency, and willing that we, his people and children, should herein be conformed and become like to our God and heavenly Father, that we might be also partakers of his inheritance and everlasting kingdom, in his holy scriptures, containing the perfect rule of righteousness, and written for our learning and direction towards his said kingdom, both by great threatenings doth continually fear[2] us from all impiety and wickedness, so displeasant to him, and also by most large and gentle promises, like a loving father, doth provoke and entice us to righteousness and holiness, so acceptable unto him; and so leaveth nothing unassayed, no way unproved, whereby he might save us from perpetual destruction, and bring us to life everlasting. To this end all those threatenings of temporal punishments and plagues, whereof the scriptures be so full, are to be referred; that we, for fear of temporal punishments refraining from all unrighteousness, might also escape eternal pain and damnation, whereunto it would finally bring us, if we should not by repentance turn from the same, and return unto our God and most merciful Father, who would not the destruction and death of sinners, but rather that they should convert and be saved.

<small>Gen. xii.
Job xxxvi.
Psal. vii. xii.
cxix.
Isai. xxvi.
Jer. xxx.
Job v.</small>

<small>Tob. iii.
2 Pet. iii.</small>

But when he perceiveth that neither gentleness can win us, as his loving children, neither fear and threatenings can amend us, as being most stubborn and rebellious servants, at the last he performeth in deed that which he hath so oft threatened, and of fatherly sufferance and mercy so long, upon hope of amendment, deferred, his longanimity and patience being now

[1 This homily was composed expressly for the occasion of the plague, by Alexander Nowel, Dean of St Paul's, and was printed and circulated together with the preceding form. (See above, p. 79.) For this reason it seemed desirable that it should still retain its position as part of the service.]

[2 Fear: affright.]

overcome with our stony hardness and obstinate impenitency. After this sort we shall find by the holy scriptures and histories ecclesiastical that he hath dealt with his people of all ages, namely the Israelites, whom in sundry other places, but especially in the 26th of Leviticus and 28th of Deuteronomium, as well by fair promises as by menaces, he laboureth to bring to due obedience of his law, which is perfect righteousness. "If (saith he) thou hear the voice of the Lord thy God and keep his commandments, all these blessings shall come upon thee: Thou shalt be blessed in the city and in the field: the seed of thy body, the fruit of thy earth, the increase of thy cattle, shall be blessed, &c. Thou shalt have seasonable weather, fruitful ground, victory of thy enemies, and after, quiet peace in thy coasts; and I will be thy loving Lord and God, thy aid and defender, and thou shalt be my beloved people. But if thou wilt not hear the voice of the Lord thy God, nor keep his commandments, but despise his laws, &c., all these curses shall come upon thee: Thou shalt be cursed in the city and in the field; thy barn, all thy storehouses shall be cursed; the fruit of thy body, of thy cattle, and of thy ground, shall be cursed: thou shalt be cursed going out and coming in. The Lord shall send thee famine and necessity; he shall strike thee with agues, heats and colds, with pestilences and all other evil diseases; yea, and with all the botches and plagues of Egypt. He shall make heaven over thee as it were of brass, and the earth which thou treadest on as it were iron. He shall send thee unseasonable weather, &c.; wars; and overthrow thee at thine enemies' hands, and thy carrion shall be a prey to the birds of the air and the beasts of the earth, and there shall be no man to drive them away." And so forth, many more most horrible evils and mischiefs, written at large in those two chapters; where ye may see how lovingly on the one part he promiseth to the obedient, and how terribly on the other part he threateneth the disobedient, and how largely and at length he prosecuteth the matter, specially in the threatenings and menaces most meet for the Jews, a people ever stiff-necked and rebellious. And indeed the whole writings of the prophets, and universally of all the scriptures, be nothing else but like callings to true obedience, and to repentance from our transgressions, by like promises and threatenings; yea, and greater also, as by promise of life everlasting to the faithful, obedient, and penitent,

Levit. xxvi.
Deut. xxviii.

Levit. xxvi.

Levit. xxvi.
Deut. xxviii.

and contrarily, of everlasting damnation and death to the stubborn, rebellious, and impenitent sinners.

And to prosecute this matter, when the Jews were monished, remonished, prayed, threatened so oft by so many prophets, and in all in vain, did not the Lord at the last bring upon them all those evils which he had threatened, namely, famine, war, and pestilence?—as ye may read at large in the books of Judges, Kings, and Chronicles, in the Lamentations of Jeremy, namely the 2nd, 4th and 5th chapters, and in other places of the prophets and the Old Testament, containing the descriptions of extreme famines, horrible wars and captivities, and dreadful plagues, whereby God punished and afflicted his people for their sins and rebellion against him most sharply. Yea, and when all this could not amend them, but that they waxed worse under the rod and correction, did he not at the last, which is most horrible, utterly destroy them with famine, war and pestilence, and carried the rest into captivity, and destroyed utterly their cities and countries, according to the prophecy of Esay, and as our Saviour Christ likewise in the gospel foresheweth of the miserable destruction and ruin of their cities and temple, so horrible that one stone should not be left upon another?

<small>Jer. xx. v.</small>

<small>Isai. v.</small>
<small>Matt. xxiv.</small>
<small>Mark xiii.</small>

In like manner, the same immutable God proceeded aforetime with the Christians of Asia, Afric, and Greece. He sent them like prophets, learned doctors, and holy saints; saint Clement, Ignatius, Tertullian, Cyprian, Origene, Gregorius, Basil, Chrysostome, Augustine, and many more; who, out of holy scriptures, likewise warned and warned them again to turn from their sins and to return to God; unto whom after, when they would not be warned with words, he sent them the swords of the Goths, Huns, Vandals, Saracens, and Turks; he sent them likewise famines and pestilences; and finally, when neither threats nor punishments could amend them by those nations, and especially the Saracens and Turks, he hath either utterly destroyed them, or else made them most miserable captives of the miscreant Turks, under them to be in all unspeakable slavery and misery, and (that which is most horrible of all) where their forefathers worshipped Christ the Saviour of the world, to serve in his stead filthy and damned Mahomet, the deceiver of the world.

<small>Goths.</small>

Now to come to our times, most dearly beloved in our

Saviour Christ, hath not God likewise begun this order of proceeding with us Christians of this age? Hath he not sent amongst us his prophets and preachers, who out of God's holy word have continually called us to repentance, continually denounced unto us that he is the same immutable God, of the same justice that he will, and of the same power that he can, persecute the same wickedness and impenitency with like punishments and plagues? In the which also he hath used his wonted clemency in denouncing evils before he bring them upon us, that by speedy repentance we might avoid and escape them. And hath he not, I pray you, prosecuted the same his proceedings with us also, continuing in impenitency, by sending us sundry plagues at sundry times, wars, famines, exiles, horrible fires? And hath he not now at the last, after almost twenty years' patience and forbearing of us, sent us the pestilence, which of all sicknesses we most fear and abhor, as indeed it is to be feared? Seeing we have so long despised his justice requiring our innocency, he cannot but visit with his justice punishing our iniquity; and that he doth more justly execute upon us, than he did upon his people of any time before us, for that we, besides the warning of his scriptures and preachers of his word, by so many examples of the punishments of all former ages for like vices have not been amended or moved to any repentance.

Wherefore now at the last he hath sent to us, that could never in health by any means be brought to the obedience of him, horrible sickness and the dreadful fear of death, present at our doors and before our eyes. We, that could never skill of compassion towards the misery of others, are now ourselves by his just judgments fallen into extreme misery. We, that have not visited and comforted the sick according to God's will, are now fallen into such sickness that the nearest of our friends refuse to visit us. We, that could never be brought from the love of this world, are now most justly brought in fear suddenly to leave and depart out of this world. We, that loved our wicked mammon so much, that we could not find in our hearts to bestow any part thereof upon the relief of our poor brethren and sisters, are now brought in fear suddenly to lose it altogether, and ourselves also with it, by sudden and dreadful death of our bodies, and, for the abusing of it, in danger and dread to lose our souls also everlastingly. We, that set all our delight in gathering together and heaping of worldly muck, in building of fair houses, and purchasing of lands, as though we should live for ever, are now justly put in fear of loss of life and all with it, at the short warning of two or three days, and often not many more hours. All those doctrines of the vanity of this transitory life and world, set out in the scriptures in so many places, preached unto us in so many sermons, which we yet could never hitherto by hearing believe, are now put in practice in deed, and set before our eyes and all our senses to see and perceive most certainly. Wherefore, unless we now at the last repent, I see not what time is left for repentance. It had been the best indeed, as we have been oft forewarned, to have turned to our heavenly Father in time of quietness, for love of our Father, rather than fear of the rod; for that had been indeed the part of loving and good children: but not to be mended with stripes, is now the part not of servants that be corrigible, but of indurate and desperate slaves. Let us not, O dearly beloved, fall into the uttermost of all mischiefs, that we should be incorrigible with punishment also, and worse under the scourge; as were those stiff-necked Jews, who when, first after threatenings, and then after plagues of war, famine, and pestilence, they remained indurate and incorrigible, lastly, as he by his holy prophets had threatened them, he overthrew them as a high wall down to the ground, and dashed them all to pieces as an earthen vessel, that their ruin might be without help, and their destruction remediless. Which most horrible mischief that we may avoid, let us avoid the cause thereof, contempt, obstinacy, and hardness of heart in God's most just wrath and scourge now used for our correction. There is yet no cause, for all this, why we should despair or distrust; but rather that we should turn from our sins, and return to our merciful Father, craving pardon and deliverance at his hand.

For the declaration whereof, it shall be shewed out of the scriptures, First, that God doth not punish us in this world, and send us these miseries and sickness, of hatred, to destroy us, but of love, mercifully to correct us. And out of infinite places, it shall suffice to rehearse a few notable, serving for

Marginal references: 2 Chron. xxviii. Jer. ii. & v. Ezek. xxiv. Hagg. ii. Zeph. iii. Prov. i. & xxix. Isai. xxx. Levit. xxvi. xl. Deut. viii. Psal. cxviii. Judith viij.

this purpose. And here the testimony of Job, a man both sore punished and most favoured of God, hath a worthy place; who, well understanding God's goodness and mercy, even in his grievous punishments, "Blessed or happy (saith he) is the man whom God punisheth. Therefore refuse not thou the chastening of the Almighty: for though he make a wound, he giveth a plaster; though he smite, his hand maketh whole again. He shall deliver thee in six troubles, and in the seventh there shall no evil come unto thee. In hunger he shall feed thee from death, and in the wars he shall deliver thee from the power of the sword;" and so forth, how God in dearth and destruction will help and save, and how that such correction keepeth us from sinning. And again in the 36th chapter, God by punishing and nourtring[1] of men roundeth them (as it were) in the ears, warneth them to leave off their wickedness, and to amend: "If they now take heed and serve him, they shall wear out their days in prosperity, and their years in prosperity and joy." And Toby, a man likewise exercised in afflictions, saith: "Blessed is thy name, O God of our fathers, who when thou art angry shewest mercy, and in time of trouble forgivest the sins of them that call upon thee." And by and by after: "This may every one that worshippeth thee look for of a certainty, that if his life be put to trial, he shall be crowned; if he be in trouble, he shall be delivered; if he be under correction, he shall come to thy mercy; for thou delightest not in our destruction, for after tempest thou sendest calm, and after mourning and weeping thou bringest joy and rejoicing: thy name, O God of Israel, be blessed for ever." And in the 6th chapter of Osee God saith: "In their adversity they shall seek me and say, Come, let us turn again unto the Lord, for he hath smitten, and he shall heal us; he hath wounded us, and he shall bind us up again. After two days shall he quicken us, and the third day shall he raise us up, so that we shall live in his sight. Then shall we have understanding, and endeavour ourselves to know God." And in the third chapter of the Proverbs: "My son, (saith Salomon,) despise not the chastening of the Lord, neither faint when thou art rebuked of him: for whom the Lord loveth, him he chasteneth; yea, and delighteth in

Job v.

Job xxxvi.

Tob. iii.

Hosea vi. Isai. xxvi.

Prov. iii.

[1 Nourtring: nurturing, chastening; as also in the next page.]

him, even as a father in his own son." The apostle to the Hebrews hath the like most comfortable doctrine, which he yet amplifieth more, saying: "Ye have forgotten the exhortation which speaketh unto you as unto children: My son, despise not thou the chastening of the Lord, neither faint when thou art rebuked of him; for whom the Lord loveth, him he chasteneth, yea, and scourgeth every son that he receiveth. If ye endure chastening, God offereth himself unto you as unto sons. What son is he whom the Father chasteneth not? If ye be not under correction, whereof all are partakers, then are ye bastards and not sons. Therefore, seeing we have had fathers of our flesh, which corrected us, and we gave them reverence, shall we not much rather be in subjection unto the Father of spirits, and live? And they verily for a few days nourtered us after their own pleasure; but he nourtereth us for our profit, to the intent that he may minister of his holiness unto us. No manner chastening for the present time seemeth to be joyous, but grievous; nevertheless afterward it bringeth the quiet fruit of righteousness unto them which are exercised thereby." And in the third of the Revelation Christ saith: "As many as I love, I rebuke and chasten: be zealous therefore, and repent." And St Paul declareth that neither trouble nor peril, neither life nor death, nor any other thing can separate us from the love of God, if we through Christ trust in his mercy. And [in] the first to the Corinthians he teacheth, that God doth punish and correct us in this wretched world, that we should not be condemned with the wicked world.

<small>Heb. xii.</small>

<small>Rev. iii.</small>

<small>Rom. viii.</small>

<small>1 Cor. xi.</small>

Secondly, it is most comfortable to call to remembrance such places of the scriptures as contain God's merciful promises, made to all such as in their trouble unfeignedly call unto him for help; whereof certain be hereunder noted, for the more readiness to have them before our eyes. In the 4th of Deuteronomy, as God threateneth to bring the Jews into all miseries, if they do disobey him, so, saith he, "if thou then in thy greatest distress do turn unto the Lord thy God, and hear his voice, and seek him, thou shalt find him, if thou seek him with all thy heart and soul: for the Lord thy God is a merciful God; he will not forsake thee, nor destroy thee." And in the 30th chapter of the same book: "If," saith the

<small>Deut. iv.</small>

<small>Deut. xxx.</small>

Lord, "for thy sins the curses written in this book do light upon thee, and thou, moved with repentance of thy heart, turn unto the Lord, and obey his commandments with all thy heart and with all thy soul; the Lord thy God shall bring thee again out of captivity, and will have compassion upon thee, and will turn and set thee again from all the nations among which the Lord thy God shall have scattered thee. Though thou were cast unto the extreme parts of heaven, even from thence will the Lord thy God gather thee, and from thence will he set thee. And the Lord thy God will bring thee into the land which thy fathers possessed, and thou shalt enjoy it. And he will shew thee kindness, and multiply thee above thy fathers. And the Lord thy God will circumcise thine heart, and the heart of thy seed, that thou mayest love the Lord thy God with all thy heart, and with all thy soul, that thou mayest live. And the Lord thy God will put all these curses upon thine enemies, and on them that hate thee and that persecute thee. But thou shalt turn and hearken unto the voice of the Lord, and do all his commandments which I command thee this day. And the Lord thy God will make thee plenteous in all the works of thy hands, in the fruit of thy body, and in the fruit of thy cattle, and in the fruit of thy land, for thy wealth; for the Lord will turn again and rejoice over thee, to do thee all good, as he rejoiced over thy fathers." The book of Psalms is very plentiful of such comfortable promises. Psalm 50, "Call upon me in the time of thy trouble, and I will deliver thee, (saith the Lord,) and thou shalt honour me." Psalm 86, "Thou, Lord, art good and gracious, and of great mercy unto all them that call upon thee." And by and by: "In the time of my trouble I will call upon thee, for thou hearest me." In the 91st psalm be large promises of God's help and deliverance, yea, and that expressly from the plague and pestilence, and all other evils. Psalm 145, "The Lord is nigh unto all them that call upon him, yea, all such as call upon him faithfully." And Salomon, in dedicating of his temple, testifieth that if either in war, or famine, or pestilence, or any other plague for our sins, we do convert unto God, and ask mercy, that we shall obtain it. And God, appearing unto him, doth promise and assure the same; Psal. l.

Psal. lxxxvi.

Psal. xci.

Psal. cxlv.

1 Kings viii.

2 Chron. vi.

which promise of God the good king Jehosaphat doth repeat in the 2nd of Paralipomenon and the 20th chapter, and according to the same, in his distress obtaineth God's mercy and help. And the Lord by his prophet Jeremy saith: "If that people, against whom I have thus devised, convert from their wickedness, I will repent of the plague that I devised to bring upon them." Again, "When I take in hand to build or to plant a people or a kingdom, if the same people do evil before me, and hear not my voice, I will repent of the good that I devised to do for them." And in another place: "Ye shall cry unto me, ye shall go and call upon me, and I shall hear you: ye shall seek me and find me, yea, if so be that you seek me with your whole heart, I will be found of you, (saith the Lord,) and will deliver you." And again, in another place: "I heard Ephraim that was led away captive complain on this manner: O Lord, thou hast corrected me, and thy chastening have I received as an untamed calf: convert thou me, and I shall be converted; for thou art my Lord God; yea, as soon as thou turnest me, I shall reform myself; and when I understand, I shall smite upon my thigh." And by his prophet Ezechiel he saith: "If the ungodly will turn away from all his sins that he hath done, and keep all my commandments, and do the thing that is equal and right, doubtless he shall live and not die. As for all his sins that he did before, they shall not be thought upon; but in his righteousness that he hath done he shall live. For have I any pleasure in the death of a sinner, saith the Lord God, but rather that he convert and live?" And shortly after again: "When the wicked man turneth away from his wickedness that he hath done, and doth the thing which is equal and right, he shall save his soul alive. For in so much as he remembereth himself, and turneth him from all the ungodliness that he hath used, he shall live and not die." And again: "Wherefore be converted, and turn you clean from all your wickedness; so shall there no sin do thee harm. Cast away from you all your ungodliness that ye have done; make you new hearts, and a new spirit. Wherefore will ye die, O ye house of Israel? seeing I have no pleasure in the death of him that dieth, saith the Lord God: turn you then, and ye shall live." And likewise by his prophet Joel: Although an horrible destruction be threatened to be at hand, " yet (saith the Lord) turn unto me with all your hearts, with fasting, weeping, and mourning; rend your hearts and not your clothes, turn you unto the Lord you God; for he is gracious and merciful, and of great compassion, and ready to pardon wickedness." And anon: " Every one that calleth upon the name of the Lord shall be saved." And the Lord himself testifieth, that he hath performed these his promises accordingly, saying, " Thou calledst upon me in troubles, and I delivered thee, and heard thee, what time as the storm fell upon thee." Yea, and it is so accustomed unto God to help those that in their troubles flee unto him for succour, that he is, as it were, by a special name called in the scriptures the helper and refuge in the day of trouble, the Father of mercies, the God of all comfort; that thereby we might in our distress be the more encouraged to sue to the throne of his heavenly grace, whereunto our Saviour most lovingly calleth all such as feel the burthen of adversity, and their sins withal.

<small>Joel ii.</small>

<small>Psal. lxxxi.</small>

<small>Jer. xiv. xvi.
2 Cor. i.</small>

<small>Matt. xi.</small>

Now it remaineth, for the third part, rehearsal be made of certain examples of such as being in trouble, and trusting to God's merciful promises, called upon him and were delivered. And first, of David, a man wonderfully exercised in worldly troubles, to his eternal health and salvation; who confesseth that God was ever his helper and deliverer, when he called upon him in trouble, sickness, or any other adversity; and that in very many places of the Psalter, a number whereof are noted in the margents. Yea, when he was in desperate state concerning all worldly help, crying out that the snares and sorrows of death had compassed him round about, and that the pains of hell had come upon him, and taken hold of him; that he would yet call upon the name of the Lord, beseeching him to deliver his soul, and that God out of his holy temple would not fail to hear, and speedily to help and save him. And notably and directly to this purpose, the same king David, as is testified in the 2nd book of Kings and 24th chapter, when 70,000 were in three days slain with the plague for his and their sins, making most humble confession of his offence, and earnest prayer for mercy and pardon, obtained the same, and

<small>Psal. iv.
xxxi. xxxiv.
lxxvii.
lxxxvi.
cxviii.
cxxxviii.
cxlii. cxliv.</small>

<small>Psal. xviii.
cxvi.
2 Sam. xxii.</small>

<small>2 Sam. xxiv.</small>

the plague at God's commandment suddenly ceased. Ezechias and the people with him in their great distress, whereunto they were brought for their sins, called upon the merciful Lord, and he heard and holp them, not remembering their sins. Jonas, when by disobedience he had offended God, and was swallowed up by the whale, yet by prayer he was delivered even out of the belly of hell, as he himself speaketh; that none, even in most desperate state, should distrust in God's mercy and help. The Jews also, ever most stubborn and rebellious against God, yet when they, being afflicted most worthily, did in their distress call upon the Lord for mercy and help, he heard and relieved them, as appeareth by all the scriptures of the old testament; but especially and notably the 107th Psalm, which rehearseth the manifold rebellions of that nation against their Lord and God, and the sundry afflictions that he therefore sent upon them. But ever this verse, as it were the burden of the psalm or song, is oftentimes among rehearsed: " But they cried to the Lord in their trouble, and he delivered them from their distress." And in the end of the psalm is added, that "they that be wise will consider these examples, and thereby understand the mercies of the Lord," in like distress to flee thereunto. The like rehearsal of God's mercies, shewed unto them when they in their troubles called upon him, is in the book of Nehemias, or 2nd of Esdras, and the ninth chapter. How mercifully relieved God Ismael and his mother in their great distress! What mercy was shewed to wicked Manasses truly repenting! Likewise to Nabuchodonosor, turning unto the Lord in his trouble! How graciously is the prodigal son received of his father in his extreme misery, procured by his own wickedness! How mercifully is the thief pardoned even in the miserable end of his most wicked life! Yea, all those diseases which the gospel recordeth to be so miraculously cured by our Saviour Christ, in such as sued to him for health, and by faith trusted to obtain the same, what be they else but testimonies to us of our like relief in our grievous sickness, if with like faith we call to him for help? "For it is the same Lord of all, rich in mercy towards all that call upon him." Neither is his hand shortened or weakened, that he can not, nor his goodness abated or diminished that he will not, now help his servants that in their distress do flee to his mercy and goodness. For it is now also true, as it was then when it was written, of the sheep and penny lost and found again, and that "there is more joy in heaven upon one sinner repenting than upon ninety-nine righteous."

I have more largely prosecuted this part, for that I thought it necessary that we should be instructed by the doctrine of God's word, his merciful promises, and the comfortable examples of his saints in their troubles, that God doth punish us in this wretched world, that we be not damned with the wicked world; and that he will not refuse nor reject such as, being punished for their sins, do unfeignedly in their distress return unto him. For where[1] our negligence in coming to him heretofore in the time of our quietness might now in the day of our trouble come into our minds, to the great disquieting of our fearful consciences, I thought it expedient to stir up and erect our good hope in his mercies in the time of our troubles, by the manifold most sweet and assured comforts of the holy scriptures, written for our doctrine and consolation, both at all times, and specially in the time of affliction; for then is that heavenly medicine most necessary, when our disease doth most grieve and fear us, which we should undoubtedly receive at God's merciful hand, to our eternal health, if we, according to the above-written doctrines, promises, and examples, do unfeignedly turn to the Lord our God in these days of our affliction: unfeignedly, I say, not for the time of affliction only, as mariners in the tempest, neither as dogs returning again to their vomit; but to remain such in health and security, as in sickness and danger we promised to be; and all the days of our life hereafter, being delivered from fear of all plagues, to serve the Lord our God sincerely and continually in all holiness and righteousness acceptable to him. Wherefore I thought good to admonish us, that we do not by dissembling with God, who cannot be deceived, deceive ourselves: but that as the Lord would have this plague not to be an utter destruction unto us, but to be our fruitful correction, as by the doctrine and examples above rehearsed appeareth; so we of this cross might win that gain, and gather that fruit, which may be healthful unto us, as it was

1 Cor. xi.

Deut. iv. xxx.
Psal. cxlv.
Isai. lviii.
Jer. xxix.
Eccle. ii.

Luke i.

[1 Where: whereas.]

to those godly saints, which were before under like correction and chastisement of the Lord. Therefore let us learn by this affliction to mourn for our sins, to hate and forsake sin, for the which God doth thus shew his anger and displeasure against us. For when shall we mourn for our sins, if not now in the time of mourning? When shall we hate them, if not now when they so grievously wound us, and bring us to present danger of double death, both of body and soul, if we flee not from them? When shall we forsake sin in our life, if we cleave to it now when life forsaketh, or is most like to forsake us? And if we shall enter into particularities, when will we forsake our pride, if not now when all glory is falling into the dust? When will we leave our envy, malice, hatred, and wrath, if not now when we are going to the grave, where all these things take an end? When will we give over our gluttony, if not now when we must forego the belly and whole body also? When will we leave our fleshly lusts, if not now when our flesh shall turn to dust? When will we give over the cares of this life, if not now when we shall cease to live? When will we cease from our usury, if not now when we must lose both the increase and the stock wholly? When shall we willingly give over the love of wicked mammon, if not now when we cannot hold nor use it, but, will we nill we[1], we must part from it? Wherefore, either now let us make us friends of it, who may receive us into the heavenly tabernacles; or else there is no hope that we ever will. When shall we relieve the poor in their need, if not now, thereby to provoke the Lord to succour us in this our great distress? When will we awake, that we sleep not in death, if not now at the point of death? When shall we ever truly remember the last times, thereby to avoid sin, if not now in the last times themselves? And as we ought now in affliction to flee all wickedness, so ought we to learn the love of righteousness, whereunto of long by gentleness God hath drawn us, and now by his just punishment meaneth to drive us. Let us learn the fear of God, now punishing us, which by his long sufferance and patience heretofore was

Psal. cxlv. almost clean gone out of our hearts; for there be special

[[1] Whether we will or not.—*Nill*, not will, as *nolo, non volo*. A similar phrase in Latin is familiar: 'nolens volens'.]

promises that he will hear them that fear him. And when will we fear him, if not now when he punisheth us? Let us learn patience, "knowing that affliction in the children of salvation worketh patience, patience bringeth trial, trial hope, and hope shall not suffer us to be confounded;" "for the short evil of our troubles in this world, patiently taken, worketh in us an exceeding high and everlasting weight of glory" in the world to come. Let us learn the contempt of this wretched life and wicked world, with all her trifling and uncertain joys, and manifold and horrible evils. For when shall we understand that this life is as a vapour, as a shadow, passing and fleeing away, as a fading flower, as a bubble rising on the water, if not now in the decaying, passing, and vanishing away of it? When shall we forsake this wicked world, if not now when it forsaketh us? Let us learn the desire of heaven and the life to come, where be both many and most great and certain joys, mingled with no evils, no plagues of famine, war, pestilence, or other sickness, and miseries, whereof this wretched life is full, as we now by experience prove. Rom. v.
2 Cor. i.
James i.
2 Cor. iv.

James iv.
Job [vii.]

To conclude, let us, giving over all wickedness, now at the last, when we are in most greatest danger to give over ourselves, and helping the needy and poor, that the Lord in our necessities may relieve us; let us, I say, now at the last turn unto the Lord our God, and call for help and mercy; and we shall be heard and relieved, according to the doctrine of God's word, and his merciful promises made unto us, and after the examples foreshewed to us out of the holy scriptures afore declared, and in infinite other places, to our great comfort. For if, as God by affliction goeth about, as our heavenly schoolmaster, to teach us thus to flee from sin, and to follow righteousness, to contemn this world, and to desire the life to come, with such other godly lessons, so we, like his good disciples, do well learn the same; we shall not need much to fear this plague as dreadful and horrible, but with the blessed man of God, Job, to trust in him, yea, though he should kill us bodily, and patiently to take our sickness as God's good visitation and fatherly correction, and in it quietly and constantly to commit ourselves wholly to the holy will of our most merciful Father, by our Saviour Christ, Isai. lviii.
Dan. iv.

Job xiii.

<small>Deut. xxxii.
Wisd. xvi.
Rom. xiv.
John xviii.</small> whether it be to life or death; knowing that he is the Lord of life and death, and that whether we live or die, we be the Lord's. For it cannot perish which is committed unto him; in whom they that believe, though they die, shall live, and in whom all that live and trust faithfully in his mercy, shall not die eternally; and by whom, through our Saviour Christ, all that die in him have life everlasting; which I beseech the same our most merciful heavenly Father, for the death of our Saviour Jesus Christ, to grant unto us all: unto whom with the Father and the Holy Ghost, one eternal Majesty of the most glorious God, be all honour, glory, and dominion, world without end. Amen.

THANKSGIVING

FOR THE

ABATEMENT OF THE PLAGUE.

A Psalm and Prayer[1] to be used on occasion of the abatement of the plague.

The Psalm.

1. O praise the Lord; for it is a good thing to sing praises unto our God: yea, a joyful and pleasant thing it is to be thankful. Psal. cxlvii.

2. O give thanks unto the Lord, and call upon his name, and tell the people what he hath done. Psal. cv.

3. For it is a good thing to give thanks unto the Lord, and to sing praises unto thy name, O most Highest: Psal. xcii.

4. To tell of thy loving-kindness early in the morning, and of thy truth in the night-season.

[1 This Psalm and Prayer are given by Strype, (p. 475) as the bishop's form of thanksgiving for the *cessation* of the plague; which obviously it cannot be, the collect simply expressing thankfulness to God, that it had pleased him "*partly to mitigate* his severe rod, &c." And, moreover, it contains no reference whatever to the preservation of the queen during the time of sickness, a point which the bishop informed Sir W. Cecil he had reserved for the Collect. "The thanksgevinge for the Quene's Maj^{ties} preservation I have inserted into the Collect, wch was apter place, in my opinion, than in the Psalme. Ye shall see the probe of the printe, and afftter judge." (Vid. Letters, infra. Dati. 21 Januarii. 1563.) The bishop evidently refers to this Psalm and Collect in a letter to Cecil, 15 Dec. 1563. "I sende you herewith a Psalme and a Prayer, wch maye be sette furthe (yff ye so thinke ft goode) in this tyme off ye diminution off sicknesse; myndynge also to cawse another Psalme and Prayer off thankes to be drawen, wch maye be used, when it shall please Godde to sende us perfect deliverie." Vide infra. Letters. Dati. Decemb. 15, 1563.]

Psal. xiii.	5. We will sing of the Lord, because he hath dealt so lovingly with us; yea, we will praise the name of the Lord most Highest.
Psal. xxx.	6. We will magnify thee, O Lord; for thou hast set us up, and not made our foes to triumph over us.
Psal. xcii.	7. For thou, Lord, hast made us glad through thy works; and we will rejoice in giving praise for the operation of thy hands.
Psal. xxx.	8. For, O Lord our God, we cried unto thee, and thou hast healed us.
	9. Thou hast brought our souls out of hell; thou hast kept our life from them that go down to the pit.
Psal. lxxxvi.	10. For great is thy mercy towards us, and thou hast delivered our souls from the nethermost hell.
Psal. lxviii.	11. Praised be the Lord daily, even the God which helpeth us, and poureth his benefits upon us.
Psal. ciii.	12. The Lord is full of compassion and mercy, long-suffering, and of great goodness.
Psal. cxvi.	13. Gracious is the Lord, and righteous; yea, our God is merciful.
Psal. xxx.	14. For his wrath endureth but the twinkling of an eye, and in his pleasure is life: heaviness may endure for a night, but joy cometh in the morning.
Psal. ciii.	15. He will not alway be chiding, neither keepeth he his anger for ever.
	16. He hath not dealt with us after our sins, nor rewarded us according to our wickedness.
	17. For look how wide the east is from the west, so far hath he set our sins from us.
	18. For like as a father pitieth his children, even so is the Lord merciful to them that fear him.
	19. For he knoweth whereof we be made; he remembereth that we are but dust.
Psal. lxxxvi.	20. For thou, Lord, art good and gracious, and of great mercy unto all them that call upon thee.
Psal. lxxxv.	21. Thou hast forgotten the offence of thy people, and covered all their sins.
	22. Thou hast taken away all thy displeasure, and turned thyself from thy wrathful indignation.

23. Thou hast turned our heaviness to joy : thou hast put off our sackcloth, and girded us with gladness. Psal. xxx.

24. Turn thee again, O Lord, at the last, and be gracious unto thy servants. Psal. xc.

25. O satisfy us with thy mercy, and that soon; so shall we rejoice and be glad all the days of our life.

26. Comfort us again, after the time that thou hast plagued us; and for the *year* wherein we have suffered adversity.

27. Shew thy servants thy work, and their children thy glory; and the glorious majesty of the Lord our God be upon us. Prosper thou the work of our hands upon us; O prosper thou our handy work.

Glory be to the Father, and to the Son, and to the Holy Ghost:

As it was in the beginning, is now, and ever shall be, world without end. Amen.

The Prayer, or Collect.

We yield thee hearty thanks, O most merciful Father, that it hath pleased thee in thy wrath to remember thy mercy, and partly to mitigate thy severe rod of this terrible plague, wherewith thou hast hitherto most justly scourged us for our wickedness, and most mercifully revoked us from the same; calling us, (who in health and prosperity had clean forgotten both thee and ourselves,) by sickness and adversity, to the remembrance both of thy justice and judgment, and of our own miserable frailness and mortality; and now, lest we by the heaviness of thine indignation should have utterly despaired, comforting us again by the manifest declaration of thy fatherly inclination to all compassion and clemency. We beseech thee to perfect the work of thy mercy graciously begun in us. And forasmuch as true health is to be sound and whole in that part, which in us is most excellent and like to thy Godhead, we pray thee thoroughly to cure and heal the wounds and diseases of our souls, grievously wounded and poisoned by the daily assaults and infections of the old serpent, Satan, with the deadly plagues of sin and wickedness; by the which inward infections of our minds these outward

[GRINDAL.]

diseases of our bodies have, by the order of thy justice, O Lord, issued and followed: that we, by thy fatherly goodness and benefit obtaining perfect health, both of our minds and bodies, may render unto thee therefore continual and most hearty thanks; and that by flying from sin we may avoid thine anger and plagues, and ever hereafter in innocency and godliness of life studying to serve and please thee, may both by our words and works always glorify thy holy name. Which we beseech thee to grant us, O Father of mercies, and God of all consolation, for thy dear Son our only Saviour and Mediator Jesus Christ's sake. *Amen.*

A Short

Fourme of thankesgeuyng to

God for ceassing the contagious sicknes of the plague, to be vsed in Common prayer, on Sundayes, Wednesdayes, and Frydayes, in steade of the Common prayers, vsed in the time of mortalitie. Set forth by the Byshop of London, to be vsed in the Citie of London, and the rest of his diocesse, and in other places also at the discretion of the ordinary Ministers of the Churches.

(∴)

A

SHORT FORM OF THANKSGIVING TO GOD[1]

FOR

CEASING THE PLAGUE.

¶ After the end of the collect in the Litany which beginneth with these words, 'We humbly beseech thee, O Father,' &c. shall follow this Psalm, to be said of the minister, with the answer of the people.

Psal. lxxxv. 1. LORD, thou art become gracious unto thy land, thou hast turned away the afflictions of thy servants.

2. Thou hast taken away all thy displeasure, and turned thyself from thy wrathful indignation.

Psal. xciv. 3. For if thou, Lord, hadst not helped us, it had not failed, but our souls had been put to silence.

4. But when we said, Our feet have slipped, thy mercy, O Lord, helped us up.

5. In the multitude of the sorrows that we had in our hearts, thy comforts have refreshed our souls.

Psal. lxii. 6. Our souls waited still upon the Lord, our souls hanged upon his help, our hope was always in him.

7. In the Lord's word did we rejoice, in God's word did we comfort ourselves.

Psal. l. 8. For the Lord said, Call upon me in the time of trouble, and I will hear thee, and thou shalt praise me.

[[1] This form of Thanksgiving is taken from a printed copy in the State Paper Office, (Domestic, Anno 1564,) in all probability the identical copy sent to Secretary Cecil. Strype, it has already been observed, has fallen into an error with respect to these services. It should, however, be remarked, that that indefatigable writer was not ignorant of this Form of Thanksgiving, but he attributes it to the bishop of Ely. (See Strype, Parker, vol. III. p. 60.) It is probable, that the bishop of Ely may have adopted the form set forth by Grindal's authority in London.]

A SHORT FORM OF THANKSGIVING, &c.

9. So when we were poor, needy, sickly, and in heaviness, the Lord cared for us: he was our help and our Saviour according to his word. Psal. xl. lxix.

10. In our adversity and distress he hath lift up our heads, and saved us from utter destruction. Psal. xxvii.

11. He hath delivered our souls from death, he hath fed us in the time of dearth, he hath saved us from the noisome pestilence. Psal. xxxiii. xci.

12. Therefore will we offer in his holy temple the oblation of thanksgiving with great gladness; we will sing and speak praises unto the Lord our Saviour. Psal. xxvii.

13. We will give thanks unto the Lord, for he is gracious, and his mercy endureth for ever. Psal. cvi.

14. The Lord is full of compassion and mercy, long suffering, plenteous in goodness and pity. Psal. lxxxvi. ciii.

15. His mercy is greater than the heavens, and his gracious goodness reacheth unto the clouds. Psal. lvii. cviii.

16. Like as a father pitieth his own children, even so is the Lord merciful unto them that fear him. Psal. ciii.

17. Therefore will we praise thee and thy mercies, O God; unto thee will we sing, O thou Holy One of Israel. Psal. lxxi.

18. We will sing a new song unto thee, O God; we will praise the Lord with psalms of thanksgiving. Psal. xcviii.

19. O sing praises, sing praises unto our God: O sing praises, sing praises unto our King. Psal. xlvii.

20. For God is the king of the earth; sing praises with understanding.

21. We will magnify thee, O God our king; we will praise thy name for ever and ever. Psal. cxlv.

22. Every day will we give thanks unto thee, and praise thy name for ever and ever.

23. Our mouth shall speak the praises of the Lord; and let all flesh give thanks to his holy name for ever and ever.

24. Blessed be the Lord God of Israel for ever: and blessed be the name of his Majesty, world without end. Amen. Amen. Psal. xxi. lxxii.

¶ After this Psalm shall be said by the Minister, openly and with an high voice, the Collect following.

The Collect.

O heavenly and most merciful Father, what mind or what tongue can conceive, or give thee worthy thanks, for thy most great and infinite benefits, which thou hast bestowed, and dost daily bestow upon us, most unworthy of this thy so great and continual goodness and favour, though we should bestow all our life, power, travail, and understanding thereabouts only and wholly? When we were yet as clay is in the potter's hands, to be framed at his pleasure, vessels of honour or dishonour, of thy only goodness, without our deserving, (for how could we deserve any thing before we were any thing?) thou hast created and made us of nothing, not dumb beasts void of reason, not vile vermins creeping upon the earth, but the noblest and most honourable of all thy worldly creatures, little inferior to thy heavenly angels, endued with understanding, adorned with all excellent gifts, both of body and of mind, exalted to the dominion over all other thy earthly creatures, yea, the sun and the moon with other heavenly lights appointed to our service, enriched with the possession of all things either necessary for our use, or delectable for our comfort. And as thou hast made us so excellent of nothing, so hast thou restored us being lost, by thy son our Saviour Jesus Christ, dying for us upon the cross, both more marvellously and mercifully than thou didst first create us of nothing; besides that thou dost continually forgive and pardon our sins, into the which we do daily and hourly fall most dangerously, yea, deadly also, damnably, and desperately, were not this thy present and most ready help of thy mercy. And what have we, that we have not by thee? or what be we, but by thee? All which unspeakable benefits thou hast, like a most loving father, bestowed upon us, that we thereby provoked might, like loving children, humbly honour and obediently serve thee, our good and most gracious Father. But forsomuch as we have dishonoured thee by and with the abusing of thy good gifts, thou dost even in this also, like a father correcting his children whom he loveth, when they offend, no less mercifully punish us for the said abuse of thy gifts, than thou didst bounteously before give them unto us; scourging us sometime with wars and troubles, sometimes with famine and scarcity, sometimes with sickness and diseases, and sundry other kinds of plagues, for the abusing of peace, quietness, plenty, health, and such other thy good gifts, against thy holy word and will, and against thy honour and our own health, to thy great displeasure and high indignation. As thou now of late terribly, but most justly and deservedly, plagued us with contagious, dreadful, and deadly sickness, from the which yet thou hast most mercifully, and without all deservings on our part, even of thine own goodness, now again delivered us and saved us. By the which thy most merciful deliverance, and especially in that, amongst other thy great and manifold benefits, it hath pleased thee of thine eternal goodness, most mercifully and miraculously, not only heretofore to deliver our most gracious Queen and governor from all perils and dangers, yea, even from the gates of death; but now also to preserve her from this late most dangerous contagion and infection; like as thou hast exceedingly comforted our sorrowful hearts, so we for the same do yield unto thee, as our bounden duty is, our most humble and hearty thanks, O most merciful Father, by thy dear Son our Saviour Jesus Christ; in whose name we pray thee to continue this thy gracious favour towards us, and stay us in thy grace, defending us against the assaults of Satan, that we, continually enjoying thy favour, with the health of our souls, which is the quietness of our consciences, as a taste here in earth of thy heavenly joys, and as a pledge of thy eternal mercy, may always in this life render therefore all laud and honour to thee, and after this transitory and miserable life may ever live and joy with thee, through the same our only Saviour and Mediator Jesus Christ, thy only Son, who with thee and the Holy Ghost, one immortal Majesty of the most glorious God, is to be praised and magnified, world without end. Amen.

Psalmes whereof may be vsed, in stede of the ordinary Psalmes in the Morning Prayer, one, two, or three, in order, according to the length therof: And also one of the same, may be said or songe in the beginning or endyng of publique prayer.

34	95	96	100
103	107	116	118
145	146	147	148.

INJUNCTIONS

AND

ARTICLES OF INQUIRY,

GIVEN AT VARIOUS TIMES.

Injunctions

given by the Moste Reverende Father in Christe, Edmonde, by the Providence of God Archbishop of Yorke, Prymate of Englande and Metropolitane, in his Metropoliticall Visitation of the Province of Yorke, as well to the Clergye, as to the Laytye of the same Province,

Anno Domini,

1571.

INJUNCTIONS[1],

&c. &c.

I. FOR THE CLERGY.

1. INPRIMIS, You must travail diligently and painfully to set forth God's true religion, and adorn the same with example of godly life, being circumspect that you offend no man either by light behaviour or by light apparel.

2. ITEM, Upon every Sunday and holiday ye shall in your church or chapel at convenient hours reverently and distinctly say or sing the Common Prayer, appointed by the laws of this realm, both in the forenoon and afternoon, standing in a pulpit or seat appointed for that purpose, and so turning your face towards the people, as they may best hear the same. And upon every Wednesday and Friday in the forenoon (not being holy day) ye shall in like manner say the litany and other prayers appointed for the day, and likewise the evening prayer every Saturday and holy-even, and shall also, at all times requisite and convenient, duly and reverently minister the two holy sacraments, that is to say, Baptism and the Lord's Supper, commonly called the holy Communion, according to such order as is set forth in the Book of Common Prayer and administration of the sacraments.

3. ITEM, Ye shall minister the holy Communion every

[1] The Archbishop the next year instituted a metropolitical Visitation, beginning the 15th of May, 1571, whereof there seemed, in these parts especially, to be great need.... He gave forth his own Injunctions as well to the Clergy as to the Laity, consisting of twenty-five articles each, which are of good length; and in all of them he shewed a great zeal for the discipline and good government of the church.... By the heeding of these Injunctions one may observe how old popish customs still prevailed in these northern quarters, and therefore what need there was of this general Visitation. See Strype, Grind. pp. 246—250.
The state in which the Archbishop found his province will be seen hereafter in a letter to Sir W. Cecil, dated 29 August, 1570.]

month once at the least in every of your churches and chapels, where ministration of the sacraments is permitted. And to the intent that the people may better understand their duties, and come the better prepared to the holy Communion, ye shall monthly exhort your parishioners to come to the same, and always give them warning thereof the next Sunday before ye minister the same, declaring unto them, that by the laws of this realm every person of convenient age is bound to receive the holy Communion at the least three times in the year, and namely at Easter for once.

4. ITEM, That at all times, when ye minister the holy sacraments, and upon Sundays and other holy days, when ye say the Common Prayer and other divine service in your parish churches and chapels, and likewise at all marriages and burials, ye shall, when ye minister, wear a clean and decent surplice with large sleeves; and shall minister the holy Communion in no chalice nor any profane cup or glass, but in a Communion cup of silver, and with a cover of silver, appointed also for the ministration of the Communion-bread. Ye shall not deliver the Communion-bread unto the people into their mouths, but into their hands; nor shall use at the ministration of the Communion any gestures, rites, or ceremonies not appointed by the Book of Common Prayer, as crossing or breathing over the sacramental bread and wine, nor any shewing or lifting up of the same to the people, to be by them worshipped and adored, nor any such like; nor shall use any oil or chrism, tapers, spattle, or any other popish ceremony in the ministration of the sacrament of Baptism.

5. ITEM, Ye shall every Sunday and holy day openly in your church or chapel call for, hear, and instruct the children and servants, both menkind and womenkind, that be of convenient age within your parish (at the least so many of them at once by course as the time will serve, and as you may well hear and instruct for an hour at the least) before evening prayer, in the Ten Commandments, the Articles of the Belief, and the Lord's Prayer in English, and diligently examine and teach them the Catechism set forth in the Book of Common

Prayer. And to the intent this thing may be more effectually executed, ye shall take the names of all the children, young men, maidens, and servants in your parish, that be above six years of age and under twenty, which cannot say the Catechism, and shall call by course certain of them by name, every Sunday and every holy day, to come to the Catechism, whereby you may easily note and observe what parents or masters be negligent in sending their children and servants to be instructed, and take occasion thereof, both privately and openly, to exhort them to send their youth as they are appointed, and shall present the refusers to the ordinary.

6. ITEM, You shall not admit to the receiving of the holy Communion any of your parish, which be openly known to live in any notorious sin, as incest, adultery, fornication, drunkenness, much swearing, bawdery, usury, or such like, without due penance first done to the satisfaction of the congregation; nor any malicious person that is out of charity, or that hath done any open wrong to his neighbour by word or deed, without due reconciliation first made to the party that is wronged or maliced.

7. ITEM, You shall not admit to the holy Communion any of your parish, men or women, being above four and twenty years of age, that cannot say by heart, at the least, the Ten Commandments, the Articles of the Faith, and the Lord's Prayer in English; nor any, being fourteen years and above, and under four and twenty years of age, that cannot say by heart the Catechism that is set forth in the said Book of Common Prayer.

8. ITEM, For that purpose you shall, before Easter and all other times of the year, when the holy Communion is to be by you ministered, give warning before unto your parishioners to come unto you, either in the afternoon of some Sunday or holy day, or the day before they purpose to receive, or at some other times before, as necessity shall cause you to appoint, if there be any multitude; or (if the number be but small) in the morning, at the farthest, before they shall receive, so that it be before the beginning of the morning

prayer, so many of them as intend to receive, and not only to signify unto you their names, to the intent ye may keep a register or note of all such persons as from time to time shall communicate, but also to be by you examined whether they can say by heart the Ten Commandments, the Articles of the Faith, the Lord's Prayer, and the Catechism, according as after the diversity of their ages is above required. And such of them as either cannot, or will not, recite the same by heart unto you, ye shall repel and put back from the holy Communion, until they shall be able and willing to learn, and can by heart recite the same unto you. For your better assistance wherein, ye shall call upon and require the churchwardens and sworn men of your parish to be present (one of them at the least) at every such examination, to the intent they may help to put this good order in practice; and ye shall take a note of such wilful and negligent persons, as ye shall find faulty in this behalf, and so present the same, and the churchwardens and sworn men also, to the ordinary, if they shall refuse so to assist you.

9. ITEM, Ye shall not marry any persons, or ask the banns of marriage between any persons, which before were single, unless they can say the Catechism by heart, and will recite the same unto you before the asking of the banns. And ye shall not marry any persons without the banns be thrice, on three several Sundays or holy days, first openly asked, without any impediment or forbidding; neither shall ye marry any persons within the degrees of affinity or consanguinity, by the laws of God forbidden, so set out for an admonition in a table lately appointed to be affixed in your parish church; for the better knowledge of which degrees ye shall read unto your parishioners the said table every year twice at the least.

10. ITEM, Ye shall not admit to answer as godfathers or godmothers, at the christening of any child, any person or persons, except he, she, and they have before received the holy Communion, and can say by heart the Articles of the Christian Faith in English, and will recite the same before you at the time of ministration of Baptism, or before the minister,

if he, she, or they be thereunto required, and, being young folks, except he, she, or they can say by heart the whole Catechism, and will recite the same before you, as is aforesaid.

11. ITEM, Ye shall not church any unmarried woman, which hath been gotten with child out of lawful matrimony, except it be upon some Sunday or holy day, and except either she, before her child-birth, have done due penance for her fault to the satisfaction of the congregation, or at her coming to be churched she do openly acknowledge her fault before the congregation accordingly, and shew herself to be very penitent for the same, leaving it free for the ordinary to punish her further at his discretion.

12. ITEM, Ye shall every Sunday and holy day, when there is no sermon in your church or chapel, distinctly and plainly read in the pulpit some one of the Homilies set forth by the Queen's Majesty's authority, or one part thereof, at the least, in such sort as the same are divided and appointed to be read by the two books of the Homilies; and every holy day, when there is no sermon, ye shall, immediately after the gospel, plainly and distinctly recite to your parishioners the Lord's Prayer, the Articles of the Faith, and the Ten Commandments in English; and, being not admitted by the ordinary or other lawful authority, ye shall not expound any scripture or matter of doctrine by the way of exhortation, or otherwise, and thereby omit and leave off the reading of the Homilies.

13. ITEM, Ye shall plainly and distinctly read in your church or chapel unto the people, between the Litany and the Communion, the form of Commination against sinners, with certain prayers following the same, set forth in the latter end of the Book of Common Prayer, three times at the least in the year, that is to say, for order's sake, yearly upon one of the two Sundays next before Easter, for the first time; upon one of the two Sundays next before the feast of Pentecost, for the second time; and for the third time, upon one of the two Sundays next before the feast of the birth of our Lord, over and besides the accustomed reading thereof the first day of Lent.

14. ITEM, Ye shall read openly in your church, in time of Divine service, twice every year, upon some of the Sundays within one month next after the feasts of Easter and Saint Michael the archangel, plainly, without addition or change, a declaration of certain principal Articles of Religion[1], set forth by both the archbishops and the rest of the bishops of this realm for the unity of doctrine.

15. ITEM, Ye shall not proclaim, bid, or observe, nor willingly suffer your parishioners to observe, any holy days or fasting days heretofore abrogated, or not appointed by the new Calendar of the book of Common Prayer, to be used or kept as holy days or fasting days, nor give the people any knowledge thereof by any indirect means.

16. ITEM, Ye shall keep well the Registers of all weddings, burials, and christenings within your parish, according to the order prescribed in the Queen's Majesty's Injunctions[2], and shall present a copy of them, every year once, by indenture to the ordinary or his officers.

17. ITEM, You shall preach, or, by such as are lawfully licensed, shall cause to be preached, in the churches where you are parsons or vicars, one sermon every quarter of the year at the least.

18. ITEM, No minister or priest shall serve two cures at one time, nor say common service in any private man's house, without special license under the ordinary's seal; nor any curate shall serve any one cure within this province without letters testimonial of the ordinary of the place from whence he came, testifying the cause of his departing from thence, and of his behaviour there; nor unless he shall first obtain and have special license in writing, under the seal of the ordinary of the place whereunto he cometh, for his admission to such a cure, and shall shew the same to the churchwardens before he enter to serve any such cure.

[1 The Thirty-nine Articles.]
[2 Art. x. See Wilkins, Concil. iv. 183; or Cardwell, Doc. Ann. vol. I. p. 178.]

19. ITEM, Ye shall read openly in your churches and chapels, in time of divine service, the Queen's Majesty's Injunctions every quarter of a year once; and these our Injunctions, concerning as well the clergy as the laity, every half-year once.

20. ITEM, For the putting of the churchwardens and sworn-men better in remembrance of their duty, in observing and noting all such persons of your parish as do offend in not coming to divine service, ye shall openly every Sunday, after ye have read the second lesson at morning and evening prayer, monish and warn the churchwardens and sworn-men of your parish to look to their oaths and charge in this behalf, and to observe who, contrary to the law, do that day offend either in absenting themselves negligently or wilfully from their parish church or chapel, or unreverently use[3] themselves in the time of divine service, and so note the same, to the intent they may either present such offenders to the ordinary, when they shall be required thereunto, or levy and take, by way of distress, to the use of the poor, such forfeitures as are appointed by a statute[4] made in the first year of the Queen's Majesty's reign in that behalf. And if the churchwardens and sworn-men be negligent, or shall refuse to do their duty that way, ye shall present to the ordinary both them and all such others of your parish as shall offend, either in absenting themselves from the church, or by unreverent behaviour in the church, contrary to the same statute.

21. ITEM, Ye shall from time to time diligently call upon and exhort your parishioners to contribute and give towards the relief of the poor, as they may well spare; and specially when ye visit them that be sick, and make their testaments; and for your own parts also ye shall charitably relieve the poor to your ability.

22. ITEM, Ye shall daily read, at the least, one chapter of the Old Testament and another of the New, with good advisement: and such of you as be under the degree of a Master of Arts shall provide and have of your own, according to the

[3 Use: behave.]   [4 Cap. 16.]

[GRINDAL.]

Queen's Majesty's Injunctions[1], at the least the New Testament, both in Latin and English, conferring the one with the other, every day one chapter thereof at the least, so that upon the examination of the archdeacon, commissary, or their officers in synods and visitations, or at other appointed times, it may appear how ye profit in the study of holy scripture.

23. ITEM, Ye shall not keep, or suffer to be kept, in your parsonage or vicarage houses, any alehouses, tippling-houses, or taverns, nor shall sell ale, beer, or wine. Nor any of you shall keep any suspected woman in your house, or be an incontinent liver, given to drunkenness or idleness. Nor any of you, being unmarried, shall keep in your house any woman under the age of threescore years, except she be your daughter by former marriage, or be your mother, aunt, sister, or niece; and such an one as ye shall keep shall be of good name and fame. Nor any of you shall be a haunter of taverns, alehouses, or suspected places, or a hunter, hawker, dicer, carder, tabler, swearer, or otherwise give any evil example of life; but contrariwise, at all times, when ye shall have leisure, ye shall hear or read some part of holy scripture, or some other good authors, or shall occupy yourselves with some other honest study or exercise, and oftentimes give yourselves to earnest prayer, and shall be diligent in visiting the sick and comforting of them.

24. ITEM, You shall exhort your parishioners to obedience towards their prince, and all other that be in authority, and to charity and mutual love amongst themselves, helping to reconcile them which shall happen to be at variance at any time; and if ye cannot preach, ye shall teach children to read, to write, and to know their duties towards God, their prince, parents, and all others. And, by all means ye can, ye shall endeavour yourselves to profit the commonwealth, having always in mind, that ye ought to excel all other in purity of life, and should be examples to your people to live well and christianly, not giving any way just cause of offence.

25. ITEM, All proprietaries, parsons, vicars, and clerks,

[1 Art. xvi.]

having churches or chapels within this province, shall cause the chancels or choirs of their churches or chapels to be from time to time, according to the Queen's Majesty's Injunctions[2] in that behalf, sufficiently repaired and maintained in good estate; and all parsons, vicars, and other clerks, having mansion houses, belonging to their promotions, shall likewise repair and keep the same in good estate; and upon the same chancels or choirs and mansion houses, with buildings thereunto belonging, being in decay, shall yearly bestow, according to the same Injunctions, the fifth part of that their benefice, till they be fully repaired, and, being repaired, shall maintain the same in good estate and order.

[[2] Art. XIII.]

INJUNCTIONS,

&c. &c.

II. FOR THE LAITY.

1. FIRST, We do enjoin and straightly command, that from henceforth no parish clerk, nor any other person, not being ordered, at the least, for a deacon, shall presume to solemnize Matrimony, or to minister the sacrament of Baptism, or to deliver to the communicants the Lord's cup at the celebration of the holy Communion. And that no person, not being a minister, deacon, or, at the least, tolerated by the ordinary in writing, do attempt to supply the office of a minister in saying of divine service openly in any church or chapel.

2. ITEM, To the intent that the people may the better hear the morning and evening prayer, when the same by the minister is said, and be the more edified thereby, we do enjoin that the churchwardens of every parish, in places as well exempt as not exempt, at the charges of the parish, shall procure a decent low pulpit to be erected and made in the body of the church out of hand, wherein the minister shall stand with his face towards the people, when he readeth morning and evening prayer; provided always that, where the churches are very small, it shall suffice that the minister stand in his accustomed stall in the choir, so that a convenient desk or lettern, with a room to turn his face towards the people, be there provided by the said churchwardens at the charges of the parish; the judgment and order whereof, and also the form and order of the pulpit or seat aforesaid in greater churches, we do refer unto the archdeacon of the place or his official; provided also, that the prayers and other service appointed for the ministration of the holy Communion be said and done at the communion table, except the epistle and gospel, which shall be read in the said pulpit or stall, and also the ten commandments when there is no Communion.

3. ITEM, That the churchwardens, according to the cus-

tom of every parish, shall be chosen by the consent, as well of the parson, vicar, or curate, as of the parishioners; otherwise they shall not be churchwardens; neither shall they continue any longer than one year in that office, except perhaps they shall be chosen again. They shall not sell or alienate any bells, or other church goods, without consent of the ordinary in writing first had; nor shall put the money that shall come of any such sale to any other uses, than to the reparations of their churches or chapels, or for providing of necessaries for the same churches or chapels. And all churchwardens, at the end of every year, shall give up to the parson, vicar, or curate, and their parishioners, a just account written in a book, to be provided at the charges of the parish for that purpose, of all such money, ornaments, stock, rents, or other church goods, as they have received during the time they were in office; and also shall particularly shew what cost they have bestowed in reparations and other things for the use of the church. And going out of their offices, they shall truly deliver up in the sight of the parishioners to the next churchwardens, and note in the said church book, whatsoever money, ornaments, stock, or other church goods, shall remain and be in their hands, at the time of giving up of their accounts.

4. ITEM, That the churchwardens in every parish shall, at the costs and charges of the parish, provide (if the same be not already provided) all things necessary and requisite for common prayer and administration of the holy sacraments, on this side the 20th day of ——— next ensuing, specially the book of Common Prayer, with the new calendar, and a psalter to the same, the English Bible in the largest volume, the two tomes of the Homilies, with the Homilies lately written against rebellion, the table of the Ten Commandments, a convenient pulpit well placed, a comely and decent table, standing on a frame, for the holy Communion, with a fair linen cloth to lay upon the same, and some covering of silk, buckram, or other such like, for the clean keeping thereof; a fair and comely communion cup of silver, and a cover of silver for the same, which may serve also for the ministration of the communion-bread; a decent large

surplice with sleeves, a sure coffer with two locks and keys for keeping of the register book, and a strong chest or box for the almose of the poor, with three locks and keys to the same, and all other things necessary in and to the premises; and shall also provide, before the said day, the paraphrases of Erasmus in English upon the gospels, and the same set up in some convenient place within their church or chapel, the charges whereof the parson or proprietary and parishioners shall by equal portions bear, according to the Queen's Majesty's Injunctions[1]; all which books must be whole and not torn or unperfect in any wise. And the churchwardens also shall, from time to time, at the charges of the parish, provide bread and wine for the Communion; and for that purpose shall take some order among the parishioners, that every one may pay such a reasonable sum towards the same, as may suffice for the finding of bread and wine for the Communion throughout the whole year, so as no Communion at any time be disappointed for want of bread and wine.

5. ITEM, That the churchwardens shall see that in their churches and chapels all altars be utterly taken down, and clear removed even unto the foundation, and the place where they stood paved, and the wall whereunto they joined whited over, and made uniform with the rest, so as no breach or rupture appear. And that the altar-stones be broken, defaced, and bestowed to some common use. And that the rood-lofts be taken down and altered, so that the upper boards and timber thereof, both behind and above where the rood lately did hang, and also the seller or loft be quite taken down unto the cross-beam, whereunto the partition between the choir and the body of the church is fastened, and that the said beam have some convenient crest put upon the same. And that all the boards, beams, and other stuff of the rood-lofts be sold by the churchwardens to the use of the church, so as no part thereof be kept and observed.

6. ITEM, That the churchwardens shall, from time to time, see that their churches and chapels and the steeples thereof be diligently and well repaired with lead, tile, slate, or shingle,

[1 Art. VI.]

lime-stone, timber, glass, and all other necessaries; and that their churches and chapels be kept clean and decently, that they be not loathsome to any, either by dust, sand, gravel, or any filth; and that there be no feasts, dinners, or common drinking kept in the church; and that the church-yard be well fenced, and cleanly kept, and that no folks be suffered to dance in the same.

7. ITEM, That the churchwardens and minister shall see that antiphoners[2], mass books, grailes[3], portesses[4], processionals[5], manuales[6], legendaries[7], and all other books of late belonging to their church or chapel, which served for the superstitious Latin service, be utterly defaced, rent, and abolished. And that all vestments[8], albes, tunicles, stoles, phanons[9], pixes[10], paxes[11], hand-bells, sacring-bells[12], censers, chrismatories[13], crosses, candlesticks, holy-water-stocks[14], or fat

[[2] Antiphoners: a book containing antiphones.]

[[3] Graile: from the Latin *gradale*, or *graduale*: a book containing graduals. "*Gradale* sic dictum a gradalibus, in tali libro contentis: stricte tamen ponitur *gradale* pro eo quod *gradatim* ponitur post epistolam; hic tamen ponitur pro libro integro, in quo contineri debent Officium aspersionis aquæ benedictæ, Missarum inchoationes sive officia, Kyrie cum versibus, Gloria in excelsis, Alleluia, et Tractus, Sequentiæ, Symbolum cantandum in missa, Offertoria, Sanctus, Agnus, Communio, etc. quæ ad chorum spectant in missæ solennis decantatione." Lyndewode Provinciale, fol. 137. note.]

[[4] Portess: breviary.]

[[5] Processional: a book of litanies, &c. used in solemn processions.]

[[6] Manual: a book of the occasional services.]

[[7] Legendary: a book containing the lives and miracles of saints.]

[[8] For a description of these ecclesiastical vestments, see Palmer, Orig. Liturg. Appendix, Sects IV. V. VI., vol. ii. p. 314.]

[[9] Phanon, or fanon: a kind of scarf or napkin, worn on the left arm of the priest while celebrating mass. "Quartum vero mappula sive mantile sacerdotis indumentum est, quod vulgo *phanonem* vocant." Rabanus Maurus. de Institut. Cleric. Lib. I. c. 18. Biblioth. Patr. tom. x. col. 572. Vid. Spelman, Glossar. sub voce.]

[[10] Pix: the box in which the host was preserved.]

[[11] Pax: called also *osculatorium*, usually an image or relic which was handed round to be kissed; a custom which took its rise from the *osculum pacis*, 'the kiss of peace,' in the primitive church.]

[[12] Sacring-bell: the bell used at the elevation of the host.]

[[13] Chrismatory: a vessel for the oil used in anointing at baptism and extreme unction.]

[[14] Stone basins for holy water, usually placed at the entrance of churches.]

images[1], and all other relics and monuments of superstition and idolatry, be utterly defaced, broken, and destroyed; and if they cannot come by any of the same, they shall present to the ordinary what they cannot come by, and in whose custody the same is, to the intent further order may be taken for the defacing thereof.

8. ITEM, When any man or woman, dwelling near to the church in any city, borough, or great town, is in passing out of this life, the parish clerk or sexton shall knoll the bell, to move the people to pray for the sick person. And after the time of the departing of any christian body out of this life, the churchwardens shall see that neither there be any more ringing but one short peal before the burial, and another short peal after the burial, without ringing of any handbells, or other superfluous or superstitious ringing, either before or at the time of the burial, or at any time after the same; nor any other form of service said or sung, or other ceremonies used at any burial, than are appointed by the book of Common Prayer. And also that neither on All Saints' day after evening prayer, nor the day next after, of late called All Souls' day, there be any ringing at all then to Common Prayer, when the same shall happen to fall upon the Sunday. And that no month-minds[2] or yearly commemorations of the dead, nor any other superstitious ceremonies, be observed or used, which tend either to the maintenance of prayer for the dead, or of the popish purgatory.

9. ITEM, That the churchwardens shall not suffer any ringing or tolling of bells to be on Sundays or holy days used between the Morning Prayer, Litany, and Communion, nor in any other time of Common Prayer, reading of the Homilies, or of preaching, except it be one bell, in convenient time to be rung or knolled before a sermon; nor shall suffer any other ringing to be used upon Saints' evens, or festival

[1 Solid images, as distinguished from pictures.]
[2 Month-minds: monthly remembrances of the departed. Persons in their wills often directed that requiems should be performed for the repose of their souls at stated intervals, whether of days, months, or years; whence these reminiscenses or *memories* (as they were called) took the names of " day's minds," " month's minds," or " year's minds."]

days, saving to Common Prayer, and that moderately and without excess; nor the minister shall pause or stay between the Morning Prayer, Litany, and Communion, but shall continue and say the Morning Prayer, Litany, and Communion, or the service appointed to be said when there is no Communion, together, without any intermission, to the intent the people may continue together in prayer and hearing the Word of God, and not depart out of the church during all the time of the whole divine service.

10. ITEM, That all fathers, mothers, masters, and other governors of youth, shall in every parish cause their children and servants, both menkind and womenkind, being above seven years of age and under twenty years, which have not learned the catechism, or at the least such and so many of them as the minister shall appoint, diligently to come to the church every Sunday and every holy day, at the time appointed, and there diligently and obediently to hear, learn, and be ordered by the minister, until such time as they have learned all the said catechism by heart; and shall give to the minister the names of all their children and servants, both menkind and womenkind, being above seven years and under twenty years of age, to the intent he may well call for them to be examined and instructed in the said catechism. And if any of the said fathers, mothers, masters, or other governors of youth, shall refuse or neglect so to send their children or servants unto the minister to be examined and instructed at the times appointed, or to give their names, as is aforesaid, or if any of the said young folks shall refuse to be examined and instructed, that then the minister and churchwardens shall present such negligent persons and refusers to the ordinary, to be by him punished accordingly.

11. ITEM, That all men and women of fourteen years of age and upwards shall (as by the laws of this realm they are bound) receive in their own parish churches or chapels the holy Communion thrice, at the least, every year; and namely at Easter or thereabouts for once; and yearly before Easter, at convenient times, and namely on Sundays in Lent at afternoon, or in some of the work days next before Easter,

as the parson, vicar, or curate shall appoint, they shall, before they receive, come to the minister, and recite to him, such of them as be of fourteen years or above and under twenty-four years of age, the whole catechism by heart; and such of them as be of twenty-three years of age and upwards, the catechism, or, at the least, the Lord's Prayer, the Articles of the Faith, and the Ten Commandments, likewise by heart in English; and whosoever either cannot, or wilfully and stubbornly shall refuse to recite and say the same by heart before their minister, shall be repelled and put back from the Communion table. And the churchwardens and minister shall present all such refusers, and all others that shall not receive thrice a year the holy Communion, unto the ordinary yearly at the next visitation after Easter.

12. ITEM, The churchwardens shall not suffer any pedler or others whatsoever to set out any wares to sale, either in the porches of churches or in the church-yards, nor any where else on holy days or Sundays, while any part of divine service is in doing, or while any sermon is in preaching.

13. ITEM, That no inn-keeper, alehouse-keeper, victualler, or tippler, shall admit or suffer any person or persons in his house or backside to eat, drink, or play at cards, tables, bowls, or other games in time of Common Prayer, preachings, or reading of Homilies, on the Sundays or holy days; and that there be no shops set open on Sundays or holy days, nor any butchers or other suffered to sell meat or other things upon the Sundays or holy days, in like time of Common Prayer, preaching, or reading of the Homilies. And that in any fairs or common markets, falling upon the Sunday, there be no shewing of any wares before all the morning service and the sermon (if there be any) be done. And if any shall offend in this behalf, the churchwardens and sworn-men, after once warning given unto them, shall present them by name unto the ordinary.

14. ITEM, That the lay people of every parish (as they be bound by the laws of this realm) and especially householders, having no lawful excuse to be absent, shall faithfully and

diligently endeavour themselves to resort with their children and servants to their parish church or chapel on the holy days, and chiefly upon the Sundays, both to morning and evening prayer and other divine service, and, upon reasonable let thereof, to some other usual place where Common Prayer is used, and then and there abide orderly and soberly during all the time of Common Prayer, Homilies, sermons, and other service of God there used, reverently and devoutly giving themselves to prayer and hearing of the word of God. And that the churchwardens and sworn-men, above all others, shall be diligent in frequenting and resorting to their parish churches or chapels upon Sundays and holy days, to the intent they may note and mark all such persons, as upon any such days shall absent themselves from the church, and upon such shall examine them upon the cause thereof.

15. ITEM, That the churchwardens and sworn-men shall not suffer any persons to walk, talk, or otherwise unreverently to behave themselves in any church or chapel, nor to use any gaming, or to sit abroad in the streets or church-yards, or in any tavern or alehouse, upon the Sundays or other holy days, in the time of divine service, or of any sermon, whether it be before noon or after noon; but, after warning once given, shall punish both them and all others that negligently or wilfully shall absent themselves from divine service, or come very lately to the church upon Sundays or holy days, having no lawful let or hindrance, and those also that without any just cause shall depart out of the church before the divine service or sermon be done, according to a statute made in the first year of the Queen's Majesty's reign, printed and set forth in the beginning of the book of Common Prayer; that is to say, the churchwardens shall levy and take of every one that wilfully or negligently so shall offend the forfeiture of twelve-pence for every such offence, and shall also present them to the ordinary; which forfeitures they shall levy, according to the same statute, by distraining the goods, lands, and tenements of such offenders, and shall (as by the same statute they are appointed) deliver the money that cometh thereof to the collectors, for the use of the poor people of the same parish.

16. ITEM, That no person or persons whatsoever shall wear beads, or pray, either in Latin or in English, upon beads, or knots, or any other like superstitious thing; nor shall pray upon any popish Latin or English Primer, or other like book, nor shall burn any candles in the church superstitiously upon the feast of the Purification of the Virgin Mary, commonly called Candlemas Day[1]; nor shall resort to any popish priest for shrift[2] or auricular confession in Lent, or at any other time; nor shall worship any cross or any image or picture upon the same, nor give any reverence thereunto, nor superstitiously shall make upon themselves the sign of the cross when they first enter into any church to pray, nor shall say *De profundis*[3] for the dead, or rest at any cross in carrying any corpse to burying, nor shall leave any little crosses of wood there.

17. ITEM, That yearly, at Midsummer, the parson, vicar, or curate, and churchwardens shall choose two collectors, or more, for the relief of the poor of every parish, according to a statute made in that behalf in the fifth year of the Queen's Majesty's reign, intituled " An act for the relief of the poor," and renewed in the last parliament; which collectors shall weekly gather the charitable almose of the parishioners, and distribute the same to the poor, where most need shall be, without fraud or partiality, and shall quarterly make unto the parson, vicar, or curate, and churchwardens, a just account thereof in writing. And if any person of ability shall obstinately or frowardly refuse to give reasonably towards the relief of the poor, or shall wilfully discourage others from so charitable a deed, or shall withdraw his accustomed almose without just cause, the churchwardens and sworn-men shall present to

[1 Candlemas, Feb. 2: so called from the blessing of candles on that day. "Sacerdos indutus cum ministris procedat ad benedicendum candelas. Si vero hoc festum venerit in Dominica, sit benedictio post aspersionem aquæ benedictæ more solito. Finita benedictione, et cum inceperint distribuere candelas, a choro cantetur antiphona, 'Lumen ad revelationem gentium, &c. &c.'" Processionale Romanum. Paris, 1666. p. 263.]

[2 Shrift: from the verb *shrive*, to confess: whence Shrove-Tuesday, on which day it was customary to confess.]

[3 An antiphone in the office for the dead.]

the ordinary every such person, so refusing to give, discouraging others, or withdrawing his accustomed almose, that reformation may be made therein.

18. ITEM, That, for the retaining of the perambulation of the circuit of every parish yearly, the parson, vicar, or curate, and churchwardens, with certain of the substantial men of every parish, such as the minister and churchwardens shall think meet to require, shall in the days of the rogations, commonly called Cross-week, or Gang-days, walk the accustomed bounds of every parish; and in the same perambulation or going about, the minister shall use none other ceremony than to say in English the two psalms beginning *Benedic anima mea Domino*, that is to say, the hundred and third psalm and the hundred and fourth psalm, and such sentences of scripture as be appointed by the Queen's Majesty's Injunctions[4], with the Litany and suffrages following the same, and reading one Homily already devised and set forth for that purpose[5], without wearing any surplices, carrying of banners or hand-bells, or staying at crosses, or such like popish ceremonies.

19. ITEM, That the minister and churchwardens shall not suffer any lords of misrule[6], or summer lords or ladies[7], or any disguised persons or others in Christmas or at May games, or

[4 At which time also the same minister shall inculcate these or such sentences: "Cursed be he which translateth the bounds and doles of his neighbour." Art. XIX.]

[5 The homily for Rogation week.]

[6 "In the feast of Christmas there was in the king's house, wherever he was lodged, a Lord of Misrule, or Maister of merry disports: and the like had they in the house of every nobleman of honour or good worship, were he spiritual or temporal. Amongst the which the Mayor of London and either of the Sheriffs had their Lords of Misrule, ever contending without quarrel or offence which should make the rarest pastime to delight beholders. These Lords, beginning their rule on All-hallow Eve, continued the same till the morrow after the Feast of Purification, commonly called Candlemas; in which space fine and subtle disguises, masks and mummeries, with playing of cards for counters, nayles, and points in every house, more for pastimes than gaine." Stow's Survey, p. 79.]

[7 The lords of misrule belonged to the Christmas sports, the summer lords and ladies to the festivities of May.]

any minstrels, morrice-dancers, or others, at rushbearings[1] or at any other times, to come unreverently into any church or chapel or church-yard, and there dance or play any unseemly parts with scoffs, jests, wanton gestures, or ribald talk, namely in the time of divine service or of any sermon.

20. ITEM, That no schoolmaster shall teach, either openly or privately, in any gentleman's house, or in any other place, unless he be of good and sincere religion and conversation, and be first examined, allowed, and licensed by the ordinary in writing under his seal. He shall not teach any thing contrary to the order of religion now set forth by public authority. He shall teach his scholars the Catechism[2] in Latin lately set forth, and such sentences of scripture, besides profane chaste authors, as shall be most meet to move them to the love and due reverence of God's true religion, now truly set forth by the Queen's Majesty, and to induce them to all godliness and honest conversation.

21. ITEM, That no parish clerk be appointed against the good will, or without the consent of the parson, vicar, or curate in any parish, and that he be obedient to the parson, vicar, and curate, especially in the time of celebration of divine service or of sacraments, or in any preparation thereunto; and that he be able also to read the first lesson, the epistle, and the psalms, with answers to the suffrages, as is used; and that he keep the books and ornaments of the church fair and clean, and cause the church and choir, the Communion table, the pulpit, and the font to be kept decent and made clean against service time, the Communion, sermon, and baptism, and also that he endeavour himself to teach young children to read, if he be able so to do.

[1 The wake, or feast of Dedication in honour of the patron saint; so called from the custom of bringing rushes to strew upon the floor of the church on that day. Brand's Popular Antiq. Vol. I. p. 436. Ed. 1813. Many of these sports were afterwards expressly sanctioned by King James I. in his "Declaration about lawful sports on the Lord's day," A.D. 1603. See Cardwell, Doc. Ann. ii. pp. 191, 192.]

[2 Nowel's Catechism, approved by the convocation of 1562, but not printed until 1570. It was reprinted both in Latin and English in the year 1572. See Strype, Ann. I. i. p. 525, and Parker, II. p. 17.]

22. ITEM, That the churchwardens and sworn-men of every parish shall half-yearly, from time to time, present to the ordinary the names of all such persons of their parish as be either blasphemers of the name of God, great or often swearers, adulterers, fornicators, incestuous persons, bawds, or receivers of naughty and incontinent persons, or harbourers of women with child which be unmarried, conveying or suffering them to go away before they do any penance, or make satisfaction to the congregation, or that be vehemently suspected of such faults, or that be not of good name and fame touching such faults and crimes, or that be drunkards, or ribalds, or that be malicious, contentious, or uncharitable persons, common slanderers of their neighbours, railers, scolders, or sowers of discord between neighbours. And also all such as be usurers, that is to say, all those that lend money, corn, ware, or other thing, and receive gain therefore, over and above that which they lend.

23. ITEM, That the churchwardens and sworn-men of every parish shall likewise, half-yearly, present to the ordinary all such persons as either heretofore have married and be not divorced, or hereafter shall marry, within the degrees of affinity or consanguinity by the laws of God forbidden, so set out for an admonition in a table lately appointed to be affixed in every parish church of this province; or that, being divorced or separated for the same, do yet notwithstanding cohabit, and keep company still together; and also all persons, being married without those degrees, that have unlawfully forsaken their wives or husbands, and married others. And if any man have two wives at once, or any woman two husbands at once; or if any, being divorced or separated asunder, have married again; if any be married, that have made a precontract; if any have married without banns thrice solemnly asked in the church; if any couples be married that live not together, but slanderously live apart; or if any have married out of the parish church, where they ought to have solemnized marriage, the churchwardens and sworn-men shall likewise present the same half-yearly to the ordinary.

24. ITEM, The churchwardens and sworn-men of every parish shall likewise, half-yearly, present to the ordinary the names of all such persons whatsoever, either of the clergy or laity, that be favourers of the Romish and foreign power; letters[1] of true religion; hearers or sayers of mass, or of any Latin service; preachers or setters forth of corrupt and popish doctrines; maintainers of sectaries; disturbers of divine service; keepers of any secret conventicles, preachings, or lectures; receivers of any vagabond popish priests, or other notorious mislikers of true religion, or maintainers of the unlearned people in ignorance and error, encouraging and moving them rather to pray in an unknown tongue than in English; or that stubbornly refuse to conform themselves to unity and godly religion, now established by public authority.

25. AND FINALLY, The churchwardens and sworn-men of every parish shall likewise, half-yearly, present to the ordinary, whether all these Injunctions, given as is above, as well to the clergy as to the laity, be duly observed and kept; and if they be not, then which and how many of the said Injunctions be not kept, and by whom; and in what point any person or persons do violate and break the same.

ALL WHICH INJUNCTIONS We do charge and command to be inviolably performed and observed of all persons whom they shall concern, within our province of York, upon pain of contempt and of excommunication and other censures of the church, by the ecclesiastical laws of this realm in such like cases limited and appointed.

[1 hinderers.]

Injunctions

given by the moste Reverende Father in Christe Edmunde, by the Providence of God, Archbyshop of Yorke, Prymate of Englande and Metropolitane, unto the Deane and Chapter of the Cathedrall Churche of Yorke, in his Metropoliticall Visitations begunn in the Chapitor House of the saide Cathedrall Churche the xvth daye of Maye, Anno Domini 1571, continued and proroged from daye to daye, and tyme to tyme, untill this present, beinge the tenth of October in the yeare of our Lord God a thousande fyve hundrede seventye and two.

[GRINDAL.]

INJUNCTIONS,

&c.

<small>Archbishop Grindal's Register. York.</small> 1. IMPRIMIS, For the better setting forth of God's glory, and the edifying of his church, We will, charge, and command, that all persons having any dignity or prebend in the cathedral and Metropolitan church of York shall yearly, either in their own persons, or else by some other, who for his learning is, or shall be, by sufficient authority thereunto called and allowed, preach so many sermons within the said church, as is to them by us appointed in a schedule table or note, specially set forth for that purpose, and hereunto annexed. Which order, being also confirmed by the express consent of the dean and chapter of the said church, as plainly appeareth by a decree by them made for the same purpose, the 7th of October, 1572, we charge and command to be inviolably from time to time observed and kept, upon pain and penalty in the same order expressed, and upon pain of other censures of the church, to be published and executed against all and singular neglecting the same.

2. ITEM, By the express consent of the same dean and chapter of the said cathedral church of York, we will and enjoin, that no person or persons, having dignity or prebend within the said church, shall from henceforth demise, let, or set his capital mansion house to any lay person, or to any other person or persons, saving only to those that have, or shall have, dignities or prebends in the said church; neither shall he by any other device, directly or indirectly, defeat the good meaning of this our injunction, so that if any such person, having such house, do not inhabit the same himself, or keep it for his own repair to the said church, (which shall be every year twice at the least,) the said house and houses, according to the ancient laudable custom of this church, shall

remain to be inhabited by those that have dignities or prebends in the same, lacking houses of their own. And for the better observation of this injunction, every prebendary hereafter to be installed shall take an oath in the chapter house, before his installation, duly to observe the same.

3. ITEM, We will and enjoin, that the dean and chapter shall provide and have from time to time a fair table, whereupon and in the same shall be written, without blot or rasure, in fair letters the order, word by word, and penalty by us taken and appointed, for and concerning the sermons to be had, made, and continued in the cathedral church of York; and the same to be placed in the choir or chancel of the said church, where it may easily be seen and read; that thereby every one having any dignity or prebend in the said church may be put in mind of his duty in that behalf, for and concerning his sermons thereby appointed.

4. ITEM, We will and command, that some well learned man in divinity be with all convenient speed provided by the dean and residentiaries of the cathedral church of York, of the revenues and profits of the community of the said church; and the same learned man by us to be allowed for the reading of a divinity lecture twice a week, at the least, in the said church, at such time as the chancellor of the same church of York is not bound to read the divinity lecture there: then the said learned man to be occupied in preaching the word of God in such parish church, pertaining to the common of the said cathedral church of York, as the dean, and in his absence the president of the chapter, shall appoint him; or else in some other church within the city of York, if special occasion at any time move them so to appoint him.

5. ITEM, That all the vicars choral, and other inferior ministers within the said cathedral church of York, be daily present and give diligent care to the hearing of the divinity lecture, so that it may appear how much they profit, when they shall be examined by the chancellor of the same church, or by the reader himself, who shall examine them every month once at the least.

6 ITEM, That the holy communion may be more duly frequented than hath been heretofore, we will and enjoin, that upon certain days hereafter specified the holy communion, all excuses set apart, shall be duly and reverently ministered; and we exhort all persons having dignity or prebend within the said church, and also all other inferior ministers and officers, that they, and every of them, prepare themselves to communicate at the said times as appointed, viz: Festo Omnium Sanctorum, Natalis Domini, Epiphaniæ, Purificationis, Paschatis, Pentecostes; and in all other months, wherein none of these feast days are, then the holy communion shall be duly ministered in and upon the first Sundays of every one of those months; not minding hereby to inhibit, but that the said holy communion may be also ministered on other Sundays or holy days, as to the good disposition of the governors and ministers of the said church shall seem expedient, according to the orders set forth in the book of Common Prayer.

7. ITEM, That every person having any dignity in the cathedral church of York, prebendaries and other officers of the same, remaining within the city of York, except by occasion of office or some other special impediment, be daily present at the divine service in the said church, and that none of them at any time hereafter walk in any part of the church in time of divine service, but rather to place themselves in the choir in their own stalls by order to them appointed, or some other convenient place in the same. And also, that every Sunday and holy day they that have any dignity or prebend in the said church of York, remaining and being resident within the city of York, be there present at divine service in his surplice and hood, according to his degree, except they preach in some other place.

8. ITEM, We will and command, that there be, with all speed convenient, provided and placed so many vicars choral within the church of York, to be ministers there, as the lands of their house called Beddern[1], by the discretion of the dean and chapter, will conveniently sustain. And that every of

[1 This is now a court-yard at no great distance from the minster, inhabited by the poorer classes.]

these vicars, being under the age of forty years, do commit to memory every week one chapter of St Paul's Epistles, beginning with the first to the Romans. And such as be above the age of forty years to read the same chapters appointed so diligently, that they may be well able to recite perfectly, without help of book, the whole sum of the same chapters. And that whosoever shall make default herein, after three several admonitions, if he do not amend the same, to be displaced, and some better placed in his room. Provided always, that we reserve to ourselves, or to such as by our appointment shall be thought most meet for that purpose, the examination of the said vicars.

9. ITEM, That the vicars choral of the cathedral church of York abstain from evil company and unlawful games, neither give occasion of offence by long continuing idle in any open street; and that such as be unmarried go to commons together in their common hall within the Beddern, except those vicars which give attendance of the canons residentiaries of the said church. And that all and every of the said vicars have a Bible, either in the English or Latin tongue, to occupy themselves at times convenient in reading thereof. And also, that such as be in commons there within the Beddern shall daily by course, immediately after dinner, read one chapter of the four Evangelists; and every day, after supper, shall read one chapter of the Acts of the Apostles, or some chapter of St Paul's Epistles: and the same to be read in order, one chapter after another, unto the end of the said books.

10. ITEM, That the order and injunction taken by our late predecessor Thomas[2], by the providence of God late Archbishop of York, for and concerning a survey, and other due regard of the lands and revenues of the Church of York, be duly observed; viz. that the dean and chapter shall cause, with as convenient speed as may be, one perfect survey to be made of all the lands and revenues, as well in common, as also to the dean, any office, or prebends of the said church, belonging, and to continue the same from time to time here-

[2 Abp. Young.]

6 ITEM, That the holy communion may be more duly frequented than hath been heretofore, we will and enjoin, that upon certain days hereafter specified the holy communion, all excuses set apart, shall be duly and reverently ministered; and we exhort all persons having dignity or prebend within the said church, and also all other inferior ministers and officers, that they, and every of them, prepare themselves to communicate at the said times as appointed, viz: Festo Omnium Sanctorum, Natalis Domini, Epiphaniæ, Purificationis, Paschatis, Pentecostes; and in all other months, wherein none of these feast days are, then the holy communion shall be duly ministered in and upon the first Sundays of every one of those months; not minding hereby to inhibit, but that the said holy communion may be also ministered on other Sundays or holy days, as to the good disposition of the governors and ministers of the said church shall seem expedient, according to the orders set forth in the book of Common Prayer.

7. ITEM, That every person having any dignity in the cathedral church of York, prebendaries and other officers of the same, remaining within the city of York, except by occasion of office or some other special impediment, be daily present at the divine service in the said church, and that none of them at any time hereafter walk in any part of the church in time of divine service, but rather to place themselves in the choir in their own stalls by order to them appointed, or some other convenient place in the same. And also, that every Sunday and holy day they that have any dignity or prebend in the said church of York, remaining and being resident within the city of York, be there present at divine service in his surplice and hood, according to his degree, except they preach in some other place.

8. ITEM, We will and command, that there be, with all speed convenient, provided and placed so many vicars choral within the church of York, to be ministers there, as the lands of their house called Beddern[1], by the discretion of the dean and chapter, will conveniently sustain. And that every of

[1 This is now a court-yard at no great distance from the minster, inhabited by the poorer classes.]

able; and that the rest, which shall be thought necessary or profitable for the good government of the church of York, be collected and drawn into a book, duly to be confirmed; we will and enjoin, that the same old statutes be viewed and examined by Mr Dr Hutton, dean of York, Dr Rookbye, precentor of the same church, Mr Palmer, chancellor thereof, Dr Lakin, prebendary of Wistow, Dr Gibson, prebendary of Botevant, Mr Lynley, prebendary of Husthwaite: which statutes, after such collection and confirmation had, we will and command, that they shall yearly openly be read in the chapter house at four sundry times, viz. the Wednesdays after the feasts of Saint Martin, Purification, Whit-sunday, and Matthew.

14. ITEM, We will and enjoin, that upon the Wednesday after every of the said feasts of Martin, Purification, Whit-sunday, and Matthew, betwixt seven and eleven of the clock in the forenoon, the dean of the cathedral church of York, and in his absence the president of the chapter and canons of the same, being within the diocese of York, and thereof monished by public citation, by the space of twenty days before set upon the places for such purposes accustomed within the said church, and the proctors of those that be absent without the diocese, being canons of the same church, shall congregate themselves and meet together *capitulariter*, concerning necessary business of the same church, there to be entreated and concluded upon, or for reformation of any abuse, officer, or member of the said church. All which their decrees concerning the premises we command shall be observed, obeyed, and diligently kept, upon pain and punishment by the censures of the church, as shall be thought convenient.

15. ITEM, We will and enjoin, that all that have any dignities or prebends within the said cathedral church of York, dwelling twenty miles from the said church, shall constitute and appoint before Christmas next a sufficient proctor, either of the canons or prebends or vicars choral of the said church, who shall exhibit the same proxy, and take upon him the same to discharge all manner of duties incident to the said dignity or prebend.

16. ITEM, That the precentor of the church of York for the time being, or some other discreet person by him appointed, and the master of the choristers, provide that the said choristers of the church of York be virtuously brought up, and taught in the principles of religion; and that they cause them to be examined thrice in every quarter of a year in the English catechism, now lately set forth and enlarged[1].

17. ITEM, That the vergers of the cathedral church of York suffer no man to walk in the body of the church, or in any part thereof, in sermon time, during the abode of the preacher in the pulpit; and that if any person so contemptuously walk, then they to present them unto us and other our associates, the Queen's Majesty's commissioners for causes ecclesiastical within the province of York, to be corrected. And also that the same vergers diligently attend in the choir in time of divine service, and procure that then there be silence and quietness.

18. ITEM, That no muniment, charter, evidence, or other writing, belonging to the church of York, be taken out of the treasury, vestry, or library, except he that taketh the same write his name in a book to be provided for the same purpose, testifying the contents of the said writing, and binding himself to restore the same again.

19. ITEM, For better satisfaction and contentation of the prebendaries and canons of the cathedral church of York, which are not residentiaries, we will that monition be given in writing eight days before, publicly in the chapter house, when and at what time the accounts belonging to the common and fabric of the said church of York shall be made, that all those prebendaries that will may be there present to hear and see the same.

ALL WHICH INJUNCTIONS we do charge and command to be inviolably performed and kept, upon pain of contempt and other censures by the laws ecclesiastical of this realm in such

[1 Nowel's Catechism. See note, p. 142.]

like cases limited and appointed. In witness of all and singular the premises, we have caused our great seal to be put to these presents, and hereunto have subscribed our name. Given in the chapter house of the aforesaid cathedral and Metropolitical church of York, the tenth day of the month of October, in the year of our Lord God a thousand five hundred seventy and two, and of our translation the third year.

THESE ARTICLES FOLLOWING,

WE

EDMUND,

BY THE PERMISSION OF GOD, ARCHBISHOP OF YORK,
PRIMATE OF ENGLAND, AND METROPOLITAN, DO COMMAND
AND ENJOIN TO BE PUT IN EXECUTION WITHIN
THE ARCHDEACONRY OF YORK, BY THE
ARCHDEACON OF THE SAME, OR
HIS OFFICIAL, WITH SPEED
AND EFFECT[1].

Reg. Grind. York. fo. 124.

1. IMPRIMIS, That the form and order appointed in the printed schedule hereunto annexed[2], for taking down of *rood-lofts*, be duly and precisely observed within the said archdeaconry, as well within places exempt as not exempt.

[[1] These articles were issued by the archbishop, together with a commission, in Latin, to each of his four archdeacons, viz. of York, Nottingham, East Riding, and Cleveland, and also to the bishop of Sodor and Man, *ad deponenda et diruenda* (as the commission runs) *sollaria, cellaria, seu sustentacula illa, quæ vulgari hujus regni Angliæ lingua* Rood-lofts *appellantur, ad cujusque ecclesiæ parochialis ostium chorale posita, tanquam veteris idolatriæ et superstitionis vestigia et monumenta.* A printed copy also of an order of the queen's commissioners was annexed, as in the following note. The *Rood-loft* was a gallery, or platform, over the screen, at the entrance of the chancel, upon which was the Rood, or cross, with images of Mary and John.]

[[2] *Order of the Ecclesiastical Commissioners for the removal of Rood-lofts.* Orders taken the tenth day of October, in the third year of the reign of our sovereign lady Elizabeth, Queen of England, France, and Ireland, Defender of the Faith, &c., by virtue of her Majesty's letters addressed to her Highness' Commissioners for causes ecclesiastical, as followeth:

IMPRIMIS, For the avoiding of much strife and contention that hath heretofore risen among the Queen's subjects, in divers parts of the realm, for the using and transposing of the rood-lofts, fonts, and steps within the quires and chancels in every parish church; It is thus decreed and ordained, that the rood-lofts, as yet being at this day aforesaid untransposed, shall be so altered that the upper parts of the same, with the soller, be quite taken down unto the upper parts of the vaults and beams, running in length over the said vaults, by putting some convenient crest upon the said beam, towards the church, leaving the situation of the seats, as well in the quire as in the church, as heretofore hath been used, provided, &c.]

2. ITEM, That every parson, vicar, curate, and other minister within the said archdeaconry, as well in places exempt as not exempt, when he readeth Morning or Evening Prayer, or any part thereof, shall stand in a pulpit to be erected for that purpose, and turn his face to the people, that he may be the better heard, and the people the better edified: Provided always, that when the churches are very small, it shall suffice that the minister stand in his accustomed stall in the quire, so that a convenient desk or lectern, with a room to turn his face towards the people, be there provided, at the charges of the parish. The judgment and order whereof, and also the form and order of the pulpit to be erected, as before, in greater churches, we do refer unto the same archdeacon, or his official. Provided also, that all the prayers and other service, appointed for the ministration of the holy Communion, be said and done at the communion-table only.

3. ITEM, That every minister saying any public prayers, or ministering the sacraments, or other rites of the church, shall wear a comely surplice with sleeves; and that the parish provide a decent table, standing in a frame, for the communion-table; and that no linen cloths, called altar-cloths, and before used about masses, be laid upon the communion-table; but that new be provided, where provision hath not so been made afore.

Articles

to be enquired of, within the Prouince of Canterburie, in the Metropoliticall visitation of the most reuerende father in God, Edmonde Archbishop of Canterburie, Primate of all Englande, and Metropolitane.

In the xviij. yeare of the reigne of our most gracious souereygne Ladie Elizabeth, by the grace of God, Queene of Englande, Fraunce and Irelande, defender of the fayth. etc.

ARTICLES[1]

TO BE

INQUIRED OF WITHIN THE PROVINCE OF CANTERBURY, &c.

---

1. WHETHER Common Prayer be sung or said by your parson, vicar, or curate in your several churches or chapels, distinctly and reverently, and in such order as it is set forth by the laws of this realm, without any kind of alteration, and at due and convenient hours; and whether your minister so turn himself, and stand in such place of your church or chancel, as the people may best hear the same; and whether the holy sacraments be likewise ministered reverently, in such manner as by the laws of this realm is appointed; and whether upon Wednesdays and Fridays, not being holy days, the Litany and other prayers appointed for the day be said accordingly?

2. Whether you have in your parish churches and chapels all things necessary and requisite for Common Prayer, and administration of the sacraments, specially the Book of Common Prayer with the new Kalendar, a Psalter, the English Bible in the largest volume, the two tomes of the Homilies, the Paraphrases of Erasmus translated into English, the table of the Ten Commandments, a convenient pulpit well placed, a comely and decent table, standing on a frame, for the holy Communion, with a fair linen cloth to lay upon the

---

[1] These Articles of Inquiry are taken from a printed copy in the Cambridge University Library. They are not noticed by Strype, nor are they given by Wilkins or Cardwell. The Archbishop's sequestration, which took place in this year, seems to have interrupted the progress of this metropolitical visitation.]

same, and some covering of silk, buckram, or other such like, for the clean keeping thereof, a fair and comely Communion cup of silver, and a cover of silver for the same, which may serve also for the ministration of the Communion bread, a decent large surplice with sleeves, a sure coffer with two locks and keys for the keeping of the register book, and a strong chest or box for the almose of the poor, with three locks and keys to the same, and all other things necessary in and to the premises?

3. Whether the form of Commination against sinners, with certain prayers following the same, set forth in the latter end of the book of Common Prayer to be used at divers times in the year, be by your minister plainly and distinctly read in your church or chapel unto the people, between the Litany and the commemoration or ministration of the holy Communion, three times at least in the year, that is to say, for order sake, yearly upon one of the three Sundays next before Easter, for the first time; upon one of the two Sundays next before the feast of Pentecost, for the second time; and for the third time, upon one of the two Sundays next before the feast of the birth of our Lord, over and besides the accustomed reading thereof upon the first day of Lent?

4. Whether in your churches and chapels, all altars be utterly taken down and clean removed, even unto the foundation, and the place where they stood paved, and the wall whereunto they joined whited over, and made uniform with the rest, so as no breach or rupture appear? And whether your rood-lofts be taken down, and altered, so that the upper parts thereof, with the soller or loft, be quite taken down unto the cross beam, and that the said beam have some convenient crest put upon the same?

5. Whether your churches and chapels with the chancels thereof be well and sufficiently repaired, and kept without abuse of any thing: and whether your churchyards be well fenced, and cleanly kept; and if any part thereof be in decay, through whose default it is so?

6. Whether all and every antiphoners[1], mass-books, grailes, portesses, processionals, manuals, legendaries, and all other books of late belonging to your church or chapel, which served for the superstitious Latin service, be utterly defaced, rent, and abolished; and if they be not, through whose default that is, and in whose keeping they remain? And whether all vestments, albs, tunicles, stoles, phanons, pixes, paxes, handbells, sacringbells, censers, chrismatories, crosses, candlesticks, holy-water-stocks, images, and such other relics and monuments of superstition and idolatry be utterly defaced, broken, and destroyed; and if not, where, and in whose custody they remain?

7. Whether your parson, vicar, curate, or minister, do wear any cope in your parish church or chapel, or minister the holy Communion in any chalice heretofore used at mass, or in any profane cup or glass, or use at the ministration thereof any gestures, rites, or ceremonies, not appointed by the book of Common Prayer, as crossing or breathing over the sacramental bread and wine, or shewing

[[1] Vide supra, p. 135, notes. It is curious to find most of these articles of church furniture enjoined by a previous Archbishop of Canterbury, to be *provided* by the parishioners. Archbishop Winchelsea lived in the early part of the fourteenth century.

"Robertus Winchelsea.

"In ecclesiis parochialibus omnis supellex rei divinæ aut parochiali opportuna hic annotata reperiatur.

"Ut parochiani ecclesiarum singularum nostræ Cantuariensis provinciæ sint de cætero certiores de defectibus ipsos contingentibus, ne inter rectores et ipsos ambiguitas generetur temporibus successivis, Volumus de cætero et præcipimus quod teneantur invenire omnia inferius annotata; videlicet, *legendam, antiphonarium, gradale,* psalterium, troperium, ordinale, *missale, manuale,* calicem, vestimentum principale cum *casula, dalmatica, tunica,* et cum capa in choro cum omnibus suis appendiciis, frontale ad magnum altare cum tribus tuellis, tria superpellicia, unum rochetum, *crucem processionalem, crucem pro mortuis, thuribulum, lucernam, tintinnabulum* ad deferendum coram corpore Christi in visitatione infirmorum, *pixidem* pro corpore Christi, honestum velum, quadragesimale, vexilla pro rogationibus, *campanas* cum chordis, feretrum pro defunctis, *vas pro aqua benedicta, osculatorium, candelabrum* pro cereo paschali, fontem cum serura, *imagines* in ecclesia, imaginem principalem in cancello, etc." Lyndewode. Provinciale seu Constitutiones Angliæ. Lib. III. tit. de Ecclesiis Ædificandis, fo. 137.]

the same to the people to be worshipped and adored, or any such like, or use any oil and chrism, tapers, spattle, or any other popish ceremony in the ministration of the sacrament of Baptism?

8. Whether any holy days or fasting days heretofore abrogated, or not appointed to be used as holy days or fasting days by the new kalendar of the book of Common Prayer, be either proclaimed and bidden by your parson, vicar, or curate, or be superstitiously observed by any of your parish, and what be their names that so do observe the same; and whether there be any ringing or tolling of bells to call the people together used in any of those days, more or otherwise than commonly is used upon other days that be kept as work days?

9. Whether, when any man or woman is in passing out of this life, the bell be tolled to move the people to pray for the sick person, especially in all places where the sick person dwelleth near unto the church; and whether, after the time of his or her passing out of this world, there be any more ringing but one short peal before the burial, and another short peal after the burial, without any other superfluous or superstitious ringing: and whether on All Saints' day after Evening Prayer there be any ringing at all, or any other superstitious ceremony used, tending to the maintenance of popish purgatory, or of prayer for the dead, and who they be that use the same; and whether there be any ringing or knolling of bells on Sundays or holy days between Morning Prayer and the Litany, or in any time of the Common Prayer, reading of the Homilies, or of preaching, except one bell in convenient time to be rung or tolled before the sermon; or any other ringing used upon Saints' eves or festival days, saving to Common Prayer, and that without excess; and who doth ring or knoll otherwise?

10. Whether your parson or vicar have preached, or caused to be duly preached in your church, his quarterly or monthly sermons, as by the Queen's Injunctions he is

[¹ Arts. III. and IV.]

bound, and what be the names of such as have preached for him; and whether he hath admitted any man to preach not having sufficient licence, or hath inhibited or letted any from preaching having sufficient licence?

11. Whether any person or persons, not being ordered at least for a deacon, or licensed by the ordinary, do say Common Prayer openly in your church or chapel; or any, not being at the least a deacon, do solemnize matrimony, or administer the sacrament of Baptism, or deliver unto the communicants the Lord's cup, at the celebration of the holy Communion; and what he or they be, that so do. And whether the parson, vicar, or fermer[2] of your benefice, do cause or suffer any curate or minister to serve your church, before he be examined and admitted by the ordinary or his deputy in writing, and do shew his licence to the church-wardens; and whether any curate do serve two cures at one time, without the special licence of the ordinary, or his deputy in that behalf, in writing first had?

12. Whether your parson, vicar, or curate do every Sunday, when there is no sermon, read distinctly and plainly some part of the Homilies prescribed and set forth by the Queen's authority to be read; and every holy day, when there is no sermon, immediately after the gospel, openly, plainly, and distinctly recite to his parishioners the Lord's Prayer, the Articles of the Faith, and the Ten Commandments in English; and whether any minister not admitted by the ordinary, or by other lawful authority, do expound any scripture or matter of doctrine by the way of exhortation or otherwise, and thereby omit and leave off the reading of the Homilies?

13. Whether your parson, vicar, or curate do every Sunday and holy day, openly in the church, call for, hear, and instruct all the children, apprentices, and servants of both sexes, that be of convenient age within your parish, or at the least so many of them by course as the time will serve, and as he may well hear and instruct for half an hour at

[2 Fermer: farmer, one who farmed the tithes. Vide Spelman, Glossar. in voc. *firmarius*.]

[GRINDAL.]

the least, before or at the Evening Prayer, in the Ten Commandments, the Articles of the Belief, and the Lord's Prayer, and diligently examine and teach them the Catechism, as it is now allowed and set forth; and whether for that purpose, he doth take the names of them all, and by course call certain of them by name every Sunday and holy day, to come to the teaching of the same Catechism?

14. Whether all fathers and mothers, masters and dames of your parish, cause their children, servants, and apprentices, both mankind and womankind, being above seven years of age and under twenty, which have not learned the Catechism, to come to the church on Sundays and holy days, at the times appointed, or at the least such and so many of them as your minister shall appoint, and there diligently and obediently to hear and to be ordered by the minister, until such time as they have learned the same Catechism; and what be the names of those that do not cause their children, servants, and apprentices so to come to the church to be instructed and examined, and how many of the said children, servants, and apprentices be in your parish, which, being above seven years old and under twenty years of age, cannot say by heart the said Catechism, and what be their names and age, and with whom they dwell?

15. Whether your parson, vicar, curate, or other minister in your church or chapel, hath admitted to the receiving of the holy Communion any open and notorious fornicator, adulterer, or evil liver, by whom the congregation is offended, without due penance first done, to the satisfaction of the congregation; or any malicious person that is notoriously known to be out of charity, or that hath done any open wrong to his neighbour by word or deed, without due reconciliation first made to the party that is wronged?

16. Whether your parson, vicar, curate, or minister, hath admitted to the holy Communion any of his parish, being above twenty years of age, either mankind or womankind, that cannot say by heart the Ten Commandments, the Articles of the Faith, and the Lord's Prayer in English, and what

be the names of such as cannot say the same, or being above fourteen years and under twenty years of age, that cannot say the Catechism allowed and set forth in the said book of Common Prayer. And whether he marry any persons which were single before, that cannot say the Catechism. And whether he useth to examine his parishioners at convenient times before he administer unto them, and namely before Easter yearly, to the intent he may know, whether they can say by heart the same, which is required in this behalf, or no?

17. Whether your priests and ministers be peace-makers, and no brawlers, or sowers of discord, and exhort their parishioners to obedience towards their Prince, and all other that be in authority, and to charity and mutual love among themselves; whether they be diligent in visiting the sick, and comforting them, and do move them earnestly, especially when they make their testaments, to consider the necessity of the poor, and to give to their box or chest their charitable devotions[1] or almose?

18. Whether they neglect the study of the holy Scriptures and of the Word of God; and whether such of them as be under the degree of a Master of Arts, have of their own at the least the New Testament both in English and Latin; and whether they do every day with good advisement confer one chapter of the Latin and English together at the least; and whether they have given due account thereof, and to whom?

19. Whether any of your parsons, vicars, curates, or ministers be favourers of the Romish or foreign power, letters of true religion, preachers of corrupt and popish doctrine, or maintainers of sectaries, or do set forth and extol vain and superstitious religion, or be maintainers of the unlearned people in ignorance and error, encouraging or moving them rather to pray in an unknown tongue, than in English, or to put their trust in a certain number of prayers, as in saying over a number of beads, Lady-Psalters, or other like?

[1] Devotions: oblations *devoted* to charitable or pious purposes. See Rubric after the Offertory in the Communion Service.]

20. Whether any do preach, declare, or speak any thing in derogation of the book of Common Prayer, which is set forth by the laws of this realm, dispraising the same, or any thing therein contained?

21. Whether your parson, vicar, or curate hath or doth maintain any doctrine contrary or repugnant to any of the "Articles agreed upon by the clergy in the convocation holden at London, Anno Domini, 1562, for the avoiding of diversities of opinions, and for establishment of consent touching true religion[1]," set forth by the Queen's authority; and whether any, having been admitted to his benefice since the thirteenth year of the Queen's reign, hath not within two months after his induction publicly read the said Articles in your church in the time of Common Prayer there, with declaration of his unfeigned assent thereunto[2]?

22. Whether your parson, vicar, curate, minister, or reader, do church any unmarried woman which hath been gotten with child out of lawful marriage, and say for her the form of Thanksgiving of women after child-birth, except such an unmarried woman have either, before her child-birth, done due penance for her fault to the satisfaction of the congregation, or at her coming to give thanks do openly acknowledge her fault before the congregation, at the appointment of the minister, according to order prescribed to the said minister by the ordinary or his deputy; the same churching to be had always on some Sunday or holy day, and upon none other day?

23. Whether any of your parsons, vicars, curates, or ministers, or any other priest, or any lay man or woman, do wilfully maintain or defend any heresies, false opinions, or popish errors, contrary to the laws of Almighty God,

[1] The Thirty-nine Articles.]
[2] By a statute passed A.D. 1571, 13 Eliz., it was enacted, that every person, after the end of that session of parliament, to be admitted to any benefice with cure, should within two months after his induction publicly read the thirty-nine Articles in his parish church, with declaration of his unfeigned assent to the same, otherwise to incur deprivation immediately *ipso facto*. See Strype, Annals II. i. 105.]

and true doctrine by public authority in this realm now set forth, and what be their names; and whether any keep any secret conventicles, preachings, lectures, or readings contrary to the law, and what be their names?

24. Whether there be any in your parish that openly or privately say mass, or hear mass, or any other kind of service or prayer than is set forth by the laws of this realm?

25. Whether any popish priests, either going as priests, or disguised in other apparel, or altering their names for any cause, or any other, or runagate persons, mislikers or depravers of true religion, that do not minister or frequent Common Prayer now used, nor communicate at times appointed by the law, do resort secretly or openly into your parish; and to whom, and of whom be they received, harboured, and relieved, and what be their names and surnames, or by what names are they called?

26. Whether your parsons and vicars be resident and dwell continually upon their benefices, doing their duties in preaching, reading, and ministering the sacraments; and whether they keep hospitality, according as their livings will extend; and whether their houses and chancels be well repaired and upholden?

27. Whether they, or any of them, have more benefices than one, how many, and in what countries they be, and what be the names thereof?

28. Whether they, when they be absent from their benefices, do leave their cures to a rude and unlearned person, and not to an honest and well-learned expert curate, which can and will teach the people wholesome doctrine; and whether in their absence they do procure learned men to preach in their churches and cures, at least one sermon every quarter of a year?

29. Whether such parsons and vicars as be not resident, neither keep hospitality, do relieve their poor parishio-

ners, and what give they yearly to them; and if they be not resident, and may dispend yearly twenty pounds or above either in this diocese or elsewhere, whether do they distribute every year among their poor parishioners at the least the fortieth part of the fruits of their benefices, where they be not resident?

30. Whether your parsons, vicars, curates, and ministers, keep well their registers of all weddings, buryings, and christenings within your parish, and do present a copy of them once every year by indenture to the ordinary or his officers, and whether they read the Queen's Majesty's Injunctions every quarter of a year once, or no?

31. Whether they, or any of them, keep any suspected women in their houses, or be incontinent persons, given to drunkenness, idleness, or be haunters of taverns, ale-houses, or suspected places, or be hunters, hawkers, dicers, carders, tablers[1], swearers, or otherwise suspected of any notorious crime, or give any evil example of life; and whether they (as they ought to do) occupy themselves in the reading or hearing some part of the holy Scripture, or other good author, or in some other godly or laudable exercise, meet for their vocation?

32. Whether they, or any of them, do keep or suffer to be kept in their parsonage or vicarage-houses any ale-houses, tippling-houses, or taverns, or do sell ale, beer, wine, or any victual?

33. Whether your parsons or vicars have bought their benefices, or come to them by simony, fraud, or deceit, or by any colourable pact, or other unlawful mean whatsoever, or be vehemently suspected or defamed[2] thereof; and whether they keep in their own hands, or have demised and let to farm their parsonages and vicarages, or their glebe land, or tithes, or any part thereof, and whether any such lease be made for the performance of any simoniacal pact, made di-

[1] Players at the game of *tables* or *backgammon*.]
[2] Defamed: accused.]

rectly or indirectly between the incumbent and the patron, or between the incumbent or any other person, for the presenting of the same incumbent to that benefice?

34. Whether any minister or priest, presented to any benefice in this diocese, hath covenanted, promised, or practised to or with the patron thereof, or any other person or persons that had the advowson or gift of the same benefice, or with any other person or persons on his or their behalf, to give to him or his friend any sum of ready money for presenting him to the same, or have offered by promise or bond any lease, either of the whole benefice, limiting the rent far under the just value, or of the mansion house, glebe lands, or any portion of the tithes and fruits of the same benefice, receiving little or nothing therefor, or suffering the patron, or any other person that presented him, to have his own tithes within the benefice free unto himself, or else have granted some yearly pension, or other yearly commodity, to him, his child, servant, or friend, for preferring him to the same benefice, or otherwise have suffered him to make a gain by any colour, deceit, or simoniacal pact in bestowing the said benefice?

35. Whether the church of your parish be now vacant or destitute of an incumbent, or no; and if it be, how long it hath been so, and who is the patron; and whether he suffereth the benefice to lie vacant, and occupieth the glebe land, and taketh the tithes and other fruits to himself, during the time of the vacation; or who else occupieth and taketh the same?

36. Whether there be any lay or temporal man, not being within orders, or any child, that hath or enjoyeth any benefice or spiritual promotion?

37. Whether any priest or minister be come into this diocese out of any other diocese, to serve any cure here, without letters testimonial of the ordinary, from whence he came, under his authentic seal and hand, to testify the cause of his departing from thence, and of his behaviour there?

38. Whether, for the retaining of the perambulation of the circuit of your parish, the parson, vicar, or curate, churchwardens, and certain of the substantial men of the parish, in the days of the rogations commonly called the Gang-days[1], walk the accustomed bounds of your parish; and whether, in the same perambulation and going about, the curate do use any other rite or ceremony than to say or sing in English the two psalms beginning *Benedic anima mea Domino*, that is to say the ciii. psalm and the civ. psalm, and such sentences of Scripture as be appointed by the Queen's Majesty's Injunctions, with the Litany and suffrages following the same, and reading one Homily already devised and set forth for that purpose, without wearing any surplices, carrying of banners or hand-bells, or staying at crosses, or any such like popish ceremonies?

39. Whether the parish clerk be appointed according to the ancient custom of the parish; and whether he be not obedient to the parson, vicar, or curate, especially in the time of celebration of divine service, or of the sacraments, or in any preparation thereunto; and whether he be able and ready to read the first Lesson, the Epistle, and the Psalms, with answers to the suffrages, as is used; and whether he keep not the books and ornaments of the church fair and clean, and cause the church and choir, the Communion-table, the pulpit, and the font to be made decent and clean, against service time, the Communion, sermon, and Baptism?

40. Whether there be any man or woman in your parish that resorteth to any popish priest for shrift or auricular confession, or any that within three years now last past hath been reconciled unto the pope, or to the church of Rome, or any that is reputed or suspected so to be: and whether there be any that refuse to come to the church to hear divine service, or to communicate according to the order now established by public authority; and what be their names?

41. Whether there be any person or persons, ecclesiastical or temporal, within your parish, or elsewhere within

[1] Walking, or perambulation days: from *gang*, to walk.

this diocese, that of late have retained or kept in their custody, or that read, sell, utter, disperse, carry, or deliver to others any English books, set forth of late years at Louvain[1], or in any other place beyond the seas, by Harding, Dorman, Allen, Saunders, Stapleton, Marshall, Bristow[2], or any of them, or by any other English papist, either against the Queen's Majesty's supremacy in matters ecclesiastical, or against true religion and catholic doctrine now received and established by common authority within this realm; and what their names and surnames are?

42. Whether there be any in your parish that useth to pray in English or in Latin upon beads, or other such like thing, or upon any superstitious popish Primer, or other like book; and what be their names?

43. Whether the people of your parish, especially householders, having no lawful excuse to be absent, do faithfully and diligently endeavour themselves to resort with their children and servants to their parish church or chapel on the holy days, and chiefly upon the Sundays, to Morning and

[1 " Now were many of the English popish recusants become fugitives abroad in Flanders, and particularly in Antwerp and Louvain, and in other places in the king of Spain's dominions. Here they employed themselves in writing very dangerous and seditious books against the Queen and her government, which, when they had printed, they caused to be conveyed over hither, and privily dispersed abroad; which had perverted many of the ignorant people, and made them run into disorders." Strype, Annals, Chap. XLVI. Vol. I. part ii. p. 192. Also Chap. XXIV. Vol. I. part i. p. 410, 411. See also the Queen's Letter to the Bishop of London for seizing seditious books, &c. Appendix, No. XXXII. Vol. I. part ii. p. 529.]

[2 The above-named writers were the principal authors of the seditious books of this period; the design of which was, not only to vilify the reformed English Church, but also to draw the people from their allegiance to the Queen. Harding, Dorman, Saunders and Stapleton attacked Bishop Jewel's Apology. Dr Richard Marshall is rendered infamous by his brutal treatment of the remains of Peter Martyr's wife at Oxford, which he dug up and buried in his dung-hill. Allen, who was afterwards a cardinal, wrote various tracts in furtherance of the Spanish invasion, many of which were found in some of the ships of the Armada, ready for distribution in England. A full account of these men and their writings may be read in Strype's works, to which the reader is referred.]

Evening Prayer, and upon reasonable let thereof to some usual place, where Common Prayer is used, and then and there abide orderly and soberly during the time of Common Prayer, homilies, sermons, and other service of God there used, reverently and devoutly giving themselves to the hearing thereof, and occupying themselves at times convenient in private prayer; and who they be that either negligently or wilfully absent themselves, or come very late to the church, upon the Sundays especially, or that walk, talk, or otherwise unreverently behave themselves in the church, or use any gaming or pastime abroad or in any house, or sit in the streets or churchyard, or in any tavern or ale-house, upon the Sunday or other holy day, in the time of Common Prayer, sermons, or reading of the homilies, either before noon or after noon?

44. Whether the forfeiture of twelve-pence for every such offence, appointed by a statute made in the first year of the Queen's Majesty's reign[1], be levied and taken, according to the same statute, by the churchwardens, of every person that so offendeth, and by them be put to the use of the poor of the parish, and if it be not, by whose default it is not levied; and what particular sums of money have been forfeited that way, and by whom, since the feast of Easter in the year of our Lord 1575, until the day of giving up the presentment concerning these articles; and so from time to time, as the same churchwardens and sworn men shall be appointed to present in this behalf, and how much of such forfeitures have been delivered to the use of the poor of the parish, and to whom the same hath been delivered?

45. Whether you know any, that in the time of the reading of the Litany, or of any other part of the Common Prayer, or in the time of the sermon, or of reading the homilies, or any part of the Scriptures to the parishioners, any person have departed out of the church without just and necessary cause, or that disturb the minister or preacher any manner of ways in the time of divine service or ser-

[[1] Cap. 16. This, and other enactments of Queen Elizabeth's reign on the same subject, are given in Burn's 'Justice of the Peace,' under the head—Public Worship.]

mon; and whether any, in contempt of their parish church or minister, do resort to any other church or no?

46. Whether there be any innkeepers, ale-wives, victuallers, or tipplers, that suffer or do admit any person or persons in their houses, to eat, drink, or play at cards, tables, or such like games in the time of Common Prayer or sermon, on the Sundays or holy days; and whether there be any shops set open on Sundays or holy days, or any butchers or others, that commonly use to sell meat or other things in the time of Common Prayer, preaching, or reading of the homilies; and whether in any fairs or common markets, falling upon the Sunday, there be any shewing of any wares before the Morning Prayer be done; and whether any markets or selling of any wares be used or suffered in any churchyards?

47. Whether, for the putting of the churchwardens and sworn men the better in remembrance of their duty, in observing and noting such as offend in not coming to divine service, your minister or reader do openly every Sunday, after he have read the second Lesson at Morning and Evening Prayer, admonish and warn the churchwardens and sworn men to look to their charge in this behalf, and to observe who, contrary to the said statute, offend in absenting themselves negligently or wilfully from their parish church or chapel, or unreverently (as is aforesaid) use themselves in the time of divine service?

48. Whether the churchwardens of the last year have given to the parish a just account of the church goods and rents that were committed to their charge, according unto the custom that hath been aforetime used, and what church goods they or any other have sold, and to whom, and whether to the profit of your church, or no; and what hath been done with the money thereof coming?

49. Whether the churchwardens and sworn men of the last year have of any private corrupt affection concealed any crime, or other disorder, in their time done in your parish, and have not presented the same to the bishop, chancellor,

archdeacon, commissary, or such other as had authority to reform the same; and whether they, or any of them, at any such time as they should have been at divine service on Sundays or holy days, and should there have observed others that were absent, have been away themselves at home, or in some tavern or ale-house, or else about some worldly business, or at bowls, cards, tables, or other gaming, without regard of their office and duty in that behalf?

50. Whether any man hath pulled down or discovered[1] any church, chancel, or chapel, or any part of any of them, any church-porch, vestry, or steeple, almose-house, or such like, or have plucked down the bells, or have felled or spoiled any wood or timber in any churchyard?

51. Whether your hospitals, spitals, and almose-houses, be well and godly used according to the foundation and ancient ordinances of the same; whether there be any other placed in them than poor impotent and needy persons, that have not wherewith or whereby to live?

52. Whether any of your parish, being of convenient age, have not received the holy Communion thrice this last year at the least, and namely at Easter last or thereabouts for once, and what their names are; or, receiving, have not signified the same before to your parson, vicar, or curate, that he might conveniently examine them; or that have refused to come to him to be examined?

53. Whether there be any in your parish that hath or doth offend contrary to the statute made in the thirty-seventh year of the reign of King Henry the Eighth, for reformation of usury, and revived by an act made in the thirteenth year of the reign of the Queen's Majesty; what be the names of such offenders, and what is the manner of their usury?

54. Whether there be any in your parish that minister the goods of those that be dead without lawful authority,

[1 Discovered: uncovered.]

or any that suppress the last will of the dead, or any executors that have not fulfilled their testators' will, specially in paying of legacies given to the church, or to other good and godly uses, as to the relief of poverty, to orphans, poor scholars, poor maids' marriages, highways, schools, and such like?

55. Whether there be any which of late have bequeathed in their testaments any jewels, plate, ornaments, cattle, or grain, or other moveable stocks, annuities, or sums of money for the erection or finding of any obits, diriges, trentals, torches, lights, tapers, lamps, or any such like use[2], now by law forbidden, which are not paid out of any lands, and whereunto the Queen's Majesty is not entitled by any Act of Parliament; and if there be any such legacy or appointment, what are the names of such testators, and of the executors of their testaments, what is the quantity and quality of the gift, and to what godly and lawful use is the same converted and employed?

56. Whether there be any money or stock appertaining to your parish church or chapel, or to the poor of your parish, in any man's hands that refuseth or deferreth to pay the same, or that useth fraud, deceit, or delay to make any account in the presence of the honest of the parish for the same; and whether any such stock be decayed, by whose negligence, and in whose hands; and whether the store of the poor men's box be openly and indifferently given where need is, without partial affection?

57. Whether the schoolmasters which teach within your parish, either openly, or privately in any noble or gentleman's house, or in any other place there, be of good and sincere religion and conversation, and be diligent in teaching and bringing up of youth; whether they be examined, allowed, and licensed by the ordinary or his officer in that behalf; whether they teach the grammar[3] set forth by King Henry the

[2 Vide Queen Elizabeth's Injunctions, Art. xxv. Cardwell, Doc. Ann. i. 190.]

[3 This grammar, commonly called Lily's, was originally written in Latin for the use of St Paul's school: it was put forth by authority both by Henry VIII and Edward VI. See Cardwell, Doc. Ann. I. p. 20.]

Eighth of noble memory, and none other; whether they teach any thing contrary to the order of religion now established by public authority; and whether they teach not their scholars the Catechism[1] in Latin lately set forth, and such sentences of Scripture as shall be most expedient and meet to move them to the love and due reverence of God's true religion, now truly set forth by the Queen's Majesty's authority, and to induce them to all godliness and honest conversation; and what be the names and surnames of all such schoolmasters and teachers of youth within your parish, as well of such as teach publicly, as those that teach in the houses of noblemen, gentlemen, or other private men?

58. Whether there be any among you that use sorcery or witchcraft, or that be suspected of the same, and whether any use any charms or unlawful prayers, or invocations in Latin, or otherwise, and namely midwives in the time of women's travail of child[2]; and whether any do resort to any such for help or counsel, and what be their names?

59. Whether there be among you any blasphemers of the name of God, great or often swearers, adulterers, fornicators, incestuous persons, bawds, or receivers of naughty and incontinent persons, or harbourers of women with child which be unmarried, conveying or suffering them to go away before they do any penance, or make satisfaction to the congregation, or any that be vehemently suspected of such faults, or that be not of good name and fame touching such crimes and faults, any drunkards, or ribalds, or any that be malicious, contentious, or uncharitable persons, common slanderers of their neighbours, railers, scolders, or sowers of discord between neighbours?

60. Whether there be any in these parts that have

[1 Dean Nowel's Catechism.]

[2 "Also I will not use any kind of sorcery or incantation in the time of the travail of any woman." From the oath taken by Eleanor Pead, before being licensed by the Archbishop to be a midwife. Strype, Annals, Vol. i. part ii. p. 242.]

married within the degrees of affinity or consanguinity, by the laws of God forbidden, so set out for an admonition in a table now appointed to be affixed in every parish church within this diocese; or any that, being divorced or separated for the same, do yet notwithstanding cohabit and keep company still together; or any that, being married without those degrees, have unlawfully forsaken their wives or husbands, and married others; any man that hath two wives, or any woman that hath two husbands; any that, being divorced or separated asunder, have married again; any married that have made precontracts; any that have made privy or secret contracts; any that have married or contracted themselves without the consent of their parents, tutors, or governors; any that have married without banns thrice solemnly asked; any couples married that live not together, but slanderously live apart; any that have married out of the parish church where they ought to have solemnized their marriage?

61. Whether the minister and churchwardens have suffered any lords of misrule[3], or summer lords or ladies, or any disguised persons, or others, in Christmas or at May-games, or any morris-dancers, or at any other times, to come unreverently into the church or churchyard, and there to dance, or play any unseemly parts, with scoffs, jests, wanton gestures, or ribald talk, namely in the time of Common Prayer[4]; and what they be that commit such disorder, or accompany or maintain them?

[3 Vide supra, note p. 141.]
[4 "The wilde heades of the parish, flocking together, chuse them a graund captaine of mischief, whom they innoble with the title of my Lord of Misrule. Then marche these heathen companie towards the church and churchyard, their pipers pypyng, drummers thonderyng, their stumpes dauncyng, their belles jyngling, their handkerchefes swyngyng about their heades like madmen, their hobbie-horses and other monsters skyrmishyng amongst the throng; and in this sorte they go to the churche (though the minister be at praier or preachyng) dauncing and swyngyng their handkerchiefs over their heads in the churche, like devilles incarnate, with such a confused noise that no man can heare his owne voyce. Then the foolish people, they looke, they stare, they laugh, they fleere, and mount upon the formes and pewes to see these goodly pageants solemnized in this sort. Then, after this, about the church they go againe and againe, and so fourthe into the churcheyard, where

62. Whether the archdeacon, chancellor, commissary, official, or any other using ecclesiastical jurisdiction in this diocese, their registrars, or actuaries, apparitors, or summoners, have at any time winked at and suffered any adulteries, fornications, incests, or other faults and offences, to pass and remain unpunished and uncorrected, for money, rewards, bribes, pleasure, friendship, or any other partial or affectionate respect; or any of them have been burdensome to any in this diocese by exacting or taking excessive fees, excessive procurations, any rewards, or commodities, by the way of promotion, gift, contribution, help, redemption of penance, omission of quarter sermons, obtaining of any benefices, or office, or any other like ways or means?

63. How many adulteries, incests, and fornications are notoriously known to have been committed in your parish, since Easter, 1575; how many offenders in any such faults have been put to open penance, and openly corrected; and how many have been winked at and borne withal, or have fined and paid money to the archdeacon, chancellor, commissary, official, or their deputies, or to the deans, registrars, or sumners[1], or any of them, for to escape open punishment and correction; and what their names and surnames be?

64. Whether the deans rurals, and sumners, or any of them, do pay any annual rent, fee, or pension for their offices, and when they pay, and to whom?

65. Generally, whether there be among you any notorious evil livers, or any suspected of any notorious sin, fault, or crime, to the offence of christian people committed; any that stubbornly refuse to conform themselves to unity and godly religion now established by public authority, or any that bruiteth abroad rumours of the alteration of the same, or

where they have commonly their summer-halls, their bowers, arbours and banquetyng-houses set up, wherein they feast, banquet and daunce all that day, and, peradventure, all that night too, and thus these terrestrial furies spend the sabbath daie." Stubs' Anatomie of Abuses (A.D. 1585), p. 92.]

[1 Sumner: summoner.]

otherwise that disturbeth good orders, and the quietness of Christ's church and the christian congregation?

The tenor of the oath ministered to the churchwardens and sworn men.

Ye shall swear by Almighty God, that ye shall diligently consider all and every the articles given to you in charge, and make a true answer unto the same in writing, presenting all and every such person and persons dwelling within your parish, as have committed any offence or fault, or made any default, mentioned in any of the same articles, or which are vehemently suspected or defamed of any such offence, fault, or default; wherein ye shall not present any person or persons of any evil will, malice, or hatred, contrary to the truth, nor shall for love, favour, mede, dread, or any corrupt affection, spare to present any that be offenders, suspected or defamed in any of these cases, but shall do uprightly, as men having the fear of God before your eyes, and desirous to maintain virtue and suppress vice. So God help you.

ARTICLES

TO BE INQUIRED OF

IN THE

METROPOLITICAL VISITATION OF THE MOST REVEREND FATHER IN GOD

EDMUND,

BY DIVINE SUFFERANCE ARCHBISHOP OF CANTERBURY, PRIMATE OF ALL ENGLAND, AND METROPOLITAN, IN ALL AND SINGULAR CATHEDRAL AND COLLEGIATE CHURCHES WITHIN HIS PROVINCE OF CANTERBURY.

Grind. Reg. fol. 97.

1. FIRST, Whether your bishop and his chancellor, commissaries, and all other his officers, do minister justice indifferently and incorruptly to all her Majesty's subjects, and punish vice and public crimes with due punishment, without any corrupt commutations, neither respecting gifts nor persons; and whether any money, gift, reward, or any other temporal commodity, other than accustomed lawful fees, hath been received for justice, or any judgments or execution of laws, or for any gift, advowson, presentation, collation, institution, or induction, or for the procuring of any such to any spiritual or ecclesiastical living; what hath been received; by whom, and by whose mediation?

2. ITEM, Whether your bishop, dean, chapter, and all other your governors, do, in their several regiments, direct all their doings to seek the glory of God, the godly quietness of the Church of England, the upholding in good order of your cathedral of ——, neither suffering in the same corrupt doctrine nor offensive manners; and whether any of them hath, or doth make, or suffer any waste, ruin, decay, or dilapidation of the goods or possessions of this church; as by decay, or

not repairing the church and their several houses, alienating the stock, buildings, implements, or other moveable goods of the church; or committing any of the same to private uses, or making of leases in possession or reversion for more years, or otherways, than the statutes of your church do prescribe; or by greedy waste of timber, excessive sales of woods, advowsons, unused and unreasonable grants, patents, and reversions of offices, unwonted annuities, and such like greedy griping of things present, to the impoverishing of the church and succession; how many, and what they be; whether any such grant or advowson hath been sold for any value, by whom, to whom, and for how much, and who now enjoyeth the same?

3. ITEM, How many such grants, patents, advowsons, sales, offices, annuities, and such like, hath been confirmed by your chapter-seal, sithence the first year of her Majesty's reign, to whose use, and by whose means; and what money was received for the same, by whom, and to whose use: whether any like gift, grant, advowson, or lease for longer time than for twenty-one years, or three lives, hath been made or confirmed, antedated, or by other colourable means procured in possession or reversion, sithence the beginning of the Parliament in the thirteenth year of her Majesty's reign; what those be, and by whose means procured, and to whose use?

4. ITEM, Whether your deans, archdeacons, and other dignities of your church, be resident or not; who they be; what other promotions or livings every one of them hath, and in what diocese; and whether every one of them be ministers or not; whether they use seemly or priestly garments, according as they are commanded by the Queen's Majesty's injunctions to do?

5. ITEM, Whether your prebendaries be commonly resident, or how many of them; where every one of the rest be; what be their names; what livings every one of them hath, and in what place; what orders they be in; how or in what apparel they do commonly go; whether they do

preach in their several courses, or how often, and what times in the year; or how often they do resort to your cathedral church?

6. ITEM, Whether your divine service be used, and the Sacrament ministered in manner and form prescribed in the Queen's Majesty's Injunctions, and none other ways; whether it be said or sung in due time; whether in all points according to the statutes of your church, not being repugnant to any of the Queen's Majesty's laws or injunctions; whether all that were wont, be bound, or ought to come to it, do so still; whether every one of your church doth openly communicate in the said cathedral church at the least once in every year?

7. ITEM, Whether your grammar-school be well ordered; whether the number of the children thereof be furnished; how many do want, and by whose default; whether they be diligently and godly brought up in the fear of God and wholesome doctrine; whether any of them have been received for money or rewards, and by whom; whether the statutes, foundations, and other ordinances, touching the godly prescribed and used alms of your church, and the said grammar-school, master, or the scholars thereof, or any other having doing or interest therein, be kept; by whom it is not observed, or by whose default? And the like in all points you shall inquire and present of your choristers and their master.

8. ITEM, Whether all other officers and ministers of your church, as well within as without, do their duties in all points obediently and faithfully; and whether your dean, stewards, treasurers, bursars, receivers, or any officer, having any charge, or any ways being accountant to the said church, do make a true, perfect, and faithful account, at such days and times as be limited and appointed by the statutes and customs of the said church, making full payment yearly of all arrearages; whether any money or goods of the church do remain in any men's hands; who they be, and what sum remaineth?

9. ITEM, You shall inquire of the doctrine and judgment of all and singular head and members of your said church, as your dean, archdeacons, prebendaries, readers of divinity, schoolmasters, vicars, petty canons, deacons, conducts[1], singing-men, choristers, scholars in grammar-schools, and all other officers and ministers, as well within your church as without; whether any of them do either privily or openly preach any unwholesome, erroneous, or seditious doctrine, contrary or repugnant to any article agreed upon in any synod of the clergy of the province of Canterbury, sithence the first year of her Majesty's reign; or discourage any man, soberly for his edifying, from the reading of the holy Scriptures; or in any point do persuade or move any not to conform themselves to the order of religion reformed, restored, and revived by public authority in this church of England?

10. ITEM, You shall inquire of the names and surnames of all and singular the abovenamed members, officers, and ministers of this your said church, as well high as low: whether you know or suspect any of them to obtain his room, or living, by simony, that is, by money, unlawful covenants, gift, or reward; who presented him; whether his living be in lease; and by whom it is leased; to whom, upon what rent; whether he doth pay any pension; for what cause, what sum, and to whom; whether any of them be known or suspected to be a swearer, an adulterer, a fornicator, or suspected of any other uncleanliness; whether any of them do use any suspect house, or suspected company of any such faults, any tavern, alehouse, or tippling houses, or any inconvenient season; whether any of them be suspected to be a drunkard, a dicer, a carder, a brawler, fighter, quarreler, or unquiet person, a carrier of tales, a backbiter, slanderer, batemaker[2], or any other ways a breaker of charity or unity, or cause of unquietness by any means?

11. ITEM, Whether you have necessary ornaments and books for your church?

[[1] Conducts: *conducti*, hired chaplains; not members of the society.]
[[2] Bate-maker: maker of discord.]

12. ITEM, Whether your church be sufficiently repaired in all parts; what stock or annuity is there towards the reparations of the cathedral church; in whose hands and custody doth it remain?

13. ITEM, Finally, you shall present what you think necessary or profitable for the church to be reformed, or of new to be appointed and ordered in the same.

INJUNCTIONS

GIVEN TO THE

DEAN AND CHAPTER

OF THE CATHEDRAL CHURCH OF BANGOR, AND TO OTHER OF THE CLERGY OF THAT DIOCESE, BY THE MOST REVEREND IN CHRIST, EDMUND ARCHBISHOP OF CANTERBURY, PRIMATE OF ALL ENGLAND, AND METROPOLITAN, IN HIS METROPOLITICAL VISITATION OF THE SAID DIOCESE OF BANGOR, IN THE YEAR OF CHRIST, ONE THOUSAND, FIVE HUNDRED, SEVENTY SIX.

IMPRIMIS, That the dean and prebendaries of the said cathedral church, and every of them, which are bound by the Queen's Majesty's visitors' injunctions to preach in the said cathedral church, do and execute the said sermons in their proper persons, every of the times to them especially appointed; except for reasonable causes they obtain of the bishop of the said see, to do such sermons, and every of them, by some other learned men; upon pain of 20s. to be levied of the fruits of their livings, to the use of the cathedral church, so often as herein any of them shall offend. Grind. Reg. fol. 98.

2. ITEM, That the said dean and prebendaries shall make the said quarter sermons, and every of them, upon the days limited in a certain table hereunto annexed, upon the foresaid pain; and that the said table shall be set up in a frame within the choir of the said cathedral church, that the days of such sermons may be publicly known.

3. ITEM, That every other prebendaries, having any church or churches to his or their prebends annexed, shall make, in their proper persons, one sermon in the said cathedral church yearly upon a certain day also to be limited by the bishop there; except upon reasonable causes, to be allowed by the said bishop, he or they be permitted to do the same by some other learned man; upon the pain before mentioned.

4. ITEM, That the said dean and prebendaries diligently and carefully look quarterly, that schoolmaster, usher, and scholars of the grammar school there erected, observe and keep the statutes and ordinances of the same school; and that once every year a full and perfect account be made of all the revenues belonging to the said school, before the bishop there, or his substitute, the first week of November yearly, without any fraud, delay, or collusion.

5. ITEM, That every archdeacon of the said diocese within his jurisdiction do diligently exhort the parsons, vicars, and curates, to apply the study of holy Scripture, to avoid idleness and unseemly apparel; and the defects and disorders in that behalf from time to time, by himself or his official, to direct and present to the bishop.

6. ITEM, That every minister or priest in the said diocese, not licensed to preach, having any benefice with cure, execute in his own person, once at the least every half year, in every his benefice with cure the whole service of the church; and also then and there minister the holy Communion, upon pain to forfeit of the fruits of every such benefice 5*l*. for every such default, to be employed by the bishop to the poor of the same parish.

Here follows a table of the times appointed for the ordinary sermons, which the dean and certain prebendaries of the church are yearly bound to make in the same.

In witness and testimony of all which premises, we, Edmund Archbishop of Canterbury abovesaid, to these presents have put our seal, yeoven in our manor of Lambeth the five and twentieth of February in the year of our Lord God, after the computation of the church of England, one thousand five hundred seventy and six, and in the second year of our translation.

ARTICLES,

WHEREUPON IT WAS AGREED

BY THE

MOST REVEREND FATHER IN GOD,

EDMUND,

ARCHBISHOP OF CANTERBURY,
AND OTHER THE BISHOPS, AND THE WHOLE CLERGY OF THE PROVINCE OF CANTERBURY, IN THE CONVOCATION OR SYNOD, HOLDEN AT WESTMINSTER BY PROROGATION, IN THE YEAR OF OUR LORD GOD, AFTER THE COMPUTATION OF THE CHURCH OF ENGLAND, MDLXXV, TOUCHING THE ADMISSION OF APT AND FIT PERSONS TO THE MINISTRY, AND THE ESTABLISHING OF GOOD ORDER IN THE CHURCH[1].

(Petyt. MSS., Inner Temple Library, No. 38, fol. 217.)

FIRST, That none shall be made deacon or minister hereafter, but only such as shall first bring to the bishop of that diocese, from men known to the same bishop to be of sound religion, a testimonial, both of his honest life, and of his professing the doctrine expressed in the Articles of Religion, which concern the confession of true Christian faith, and the doctrine of the sacraments, comprised in a book imprinted, entituled, *Articles, whereupon it was agreed by the archbishops and bishops of both provinces, and the whole clergy in the Convocation holden at London, in the Year*

[1 The convocation, having been divers times adjourned, at last, on Saturday March the 17th, A.D. 157$\frac{5}{6}$, met at Henry the Seventh's chapel, where the most reverend the Archbishop, being present, commanded and caused to be read certain articles conceived in writing: which, after they had been read over, the archbishop and his brethren the bishops gave their assent and consent to, and subscribed their names with their own hands. Strype, Grindal, p, 289.

These Articles, with the exception of the twelfth and fifteenth, were published and printed by the Queen's authority. The reason of the omission in the latter case is stated in the note at that Article. The text has been corrected from the MS. copy which belonged to Whitgift, who was Prolocutor of the convocation, and which is indorsed with his own hand.]

of our Lord 1562, *for the avoiding of the diversities of opinions, and for the establishing of consent touching true religion; put forth by the Queen's authority:* and which also shall then be able to answer, and render to the same bishop an account of his faith in Latin, agreeable and consonant to the said articles; and shall first subscribe to the said articles. And every such deacon shall be of the age of three and twenty years, and shall continue in that office the space of a whole year, at the least, before he be admitted to the order of priesthood. And every such minister shall be of the full age of four and twenty years. And that neither of those orders shall be given, but only upon a Sunday or holy day, and in the face of the church; and in such manner and form, and with all such other circumstances as are appointed by the book entituled, *The form and manner of making and consecrating Bishops, Priests, and Deacons.*

2. ITEM, That no bishop shall give either of the said orders to any that be not of his own diocese, (other than graduates resiant in either of the Universities,) unless they be dimitted under the hand and seal of that bishop of whose diocese they are; and not upon letters dimissory of any chancellor or other officer to any bishop.

3. ITEM, That unlearned ministers, heretofore made by any bishops, shall not hereafter be admitted to any cure or spiritual function, according to the Queen's Majesty's injunction in that behalf[1]. For which purpose, the bishop shall cause strait and diligent examination to be used in the admission of all curates to the charge of any cure.

4. ITEM, That diligent inquisition be made in every diocese for all such as have forged or counterfeited letters of orders, that they may be deposed and punished by the commissioners ecclesiastical.

5. ITEM, That the bishops by their letters do certify one to another the names of such counterfeit ministers, to the end they be not suffered to serve in any other diocese.

[1 Art. xliii.]

6. ITEM, That from henceforth none shall be admitted to any orders ecclesiastical, unless he do presently shew to the bishop a true presentation of himself to a benefice then void, within the diocese or jurisdiction of the said bishop; or unless he likewise shew to the said bishop a true certificate, where presently he may be placed to serve some cure within the same diocese or jurisdiction; or unless he be placed in some cathedral, or collegiate church, or college; or unless the bishop shall forthwith place him in some vacant benefice or cure; or unless he be known to have sufficient patrimony or livelihood of his own.

7. ITEM, That none shall be admitted unto any dignity or benefice with cure of souls, unless he be qualified according to the tenor of the first article: and if any such dignity or benefice be of the yearly value of £30. or above, in the Queen's books, unless he shall then be a doctor in some faculty, or a bachelor of divinity at least, or a preacher lawfully allowed by some bishop within this realm, or by one of the Universities of Cambridge or Oxford; and shall give open trial of his preaching before the bishop or ordinary, or some other learned men appointed by him, before his admission to such dignity or benefice. And nevertheless, where the stipends or livings be very small, there to choose and admit of the best that can be found in such case of necessity.

8. ITEM, That all licences for preaching granted out by any archbishops or bishops within the province of Canterbury, bearing date before the 8th of February 157$\frac{2}{3}$, be void and of none effect. And nevertheless, all such as shall be thought meet for that office to be admitted again without difficulty or charge, paying not above four-pence for the seal, writing, parchment, and wax for the same, according to an article of the advertisements in that behalf. *In the printed articles it is somewhat different, viz. paying nothing for the same.*

9. ITEM, That every bishop take order, that all able preachers within his diocese do earnestly and with diligence teach their auditors sound doctrine of faith and true religion; and continually exhort them to repentance and amendment of life; that they may bring forth the fruits of faith and charity,

and be liberal in alms and other good deeds commanded by God's word. And that none be admitted to be a preacher unless he be first a deacon at the least.

10. ITEM, That every bishop in his diocese shall with all expedition take order, that the catechism allowed be diligently taught to the youth in every parish church; and that the Homilies, when no sermons be had, be duly read in order, as they be prescribed, every Sunday and holy day.

11. ITEM, That every bishop shall likewise take order within his diocese, that every parson, vicar, curate, and stipendiary priest, being under the degree of a Master of Art, and being no preacher, shall provide, and have of his own, within two months after warning given to him or them, the New Testament, both in Latin and English, or Welsh; and shall confer daily one chapter of the same, the Latin and English, or Welsh together. And that archdeacons, commissaries, and officials, in their synods and visitations, shall by their discretion appoint to every of the said parsons, vicars, curates, and stipendiary priests, some certain tax of the New Testament to be conned without book, or otherwise to be travailed in, as shall be thought most convenient to the said archdeacons, commissaries, or officials; and shall exact a rehearsal of the same, and examine them, how they have profited in the study thereof, at their next synods and visitations, or such other time or times as to them shall be thought meet.

12. ITEM, Where some ambiguity and doubt hath risen among divers, by what persons private baptism is to be ministered; forasmuch as by the book of Common Prayer, allowed by statute, the bishop of the diocese is authorized to expound and resolve all such doubts as shall arise concerning the manner how to understand, do, and execute the things contained in the said book; it is now by the said archbishop and bishops expounded and resolved, and every of them doth expound and resolve, that the said private baptism, in case of necessity, is only to be ministered by a lawful minister or deacon, called to be present for that purpose, and by none other. And that every bishop in his diocese shall take order,

that this exposition of the said doubt shall be published in writing before the first day of May next coming, in every parish church of his diocese in this province. And thereby all other persons shall be inhibited to intermeddle with the ministering of baptism privately, being no part of their vocation[1].

13. ITEM, That from henceforth there be no commutation of any penance by any having ordinary jurisdiction ecclesiastical, or any their officers or deputies, into any mulct pecuniary; unless the same be done upon great and urgent causes, by the consent of the bishop of the diocese, declared in writing under his hand and seal.

14. ITEM, That all archdeacons, and others, which have ordinary jurisdiction ecclesiastical, and their officers and deputies, shall call before them all such person and persons as shall be detected or presented before them, or any of them, of any ecclesiastical crime and fault; and shall use all means by law prescribed, to convince and punish such as be found to be offenders effectually, upon pain of suspension from his and their office.

15. ITEM, That the bishops shall take order, that it be published and declared in every parish church within their diocese, before the first day of May next coming, that marriage may be solemnized at all times of the year, so that the banns be first, upon three several Sundays or holy days in the service-time, openly asked in the church, and none impediment objected; and so that the said marriage be also publicly solemnized in the church at the usual time of Morning Prayer[2].

> "To all which Articles, and every of them, we, the said archbishop and bishops, whose names are underwritten, have assented and subscribed our several names with our proper hands, as well for ourselves, as also for other bishops, being absent; for whom in this synod we have lawful proxies."

[1 This twelfth Article is omitted in the printed book of these Articles.]
[2 This fifteenth Article also is omitted in the printed articles. "Ultimus tamen articulus typis non fuit expressus, eo quod domina regina (ut dicitur) non assensit eidem." Wilkins, Concil. IV. 285.]

MANDATUM Archiepiscopi Cantuar. ad publicandum Articulos in Convocatione, MDLXXV. stabilitos.

(WILKINS, Concil. vol. iv. p. 285.)

EDMUNDUS, divina providentia Cant. Archiepiscopus, totius Angliæ primas et metropolitanus, venerabili confratri nostro Edwino, eadem providentia London. Episcopo, salutem et fraternam in Domino charitatem. Cum in sacra Synodo provinciali sive convocatione prælatorum et cleri nostræ Cant. provinciæ, auctoritate brevis regii in ea parte emanati, in domo capitulari ecclesiæ cathedralis D. Pauli London. 9° die mensis Maii A.D. MDLXXII. ultimo præterito inchoata ac celebrata, ac de die in diem et de loco in locum continuata et prorogata, de consilio et assensu vestris, et aliorum venerabilium confratrum nostrorum, totiusque cleri dictæ nostræ Cant. provinciæ, in eadem sacra synodo sive convocatione 17° die mensis Martii A.D. (juxta computationem ecclesiæ Anglicanæ) MDLXXV. ultimo præterito congregata, inter nonnulla alia, per nos mutuo et unanimi nostro consensu, ad Dei gloriam illustrandam, divini cultus augmentum, ecclesiæ Anglicanæ utilitatem, ordinis clericalis honestatem et decentiam, ac illustrissimæ Dominæ nostræ Reginæ regnique sui Angliæ tuitionem et defensionem tendentia, ordinata et stabilita, ex certis magnis, arduis, et urgentibus causis, per nos eisdem confratribus nostris et clero dictæ nostræ provinciæ Cant. expositis, et inter nos matura deliberatione consideratis et ponderatis, quosdam articulos intitulatos "Articles whereupon it was agreed," etc. ordinaverimus et stabiliverimus; NOS igitur Articulos prædictos in et per totam provinciam nostram Cant. prædictam debitæ executioni demandare volentes, verum exemplum articulorum præsentibus annexum (ne quisquam ignorantiam prætendere possit) fraternitati vestræ committimus publicandum; eidem fraternitati vestræ præcipiendo mandantes, quatenus vera exemplaria prædictorum articulorum sub sigillo et separalibus literis vestris, universis et singulis venerabilibus confratribus nostris episcopis suffraganeis dictæ nostræ provinciæ Cant. ac custodibus spiritualitatis sedium vacantium transmittentes, ex parte nostra iis injungatis, quibus nos etiam harum serie injungimus, quatenus eorum singuli in singulis civitatibus ac diœcesibus eorundem, prout [ad] eos et eorum quemlibet respective pertinet, articulos prædictos debite publicent et denuncient, ac ab omnibus, quos concernunt, observari et debitæ executioni demandari faciant, et curent cum effectu. Ac insuper articulos memoratos per fraternitatem vestram, in et per civitatem et diœcesim vestram, prout ad vos attinet, debite et effectualiter publicari, denunciari, et executioni debitæ demandari volumus et mandamus, prout convenit. In cujus rei testimonium, etc. Dat. 20° die Aprilis, MDLXXVI.

TRANSLATION.

MANDATE of the Archbishop of Canterbury for the publication of the Articles[1] agreed upon in the Convocation, 1575.

EDMUND, by divine providence Archbishop of Canterbury, primate of all England and Metropolitan, to our reverend brother Edwin, by the same providence Bishop of London, health and brotherly love in the Lord. WHEREAS in the sacred provincial synod or convocation of the prelates and clergy of our province of Canterbury, begun and holden, under authority of a royal brief issued in that behalf, in the chapter-house of the cathedral church of St Paul in London, on the 9th day of May A.D. 1572 last past, and from day to day and from place to place continued and prorogued by the counsel and assent of you, and the rest of our venerable brethren, and the whole clergy of our said province of Canterbury, in the same sacred convocation, assembled on the 17th day of March A.D. 1575, according to the computation of the church of England, last past, amongst sundry other matters by us with our mutual and unanimous consent ordained and established, tending to the setting forth of God's glory, the increase of divine worship, the advantage of the Church of England, the honesty and decency of the clerical

[[1] The preceding Articles.]

order, and the tuition and defence of our illustrious sovereign the Queen and her realm of England, for certain great, arduous, and urgent causes, set forth by us to the same our brethren and the clergy of our said province of Canterbury, and considered and weighed amongst us with mature deliberation, we ordained and established certain Articles entituled "Articles whereupon it was agreed, etc.":—WE therefore, willing to put into due execution the aforesaid Articles in and throughout our entire province of Canterbury aforesaid, do commit to your brotherhood to be published, that no one may pretend ignorance, a true copy of the Articles annexed to these presents; strictly charging the same your brotherhood, that, transmitting true copies of the aforesaid Articles under your seal and several letters to all and singular our venerable brethren the suffragan bishops of our said province of Canterbury, and to the keepers of the spiritualities of the vacant sees, you enjoin them in our behalf, (and we ourselves also enjoin them by the tenor hereof,) that each of them in their several cities and dioceses, as respectively pertains to them and any of them, duly publish and proclaim the aforesaid Articles, and cause and effectually take care that they be observed and duly executed by all whom they concern.

And moreover, we will and command that the said Articles be duly and effectually published, proclaimed, and put into due execution, as is fit, by your brotherhood, in and through your city and diocese, as pertaineth to you.

In witness whereof, &c.

Given the 20th day of April, MDLXXVI.

DISPUTATION AT CAMBRIDGE,

A.D. 1549,

ABOUT THE

SACRAMENT OF THE LORD'S SUPPER.

[GRINDAL.]

NOTICE.

[This disputation was held in the presence of king Edward's visitors, viz. Thomas Goodrich, bishop of Ely; Nicholas Ridley, bishop of Rochester; Sir William Paget; Sir Thomas Smith; Sir John Cheke; Dr May; and Dr Wendy, the king's physician. The conclusions to be disputed were:
1. That transubstantiation could not be proved by the plain and manifest words of Scripture.
2. That it could not thereof be necessarily collected, nor yet confirmed by the consent of the ancient fathers for these thousand years past.[1]

In this disputation, holden June 20, 1549, the disputants were, on the protestant side, Dr Madew; on the Romish, Glin, Langdale, Sedgwick and Young: In the second, on June 24, Glin, affirming the corporeal presence of Christ in the sacrament, was opposed by Grindal, Perne, Guest, and Pilkington. And in the third, Perne was opposed by Parker (not Dr Matthew Parker, afterwards archbishop), Pollard, Vavasor, and Young: Bishop Ridley determined. The entire disputation may be seen in Foxe's Acts and Monuments, p. 1376. Ed. 1583. For Bishop Ridley's Determination, see Works, Parker Society Edition, p. 171. et seq.]

[1 It should rather be, "for a thousand years after Christ." See Strype, Grindal, p. 6.]

THE
SECOND DISPUTATION
HOLDEN
AT CAMBRIDGE,
THE 24TH DAY OF JUNE, 1549.

[After Perne had argued from Scripture against Glin's Conclusion in support of Transubstantiation, the narrative proceeds in p. 1383.]

Here Master Grindal beginneth to dispute.

Grindal:—Whereas you say, worshipful master doctor, that we speak not now as sometimes we thought and judged in this matter; peradventure you also judge not so now all things as you have done heretofore. But what we have once been, it forceth not, God respecteth no man's person. And whereas you say that you dare not, contrary to Christ, call it a sign, or a figure; Augustine[2] notwithstanding dareth to call it a figure, and Tertullian[3] likewise, with many more. Grindal replieth. Aug. Tertul. with many more call it a figure.

Glin:—True it is, but they called it not a sign or a figure only: but prove you, if you can, that after the consecration remaineth any other substance than the real body of Christ.

Grindal:—If the forms do nourish, as you contend, they nourish the natural and human body, for they be both as one, and are nourished alike. What the form of bread and wine do nourish.

Glin:—Your reason is mere physical, and therefore to be rejected in matters of faith; but I grant they nourish, but miraculously.

Grindal:—If you grant that the forms do nourish, then you grant that bread remaineth.

[2 S. August. de doctr. Christ. Lib. iii. c. 16. Basil, 1569. Tom. III. col. 53. Vide supra, p. 63. Also contra Adimant. c. 12, Tom. VI. col. 187.]

[3 Tertull. advers. Marcion. Lib. iv. c. 40. Paris. 1641. p. 571. Vide supra, p. 65.]

Glin:—I said even now that that is true, but the nature of it is changed, and that miraculously.

<small>It remaineth bread and wine after the consecration.</small>

Grindal:—If it be the real and substantial body of Christ, because Christ said, "This is my body;" ergo, because the Lord said, "I will not drink of the fruit of this vine," and Paul calleth it bread after the consecration, it is therefore bread and wine.

Glin:—Truly, sir, you must bring better arguments, or else you will prove nothing for your purpose. For to your reasons thus I answer: Chrysostom saith, "Christ did drink of the blood[1];" but whether this sentence, "I will not drink of the fruit of the vine," be spoken of the blood, it is not certain. And truly, Erasmus denieth that it is not to be found in all the whole scripture, that it is called bread after the consecration. Or else thus I may answer you. Even as it is called bread for the form, and kind, and accidents which remain; so, for the form and similitude which it hath, it may be called the fruit of the vine, after the consecration. And whereas Chrysostom calleth it wine, he speaketh of the nature whereof the sacrament necessarily is made. And I deny not but it may be called wine, but yet eucharistical, &c.

<small>How it is called bread, and in what respect.</small>

Rochester:—The Evangelists, Matthew, Mark and Luke, call it the fruit of the vine, and Chrysostom saith, "that the fruit of the vine is nothing else but wine:" ergo Christ gave them wine, and drank wine himself also, not blood.

<small>Christ called it wine, not blood.</small>

Glin:—Christ said twice, "I will not drink of the fruit of the vine;" once at the eating of the paschal lamb, (as Luke saith,) and then was it wine indeed; and again, after the consecration of his body and blood, he said the like, and then it was not wine; which methink I can prove by the plain words of St Luke, if we compare him with Matthew. For if it were wine, as they both affirm, then the words of Christ cannot well stand, because first (as Luke sheweth) he said at his legal supper, "I will not drink of the fruit of this vine," &c.; and again in Matthew, after the consecration of his body and blood he drank: it followeth therefore, that that which he drank was not wine by nature;

[1 S. Chrysost. Hom. $\pi\beta$. in Matth. cap. xxvi. Eton. 1612. Tom. II. p. 510. Vide supra p. 65.]

for then must Christ needs be a liar, which were blasphemy to say.

Rochester:—Augustine doth thus reconcile those places, saying, it is spoken by a figure which we call *Hysteron proteron*[2]. *Two places assoiled.*

Glin:—I know that Augustine saith so, but methink that which I have said seemeth to be the true meaning of the places.

Rochester:—Augustine seeketh no starting holes, nor yet any indirect shifts to obscure the truth.

Glin:—Say your fatherhood what you will of Augustine, I think not so.

Grindal:—"This cup is the New Testament in my blood", but here is a trope; ergo, in these words of Christ, "This is my body," is a trope also. *In these words, This is my body, is a trope.*

Glin:—I deny your argument; for whereas Luke saith, "this cup," Matthew saith, "this is my blood;" and therefore, as Augustine saith, "Places that be dark, are to be expounded by other that be light[3]."

Rochester:—All of your side deny that Christ ever used any trope in the instituting of sacraments.

Glin:—For my part, I hold no opinion but the truth, whereof you yourself also do pretend the like.

Rochester:—What understand you by this word *hoc*, (this), and in what words standeth the force or strength of the sacrament? In this pronoun *hoc* (this), or in this verb *est* (is), or else in this whole sentence, "this is my body"? *A question wherein consisteth the strength of the sacrament.*

Glin:—It is not made the true body, except all the words be spoken, as in baptism, "I baptize thee in the name of the Father, of the Son, and of the Holy Ghost." For neither doth baptism consist in this word *ego* (I), or in *baptize*, or in this word *te* (thee), or in these words, *in nomine* (in the name), &c. but in all the words spoken in order.

[2 Quod enim Lucas de calice bis commemoravit, prius antequam panem daret, deinde posteaquam panem dedit, illud quod superius dixit præoccupavit, ut solet; illud vero quod ordine suo posuit non commemoravit superius. S. August. de consensu Evangelist. Lib. iii. cap. 1. Tom. IV. col. 471.]

[3 Quibusdam enim scripturarum locis apertius aliquid exponitur, quod diligens et pius lector etiam in aliis locis, in quibus minus aperitur, intelligat. S. August. de diversis quæstionibus. Quest. liii. Tom. IV. col. 553.]

Grindal:—If to eat the body of Christ be a figurative speech, as Augustine saith it is, ergo, then these words, "this is my body," is a figurative speech also.

Glin:—It is a figurative speech, because we eat not the body of Christ after the same manner that we do other meats, &c.

Grindal:—Cyprian understandeth this of those that come unworthily, and make no difference of the Lord's body, speaking of the dijudication of the sacraments, and not of the body of Christ.

Glin:—Truly he speaketh of the true body of Christ.

Rochester:—They receive unworthily, who neither judge themselves, nor yet the sacraments, taking them as other common bread.

Grindal:—Augustine, upon the thirty-third psalm[1], saith, "Christ bare himself in his own hands after a sort, not indeed or truly," &c.

Glin:—You omit many other things which Augustine saith; and I confess that he carried himself in his own hands after a sort. But Augustine delivereth this unto us, and as a great miracle; and you know it was no great miracle to carry a figure of his body in his hands. And whereas you say that Christ carried himself after a sort in his own hands, it is very true, but yet diversly; for he sat after one manner at his supper, and after another manner he carried himself in his hands: for Christ in the visible figure bore himself invisibly.

Grindal:—Tertullian calleth it a figure, ergo, it is so.

Glin:—It is, as I have said, a figure, but not a figure only. But hear what Tertullian saith[2], "He took bread and made it his body, saying, This is my body," &c.

Grindal:—Hear what Chrysostom saith upon Matthew[3], Homil. II. sup. cap. 5, "If vessels sanctified to holy uses," &c.

Glin:—That work is received not as Chrysostom's, but some man's else, as you know: or thus I answer, it is not the true body in proper and visible form.

[1 S. August. in Psalm. xxxiii. Tom. viii. col. 234. Vide supra p. 61.]

[2 Advers. Marcion. Lib. iv. c. 40.]

[3 Opus imperf. in Matth. Hom. xi. Paris. 1724. Tom. vi. ad finem p. 63. Vide supra p. 67.]

THE EXAMINATION

OF

CERTAIN LONDONERS

BEFORE THE

ECCLESIASTICAL COMMISSIONERS.

JUNE 20, 1567.

THE EXAMINATION

OF

CERTAIN LONDONERS

BEFORE THE

ECCLESIASTICAL COMMISSIONERS.

JUNE 20, 1567.

The true report of our examination[1] and conference (as near as we can call to remembrance) had the 20th day of June, Anno 1567, before the Lord Mayor, the Bishop of London, the Dean of Westminster[2], Master Watts[3], and other Commissioners[4].

WHEN we were come in, we did our obeisance, and they bade us come near, and the bishop's registrar called us by name, John Smith, William Nixson, William Wh. [White], James Ireland, Robert Hawkins, Thomas Boweland, and Richard Morecraft. The bishop said, Is here all? One answered, No, there are ten or eleven in the Compter.

[1 This narrative is taken from that 'very rare' book, entitled "A parte of a Register, contaynyng sundrie memorable matters, &c.", supposed to have been published at Edinburgh about A.D. 1593. For an account of which, and the circumstances connected with its suppression, see Herbert's Ames. Vol. III. p. 1514. The 'report' is of course an ex parte statement, and must be received accordingly.]

[2 Dr Gabriel Goodman.]

[3 Chaplain to Bishop Grindal.]

[4 "Some of this sort (the more violent separatists) had hired Plumbers' Hall, upon pretence of keeping a wedding there, but in truth for a religious meeting. Here, on the 19th of June, about an hundred persons met, but were disturbed by the sheriffs, and about fourteen or fifteen of the chief of them taken, and sent to the Compter for disobedience. The next day several of them were sent for before the Lord Mayor, (Sir Christopher Draper,) the bishop of London, and others the queen's commissioners. Strype, Grindal, p. 169.]

Bishop:—I know that well enough.

The bishop said unto the mayor : My lord, will you begin? The mayor said unto him, I pray you begin.

Bishop:—Well then, here you have shewed yourselves disorderly, not only in absenting yourselves from your parish churches, and the assemblies of other Christians in this commonwealth, which do quietly obey the Queen's proceedings, and serve God in such good order, as the Queen's grace, and the rest having authority and wisdom, have set forth and established by act of parliament; but also you have gathered together and made assemblies, using prayers and preachings, yea, and ministering the sacraments among yourselves; and thus you gather together many times, yea, and no longer ago than yesterday you were together to the number of an hundred; whereof there were about fourteen or fifteen of you sent to prison. And our being here is to will you to leave off, or else you shall see the Queen's letter, and the council's hands at it. (Then he opened it, and shewed it us, but would not read it. The effect of it, he said, was to move us to be conformable by gentleness, or else at the first we should lose our freedom of the city, and abide that would follow.) And moreover, you have hired the Plumbers' Hall, saying, you would have it for a wedding. Where is Boweland?

Boweland:—Here I am, and if it please you.

Bishop:—Did you hire the hall?

One of us said: " In that we said to the sheriffs, it was for a wedding, we did it to save the woman harmless, and at her request."

Bishop:—Yea, but you must not lie; that is against the admonition of the apostle : " Let every man speak the truth to his neighbour." And herein you have put the poor woman to great blame, and enough to lose her office : this is against the order of charity.

Here we would have answered, but he would not suffer us, but said, You shall be heard anon.

Bishop:—But to the matter. In this severing yourselves from the society of other Christians, you condemn not only us, but also the whole state of the church reformed in King Edward's days, which was well reformed according to the word of God, yea, and many good men have shed their blood for the same, which your doings condemn.

Hawkins:—We condemn them not, in that we stand to the truth of God's word.

But he would not suffer us to answer to it.

Bishop:—But have you not the gospel truly preached, and the sacraments ministered accordingly, and good order kept, although we differ from other churches in ceremonies, and in indifferent things, which lie in the prince's power to command for order's sake? How say you, Smith? You seem to be the ancientest of them; answer you.

Smith:—Indeed, my lord, we thank God for reformation; and that is it we desire, according to God's word. (And there he stayed.)

White:—I beseech you, let me answer.

Bishop:—Nay, W. W. hold your peace, you shall be heard anon.

Nixson:—I beseech you, let me answer a word or two.

Bishop:—Nixson, you are a busy fellow, I know your words; you are full of talk; I know from whence you came.

Hawkins:—I would be glad to answer.

Bishop:—Smith shall answer. Answer you, Smith.

Smith:—Indeed, as you said even now, for preaching and ministering the sacraments, so long as we might have the word freely preached, and the sacraments administered without the preferring of idolatrous gear about it, we never assembled together in houses. But when it came to this point, that all our preachers were displaced by your law, that would not subscribe to your apparel and your law, so that we could not hear none of them in any church by the space of seven or eight weeks, except Father Coverdale, of whom we have a good opinion, and yet (God knoweth) the man was so fearful, that he durst not be known unto us where he preached, though we sought it at his house;—and then were we troubled and commanded to your courts from day to day, for not coming to our parish churches:—then we bethought us what were best to do; and we remembered that there was a congregation of us in this city in Queen Mary's days; and a congregation at Geneva, which used a book and order of preaching, ministering of the sacraments and

Marginal notes: Blood shed for King Edward's reformation. — Displacing good preachers, cause of private meetings.

discipline, most agreeable to the word of God; which book is allowed by that godly and well learned man, Master Calvin, and the preachers there; which book and order we now hold. And if you can reprove this book, or any thing that we hold, by the word of God, we will yield to you, and do open penance at Paul's Cross; if not, we will stand to it by the grace of God.

Bishop:—This is no answer.

White:—You may be answered, if you will give leave.

Bishop:—White, you shall speak anon; let the elder speak first.

Smith:—Would you have me go back from the better to such churches, that I had as leave go to mass as go to them,—they are so evil-favouredly used?—as the parish church where I dwell is one. He is a very papist that is there, and yet he hath another place too.

Dean:—Lo! he counteth the service and reformation in King Edward's days as evil as the mass.

Bishop:—Lo! because he knoweth one that is evil, he findeth fault with all. But you may go to other places, as at St Laurence.

White:—You say we find fault with all for one papist. If it were well tried, there should a great company of papists be found in this city, whom you do allow to be preachers and ministers, and thrust out the godly for your pleasure's sake.

Roper:—I know one that in Queen Mary's time did persecute God's saints, and brought them forth to Bishop Bonner, and now he is minister allowed of you, and never made recantation.

Bishop:—Can you accuse any of them of false doctrine, and shew us of it?

Nixson:—Yea, that I can, and he is even now in this house that I can accuse of false doctrine. Let him come forth and answer his doctrine that he preached upon the 10th of John. (And so I looked back upon Bedell, and Bedell hung down his head, and the bishop looked upon the dean, and one looked upon another.)

<small>A B. chapl. challenged of false doctrine.</small>

Dean:—You would take away the authority of the prince, and liberty of a Christian man.

Bishop:—Yea, and therefore ye suffer justly.

Hawkins:—But it lieth not in the authority of the prince, and liberty of a Christian man, to use and to defend that appertaineth to papistry and idolatry, and the pope's canon law, as we may plainly see in the 7th of Deuteronomy, and other places of the Scriptures.

Dean:—When do you hear us maintain such things in our preachings?

Hawkins:—Though you do it not in your preachings, yet you do it in your deeds and by your laws.

White:—The prophet saith, That the foolish say not with their mouths, There is no God, but in their hearts; their doings are corrupt and vain.

Hawkins:—You preach Christ to be priest and prophet, but you preach him not to be king, neither will you suffer him to reign with the sceptre of his word in his church alone; but the pope's canon law and the will of the prince must have the first place, and be preferred before the word and ordinance of Christ.

Dean:—You speak unreverently here of the prince before the magistrates: you were not bidden to speak, you might hold your peace.

Hawkins:—You will suffer us to make our purgation, seeing that you persecute us.

Bishop:—What is so preferred?

Nixson:—Why, that which is upon your head and upon your back, your copes and your surplices, and your laws and ministers; because you will suffer none to preach nor minister, except he wear them, or subscribe to them.

Bishop:—No? how say you to Sampson and Lever[1], and others? do not they preach?

White:—Though they preach, you have deprived them and forbidden them, and the law standeth in force against them still, howsoever you suffer them now. And for what purpose you will not suffer other, whom you cannot reprove by the word of God, I know not.

Bishop:—They will not be preachers, nor meddle with you.

[[1] Who, with Coverdale, were then connived at in their non-conformity as to the habits.]

White:—Your doings is the cause.

Hawkins:—They will not join with you. I heard one of them say, that he had rather be torn in a hundred pieces than to communicate with you. We hold nothing, nor allow any thing, but that which is maintained by the word of God; the which word, saith Esay, shall come forth of Sion, and give sentence among the heathen, and reform the multitude. And Christ saith, "The word that I have spoken, shall judge in the last day," when both the prince, and you, and we shall stand naked before the judgment-seat of Christ. And if you can prove that we hold not the truth, shew it, and we will leave it.

<small>Isai. ii. iii. iv.</small>

<small>John xii. 48.</small>

<small>Truth punished by the B.</small>

Smith:—And if you cannot, we pray you, let us not be thus used.

Dean:—You are not obedient to the authority of the prince.

White:—Yes, that we are; for we resist not, but suffer that the authority layeth upon us.

Bishop:—So do thieves suffer that the law layeth upon them

White:—What a comparison is this! They suffer for evil doing, and you punish us for seeking to serve God according to his word.

Nixson:—Both the prince and we must be ruled by the word of God, as we read in the first book of Kings, the 12th chapter, that the king should teach only the word of God.

Bishop:—What? that the king shall teach the word of God? Lie not.

Nixson:—It is that both king and people should obey the word of God, or else they shall perish.

Bishop:—Indeed it is true in effect, that the prince should and must obey the word of God only. But I will shew you this consisteth in three points.

The *first* is, that which God commandeth may not be left undone.

The *second* is, that which God forbiddeth may not be done.

And the *third* consisteth in things which God neither commandeth nor forbiddeth, and they are of the middle sort, and are things indifferent. And such things princes have authority to order or to command.

Prisoners:—Prove that, said one. Where find you that? said another.

Bishop:—I have talked with many men, and yet I never saw any behave themselves so unreverently before magistrates.

White:—I beseech you, let me speak one word or two.

Bishop:—White, stay a little, you shall speak anon.

Hawkins:—Kings have their rule and commandment in the 17th of Deuteronomy, not to decline, neither to the right hand nor to the left, from the word of God, howsoever you make your distinction.

Smith:—How can you prove that indifferent, which is abominable?

Bishop:—What? you mean of our caps and tippets, which, you say, came from Rome.

Ireland:—It belongeth to the papists; therefore throw it to them.

Watts:—You would have us use nothing that the papists used; then should we use no churches, as the papists have used.

Hawkins:—Churches be necessary to keep our bodies from the rain, but surplices and copes be superstitious and idolatrous.

White:—Christ did cast out the buyers and sellers in the temple and their ware, and yet the temple was not overthrown for all that.

Bishop:—Things not forbidden of God may be used for order and obedience' sake: you shall hear the mind and judgment of a well learned man, whom you like of, namely, Master Bullinger; (then he read out of a book this in effect): "It is not yet proved that these garments had their first original from Rome. And though we use them not here in our ministry, yet we may lawfully use them as things that have not yet been removed away." These be Bullinger's words: therefore we desire and wish you to leave off and to be conformable. [See the table for M. Beza's and R. Gualter's letters.]

Smith:—What, if I can shew you Bullinger against Bullinger in this thing?

Bishop:—I think not, Smith.

Smith:—Yes, that I can.

Bishop:—Well, all reformed churches do differ in rites and ceremonies, and we agree with all reformed churches in substance of doctrine.

Watts:—Yea, that we do.

Hawkins:—Yea, but we should follow the truest and best way. Christ saith, "Go you forth and preach to all nations, baptizing them in the name of the Father, of the Son, and of the Holy Ghost, teaching them to observe all things that I have commanded you." But you have brought the gospel and sacraments into bondage to the ceremonies of antichrist, and you defend idolatry and papistry. There is no ordinance of Christ, but you have mingled your own inventions withal. How say you to godfathers and godmothers in baptism?

<small>Matt. xxviii. 20.</small>

Watts:—O! a wise reason!

Bishop:—How say you to the church of Geneva? They communicate with wafer cakes, which you are so much against.

Nixson:—Yea, but they do not compel to receive so, and with none other.

Bishop:—Yes, in their parish churches.

White:—The English congregation did minister with loaf bread there.

Bishop:—Because they were of another language.

White:—It is good to follow the best example; but we must follow them as they follow Christ.

Dean:—All the learned men in Europe are against you.

Watts:—Ye will believe no man.

<small>A lie, see the letters of M. Beza and M. Gualter.</small>

Smith:—Yes, we reverence the learned in Geneva, or in other places wheresoever they be; yet we build not on them our faith and religion.

Bishop:—Will you be judged by the learned in Geneva? They are against you.

Hawkins:—We will be judged by the word of God, which shall judge us all at the last day, therefore sufficient to judge now. But how can they be against us, seeing they know not of our doings, also holding of the same truth that they do, except they will be against the truth and against themselves?

Bishop:—Here is the letter that came from Geneva, and

they are against you and your doings and going from us, in these words.—Then he turned to this place, which is: "That against the prince's and bishops' wills they should exercise their office, we do so much the more tremble at, because of these reasons, which of themselves are plain enough, albeit we do not utter them[2]." Mark how that he saith he doth tremble at your cause.

^{See the letter from M. Beza in the table.}

Hawkins:—Why, the place is against you; for they do tremble at the prince's case and yours, because that you, by such extremities, should drive us against our wills to that which of itself is plain enough, albeit they would not utter them.

Then the bishop wrung himself and said: See, ye enter into judgment against us.

Hawkins:—Nay, we judge not; but we know the letter well enough, for we have it in our houses; it maketh nothing against us.

Bishop:—We grant it doth not: but yet they count this apparel indifferent, and not impious and wicked in their own nature: and therefore they counsel the preachers not to give over their function or flocks for these things.

Hawkins:—But it followeth in the same letter, that if they should be compelled to allow it by subscription or silence, that they should give over their ministry.

Nixson:—Let us answer to your first question.

Bishop:—Say on, Nixson.

Nixson:—We do not refuse you for preaching the word of God, but because ye have tied the ceremonies of antichrist to it, and set them before it, so that no man may preach or minister the sacraments without them. For before you compelled them by law all was quiet.

Bishop:—See how ye be against indifferent things, which may be borne withal for order and obedience' sake.

Mayor:—Well, good people, I would you would wisely consider these things, and be obedient to the Queen's Majesty's good laws, as I and other of the Queen's subjects

[2 Tertium enim illud, nempe ut contra regiam majestatem et episcoporum voluntatem ministerio suo fungantur, magis etiam exhorrescimus propter eas causas, quæ tacentibus etiam nobis satis intelligi possunt. Bezæ Epist. xii. Ad fratres quosdam, &c. Genev. 1573. p. 105.]

are, that you may live quietly and have liberty, as my lord here and masters have said. And as for my part, I would you were at your heart's ease, and I am sorry that ye are troubled; but I am an officer under my prince, and therefore blame not me. I cannot talk learnedly with you in celestial matters; but I have a mother wit, and I will persuade the best that I can. The Queen hath not established these garments and things for any holiness' sake or religion, but only for a civil order and comeliness; because she would have the ministers known from other men, as the aldermen are known by their tippets, and the judges by their red gowns, and sometimes they wear coifs; and likewise lords' servants are known by their badges. I will tell you an example. There was an alderman within this year, that went in the street, and a boisterous fellow met him, and went between him and the wall, and put him towards the kennel; and some that were there about him said to him, "Knowest thou not what thou doest? He is an alderman." And he said, "I knew him not, he might have worn his tippet." Even so, when the ministers began to be despised, the Queen's grace did ordain this priests' apparel; but the people cannot be content and like it. Now what may the papists say? Some of them goeth to the court whispering, saying, that ye cannot be content that the Queen should command any thing in the church, not so much as a cap or a tippet; whereupon the Queen may have occasion to say: "Will they not be content that I should rule in the church? I will restore that my forefathers have followed;" and therefore, masters, take heed.

A simple meaning.

Hawkins:—I beseech you to let me answer your lordship before all your wisdoms. Philip Melancthon, writing upon the 14th chapter to the Romans, hath these words: "When the opinion of holiness, of merit, or necessity, is put unto things indifferent, then they darken the light of the gospel, and ought by all means to be taken away."

Merit, holiness, or necessity maketh indifferent things intolerable.

Bishop:—It is not commanded of necessity in the church, or of heavenly things.

Hawkins:—You have made it a matter of necessity in the church, and that many a poor man doth feel.

Nixson:—Even so, my lord, as you do say that the alderman is known by his gown and tippet, even so by this apparel, that these men do now wear, were the papist mass-priests known from other men.

Dean:—What a great matter you make of it!

Hawkins:—The apostle Paul would not be like the false apostles in any thing, and therefore you have the apostle against you.

Bishop:—There be good men and good martyrs that did wear these things in King Edward's days; do you condemn them?

Nixson:—We condemn them not: we would go forward to perfection; for we have had the gospel a long time amongst us: and the best of them that did maintain it, did recant for it at their death, as did Ridley, sometime bishop of London, and doctor Taylor. Ridley did acknowledge his fault to Hooper; and when they would have put on the same apparel upon him, he said[1], they were abominable and too fond for a vice in a play[2]. Ma. Ridley's judgment of po[pish] apparel.

Bishop:—Where find you that in the book of letters of the martyrs?

Hawkins:—It may be shewed in the book of the monuments of the church, that many which were burned in Queen Mary's time, died for standing against popery as we now do.

Bishop:—I have said mass; I am sorry for it.

Ireland:—But you go like one of the mass-priests still.

Bishop:—You see me wear a cope or a surplice in Paul's. I had rather minister without these things, but for order's sake and obedience to the prince.

Roper:—Master Crowley saith, "He could not be persuaded to minister in those conjuring garments of popery."

Nixson:—Your garments are accursed, as they are used.

Bishop:—Where do you find them forbidden in the scriptures?

Nixson:—Where is the mass forbidden in the scriptures?

Bishop:—The mass is forbidden in the scripture, as thus: It was thought to be meritorious, it did take away free justifi-

[1 In saying of these words, they put upon the said Dr Ridley the surplice, *with all the trinkets appertaining to the mass.* And as they were putting on the same, Dr Ridley did vehemently inveigh against the Romish bishop and all that foolish apparel, calling it "antichrist, and the apparel foolish and abominable, yea, too fond for a vice in a play." Ridley's Last Examination and Degradation. Works, Parker Society, p. 289.]

[2 The *vice* of the old Moralities was a buffoon or fool, who was fantastically dressed. See Nares's Glossary.]

cation, it was made an idol; and idolatry is forbidden in the scriptures.

Hawkins:—By the same argument I will prove your garments forbidden in the scriptures.

Bishop:—Let us hear.

Hawkins:—I do prove it out of the 138th psalm, and out of the 10th chapter of the second to the Corinthians. In the psalm the prophet saith that "God hath exalted his word according to his great name:" the epistle saith, that "the weapons of his warfare are not carnal things, but things mighty in God to overthrow strong holds and imaginations of men, and to bring into captivity all imagination that exalteth itself against the knowledge of God." But you have brought the word of God into captivity to the pope's garments and his canon law; and therefore they are idols, and forbidden in the scripture. "Whatsoever," saith Christ, "is highly esteemed before men, is abominable before God."—Luke xvi. 15.

<small>Ceremonies become idols.</small>

White:—Reprove that we hold by the scripture, and prove that you would have us come to by the scripture, and we will yield to you. And if you cannot, why do you persecute us?

Bishop:—You are not obedient to the prince.

Dean:—Doth not Saint Peter say, "Be obedient to all manner ordinance of man?"

White:—Yea, as they obey God.

Nixson:—This hath been always the doings of popish bishops: when as they cannot maintain their doings by the scriptures, nor overcome them, then they make the mayor and the aldermen their servants and butchers, to punish them that they cannot overcome by scripture. But I trust that you, my lord, seeing you have heard and seen it, will take good advisement.

Mayor:—Good lord! how unreverently do you speak here before my lords and us in comparing so!

Bishop:—Have not we a godly prince? answer, Is she evil?

White:—What a question is that! the fruits do shew.

Bowland:—No: but the servants of God are persecuted under her.

Bishop:—Yea, go to; mark this, my lord. (Reader, see Luke xix. 7.)

Hawkins:—Why, this question the prophet may answer in the psalm: "How can they have understanding that work iniquity, spoiling my people, and that extol vanity?"

Dean:—Do we hold any heresy? Do we deny any article of the faith, as "I believe in God the Father Almighty, and in Jesus Christ his Son?" Do we deny any of these articles? Do we maintain purgatory or pilgrimages? No, we hold the reformation that was in King Edward's days. [See Ma. Janson's letter in the table.]

One of us said, No more did the papists in words.

White:—You build much of King Edward's time. A very learned man as any is in the realm, (I think you cannot reprove him,) writeth these words of King Edward's time: "I will let pass to speak of King Henry's time, but come to King Edward's time, which was the best time of reformation: all was driven to a prescript order of service, pieced and patched out of the popish portass[1], of mattins, mass, and even-song; so that when the minister had done his service, he thought his duty done. To be short, there might no discipline be brought into the church." [K[ing] E[dward's] days.]

Nixson:—Yet they never came so far as ye have done, to make a law that none should preach or minister without these garments.

Bishop:—St Paul saith, that "to the clean all things are clean:" that which other have evilly abused we may use well, as not receiving them for any such purpose of holiness or religion.

Nixson:—Howsoever ye received them, we see now you have exalted them, and brought the word of God in subjection and slavery to them.

Hawkins:—It cannot be proved, that the ceremonies of antichrist, works of darkness, and the pope's canon law, may be clean to a true christian; for the apostle saith, "There is no fellowship between Christ and Belial, light and darkness." 2 Cor. vi. 14, 15.

Dean:—All the learned are against you.

White:—I delivered a book[2] to Justice Harris, which is

[1] Portass, portesse, or portues: breviary.]
[2] Probably the Geneva book, entitled 'The Form of Prayers and Administration of the Sacraments used in the English church at Geneva, &c. &c.' See Strype, Parker, I. p. 479.]

the order that we hold. Reprove the same by the word of God, and we will leave it and give over.

Bishop:—We cannot reprove it. But to gather together disorderly, to trouble the common quiet of the realm against the prince's will, we like not the holding of it.

White:—We hold nothing that is not warranted by the word of God.

<small>Cause of separation.</small> *Hawkins*:—Why, that which we do, we do it by the commandment of God: we have the example of the first and apostolic church for our warrant, as in the 16th to the Romans, v. 17. "I beseech you, brethren, mark them that cause divisions, and give occasions of evil, contrary to the doctrine which ye have learned, and avoid them."

Dean:—Yea, but the manner which ye hold is unorderly, and against the authority of the prince.

Hawkins:—Why, the truth of God is a truth, wheresoever it be holden, or whosoever doth hold it; except ye will make it subject to places and persons, and to the authority of the prince. It had been better we had never been born, than to suffer God to be dishonoured, and his word defaced for princes' pleasures.

<small>This note three times sung.</small> *Bishop*:—All the learned are against you; will you be tried by them?

White:—We will be tried by the word of God, which shall judge us all at the last day.

Dean:—But who will you have to be judge of the word of God?

Hawkins:—Why, that was the saying of the papists in Queen Mary's time. I have heard it: when the truth was defended by the word of God, then they would say, "Who shall judge of the word of God? The Catholic church must be judge."

White:—We will be tried by the best reformed churches. The church of Scotland hath the word truly preached, the sacraments truly ministered, and discipline according to the word of God; and these be the notes by which the true church is known.

Dean:—We have a gracious prince.

We said, "God preserve her grace and the council!"

White:—I would have answered to a thing that hath been said: That which God commandeth to be done, that ought to be done; and that which God forbiddeth to be done, that ought not to be done.

Bishop:—Yea, I said so.

White:—Now it is manifest, that that which God commandeth to be done is left undone, and that which God forbiddeth to be done, that is done by authority; as this: God saith, "Six days thou shalt labour and do all that thou hast to do: but the seventh day is the sabbath of the Lord thy God, &c." But the prince's law saith, "Thou shalt not labour seven [six] days, but shall keep the popish holy-days." And again, Christ commandeth discipline in the 18th of Matthew, and it was put in practice of the apostles: but in the church of England there is none but the pope's discipline. And Christ saith in the last chapter of the Revelation: "If any man shall add to the prophecy of this book, God shall add unto him all the plagues that are written in this book; and if any man shall diminish, God shall take his part out of this book of life, and from the holy city." How will you avoid this? _(margin: God's commandments broken.)

Bishop:—Why, is it not a good work, to hear a good sermon or two upon the holy-days?

White:—We are not against that. But what shall we do when the sermons be done? If we do any work, we are commanded to your courts.

Bishop:—You may well be occupied in serving of God.

White:—So we are all occupied, when we are at our work that God commandeth. The sabbath is appointed to rest in, and to serve God. Exod. xx. 10.

Dean:—Why, then you would have no sermons nor prayer all the week.

White:—Who is not against that? I think him to be no christian, that doth not pray and serve God every day, before he begin his work.

Nixson:—You can suffer bear-baiting and bowling and other games to be used on the sabbath day, and on your holy-days, and no trouble for it.

Dean:—Then you would have no holy sabbath days, because the papists have used them.

White:—We ought to do that God commandeth.

Dean:—Why, then you must not use the Lord's prayer, because the papists used it, and many other prayers, be-

<small>Herbs twice chopt.</small> cause the priests used them; you would have nothing but the word of God. Is all the psalms you sing the word of God? They were turned into metre.

White:—Is every word that is preached in a good sermon the word of God?

Dean:—No.

White:—But every word and thing agreeing with the word of God is as the word of God.

Bishop:—There hath been no heretic, but he hath challenged the word to defend him.

White:—What is that to us? If you know any heresy we hold, charge us with it.

Bishop:—Holy-days may be well used.

Hawkins:—Well, master Hooper saith in his commentary upon the commandments, that holy-days are the leaven of antichrist.

Here they entered into a question of ministering the sacrament in a private house; and further is not come unto my hands.

From hence to prison they went all or most part of them. Such was the great charity of the bishops! And till their day of deliverance they never knew one good word they spake for them, though divers of them had wives and children, and were but poor men[1].

[[1] This statement appears to be incorrect. Strype says, "There were divers separatists kept in the prison of Bridewel, for holding private assemblies, and using a form of prayer different from that allowed and enjoined by law; and here they had lain for about a twelvemonth. Their great opinion was, that certain of the ceremonies used in the public service were popish, having been used by the papists, and therefore that they ought in conscience not to be present at it. Nor could all the bishop's endeavours reclaim them. And therefore pitying their condition, he moved the secretary (Cecil), that clemency might be used towards them, that so by giving them freely their liberty, only with an admonition, they might be more prevailed withal to comply with the laws, than by severity; and praying the secretary to obtain from the lords of the council an order to him, the bishop, to release them. Accordingly the lords approved of Grindal's counsel, and in April sent him a letter with a warrant for that purpose; but withal, &c." Strype, Grindal, p. 200. Upon this, by a warrant from himself to the governor of the prison, he discharged them to the number of twenty-four, besides seven women. The names of all the parties concerned in the above Examination occur in the list of persons released. See Lansdown MSS. 12. No. 28. British Museum. See also below, Letters, date Jan. 4, 1569.]

VARIOUS LETTERS

OF

EDMUND GRINDAL,

FROM A.D. 1555 TO A.D. 1583.

COLLECTED FROM DIFFERENT SOURCES.

LETTERS
OF
EDMUND GRINDAL
TO JOHN FOXE[1].

[These letters are taken from Foxe's papers, preserved amongst the Harleian MSS. in the British Museum.]

LETTER I.

Doctissimo viro D. Johanni Foxo, *Anglo, et fratri in Christo carissimo. Basileæ.*

May 10, 1556.

[Ex Harl. MS. 417, fo. 113.]

Salutem in Christo Servatore. Accepi literas tuas quas 4to Maii ad me dedisti, frater amicissime, in quibus meam operam in vita et obitu D. Cantuariensis describendo postulas. Qua de re sic paucis accipe, quia, cum hæc scriberem, iter ad Badensem civitatem ut amicos quosdam inviserem adornabam. De tota ratione mortis D. Cantuariensis scripsit nuper exactissime ad D. P. Martyrem vir quidam doctus æque ac pius. Eum commentariolum mihi nondum contigit videre: audio tamen ab iis qui legerunt, eleganter et vere esse conscriptum; atque adeo non plene constitutum esse audio, an brevi sit seorsim typis excudendus. Quod si fiat, nihil impediet quo minus possis publicis pro tuo jure uti. Sin vero publicare nolunt, dabo operam pro mea virili ut exemplar aliquod ad te mittatur, quum res postulaverit: neque enim credo te tantum opus in tantis occupationibus adhuc absolvisse. Quod autem scribis de Wendelino sollicitando, ut ingenue quod sentio loquar, non audeo illum de hoc negotio interpellare: vir est morosus; deinde etiam sententiæ illius

A.D. 1556.

[1 The following letters relate chiefly to Foxe's celebrated work, 'The Acts and Monuments;' in compiling parts of which Grindal rendered much valuable assistance, both by his continual advice, as well as by supplying materials. Foxe had removed from Frankfort, where he had at first settled, and was now residing at Bâsle. Grindal was resident at Strasburgh. See Strype, Grind. p. 16, et seq.]

A.D. 1556. [illi], quam Luthero ascribunt, de re sacramentaria, vehementer addictus, ut omnino nihil spes [spei] sit illum accepturum in manus. Est hic alius quidam, Augustinus Frisius, typographus, sed pauper admodum. Is, si alienis sumptibus res gereretur, non dubito quin strenue rem administraret. Sed meo quidem judicio Froschoverus omnium esset aptissimus, cui hoc committas. Nam et is est satis dives, et D. Bullingerus (credo) rogatus hominem instigaret. De ceteris alias copiosius; nunc propero. Saluta, quæso, D. Baleum, Pet. Morvinum, et ceteros Anglos. Vale. Argentinæ, 10 Maii, 1556.

EDM. GRINDALLUS, tuus.

Translation.

GRINDAL TO FOXE.

HEALTH in Christ our Saviour. I have received your letter, my very dear brother, which you sent to me on the 4th of May, in which you request my help in describing the life and death of my Lord of Canterbury. On which subject these few words must suffice, because while I am writing them I am preparing for a journey to Baden, to visit some friends. A certain person, both learned and pious, has lately written to Master Peter Martyr an entire and exact account of my Lord of Canterbury's death. I have not yet had an opportunity of seeing this little work: but I hear from those who have read it, that it is elegantly and faithfully written; and I hear moreover, that it is not yet fully decided, whether or not it is shortly to be printed by itself. Should this be the case, there will be nothing to hinder you from making what use of it you please, when published. If, however, they do not intend to publish it, I will do my utmost endeavours to send you a copy, when occasion requires it; for I do not think, that in the midst of such great occupations you have already finished so great a work. As to what you write about treating with Wendelin[1], to tell you candidly what I think, I dare not address him on this matter. He is a morose man, and moreover strongly addicted to that opinion on the sacramental question, which

[[1] A printer at Strasburgh, with whom Foxe had requested Grindal to treat about the printing of Cranmer's controversy with Gardiner on the Eucharist.]

they attribute to Luther; so that there is no hope at all that he will take the work in hand. There is here another printer, one Augustine Frisius; but he is very poor. He, I doubt not, if the matter could be carried on at the charges of others, would strenuously set about it. But in my judgment Froschover is the fittest man of all to commit the business to. For he is rich enough; and Master Bullinger, I believe, if he were asked, would urge him to it. As to the other matters, I will write more fully at another time; I am now in haste. Salute Bale, Peter Morwin, and the rest of the English[2]. Farewell. Strasburgh, 10 May, 1556.

Yours,
EDM. GRINDAL.

LETTER II.

GRINDALLUS AD FOXIUM.
Aug. 1, [1556.]
[Ex Harl. MSS. 417, fo. 112.]

GRATIAM et pacem. Maximas tibi gratias ago, Foxe amicissime, quod me istis laborum tuorum primitiis dignatus sis. Valde quidem dolet, quod isto tam intempestivo edicto retardatus sis ab edendo. Sed fortasse magistratus vestri, principum Germaniæ rogatu, hoc faciunt, ne recandesceret pugna sacramentaria, si plures hujus argumenti libri imprimerentur. Aiunt enim, principes in hoc totos esse ut componatur hæc controversia; interea fortassis volunt justitium quoddam esse. Exspectemus igitur, quando ita est necesse, et videamus quid secum adferet boni tempus: postea, si non potes impetrare ut istic perficiatur, mea non deerit opera, si quid precibus aut gratia perficere possim, ut ad alios locos tentandos viaticum tibi suppeditetur.

De Philpotti examinationibus hoc tibi dicam quod sentio. Sunt in illis quædam quæ lima opus habent. Videtur sese nescio quomodo irretire in vocabulis quibusdam non satis approbatis, quod Christus sit realiter in coena, etc. Si liber Anglicus non fuisset divulgatus, potuissent quædam in eo mitigari. Deinde citat veteres aliquando memoriter, destitu-

[2 Exiles for religion.]

tus præsidio librorum, qua in re facilis est lapsus: ut quod Athanasium dicit præfuisse concilio Nicæno; quamvis tantum eo tempore esset Alexandrini episcopi (si bene memini) diaconus; etiamsi disputando etc. plus quam alii laboraverit, atque ita possit dici præfuisse; sed ibi de honore et primatu controversia est. Fortasse tu etiam alia similia reperisti; nam hæc exempli causa adduxi: utere judicio tuo. Audivi etiam D. Martyrem et D. Bullingerum, in illis scriptis D. Hooperi, optasse illi fuisse [aliquid] temporis et otii ad illa recognoscenda. Nam quæ erant subito et in carcere scripta, non satis munite caussam tum multorum disputationibus exagitatam, pro ratione hujus exulcerati sæculi, scripsisse. Non arrogo mihi partes criticas, sed candide, pro meo more, animi mei sensa communico. Non dubito quin, si tu emittas in publicum, censoriam notam ubi opus fuerit adhibebis. Sunt hic apud nos quædam de ipsius historia, sed plura exspectantur: ea fortasse commodissime inter ceterorum gesta poterunt collocari. Ac fortassis, etiamsi separatim Philpotti examinationes emittas, poterunt eadem denuo magno operi inter acta inseri. Invenies hic involutos duos dolleros, quos ad tuos usus assumere possis: qua autem ratione ad te perveniant, alias fortasse scribam; interea istis fruere; quam vellem essent ducenti! Oro ut diligenter cures de literis istis Tigurum transmittendis, idque quamprimum potes. Opto te in Domino valere. Salutes, quæso, Dominum Baleum, Pilkingtonum, Benthamum, et ceteros fratres.

Argentinæ, calend. Augusti, [1556].

ED. GRINDALLUS, tuus.

Translation.

GRINDAL TO FOXE.

GRACE and peace. I give you my best thanks, my very dear friend Foxe, that you have honoured me with those first-fruits of your labours. I am much grieved indeed, that you are delayed in editing by that so unseasonable edict[1]. But perhaps your magistrates do this at the request of the German princes, lest the sacramental controversy should break forth afresh, if more books on this subject should be printed. For it is said, that the princes are wholly bent

[1 An edict forbidding the printing of any books in those parts.]

upon composing this controversy. In the mean time, perhaps, they wish that there should be some intermission. Let us wait therefore, since we must needs do so, and see what good issue time may bring with it: afterwards, if you cannot obtain that the work be perfected there, you shall not want my help, if I can accomplish any thing by entreaties or interest, that means may be supplied to you to enable you to try other places.

With regard to the examinations of Philpot, I give you my opinion, that there are some things in them which need correction. He seems somehow to entangle himself in certain words not so well approved; as for instance, that Christ is *really* in the supper, &c. If the English book had not been published, some things in it might have been modified. Then again he cites the ancients sometimes from memory, being deprived of the safeguard of books, wherein one may easily slip: as when he says that Athanasius was at the head of the Nicene council; whereas at that time, if I remember rightly, he was only deacon of the bishop of Alexandria; although in disputing he laboured more than others, and so may be said to have taken the lead. But there the controversy is concerning honour and primacy. Perhaps you also have discovered others of a similar kind, for I have adduced these for the sake of example: use your own judgment. I have heard also that Master Martyr and Master Bullinger have expressed a wish, with respect to the writings of Master Hooper, that he had had time and leisure to revise them: for that, being composed suddenly and in prison, he had not written on a subject, agitated at that time by the disputations of many, with the guardedness which such an ulcerated age as ours requires. I do not arrogate to myself the part of a critic; but candidly, after my manner, communicate to you the convictions of my mind. I doubt not but that, if you publish them, you will where there is need subjoin a critical note. There are here with us some documents relating to his history, but more are expected. These perhaps may be most conveniently placed amongst the Acts of the rest. And perhaps even if you should publish Philpot's examinations separately, the same may be again inserted in the great work among the Acts[2]. You will find inclosed herein

[[2] The Acts and Monuments.]

two dollars, which you may take to your own use: but how they come to you, I may perhaps write hereafter: in the mean time enjoy them: I would they were two hundred[1]. I pray you to take care that those letters be sent to Zurich, and that with all speed. Fare you well in the Lord. Salute, I pray you, Bale, Pilkington, Bentham, and the rest of the brethren.

Strasburg, August 1, 1556.

Yours,

EDM. GRINDAL.

LETTER III.

GRINDALLUS AD FOXIUM.
June 18, 1557.

[Ex Harl. MSS. 417, fo. 102.]

SALUTEM in Christo Servatore. Gaudeo te tandem opus illud Domini Cantuariensis ad exitum perduxisse. Longum opus fuit, et in quo necesse erat multis cum difficultatibus luctari. De Martyrum Historia quod scribis, tam gaudeo te ad illud aggrediendum animo esse prompto, quam doleo illius operis materiem non posse de modo tibi subministrari, quo ego ante annum subministrandam iri existimabam. Tum enim temporis putavi nos ante hunc diem Historiam Martyrum nostro sermone conscriptam habituros fuisse, eamque, si non excusam, saltem ad prælum paratam, ut pene eodem tempore et Anglice et Latine (quod tua opera fieret) historia illa publicaretur. Sed cessatum est nonnihil hac in re; partim quod actorum exemplaria tam tarde admodum et maligne, saltem quæ alicujus fidei essent, subministrarentur; partim propter peregrinationes et occupationes quorundam, qui in hoc negotio laborant. Nam ita erat comparatum, ut, partitis inter se laboribus, quidam hoc agerent. Ita fit ut

[[1] There were monies secretly conveyed over from England, by persons well disposed, to private hands, to be distributed among these exiles; especially preachers and students, who were not able to subsist of themselves. And Grindal, I suppose, had some of this charitable money consigned to him, to bestow according to his discretion. And a share of it was this which he now sent to Fox; who was very poor, and had, besides himself, a family to maintain. Strype, Grind. p. 30.]

nunc nihil habeamus præter sylvam, et illam pene rudem, A.D. 1557. sed tamen hujusmodi, quæ præclaro ædificio materiam non contemnendam præbere possit; præsertim si ab illis aliquantulum expoliretur, qui scripta illa habent, quique etiam alias circumstantias, non scriptas, utiles tamen ad rem illustrandam, adjicere norunt. Sunt igitur hic apud nos qui nondum prorsus desperant se, si non statim, saltem post aliquod temporis spatium, Anglice scriptam historiam concinnare posse. Id eos male habet, quod nunc, cum tu tam paratus sis ad hoc suscipiendum, ipsi imparati non possunt tibi sua scripta communicare, nisi velint eos labores quos hactenus sustinuerunt prorsus perdere. Quam autem hoc esset optandum, ut, si utraque lingua publicetur historia, summus esset consensus utriusque, nemo est qui non videt. Et profecto existimo nusquam neque plura neque certiora reperiri posse, quam quæ apud nostros habentur, et brevi habebuntur. Quum nostros dico, neminem nomino; nam fortassis ipsi nollent se adhuc nominari. Gratum igitur mihi feceris, si proximis tuis literis mihi significes, quidnam in istis angustiis optimum factu putes, ut neque tua industria retardetur, neque illorum conatus irriti fiant. Mihi videretur non omnino malum, si hoc impetrari possit ab illis, ut ipsi quam maxime possint festinarent, et quamprimum aliqua pars absoluta esset, ad te mitterent; mox progrederentur, et in ceteris partibus idem fieret. Egi cum illis hac de re, et postquam ad me scripseris agam aliquanto vehementius. Nihil certi responsi retuli. Tantum videbar mihi ex illorum dictis colligere, optare se ut hoc, qualecunque esset, volumen separatim ederetur, scilicet de totius quadriennii[1] persecutione; in quo sane et me consentientem habent. Quare si quid in promptu habes, quod faceret ad absolvendum alterum tomum ecclesiæ tuæ historiæ, illud separato libello prosequi possis usque ad annum ultimum Henrici octavi: interea hujus persecutionis historiam ipsi possent bene concinnare, et fortassis circa Michaelis absolvere. Oro itaque ut, quid tibi maxime probetur in toto hoc negotio, quamprimum significes. Me habebis ad omnia quæ potero tua causa præstanda paratissimum.

[1 The text is obviously corrupt in the MS.: the editor has ventured to insert what he conceives to be the true reading. In the MS. the words are *de trinis quadriennis*.]

A. D. 1557. Basileam commigrare hactenus non constitui. Statueram quidem aliquoties data occasione vestram urbem et Tigurinam, quique in iisdem sunt viros doctos, invisere; sed id faciam, volente Deo, quum sese justa occasio obtulerit; quod hactenus non evenit. Dominum Baleum, et Pilkingtonum, ceterosque nostros amicos et fratres, oro ut meo nomine salutes. Bene vale, frater in Domino carissime.

Argentinæ, 18° Junii, 1557.

Tuus in Christo,
EDM. GRINDALLUS.

Translation.

GRINDAL TO FOXE.

HEALTH in Christ our Saviour! I am glad that you have at length brought that work of my lord of Canterbury to an end. It was a tedious work, and one in which you must needs have had to contend with many difficulties. As to what you write concerning the history of the Martyrs, I am as glad that you are forward to undertake it, as I am sorry that the materials of that work cannot be supplied to you after the manner in which a year ago I thought they would be supplied. For I then thought that before this time we should have had the history of the Martyrs written in our own language, and, if not printed, at least prepared for the press; so that the history might be published nearly at the same time both in English and Latin, the latter being done by your assistance. But there has been some delay in this matter; partly because copies of the Acts, at least such as could at all be relied on, were so slowly and grudgingly supplied; partly on account of the travels and engagements of some who are labouring in this business. For so it was arranged, that by a division of labour certain persons should manage this business. Hence it is that we have now nothing but a somewhat rude quantity of matter, but yet of such sort, as may afford no despicable material for constructing a noble edifice; especially if it should be polished a little by those who possess those writings, and who also know how to add other circumstances not written, but useful for illustration. There are therefore some here amongst us, who do not yet altogether despair, that if not immediately, at least after some little time, they may be able to compile a history in English. This vexes them, that now, when you are so prepared for this undertaking, they, being unprepared, cannot communicate their writings to you, without making up their mind altogether to throw away the labours which they have hitherto bestowed. Every body however must perceive how desirable it is, that, if the history be published in both languages, there should be the utmost possible agreement between the two. And truly I think, that nowhere can more abundant or more authentic relations be found, than those which are now, or shortly will be, in the possession of our friends. When I say *our friends*, I mention none in particular; for perhaps they would be unwilling as yet to be named. You will do me a favour therefore, if in your next letter you will signify to me what you think best to be done in these straits; so that neither your industry may be retarded, nor their attempts be rendered futile. It would seem to me to be not altogether a bad arrangement, if they could be prevailed upon, to make as much haste as possible, and as soon as any part is finished to send it to you: they might then proceed farther, and deal in the same way with the rest. I have had some negociation with them respecting this matter, and as soon as you have written to me, will press it somewhat more earnestly. I have received no definite answer. This only I seemed to gather from what they said, that it was their wish that this volume, whatever it might be, should be published separately, namely, on the persecution of the whole four years[1]; in which they have my concurrence. If therefore you have anything ready, which would do to complete another volume of your Ecclesiastical History, you may prosecute that in a separate book as far as to the last year of Henry the Eighth. In the mean time, they would be able to arrange well the history of this persecution, and perhaps to complete it about Michaelmas. I pray you there-

A.D. 1557.

[[1] Namely, from 1555 to 1558. There were burned during these four years 288 persons, " besides those that dyed of famyne in sondry prisons." MSS. Cecilian. See Strype, Mem. III. part 2, pp. 554—556.]

fore to signify to me, as soon as possible, what most meets your approbation as to the whole of this matter. You will find me most ready to render all the help I can for your sake. I have not yet resolved to remove to Bâsle. I had indeed several times determined, when opportunity served, to visit your city and Zurich, and the learned men who are in them; but I will do this, God willing, when a fair occasion presents itself, which has not yet fallen out. I beg you to salute in my name Bale, and Pilkington, and the rest of our friends and brethren.' Farewell, brother most dear in the Lord.

Strasburgh, 18 June, 1557.

Yours in Christ,
EDM. GRINDAL.

LETTER IV.

GRINDALLUS AD FOXIUM.
Nov. 28, 1557.
[Harl. MSS. 417, fo. 119.]

SALUTEM in Christo. Equidem aliquandiu Argentina abfueram, atque ideo tamdiu tacui. Nunc vero, ne tot meas promissiones inanes esse existimes, mitto ad te una cum istis examinationes Bradfordi, et quædam alia ipsius scripta, uti in his vertendis te exercere poteris uti velis. Ubi hæc absolveris, remitte ad me per fidelem nuntium, et plura mittam. Multa quidem desideramus; sed quæ habemus bonæ fidei sunt, et fortassis haud facile alibi tam multa reperias. Equidem libenter cognoscere vellem, an adhuc cum aliquo typographo transegeris de editione Cantuariensis. Valde mihi placuit gustus operis quem ad me misisti. Ego exemplar habeo disputationum Oxoniensium Cranmeri et Ridleii, ab ipsismet conscriptum, ubi et adversariorum objecta et sua responsa, quantum memoria consequi potuere, consignarunt. Contuli cum exceptis a notariis. De summa rei satis convenit; nisi quod in meo exemplari brevius omnia recensentur, omissis conviciis et inanibus repetitionibus. Ubi longius progressus fueris, mittam ad te una cum aliis quibusdam, ut in historiæ seriem, si videbitur, conjicias. Cupio equidem omnibus modis quibus potero institutum tuum promovere, ut hujus Anglicanæ persecutionis historiam ad exitum qualem optamus perducere possis. Opto te in Domino quam optime valere, carissime frater.

Argentinæ, 28° Novembris, 1557.

EDMUNDUS GRINDALLUS tuus.

Translation.

GRINDAL TO FOXE.

HEALTH in Christ! I was absent for some time from Strasburgh, and therefore have been so long silent. But now, lest you should think my many promises to be empty, I send to you together with them the examinations of Bradford, and some other of his writings, that you may employ yourself as you please in translating them. When you have finished these, send them back to me by a trusty messenger, and I will send you more. We want many things, but what we have may be relied on; and perhaps you may not easily find so many elsewhere. I would gladly be informed, whether as yet you have arranged with any printer about publishing the archbishop of Canterbury's work. I was much pleased with the sample of the work which you sent me. I have a copy of the disputations of Cranmer and Ridley at Oxford, written by themselves, wherein they have set down both the objections of their opponents and their own answers, as far as they could recall them to their memories. I have compared them with what was taken by the notaries. There is sufficient agreement in the main, except that in my copy every thing is more briefly related, reproaches and vain repetitions being omitted. When you have made further progress, I will send it to you with some other things, that, if you think fit, you may cast them into the series of your history. I wish by all means in my power to promote your undertaking, that you may be able to bring to such an end as we desire the history of this English persecution. I wish you, dearest brother, most heartily farewell in the Lord.

Strasburgh, 28 November, 1557.

Yours,
EDM. GRINDAL.

LETTER V.

FOXIUS AD GRINDALLUM[1].
[Ex Harl. MSS. 417, fo. 113.]

SALUTEM in Christo. Recepi cum literis tuis historiam Bradfordianam cum variis illius alio atque alio missis epistolis. Qua in re video, mi Edmunde, quam bonæ fidei sponsor sis, citraque noxam, quod aiunt. Utinam ad eandem diligentiam cetera omnia τὰ μαρτυρικὰ congesta habeamus! Atque ut non dubito, quin magnam harum rerum farraginem (ut scribis) jam etiamnum habeatis, ita nec diffido in ceteris conquirendis vigilantiam vestram fidemque non defuturam. Jam ante, te absente, binas ad te misi literas, quas an receperis ideo subdubito, quod nullam video in literis tuis de libris Cantuariensis mentionem. Jamdudum transactum est cum Froschovero, jamque mense Octobris primum librum, meo magno tædio iterum descriptum, illis in gustum miseram: interim autem, dum exspecto ab illis responsum, delatum mihi est negotium a Frobenio et Episcopio Chrysostomi exemplaria cognoscendi et conferendi; eramque tum omnibus plane exutus pecuniis, adeoque pene ad extremum assem redactus. Itaque in ea movenda farina perierunt mihi duo menses. Interea temporis venit ad me Froschoverus cum literis D. Elmeri et Bullingeri, paciscens mecum inducias ob certa negotia in proximas nundinas, quas nec minus libenter ipse accepi: scis enim in hieme ubique fere conquiescere τὰ πολεμικὰ, ducibus se in hiberna recipientibus. Habes itaque integrum hujus negotii statum.

[1 This portion of a letter, though without a date, seems to be a part of Foxe's reply to the foregoing. And as it is closely connected with the subject of this series of letters, it is here inserted.]

Translation.

FOXE TO GRINDAL.

HEALTH in Christ! I received with your letter the narrative of Bradford, together with sundry of his letters addressed to different persons. I see, my Edmund, in this business, how faithful a performer of your promise you are, and (as they say) without fault. I would that we had all the rest of the martyrs' remains collected with the same diligence. And as I do not doubt, but that (as you write) you have still a great *farrago* of these papers, so neither have I any distrust, that your vigilance and fidelity will be wanting in collecting the rest. I have already, during your absence, sent you two letters; whether you have received them or not I have some doubt, for this reason, that I see no mention in your letters of the archbishop of Canterbury's books. The matter has been for some time arranged with Froschover; and I had already in the month of October sent the first book, written out again to my great weariness, as a sample of the work. But in the mean time, while I was waiting for an answer, there was laid upon me by Frobenius and Episcopius the employment of reading and collating copies of Chrysostom: and I was then altogether destitute of money, and so almost reduced to the last farthing. Thus two entire months were lost by me in that tedious employment. In the mean time Froschover came to me with letters of Master Elmer and Master Bullinger, to arrange a truce with me, on account of some business, until the next fair, which I no less willingly accepted; for you know that military operations almost every where cease during the winter, the commanders retiring into winter-quarters. You have thus the whole state of the matter.

LETTER VI.

GRINDALLUS AD FOXIUM.
Dec. 28, 1557.
[Ex Harl. MSS. 417, fo. 114.]

A. D. 1557. SALUTEM in Christo Servatore. Archiepiscopi Cantuariensis librum[1] jam te in manibus habere gaudeo. Sin autem me Theseum tibi exoptas, erras in delectu. Quanquam, si mihi Basiliæ sedes esset, (et fuisset quidem, nisi quod inopinatum quiddam ante aliquot menses intercidit,) nihil esset quod ego libentius facerem, quam ut studium et operam meum quantumcunque ad hoc tam pium negotium, si opus esset, conferrem. Sed habetis Anglos nonnullos, (ut dicis,) et inter hos Jacobum Pilkingtonum, exactissimi judicii virum, quocum aliquando communicare consilia poteris. Is (uti spero) non illibenter id faciet.

Quod ad judiciorum varietatem attinet, non est cur multum labores. Boni de te bene loquentur, mali male. Satis est laudari a laudatis viris; omnibus placere nemini unquam datum est. De ratione vertendi nemo melius judicabit quam tu ipse, cui non est incognita fidi interpretis libertas. Verbum verbo reddi qui exigerent, seipsos statim proderent, quam nullius essent judicii. Sensum sensu reddidisse semper in laude fuit, modo scriptoris mentem, non suam, explicuisse appareat. In his omnibus mediam quandam viam tenuisse, ut fere etiam in ceteris, tutissimum erit. Idemque etiam judico de stylo. Nam neque ecclesiasticus stylus cum fastidio rejiciendus est, (quod faciunt quidam,) præsertim quum capita controversiarum sine eo nonnunquam perspicue explicari non possunt; neque e diverso tam superstitiose consectandus est, ut orationis lumen

[1] Archbishop Cranmer's controversy with Gardiner, bishop of Winchester, upon the Eucharist. Foxe translated this work into Latin; and finding many difficulties, arising from Gardiner's style and mode of dealing with his opponent's arguments, as well as apprehending severe criticism, he wrote to Grindal for his advice, which is given in this letter. It seems that this work was never completely printed. Froschover, a printer at Zurich, indeed undertook the work, and a part of it was printed; but it does not appear that it was finished. See Strype, Grind. p. 23.]

aliquando aspergere non possimus. Hujus rei egregium nobis A.D. 1557.
exemplum ob oculos posuit D. Calvinus, quem honoris causa
nomino, qui et styli ornatum non neglexit, et ecclesiasticas
loquendi formulas, tanquam civitate donatas, sæpenumero
usurpat. De librorum inversione, qua utitur Wintoniensis,
meum quidem hoc est judicium; ut omnino permittatur ille
suo arbitratu uti atque ordine, neque moveas quicquam. Duo
sunt quæ me præcipue movent. Primum, vociferabuntur adversarii, fraude et dolo malo mota esse argumenta loco suo.
Nam ut in præliis non semper eodem ordine pugnam ineunt
imperatores, sed aliquando primam aciem invadunt, aliquando
in cornua impressionem faciunt, nonnunquam equestri pugna,
sæpius etiam tenui armaturæ velitatione hostes primum aggrediuntur, (iniquissimum enim esset de ordine pugnæ ineundæ
ab hostibus leges accipere); ita et de vobis queritabuntur, si
Wintonienses copiæ alia ratione, quam ipsemet instruit, in
aciem producantur. Deinde et hoc mihi videtur ad auctoris
ingenium patefaciendum pertinere. Nam qui in tota vita
præposterissimus (ut ita dicam) fuit omnium rerum humanarum et divinarum inversor, consentaneum est ut in scribendo
etiam præposterum sese ostentet, et, ut vulgo dici solet, *Joannem ad oppositum*.

Hæc mea est sententia; tu pro tuo candore aliter consulas.
Quod ad titulum libri, nemo melius adaptabit quam interpres,
qui non modo singulas sententias, sed et verba etiam et apices
pene excussit.

Mihi impræsentiarum libri copia non fuit: itaque nunc
nihil habeo quod in medium proferam. Si posthac aliquid
occurrerit, quod acuminis aut gratiæ aliquid in se habeat, non
illibenter communicabo. Verum quiddam est quod nunc scribenti mihi in mentem venit, cujus tuam prudentiam admonere
non inutile fore existimavi. Audivi hoc mussitatum aliquando
in Anglia, Cantuariensem aliquando papistis affingere, quod
ipsi non profitentur. Et, si bene memini, habet quasdam antitheses inter papisticam et doctrinam nostram, hac formula,
Illi dicunt, Nos dicimus. Ibidem credo habet, *Papistas corpus Christi ubique esse asseverare:* quod illi nusquam docent,
sed in omni altari pertinaciter esse contendunt. Siqua similia
inter vertendum repereris (nam illud exempli causa tantum
affero), aut sicubi tuo ipsius judicio non plene satisfiat, faceres

A.D. 1557. meo quidem judicio non male, si ad D. Petrum Martyrem catalogum hujusmodi locorum mitteres, et illius consilium in amantissimi sui patroni opere requireres. Communicaret, sat scio, libentissime, et fortasse siqua ipse præterea annotaverit similia subindicaret.

Hæc ita a me scripta sunto, ut tuo tamen judicio omnia geri vellem; tantum meæ mentis sensa apud amicum et fratrem, candidius fortasse quam prudentius, in medium profero. Saluta D. Baleum, et ceteros amicos. Opto te in Domino quam optime valere.

Argentinæ V. calend. Jan. 1557.

EDMUNDUS GRINDALLUS tuus.

Translation.

GRINDAL TO FOXE.

HEALTH in Christ our Saviour! I am glad that you have the archbishop of Canterbury's book already in hand. But if you wish me to be your helper[1], you are mistaken in your choice. Although, if my residence were at Bâsle (as indeed it would have been, had not an unexpected circumstance some months ago prevented me), there would be nothing which I should be more willing to do than to contribute, if need be, my study and assistance, however great, to promote so pious an undertaking. But you have with you, as you say, some English, and amongst them James Pilkington, a man of most exact judgment, with whom you may occasionally interchange counsels. He, as I hope, will not be unwilling to do so.

As to variety of opinions, you need not be much concerned. Good men will speak well of you, bad men ill. It is enough to be praised by men of reputation; to please all men falls to the lot of none. As to the mode of translating, no one is more competent to judge than yourself; for you well know the licence which is allowed to a faithful translator. Those who would require you to translate word for word would instantly betray their want of judgment. It has always been the approved

[[1] "Your Theseus"—probably alluding to the aid afforded by that hero to his friend Pirithous.—After this word in the original MS. there is a blank space.]

mode to render the sense, provided the translator manifestly express his author's mind, and not his own. In all these matters, as also in most others, it will be safer to hold a middle course. My judgment is the same with regard to style. For neither is the ecclesiastical style to be fastidiously rejected, as it is by some, especially when the heads of controversies cannot sometimes be perspicuously explained without it; nor, on the other hand, is it to be so superstitiously followed, as to prevent us sometimes from sprinkling it with the ornaments of language. A remarkable illustration of this is presented to us by Master Calvin, whom for honour's sake I mention, who has not neglected the grace of style, and yet frequently adopts ecclesiastical forms of speech, as if naturalized. As to the inversion of books, which the bishop of Winchester practises, this is my judgment; that he should be allowed to follow his own discretion and order, and that you should transpose nothing. There are two reasons which principally prevail with me. First, the adversaries will cry out, that the arguments are moved out of their position with a fraudulent intention. For as in battles commanders do not always commence the engagement in the same order, but sometimes attack the front, at other times assail the wings; they make the first charge upon the enemy sometimes with cavalry, frequently also with light-armed skirmishers, (for it would be a most unreasonable thing to be dictated to by the enemy as to the order of commencing the conflict;) so also they will complain of you, if the forces of the bishop of Winchester are drawn up in array after any other plan than that according to which he himself has arranged them. Again, this method seems to me to tend to the exhibition of the author's character. For it is but meet, that one who all his life long has been, so to speak, the most preposterous inverter of all things human and divine, should shew himself to be preposterous also in writing, and, as the saying is, *Joannes ad oppositum*[2].

This is my opinion; you in your candid judgment may come to a different conclusion. As to the title of the book, none will give a more fitting one than the translator, who has considered not only every sentence, but almost the very words and points.

[[2] The Editor is unable to discover the allusion in these words.]

A.D. 1557. At present I have not many books; so that I have nothing now to bring forward. If hereafter any thing should occur to me, which has any cleverness or elegance, I will most gladly communicate it to you. But there is something which comes into my mind while I am writing, of which I think it may not be without advantage to advise your prudence. I have heard it sometimes muttered in England, that occasionally the archbishop of Canterbury[1] falsely attributes to the papists what they do not hold. And, if I rightly remember, he has certain contrasts between the popish doctrine and ours, expressed in this form: 'They say'—'We say.' He states, I believe, in the same place, that the papists affirm the body of Christ to be every where: which they nowhere teach; but earnestly maintain, that it is upon every altar. If in course of translating you should find things of this kind, (for I bring forward this merely for example,) or if any where he does not fully satisfy your own judgment, you would, in my opinion, do well, if you were to send to Peter Martyr a list of such places, and ask his advice on the work of his most loving patron. He would communicate it, I well know, most willingly; and perhaps, if he has himself marked any similar passages besides, would point them out to you.

Consider these things to be so written by me, as that I wish, notwithstanding, every thing to be done according to your own judgment. I merely put these thoughts of my own mind before you, my friend and brother, more candidly perhaps than wisely. Salute Bale and the rest of my friends. Fare you right well in the Lord.

Strasburgh, December 28th, 1557[2].

Yours,

EDMUND GRINDAL.

[1 Abp. Cranmer.]
[2 Throughout these letters the old calendar is observed by Grindal, which reckoned the year to end March 24. Hence V. Cal. Jan. 1557, is still in 1557 in our style.]

LETTER VII.

GRINDALLUS AD FOXIUM.
Dec. 19, 1558.

[Harl. MSS. 417, No. 102.]

Salutem in Christo. Mutationes temporum meum etiam institutum mutarunt, doctissime et carissime Foxe: ego jam cogor urgentibus amicis in Angliam iter instituere, qui alioqui Basileam ad vos transvolassem. Jam quod ad historiam Martyrum attinet, Sampsonus et ego existimamus optimum fore, ut ad aliquod tempus premeretur, donec ex Anglia et certiora et plura comparemus. Dubium enim non est, quin multa tum in lucem prodibunt, quæ antea in tenebris delitescebant. Si tibi etiam idem videatur, bene est. Nos quæcunque possumus ibi corrademus, et ad te transmittenda curabimus. Levis erit jactura temporis, si rerum copia et certitudine compensetur. Vale in Christo quam optime.

Argentinæ, raptim, 19° Decemb. 1558.

EDMUNDUS GRINDALLUS tuus.

Translation.

GRINDAL TO FOXE.

Health in Christ! Changes of times have changed also my purpose, most learned and dear Foxe: I am now compelled by the urgency of my friends to set out for England[3], when otherwise I should have passed over to you at Bâsle. As to the history of the Martyrs, Sampson and I think it will be best that it should be delayed for a time, until we can procure from England more certain and more copious intelligence. For there is no doubt, but that many things will then come to light, which before were lying hid in darkness. If you should be of the same mind, well. We will there collect together what we can, and transmit

[3 As soon as tidings of Queen Mary's death, 17 Nov. 1558, reached the exiles, Grindal with many others lost no time in preparing to return to England.]

A.D. 1558. them to you. The loss of time will be a trifling consideration, if it be compensated by the fulness and certainty of the accounts. Fare you right well in Christ.

Strasburgh, in haste, 19 Decemb. 1558.

Yours,

EDMUND GRINDAL.

LETTER VIII.

GRINDAL TO BISHOP RIDLEY[1].
(COVERDALE.)

GRATIAM et consolationem a Domino et Servatore nostro Jesu Christo[2]. Sir, I have often been desirous to have written to you, and to have heard from you; but the iniquity of the times have hitherto always put me forth of all hope and comfort. Now at this present God seemeth to offer some likelihood that these might come to your hands, which I thought to use, referring the rest to God's disposition. Your present state not I only, (who of all other am most bound,) but also all other our brethren here, do most heartily lament, as joined with the most miserable captivity that ever any church of Christ hath suffered. Notwithstanding, we give God most humble thanks, for that he hath so strengthened you, and others your concaptives, to profess a good profession before so many witnesses. And I doubt nothing, but he that hath called you and them, not only to believe upon him, but also to suffer for him, doth not leave you destitute of that unspeakable comfort, which he useth to minister abundantly to his in the school of the cross. He grant that his name may be glorified in you, whether it be by life or death, as may be most to 'his honour, and your everlasting consolation.

Sir, I thought it good to advertise you partly of our state in these parts. We be here dispersed in divers and several places. Certain be at Tigury[3], good students of either

[1 Bp. Ridley was at this time a prisoner at Oxford.]
[2 Grace and consolation from our Lord and Saviour Jesus Christ.]
[3 Zurich.]

University a number, very well entreated of Master Bullinger, of the other ministers, and of the whole city. Another number of us remain at Argentine[4], and take the commodity of Master Martyr's lessons, who is a very notable father. Master Scory and certain other with him be in Friesland, and have an English church there, but not very frequent[5]. The greatest number is at Frankfort, where I was at this present by occasion; a very fair city, the magistrates favourable to our people, with so many other commodities as exiles can well look for. Here is also a church, and now (God be thanked!) well quieted by the prudence of Master Coxe, and other which met here for that purpose[6]. So that now we trust God hath provided for such as will flee forth of Babylon a resting-place, where they may truly serve him, and hear the voice of their true pastor. I suppose, in one place and other dispersed, there be well nigh an hundred students and ministers on this side the seas. Such a Lord is God to work diversely in his, according to his unsearchable wisdom, who knoweth best what is in man.

Primus est victoriæ titulus, gentilium manibus apprehensum Dominum confiteri. Secundus ad gloriam gradus est, cauta secessione subtractum Domino reservari. Illa publica, hæc privata confessio est. Ille judicem sæculi vincit; hic, contentus Deo suo judice, conscientiam puram cordis integritate custodit. Illic fortitudo promptior, hic solicitudo securior. Ille appropinquante hora sua jam maturus inventus est, hic fortasse dilatus est: qui patrimonio derelicto idcirco secessit, quia non erat negaturus, confiteretur utique si fuisset et ipse detentus[7].

[4 Strasburgh.]   [5 Numerously attended.]
[6 Yet afterwards, in April or May 1555, he [Grindal] was at Frankfort again, with Cox, Chambers, and some others of chief account; and there, by their prudence, quieted these differences. Strype, Grind. p. 15.—For an account of Grindal's concern in quieting the unhappy dissensions amongst the English exiles at Frankfort, see Strype, ibid.; and for a full detail of those troubles, see Collier, Eccles. Hist. Vol. vi. pp. 144—153. Ed. 1840.]
[7 S. Cyprian. de Lapsis. Opera Oxon. 1682, p. 122. "The first title of victory, is for one apprehended by the hands of the heathen to confess the Lord. The second step to glory is for one withdrawn by a cautious retirement to be reserved for the Lord. The one is a public, the other a private confession. The one overcomes the judge of this world; the other, contented with God as his judge, preserves a pure conscience in the integrity of his heart. In the one case there is a more

A.D. 1555. We have also here certain copies of your answers in the disputation; *Item, Antoniana objecta cum responsione:* the treatise in English against transubstantiation, which in time shall be translated into Latin. It hath been thought best not to print them till we see what God will do with you, both for[1] incensing of their malicious fury, and also for restraining you and others from writing hereafter; which should be a greater loss to the church of Christ, than forbearing of these for a time. If I shall know your will to be otherwise in it, the same shall be followed. Thus much I thought good to let you understand concerning these matters, and concerning the poor state of men here, who most earnestly and incessantly do cry unto God for the delivery of his church, to behold the causes of the afflicted, and to hear the groans of his imprisoned; knowing that you, who in this state have more familiar access unto God, do not forget us.

God comfort you, aid you, and assist you with his Spirit and grace, to continue his unto the end, to the glory of his name, the edification of his church, and the subversion of Antichrist's kingdom! Amen[2].

From Frankfort, the 6. of May, 1555.

E. G.

LETTER IX.

BISHOP GRINDAL TO THE ARCHDEACON OF ESSEX.
May 13, 1560.

[Ex Registr. Grind.]

For avoiding of superstitious behaviour, and for uniformity to be had in the Rogation-week[3], now at hand; these

ready fortitude, in the other a more secure solicitude. The one as his hour approaches is already found prepared; the other is perchance delayed. He who, leaving his patrimony, retired for the express purpose that he might not deny, would doubtless have confessed, had he also been detained.]

[1 For fear of.]

[2 For Ridley's reply to this letter, see his Works, Parker Soc. Ed. pp. 388—395.]

[3 The Rogation time drawing on, when many superstitious processions were wont to be used in London and other places, the Bishop took care, as to allow of the ancient useful practice of perambulations

shall be to require you to give notice and commandment within your archdeaconry, that the ministers make it not a procession, but a perambulation; and also that they suffer no banners, nor other like monuments of superstition to be carried abroad; neither to have multitude of young light folks with them; but the substantial of the parish, according to the injunctions; the ministers to go without surplices and lights; and to use no drinkings, except the distance of the place do require some necessary relief; and to use at one or two convenient places the form and order of prayers and thanksgiving appointed by the queen's majesty's Injunctions[4]. Thus fare ye well. From my house in London, the xiii. of May, anno 1560.

To Mr Cole, Archdeacon of Essex:
this be delivered with speed.

LETTER X.

TO THE SUFFRAGAN BISHOPS.

[E Registr. Grind. fo. 7.]

AFTER my very hearty commendations, these are to signify unto your lordship, that I have received a letter[5], directed

for the asserting of the bounds of each parish, so to check and restrain the superstitions thereof: therefore he prescribed this order to the archdeacons, to be by them communicated through the diocese.... But though our bishop took this care of his diocese, yet I find in many places of the realm this year *gang-week*, as they called it, was observed. And in divers places, of Bucks and Cornwall especially, the people went in procession with banners, and had good cheer after the old custom. See Strype, Grindal, pp. 55, 56.]

[4 Arts xviii. and xix. Cardwell, Documentary Annals, i. 187.]

[5 "The next month an order came, directed to the bishop from the metropolitan, to forbear ordaining any more artificers, and others that had been of secular occupations, that were unlearned; which they, the bishops, had been forced to do at first, if they were qualified with sobriety and good religion and skill in reading, for the supply of the vacant churches: and that all henceforth should be excluded from taking holy

[GRINDAL.]

me from my lord of Canterbury's grace, containing an advertisement to be communicated unto you, and the other of our brethren within his grace's province: and for that intent I have caused the copy of the said letters to be inserted and inclosed herein; the which now I do send by this bearer unto you, not doubting but that your lordship will consider the same, and have such regard thereunto as appertaineth. And thus wishing unto your lordship prosperous health and felicity, to the pleasure of Almighty God, I bid you most heartily farewell. From my house at Fulham, the 17th day of August, Anno Domini 1560.

By your loving brother,
EDM. LONDON.

LETTER XI.

AD DOMINUM PETRUM DE LŒNUM ET DOMINUM JOHANNEM UTENHOVIUM.

Sept. 4, 1560.

[Ex Biblioth. Eccles. Belgic. Lond.]

SALUTEM in Christo. Mitto exemplar supplicationis cujusdam ad me missæ per quosdam (uti apparet) anabaptistas, sed anonymos. Curavi Latine vertendam. Archetypon ad vos misi, quod diligenter uti asservetis oro. Nondum respondi, quia nescio quibus responderem. Sunt qui Adrianum auctorem existimant: is enim (uti audio) quodam tempore quibusdam audientibus dixit, se velle anabaptistarum nomine supplicem libellum ad me conscribere. Itaque puto compendio me facturum, si ad ipsum Adrianum responsionem meam destinarem, ut is fratribus illis anonymis tradendam curaret. Sed tamen decrevi nullo illos responso dignari, nisi prius communicato cum vobis consilio, qui hujus sectæ profunditates melius novistis quam ego propter diuturnam

orders, but such as had good testimonials of their conversation, were exercised in learning, or at least had spent some time in teaching school." See Strype, Grind. p. 60, and Parker, i. p. 180.]

experientiam. De ceteris fratres quos ad me misistis certiores vos reddent. Opto vos in Domino quam optime valere. Fulhamiæ, 4 Septembr. 1560.

A. D. 1560.

Vester in Christo,
EDMUNDUS GRINDALLUS,
Lond. Ep.

Domino Petro de Lœno et domino Joanni Utenhovio, fratribus et amicis in Domino carissimis, Londini.

Translation.

TO PETER DE LŒNE, AND JOHN UTENHOV,
MINISTERS OF THE DUTCH CHURCH, LONDON.

HEALTH in Christ. I send you a copy of a certain supplication[1] sent to me by some anabaptists, as it appears, but anonymous. I have had it translated into Latin. I have sent the original to you, which I beg you to preserve carefully. The author is supposed by some to be Hadrian [Hamsted]: for he, as I am informed, was once heard to say, that he wished to write a supplication to me in the name of the anabaptists. I think, therefore, that I shall be taking the shortest method, if I direct my reply to Hadrian himself, that he may have it delivered to those anonymous brethren. I have determined however to vouchsafe no reply to them, without first consulting you, who know the depths

[[1] This supplication was for the free exercise of their religion. The opinions of these men were sufficiently dangerous and heretical, though they appear to have been outwardly sober and quiet. One of their principal doctrines was, that Christ took not flesh of the Virgin, but brought it down from heaven. Hadrian Hamsted became their apologist, and for some unsound statements was cited before the bishop of London, and openly censured. The entire matter was related by the Dutch congregation to Peter Martyr, who gave his decided opinion against the writings and conduct of Hadrian. The letter of P. Martyr, entitled "Ecclesiæ peregrinorum Londini," is extant among his epistles. Loci Communes, Zurich, 1587, pp. 1128—1133. Bishop Grindal drew up a form of retractation in Latin, to be subscribed by Hadrian Hamsted in order to his absolution and restoration; but he refused to subscribe it. This form, with Strype's translation, will be found in the Appendix.]

of this sect better than I do, by reason of your long experience of them. As to the other matters, the brethren whom you sent to me will inform you. I wish you heartily well to fare in the Lord. From Fulham, 4 September, 1560.

Yours in Christ,
EDM. GRINDAL,
Bishop of London.

To Mr Peter de Lœne, and Mr John Utenhov, my very dear brothers and friends in the Lord, at London.

LETTER XII.

TO SIR W. CECIL.
Aug. 11, 1561.
[State Paper Office.]

SALUTEM in Christo. Sir, I received your letters yesternight late, which I signify, lest you should have cause to think me slack in answer. The French minister, Mons. Saül, was with me on Monday last past, and shewed me the admiral of France his letters with other; whom I exhorted by all means to make haste, adding thereunto, that you one time, in private talk with me, marvelled that the said Mons. Saül went not into France long ago. Whereupon he determined with me to be gone four days ago at the longest: and I have written to my chaplain at London to know the day certain, and to put into these a schedule declaring the same.

I am of your judgment, that no man alive is more fit than Peter Martyr for such a conference[1]; and my lord of

[[1] The conference at Poissy between the papists and the French protestants. P. Martyr attended this conference under a safe conduct, but Beza was the chief speaker on the protestant side. In a letter to Bullinger, dated from St Germain's, 12th Sept. 1561, P. Martyr says: *Colloquium habebitur lingua Gallica, quoniam rex et regina et principes volunt interesse atque audire. Ego itaque non interloquar, sed consulam,*

Canterbury, I trust, will communicate his opinion herewith: but forasmuch as the king's proclamation giveth surety only to his born subjects, Mr Martyr cannot come unless he be called. I think therefore it were very good, if means were made by the queen's majesty, or your honours of the council, that Mr Martyr might be called by the French king, or the council of France. And then assure yourself, the papists can win no honesty in any indifferent[2] hearing; for he is better seen in old doctors, councils, and ecclesiastical histories than any Romish doctor of christendom: he is also himself well seen in the civil and canon laws. But for assistance herein Dr Francis Baldwin[3], who is the reader at Heidelberg in Almayne, were very fit. He is a Frenchman born, and if he is zealous, having this liberty, he will go uncalled; but if he were relieved by some prince's liberality for his charges, then I am sure he would go.

You and all good men have just cause to complain of the unthankfulness of our age. I trust God will make us better one day. In the mean time, our unthankfulness commendeth his mercy; that he may again say, *Inventus sum ab iis, qui me non quærebant*[4]; and again, *Tota die expandi manus meas ad populum non credentem et contradicentem*[5]. I must say with St Paul, *Bene faciendo ne defatigemini*[6]. God keep you! From my house at Fulham, 11 Augusti, 1561.

Yours in Christ,
EDM. LONDON.

To the Honourable Sir William
Cecil, Knight, Secretary to
the Queen's Majesty.

juvabo, et suggeram collegis quæ videbuntur. After the conference, the issue of which was unsatisfactory, he left Paris Oct. 31, and arrived at Zurich Nov. 21. An interesting account of this conference is given by P. Martyr in letters to Bullinger, Calvin, and Lavater. See his letters at the end of the Loci Communes. Zurich, 1587. pp. 1136—1144.]

[2 Indifferent: impartial.]

[3 A professor of civil law. See Strype, Cranmer, I. 474.]

[4 I am found of them that sought me not. Isai. LXV. 1, and Rom. X. 20.]

[5 All day long have I stretched forth my hands unto a disobedient and gainsaying people. Rom. x. 21.]

[6 Be not weary in well-doing. 2 Thess. iii. 18.]

LETTER XIII.

TO THE ARCHDEACONS OF THE DIOCESE OF LONDON[1].

Sept. 6, 1561.

[E Registr. Grind. fo. 25.]

AFTER my hearty commendations: These are to certify you, that I have received my lord of Canterbury his grace's letters, the copy and tenor whereof, with the copy also of the queen's majesty's letter to his grace directed, I do send to you herein inclosed; by virtue whereof I require you, that with all expedition ye call before you all the whole clergy within your archdeaconry, as well those that be exempt as not exempt, opening and declaring to them, as well the queen's majesty's pleasure, as also the advice and commandment of my lord Canterbury's grace, about the contribution concerning the re-edifying of the cathedral church of St Paul's in London; viz. that ye, and every parson and vicar within your archdeaconry, not being in first-fruits, do contribute and pay the twentieth part, and, being in first fruits, the thirtieth part of your and their spiritual promotions: and every stipendiary and curate two shillings and sixpence. Desiring you also to use, in my name, all the persuasion ye can to every of them, so to extend their benevolence, that of their voluntary contribution they may rather exceed their several rates in so reasonable a circumstance; whereof I hope ye shall find a good number. Praying you to make one or two good, grave, beneficed men, in every your deaneries, to be collectors of this contribution, and to deliver the same to you or your deputies on this side the

[1 On Wednesday the 4th of June, 1561, St Paul's Cathedral was set on fire by lightning, and a great part of it consumed. "The queen, (says Strype, Grind. p. 81) was deeply affected with this misfortune, and resolved therefore to have the damage speedily repaired." She issued her letters to the archbishop of Canterbury, bidding him to consult with the other bishops and the chief of the clergy, to devise some expedient for laying a contribution upon the clergy of the province; which was done accordingly. See Bp. Pilkington's Works, p. 480. et seq.]

last day of November next, and thereof to certify me accordingly. And thus I bid you farewell. From my manor at Fulham, the sixth day of September, 1561.

LETTER XIV.

AD MAGISTRATUS FRANCFORTI.
Nov. 12, 1561.

[Ex Biblioth. Eccl. Belgic. Lond.]

GRATIAM et pacem in Christo. Rogarunt me fratres Flandrenses, qui religionis nomine hic apud nos exulant, ut et Gotfridum Wingium, qui istas defert, et ecclesiolam Flandricam, quæ in urbe vestra collecta est, quæque jam per aliquot annos benignissime apud vos hospitium invenit, vestræ amplitudini commendarem. Ego vero, clarissimi atque amplissimi viri, hanc scribendi occasionem libenter arripui, non solum ut illis gratificarer, verum etiam ut meo, atque adeo omnium Anglorum exulum nomine, vestræ amplitudini pro vestra summa erga nos, afflictissimis nostris temporibus, benignitate ac pietate gratias agerem. Nulla unquam dies hoc vestrum beneficium Anglorum animis eximet. Argentinensi, Tigurinæ, Basiliensi, Wormaciensi, sed ante omnes vestræ inclytæ reipublicæ debet Anglia, quod tot habeat episcopos ceterosque verbi divini ministros, qui hodie puram evangelii doctrinam annuntiant. Vos illos hospitio excepistis, exceptos summa humanitate complexi atque auctoritate tutati estis. Nisi igitur istam vestram pietatem gratis animis agnosceremus et prædicaremus, essemus omnium mortalium ingratissimi.

De Gotfrido Wingio hoc habeo quod scribam, hominem esse doctum, pium, ingenio moderato ac pacifico, quique diu in Flandria sub cruce, et quasi perpetuo animam in manibus habens, Christi evangelium prædicavit. Quo nomine non dubito quin vestræ pietati erit acceptissimus. Oro etiam, idque in visceribus Christi, ut Flandrensis ecclesiæ, jam integrum septennium apud vos agentis, nunc vero de ejectione nonnihil sollicitæ, tutelam et patrocinium perpetuetis. Valeat in illos caritas vestra. Nihil enim vel apud homines gloriosius, vel apud Deum acceptius facere potestis, quam si tot membra Christi in pristino suo hospitio retineatis. Quamquam fortassis in uno articulo, jam per multos annos inter doctissimos alioqui viros controverso, cum quibusdam per omnia non consentiant; tamen si ecclesiarum vestrarum pacem non perturbent, quod spero eos neque fecisse hactenus, neque postea facturos, orandi estis ne ad extrema remedia descendatis; sed potius ut Christiana lenitate et mansuetudine in suo sensu ipsos toleretis. Christi Domini præsentiam in sua sacra cœna, eamque veram et salvificam, omnes fatemur; de modo tantum est disceptatio. Nos in nostris ecclesiis, quanquam eandem cum Flandrensibus istis doctrinam et apud vos professi sumus, et etiamnum hic profitemur, nunquam tamen aliquem qui cum Luthero sentiret, si pacifice se gereret, pro hæretico aut nefario homine persecuti fuimus. Utinam conditionibus in Marpurgensi colloquio conclusis statum fuisset, ut pacem utraque pars coleret, donec utrisque Dominus aliud revelaret! Sed præterita facilius defleri possunt, quam corrigi.

Si vos fratres istos ejeceritis, necesse est in antichristi carnificum manus eos incidere. Quo enim miseri fugient? In Germania, a vobis ejecti, nusquam recipientur. In Gallia nondum sunt res constitutæ. Si ad nos penetrare vellent, ubi obviis ulnis reciperentur, media in via tantam multitudinem intercipi necesse est. Nuper enim aliquot fratres ecclesiæ nostræ Londino-Germanicæ, in Flandriam quam poterant occulte atque pacifice profecti, comprehensi sunt atque incendio absumti.

Reputate animis vestris, clarissimi ac pientissimi viri, quam triste esset spectaculum tot Christi membra omnium ætatum ac sexuum simul uno incendio conflagrantia conspicere. Tale autem aliquid futurum sine dubio existimare poteritis, si illos portis vestris excluseritis. Sed hoc quam longissime a vestra pietate abfuturum certissime mihi persuadeo.

Iterum igitur ad preces conversus, oro vestram pietatem quam possum demisissime, ut quorum patrocinium et tutelam tamdiu benignissime suscepistis, quosque et misera et crudeli antichristi tyrannide salvos et incolumes Dei Opt. Max. beneficio conservastis, tantaque cum clementia et humanitate hactenus fovistis, pro vestro in Christum ejusque religionem sincero studio retineatis, ac hospitio dignos, licet non propter se, propter eundem tamen Christum, ducatis. Quo fiet, ut non solum veritatis evangelicæ in gentem Flandricam propagandæ tanquam auctores futuri sitis, gloriæ Christi singularem in ea parte operam navaturi; verum etiam cum in hoc seculo benedictionem Domini quam amplissimam, omni bonorum genere locupletati, (pietas enim, teste D. Paulo, etiam præsentis vitæ promissionem habet,) experiamini, tum in futuro a Christo Domino hospites, ut qui eum collegistis et hospitio excepistis, agnoscamini.

Hæc in Flandricæ gentis, quæ apud vos exulat, gratiam, evangelii propagandi studio, ad vos, clarissimi viri, pietate vestra fretus, scribere sustinui; non dubitans quin, pro vestra in Christi afflicta membra humanitate et clementia, benignitatem vestram in ipsos largiter effusam sentient. Siqua vero in re ego vobis aut reipublicæ vestræ opera vel studio gratificari aut usui esse potero, diligentiam promptamque in ea parte voluntatem vobis ipsi de me polliceri poteritis. Deus amplitudinem vestram et civitatis vestræ statum quam florentissimum diutissime conservet.

Londini, duodecimo Novembr. 1561.

Translation.

TO THE MAGISTRATES OF FRANKFORT[1].

GRACE and peace in Christ! The Flemish brethren, who are living here in exile for the sake of religion, have requested me to commend to your honours Gotfrid Wing, who is the bearer of this letter, and also the little Flemish church which is gathered together in your city, and which has now for several years received the kindest hospitality amongst you. I indeed, most illustrious and worshipful sirs, have willingly seized this opportunity of writing, not only for the sake of

[[1] In behalf of the congregation of Dutch protestants there, who were threatened with expulsion from the city, on account of their refusing the Augustan confession in the matter of the Eucharist. See Strype, Grind. p. 74.]

A.D. 1561. gratifying them, but also that in my own name, and the name of all the English exiles, I might return thanks to your honours for your great kindness and piety towards us in the time of our greatest affliction. No time shall ever remove this your benefit from the minds of Englishmen. England owes it to Strasburg, Zurich, Bâsle, Worms, but above all to your renowned republic, that she has so many bishops, and other ministers of God's word, who at this day are preaching the pure doctrines of the gospel. You hospitably received them, and having received you embraced them with the utmost benevolence, and protected them by your authority. Did we not therefore with grateful minds acknowledge and proclaim that your piety, we should be of all men most unthankful.

Concerning Gotfrid Wing I have this to write, that he is a learned and pious man, of a moderate and peaceable disposition, and one who in Flanders has long preached Christ's gospel, bearing the cross, and, as it were, continually having his life in his hands. On this ground, I doubt not but that he will be most acceptable to your piety. I pray also, and that in the bowels of Christ, that you will continue your protection and patronage to the Flemish church, which has now been amongst you full seven years, but is at present in no small anxiety about their ejection. Let your charity prevail towards them. For you can do nothing either more glorious before men, or more acceptable with God, than to retain in their former hospitable refuge so many members of Christ. Although perhaps in one article, now for many years controverted amongst men in other respects most learned, they do not in all points agree with some; yet, if they do not disturb the peace of your churches, which I hope they have not hitherto done, nor will do hereafter, you are to be entreated not to proceed to extreme remedies, but rather with christian forbearance and mildness to tolerate them in their opinion. The presence of Christ the Lord in his holy Supper, and that a true and saving presence, we all confess; the dispute is only respecting the mode. We in our churches, although amongst you we professed, and even now here also profess, the same doctrine with those Flemings, yet have never persecuted as a heretic or an impious man one who held Luther's opinion, if he conducted himself peaceably. I wish it had been stated in the terms agreed upon at the conference of Marpurg[1], that each side should cultivate peace, until the Lord should reveal otherwise to each. But what is past is more easily lamented than corrected.

If you should eject these brethren, they must of necessity fall into the hands of the butchers of antichrist. For whither, miserable men, shall they fly? Cast out by you, they will nowhere in Germany be received. In France things are still unsettled. If they should wish to come through to us, where they would be received with outstretched arms, such a multitude must needs be intercepted in the way. For but lately some brethren of our German church in London, who had set out for Flanders as secretly and quietly as possible, were caught and burnt to death.

Reflect upon it in your minds, most illustrious and pious sirs, how sad a sight it would be to behold so many members of Christ, of all ages and sexes, burning together in one fire. But you may undoubtedly be assured that something of this kind will ensue, if you should shut them out of your gates. But I most fully persuade myself, that it will be very far from your piety to do this.

Again therefore turning to entreaty, I beseech your piety with all possible humility, that according to your sincere zeal for Christ and his religion, you would still retain and deem worthy of your hospitality, if not for their own sakes, at least for the sake of Christ, those, the patronage and protection of whom you have so long most kindly undertaken; whom you have, through the help of Almighty God, preserved safe and unhurt from the miserable and cruel tyranny of antichrist, and have hitherto cherished with so great clemency

[[1] To terminate this controversy (concerning the Eucharist), Philip, Langrave of Hesse, invited in 1529 to a conference at Marpurg Luther and Zuingle, with some of the most eminent doctors who adhered to the respective parties of these contending chiefs.... The principal champions in these debates were Luther, who attacked Œcolampadius, and Melancthon, who disputed against Zuingle.... The only advantage that resulted from this conference was that the jarring doctors formed a sort of truce, by agreeing to a mutual toleration of their respective sentiments. Mosheim, Ecc. Hist. Cent. xvi. sect. i. c. 28. For an account of this conference, see Sculteti Annal. Evang. Heidelberg, 1620. pp. 197—229.]

and kindness. By which means, not only will you be, as it were, authors of the propagation of evangelical truth amongst the Flemish people, rendering singular assistance in that behalf to promote the glory of Christ; but also will both experience in this life the largest blessing of the Lord, being enriched with all manner of good gifts (for godliness, as St Paul witnesseth, hath the promise even of this present life), and in the next will be acknowledged by Christ the Lord as his hosts, inasmuch as you took him in and hospitably entertained him.

Relying upon your piety, most noble sirs, I have been so bold, in my zeal for the propagation of the gospel, as to write these things to you in behalf of the Flemish people who are exiles amongst you; not doubting but that, according to your benevolence and kindness towards Christ's afflicted members, they will experience your benignity plentifully flowing out towards them. And if in any matter I can gratify or benefit you or your commonwealth by my service or zeal, you may promise yourselves on my part diligence and a ready good will in that behalf. May God very long preserve your honours and the state of your city in the most flourishing condition!

London, 12 November, 1561.

LETTER XV.

TO ARCHBISHOP PARKER.

Oct. 3, 1562.

[Lambeth Library, MS. No. 959, 43.]

PLEASE it your grace, your whole province is shrewdly troubled at this present by exacting a remnant of the last subsidy. There is a blind clause, the which I understand not, in the grant of the said subsidy, A° 4 et 5 Phil. et Mariæ, that if by exility or decay of benefices, &c. any arrearages be, they are to be answered the next year. I would Dr Kennell, Dr Harvey, and such like, that were then in the convocation, were called to expound their meaning.

If, because the queen's majesty, at your grace's suit, pardoned the components, that sum be now cast into the arrearage, it were an unreasonable matter. If your grace could help to ease your province, it were well done. If your grace also sent for Godfrey[1], he might open some matter.

On Monday afternoon I intend to see your grace in my returning hither from London. God keep your grace!

Octr. 3, 1562.

Your grace's in Christ,
EDM. LONDON.

LETTER XVI.

TO SIR W. CECIL.
Oct. 28, 1562.
[State Paper Office.]

I PRAY you let me understand, whether it may be certainly avouched that the king of Navarre, the second Julian, is killed[2]. I intend (God willing) to preach at the cross the next Sunday, and upon occasion offered would peradventure make some mention of God's judgments over him, if the same be true and certain; else not. If there be any other matter which ye wish to be uttered there for the present state, I would be pleased to know it in time, if your leisure will serve. God keep you!

Octr. 28, 1562.

Yours in Christ,
EDM. LONDON.

[1 Probably an officer of the Exchequer. See Strype, Annals, II. ii. 51.]
[2 Antoine de Bourbon, king of Navarre, and brother of the prince of Condè, had joined the Huguenot party, but after the conference of Poissy (see above p. 244, note) he abandoned their cause. Hence Grindal calls him 'the second Julian.' He was mortally wounded at the siege of Rouen, A.D. 1562, while commanding the royal forces against the Protestants, who defended that town. It was however afterwards taken and sacked the same year by the duke of Guise.]

LETTER XVII.

TO SIR W. CECIL.

[1563.]

[State Paper Office.]

Sir, I will send my man to Velsius'[1] lodgings, and to bring him to you, if he can be found. I am sorry I cannot be present myself. I took physic yesterday, and it worketh on me this day, so as I dare not go abroad. It is not needful to describe the qualities of this Velsius; he bewrayeth himself in his own writings, if ye have leisure to wade and weigh them.

First, he confessed before me that he never joined himself with any church, because hitherto he findeth none rightly to be called a church of Christ. What church soever he cometh to, he moveth dissensions in the same, and always opposeth himself against governors thereof; as at Strasburg, he contended with Bucer; at Frankfort, with Lasco[2] and Calvin; and therefore everywhere ejected. He is, in my judgment, (as he uttereth himself in those writings,) a justiciary and a Pelagian, and therefore cannot explicate himself how *justitia* shall be *imputativa*, and yet men be without sin. For indeed he holdeth that *justitia nostra* is only *essentialis*, as the papists, Pelagians, and Osiandrians[3] do: and for sure proof

---

[[1] Justus Velsius was a sectary, from the Hague, who caused much trouble to Bishop Grindal. He was a man of some learning, but an enthusiast, pretending to illuminations from heaven. Strype gives an account of his factious doings in the Dutch church at Austin Friars. (See Annals I. part ii. pp. 8—14.) He wrote an insolent and conceited letter to Queen Elizabeth, which is preserved in the State Paper Office, together with the bishop's letter, of which the above is a copy.]

[[2] John à Lasco, who was the first minister of the foreigners' church at Austin Friars, London, in King Edward's reign. Upon the accession of Mary he retired to Frankfort, where he died, A.D. 1569.]

[[3] Andrew Osiander was a German divine, who excited much controversy about the year 1550 on the doctrine of Justification. Mosheim observes, that "in his discussion of this important point, we shall find it much more easy to perceive the opinions he rejected, than to understand

that this is his meaning, in his letter to the queen's majesty he reprehendeth the prayers used in all reformed churches, wherein we continually confess our sins.

A.D. 1563.
Vide locum notatum.

Such of late were in our realm, that thought a Christian ought not to say the Litany, to confess himself a miserable sinner. This pharisaical spirit is ever joined with pride, and therefore ye see how he boasteth himself, and with what contempt he speaketh of the bishop of Winton and me; whom for our calling's sake he might have termed somewhat more modestly. I did object unto him, that he came hither *in alienam ecclesiam sine vocatione*[4]. I pray you read in the end of his letter to the queen's majesty, where he affirmeth his vocation now to be confirmed by a miracle wrought upon one Cosmus, a servant to the ambassador. This Cosmus fasted five or six days by Velsius' persuasion, in his lectures upon Dionysius Areopagita, that after his abstinence he might receive *illuminationes a cœlo*[5]; but in the end he fell mad: so that Christ's miracles were to cure men of madness, and Velsius' miracles are to make men mad.

Hoc signo*.

Read his letter to the ambassador.

To conclude, he is altogether fanatical, and a dangerous man to be in any commonwealth. If in any town in Germany he should thus use himself, I mean, to teach, to dispute, to gather conventicles, as he doth here, he should be severely looked to.

the system he had invented or adopted." Cent. xvi. Sect. iii. c. 35. The leading principle of that system seems to have been, that justifying righteousness is inherent; and that man becomes a partaker of this righteousness by the indwelling of Christ in the soul, or by the union of the soul with Christ; in other words, that man is justified by the indwelling divinity of Christ. See Mosheim. Ibid.

Calvin states the doctrine briefly in these words: "*Ut justificari sit, non solum reconciliari Deo gratuita venia, sed etiam justos effici: ut justitia sit non gratuita imputatio, sed sanctitas et integritas quam Dei essentia in nobis residens inspirat,* etc. And again: *Quia re ipsa ad colendam justitiam renovat Deus quos pro justis gratis censet, illud regenerationis donum miscet* [Osiander] *cum hac gratuita acceptatione, unumque et idem esse contendit....Ubi Paulus dicit reputari fidem ad justitiam non operanti, sed credenti in eum qui justificat impium, exponit, justum efficere.*" Calv. Inst. lib. iii. c. 11. Sect. 6. et seq. See Bishop Grindal's animadversions upon a work of Velsius, in the Appendix.]

[4 Into a strange church without a call.]

[5 Illuminations from heaven.]

A.D. 1563.   I assure you, if he be suffered to remain here, I look to have the city swarm with sects, ere a year go about. Such another was Rotman, that began the business at Münster[1]. I wish therefore he were commanded to depart. Here is no calling for him. I conferred with you before I sent for him; and after, with my lord of Canterbury's assent, by virtue of the commission, willed him to depart. I trouble you too long. God keep you![2] [1563.]

Yours,
EDM. LONDON.

LETTER XVIII.

TO SIR W. CECIL.
May 17, 1563.
[Lansdown MS. 6. No. 51.]

SIR,—I understand a gentleman, one Skelton, very near my native town, is departed, and doubt nothing but my countrymen made good speed for the wardship. My meaning is not at this time to hinder any particular suit; but I have often thought to make a general suit to you for regard to that little angle where I was born, called Cowpland[3], parcel of

[[1] In the year 1533 some Anabaptists seized the city of Münster, and committed atrocities, which, as Mosheim observes, "would surpass all credibility, were they not attested in a manner that excludes every degree of doubt and uncertainty......They made themselves masters of the city, deposed the magistrates, and committed all the enormous crimes and ridiculous follies, which the most perverse and infernal imagination could suggest." For an account of these proceedings, see Mosheim, Eccles. Hist. sect. III. part ii. c. 7.

"Bernard Rothman, an ecclesiastic of Münster, had introduced the reformation into that city, but afterwards was infected with the enthusiasm of the Anabaptists; and though in other respects he had shewn himself to be neither destitute of learning nor virtue, yet he enlisted himself in this fanatical tribe, and had a share in their most turbulent and furious proceedings." Ibid. note.]

[[2] This letter is without a date.]

[[3] The part of the county in which St Bees is situated.]

Cumberland; the ignorantest part in religion, and most oppressed of covetous landlords, of any one part of this realm, to my knowledge. I intend, at my next coming to you, to discourse more largely of the state thereof, which, God willing, shall be shortly. I have no more to say for this matter, but only to pray you, if your grant be not fully past, to take order both for the good education of the ward, and not to leave the poor tenants subject to the expilation[4] of these country gentlemen, without some choice; wherein if it please you to understand mine opinion, I will utter it simply according to my understanding

God keep you! 17th Maii, 1563.

Yours in Christ,

EDM. LONDON.

To the Honourable Sir William Cecil, Knight, Secretary to the Queen's Majesty.

LETTER XIX.

TO SIR W. CECIL[5].

July 17, 1563.

[Lansdown MS. 6. No. 59.]

SIR,—I SEND you at length the catalogue of names of the late Convocation[6]. Few of these named were absent: and I think not one that was present refused to subscribe the Articles, as they were first offered to the queen's majesty, no, not D. Whyte of Oxford[7].

[[4] Expilation: spoliation—from *expilo*, to pluck out the hair.]
[[5] The following letters, chiefly relating to the offices for the Plague, are for convenience sake placed consecutively; other letters, belonging to this year, are placed after them.]
[[6] The celebrated convocation of 1562, at which the Thirty-nine Articles were agreed upon.]
[[7] The name of "Tho. White, Archid. Berks." occurs in the list of subscriptions to the Articles. Strype, Ann. I. i. p. 489.]

[GRINDAL.]

A.D. 1563. Some that bear good zeal and dutiful affection to the queen's majesty, do marvel that her highness removeth not. The Germans give these precepts in a plague-time: *Cito, procul, sero;* and expound the enigma thus, *Cito fuge, procul fuge, sero revertere*[1]. I am bold sometimes in these things *quæ sunt supra me*[2] to utter mine affection to you. God keep you! From Fulham, 17th Julii, 1563.

Yours in Christ,
EDM. LONDON.

*To the Honourable Sir William
Cecil, Knight, Secretary to
the Queen's Majesty.*

LETTER XX.

TO SIR W. CECIL.
July 30, 1563.
[Lansdown MS. 6. No. 63.]

I HAD somewhat thought of some preparations for common prayer, &c., afore I received your letters, and had written to Mr Dean of Paul's[3] to write an homily meet for the time, which he hath done; but I meant it then for mine own cure. Now, upon your admonition, by help of Mr Dean, who was luckily with me at the receipt of your letters, I have proceeded further, and send you herewith a copy of that which is done.

After ye have considered it, if ye think so good, it may be sent speedily to my lord of Canterbury, by one of Jugg's[4] men, and so returned to the printer.

1. It is to be considered by you, in what form the fast is to be authorised, whether by proclamation, or by way of injunction, or otherwise; for it must needs pass from the queen's majesty.

[1 Fly quickly: fly far off; return late.]
[2 Which are above me.]
[3 Alexander Nowel.]
[4 The printer of the offices for the plague.]

2. Item, Whether any penalty is to be prescribed to the violators thereof, or no.

3. Item, Whether ye will have it general through the realm, or but in this province.

4. Item, To add, diminish, or amend the form and circumstances of fast devised here.

The last week I sent order to London for exhortations of diligent coming to their parish churches on these days, and also for private prayer and abstinence: but some are offended that we have not general assemblies, as we did in the time of unseasonable weather; which I think not meet, for fear of spreading the infection. If it seem so to you, it were not amiss that an admonition were annexed, that in cities infected general concourses be forborne; and moderate assemblies, as of those that be of one parish, to meet at their parish churches, to be more commendable.

The sentences or psalm, which ye wished to be revised, are not altogether ready; they shall be finished this night.

The homily is also not fair written; but of that ye cannot doubt, knowing the author.

If this fast be concluded, I doubt not but the court will give good example. I could also wish a good portion of that which should be spared hereby in weekly provision should be bestowed in the back lanes and alleys of London, and amongst the poor strangers;[5] for these are the sorest visited.

If ye send any order to my lord of Canterbury, if the messenger come by me, I shall deliver him the homily, and the sentences; or else send them to you to-morrow morning. God keep you!

From Fulham, 30 Julii, 1563.

Yours in Christ,
EDM. LONDON.

To the Honourable Sir William
Cecil, Knight, Secretary to
the Queen's Majesty.

[5 Foreigners.]

LETTER XXI.

TO SIR W. CECIL.
August 1, 1563.

[Lansdown MS. 6. No. 65.]

I THINK we are bound to God (his visitation at Newhaven[1] considered), if we have tolerable conditions; much more if they be honourable. I pray you, among your weightier affairs (as ye may) remember to give to my lord mayor, and some other godly honest persons, order for the poor afflicted French, exiled for religion, that they be not taken as prizes[2] (as they now are at London) by virtue of your late proclamation, wilfully wrong understood. Let that be one mean to mitigate God's ire. I have sent to Quintin, your man, to remember you of poor Leach's case.[3]

I set forward to-morrow to Farnham, having left the book in some readiness, and willing Jugg to wait upon you with it. I carry Mr Dean with me.

I am bound to you and my lady, that it pleased her to use my rude house so friendly: her coarse cheer deserved no thanks. God keep you!

1° Augusti, late, 1563.

Yours,
EDM. LONDON.

To the Honourable Sir William
Cecil, Knight, Secretary to
the Queen's Majesty.

[[1] Newhaven (Havre de Grace) was in the month of July surrendered to the French, the English being unable longer to maintain its defence, on account of the plague which raged there.]

[[2] It seems that a proclamation had been made for reprisals upon the French residents in London, in consequence of the seizure of Englishmen's goods in France. This proclamation had been taken advantage of by some ill-affected persons to oppress the French protestants, who had fled hither from persecution in their own country. In this month (August) Sir Nicholas Throgmorton, the queen's ambassador in France, was put under restraint, and retaliation was made upon the French ambassador in London. See Strype, Ann. I. ii. p. 94.]

[[3] See Letter XXXII.]

LETTER XXII.

TO SIR W. CECIL.
Aug. 12, 1563.
[Lansdown MS. 6. No. 69.]

AMONGST your many and weighty affairs, (wherein I pray God send you the assistance of his Spirit, and good success,) I am bold to crave a piece of your advice touching the common prayer and fast: which is, Whether ye think it convenient, notwithstanding the infection, that I send to my lord mayor to have common assemblies twice or once a week, with his brethren and liveries in London, whereat I shall see sermons made accordingly; or that ye think it better to be used in every parish church privately, and no common assemblies to be had. Because the matter is mixed with religion and policy, I am the bolder to ask[4] your counsel, praying you to write me two or three words. My lord Robert[5] wrote to me earnestly for Sebastian, to whom I have written a long letter, much like an apology, the copy whereof I send you herewith.

I hear it will be Sunday at night, or Monday, afore Jugg make an end of printing. The things you wished to be added are partly in the homily, and partly may more conveniently be prosecuted by preaching. God keep you!

From Fulham, 12 Augusti, 1563.

  Yours,   EDM. LONDON.

LETTER XXIII.

TO THE LORD ROBERT DUDLEY.
Aug. 1563.
[From Strype. Grind. pp. 113—116.]

PLEASE it your good lordship. Being at Farnham with my lord of Winton[6], I received your lordship's letters for

---

[4 MS. *axe*. Here and elsewhere the modern form is adopted.]
[5 Lord Robert Dudley, afterwards earl of Leicester. See the following letter.]
[6 Bishop Horn.]

A.D. 1563. Sebastian[1], who at this present standeth excommunicate. I will open to your lordship some circumstances of the matter, and then I doubt not but your lordship will well approve my doings therein. Sebastian was complained of in my visitation, now more than two years past; and that not by one or two, but by a good number of the best learned of my church, that he utterly abstained from the communion. The said Sebastian, being examined by me, confessed the same; and alleged, partly that his conscience was not fully satisfied, but chiefly, that he was not in charity, because of certain actions of debt and suretyship between him and Sir William Garret, &c. I answered, that the latter allegation was merely frivolous, as it was indeed. The first was worthy of consideration: and therefore I gave him a good long day for the better instructing of his conscience; willing him in the mean space to frequent sermons, and to confer with Mr Dean, and others of the church, offering also mine own labour therein.

When his day appointed came, I found him as far off as at the first. That notwithstanding, I gave him a longer day: and so from day to day, till July last past. I also one day conferred with him myself: and perceiving that he sticked much at the matter of transubstantiation, I shewed him testimonies not only of the scriptures, but also of the old fathers, most evidently against that error; and gave him then time to think upon the matter. But all in vain. And therefore I was at length compelled to pronounce him excommunicate, who afore in doings had excommunicated himself. And these were the causes that moved me so to do:—

First, the discharge of mine own duty and office, to whom not only the word of exhortation, but also the sword of ex-

[1] This Sebastian, whose surname was Westcote, "belonged to the choir of St Paul's, being the first minor canon, and master of the choristers there; but being a papist, came not to the communion, and held transubstantiation, and perhaps not without other faults: and persisting therein after divers complaints, the bishop had excommunicated him. But it seems he was favoured by the Lord Robert Dudley, a great courtier and favourite, who wrote an earnest letter to the bishop in his behalf, shewing that he was not obstinate, and that what he did was out of zeal; and that haste in such cases might be hurtful. The bishop well knew what a man he had to deal with, being very haughty and impatient of denial, and apt to resent; and therefore he composed an answer at good length." Strype, Grind. 113.]

communication is committed; whereof neither can be omitted in his time and place, without offence against God. [A.D. 1565.]

Secondly, I seek herein his reformation: for excommunication in such disobedient persons is the ordinary mean taught by the Holy Ghost to reduce men to God. Therefore, saith St Paul, *Tradatur Satanæ ad interitum carnis, ut spiritus salvus sit in die Domini Jesu.* [1 Cor. v. 5.]

Thirdly, He hath been of long time very offensive, not only to the godly of my church, but also to all other well affected persons frequenting common prayer there; seeing such an one joined with us in common prayer, which refused to join with us in the Lord's supper, as one accounting our form of administration heretical and schismatical. Whereas communion of prayer and sacraments ought to be one, saith Chrysostom.

Fourthly, (which is a matter of great moment,) There is committed unto him the education of the choristers, or singing children: he remaining therefore in the mind he doth, with what conscience can I commit youth to his instruction?

Your lordship thinketh him not to be obstinate; but I pray you remember, that obstinacy is better known by doings than by sayings. Ye think also he doth it of zeal. Admit it be so, he is not therefore excusable, especially after so long toleration: though not communicating with God's church in Christ's institution ceaseth not to be a grievous sin against God, although it do proceed from an erroneous zeal. And yet I assure your lordship I doubt much of his zeal: for now after so long trial, and good observation of his proceedings herein, I begin to fear, lest his humility in words be a counterfeit humility, and his tears crocodile tears, although I myself was much moved with them at the first.

Last of all, where your lordship thinketh, that haste in such cases might be hurtful, and time might win him, it may please your lordship to understand what time he hath had already, and how long I have borne with him; which is no less than all the time since my first entry, being now almost four years: and therefore I am afraid I have rather been too slow than too hasty; and that I have an account to give to God for all those corrupt lessons of false religion, which he the space of two or three years hath instilled into

A.D. 1563. the ears and minds of those children committed unto him. Wherein, no doubt, he hath been too diligent, as hath appeared by his fruits.

If Sebastian will acknowledge his fault and amend, I am ready most willingly to receive him. If no, I dare not absolve an impenitent sinner; for that were to loose him whom God bindeth, and to abuse the keys of the church. I am content, because your lordship writeth so earnestly for him, to forbear prosecuting the penalties of the laws against him, till after Michaelmas, or Halloweentide; that he may yet have more time to search and to understand, praying God in the mean time to open his eyes. Thus being bold to trouble your lordship with a long letter, because I wish your lordship should be fully satisfied in this matter, I commit the same to Almighty God. [August, 1563.]

LETTER XXIV.

TO SIR W. CECIL.

Aug. 21, 1563.

[Lansdown MS. 6. No. 68.]

SIR,—I HAVE sent the queen's majesty's letters directed to the archbishop of York, inclosed in a letter of mine, (for that I was compelled to break it up by occasion of your letter, that Jugg might print the copy of it,) to the ordinary post at London, to be set forward with half a dozen copies annexed, that he may begin in the city of York, and the impression for his province shall follow with convenient speed. I have been bold to use your name to the post, thinking that I have not therein offended your meaning. For the copies to be printed in form of a Manual, you and I were of one mind; and I talked with Jugg of it six days ago, and think them to be in a forwardness. There was committed also to the print a short Meditation[1] to be used in private houses,

[[1] In the Appendix will be found "A forme of Meditation, very meete to be daylye used of house holders in their houses, in this daungerous and contagious time. Set forth accordyng to the order in the Quenes Majesties Injunction;" which, although without a date, is in

which I suppose is abroad. I marvel the book came to you so late. Jugg said he delivered it on Monday to the post. It was exercised in London on Wednesday last, and the same day here at Fulham I had a convenient assembly. By outward appearance, it seemeth that this order of fast is generally embraced. Surely my opinion hath been long, that in no one thing the adversary hath more advantage against us, than in the matter of fast, which we utterly neglect; they have a shadow. That made me put in these words, "For some beginning of redress herein[2]." The hope of peace[3] hath somewhat exhilarated me, considering the circumstances of the present time. I have willed the eighth verse to be omitted. God keep you! From Fulham, 21° Augusti, 1563.

Yours in Christ,
EDM. LONDON.

To the Honourable Sir William
  Cecil, Knight, Secretary to
  the Queen's Majesty.

LETTER XXV.

TO SIR W. CECIL.
Dec. 21, 1563.
[Lansdown MS. 6. No. 82.]

I SEND you herewith a psalm and a prayer, which may be set forth, (if ye so think it good,) in this time of the diminution of sickness, minding also to cause another psalm and prayer of thanks to be drawn, which may be used when it shall please God to send us perfect delivery. I intend also at that time to have a sermon and some solemn assembly of the companies at Paul's on some Wednesday, to give God thanks; and so to end *jejunium nuper indictum*[4], if you do not otherwise advise me. But I suppose this latter cannot be done till the number of the plague be under a hundred a week.

all probability the form here alluded to. It is curious and interesting as an early specimen of family devotion.]
[2 See the conclusion of the office for the plague in this volume.]
[3 With France.]
[4 The fast lately enjoined.]

A.D. 1563. I have signified the effect of your letter to Mr Utenhov[1]. He said he would write to know, how long ye thought it good that he deferred his answer to the chancellor. I am of opinion, that the opportunity of that place[2] is better for us, than any oversea part that I know. For intercourse of merchandise I doubt more, because they cannot thence be well conveyed into High Germany, but through West Friesland, or the borders of Holland, by water, which are King Philip's countries, and therefore upon abstinence from Antwerp questions might grow. I have caused money to be delivered to my man the bringer, to pay for Foxcroft's seals, if they be passed. I will write myself to the bishop of Lincoln[3] for his institution: there is no doubt of retaining the benefice, if the presentation be obtained; for the law is against D. Dallyson.

I would thank my lord of Oxford, or you, or both, if ye would give me a warrant for a doe in the park at Castle Camps in Cambridgeshire, which is not far from Hadham. My keeper of Hadham-house would bring it me up against Christmas. Thus ceasing to trouble you, I commend you to God.

From Fulham, 15 Decemb. 1563.

Yours in Christ,

EDM. LONDON.

For Barton's matter, he is *dedecus nostri ordinis*[4], and slanderous to all good men that know his vile doings. Therefore I said to Locke, that he, being of you esteemed an honest man, should not be so importune for a man not honest.

To the Honourable Sir William
  Cecil, Knight, Secretary to
  the Queen's Majesty.

[1 Minister of the Dutch Church, London. See p. 242.]

[2 Allusion is made to a political transaction in which the bishop was engaged, viz. the settling of some English merchants at Embden, in East Friesland. See Strype, Grind. pp. 126—132.]

[3 Bishop Nicholas Bullingham.]

[4 "A disgrace to our order." Barton was an infamous clergyman, parson of Abchurch in London, whom the bishop had deprived or suspended. Intercession had been made with Cecil in his behalf by one Locke. See Strype, p. 133.]

LETTER XXVI.

TO ARCHBISHOP PARKER.
Jan. 2, 1563.
[Petyt MSS. 47, fo. 525.]

I sent your books yesterday to my lord of Ely[5], who returned me them this day with some notes of his opinion. It were good we had a time of some further conference. If the communion be ministered in Paul's[6], it will be done so tumultuously and gazingly, by means of the infinite multitude that will resort thither to see, that the rest of the action will be disordered: and therefore I think it shall be good to remain in suspense, till we talk with more. God keep your grace!

2° Januarii[7], 1563. [1564.]

Your grace's in Christ,

EDM. LONDON.

P. S. I send your grace herewith the temporal man's[8] draught for two statutes to be considered.

LETTER XXVII.

TO SIR W. CECIL.
Jan. 21, [1563.]
[Lansdown MS. 7. No. 57.]

Sir,—I have committed the prayers to the print, and hope to proceed at London to the publication thereof on Wed-

[5] Bishop Cox.]
[6] The archbishop advised that, seeing the office for the cessation of the plague was an eucharistic office, the holy Communion should be then celebrated; that those of the church of St Paul's, the magistrates of the city, and others, might communicate. See Strype, p. 121.]
[7] It will be borne in mind that the beginning of the year was reckoned from the 24th of March. Consequently January, February, and part of March, in the year 1564, according to modern reckoning, would then be considered as belonging to the year 1563. The same observation will apply to other dates in this collection of letters.]
[8] Lawyer, or civilian.]

A.D. 1563. nesday next. The thanksgiving for the queen's majesty's preservation I have inserted into the collect, which was apter place, in my opinion, than in the psalm; ye shall see in the probe[1] of the print, and after judge. The heads of colleges in Cambridge made me privy of their suit, which they now make to the queen's majesty by you, for a good order concerning the election of the vice-chancellor. In my judgment it is a very necessary suit. I pray you, be good to my lord of Carlisle[2] the bringer. There be marvellous practices to deface him in my lawless country, and by him the cause. If those two of whom he now complaineth were touched by the authority of my lords, it would be a terror to the rest. God keep you!

From Fulham, 21 Januarii, [1563.]

Yours in Christ,

EDM. LONDON.

To the Honourable Sir William Cecil, Knight, Secretary to the Queen's Majesty.

LETTER XXVIII.

TO SIR W. CECIL.

Feb. 22, 1563.

[Lansdown MS. 7. No. 62.]

MR CALFHILL[3] this morning shewed me your letter to him, wherein ye wish some politic orders to be devised against infection. I think it very necessary, and will do mine endeavour, both by exhortation and otherwise. I was ready to crave your help for that purpose afore, as one not unmindful of the peril.

[1 Probe: proof.]

[2 "Best, bishop of Carlisle, had met with very ill dealings in that country, replenished with papists and such like: which perhaps was the cause that Bernard Gilpin prudently declined this bishoprick." Strype, Grind. p. 126. See infra, Letter, date 27 Dec. 1563.]

[3 Prebendary of St Paul's.]

By search I do perceive, that there is no one thing of late is more like to have renewed this contagion, than the practice of an idle sort of people, which have been infamous in all good commonweals; I mean these *histriones*, common players, who now daily, but specially on holy-days, set up bills, whereunto the youth resorteth excessively, and there taketh infection: besides that God's word by their impure mouths is profaned and turned into scoffs. For remedy whereof, in my judgment, ye should do very well to be a mean, that a proclamation were set forth to inhibit all plays for one whole year (and if it were for ever, it were not amiss) within the city, or three miles compass, upon pains, as well to the players, as to the owners of the houses where they play their lewd interludes.

A. D. 1563.

I wrote to Mr Dr Humfrey of Oxford, to keep the day appointed him by my lord of Rochester[4], which he will observe, I doubt not. As I counselled Mr Calfhill to know your pleasure for his repair to court, so I shall pray you to let me understand your advice for mine own case concerning my sermon, whether I, remaining here, may be admitted; and the like for my chaplain, Mr Watts. I was compelled to remove hither, both for the better discharge of mine office, and also for that I was destitute of necessary provision at Fulham. Yet I thought then the city would have been clean ere now. God keep you!

From my house at Paul's, 22 Febr. 1563.

Yours in Christ,
EDM. LONDON.

To the Honourable Sir William
Cecil, Knight, Secretary to
the Queen's Majesty.

[4 Bp. Guest.]

LETTER XXIX.

TO SIR W. CECIL.
March 7, 1563.
[Lansdown MS. 7. No. 63.]

Sir,—I have conferred with my lord mayor concerning my lord's letters lately directed to him and me: wherein were two things contained appertaining to mine office, one for refraining of preachers, which are said to have persuaded the people to break the orders set forth, &c.; the other for setting forth an admonition to be read in churches. This letter I send you inclosed herein. And for the first, I asked my lord mayor if he knew any such preacher by name; and he answered, No. Since, I have called them all before me, and they deny that either they have done it heretofore, thinking it a matter very unfit, or that they intend to do it hereafter.

Only one man spake something in summer concerning the fires[1] then commanded; but he himself hath been sick ever since of the plague, and hath had three or four (saving your honour) plague-sores, one after another: so that God hath sufficiently corrected him. What his manner of utterance was then, I cannot tell; and now he is not in case to be talked withal. My lord mayor (I doubt not) will also certify what he doth in matters pertaining to his office. Thus I cease, and commend you to the grace of God.

From my house in London, 7 March, 1563.

Yours in Christ,
EDM. LONDON.

To the Honourable Sir William
  Cecil, Knight, Secretary to
  the Queen's Majesty.

THE BISHOP'S ADMONITION, TO BE READ BY MINISTERS TO THEIR PEOPLE.

According to a certain order sent of late from the queen's majesty's most honourable privy council, to the reverend

[1 Fires in the streets, supposed to be a preventive of infection.]

father in God the bishop of London, our ordinary; I am by the said bishop willed to exhort and admonish you that be of this parish, diligently to observe, and obediently to keep those good orders, which lately have been set forth by the lord mayor of this city, for avoiding the danger of the infection of this contagious sickness, wherewith God hath of late visited this city, and which as yet is not clearly taken away. And further, on the behalf aforesaid, I do most earnestly exhort and beseech those, whom it hath pleased God to visit with this sickness, and are in the way of recovery, to forbear to company with the whole, for such convenient time as is by order of the said lord mayor appointed in this behalf, or longer, if need so require; that thereof no infection increase to others by their occasion; considering that even by the rule of charity all men are bound in conscience not to do any thing that by common judgment and experience may bring a manifest peril and danger to their brethren or neighbours, as may well appear by the law of God, in separating the leprous persons from the clean; wherein Ozias[2], being a king, was not spared; the disease of leprosy being nothing so dangerous for infection as this is. *Levit. xiii. 2 Chron. xxvi.*

And likewise I exhort, as afore, those that be whole to use convenient means and helps, being not against God's word, to keep themselves from infection, and not to resort to places infected, whereunto by their duty and vocation they are not bound to resort; lest, by rash and wilful entering into companies or places of danger, they tempt God, casting themselves into unnecessary perils, which is against his express commandment; "and by loving peril," as the wise man saith, "perish in the same." *[Ecclus. iii. 26.]*

This thing therefore being both so charitable and godly, and also very like to be profitable for this afflicted city, I trust all godly men will gladly embrace and receive, the rather for that it may be easily observed, the number of the sick (thanks be to God!) being now but small; and for that also by the godly order now set forth by the said lord mayor, those that be not of ability are sufficiently provided for in this case.

4º die Martii an. Dom. 1563.

[² Uzziah.]

LETTER XXX.

TO SIR W. CECIL.
July. 3, 1563.
[Lansdown MS. 6. No. 55.]

BECAUSE some have died lately near my house here, I dare not come to the court to speak with you: notwithstanding I shall pray you to have your furtherance in this matter following, which I have communicated with my lord Keeper[1], who seemeth not to mislike of it. St Bartholomew's church, adjoining to my lord Rich's[2] house, is in decay, and so increaseth daily[3]: it hath an heavy coat of lead, which would do very good service for the mother church of Paul's[4]: I have obtained my lord Rich's good will, and if I could obtain my lord Chief Justice of the King's Bench and Sir Walter Mildmay's[5] assent, I would not doubt to have the assent also of the whole parish, that the lead might go to the covering of Paul's. There remaineth only this scruple, How shall the parish be provided of a church? That is thus answered. There is a house adjoining, which was the Fratrie[6]

[1 Sir Nicholas Bacon.]
[2 "Here (in the priory of Great St Bartholomew's) after the dissolution of the priory lived Sir Richard Rich, Lord Rich, and Lord Chancellor in the beginning of King Edward VI. Here also dwelt another great counsellor of Queen Elizabeth's, Sir Walter Mildmay, Chancellor of the Exchequer." Stow's Survey of London, p. 716.
"This church (i.e. the priory-church) being pulled down to the choir, the choir was annexed to the old parish church adjoining, and after the 1st of Elizabeth was given by act of parliament to the parishioners." Ibid.]
[3 "The parochial church (now called Great St Bartholomew's) was an old parish church, and stood next adjoining to the priory-church. The old parish church was pulled down except the steeple of rotten timber, which was ready to fall of itself, which in 1628 was pulled down to the very foundation, and a new one re-built of brick and stone." Newcourt's Repertorium of the Diocese of London.]
[4 Which had been recently burned. See above, p. 246.]
[5 "A monument to Sir Walter Mildmay, who died May 1589, in St Bartholomew's church." Maitland's History of London, p. 1069.]
[6 "Refectories or Fratries, large wainscoted halls, with a crucifixion above the boards, a dresser, almories or cupboards, windows opening into the kitchen, through which the meal was served, and desk with a bible

(as they termed it), a very fair and a large house, and in- A.D. 1563.
deed already, if it was purged, lacketh nothing but the name
of a church; well builded, of free-stone, garnished within round
about with marble pillars, large windows, &c. I assure you
without partiality, if it was dressed up, it were far more
beautiful and more convenient than the other. It is covered
with good slate. If we might have the lead, we would compound with my lord Rich for converting the said Fratrie to
a church; and we will also supply all imperfections of the
same, and not desire the parish to remove, till the other be
meet and convenient to go to. Methinketh the matter is
very reasonable; for what is more reasonable, than that the
children should clothe their naked parents? Our church is
matrix ecclesia, (as the canons term such churches,) which is
all one with *mater*. I pray you, let us have your help in it
to my lord Chief Justice and Mr Mildmay, if they be *difficiles*;
and also, if ye shall think it convenient to move the queen's
majesty, (which my lord Keeper thinketh not amiss,) let us
have your help that way also. I will repair to you when
the court cometh to Richmond, or at some other convenient
time, to understand what ye think good. God keep you!
From London, 3 Julii, 1563.

      Yours in Christ,   EDM. LONDON.
To the Honourable Sir William
 Cecil, Knight, Secretary to
 the Queen's Majesty.

LETTER XXXI.

TO SIR W. CECIL.
July 12, 1563.
[Lansdown MS. 6., No. 56.]

I RECEIVED yesternight, being the 11th of this July, a
letter from my lords for making a certificate of the state of

for reading during dinner." Fosbroke's Encyclopædia of Antiquities,
Vol. I. p. 108. See also Fosbroke's British Monachism, v. Refectory.

 The fratry at St Bartholomew's the Great adjoined the south transept of the church. See the plan of the old priory in Londina Illustrata,
Malcom's Lond. Rediviv. and Brayley's Beauties of London, Part III.]

[GRINDAL.]

A.D. 1563. my diocese, which I will answer (God willing) with all possible speed.

1. I have received also from you three letters: the first was concerning St Bartholomew's[1], and a certificate of the convocation. For St Bartholomew's, I mean not to pull down but to change a church, more commodious than the other, unless some strange opinion should arise, that prayer were more acceptable under lead than under slate.

For the convocation, I sent to Mr Saye, registrar thereof, and he with all his clerks are in the country; but I send again with more strait charge, and hope to certify you within a day or two.

2. Your second letter was for Sir Thomas Fitzharbert. He is a very stiff man. We had a solemn assembly of commissioners in the end of the term only for his case, where Mr Chancellor of the dutchy was present, and there concluded to let Mr Fitzharbert be abroad upon sureties, if he would be bound in the mean time to go orderly to the church, without binding him to receive the communion. That Sir Thomas refused. We will have a new conference upon occasion of your letter, and consider the circumstances of his case, and after certify you of the same.

3. Your third letter was for Barton's[2] case, the parson of Abchurch. I suppose that he which offered the supplication to you, although he allege that I understood not the case, did not truly understand it himself. Although the act was not finished, yet *per ipsum non stetit*[3], and the circumstances were too vile; and therefore severity must be used, or else God will be offended, and the mouth of the adversary opened. I commit you to God.

From Fulham, 12 Julii, 1563.

Yours in Christ,

EDM. LONDON.

To the Honourable Sir William
Cecil, Knight, Secretary to
the Queen's Majesty.

[1 See the preceding Letter.]
[2 See Letter XXV.]
[3 It was no fault of his.]

LETTER XXXII.

TO SIR W. CECIL.
July 31, 1563.
[Lansdown MS. 6. No. 64.]

SIR,—I SEND you inclosed a letter writ (as I am informed) by one Leach[4], a Scotchman, now in Ireland. I am informed that he is in prison, and great matters objected against him. I can affirm nothing of his case; but this I can say, I know the man well: he was mine host at Spires in Germany: he is of good religion, honest, and one that ever wished to live to see the queen's majesty come to the crown; and for declaration of his affection herein he forsaked Germany, where he was in good estimation, and good case to live, and came over among us exiles. I cannot believe he would speak any dishonour of the queen's majesty; and therefore, if I should die this hour, I think he is wrongfully accused. I pray you therefore, be good to him; and help that the matter be not hastily judged, but may be throughly examined. I fear me it is too easy a matter, either in Ireland or in Wales, to get false witnesses to swear. I pray you, be good to the poor man, and obtain him at least some time. God will reveal the truth, I doubt not. God keep you!

Ult°. Julii, 1563.

Yours in Christ,
EDM. LONDON.

To the Honourable Sir William
Cecil, Knight, Secretary to
the Queen's Majesty.

[4 " This man's occasions led him to Ireland; where this year were great and dangerous matters laid to his charge, as though he had spoken treason against the queen. For this he was laid up in prison, and in danger of his life; being prosecuted and sworn against by some Irish, whether out of some private grudge or hatred to him for his good-will to the reformed religion, or no, I cannot tell.' Strype, Grind. p. 109.]

LETTER XXXIII.

HIERONYMO ZANCHIO.

[Zanchii Epist. lib. II.]

Augusti 23, 1563.

S. D.[1] Quod tam copiose ad me [de] dissidii vestri compositione scripsisti, clarissime D. Doctor Zanchi, gratias ago: quod autem petis, ut meam aliorumque amicorum tuorum sententiam ea de re perscribam, id hoc tempore plene præstare non potui. Amici enim illi tui, quos nominasti, Londino jam diu abfuere propter pestem ibi grassantem. Quod ad me attinet, tantum tribuo pietati ac prudentiæ tuæ, ut de omnibus actionibus tuis bene sentiam. Accedit etiam (uti ais) Domini Calvini calculus, qui subscriptionem tuam cum illis conditionibus et exceptionibus approbavit; quod me multum confirmat: nam illius judicio multum soleo tribuere. Hoc unum metuo, ne priores adversarii, nisi tu tibi in istis controversiis silentium prorsus indixeris, (quod hoc tempore, cum veritas a quibusdam libris editis, oppugnatur, durum esset,) ex hac compositione gradum sibi struant ad novas turbas excitandas, ac tum simplicem subscriptionem, quæ literis consignata est, urgeant, exceptiones vero illas et protestationes, quæ viva voce tantum factæ sunt, non agnoscant. Sed de futuris incertum est judicium: ea igitur Domino commendemus, qui tibi etiam (non dubito) os et sapientiam dabit, cui non poterunt resistere adversarii veritatis. Vale in Domino quam optime. Ex suburbano meo Fulhamiensi ad ripam Thamesis, 23 August. 1563.

Tuus in Christo,

EDMUNDUS GRINDALLUS,

Episcopus Londinensis.

[1 Salutem dico.]

Translation.

TO HIEROME ZANCHIUS[2].

I WISH you health. I thank you, most famous Master Doctor Zanchius, for writing to me so fully concerning the settlement of your dispute: but whereas you ask me to write my own opinion and that of the rest of your friends upon that question, this request at the present time I have been unable fully to execute. For those your friends, whom you named, have now for some time been absent from London, on account of the plague now raging there. For my own part, I attribute so much to your piety and prudence, that I have a good opinion of all your actions. The opinion of Master Calvin, moreover, as you say, is with you, who approved of your subscription under those conditions and exceptions; which much confirms me: for I am wont to pay much deference to his opinion. This one thing only I fear, lest your former adversaries, unless you impose a silence upon yourself in these controversies, (which it would be hard to do at this time, when the truth is assailed by some in certain published books,) should from this composition make a way for stirring up new commotions, and

[2 " Hierom Zanchy, an Italian by birth, was now public reader of divinity at Strasburgh: with him Grindal was acquainted ever since himself lived there, and since his departure kept a correspondence with him. This year letters happened between them upon this occasion. The Augustan Confession about this time began to be pressed vigorously, and particularly in the said town of Strasburgh, upon all the reformed there, or no abiding for them. This was the cause of great contests and debates between the learned Lutherans in the school there, and Zanchy, who in the matter of the sacrament, and predestination, and some other things, could not accord with their Confession. But at last for peace sake, this year, the difference was composed, and he did subscribe (yet with some exceptions and conditions) in these words, *Hanc doctrinæ formulam ut piam agnosco: ita etiam recipio ego Hieronymus Zanchius.*

This being so large a concession to the Lutheran doctrine, he saw, might justly make the reformed in other parts to wonder at his subscription. And therefore in an epistle he at large declared the reason of what he had done to our bishop, adding, that he had also the opinion of Calvin therein. And he believed, he said, that Grindal, such was his piety and prudence, would have done no otherwise than he had done, had he been in the like circumstances. Yet herein he desired to know the bishop's thoughts." Strype, Grind. p. 111.]

A.D. 1563. urge this naked subscription, which appears under your hand, and not acknowledge those exceptions and protests, which were made only *viva voce*. But our judgment of the future is uncertain; let us leave those things therefore to God, who will give to you also, I doubt not, a mouth and wisdom which the adversaries of the truth shall not be able to resist. Fare you right well in the Lord. From my country house at Fulham on the banks of the Thames, 23 August, 1563.

Yours in Christ,

EDM. GRINDAL, bishop of London.

LETTER XXXIV.

HIERONYMO ZANCHIO.

[Zanchii Epist. lib. II.]

SALUTEM in Christo. Gratulabaris mihi proximis tuis literis novam dignitatem, seu potius (ut vere scribis) officium et onus, cui me valde imparem ingenue agnosco. Ego vero tibi gratulor, clarissime D. Doctor Zanchi, istam tuam magnanimitatem et constantiam in optima causa defendenda. Audivimus enim quot et quantos labores ac certamina sustinueris, in vera sententia tuenda de eucharistia ac prædestinatione. Est hoc quidem veri doctoris, tenacem esse fidelis illius sermonis, qui ad doctrinam facit, atque a veritate ne latum quidem unguem discedere. Equidem non dubito, quin magistratus vestri, pro ipsorum prudentia, satis moderate judicabunt, etiamsi multa (ut nosti) quorundam importunitati concedere cogantur. Sed si ad extrema ventum fuerit, Dominus ubique ostium satis amplum aperit: *Domini etiam est terra et plenitudo ejus*, &c.

Nos hic, Dei beneficio, utcunque pacatam habemus ecclesiam. Habemus episcopos in vera doctrina consentientes, non otiosos, sed in vinea Domini laborantes. Augetur etiam indies numerus fidelium, etiamsi non desunt (ut fit) hostes clancularii: sed hi angulos quærere coguntur; palam virus suum prodere non audent. Faxit Deus, ut motus Gallici felicem habeant exitum, quod hostibus nostris omnem spem præcideret! In Scotia etiam hactenus summa procerum contentione bene successit. Sola regina apud illos sacra papistica admittit, quæ alioqui senatus-consulto per totum regnum haberi non permittuntur. Quanquam autem dubium non est, quin Antichristi satellites in illo regno huic libertati insidiabuntur, præsertim si Guisiani, ex quorum familia est Scotiæ regina, superiores evadant; tamen speramus Dominum causæ suæ non defuturum, et optimis illis regni proceribus non solum animos, sed et vires suppeditaturum, ut hoc tam sanctum negotium perficere possint. D. Coocus, D. Wrotus, D. Hetonus, ceterique amici ac noti, vivunt valentque, ac te plurimum salutant. Vale. Londini.

Tuus in Christo,
EDMUNDUS GRINDALLUS,
Episcopus Londinensis.

Translation.

TO HIEROME ZANCHIUS.

HEALTH in Christ. You congratulated me in your last letter upon my new dignity, or rather (as you truly write) my duty and burden, for which I candidly confess myself very insufficient. But I congratulate you, most famous Master Dr Zanchius, upon your magnanimity and firmness in the defence of a most worthy cause. For we have heard how many and how great labours and contests you have sustained, in defending the true opinion concerning the Eucharist and Predestination. This is indeed the part of a true doctor, to hold fast that faithful word, which is profitable for doctrine, and to depart from truth not even a nail's breadth. I do not doubt, but that your magistrates, according to their prudence, will judge with moderation, although (as you know) they may be compelled to make many concessions to the importunity of some persons. But if things come to the worst, the Lord everywhere opens a sufficiently wide door. "The earth, too, is the Lord's and the fulness thereof," &c.

We have here, through God's goodness, a church to a certain extent tranquillized. We have bishops agreeing in true doctrine, not idle, but labouring in the Lord's vineyard. The number of the faithful too is daily increasing, though there are not wanting (as is usual) secret enemies: but these are compelled to lurk in corners; they dare not openly put forward their venom. God grant the movement in France[1] may have a happy issue, which would cut away all hope from our enemies! In Scotland also hitherto matters have succeeded well through the earnest zeal of the nobles. The queen alone amongst them admits the popish rites, which otherwise are forbidden by Act of Parliament to be performed throughout the whole realm. Although there is no doubt, but the abettors of Antichrist in that kingdom will plot against this liberty; especially if the Guise party, of whose family is the queen of Scots, should get the better: yet we trust that the Lord will not fail his own cause, and will supply not only courage, but strength also, to those excellent nobles of the land, so that they may be able to accomplish this so holy work. Master Cook, Master Wroth, Master Heton, and the rest of your friends and acquaintances, are alive and well, and greet you most heartily. Farewell. From London.

Yours in Christ,

EDM. GRINDAL,
Bp. of London.

LETTER XXXV.

TO SIR W. CECIL.
Oct. 15, 1563.
[Lansdown MS. 6. No. 77.]

SALUTEM *in Christo Servatore.* As I am glad to hear that your disease diminisheth, so I am sorry it hangeth on you so long. It is said your pain is in your back: I will be bold to communicate unto you my conjecture of the cause thereof, and of the means to avoid the like hereafter; not by any art of physic, but upon some experience of mine own body in the like case. When I came first from beyond seas, I felt great heat in my back, and feared the stone: I cut my doublets, my petticoats, in the back; I went ungirt; I could

[1 Of the protestants under the prince of Condé and others.]

not abide to sit on a cushion, &c. In continuance, I strived so to cool my back, that I fell into the contrary, so that a small cold taken on that part by going single, and specially by riding single, to this day casteth me into a stitch; which beginneth under the point of one shoulder or both, and suddenly claspeth on the small of my back, and there remaineth fifteen or twenty days. I do remember one morning, a year and more agone, ye shewed me your doublets cut and voided in the back, and that ye feared the stone. I am surely persuaded, that by resisting heat (which might come then by some accident) ye have cooled your back too much, ridden and gone single, and so have brought those parts to great imbecility. Surely, I think, the only way to avoid it hereafter is to go warm, and namely on your back; but specially when ye ride, though it be in the midst of summer. I begin every day to like better and better Sir Rich. Sackvill's physic, with store of clothes and furs. *Frigus nunquam sensi*[2] was a piece of his physic that said, *Centum annis vixi*[3]. I have sent you herewith a glass, sealed *Sigillo Hermetis*, of Thomas Gybson's Balsam. It is to be used outwardly, as an ointment. I dare not advise you to use it without the counsel of the physicians, for it is very hot; but it may stand by you, for it is very good in aches that come of cold causes. I have seen the proof of it. Thus much of physic, whereof all sick men love to hear, be it never so slender.

I thank you that in your most pain ye remembered to ease me of one guest[4]. My Lord of Ely received him on Sunday last past, and writeth that he is welcome for their sakes that send him, otherwise not. I signified to Dr Watson, that, if he had tarried, I was willing to have conferred with him in divers points; but he answereth, that he will not enter in conference with no man; the reason is, he will not incur penalties of laws. I said only one law was penal[5],

[2 I never felt cold.]
[3 I have lived a hundred years.]
[4 Watson, late bishop of Lincoln, was for some time under restraint in Grindal's house. In the month of October he was, by order of council, transferred to the care of Cox, bishop of Ely. See Strype, Grind. p. 116.]
[5 For denying the queen's supremacy.]

that might be forborne; but he persisted in his opinion. I hear said, Mr Fecknam[1] is not so precise, but could be contented to confer. The Bishop of Winton, when he was with me, said that if he should have any, he could best deal with Fecknam; for in king Edward's days he travailed with Fecknam in the tower, and brought him to subscribe to all things, saving the presence, and one or two more articles. Ye might do very well (in my opinion) to ease the poor Dean of Westminster, and send the other also to some other bishop, as Sarum, or Chichester, &c. It is more reason that we bishops should be troubled with them than the poor dean. Thus ceasing, I wish you in God ever well to fare. From Fulham, 15 Oct. 1563.

Yours in Christ,

EDM. LONDON.

I pray you hurt not your health with too much cogitation of evil successes of things[2], which are in God's hands, and without our compass. He knoweth how to direct them to the best end.

To the honourable Sir William Cecil, Knight, Secretary to the Queen's Majesty.

LETTER XXXVI.

TO SIR W. CECIL.

Nov. 12, 1563.

[Lansdown MS. 6. No. 79.]

Mr SAMPSON[3] of late sent unto me the copy of certain injunctions delivered him by my lord Keeper, (who is visitor of his house,) to be observed in the same till their book of

[1 Fecknam, late abbot of Westminster, was now under the care of Goodman, dean of Westminster.]

[2 The late miscarriage at Newhaven, and the plague which was now raging.]

[3 Dean of Christ Church, Oxford.]

statutes be fully finished⁴; but withal signified, that some of his house take exceptions against the said injunctions, as not being of sufficient authority, because they come not directly from the queen's majesty. The injunctions themselves are in my opinion very good; and are (so far as I can call to remembrance) an epitome of the best and most necessary orders, which my lord of Canterbury, I, and others have (as for the first view) allowed in their book of statutes. If your opportunity will serve, I suppose ye should do a very good act, when Mr Sampson repaireth unto you, to help him, that he may with sufficient authority from the queen's majesty or otherwise, as to your wisdom seemeth good, put these injunctions in execution. And when God shall send my lord of Canterbury and others to come to London, I trust we shall soon finish their book of statutes, which already is in a good forwardness. Thus, referring the rest to Mr Sampson's own report, I cease, and so commend you to the grace of God. From Fulham, 12 Novemb. 1563.

Yours in Christ,
EDM. LONDON.

To the Honourable Sir William
Cecil, Knight, Secretary to
the Queen's Majesty.

LETTER XXXVII.

TO SIR W. CECIL.
Dec. 20, 1563.
[Lansdown MS. 6. No. 85.]

I PRAY you, if it chance any suit to be made for one Evans to be bishop of Llandaff, help to stay it, till some

[⁴ "His church [Christ church, Oxford] as yet had no fixed statutes: the want of which created great disorders there, and occasioned too much liberty to such as were popishly affected in that college. Which was so well foreseen, that by the queen's orders before now the archbishop, our bishop, and some other civilians of the ecclesiastical commission, were appointed to frame statutes for the said church: wherein he and they had made some good progress; but the archbishop being

examination be had of his worthiness. If any means might be found, that things wickedly alienated from that see might be restored, it were well. If any competency of living might be made of it, I would wish it to Father Coverdale[1], now lately recovered of the plague. Surely it is not well that he, *qui ante nos omnes fuit in Christo*[2], should be now in his age without stay of living. I cannot herein excuse us bishops. Somewhat I have to say for myself; for I have offered him divers things, which he thought not meet for him. Your gone the last year to his diocese in visitation, and other businesses intervening, the work was not gone through with." Strype, Grind. p. 119.]

[1 Miles Coverdale wrote the following letter to Cecil upon his appointment by Bishop Grindal to St Magnus, London:

(Lansdown MS. 7. No. 60.)

My duty considered in right humble wise unto your honour. These are in like manner to beseech the same, that whereas my lord of London, tendering as well mine age, as my simple labours in the Lord's harvest, hath very gently offered me the pastoral office and benefice of St Magnus in London; even so it may please your honour to be means for me to the queen's most excellent majesty, that, in favourable consideration, not only how destitute I have been ever since my bishoprick was taken from me, and that I never had pension, annuity, or stipend of it these ten years and upward, but also how unable I am, either to pay the first fruits, or long to enjoy the said living, I going upon my grave, not able to live over a year; her majesty at the contemplation hereof, may most graciously grant[3] me the first fruits of the said benefice, which her highness, nevertheless, might needs have again anew when I am gone. Heretofore, (I praise God for it) your honour hath ever been my special help and succour in all my rightful suits. If now, that poor old Miles may be provided for, it please your honour to obtain this for me, I shall think this "enough" to be unto me "as good as a feast." Thus most humbly beseeching your honour to take my boldness in good part, I commit you and all yours to the gracious protection of the Almighty.

From London, 6 Februarii, [1564.]

MILES COVERDALE, *quond. Exon*[4].

To the Right honourable Sir Willliam Cecil, Knight, Chief Secretary to the Queen's most excellent Majesty, and of her highness' most honourable council.]

[2 Who was in Christ before us all.]

[3 Grant: forgive, remit.]   [4 Formerly Bishop of Exeter.]

warrant in Hatfield park, or Enfield chase[5], would serve my turn very well. God keep you!

From Fulham, 20 Decembr. 1563.

Yours in Christ,
EDM. LONDON.

*To the Honourable Sir William
Cecil, Knight, Secretary to
the Queen's Majesty.*

LETTER XXXVIII.

TO SIR W. CECIL.
Dec. 27, 1563.
[Lansdown MS, 6. No. 86.]

THE bishop of Carlisle[6] hath often complained to me for want of preachers in his diocese, having no help at all of his cathedral church. Sir Thomas Smith is his dean, occupied in the queen's majesty's affairs, as ye know[7]. All his prebendaries (Sewell only excepted, who is discredited by reason of his inconstancy) are ignorant priests, or old unlearned monks. One of the said unlearned prebendaries is lately departed, and the bishop writeth to me to help, as I may, the bringer Mr Scot, being that countryman born, well learned, and of good zeal and sincerity, as partly I know by mine own experience. And therefore, bold to trouble you in all such cases, and thinking that this man shall do much good in my country, I commend his cause unto you, which indeed is God's cause. I know the nature of my countrymen. I believe horse-flesh hath not been spared for prevention; but if it may be stayed for this man, I believe he shall do the most good. I have also been bold to commend him to my lord Keeper, doubting whether the presentation pertain to his office, being a prebend of the new erection, and in value just £20, as I am informed. As I trust his

[5 For venison. See Letter XXV.]
[6 Bishop Best.]
[7 Sir T. Smith was at this time ambassador in France.]

A.D. 1563. lordship will be good, if it pass from him, so I pray your help, if it pass from the queen's majesty; and so commend you to the grace of God.

From my house at Fulham, 27 Decemb. 1563.

Yours in Christ,

EDM. LONDON.

To the Honourable Sir William Cecil, Knight, Secretary to the Queen's Majesty.

LETTER XXXIX.

AD UTENHOVIUM[1].

Martii 25, 1564.

[Ex Biblioth. Londino-Belg.]

SALUTEM dico. Martinus iste famulus meus in vestram ecclesiam recipi cupit, ut qui nostram linguam non satis calleat, quum sit Coloniensis. Quid intelligat de religionis nostræ principiis, vos examinatione facile potestis cognoscere. Quod ad vitam et mores attinet, plane vixit apud me jam integrum fere annum satis honeste ac temperanter, ut nihil in illo criminis aut ipse aut mei unquam deprehenderent. Oro igitur ut in cœtum vestrum recipi possit. Vale.

Ex ædibus nostris Paulinis, 25° Martii, 1564.

EDM. LONDON, tuus.

Translation.

TO UTENHOV.

MINISTER OF THE DUTCH CONGREGATION.

I WISH you health. Martin, my servant, desireth to be received into your church, as not well enough understanding our language, being a man of Cologne. What he under-

[1 "Having an honest servant, a German by birth, who could not well understand English, the bishop by a letter to Utenhovius recommended him to be received into their congregation, upon his said servant's desire." Strype, Grind. p. 140.]

standeth of the principles of our religion, you may easily know by examination. As to his life and manners, indeed he hath now lived with me almost a whole year honestly and soberly; so that neither I nor mine have ever seen any crime in him. I pray therefore that he may be received into your congregation. Farewell.

From my house at Paul's. Mar. 25, 1564.

Yours,

EDM. LONDON.

LETTER XL.

TO SIR W. CECIL.

Oct. 12, 1565.

[State Paper Office.]

Sir,—I have received from my lord of Canterbury certain advertisements concerning Malta, &c[2]. I perceive you wish some public thanksgiving to be had on Sunday next. I am of opinion, that it were good to defer it eight days longer; and that for two causes: one is, that more certainty

[[2] "The Turks, with a great army, had long besieged Malta by sea and land; a place of great import, lying near Sicily and Italy, and was, as it were, the key of that part of Christendom. Therefore a form of prayer was used every Wednesday and Friday, in the city and diocese of London, for the deliverance of that place and those Christians. Now about the month of October joyful news was brought, that the Turks, with all their forces, were beaten off, and gone with great loss, shame, and confusion. This occasioned great joy and triumph in Christendom; and England joined with the rest in its resentments of this good news. The archbishop had given the secretary certain advertisements about it; as that it were convenient to turn their prayers now into praises, and that some public thanksgivings should be made to God in St Paul's church; and that the bishop of London should, against the next Lord's day, appoint an office to be used for that occasion. And of the same judgment was the secretary. And so he wrote to our bishop. But the grave man was not for doing it in such haste, for fear of some after-clap of news, which might clash with and confute the first tidings." Strype, Grind. p. 152.]

of the news may be known, which by this advertisement seemeth to me uncertain. It were less inconvenient to defer a week, than to make solemn gratulations, if the matter hereafter prove untrue; as in this case of Malta, and the birth of queen Mary's first son[1], hath heretofore appeared. Another cause is, for that nothing in this short time can be devised and printed for that purpose. If you resolve otherwise with Mr Watts the bringer, I will do what I can; but I distrust the news. God keep you!

From my house at Paul's, 12 Oct. 1565.

Yours in Christ,
EDM. LONDON.

LETTER XLI.

TO SIR W. CECIL.
May 4, 1566.
[State Paper Office.]

SIR,—I HAVE thought good to advertise you of things passed of late. One Bartlett, a reader of a divinity lecture in St Giles' parish without Cripplegate, notwithstanding he was suspended with the rest, took upon him to read again without licence. I sent for him, and willed him to surcease, seeming to offer impunity for the matter past, so he would promise silence for the time to come. He refused so to promise, alleging that in conscience he was forced to instruct the ignorant desirous to learn, and now destitute, &c. Whereupon I, with two other commissioners, yesterday afternoon committed him to his own house, where he still remaineth. This day before noon came into my house three-score women of the same parish to make suit for him: to whom I sent answer, that I would not in such case deal with such numbers of women, as much misliking such kind of assembling; but willed them to send me half-a-dozen of their husbands, and with them I would talk.

[1 See Strype, Memor. III. i. 343.]

One Mr Philpott, who is also suspended, but of more quiet disposition than some other, hearing of it came to my house, and persuaded them to depart. His authority was greater with them than mine could have been; otherwise I feared I should have prayed aid of some magistrate of the city: but by Mr Philpott's persuasion they went away quietly, but yet so as with tears they moved, at some hands, compassion.

By this beginning I suppose ye will consider of that I moved you; which is, that some assistance of the council must be had in execution of these matters, if ye will have them to take effect. On Wednesday next 1 hope to see you at the Star-chamber, or sooner, if ye come to your house at the Strand. I shall then further open mine opinion herein. God keep you! From my house at Paul's, 4° Maii, 1566.

Yours in Christ,
EDM. LONDON.

LETTER XLII.

TO SIR W. CECIL.

June 4, 1566.

[State Paper Office.]

Sir,—I send this bringer unto you to declare a womanish brabble that happened yesternight in a church in London, so far forth as I can yet understand of it. This afternoon I will examine the matter further. I pray you, send me your warrant for a buck in Camps park[2]. If my name be in the warrant, and not the scholars, peradventure it will be the better served. I pray you also be a mean to the Queen's majesty, at some convenient time, that all ministers, now to be deprived in this querele[3] of rites, may be pardoned of all the payments of first-fruits, due after deprivation. The statute pardoneth fruits only upon evection, and not upon resignation or deprivation. This suit seemeth to me reasonable and charitable. 1. For first the Queen's majesty shall be

[2 See Letter XXV.]   [3 *querela*: complaint.]

intituled to new fruits of the successors. 2. The deprived must needs confess, that great clemency is used towards them. 3. Some evil tongues shall be bridled thereby, which otherwise, peradventure, would say that the prosecuting of this matter is for some gain, to get double fruits, both of the predecessors and successors. I pray you consider of the matter as you think good. God keep you! 4° Junii, 1566.

Yours in Christ,
EDM. LONDON.

LETTER XLIII[1].

TO ARCHBISHOP PARKER.

Jan. 13, 1567.

[Strype, Grind. p. 153.]

SALUTEM in Christo. Whereas your grace putteth me in remembrance for the state of my cure[2], I heartily thank your grace. In very deed my purpose was, after this week ended, (wherein I take some physic for my health,) to have

[1 The reader is referred to the volume of the Zurich Letters, Parker Society, for several letters of Grindal of the dates undermentioned.

Letter		
73	To H. Bullinger	27 Aug. 1566.
75	To ditto	6 Febr. 1567.
76	To ditto	8 Febr. 1567.
79	To ditto	21 June, 1567.
81	To ditto	29 Aug. 1567.
82	To ditto	11 June, 1568.
85	To ditto	13 Aug, 1569.
87	To ditto	18 Febr. 1570.
90	To ditto	31 July, 1570.
100	To ditto	25 Jan. 1572.
112	To ditto	31 July, 1573.
113	To Rodolph Gualter	31 July, 1573.]

[2 Notwithstanding the clergy of London had been the last year so spurred up to conformity, many of them were still backward towards it. Insomuch that the archbishop warned the bishop about this matter; and giving him notice of a session of the ecclesiastical commission at Lambeth, advised him to be there; and the rather, in order to the dealing with some ministers of his own diocese. Strype, Grind. p. 153.]

prayed your grace's advice and aid for the same. For I must confess, that I can hardly reduce things to conformity, if I deal in it alone. On Friday afternoon, by God's grace, I will attend; wishing that my lords of Winton and Ely may be there. I suppose it best to have no appearance that day, but only to confer *de modo rei peragendæ*[3]. I wish your Chancellor present to direct us in matters of law. Wood the Scotchman is a factious fellow, as I shall declare to your grace at my next coming.

God keep your grace! 13 January, 1566. [1567.]

Your grace's in Christ,

EDM. LONDON.

LETTER XLIV.

TO SIR W. CECIL.
May 30, 1567.

[State Paper Office.]

SIR,—I HAVE caused the book which the stranger brought me to be considered. It containeth thirty Homilies of Chrysostom, upon the eleven first chapters of Genesis. I take the book to be of Chrysostom's writing undoubtedly; for it agreeth with the Latin translation set forth by Œcolampadius, in the 5th tome of Chrysostom's works in Latin. This difference there is; the Latin book hath sixty-seven Homilies, and this Greek book but thirty[4].

I think the book worthy to be presented to the Queen's majesty, both for the author's sake, and for the rarity, (seeing the Greek copy is not in print to my knowlege,) and for the fair writing, &c. For recompensing of the party, I cannot say much. That resteth much in her Majesty's estimation of such presents, and her good inclination to mag-

[3 As to the mode of conducting the matter.]

[4 There are extant sixty-seven Homilies in Greek, but many of the MSS. contain only the first thirty. This is the case in one MS. in New Coll. Libr. Oxford, and also in another, and that the most valuable, in the Bodleian. See Eton Edition of Chrysost. 1613. Tom. VIII. notes, p. 1.]

nificency. I suppose my lord of Canterbury will not extend his liberality so far as shall satisfy the bringer, if the book were presented to him. And thus having uttered mine opinion, as ye willed me, I commend you to the grace of God. 30 Maii, 1567.

Yours in Christ,
EDM. LONDON.

To the Honourable Sir William Cecil, Knight, Secretary to the Queen's Majesty.

LETTER XLV.

TO SIR W. CECIL.
Nov. 19, 1567.
[State Paper Office.]

Sir,—This poor scholar, bringer hereof, being an Irishman, and zealous towards his country, hath heard say that one Mr Dorrell is like to be primate of Armagh, which he thinketh will hinder the course of religion in that country. Surely I myself am of the same opinion; for the said Dorrell hath been heretofore convented before me and other commissioners for sundry his misdemeanours, and therefore I know him to be an unfit man for so high an office. I pray you therefore be a means, as much as you may, that some learned man, of grave and godly disposition, may be placed there, who by doctrine and good example may win people to Christ. I once commended unto you Doctor Spencer, parson of Hadley. If it pleased the Queen's majesty that my lord of Canterbury were sent to, he might bill three or four grave men, whereof her Majesty might make choice. Those men that sue for bishoprics do in that declare themselves unmeet for the room. I refer the whole matter to your further consideration.

God keep you! 19° Novemb. 1567.

Yours in Christ,
EDM. LONDON.

To Sir William Cecil, Knight, Secretary to the Queen's Majesty.

P. S. If it would please you to talk a little with the bringer, it might somewhat encourage him. I have good hope that he shall one day be a profitable minister in his country.

LETTER XLVI.

TO MR EARL,
MINISTER OF ST MILDRED'S, BREAD STREET.
Jan. 10, 1568.
[Strype, Grind. p. 178.]

WHEREAS we understand that divers disordered persons[1], not regarding their due obedience to the Queen's majesty and her laws, have heretofore, and yet do presume to preach in the city of London, not being thereunto licensed, neither by the most reverend father in God, Matthew archbishop of Canterbury, nor me the bishop of London: notwithstanding also, that divers of the said unruly preachers have been by us, the Queen's majesty's commissioners for causes ecclesiastical, expressly commanded in her highness's name to forbear the office of preaching, until such time as they were thereunto licensed by ordinary authority: forasmuch as this contemptuous and licentious behaviour tendeth to a very evil example, and also may breed division and tumults among her highness's subjects; which appeareth to be specially sought by these disobedient persons:

We have therefore thought good by these presents, in her Majesty's name, straitly to charge and command you, that from henceforth ye permit not any person to preach in your church, but such as shall have licence in writing from

[1 " Some ministers, who, for their refusal of conformity, were not permitted any longer to preach or officiate publicly, did notwithstanding take the liberty to do both, and that in private assemblies; whereby a breach was made in Christian communion. For the better preventing of this, it was thought fit to permit none to preach in London, without licences taken forth from the archbishop of Canterbury, or bishop of London. And all the ministers in the city, who had benefices therein, were enjoined by letters from the bishop not to suffer any unlicensed preachers to come into their pulpits." Strype, Grind. p. 178.]

the said most reverend father, or me the bishop of London; and the same licence to be dated upon or since the first day of March, 1564, as you and every of you will answer to the contrary. And that forthwith, upon the receipt hereof, you cause a vestry to be had in the church, and then and there to give knowledge thereof among the rest of the parishioners: so as from time to time, at any alteration of churchwardens, they may have knowledge thereof, and the like charge given unto them. And hereof fail ye not. Given the 10th day of January.

<blockquote>
Your friends,
EDM. LONDON,   D. HUGHS.
D. LEWIS,   THO. YALE.
THO. HUYCKE[1].
</blockquote>

LETTER XLVII.

TO ARCHBISHOP PARKER.
Feb. 23, 1568.
[MSS. Corp. Christ. Coll. Camb. cxiv. 194.]

AFTER my most hearty commendations to your grace. Whereas the bearer hereof, Thomas Walker, parson of Shadwell in Essex, lying upon Thames side, by reason of the evil air of the marshes and oozes there, being sometimes fresh and sometimes salt, hath been for more than five years past much afflicted and troubled, for that he, his wife, or some of his children or family continually have been, two or three of them at once, sick both of quartan and tertian agues, and also of other diseases and infections which have grown of the corrupt air there; and therefore of necessity shall be compelled to remove his wife and children from thence, and himself to be a perpetual sickly man, if he should, as he is bound by law, continually reside there: his suit therefore unto your grace is, that ye will be so good lord unto him, as to grant him a licence of non-residence for six or seven years, if he live so long, that he may lie here in

[1] Ecclesiastical Commissioners.

London, from whence he may at all times have daily passage by water to his benefice. And he will be bound unto your grace (if ye shall require it), that he shall (if he be able by reason of his health) every month once, at the least, go to and visit his said benefice, and instruct his parishioners there, and shall procure his church by a meet minister to be duly served. The man is very well known unto me to be honest, godly, and one that of conscience will have regard to his cure, and is able sufficiently well to exhort and instruct the same.

Wherefore I desire your grace favourably to consider of his suit, the rather at my request. And he shall be bound to pray for your grace during his life. Thus I commend your grace to Almighty God. From my house at London, the 23rd of February, 1567. [1568.]

Your grace's in Christ,
EDM. LONDON.

LETTER XLVIII.

TO SIR W. CECIL.
May 8, 1568.
[Lansdown MS. 10. No. 44.]

Sir,—I send you herewith letters from Mr Dean of Paul's. My man shall attend for answer as you shall appoint. Our men are all returned out of Scotland[2]; and, so far as I can learn, make no preparation to go thither again. In the mean time they cease not here from their old practices and assemblies. It may please you to consider, whether they are to be called again before you to know their meaning. One of them, named Evans, who is thought a man of more simplicity than the rest, hath reported (as I am credibly informed) that at Dunbar, on Good-Friday, they saw certain persons go bare-footed and bare-legged to the church, to creep to the cross. If it be so, the church of

[2 Some of the puritans, who could not be prevailed upon to conform, had gone into Scotland. They shortly however returned, not finding things there to their minds. See Strype, Grind. p. 179.]

Scotland will not be pure enough for our men. They are a wilful company. God grant them humble spirits!

God keep you! 8° Maii, [1568.] From my house at Paul's.

Yours in Christ,
EDM. LONDON.

*To the Honourable Sir William
Cecil, Knight, Secretary to
the Queen's Majesty.*

LETTER XLIX.

TO SIR W. CECIL.
May 11, 1568.
[Lansdown MS. 10. No. 45.]

Sir,—I send you herewith the articles inquired of the last search for strangers; and a remembrance what I wish to be considered now.

I send also a proclamation, set forth in the second year of the Queen's majesty's reign; all which peradventure may minister occasion of matters to be thought upon now.

It appeareth also by these, that the matters now complained of have heretofore from time to time been regarded.

God keep you! 11mo Maii, 1568.

Yours in Christ,
EDM. LONDON.

To Mr Secretary.

THE ARTICLES OF INQUIRY FOR STRANGERS.
[Lansdown MS. 10. No. 46.]

Articles inquired of in the search for the number of strangers within the city of London, and about the same, in the months of November and December last past, viz. in anno Domini, 1567.

1. First, You shall inquire how many strangers and aliens, as well men, as women and children, are dwelling and

resident, or abiding within your several parishes; and of what nation they be.

2. Item, How long every of them have been dwelling or abiding there; and what the names of every of them are; and about what time every of them came first hither.

3. Item, Of what trade, living, or occupation they be of; and how many of them are vehemently suspected or defamed of any evil living, or to be setters forward or favourers of any naughty religion or sect.

4. Item, Whether they do resort to their parish churches, to hear divine service, and to receive the sacraments, as others of the parishioners do, or are bound to do.

5. Item, How many of them absenteth themselves from their said several parish churches; and what their names be.

6. Item, How many of them resort to their churches appointed for strangers here in the city of London.

THE BISHOP'S REMEMBRANCE CONCERNING STRANGERS.

I wish that the conclusion of this order of strangers may be, that all such as shall be found culpable, or vehemently suspected either of heresies or errors, or of other grievous crimes, as treasons, murders, felonies, or other such like, committed before their coming over into this realm; and also all others of the French and Dutch nation (those only excepted which are known merchants, and intend not continually to remain here), which adjoin not themselves to the French or Dutch church in London, or else, understanding our language, do not orderly resort to the parish church where they dwell, shall be commanded to depart the realm within twenty days next after warning given to them by the archbishop, or mayor, &c.

THE QUEEN'S PROCLAMATION AGAINST STRANGERS.

The Queen's majesty, understanding that of late time sundry persons, being infected with certain dangerous and pernicious opinions in matters of religion, contrary to the faith of the church of Christ, as Anabaptists, and such like,

A.D. 1568. are come from sundry parts beyond the seas into this her realm, and specially into the city of London and other maritime towns, under the colour and pretence of flying from persecution against the professors of the gospel of Christ: whereby, if remedy be not speedily provided, the church of God in this realm shall sustain great danger of corruption, and sects to increase contrary to the unity of Christ's church here established:

For redress whereof, her Majesty, by advice of her council, having commanded the archbishop of Canterbury, bishop of London, and other bishops to see the parishes in London, and other places herewith suspected, to be severally visited, and all persons suspected to be openly tried and examined, touching such fanatical and heretical opinions; willeth and chargeth all manner of persons born either in foreign parts or in her Majesty's dominions, that have conceived any manner of such heretical opinion as the Anabaptists do hold, and meaneth not by charitable teaching to be reconciled, to depart out of this realm within twenty days after this proclamation, upon pain of forfeiture of all their goods and chattels, and to be imprisoned, and further punished, as by the laws either ecclesiastical or temporal in such case is provided.

And her Majesty also chargeth and commandeth upon pain of imprisonment, that no minister, nor other person, make any conventicules or secret congregations, either to read or to preach, or to minister the sacraments, or to use any manner of divine service; but that they shall resort to open chapels or churches, and there to preach, teach, minister, or pray, according to the order of the church of England, except it be in cases of sickness, or where noblemen, and such others, that have in all former times been accustomed to have divine service said in their oratories within their houses, for divers necessary respects; upon pain that whatsoever persons or company shall make such secret conventicules, every person to be imprisoned without bail or mainprize, until the coming of the justice for delivery of the same gaols, and then to be punished by their directions.

Yeven at our castle of Windsor, the 22nd day of September, the second year of our reign, MDLX.

LETTER L.

TO ARCHBISHOP PARKER.
July 2, 1568.
[MS. C. C. Coll. Camb. cxiv. 195.]

SALUTEM in Christo. I am desired by my very good friends, Sir Peter Carew and Sir John Chichester, to pray your grace to grant dispensation of non-residence to one John Wolton[1], preacher. I hear very good of the man, and his desire is to have dispensation, not for that he intendeth to neglect his cure, (for he is reported to be a man of very good conscience,) but that he may more freely preach abroad in your grace's province, and elsewhere, and yet to avoid the danger of the promoters[2], who are most busy against the best men. In consideration whereof, I pray your grace to shew favour to the said Wolton concerning the premises, which I nothing doubt but he will use to the more ample setting forth of God's glory. God keep your grace!

From my house at London, this second of July, 1568.

Your grace's in Christ,
EDM. LONDON.

LETTER LI.

TO SIR W. CECIL.
Sep. 15, 1568.
[State Paper Office.]

SALUTEM in Christo. I thank you that you disposed otherwise for the cardinal Châtillon[3]. No man could have

[1] In all probability the same individual, who was afterwards bishop of Exeter. Grindal ordained him both deacon and priest in the first year of his episcopate, and afterwards consecrated him to the see of Exeter, August 2, 1579. See Strype, Grind. p. 359.]

[2] Informers. See Strype, Ann. II. i. 92.]

[3] Odet de Coligni, brother of the admiral of France. He fled to England on account of religion, being a favourer of the protestant faith. He

been more welcome unto me; but surely I lack provision of lodging for him, or any other guest of like honour. I observe one canon well of the council of Carthage: "*Oportet Episcopum habere vilem supellectilem*[1]." If he be to be further assigned, I pray you spare me; for surely I lack convenient furniture. To-morrow I intend to go to London to salute him. I trust the Queen's majesty will draw nearer London shortly, that I may write to you and send to you oftener. The next week (God willing) I intend to visit my lord Keeper. God keep you! From Fulham, 15°. Septemb. 1568.

Yours in Christ,
EDM. LONDON.

To the Honourable Sir William Cecil, Knight, Secretary to the Queen's Majesty.

LETTER LII.

TO SIR W. CECIL.

Oct. 25, 1568.

[State Paper Office.]

SIR,—I HEAR that the Portugal Ambassador hath sent to the Court to inform of matters done in and about his house yesterday; and fearing least he have not uttered all the truth, I have thought good to advertise you, both of

---

He arrived at the Tower Wharf, Sept. 13, 1568, in company with the bishop of Arles, and was honourably received by Sir Thomas Gresham, and some eminent citizens of London. He lodged the first night with Sir Thomas, and probably Grindal had received some communication from Cecil relative to his further entertainment. In the year 1570 he was poisoned by his own servant, and was honourably buried in Canterbury Cathedral. See Strype, Annals, II. i. p. 353. See also Thuani Histor. Lib. L. c. 13. Tom. III. p. 65.]

[1 'A bishop ought to have mean furniture.' Concil. Carthag. iv. (A.D. 398.) Can. xv. Ut episcopus vilem supellectilem et mensam ac victum pauperem habeat, et dignitatis suæ auctoritatem fide et vitæ meritis quærat. Concilia, Tom. II. col. 1201, Paris, 1671.]

mine own doings, and of the constable's doings, so far as I can learn by examining of the said constable. For the first, I and other commissioners, hearing of resort of English men and women to mass there, gave a warrant to the constable to apprehend such English persons as should be vehemently suspected to come from mass, not authorising him to enter into the house; and therefore his going into the house (the circumstances whereof appear by his own confession sent herewith) was more of zeal than good discretion.

Afterwards, when the Ambassador kept all the Englishmen secretly in his house, the mass ended, being certified thereof, I willed the constable to watch aloof from the house, till I had sent to my lord Keeper to know his pleasure; which I did. My lord Keeper sent two of his gentlemen to the ambassador, requiring him to send all the English persons in his house to his lordship, and then the said ambassador (as the said gentlemen in their return by my lord's order informed me), the Ambassador denied that there were any English folks in his house; how truly, I cannot tell. And so about four o'clock in the afternoon the said constable and his watch were willed to depart, every man to his house. Thus much concerning myself and the commissioners. The constable's doings with the circumstances thereof cannot be better known than by his own confession upon the examination of him and other. This is the fact, so far as I can learn; the judgment thereof I refer to your wisdom[2]. The poor constable standeth in great fear of his life: it may please you to have consideration thereof, as you shall think good. God keep you! From my house at Paul's in London, 25º. Octob. 1568.

Yours in Christ,

EDM. LONDON.

To the Honourable Sir William
   Cecil, Knight, Secretary to
   the Queen's Majesty.

[[2] A similar occurrence took place at the Ambassador's house in the year 1576. See Strype, Ann. II. 24—30.]

LETTER LIII.

TO SIR W. CECIL.
July 24, 1569.
[State Paper Office.]

Sir,—I moved her Majesty yesterday for the Savoy[1], where we have appointed to sit on Wednesday next. I declared to her Highness, that the master of the Savoy had converted great sums of money to his own private use, which ought to have gone to the relief of the poor. I prayed her Majesty, that we might proceed to the removing of the master; because I would be loth that the cry of the poor should [James v. 4.] "enter into the ears of the Lord of Sabaoth." Her Majesty was desirous to be informed more particularly in the matter, and then I should understand further of her pleasure. I told her Highness, I had sent a note thereof to you, which she said she was desirous to see. I pray you, therefore, shew her Majesty the notes and letter, which I wrote to you about ten or twelve days ago concerning that matter. I doubt

[[1] The Savoy hospital in the Strand had once been a foundation for the relief and entertainment of poor travellers. It was first built by Peter, duke of Savoy; and, having been destroyed by the rebels of Kent, it was founded anew by Henry VII. It was afterwards suppressed in the reign of Edward VI., and again restored and supplied with beds and furniture for the use of the poor in the 4th year of queen Mary. The rules and statutes of this last foundation are extant among the MSS. in the British Museum. The master, Thurland, had grievously abused his trust by fraudulent sales of goods, illegal leases, and alienation of lands, overcharges, neglect of the poor, besides being guilty of dissolute living and contempt of divine service. In consequence of these irregularities, a commission was appointed to visit the hospital, and to investigate the charges brought against the master. This commission, after due examination, proceeded to deprive him, July 29th, 1570. Still the matter was not entirely settled. For Thurland seems to have had some powerful interest at court, and in the year 1574 was in expectation of recovering the mastership; on which occasion Grindal, then archbishop of York, wrote to the secretary, earnestly praying his interference. See Strype, Grind. pp. 234—239, and 531—534.

This and the two following letters are, for the sake of convenience, placed together, although not belonging to the same year. See also another letter on the same subject, dated April 26, 1574.]

not but they remain among your bills. I pray you take some pains in it. The poor people shall pray to God both for the Queen's majesty and for you, if a better patron be provided for them.

I send the bringer also to attend upon your leisure for my commission. God keep you, and send you health! From Barnet, this Monday morning, being 24º. of July, 1569.

Yours in Christ,

EDM. LONDON.

Postscript. I perceive her Majesty is very favourably inclined towards the master of the Savoy; but I wish the same should appear some other way than by retaining him in that room.

LETTER LIV.

TO SIR W. CECIL.
April 21, 1570.
[Lansdown MS. 12. No. 81.]

Sir,—I HAVE sent my servant Richard Ratcliff, bringer hereof, to attend upon you from time to time, and to solicit for prosecution of the matter intended toward me[2]; referring the whole to your order, as your leisure and opportunity shall serve.

I send also herewith a bill exhibited unto me touching the abuse of the Savoy. If the matters be true (as they are by some of the fellows of that house affirmed to be), it were good some reformation were had. God keep you!

From London, 21º Aprilis, 1570.

Yours in Christ,

EDM. LONDON.

*To the Honourable Sir William
   Cecil, Knight, Secretary to
   the Queen's Majesty.*

[[2] His translation to the see of York, which in his register is dated May 1st.]

LETTER LV.

TO SIR W. CECIL.
July 27, 1570.
[State Paper Office.]

Sir,—I have yet deferred the final order of the Savoy till Saturday next, hoping that the master (whose conscience I have sore burdened with expectation of God's indignation, if he shew not himself penitent for spoiling Christ in his poor members) will on Saturday next resign. If not, we will either proceed to a conditional deprivation, leaving the confirmation thereof to her Majesty, or else continue the visitation, till my lord of Canterbury, who is now at Lambeth, may deal with her Majesty in it, or otherwise. If your opportunity serve to move her Majesty's conscience in it, *ut fiat justitia*[1], especially in such a pitiful case, ye should do a very godly act.

I must depart northward on Wednesday next[2], and can no more in the mean deal with any public cause. I have caused my lord of Carlisle's bill for the benefice in reversion to be drawn by advice of some learned in the law, which I pray you to prefer. I pray you also obtain a small vicarage for a good preacher: the presentation is sent herewith. I have also sent herewith the survey of Broxburn, which came yesterday first to my hands.

I most heartily thank you for your good prayer to God for me in discharge of mine office: and I beseech God give me grace so to do; for I perceive I have to do with a strange people. I suppose I may say with St Paul, *Ostium mihi magnum apertum est, et adversarii multi*[3]; but I refer myself wholly to God's good providence. [1 Cor. xvi. 9.]

In the business moved by Dr Youngman of Cambridge, my lord of Canterbury shall be able to ease you well. Mine opinion is (as I have written unto you before) that they are only to be bridled by authority. And if they do not revoke

[1 That justice may be done.]
[2 Viz. to York, to which diocese the bishop had recently been appointed.]
[3 A great door is opened unto me, and there are many adversaries.]

their factious assertions, let them be expelled the University, for terror to others. And although Cartwright would revoke, he is never to be permitted to read again in the University; for he hath a busy head, stuffed full of singularities.

Thus I cease at length to trouble you, and commend you most heartily to the grace of God.

From Westminster, 27° Julii, 1570.

To the Honourable Sir William Cecil, Knight, Secretary to the Queen's Majesty.

Yours in Christ,
EDM. LONDON.

LETTER LVI.

TO SIR W. CECIL.

Aug. 3, 1569.

[Lansdown MS. 11. No. 61.]

SIR,—I HAVE sent inclosed letters to certify my lords and you of the council, that I can do no good with Sir John Southworth[4] for altering his opinion in religion. Besides my travail with him, Mr Dean of Paul's, requested by me, hath conferred with him very oft, and hath also used much courtesy and humanity towards him, and not without charge; which in reason might be a mean to move the said Sir John somewhat to relent. But the man is altogether unlearned, carried with a blind zeal without knowledge. His principal grounds are: "he will follow the faith of his fathers: he will die in the faith wherein he was baptized, &c." At the instant request of the said Sir John Southworth I have licensed him to repair to the court, to sue unto your honours that he may be employed in some service. My lord of Ely, at the instant suit of me and others, hath granted the use of his house in Holborn to Mons. Vidame[5] till Michaelmas,

[4 A Lancashire knight, a papist, and concerned in seditious movements about this time. See Strype, Grind. 204, and Parker I. 525—527.]

[5 John de Ferriers, Vidame of Chartres. He narrowly escaped in the massacre at Paris in 1572. Strype describes him as "a great nobleman of France, and of chief account among the protestants, a learned and very good man." Strype, Grind. p. 206. See also Annals II. i. 249, and Parker II. 125.]

[GRINDAL.]

A.D. 1569. that he come himself. If anything be said in it, I pray you let us have your patrociny[1]. I have received two packets of letters from my lords, one for search of certain Irishmen[2], which now is in hand; the other for examinations about the supposed monster[3], which shall be prosecuted with as much speed as may be. God keep you!

From Fulham, 3° Augusti, 1569.

Yours in Christ,

EDM. LONDON.

*To the Honourable Sir William
   Cecil, Knight, Secretary to
   the Queen's Majesty.*

LETTER LVII.

TO SIR W. CECIL.
Aug. 15, 1569.

[Lansdown MS. 11. No. 63.]

SIR,—HEARING that ye would repair to London this day, I am bold to send you answers to certain letters sent me from my lords and you of the council.

1. For the monster, it appeareth plainly to be a counterfeit matter; but yet we cannot extort confession of the manner of doings.

2. For Whyte and Creygh the Irishmen I caused search to be made, but they were gone afore.

3. The mayor of Winchelsea, being found conformable in religion, was set at liberty, and referred for other matters to my lord Cobham.

4. Mr Dean of Paul's would not gladly be troubled any more with Sir John Southworth; for he will neither come at prayer nor sermon. I am bold in my letters to make a motion to my lords to spare his imprisonment for a time; for the prison sicknesses reign usually at this time of the year.

[1 Patrociny: *patrocinium*, patronage.]

[2 Suspicious persons, at this juncture especially, when there were jealousies of some insurrections at hand. Strype, ubi supr.]

[3 Set up, as it seems, by some papists, the more at this time to amuse the people. Ibid.]

Milerus, the Irishman in my custody, is very sick of an ague: this letter inclosed[4] he wrote to you thirteen days ago, but I forbare to send it you till now. Thus ceasing to trouble you, I commend you to Almighty God. From my house at Fulham, 15° Augusti, 1569.

A.D. 1569.

Yours in Christ,
EDM. LONDON.

LETTER LVIII.

TO SIR W. CECIL.
Sept. 9, 1569.

[Lansdown MS. 11. No. 64.]

SIR,—As I doubt not but ye have heard of Dr Bonner's[5] death, so think I it good to certify you of the order of his burial. The said Dr Bonner had stand excommunicate by a sentence in the Arches eight or nine years, and never desired absolution. Wherefore by the law christian sepulture might have been denied him: but we thought not good to deal so rigorously, and therefore permitted him to be buried in St George's church-yard[6]. And the same to be done not in the day solemnly, but in the night privily: which I and some others, with whom I conferred, thought requisite in that person, for two causes. One was, I heard that divers his popish cousins and friends in London assembled themselves, intending to honour his funeral so much as they could: of which honour such a persecutor was not worthy, and specially in these days. Another was, for that I feared that the people of the city (to whom Bonner in his life was most

[4 Milerus was an Irish priest, committed to the custody of the bishop of London. The letter was written in Latin with this title, "Preclarissimo domino Willielmo Cecilio primario secretario Regiæ Majestatis, domino meo semper observatissimo." See Strype, Grind. p. 207.]

[5 Edmund Bonner late bishop of London. See Strype, Annals I. ii. 298.]

[6 In Southwark.]

A.D. 1569. odious) if they had seen flocking of papists about his coffin, the same being well decked and covered, &c., they would have been moved with indignation, and so some quarrelling or tumult might have ensued thereupon. By his night-burial both the inconveniences have been avoided, and the same generally here well liked. What shall be judged of it at the court, I cannot tell; it is possible the report of his burial shall not there be made truly: but this I write unto you is the very truth.

I pray you, be so good as to hear what the bringer hereof, Mr Colpotts, fellow of the King's college in Cambridge, can say concerning the miserable state of that house, through the misgovernment of an evil provost[1]. He hath of late, contrary to the orders of all the houses of the town, set up a junior regent to be proctor, and repelled a senior, much more meet both for religion, learning, wisdom, and experience. And furthermore, because four of the youngest fellows would not give their voices at his appointment, he denieth them their grace in the house to be bachelors of art, notwithstanding that they are very well learned; and so be-like intendeth to expel them the college. All his study is to oppress learning and religion. Truly it grieveth my heart, that such an honourable foundation should be so abused. I pray you be a mean one day that it may be reformed. And for the particular case of the proctorship, if the University at the election should choose the senior regent to be proctor, and so restore him to his place, which the provost and his adherents had

[[1] The provost was Dr Philip Baker, against whom certain grave misdemeanours were objected, viz. that he was a papist himself, and a harbourer of notable papists; that he had declined to obey the injunctions given by the bishop of Lincoln in a visitation, A.D. 1565, preserving some relics of popish superstition, which by those injunctions he was bound to remove and destroy; that he discouraged the study of divinity, and was negligent of his own duties in the college; that he never preached, neither at home nor abroad, weltering in idleness, and wholly serving mammon; that he dealt fraudulently with the property of the college, &c. &c. He was deprived by the Queen's commissioners on the 22nd of February in this year; and through Grindal's intercession was succeeded by Roger Goad, B.D. Baker was said to have fled to Louvain, then the great receptacle for the deprived English clergy, who adhered to the papacy. See Strype, Grind. pp. 210—216, and Whitgift I. 34, 35.]

by wrong taken from him in his college, it should not be against the good meaning of the composition², in mine opinion. And I pray you to shew favour to the senior, as occasion may serve. God keep you! From Fulham, 9° Septembr. 1569.

A.D. 1569.

Yours in Christ,
EDM. LONDON.

P. S. My grapes this year are not yet ripe: about the end of the next week I hope to send some to the Queen's majesty.

To the Honourable Sir William
Cecil, Knight, Secretary to
the Queen's Majesty.

LETTER LIX.

TO SIR W. CECIL.
Sept. 20, 1569.
[Lansdown MS. 11. No. 65.]

SIR,—ACKNOWLEDGING myself always most bounden unto you, I will, according to the request of your late letters, labour to compound and finish the controversy between the Spanish and French preachers so soon as possibly I can. There are some impediments of expedition at this present; partly because I cannot well finish this matter, except I myself remained at London two or three days, whither I am somewhat loath to go hastily, for that the plague is most stirring near my house there; and partly because the French preacher buried one out of his house of the plague, the 15th of this month. I will send for Corranus³, the Spanish preacher, and talk with him first, and after with the other parties. If any thing be offered

[² i. e. the composition between King's college and the University.]

[³ "There was now in London one Corranus, a Spaniard, and native of Seville, preacher to an assembly of Spanish protestants, though he himself was a member of the Italian congregation, to which one Hieronymus was preacher....A contest this year arose between this man and Hieronymus; the occasion whereof seemed in part to be this. Corranus of late had caused a table, entitled *De Operibus Dei*, wrote by him in French, to be printed in Norwich, not offering the same to be examined

A.D. 1569. to Corranus on my part that is too hard, I am well contented to refer the moderation thereof to your judgment. True it is that Corranus hath good learning; but I have no good liking of his spirit and of his dealings, whereof I have had good experience. And because I perceive ye have not been informed where the original fault was, so soon as I can, I purpose to send you some notes of the beginning and process thereof[1]; thus much only signifying in the mean time, that

here before it was printed. But the minister and seniors of the Italian church had misliked certain doctrines contained in the said table, wavering, as it seems, somewhat from the opinions of Calvin; and therefore they had admonished Corranus to answer the same before them....The French church also before this had contested with him, and many high words had passed between them. Hereupon sprang up a great dissension between the said Spaniard, and Cousin the French preacher, and the elders of that church: for they gave him no countenance, but required his revocation of his principles, and submission. But Corranus thought himself injured by the minister and some of the elders, and refused them....He wrote no less than seven letters to Beza, together with an apology, relating his own case, and foully accusing not only the French minister Cousin, and divers of the members of that church, but the whole bench of elders....Beza did not like the hot accusing spirit of this Spaniard, nor did he think fit to take the deciding of the case to himself; but in the beginning of March laid the business open to the bishop of London, and withal sent him Corranus's letters," referring the matter wholly to his judgment. This happened in the year 1568. The bishop was again disturbed by the controversy in the following year. Corranus had found influential friends at court, and amongst the number secretary Cecil, who in a letter to the bishop commended his learning, and hinted that he thought too hard terms were put upon him, and prayed him to compound the controversy as soon as possibly he could. See Strype, Grind. pp. 185 and 218.]

[1 "The beginning and rise of the controversy between Corranus and the French church was not so plain to the secretary. Of which therefore the bishop sent him this account, viz. Anno Dom. 1563 a packet of letters was directed to a French merchant of London, being a member of the French church: and under the direction were written words to this or like effect; *For matters of great importance touching the church of God.* In the said packet was found a letter from Antonius Corranus, the Spanish preacher, then being in France, written to one Cassiodorus, another Spanish preacher, not long before remaining in London. The said Cassiodorus, being accused of a grievous crime, fled the realm upon the accusation, no man knew whither. The said packet directed as above was brought to the minister and seniors of the French church, who after some consultation, considering that the title was, *For matters*

upon sundry judicial hearings of the matter the fault was by sentence pronounced to be in Corranus. For restitution of Corranus to his preaching or reading, there is now lately a new difficulty arisen. Corranus of late hath caused a table, which he wrote in the French tongue, intituled *de operibus Dei*[2], to be printed at Norwich; not offering the same to be examined here before it was printed.

The minister and seniors of the Italian church in London, (whereof Corranus is a member,) mislike the doctrine contained in the said table, and therefore have monished the said

of God's church, concluded to open the said packet, and also to break up the letter directed to Cassiodorus. And finding no public matter in it, but only for the impression of the Spanish bible, they wrote answer to Corranus, that Cassiodorus was departed out of this realm, and, as they thought, was gone into Germany. And by chance, (as should seem,) rather than of any purpose, they kept still Corranus's said letter in their custody. After the great troubles in Antwerp, Corranus came to London, and desired to be admitted into the French church. The consistory called him before them, and burdened him with the said letters; which ministered great occasion of suspicion, (as they thought,) that the said Corranus did not think well in some principal articles of Christian religion. He answered, that his letter was written by way of questioning, and not of affirmation. They replied, that such kind of questioning was not meet in these times for a minister of God's church; but in the end offered, that if he would subscribe to true doctrine, and acknowledge that those letters were *imprudenter scriptæ*, he should be received into the church. Corranus answered, that the letters were written in good and lawful manner; and that he did not repent the writing of them; and that he would (if need were) set them out in print, with a defence or apology annexed. Whereupon the minister and seniors of the French church would not receive him. Corranus thinking himself injured herewith, and offended with certain speeches uttered by some of the French church in Lombard-street, [where merchants met before the Exchange was built,] and at tables in London, (as he often declared unto the bishop, who always advised him to contemn them,) wrote a pamphlet, which he called *an Apology*, but indeed a sharp invective, containing many slanders against the ministers and seniors of the French church, and also sundry untruths of the bishop's own knowledge. Which Apology was communicated unto divers, and a copy thereof sent to Beza, to Geneva. It was long and tedious; and the principal points of it were contained and answered in a letter of Beza to Corranus; which is published among his epistles. Whereupon the ministers and elders complained against Corranus, before the bishop and commissioners ecclesiastical, for defamation, as was said before." See Strype, Grind. pp. 219, 220.] [2 On the works of God.]

A.D. 1569.

A.D. 1569. Corranus to answer for the same before them. Thus much Hieronymus, the Italian preacher, told me sithence the receipt of your letters. If the controversy with the French (which is only about offence in manners) be compounded, I cannot see but his restitution to reading or preaching must be deferred, till he have cleared himself before the governors of his own church in matters of doctrine, which is a matter of far greater moment. I do not yet know the particular matters; but I have willed Hieronymus, the Italian preacher, to translate the said table into Latin, and to send me a copy, that some conference may be used in it. Thus much for Corranus[1].

I hear that some fault is found with me abroad, for sending my servant lately to the court with grapes, seeing one died in my house of the plague, (as they say,) and three more are sick. The truth is, one died in my house the 19th of this month, who had laid but three days; but he had gone abroad languishing above twenty days before that, being troubled with a flux, and thinking to bear it out, took cold and so ended his life. But I thank God there is none sick in my house; neither would I so far have overseen myself, as to have sent to her majesty, if I had not been most assured that my man's sickness was not of the plague; and if I suspected any such thing now, I would not keep my household together, as I do. Thus much I thought good also to signify unto you.

God keep you! From Fulham, 20 September, 1569.

Yours in Christ,

EDM. LONDON.

To the Honourable Sir William
Cecil, Knight, Secretary to
the Queen's Majesty.

[1 "At length, by the favour chiefly of the earl of Leicester, but not before Grindal was removed to York, Corranus brake through these clouds. For in the year 1571 he was preferred to be reader of divinity in Latin at the Temple; and some years after he read divinity at Oxford, having first purged himself of certain doctrines formerly charged upon him: and becoming a member of the church of England, obtained a prebend of St Paul's church, London; and having published several tracts, died, and was buried in London about the year 1591." See Strype, Grind. p. 221.]

JUDICIUM EPISCOPI LONDINENSIS,

DE ANTONIO CORRANO[2].

Junii 5º, 1567.

QUIA ad nonnullos (uti accepimus) fama pervenit, quosdam occasione literarum quarundam privatim scriptarum suspiciones concepisse de domino Antonio Bellerivo Corrano Hispano, nuper ecclesiæ Montargiri erectæ in Galliis ministro, et postea ab ecclesia Antverpiana accersito; quæ quidem suspiciones, post dicti domini Antonii ad nos adventum, multorum sermonibus in nostris pariter ac transmarinis ecclesiis jactatæ, non nihil creverunt: Nos, concordiæ et pacis ecclesiasticæ conservandæ, et famæ dicti domini Antonii tuendæ studio permoti, eum accersivimus, et cum eo, adhibitis aliquot piis ac doctis viris, de illis christianæ religionis capitibus, de quibus in suspicionem aliquam venerat, diligenter contulimus; et ex collatione cum illo habita plane intelleximus, dictum dominum Corranum ab omnibus impiis dogmatibus alienum esse, et de religione christiana bene ac pie sentire, puramque evangelii doctrinam, quam nostra aliæque ecclesiæ reformatæ profitentur, ex animo amplexari. Et quia nobis abunde satisfecit, ut et aliis etiam omnibus satisfiat, dominoque Corrano fama sua maneat integra, conceptæque suspiciones omnium animis eximantur, isti [ista] hoc scripto, apud omnes qui illud lecturi sunt aut audituri, testata esse volumus. Dato quinto die mensis Junii, 1567. Anno regni sereniss. Elizabethæ, Angliæ, Franciæ, et Hiberniæ Reginæ, nono.

EDM. LONDON.

(Appenso magno sigillo, cum effigie D. Pauli, cera rubra.)

[[2] This document is taken from a very rare tract, entitled "Acta Consistorii Ecclesiæ Londino-Gallicæ, cum Responso Antonii; ex quorum lectione facile quivis intelligere poterit statum controversiæ inter Jo. Cusinum, ejusd. Ecclesiæ Ministrum, et Ant. Corranum Hispanorum peregrinorum Concionatorem. Anno 1571." This tract contains the letter of Corranus to Cassiodorus, alluded to in a former note, p. 310, which occasioned the suspicions of the orthodoxy of Corranus, and which Bishop Grindal alludes to in this judgment. It would seem that the bishop had judged too favourably of Corranus.]

Translation.

THE BISHOP OF LONDON'S JUDGMENT IN THE MATTER OF CORRANUS.

A. D. 1567. WHEREAS it has been reported to sundry persons, as we have heard, that some, on account of a certain letter privately written, have conceived suspicions concerning master Antonius Bellerivus Corranus, a Spaniard, lately minister of the church at Montargis in France, and afterwards called by the church at Antwerp; which suspicions, after the arrival of the said master Antonius amongst us, being talked of by many in our own, as well as in the churches beyond sea, have considerably increased: We, moved with the desire of preserving the concord and peace of the church, and of defending the good fame of the said master Antonius, have cited him before us, and have diligently conferred with him, in the presence of some pious and learned men, on those points of christian religion, concerning which he had fallen under some suspicion; and, from the conference had with him, we have plainly understood, that the said master Corranus is averse from all impious opinions, and that he entertains right and pious sentiments concerning christian religion, and embraces from his heart the pure doctrine of the gospel, which our own and other reformed churches profess. And since he has abundantly satisfied us, that all others also may be satisfied, and that his character may remain unimpeached, and the suspicions which had been conceived may be removed from the minds of all, we wish these things to be testified by this writing unto all who may read or hear it. Given on the 5th day of June, 1567, in the 9th year of the reign of her most serene majesty, Elizabeth, queen of England, France, and Ireland.

EDM. LONDON.

(The great seal was appended, with the image of St Paul, in red wax.)

LETTER LX.

TO SIR W. CECIL.
Oct. 22, 1569.
[Lansdown MS. 11. No. 68.]

SIR,—I THANK you that ye are desirous to hear of my health. I thank God, I am well, *pro meo more*[1]: and my household is also well. I have not written to you of late, because I would not trouble you, being otherwise occupied in affairs of greatest importance. I, and such other poor men, pray daily unto God, that he may give unto my lords and you of the council the spirit of wisdom and fortitude, that ye may *bene explicare consilia*[2], for the Queen's majesty's safety and surety. Yesternight I received a letter from London, wherein were written these words following:

"The bishop of Ross[3] mustered this day in Paul's church, in a gown of damask, with a great rout about him, and attending upon him, as it were to be seen and known to the world, &c."

What may be gathered of such doings, I refer to your judgment.

I have done for the chancellor of Peterborough as you wished me. I pray you, help to get me discharged of mine Irish guest[4], whose petition I send you herewith. In mine opinion (under your correction) it were good he were sent by a pursuivant at his charge to my lord deputy, there to be ordered as you shall send instructions, or as my lord deputy and the lord chancellor and bishops of the council there shall think requisite. Cyprian would have things judged in the countries where the faults be committed. God keep you! From my house at Fulham, 22° Octob. 1569.

Yours in Christ,
EDM. LONDON.

To the Honourable Sir William
Cecil, Knight, Secretary to
the Queen's Majesty.

[1 After my manner.] [2 Successfully accomplish your counsels.]
[3 John Leslie, queen Mary's agent in England. He was continually endeavouring to promote her cause by fomenting rebellions in England, and kept up a secret correspondence with the pope for that purpose. Strype, Grind. 222.]
[4 Milerus. See p. 307.]

LETTER LXI.

TO THE LORDS AND OTHERS OF THE PRIVY COUNCIL.
Jan. 4, 1569.
[Lansdown MS. 12. No. 28.]

It may please your lordships to be advertised, that I have received your letters of the 29th of December last, and withal a bill exhibited to your lordships for maintenance of singularity in religion, in certain disordered persons[1]. In which

[1 The chief teachers of these separatists were Bonham and Crane; who at these house-meetings did use to preach and expound the scriptures, to baptize, administer the communion, marry according to the Geneva book, and withal very vehemently would inveigh against the government and religious usages of the Church of England: for which they had been taken up, but obtained their liberty again; yet with some promise to carry themselves with more moderation and forbearance for the future. This promise they broke: whereupon Bonham was taken up again by the bishop's order, and Crane was forbid to preach any more in his diocese.

Upon this, the Londoners of their party were much displeased with Grindal, and took the confidence to make a complaint against him to the Privy Council, as though he had broke his word with them. To this tenor ran their supplication to the council:

"We beseech your honours for God's cause favourably to consider of these few lines. The effect is to certify you, that whereas a certain of us poor men of the city were kept in prison one whole year for our conscience sake, because we would serve our God by the rule of his holy word, without the vain and wicked ceremonies and traditions of papistry; and being delivered forth the 23d of April last past, by authority of the honourable council's letter, as the bishop declared to us all at his house the third of May, saying, that means had been made to your honours for our liberty; the effect thereof, he said, was, that we were freed from our parish churches, and that we might hear such preachers whom we liked best of in the city: also, whereas we requested to have baptism truly ministered to our children according to the word and order of the Geneva book; he said, that he would tolerate it, and appoint two or three to do it; immediately after, at our request, he appointed two preachers, called Bonham and Crane, under his hand-writing to keep a lecture.

"But now of late, because Bonham did marry a couple, and baptize one of our children by the order of the said book, which is most sincere, he hath commanded him to be kept close prisoner; and Mr Crane also he hath commanded not to preach in his diocese.

"By these means were we driven at the first to forsake the churches,

letters also your lordships require to know, in what sort I A.D. 1569.
have heretofore proceeded towards them, and also to know,
what order in mine opinion is best to be taken with them.

For the first. In April last past, I wrote my letters to
Mr Secretary, declaring unto him, that if the said disordered
persons were then after a year's imprisonment, simply and
without condition, set at liberty, saving only an earnest admonition to live in good order hereafter; both I, and many
other that were their friends, and yet conformable subjects,
had conceived very certain hope, that taste of liberty and
experience of your clemency should in time work good
obedience in them, which by compulsion of imprisonment
could not be wrought; and that, if by trial it were found, that
this proceeding did no good, then might they easily be committed again. The motion of these letters shewed unto your
lordships was approved by the same, as appeareth in your
letters of the 28th of the said April; wherein also your
lordships referred the order of them to my discretion. I
thereupon, calling the principals of them, read unto them your
letters, wherein, amongst other things, is contained this admonition following:

"*Letting them understand, when you shall release them, that
if any of them, after their enlargement, shall behave
themselves factiously or disorderly, they shall not fail
to receive such punishment, as may be an example to
others of their sort hereafter: and so with such further*

and to congregate in our houses. Now we protest to your honours, we
never yielded to no condition in our coming forth of prison, but minded
to stand fast in the same sincerity of the gospel, that we did when we
were in prison, approved and commanded of God in his word. And
therefore we humbly beseech your honours to let us have your furtherance and help in so good a cause: that our bodies and goods be no more
molested for standing in this good purpose, which we most heartily
desire to see flourish throughout this realm, to God's high honour, the
preservation of your honourable personages, and safeguard of this realm."

Hereupon the lords wrote a letter to the bishop, and sent withal the
said supplication. The accusation wherewith they had charged him in
their supplication touched the reverend father somewhat closely: for
therein he saw they had wrongfully represented his doings with them,
and thereby dealt very ingratefully with him, who had used gentleness
and mercy towards them; hoping by that means the better to bring
them off from their singularity. See Strype, Grind. pp. 226—228.]

A.D. 1569. *admonition as you shall think convenient, your lordship may deal with them, as you shall see cause."*

And after the reading of your said letters, with further and earnest admonition by me given to like effect, in the presence of a good number, I caused them to be enlarged.

And herein your lordships may easily perceive how untruly these men burden me. For how could I say, that your lordships had exempted them from the laws, when as by your letters, read unto them openly at that very instant, the contrary did manifestly appear? And whether I licensed Bonham or Crane to preach to them according to their phantasies, it may appear also by a promise made by the said Bonham[1], sent herewith in writing, before he had my license to preach; the said license being granted afore their enlargement, and not after, as they suggest. And furthermore, Crane was admitted only by word of mouth upon like promise. But now of late, perceiving that these disordered persons, and their preachers, did keep no promise, but began to enter into open breach of the laws and disturbance of good order, I have imprisoned and discharged some of them, as is alleged; and was appurposed now in the end of these holidays to deal with more of them to like effect, though your letters had not come. Wherein my lord of Canterbury and I have had divers conferences.

[1 A promise made by William Bonham, preacher:
"Memorandum, That I, William Bonham, do faithfully promise, that I will not at any time hereafter use any public preaching, or open reading, or expounding of the scriptures; nor cause, neither be present at, any private assemblies of prayer, or expounding of the scriptures, or ministering the communion, in any house or other place, contrary to the state of religion, now by public authority established, or contrary to the laws of this realm of England. Neither will I inveigh against any rites or ceremonies used or received by common authority within this realm."

"This promise was read and declared by the said William Bonham, before Thomas Huick, doctor of law, and vicar general to the right reverend father in God, Edmund, bishop of London, at his house in Pater-noster Row, in London, the first day of May 1569. For the performance whereof, the said William Bonham hath faithfully promised for to observe the same; being also at present at the reading thereof, Thomas Jones, deputy to Mr Bedell, clerk to the Queen's majesty's commissioners for causes ecclesiastical."]

But now that the matter is opened unto your lordships, and that by their own means, mine opinion is, that all the heads of this unhappy faction should be with all expedition severely punished, to the example of others, as people fanatical and incurable: which punishment, if it proceed by order from your lordships, shall breed the greater terror. And because all prisoners, for any colour of any religion, be it never so wicked, find great supportation and comfort in London, in my opinion, (under your lordships' correction,) it were not amiss that six of the most desperate of them should be sent to the common gaol of Cambridge, and six likewise to Oxford, and some other of them to other gaols near hereabouts, as to your wisdoms shall be thought expedient. The names of those that were enlarged by me, I send to your lordships in a schedule annexed. And thus, praying pardon for troubling your lordships with so long a letter, I commend your good lordships to Almighty God, who ever have you in his blessed keeping! From my house at Paul's in London, this 4th of January, 1569.

A.D. 1569.

Your lordships' in Christ,

EDM. LONDON.

To the Right Honourable my very good Lords, my Lords and others of the Queen's Majesty's most Honourable Privy Council.

LETTER LXII.

TO THE LORDS OF THE PRIVY COUNCIL.

Jan. 14, 1569.

[Lansdown MS. 12. No. 30.]

It may please your good lordships to be advertised, that Michael Hare, Esq.[2], by order from your lordships, hath

[[2] Another Popish guest, put upon our bishop by the council about this time, was Michael Hare, Esq. whom they sent to him, November 15, with an order prescribed by them, and brought by those that were the

A.D. 1569. remained in my house sithence the 15th of November last, in which time I have conferred and travailed with him, (as my other businesses would permit me,) to persuade him to resort to common prayer, to communicate with us in the Lord's supper, and generally to assent to all points of godly religion by law established in this realm. Notwithstanding, finding the said Mr Hare in all other matters very courteous and tractable, I cannot yet persuade him hereunto, alleging always that he is not yet satisfied in conscience, and that for conscience sake only he doth forbear so to do, and not of malice. The principal ground whereon he most stayeth himself in all conferences is the long continuance of the contrary religion, in the times that have gone before; notwithstanding sundry allegations by me made, and divers authorities shewed, that the most ancient times agree with us. Thus much I thought it my duty to signify to your good lordships, according to the order prescribed me in your letters sent by those that brought the said Mr Hare unto me. Referring the rest to your wisdoms, and so ceasing further to trouble your lordships, I commend the same to the grace of Almighty God.

From my house at Fulham, this 14th of January, 1569.

Your Lordships' in Christ,

EDM. LONDON.

LETTER LXIII.

TO SIR W. CECIL.

Feb. 3, 1569.

[Lansdown MS. 12. No. 32.]

SIR,—I pray you most instantly to be a mean that I be not troubled with the bishop of Ross. He is a man of such quality as I like nothing at all. If needs I must have a guest, I had rather keep Mr Hare still. The dean of St Paul's, his wife and household, is at Hadham. He

bringers of the said Hare; which was to this effect; that the bishop should according to his prudence and learning deal with him to bring him to conformity in the religion established. Strype, Grind. p. 223.]

himself is commonly with me at meals. And if it please you to know mine opinion *in genere*, surely I think it were good that such as deserve to be committed should be sent *ad custodias publicas*[1]. Experience declareth, that none of those are reformed which are sent to me and others; and by receiving of them the punishment lighteth upon us.

God keep you! From my house at Paul's, this Sunday morning, between eight and nine, immediately after the receipt of your letter. 3° Febr. 1569. [1570.]

Yours in Christ,
EDM. LONDON.

To the Honourable Sir William
Cecil, Knight, Secretary to
the Queen's Majesty.

LETTER LXIV.

TO SIR W. CECIL.
Feb. 27, 1570.
[Lansdown MS. 12. No. 34.]

SIR,—I pray you give me leave to trouble you with a suit of such nature, as I have not used to trouble you heretofore; whereunto I am by necessity enforced for the benefit of three orphans, very near unto me in blood; praying you also to give me leave to open some part of the circumstances of my said suit, for the plainer understanding thereof.

So it is, that my only brother, Robert Grindal, of St Bees[2], in the county of Cumberland, and Elizabeth his wife, and Edmund Grindal, their only son, died all three within the space of three weeks, to my no small grief, about eighteen months ago. My said brother left four daughters orphans, and by testament made the second daughter, whose name is Anne Grindal, his sole executrix: wherein she had the possession of two leases, both by me obtained of Sir Thomas Challoner, knight, for the which also I paid the fines. The one lease is of the house wherein I was born, and the lands

[1 To the public prisons.] [2 MS. St Beghes'.]

A. D. 1570. pertaining thereto, being a small matter, under twenty shillings rent, but well builded at the charges of my father and brother. The other lease is of certain tithes of the parsonage of St Bees aforesaid. Now the said Anne Grindal, notwithstanding her father in his testament willed her in all things to be directed by me, clean contrary to my mind, and utterly against my will, married with one William Dacres, son of Richard Dacres, who dwelleth beside Carlisle, gentleman; which William Dacres (as I hear repeated, for I know no certainty thereof,) hath combined himself with Leonard Dacres, and others, in the late traitorous rebellion[1], moved in those parts. Now my suit is this, that if it fall forth that the said William Dacres, who married my niece, as is aforesaid, do forfeit his goods and chattels (for lands he hath none) to the Queen's Majesty, that you would be a mean to her Highness aforehand, for avoiding of prevention[2], that her Majesty would, of her gracious inclination, grant that the portions and interests, which the other three sisters, orphans, have, or ought to have, in the said two leases, may be reserved unto them. And also whatsoever may accrue to her Majesty by forfeiture or attainder of the said William Dacres, concerning the said two leases of the house and tithes aforesaid, that it would please her Majesty to grant me preferment of the same before another; paying to her Majesty, or any other by her Highness to be assigned, as much (and more) as the thing is worth. How much I am bound both in nature and in charity to make this suit, I trust you will consider. I pray you be a mean for me in it to her Majesty.

God keep you! From my house at Fulham, this 27th of February, 1569. [1570.]

Yours in Christ,
EDM. LONDON.

P. S.—I perceive the common opinion at St Bees is, that the forfeiture should fall to Sir Thomas Challoner's

[1 This Leonard was a younger son of William, lord Dacres, of the north. He raised a rebellion A.D. 1569, ostensibly to deliver the Scottish queen; but, as Strype asserts, in reality to gain possession of the estates of his elder brother. He was defeated by lord Hunsdon. See Strype, Annals I. ii. pp. 324—327.]

[2 Anticipation by others.]

executors, whereof I suppose you are one, by reason of charter of liberties, which the abbey there had, and Sir Thomas purchased: but I think no such liberty hath traitor's goods. If it fall with you, I pray you let me compound with you.

To the Right Honourable Sir William
Cecil, Knight, principal Secretary
to the Queen's Majesty.

LETTER LXV.

TO SIR W. CECIL.
June 24, 1570.
[State Paper Office.]

Sir,—I am to move you for the University of Cambridge, which if you help not speedily, your authority will shortly grow to great disorder. There is one Cartwright, B.D.[3], and Reader of my Lady Margaret's Divinity Lecture, who, as I am very credibly informed, maketh in his lectures daily invections against the extern policy and distinction of states in the ecclesiastical government of this realm. His own positions, and some other assertions which have been uttered by him, I send herewith[4]. The youth of the University, which is at this time very toward in learning, doth frequent

[3] Thomas Cartwright, of Trinity college, and reader of the lady Margaret's lecture, had carried away a considerable number of scholars with him, and brought them to a dislike of the present settlement of the ecclesiastical state: insomuch that the graver sort, and heads of the university, were mightily disturbed, and had convented him before them. Some of them thought it convenient also to make their application to the archbishop; who hereupon wrote thus earnestly to the secretary of state, their chancellor, shewing also particularly what his doctrines were. Strype, Grind. p. 240.]

[4] Cartwright's positions, written and delivered by him to the vice-chancellor, were as follows:
Archiepiscoporum et archidiaconorum nomina suspecta sunt.
1. Archiepiscoporum, archidiaconorum, cancellariorum, commissariorum, etc. (ut hodie apud nos sunt) munera apostolica institutione non nituntur, cui restituendæ quisque pro vocatione sua studere debet; intelligo autem id 'pro vocatione sua,' ut magistratus auctoritate, ecclesiæ

his lectures in great numbers; and therefore in danger to be poisoned by him with love of contention and liking of novelties, and so become hereafter not only unprofitable, but also hurtful to the church. The Vice-chancellor and heads of houses proceed not so roundly in this case as were requisite, in my judgment. For reforming whereof, if it please you to know my opinion, I wish you wrote your letters to the Vice-chancellor with expedition, willing him to command the said Cartwright with all his adherents to silence, both in schools and pulpits; and afterward, upon examining and hearing the matters past, before him and some of the heads, or all, either to reduce the offenders to conformity, or to proceed to their punishment, by expulsion out of their colleges, or out of the university, as the cause shall require: and also, that the Vice-chancellor do not suffer the said Cartwright to proceed doctor of divinity at this commencement, which he now sueth for: for, besides the singularity above rehearsed, the said Cartwright is not conformable in his apparel; contemning also many other laudable orders of the university. Thus I cease to trouble you, and commend you heartily to the grace of God.

From St Paul's, June 24, 1570.

Yours in Christ,

EDM. EBOR[1].

To the Honourable Sir William
Cecil, Knight, Secretary to
the Queen's Majesty.

ministri verbo, singuli eam promoveant. Ita tamen ut nihil tumultuarie aut seditiose fiat.

2. Ministrorum electio quæ apud nos est ab institutione apostolica deflexit: cui restituendæ, sicut prædictum est, singuli studere debent. Nolim autem me putet quispiam omnes damnare, tanquam a ministerio alienos, qui ad illam institutionem hactenus non fuerint cooptati.

Other assertions uttered at other times by the said Cartwright:

1. That he himself, being a reader of divinity, is a *Doctor* exercising the office named, Ephes iv., and therefore must only read, and may not preach.

2. No ministers are to be made, nor no pastors to be admitted, without election and consent of the people.

3. He that hath a cure may not preach, but only to his own flock. With many other such falsities.

[[1] Grindal was translated to the see of York May 1st, 1570, and was installed by proxy, June 9th.]

LETTER LXVI.

TO SIR W. CECIL.
Aug. 29, 1570.
[State Paper Office.]

SALUTEM in Christo.—The 17th of this month I came to this house, clearly delivered of mine ague, and so continue at this present in good health, I thank God. I stand in doubt of this air of Cawood[2], for it is very moist and gross. Bishopsthorp is said to be an extreme cold house for winter; yet, because I would be near York, to deal in matters of commission, I purpose to remove thither at Michaelmas. I was not received with such concourse of gentlemen at my first coming into this shire, as I looked for. Sir Thomas Gargrave, with his son, Mr Bunnie, Mr Watterton, one of the Savyls, and four or five more gentlemen, met me near unto Doncaster, and brought me unto Sir Thomas his house, where I lodged one night; and the next day met me all my church, Mr Ask, Mr Hungate, and four or five more inferior gentlemen, and brought me to Cawood. Notwithstanding, divers have come to me sithence, and excused themselves for sickness of themselves or their families; as Sir William Babthorp, Mr Slingsby, Mr Goodrick, Mr Beckwith, and some others. And indeed agues are universal throughout all this country. Sir Henry Gates was then with my lord lieutenant in the north, and will be with me this night.

I cannot as yet write of the state of this country, as of mine own knowledge; but I am informed that the greatest part of our gentlemen are not well affected to godly religion, and that among the people there are many remanents of the

[2 "On the 1st of August, 1570, I left London; two days after I was seized on my journey with a tertian ague, arising from fatigue, (for during my residence in London I had not been accustomed to riding on horseback,) on which account I was forced to rest ten days in the midst of my journey. At length, on the 17th of August, I arrived at Cawood, where I have a palace on the banks of the Ouse, about seven miles from the city."—Grindal to Bullinger. Zurich Letters, No. C. p. 258. Parker Soc.]

A.D. 1570. old¹. They keep holydays and fasts abrogated: they offer money, eggs, &c. at the burial of their dead: they pray on beads, &c.: so as this seemeth to be, as it were, another church, rather than a member of the rest. And for the little experience I have of this people, methinketh I see in them three evil qualities; which are, great ignorance, much dulness to conceive better instructions, and great stiffness to retain their wonted errors. I will labour, as much as I can, to cure every of these, committing the success to God. I forbear to write unto her Majesty of these matters, till I may write upon better knowledge. In the mean time I shall not cease in my daily prayers to commend her Majesty to Almighty God.

God keep you! From Cawood, this 29th August, 1570,
Yours in Christ,
EDM. EBOR.

To the Honourable Sir William
Cecil, Knight, Secretary to
the Queen's Majesty.

LETTER LXVII.

TO ARCHBISHOP PARKER.
Aug. 28, 1571.
[Petyt MSS. 47. Fo. 38.]

SALUTEM in Christo.—According to the letters sent from your grace and my lords of Winton and Ely, I have sent for Mr Whittingham², and look for his appearance here within

[¹ Compare Letter C, of the Zurich collection, Parker Soc., p. 259, in which Grindal makes a similar statement to Bullinger.]

[² The archbishop of Canterbury, together with the bishops of Winton and Ely, chief of the ecclesiastical commissioners for the province of Canterbury, had been called upon by the queen to have regard to uniform order in the church, and to reform abuses of such persons as sought to make alteration in what was established. Many of these were ministers who enjoyed benefices and places of profit in the church, and yet lived not in obedience to the rules and injunctions of it. The men of this rank of the most fame were, Goodman, Lever, Sampson, Walker, Wyburne, Goff, Whittingham, Gilby. These the said commissioners thought very fit to convent before them, and to press their duty upon them; and if they persisted in refusal of it, to deprive them. Some part of this work would lie upon the archbishop of York: for Lever, Whit-

these three days; and I will not fail to advertise you what his answers shall be to the matters objected, trusting to find conformity in him, because he subscribed concerning apparel in my predecessor's days, as I take it.

But as for Mr Gilby, I cannot deal with him; for he dwelleth at Leicester, out of this province, and much nearer to London than to York. I would gladly see Mr Goodman's book[3]. I never saw it but once, beyond seas; and then I thought, when I read it, that his arguments were never concludent, but always I found more in the conclusion than in the premises. These articles that your grace hath gathered out of it are very dangerous, and tend to sedition.

I thank your grace for the Book of Articles and Discipline[4]. I stand in doubt, whether they have *vigorem legis*[5], unless they had either been concluded upon in synod, and after ratified by her Majesty's royal assent, *in scriptis*, (for words fly away as wind, and would not serve us, if we were impleaded in a case of *premunire*,) or else were confirmed by act of parliament. I like the book very well; and if hereafter I shall doubt in any point, or wish it enlarged in any respect, I shall signify to your grace hereafter. If there be want of sufficient authority, it is yet well that the book is ready, and may receive more authority at the next parliament.

tingham (Dean of Durham), and Gilby, being of the north, and so of his province, were thought to fall under his cognizance. These two last had been exiles at Geneva in the days of queen Mary, and the heads of those that then opposed the Communion book. Whittingham was he that had wrote a preface before that dangerous wild book of Goodman, against the lawfulness of women's government, and exciting the deposing of queen Mary. Strype, Grind. p. 252.]

[3 The title of this book was, "How superior powers ought to be obeyed of their subjects, and wherein they may lawfully be disobeyed and rejected; wherein also is declared the cause of all this present misery in England, and the only way to remedy the same. By Chr. Goodman. Printed at Geneva, by John Crispin, MDLVIII." For an account of this tract, see Strype, Ann. I. i. 181—185.]

[4 Liber quorundam canonum disciplinæ ecclesiæ Anglicanæ. See Sparrow's collection, p. 240. "These canons, though subscribed by the bishops of both provinces, wanted the queen's ratification. The queen was acquainted with what passed in the synod, and approved the proceedings; but, as it happened, the royal assent was not given in form." Collier, Eccl. Hist. Vol. II. p. 500. Ed. 1840.]

[5 The force of law.]

A. D. 1571.   The day of Nevill's feast[1] I cannot yet learn. The records here have been kept very negligently; but I will cause further search to be made. I suppose my lords of Winton and Ely will be gone home before the receipt hereof: if not, I pray your grace that I may be heartily commended unto them.

I received a written book from Mr Bullinger against the Bull[2]. Like copies, I perceive, were sent to my lords of Ely and Sarum[3]. I doubt not but your grace hath seen it. I stand in doubt whether her Majesty and the council would be contented that it were published in Latin or English, or both. It is possible they would not have the multitude to know, that any such vile railing bull had passed from that see. I would be glad to know your grace's opinion in it. Thus I end, commending your grace to the custody of the Almighty.

From Cawood, being here to sit upon the subsidy. The 28th of August, 1571.

Your grace's in Christ,

EDM. EBOR.

[1 Archbishop Parker wanted now to know a particular (and one would think a slight) piece of history of the church of York: but such was his exactness in this kind of knowledge, that he sent twice to our archbishop to be informed about it; viz. what the punctual day was of that great and celebrated installation feast of archbishop Nevyl, brother to the great earl of Warwick, in Edward the Fourth's time, which was so extravagantly sumptuous and expensive, that the like had hardly ever been heard of. Perhaps the most splendid entertainments that that brave prelate had, or was about to make at Canterbury, occasioned this his inquisitiveness. Strype, Grind. p. 254.

Some idea of the sumptuousness of Nevyl's feast may be formed from the following specimen: "Fatted oxen, 80; sheep, 1004; calves, 400; geese, 3000; peacocks, 100; pigeons, 4000; roes, 400, &c. &c." Vid. Godwin, de præsulibus, ii. 275. Cambridge, 1743.]

[2 The celebrated bull of pope Pius V., in which he deposed the queen, absolving her subjects of their allegiance, and authorising them and all christian princes to take up arms against her. For a copy of the bull, see Cardwell, Doc. Ann. No. LXXIV. Vol. I. p. 328.]

[3 Bishops Cox and Jewel, who were well acquainted with Bullinger during their exile in queen Mary's days.]

LETTER LXVIII.

TO THE LORD TREASURER BURLEIGH[4].
Jan. 29, 1572.
[State Paper Office.]

SALUTEM in Christo.—My very good lord, your letters, dated the 15th of this instant January, I received at the hand of Anthony Stringer the 22nd of the same; by whose order I send you these of mine. The beginning and ending of your said letters, declaring the continuance of your old assured friendship towards me, were much to my comfort, and put me in assured hope, that I shall easily satisfy you for matters contained in the midst of the same, which are in number two; the one for Mr Webster's case[5], the other for Broxburn parsonage. I must crave pardon of your lordship, if I be longer in making mine answer, for plainer declaration of my mind in the said matters, than otherwise in reason I ought to be, your business in most weighty affairs considered.

First, for Mr Webster's case. I must plainly confess unto your lordship, that sithence I was called to the office of a bishop, and long before, I never liked the granting out of advowsons, or (as the ecclesiastical law termeth them) *expectationes*, and especially by ecclesiastical persons, for that they are by the said laws, very agreeable to reason, condemned

[4 In 1571, Sir W. Cecil was created Baron Burleigh, and shortly afterwards, lord high treasurer.]

[5 Toward the latter end of the year, the archbishop shewed his resolution, as well as his care of providing his church of York with worthy men. For a good prebend there this year falling void, the presentation to which fell in contest between three; viz. the archbishop, Webster, and Woodroff. The title Webster (who was by calling a cook) claimed by, was some pretended right of the next advowson made over to him by Young, the last archbishop; which, whatever it were, was lodged in Woodroff, by some conveyance from Webster to him. And perhaps neither of them were innocent of some unlawful dealings herein. But now Webster and Woodroff were themselves fallen to pieces about the right of presenting. The archbishop notwithstanding esteemed the true right to be in himself: and for this he had the judgment of the best lawyers. For whatsoever the former archbishop had done to the contrary, it was not in his power to grant away the advowson. Strype, Grindal, p. 254.]

A.D. 1572. as occasions of uncharitable affections and simoniacal pacts, and first practised in papacy, when it was grown to the greatest corruption. Secondly, for Mr Webster's advowson in particular, I did ever think that my predecessor did in that, as in some other things, *præter officium*[1], in taking away, as much as in him was, the nominating and presenting of a canon in his church from himself and his successors, bishops, who by common supposition are thought to be men learned, and most able to judge in such cases, and to grant the same to a master-cook, unlearned, and therefore less able to judge. It were more reason that every man should deal in his own faculty, according to the old proverb, *Tractent fabrilia fabri*[2]; and so likewise, *Tractent culinaria coci*[3]. So as Mr Webster's case, being both against a reasonable and good law, and having a corrupt original, both in my predecessor and himself, is a cause odious, and deserveth no favour before any judge. If Mr Webster be only desirous, as he ought to be, that a very good preacher should be placed in the prebend, then I have satisfied his good meaning; for I have placed a better preacher in it than he presented unto me, and such a one as, if he seek both the universities, he will hardly (of those that be unpreferred) find his like. If he have other indirect meaning, the same is not to be favoured. I was not ignorant that there was no great friendship between Mr Webster and Woodroff. But when Woodroff, (who neither hath, nor shall have, any commodity of the said prebend,) after I had refused one or two of his clerks, did simply offer to present such a one as I should nominate; then I thought that by God's providence that thing was restored unto me, which my predecessor, against all good order, had taken from me; and so (as I wrote in my last letters) I was content to follow St Paul's counsel, which is, to take benefit of all occasions, whereby [Phil. i. 18.] Christ may be the better preached; and yet for all that no injury done to Mr Webster. For if a man may trust either spiritual or temporal lawyers in these parts that I have talked withal, besides the common practice used here in like cases, Woodroff's presentation is good in law; and then, *qui suo jure*

[[1] Beside his duty.]
[[2] Let carpenters handle carpenters' tools.]
[[3] Let cooks deal with culinary affairs.]

utitur nemini facit injuriam[4]. And as for equity, it is all on my side, both for nominating the best, and for other causes before alleged. Thus much for Mr Webster's title.

Now, as touching the consideration of your lordship's request; surely, my Lord, the Queen's Majesty only excepted, there is no creature's request upon earth can weigh more with me than yours. And therefore, in all your requests made unto me, either at London or here before this, (which I confess have not been many,) I either did that you requested, or else satisfied your lordship by answer to your contentation, as I trust I shall do in this. In this matter your lordship's first letter came *quum res non erat integra*[5]: for Mr Roo, my chaplain, was then presented, and also under my hand and seal instituted; and so there was a right grown unto him, till law reverse it. How could I know aforehand that you would write for Mr Webster, much less that you would so earnestly write? The poor man that hath the possession of the prebend, fell into a double quartan about Hallowe'en-tide, and hath the single quartan still, and like to have till Midsummer, as a fruit of earnest study. He is studious, godly, learned, and eloquent. If your lordship knew him as I do, you would favour his case. I myself, in honesty and credit, cannot do and undo, nor in conscience remove the better and take the worse. Wherefore I am earnestly and heartily to pray your lordship, that ye will also have consideration of me in this matter, as well as of Mr Webster. Let it be his own matter, and none of your lordship's. He hath presented within the time of lapse; let him ask counsel of law above; it is a matter of short resolution and small suit. If this man be removed by order of law, both he and I will give place; and I will take order that every farthing of the profits shall be answered to him that prevaileth. My suit is, that your lordship will not require me to undo mine own act, which I am surely persuaded to be lawful, both in law and conscience, and that at Mr Webster's request.

For Broxburn, truly my lord, *coram Domino*[6], to the uttermost of my remembrance, (and I think I should not forget

A.D. 1572.

[4 He who uses his own right does injustice to no man.]
[5 When the matter was settled.]
[6 Before the Lord.]

any matter that so much pertaineth to yourself,) ye never moved me for any lease of Broxburn parsonage; for if ye had, or if I could but have conjectured that ye had been desirous of it, ye should have had all my furtherance to the uttermost. A terrier only ye desired of me, which I procured to be made for you of new, for old I had none. But it is well in one respect; for I have done nothing in it, that can prejudice your lordship. Thus standeth the case. Upon importune suit of Sir George Penruddock, and from the old Earl of Pembroke, I granted to the said Sir George twenty-one years in reversion, to begin after twenty-six or twenty-seven years of a lease, then in possession, were expired. I told Mr Penruddock oftentimes, that my grant in that case was void by statute, as it was, and is in deed. He was still importune to have it, with all faults; and so in the end I passed unto him a void grant. I think he hath yet twenty-four years to come in his old lease, granted by Bonner: if a reversion after that term may do your lordship pleasure, there be ways enow to bring it to pass; and sure I am, that my grant to Sir George cannot hinder the same by any means. My long writing in these matters argueth, that I am very desirous that your lordship should be fully satisfied.

My Lord, I am advertised from London, that certain are apprehended which had conspired your death[1]. God be thanked for your delivery! As this may be a warning for you to use all wariness and ordinary means for avoiding the like danger hereafter, as your own wisdom can well consider, so I take it to be a necessary warning for her Majesty. For she is the mark they shoot at, and at you and other of her council, for her sake. The number of obdurate papists and Italianate atheists is great at this time, both desperate and grown, as it evidently appeareth, to the nature of assassins. Wherefore I would wish that her Majesty should not be *tam facilis aditu*[2], as

[[1] The said lord Burghley, that wise statesman and sound counsellor of the queen's, in this dangerous juncture, was so hated by her enemies, but especially the Spaniard, that Borgest, that ambassador's secretary, had hired two desperate men, viz. Mather and Berny (alias Verny), to murder him; nay, and the queen too. They were executed in February, being hanged, drawn, and quartered. See Strype, Annals II. i. p. 124.]

[[2] So easy of access.]

she has been, especially to mean strangers; nor walk abroad so slenderly accompanied as she was wont; nor her privy gardens to be so common as they have been. I pray your lordship give me leave to be so bold, as to desire you to signify so much of my poor opinion to her Majesty; for whose preservation I daily pray to the Almighty; to whose grace and protection I also heartily commend your lordship.

From Cawood, 29° Januarii, 1571. [1572.]

Your lordship's in Christ,

EDM. EBOR.

LETTER LXIX.

AD HIERONYMUM ZANCHIUM FRAGMENTUM EPISTOLÆ.

[Harl. MSS. 416. No. 166.]

S. Ex postremis meis ad te literis, ad decimum octavum Decembris datis, intelligere potuisti, doctissime Zanche, causas extitisse justas et graves, cur de tuis ad regiam majestatem reddendis literis deliberationem mihi cum viris piis et doctis suscipiendam statuissem. Quamobrem liberatus illa, qua tum me impeditum dixi, prælonga et plena sollicitudinis circa Hispaniensem legatum cura, probatissimos quosque capiendi consilii causa adibam, exque iis, re coram explicata, quid ipsis videretur diligenter exquirebam. In iis et ecclesiastici ordinis viri lectissimi longeque principes, et regiæ majestatis consiliarii aliquot, et alii quidam magni judicii viri Deumque timentes, sententiam rogati, de literis minime exhibendis, pluribus in medium adductis rationibus, ad unum omnes statuerunt. Eorum autem ad quos nuperrime datis ad me literis scripsisti neminem prætermisi, cujus vel consilium diligenter percontando non petiverim, vel a quo, sive per literas, sive in congressu familiari, responsum in eandem sententiam non tulerim. Quas autem singuli sui judicii attulerunt rationes, eas sigillatim referre omnes et longum esset, nec fortasse expedit. Sunt qui dissentientium inter se partes non te recte perspexisse, alii ne rei quidem controversæ statum plene te percepisse, ex illis quas ad amicos quosdam scripsisti literis

A. D. 1572. non temere conjecturam facere videntur. Sed nec facilis forte erit explicatio.

Verum quo certius et melius e re nata negotii certitudinem, varietatem, magnitudinem, ipse tibi expiscari possis, conabor quidem sedulo, ut ab ipsis fundamentis, re paulo altius repetita, omnia tibi reddam quam explicatissima. Sic ergo habeto.

Quo primum tempore serenissima Elizabetha felicissimis auspiciis regni gubernacula susceperat, doctrina cultuque profligato papistico, ad eam administrandi verbi Dei sacramentorumque et totius religionis normam, quæ, regnante beatæ quidem sed et luctuosissimæ memoriæ Edwardo Sexto, in nostris ecclesiis descripta constitutaque fuerat, omnia revocavit. In hanc celeberrimo convocato concilio, quod pervulgata sermonis consuetudine *Parlamentum* vocamus, ab omnibus regni ordinibus plenis suffragiis assensum est. Hujus tanta est auctoritas concilii, ut quæ in eo scribuntur leges, illæ, nisi jubente eodem, dissolvi nulla ratione poterunt. Quare cum in hac ipsa, de qua jam dixi, olim a Rege Edwardo conscripta religionis forma, multa de vestiendi ratione ad ecclesiæ ministros proprie accommodata præcipiantur, deque rebus aliis, quæ vel aboleri vel emendari nonnulli viri boni cuperent, quo minus huic operi manum quispiam admovere potuit, legis auctoritate prohibebatur. Regiæ vero majestati, ut ex episcoporum quorundam consilio quædam immutare possit, lex ipsa concedit. At vero de lege nihil nec mutatum nec imminutum est. Nec sane episcoporum, quod sciam, quisquam reperitur, qui non et ipse præscriptis pareat institutis, et ceteris, ut idem faciant, ducem se suasoremque præbeat. Quamobrem, in quo ipsi tibi jam ante ultro concesserint, non est quod persuadendo magnopere labores, ut scilicet vel ipsi in sua maneant statione, vel Regina erga eosdem tergiversantes mitius se gerat. In eandem cum episcopis sententiam ceteri quoque ecclesiarum ministri, docti indoctique fere omnes, non invite concedere sane videntur.

Quædam desiderantur.

Doctrinam inconcussam hactenus illibatamque in nostris ecclesiis tenemus. A disciplina igitur cum omnis nostra defluxerit controversia, ista sunt de quibus queri plerumque

solet. In vestitu ministrorum communi ex præscripto requi- A. D. 1572.
ritur vestis talaris, pileum quadratum, colloque circumducta
stola quædam ab utroque humero pendula, et ad talos fere di-
missa. In publicis precibus omnique administratione sacra,
præter ista communia, lineum quoddam indumentum, quod
novo vocabulo *superpelliceum* dici solet, ministrantibus ut ac-
commodetur, ecclesiastica jubet disciplina. Ex quibus cum
depravatæ religionis sacerdotes ab iis qui evangelii lucem ad-
ministrent, quasi tesseris quibusdam, discriminari causentur
nonnulli, talibus obsequiis vel idololatrarum probare hypocrisin,
vel suum fœdare ministerium, non sibi licere dicunt. Mo-
deratiores vero, licet ut edictis pareant ritibus nullo se modo
cogi patiantur, tamen nec aliis, quod obedientiam præstent,
vitio verti volunt, nec rerum illarum usum ut impium haben-
dum ducunt. Sunt autem nonnulli, qui peculiarem illum vestiendi morem sic tuentur, ut eo remoto et sacra omnia tantum
non profanari, et magno cum ministerium ornamento, tum
populum documento fraudari, acriter contendant. At enim
ordinis ecclesiastici, ut dixi, pars major in ea persistere videntur sententia, ut quantumvis aboleri ista posse putent, (et
plurimi certe desiderant,) tamen cum in deserta statione, quam
in suscepta veste, plus inesse statuant peccati, tanquam ex
malis minimum, parere jussis quam loco cedere satius ducunt.
Atque in tanta sententiarum varietate, sui cujusque animi
sensa solidis se rationibus probe munita tenere quisque con-
fidit. Sed mitto rationes: res enim nudas commemorare
statui.

In Baptismi sacramento administrando interrogationes
responsionesque, quæ de more adhiberi solent, alii ut e mero
papatu deductas, alii ut infantibus inutiles, ipsis autem sus-
ceptoribus duriores quam ut præstando pares esse poterint,
severe criminantur. Item, ejusdem administrandi sacri quædam ratio præscribitur, quam et privatam dicunt, et de vita
periclitantibus nominatim conceditur: hæc cum ad mulieres,
quibus adesse solis parientibus licet, verbis non apertis sed
tacitis devolvi videatur, multorum reprehensione non caret.
In Cœnæ celebratione genuflexio præcipitur; deque pane
azymo nonnihil controversum est. Ordines ecclesiastici petentibus ex solius episcopi arbitrio dispensantur. Qui autem
per manuum impositionem ad sacrum ministerium consig-

A. D. 1572. nantur, iis preces publicas ceteraque administrare sacra licet; evangelium autem, nisi nova aliunde accersitæ potestatis impetrata accessione, annunciare non licet. Episcopi nisi ex mandato regio nec eliguntur nec ordinantur; iique, ut suo quisque archiepiscopo obedientiam præstent, sacramento obligantur. Sunt autem qui archiepiscoporum, archidiaconorum, et similium nomina auctoritatemque, quasi quæ dominatum quendam in ecclesia sacris libris vetitum constituant, aboleri, presbyterium autem per singulas ecclesias ex apostolorum præscripto instaurari, oportere contendant. Ad summam, ne singula persequar, ita per omnes partes nostram isti disciplinam et mancam et corruptam esse queruntur, ut de totius etiam ecclesiæ (quam, disciplina remota, nullam esse volunt) incolumitate certitudineque dubitationes aspergere subobscure videantur.

Quæ cum ita sint, auctoritate quadam ecclesiastica cavetur, nequis sacrum administrandi evangelii munus suscipiat, susceptamve retineat, qui non et ista, de quibus jamdiu loquimur, generisque ejusdem alia, libro quodam comprehensa, pro ratis habeat, et nihil eo libro contineri, quod cum verbo Dei pugnet, suo quisque ascripto chirographo profiteatur. Nec vero, siquis, quo minus id sibi facere liceat, conscientiæ queratur aculeos, vel siquid aliud contra afferat, ad causæ præsidium valere ea quicquam possunt; rectene an secus in medio relinquo. Neque enim alicujus vel factum vel institutum improbandi causa hunc mihi laborem susceptum putes: ipsos enim homines sententiis inter se variantes, propter summam eorum pietatem, doctrinam, auctoritatem, utrobique colo venerorque. De rebus nullum meum interpono judicium. Siquid inter narrandum in alteram partem præponderare videbitur, id ad rei majorem explicationem accommodatum, non affectibus indultum, existimabis. Ego enim ad ista scribenda, non animi aliqua perturbatione, sed officio ducor. Nam cum et hanc tibi, de qua scriberes, materiem suscepisses, et meum aliquod in eo desiderasses officium; cum quas ob causas tuo minus satisfecerim rogatui, reddendam mihi rationem putavi, tum nequa via per errorem a recto propositi argumenti scopo calamum deflecteres, qua potui cura et diligentia adesse tibi volui; ita tamen ut ego tibi ad eam quam instituisti scribendi provinciam auctor esse nolim; multo minus, ut, nullo præeunte ad parandam gratiam adjumento, principis animum rei novitate percellas. Res enim lubrica incertique est eventus, ut quæ non semel ante prætentata ex parvis scintillulis magnas sæpe flammas excitaverit.

Sin omnino hoc vobis curæ erit, ut ope aliqua vestra consiliisque nostras juvetis ecclesias, alia vobis ingrediendum esse via videtur. Primum enim, ipsos episcopos per literas excitandos esse, ut cum regiæ majestati ad ea emendanda quæ offensiones pariant, cursumque impediverint evangelii, quibus poterint modis accommodatissimis suasores impulsoresque se præbeant, tum etiam, si quæ volent minus impetraverint omnia, ut in pœnis exequendis erga fratres et comministros suos, præsertim eos quibus grave conscientiæ onus incumbet, aliquanto leniores esse velint, et ad tolerantiam propensiores. Non quod viros tantos vero pietatis erga fratres affectu carere cuiquam unquam in mentem venerit: nam et aliis laudatissimis in amplificanda fovendaque Christi ecclesia amoris sui testimoniis abundant; et severitatem illam, qua in tuenda legum auctoritate uti plerunque solent, ad vitandam in ecclesiis ἀταξίαν, qua pestis nulla major esse potest, a piis patribus......

Cetera (heu!) desiderantur.

Translation.

TO HIEROM ZANCHIUS,

GIVING HIM AN ACCOUNT OF THE PRESENT DIFFERENCES IN RELIGION.

HEALTH. From my last letter to you, dated the 18th of December, you would understand, most learned Zanchius, that there existed just and weighty reasons, why I resolved to hold a consultation with some pious and learned men concerning the delivery of your letter to the Queen's majesty[1].

[1 There is another excellent letter in my possession, of the said bishop to Zanchy about the present controversy, writ about 1571 or 1572. Therein it appeared, that Zanchy had intended to send a letter to the Queen in behalf of these refusers, to entreat that she would not enforce the use of these rites. This intention of his he communicated to Grindal, with whom, as we have seen, he held a correspondence, requiring his advice thereupon; and, as it seems, sent his letter for her Majesty to him to deliver. To which Grindal, December the 18th, wrote

A.D. 1571. Accordingly, when I was set free from that over-long and anxious business respecting the Spanish ambassador, in which, as I told you, I was then involved, I applied myself to those of the highest character for advice, and laying the matter open before them, diligently inquired their sentiments thereupon. Amongst them were the most distinguished ecclesiastics of the highest rank, and some privy councillors, and certain others of excellent judgment, men fearing God; who, being asked their opinion, all to a man agreed, assigning many reasons, that it were better not to present your letter. But of those, to whom you very lately wrote in letters sent to me, I have omitted none, whose opinion I have not diligently sought by inquiry, or from whom I have not received a reply to the same effect, either by letter or in familiar conversation. The several reasons which each assigned for his opinion it were long, and perhaps inexpedient, to relate. Some, not without reason, seem to conjecture, from the letters which you have written to some friends, that you have not rightly understood the parties of the dissentients; others, that you have not fully apprehended even the state of the matter in controversy. And, perhaps, it will not be easy to explain it. But that you may yourself more surely and correctly find out from the circumstances the certainty, and variety, and magnitude of the business, I will diligently endeavour, by recounting the matter from its very foundation, to make things as plain to you as possible. This then is the state of the case.

When first her highness Elizabeth, under most happy auspices, began her reign, the popish doctrine and worship being cast off, she restored all things to that standard of the administration of the word of God, and the sacraments,

him this answer: "That he would speedily consult with learned and godly men for their thoughts thereof." And accordingly soon after he applied himself to men of the best rank both for learning and godliness, and some of high quality; some whereof were in the highest place in the church, and some privy councillors: among whom we may conclude the archbishop of Canterbury and secretary Cecil to be two. And all these did unanimously conclude it best to present no letter to the Queen upon this argument. See Strype, Grind. p. 157. The letter of Zanchius to queen Elizabeth is extant in his printed works. Epist. Lib. I.]

and the whole of religion, which had been drawn up and established during the reign of Edward VI. of happy, but also of most lamented memory. To this all the states of the kingdom with full consent gave their voices in the great council of the nation, which in our vernacular language we call the Parliament. The authority of this council is so great, that the laws made therein cannot by any means be dissolved, except by the sanction of the same. Whereas, then, in this form of religion of which I have spoken, drawn up by king Edward, there were many commands respecting the habits properly adapted to ministers of the church, and also concerning other things which some good men wish to be abolished or amended, it was forbidden by the authority of the law that any one should meddle with this matter. Yet the law itself allowed the Queen's majesty, with the advice of some of the bishops, to alter some things. Nothing however of the law is either altered or diminished; nor, as far as I know, is there a bishop, who does not himself obey the prescribed rules, and also lead or persuade the rest to do the same. Wherefore there is no reason why you should give yourself the trouble to persuade what they themselves have some time ago willingly yielded to you, viz. either that they should remain in their several posts, or that the Queen should deal more gently with those who decline conformity. Almost all the other ministers of the church also, learned and unlearned, seem not unwillingly to give in to the same opinion with the bishops.

[A part of the letter is here wanting.]

As for *doctrine*, hitherto we retain it unshaken and unadulterated in our churches. And therefore, since all our controversy has flowed from *discipline*, these are the usual grounds of complaint. Ministers are required to wear commonly a long gown, a square cap, and a kind of tippet over the neck hanging from either shoulder, and falling down almost to the heels. In public prayers and every sacred administration, besides this ordinary dress, the ecclesiastical discipline requires the ministers to wear a linen garment, called, by a new appellation, a *surplice*. And since the priests of corrupt religion are distinguished from those who administer the light of the gospel by these things, as it were by certain tokens, some allege that it is not lawful for them by such compliances either to approve the hypocrisy of idolaters, or to pollute their own ministry. The more moderate, though they will by no means allow themselves to be compelled to obey the prescribed rites, yet neither are willing to censure others as sinful for yielding obedience, nor esteem the use of these things as impious. But some there are who so defend that peculiar mode of dress, that without it they eagerly contend that all sacred offices are all but profaned, and both the ministry deprived of a great ornament, and the people of instruction; but the greater part, as I have said, of the ecclesiastical order seem to persist in this opinion, that however they think that these things may be abolished, (and many certainly desire it,) yet, whereas they conceive that there is more sin in deserting their posts than in taking the garments, they think it better, as the smallest of evils, to obey the commands than to give up their places. And in so great a variety of sentiment, each man is confident that he holds his own opinions well supported by solid arguments. But I let arguments pass; for I resolved to relate naked facts.

In the administration of the sacrament of Baptism, the interrogatories and answers, which are accustomed to be put, are severely censured by some, as derived from mere popery; by others, as useless to the infants, and too hard to be performed by the sponsors themselves. Moreover, there is prescribed a certain form of administering the same sacrament, which is called *private;* and it is expressly conceded to those who are in danger of death. This does not escape the reprehension of many, since it seems, not indeed in plain terms but by implication, to be devolved upon women, who alone are allowed to be present at child-birth. In the celebration of the Lord's Supper kneeling is enjoined; and there is some controversy about unleavened bread. Ecclesiastical orders are conferred upon those who seek them at the discretion of the bishop alone. But those who are ordained to the sacred ministry by imposition of hands may conduct public prayer and other holy rites: they may not however preach the gospel without obtaining an additional authority derived from another source. Bishops are neither chosen nor consecrated but by royal mandate; and these are bound by an oath, each A.D. 1571. to render obedience to his archbishop. There are some who contend, that the names and authority of archbishops, archdeacons, and the like, should be abolished, as if they constituted a kind of lordship in the church forbidden by holy scripture; but that a presbytery ought to be established in every church according to the ordinance of the apostles. In short, that I may not follow out every particular, they complain that our discipline is in all respects so lame and corrupt, that they seem darkly to scatter abroad doubts as to the soundness and certainty of the entire church, which, they say, without discipline is no church at all.

Such being the case, it is ordained by ecclesiastical authority, that no man shall take upon himself the sacred office of the ministry of the gospel, or shall retain it when received, who shall not allow of those things of which I have spoken, and others of the same kind, contained in a certain book, and acknowledge, each under his own hand subscribed, that nothing is contained in that book which is contrary to the word of God. Nor, should any one plead compunctions of conscience as a barrier to his doing this, or allege any other objection, would these things avail aught as a defence of his cause; whether justly or otherwise, I do not determine. For do not think that I have undertaken the task of writing to you for the sake of impugning either the act or the purpose of any man. I respect and venerate the men themselves on either side, for their piety, learning, and authority, although differing in opinion amongst themselves. I do not interpose my own judgment in these matters. If in my narration any thing seems to preponderate in favour of one side or the other, you will reckon that to be intended for the fuller explication of the matter, not for an indulgence of party spirit; for I am induced to write these things, not by any bias of mind, but by a sense of duty. For when you had undertaken to write on this subject, and also had desired my assistance therein, I thought myself bound both to render an account to you, why I could not fully satisfy your request; and I also wished with the utmost care and diligence to assist you, lest in any way through mistake you should miss the exact scope of the proposed argument; yet so, that I am unwilling to persuade you to the office of writing which you have undertaken, much less that, without any previous arrangement for securing a gracious reception, you should alarm the Queen's mind by the novelty of the matter. For it is a slippery thing and of doubtful issue, as one which, having been more than once attempted before, has often from small sparks kindled a great fire.

But if you will make it your study to assist our churches by your help and counsels, it seems that you must proceed in some other way. For first, the bishops should be stirred up by letter to persuade and urge the Queen's majesty, by all convenient methods, to amend those things which breed offences, and hinder the course of the gospel; and also, if they cannot obtain all they wish, that in inflicting penalties upon their brethren and fellow-ministers, especially those whose consciences are heavily burdened, they would be somewhat more gentle, and more disposed to toleration. Not that any one should suppose that these great men are destitute of the true spirit of pious affection towards their brethren; for they abound in other notable testimonies of their love in enlarging and cherishing the Church of Christ[1].

[No date, probably 1571-2.]

LETTER LXX.

TO LORD BURLEIGH.

Jan. 24, 1572.

[Lansdown MS. 16. No. 24.]

SALUTEM in Christo. My lord, I have written to her Majesty for renewing of our ecclesiastical commission for this province, both for that it is requisite (as I think) that my lord President[2] be in the said commission, and also for that some of the old commissioners are dead, and some removed out of this province. My lord President's good government

[1 The last sentence, being unfinished, has not been translated; the manuscript ends here abruptly.]

[2 Henry, earl of Huntingdon.]

here among us daily more and more discovereth the rare A.D. 1572.
gifts and virtues which afore were in him, but in private life
were hid from the eyes of a great number. The old proverb is well verified in him, *Magistratus probat virum*[3]. I
wish still that some of her Majesty's houses and grounds
in these parts might be procured for him, towards his necessary provision; for surely, without that, I cannot see but his
lordship shall far overcharge himself. I know your lordship
is his good friend: that maketh me bold sometimes to put
your lordship in mind hereof. Thus I cease further to trouble
your lordship, heartily commending the same to the grace of
God. From Cawood, this 24th of Jan. 1572.

Your lordship's in Christ,
EDM. EBOR.

*To the Right Honourable my
very good lord, the Lord
Burleigh, Lord high Treasurer of England.*

LETTER LXXI.

TO THE LORD TREASURER BURLEIGH,

COMPLAINING OF INJURIES OFFERED TO THE CLERGY BY THOSE THAT
WERE SENT DOWN UPON CONCEALMENTS[4].

June 29, 1573.

[Lansd. MS. 17. No. 36.]

AFTER my very hearty commendations to your good lordship. I can be very well contented, that the gentlemen pensioners, in whose behalf your lordship wrote unto me, may

[3 The office of a magistrate puts a man to the test.]
[4 The archbishop had now observed great abuses offered to the clergy of his diocese by a parcel of needy, unjust men, who pretended commissions from the Queen, to recover from them penalties incurred. She had indeed granted, by her letters patent, to her gentlemen pensioners penalties forfeited by the clergy, under pretence of concealment of lands and rents given for superstitious uses, belonging now by act of

have the penalties, forfeited by the clergy of my diocese, according to their letters patents; neither did I ever mind to abridge them of any part thereof. But I find fault with the manner of proceeding, which hath been used here, about the levying of the same. For first, their deputies have been bare men, and noted for evil dealing heretofore, and so the liker to commit extortions and briberies. Whereof some, as I hear, have been opened in the Star-chamber; and of some we have suffered in these parts. Secondly, their manner of dealing, by composition for offences past and to come, tendeth not to the restraint of abuses, but is rather a mean to increase the same. Moreover, (as they use the matter,) men of good worship and calling, which are no way culpable, and generally all the whole clergy, as well the innocent as the faulty, are compelled to appear before the said deputies, being men qualified as before, and to attend upon them as commissioners (where indeed they have no such commission), to their great charge, molestation, and discredit.

Wherefore, if the said gentlemen would send me down in articles a form of proceeding to be observed by their deputies, whereby the said inconvenience, and some other now for brevity omitted, may be avoided, I shall be willing, in all reasonable order, to further their commodity, or otherwise leave them to the execution of their commission according to their own discretion, so as no injury be offered to my clergy and me: which I assure myself was not meant at their granting of their said letters patents. And thus, ceasing further to trouble your lordship at this time, I heartily commend the same to the grace of God. From Bishopsthorp, this 29th of June, 1573.

Your lordship's in Christ,

EDM. EBOR.

To the Right Honourable my very good lord, the Lord Burleigh, Lord high Treasurer of England.

parliament to the crown. Whereupon they sent their deputies about through the kingdom; who, being indigent men, used great extortion, and wofully oppressed and vexed the poor clergy. Strype, Grind. p. 264.]

LETTER LXXII.

TO LORD BURLEIGH.
Oct. 21, 1573.
[Lansdown MS. 17. No. 50.]

SALUTEM in Christo. My lord, I am bold to send to your lordship this letter inclosed[1], concerning Sir Rowland Stanley, not in respect of any private querele of mine own, nor upon any extraordinary credit of the informer, because I know enmity to be between the parties; but rather to offer to your lordship's consideration, whether the said Sir Rowland be a meet man to supply that office this year: for that now lately he hath contemned divers and sundry processes, proceeding from my lord President and me by virtue of the ecclesiastical commission[2]; of which contempts we have determined about the end of the term to certify the whole board of your council, and to pray assistance. The said Sir Rowland would not vouchsafe to salute my lord President, at his late being in Cheshire to take his *vale*[3] of my lord of Essex[4]; burdened (belike) with a guilty conscience. I know it is odious to hinder any man's preferment; but yet I know also, that it is good to let the highest magistrates understand of the conditions of those that are to be preferred, that they may consider whether they be worthy of preferment, according as circumstances may minister occasion. He is seldom a good sheriff, that setteth to be a sheriff. Many sheriffs abuse their offices, to the bolstering

He desireth to be sheriff of Cheshire.

[1 A letter written to archbishop Grindal by one Mr Robert Fletcher, a gentleman of Cheshire, containing heavy complaints against Sir Rowland Stanley. The letter is preserved in the British Museum with the archbishop's letter.]

[2 Upon some disagreement between him and his wife, divers and sundry processes were issued out from the lord President and our archbishop, by virtue of the ecclesiastical commission; all which he had contemned. Strype, Grind. p. 265.]

[3 Farewell.]

[4 Then on his way to Ireland.]

out of their own evil private causes. The whole matter I refer to your lordship's good consideration; and so commend the same to the grace of God. From York this 21st of October, 1573.

Your lordship's in Christ,

EDM. EBOR.

Of Myrrick and Gilpin[1].

P. S. Myrrick is an unlearned Welsh doctor of law, that lived long *in concubinatu*, and was presented to a benefice in Cheshire by Sir Rowland Stanley's means, of purpose that Sir Rowland might have the profits, &c.

Mr Gilpin of Cambridge was also, at my suit to Mr Fletcher, presented to the same benefice by one of the feoffees in the same advowson that presented Myrrick, in which case the choice is free to the ordinary.

I chose Gilpin, as the better learned. Sir Rowland sueth *Quare impedit* at Chester.

Some fear there is of indifferent justice in those particular jurisdictions, especially when a stranger is one party.

To the Right Honourable my
  very good lord, the Lord
  Burleigh, Lord high Trea-
  surer of England.

[1 There was a suit depending between Sir R. Stanley and the archbishop and his court: and he thought that by being sheriff he might have power in his hands to obtain his will the better against the archbishop; and therefore it was, that his friends sought that place now for him. The cause was this: Bebington, a benefice in Cheshire, being void, and the presentation being in certain feoffees, Sir Rowland laboured to get one Myrrick to be preferred to it, on purpose that Sir Rowland might have the profits of it. But to prevent Myrrick's coming in, one Mr Robert Fletcher, a gentleman in those parts, (either one of the feoffees of this advowson, or that had an interest with them,) procured one Mr Gylpin of Cambridge to be presented. By which means the choice became free to the ordinary; and he presented Gylpin, as the best learned. Strype, Grind. p. 266.]

LETTER LXXIII.

TO ARCHBISHOP PARKER.
Dec. 9, 1573.
[Petyt MS. 47, fo. 26.]

SALUTEM in Christo. Your grace's so large description of the entertainments at Canterbury[2] did so lively set forth the matter, that in reading thereof I almost thought myself to be one of your guests there, and, as it were, beholding the whole order of all things done there. I think it shall be hard for any of our coat to do the like for one hundred years, and how long after God knoweth.

The late proclamation and the council's late letters seem to lay a very heavy burden upon our shoulders, and that generally and equally, without respect of difference, whereas indeed there is not like occasion of offence given of all. I assure your grace, it was to me a great grief, and should have been tenfold greater, had they not thereby so well beaten down the other arrogant innovating spirits: which I trust shall work some benefit to the church, if the captains be not countenanced (as they have been) by those that are no bishops[3]. In very deed, in my diocese the uniform order allowed by the book[4] is universally observed. I think some of my province have some novelties. I have written to them to reform them without delay, or else I will. If my successor at London[5] have ministered any occasion of his own disquiet, I am sorry. But surely he, the bishop of London, is always to be pitied; for if burning were the penalty of these curiosities, yet should he never lack a number of that generation. I hear say that Cartwright is lodged in Cheapside, at Mr

[2 For the archbishop's account of these festivities, see Strype, Parker, II. 296.]
[3 "Meaning undoubtedly some of the great men of the court." Strype, Grind. p. 268.]
[4 Of Common Prayer.]
[5 Bishop Sandys, afterward archbishop of York.]

A. D. 1573. Martyn's house, the goldsmith. His wife was the stationer for all the first impressions of the book[1].

I marvel that Dr Penny, (who is a chief doer in these matters,) and who is become of a preacher a layman and a physician, should be suffered to enjoy a good prebend in Paul's. And the like is to be said of Wiburn, Johnson[2], &c. They are content to take the livings of the English church, and yet affirm it to be no church. *Beneficium datur propter officium*[3]. If they will do no office, let them receive no benefit.

I think long to hear what shall follow after the great inquisition at London[4]. God send us all humble and quiet spirits, and thankfully to acknowledge God's great mercy towards us; to whose tuition I heartily commend your grace.

From Bishopsthorp, 9° Decemb. 1573.

Your grace's in Christ,
EDM. EBOR.

LETTER LXXIV.

TO LORD BURLEIGH.
April 12, 1574.
[Lansdown MS. 19. No. 2.]

My very good lord, I have nothing to write to your lordship at this time, but only by occasion of my good lord President's repair to the court, to salute you. Of my lord President's good government here I need not to write: your lordship hath daily experience of it by his advertisements from hence. We are in good quietness (God be thanked!) both for the civil and ecclesiastical state. My lord President

[1 " The Admonition to the Parliament," of which Cartwright was the principal author. For an account of this book, see Strype, Whitgift, i. pp. 54, seq.]

[2 Leading men amongst the puritans.]

[3 A benefice is given for the performance of duty.]

[4 This " great inquisition" was that inspection, that was now set on foot in London, into the order and conformity of the ministers there, upon the council's letters to the bishop for that purpose. See Strype, Parker, ii. 238—241.]

serveth here very honourably and chargeably, as I have heretofore signified to your lordship. I fear he surchargeth himself: I know not; but if it be otherwise, I may say, *Amice timui*[5]. Surely I trust God hath prepared him to be a special good instrument for this commonwealth. Thus I take my leave of your good lordship, heartily commending the same to the grace of God.

From Bishopsthorp, 12° Aprilis, 1574.

Your lordship's in Christ,
EDM. EBOR.

To the Right Honourable my very good lord, the Lord Burleigh, Lord high Treasurer of England.

LETTER LXXV.

TO LORD BURLEIGH.
April 26, 1574.

[Lansdown MS. 19. No. 4.]

MY very good lord, I and others, by virtue of her Majesty's commission, obtained by your lordship's good means, took pains, visiting the hospital of Savoy almost four years ago; and finding the said hospital to have been universally spoiled by parson Thurland, then master there, we proceeded to his deprivation by sentence according to the law, and agreeable to the statutes of the house. Now I am informed, that the said Thurland maketh earnest suit, and is in some hope, to be restored to his place again; which were a pitiful case. I moved her Majesty in it at my last being at the parliament; praying her Majesty to remember, that it was her grandfather's foundation, and that it was the case of the poor, and therefore Christ's own cause. Her Highness was then resolutely determined, that Thurland should never be restored to that room any more. I pray your good lordship, finish that good work which ye began, and move her Majesty, that some other fit man (as Mr Wickham, her chaplain, or one of like godly zeal towards the poor members

[5 I feared as a friend.]

A.D. 1574. of Christ) may be admitted to that place, and that the other spoiler may be put out of all hope to recover that room; and then, by reforming of some imperfections in the statutes, which were incident to all foundations of that age, the house may be employed to a great relief of the poor, and her Majesty shall do as good a deed in it, as if her Highness should erect a new one of her own foundation. Thus ceasing any further to trouble your lordship, I heartily commend the same to the grace of God. From Bishopsthorp, this 26th of April, 1574.

Your lordship's in Christ,
EDM. EBOR.

To the Right Honourable my very good lord, the Lord Burleigh, Lord high Treasurer of England.

LETTER LXXVI.

TO LORD BURLEIGH,

CONCERNING PROCEEDINGS IN THE ECCLESIASTICAL COMMISSION WITH PAPISTS IN THE NORTH.

Nov. 13, 1574.

[Lansdown MS. 19. No. 13.]

My very good lord, We of the ecclesiastical commission here have sent a certificate to my lords of the council, of our proceedings this term. Only five persons have been committed for their obstinacy in papistical religion. For the number of that sect (thanks be to God!) daily diminisheth, in this diocese especially. None of note was committed, saving only your old acquaintance Doctor Vavasor, who hath been tolerated in his own house in York almost three quarters of a year. In his answer, made in open judgment, he shewed himself the same man which you have known him to be in his younger years: which was sophistical, disdainful, and eluding arguments with irrision, when he was not able to solute the same by learning. His great anchor-hold was in urging the literal sense of *hoc est corpus meum*, thereby to prove *transubstantiation*: which to deny (saith he) is as great an heresy as to deny *consubstantiation*, decreed in the Nicene council. The diversity was sufficiently declared unto him by testimonies of the Fathers. *Sed ipse sibi plaudit*[1]. My lord President and I, knowing his disposition to talk, thought it not good to commit the said Dr Vavasor to the castle of York, where some other like affected remain prisoners; but rather to a solitary prison in the Queen's majesty's castle at Hull, where he shall only talk to walls.

The imprisoned for religion in these parts of late made supplication to be enlarged; seeming, as it were, to require it of right, by the example of enlarging of Fecknam, Watson, and other papists above. We here are to think, that all things done above are done upon great causes, though the same be to us unknown. But certainly my lord President and I join in opinion, that if such a general *jubilee* should be put in use in these parts, a great relapse would follow soon after. Your lordship, and other of my lords, may consider of it, if any such suit should be made.

I am glad to understand by your chaplain, Mr Ramsden, that your lordship hath of late been better than afore. My fits of colic, stone, and strangury are very grievous when they come; but God sendeth me some *intervalla*, else they were intolerable. From York, 13th Nov. 1574.

Your lordship's in Christ,

EDM. EBOR.

To the Right Honourable my very good lord, the Lord Burleigh, Lord high Treasurer of England.

LETTER LXXVII.

TO LORD BURLEIGH.
Feb. 3, 1575.
[Lansdown MS. 19. No. 62.]

AFTER my right hearty commendations. I am moved to commend to your good lordship Mr Lever's suit, for the

[1 But he is self-satisfied.]

A.D. 1575. hospital of Sherborne house[1], whereof he is governor. The said hospital, which hath been, and now is, by him very well ordered, both for corporal and spiritual nutriment of the poor members thereof, is like to go to utter decay, by means of unreasonable leases and grants made by his popish predecessor, whom I deprived for papistry in the beginning of her Majesty's reign[2]; unless her Majesty's confirmation of an instrument, made by the now bishop of Durham[3], for the benefit of the said hospital, may be obtained; which confirmation, upon hearing of the cause before my lord President and the council here, is thought by learned in the laws (as I am informed and am fully persuaded to be true) to be the only mean to preserve that hospital from utter ruin, which were a case pitiful. I pray your lordship therefore, among your manifold weighty businesses, to take opportunity to further this suit, for the relief of Christ's poor members, according to your accustomed goodness in all such cases. For mine own part I think often, that those men which seek spoil of hospitals, be it by lease or any other fetch of law, did never read the twenty-fifth chapter of Matthew; for if they did, and believed the same, how durst they give such adventure? If any hospitals be abused, (as I think some are,) it were a more christian suit to seek reformation than destruction: but I refer these matters to your lordship's good consideration, and so commend the same to the grace of God.

From Bishopsthorp, beside York, this third of February, 1574 [1575.]

Yours in Christ,

EDM. EBOR.

To the Right Honourable my very good lord, the Lord Burleigh, Lord high Treasurer of England.

[1 Sherborn hospital, near Durham, founded by Pudsey, bishop of Durham, for sixty-five poor lepers. Thomas Lever, though deprived of his stall at Durham for non-conformity, yet retained the mastership of the hospital until his death.]

[2 Grindal was one of the queen's commissioners for the visitation of the north, A.D. 1559.]

[3 Bishop Pilkington.]

LETTER LXXVIII.

TO ARCHBISHOP PARKER.
March 4, 1575.
[Petyt MS. 47, fo. 21.]

SALUTEM in Christo. It is too long to trouble your grace with Lowth's disordered dealings[4]. He writeth out letters full of slander, terming my doings and the other commissioners' to be like the Spanish Inquisition. I think it will fall forth that he was never ordered priest or minister; and yet hath he these fifteen or sixteen years exercised that function. I hear that he maketh suit for a pardon from the Queen's majesty, or your grace, for this offence, which is very intolerable. I pray your grace, stay it if you can.

Mr Aylmer[5] was a fit man to answer the Latin book of Discipline[6]; but I think neither he nor Mr Dean[7] will take the pains: of the latter I am sure. Some think that Mr Still[8] were a fit man to do it. Sure I wish it were done, and that Mr Dean of Paul's and Mr Watts[9] had a view of it afore it were published.

There is a great talk here of new sects and heresies sprung about London[10], of Judaism, Arianism, &c. I would be glad

[4 Though there were not so many puritans in these northern quarters as in the south, (the ecclesiastical commissioners being chiefly employed in taking cognizance of papists,) yet some there were; whereof one was named Lowth, of Carlisle side, who for many disorders was had up before the commissioners. He was one of those that varied from the orders of the church, and neglected the rules of it. See Strype, Grind. 275, and Parker II. 400.]

[5 Archdeacon of Lincoln, afterwards bishop of London.]

[6 Towards the latter end of this year (1574) came forth a Latin book *De Disciplina*, in behalf of the puritans' way of discipline. Strype, Parker, II. p. 399.]

[7 Nowell, dean of St Paul's.]

[8 Afterwards master of Trinity College, Cambridge, and bishop of Bath and Wells.]

[9 Thomas Watts, archdeacon of Middlesex.]

[10 Next, as to the reports of strange sects and heresies sprung up in London, which our archbishop had inquired after; the archbishop of Canterbury discovered that to be occasioned from Corranus, a Spanish divine and reader in the temple; who spake not wisely, he said, of predestination, and suspiciously of Arianism: but that this was all he

[GRINDAL.]

A.D. 1575. to understand the truth. We are here now in certain expectation of her Majesty's progress into these parts the next summer. The lord Treasurer hath so signified to my lord President. It shall be a great comfort to us all to see her Majesty among us, and to me especially; only I am sorry that my ability is so small as it is. I shall strain myself to the uttermost, trusting that my good will shall be accepted, where ability faileth. I am to pay in Michaelmas term next, for the last payment of my first-fruits, no less than £380; which how well it will stand with a progress, your grace may consider, especially in one that hath not, *communibus annis*[1], above £1300. clear yearly value. I pray your grace, send me some notes of instruction, both of charges for one or two days' diet, &c., and for other circumstances, especially at what place her Highness is to be met by me; at the entry of my diocese, or otherwise. We have had here the 26th of February last, about 5 o'clock at night, an earthquake, which (as is certified) passed through this shire, Nottinghamshire, Derbyshire, and Leicestershire, and we suppose it extended into the south parts also. It was not very great; for in York it shaked not down so much as a tile; yet it putteth us in great fear of some great matter to follow[2]. I remember there was the like at Croydon, in bishop Cranmer's time, in king Edward's days, not long before his death, as I suppose. The certain time would be learned. God be merciful to us! to whose protection I remit your grace. From Bishopsthorp, 4 Martii, 1574 [1575].

It lasted not a minute of an hour.

Your grace's in Christ,
EDM. EBOR.

P.S. The bishop of Carlisle hath *in commendam* a benefice of my patronage, named Stokesley, till the first of August next: if he make suit to have his *commendam* renewed, I pray your grace stay for Stokesley. It is a market town, and hath been very evil served ever sith he had it. I would place a preacher to be resident upon it.

knew, that gave occasion of those reports that came thither to York, except the Precisians in London. Strype, Grind. 278.]

[1 One year with another.]

[2 Archbishop Parker, in his reply, observed: "As for the prognostications, *Dominus est; faciat quod bonum est in oculis suis.*"]

LETTER LXXIX.

TO LORD BURLEIGH.
Oct. 17, 1575.
[Lansdown MS. 20. No. 65.]

I COULD not omit to salute your good lordship, now upon my lord President's repair to the court. I think your lordship findeth true by experience that which I wrote unto you at my lord's first entry to this office[3], which was thus much in effect; that this office hath made manifest to many those excellent virtues and good gifts which afore were in a manner hid in him. This last service towards Scotland[4], in my opinion, hath made a good proof thereof; wherein, although the highest commendation is to be ascribed to her Majesty as the fountain, yet his lordship, as a good instrument, is not to be defrauded of his praise. And surely, so far as I can learn, all good men in these parts do much rejoice in so happy an end of so unfortunate an accident. If any mislike,

[3 See Letter LXX. p. 343.]
[4 In the Middle March towards Scotland a sudden bickering happened, about July, 1575, between the borderers, Sir John Forster, Warden of the Middle March, meeting with Carmichel, Warden of Liddisdale in Scotland; both were attended with a rabble of thieves and malefactors belonging to the borders, who took some occasion to quarrel, bearing a deadly feud one to another; where the English first beat back the Scots, and took Carmichel prisoner. Afterwards a fresh company of Scots coming on, the English were put to flight, and Sir George Heron, knight, Warden of Tindal, and others, were slain; Forster himself, the governor, and the earl of Bedford's eldest son, and other gentlemen, taken prisoners, and carried into Scotland. Murray the regent was hereupon so threatened by the queen, that he came unarmed to the very borders of both kingdoms, and there met the earl of Huntingdon, the foresaid lord president of the north, and the English commissioner: and by his prudent managery this scurvy accident was wisely made up, and the regent brought to promise to repair the honour of the English nation by the best offices he could; and sent Carmichel into England, who was kept awhile at York a prisoner, and after sent home with honour and certain presents: and thus amity was renewed between the queen and the regent, by the earl's good and dexterous management of this affair. Strype, Grind. p. 280.]

they be of the worst sort of men, who in all commonwealths are *cupidi rerum novarum*[1]. But this is more than needeth to your lordship, to whom my said lord's good service and godly wisdom is very well known; and yet I thought it not amiss, that your lordship should partly understand what I and others of these parts unfeignedly think of his lordship's good government among us; fearing nothing but that his lordship surchargeth himself in serving her Majesty in so honourable and chargeable wise as he doth. But I cease further to trouble your lordship, and heartily commend the same to the grace of God. From York, this 17th of October, 1575.

Your lordship's in Christ,
EDM. EBOR.

To the Right Honourable my very good lord, the Lord Burleigh, Lord high Treasurer of England.

LETTER LXXX.

TO LORD BURLEIGH.
Dec. 10, 1575.
[Lansdown MS. 20. No. 69.]

I UNDERSTAND by your lordship's letters of the 25th of November last, which I received the 26th thereof, what your lordship thinketh of her Majesty's inclination for my remove[2].

[1] Desirous of revolution.]
[2] The archbishopric of Canterbury lay now void since the decease of the most pious and reverend Matthew Parker, who died in May, 1575. The queen, after three months' deliberation who was the fittest to succeed in that metropolitical station, pitched upon Grindal, recommended to her by the lord treasurer, his friend; who therefore gave him the first notice of it in a letter, dated Nov. 25, in these words: "I do let your grace understand, that I do think assuredly her majesty will have your grace to come to this province of Canterbury, to take care thereof; and that, now at this parliament." Strype, Grind. p. 282.
This honour was not of our archbishop's own ambitious seeking: nay, he had many inward motions to decline it. He was possessed with

If her Majesty should so resolve, although I have had heretofore many conflicts with myself about that matter, yet have I in the end determined to yield unto the ordinary vocation; lest in resisting the same I might with Jonas offend God, occasion a tempest, &c.; beseeching God to assist me with his grace, if that weighty charge be laid upon me, to the sustaining whereof I find great insufficiency in myself. And I most heartily thank your good lordship, that it pleaseth you to have such a care over me, and to take such pains in giving direction for the extern commodities[3] pertaining to that place. I have appointed one William Marshall, my servant, to attend upon your lordship from time to time, and to follow your lordship's direction in all things, as the case shall require. And thus ceasing further to trouble your lordship at this time, I heartily commend the same to the grace of God.

From Bishopsthorp, Decimo Dec. 1575.

Your lordship's in Christ,
EDM. EBOR.

To the Right Honourable my very good lord, the Lord Burleigh, Lord high Treasurer of England.

an humble spirit, and low conceit of his own abilities for so high a function in the church; but was swayed by the vocation thereto, and the fears of giving offence. Ibid. p. 283.]

[3 In the letter alluded to in the former note the treasurer added: "That he meant to give order to the officers of the temporalties to take care of the preserving thereof; and where the officers would be felling of woods, that they should not. He told him that the last archbishop was wont at Christmas to fell wood for his fuel and coal; and so were it necessary to be done for his grace, if he should have that place. He therefore desired him, by his letters or otherwise, to appoint somebody near at hand to attend on him for this and such like cause; so as when her majesty should certainly resolve, as he meant to procure her to do within three or four days, he might direct order for his benefit." Ibid.]

LETTER LXXXI.

TO LORD BURLEIGH.
April 23, 1576.
[Lansdown MS. 23. No. 7.]

I AM to move your lordship on the behalf of your old nurse, I mean St John's College in Cambridge. That famous college hath been long, and yet is, (as I am informed,) troubled with factions and contentions[1]. Some of that university, which be of credit, think the readiest way of reformation to be, if a visitation by her Majesty's commission may be procured, and the statutes of the college reduced to some certainty, and in some things altered by the report of the visitors, understanding the state of the house. I am informed that there is no original authentic book of statutes in the treasury of that college, as by statute ought to be, and is in all other colleges duly observed. The copies of the statutes which are now abroad in that house are rased, blotted, interlined, and corrupted with marginal additions, so as indeed no man can certainly affirm what is statute, what not. I think therefore your lordship might do a very good deed, at your convenient

[1 The bishop of Ely, their visitor, had perceived how contentions grew and were nourished here, and, in a visitation he had made, contrived means for the putting an end thereunto; but his power was not strong enough without some greater influence from above: he therefore employed Dr Ithel, master of Jesus college, and his chancellor, who knew well how the matters of the college stood, to acquaint the lord treasurer with a full and particular account how things were found. As, that there was in the house great bandying against government; that they professed openly to maintain a popular state in the college; and for that purpose the seniors held together, without whom the master could do nothing. That when disorder was to be punished, they would hardly, and sometimes not at all, be brought to consent to the inflicting of any punishment, but would maintain their old liberty, as they termed it. For these causes the bishop of Ely desired a commission, to reform the statutes of the house in some points; and that the commissioners might have authority to hear and determine all controversies during the time of the imperfection of the statutes that then they had. See Strype, Grind. p. 297.]

leisure, to procure such a visitation from her Majesty, with A.D. 1576. such good instructions as your lordship shall think requisite in such a case². I refer the matter to your lordship's good consideration. I have inclosed the names of some, who in my opinion are fit to be visitors. Your lordship may alter and add, as you think good. God keep your lordship!

From Lambeth, 23º Aprilis, 1576.

Your lordship's in Christ,

EDM. CANTUAR.

Visitors for St John's college in Cambridge:
1. The lord Treasurer.
2. The bishop of Ely.
3. Dr Whitgift.
4. Dr Watts.
5. Dr Hawford.
6. Dr Ithel.
7. Dr Bing.
8. Mr Goade, provost of the King's college.

To the Right Honourable my very good lord, the Lord high Treasurer of England.

LETTER LXXXII.

TO LORD BURLEIGH.

May 2, 1576.

[Lansdown MS. 23. No. 1.]

I SEND to your lordship the order taken for David Thickpenny³, the bishop of Chichester then being present. I heard

[² Accordingly in the latter end of the year a commission was sent down to the college, and the matters rectified, and some of the college punished. Ibid.]

[³ This man was curate of Brighthelmstone. The bishop of Chichester (Curtis) had suspended him from his office for some irregularities, and chiefly on suspicion of his favouring the sect called *the family of love.* Thickpenny appealed to the council against his bishop, and they referred the matter to archbishop Grindal. Upon inquiry into all the circumstances of the case, the archbishop came to the resolution of restoring him, on condition of his submissively purging what my lord of Chichester could object against him; and indeed it was nothing in effect, saving only that he suspected Thickpenny to be one of the *family of love*[1], and yet my said lord shewed no sufficient ground of his said suspicion: and moreover the said Thickpenny, by open protestation and offering of his oath, did utterly deny that he was of that faction, &c. Whereupon I moved my lord, that he would restore the said Thickpenny (being indeed well learned, and having a very good testimony of his parishioners) to the serving of his cure again, by my lord's own authority; which he refused to do. Whereupon, considering the sufficiency of the said Thickpenny, and finding that my lord rather upon some private affection, than any just ground, had displaced the said Thickpenny, I took order as is inclosed, oftentimes monishing the said Thickpenny, that he should use all dutiful submission towards his ordinary, &c. I will send for the said Thickpenny hither again, to answer to the objections sent by my lord of Chichester.

I pray your lordship's help that Mr Redmayn, who made a very good sermon before her Majesty, may be archdeacon of Canterbury. He is a very sufficient man; and the annexing of that office to the see of Rochester hath done very much harm in the diocese of Canterbury[2]. I have moved her Majesty twice for Mr Redmayn myself, and Mr Secretary Walsingham hath done the like: your lordship's good liking

himself in writing of the suspicions under which he lay, and solemnly promising to set forth God's true religion and doctrine according to the thirty-nine articles. He was required also, on two several Sundays, publicly in church to preach against and confute the errors of that sect. Thickpenny, having done this, was reinstated. But the archbishop was deceived in the matter; for immediately after his restoration Thickpenny conducted himself with so much irregularity, that he was again, at the instance of the bishop of Chichester, cited before the archbishop. See Strype, Grind. pp. 293—296.]

[1 The founder of this sect was Henry Nicolas, from Holland. For an account of their wild opinions, see Fuller, Ch. Hist. Bk. IX. pp. 112, 113; also Strype, Ann. II. i. 556—562, and II. ii. 282—290.]

[2 The bishops of Rochester hitherto during the queen's reign had held the archdeaconry of Canterbury *in commendam*. Now Freke, the present bishop, being to be removed to another see, the archbishop laboured to break that custom, which he saw had great inconvenience in it. Strype, Grind. p. 312.]

of this suit, known to her Majesty, would much further the cause³. God keep your lordship!

From Lambeth, 2° Maii, 1576.

Your lordship's in Christ,
EDM. CANTUAR.

*To the Right Honourable my very
good lord, the Lord Burleigh,
Lord high Treasurer of England.*

LETTER LXXXIII.

TO THE OFFICERS OF THE ARCHBISHOP'S COURTS[4].

Nov. 7, 1576.

[Regist. Grindal.]

SALUTEM in Christo. I perceive by the complaints of my brethren, the bishops, and other inferior ordinaries, that the ready unadvised inhibitions from my courts do not only hinder the correction of sins, but very slanderously discredit the courts, injuriously molest, and much discourage the judges, the churchwardens and others, by order and oath detecting faults. I require you therefore, that in matters of correction you temper your inhibitions, neither suffering judges by lewd bodies to be abused, nor sworn-men for their presenting to be troubled: but rather assist them in all justice, and by all means further the just correction of the evil, nowise discharging offenders by nullities of process, where faults

[³ The application was successful. Dr William Redmayn, who afterwards became bishop of Norwich, being made archdeacon.]

[⁴ In November he had occasion given him to look into a particular abuse of his courts; which the rest of the bishops, and other ordinaries of his province, had much complained of: which was that of inhibitions, taking cognizance of causes that lay before their courts, and bringing them into his own; which was ordinarily done to the vexation of many, and the stopping the execution of justice: for churchwardens were troubled for presenting, and offenders escaped by commutations. This the archbishop liked not, and perceived it to be an abuse done by his officers; and therefore despatched this mandate to the officers of his courts. Strype, Grind. p. 323.]

A.D. 1576. punishable do appear, but minister due punishment without any commutation.

I will you further, that you send out no double quarrel for admission to any benefice that is not void, both *de jure* and *de facto*; willing you to give public notice at your next court for the premises, that the same may be by all men the better observed. From Lambeth, the 7th of November, 1576.

EDM. CANTUAR.

LETTER LXXXIV.

TO THE DEAN AND CHAPTER OF OXFORD.
Nov. 18, 1577.
[Grind. Regist. fo. 158.]

SALUTEM in Christo. I have received letters from the lords of her Majesty's most honourable privy council; the tenor whereof ensueth: "After our right hearty commendations unto your good lordship, &c." These are therefore to require you, taking unto you such assistance as you shall think convenient in that behalf, to make diligent inquisition, as well by the searching of the records, as by the public fame in the country, and by all other convenient ways and means that you can, of the names of all such persons within the diocese of Oxford, as refuse to come unto divine service, and also of the value of their lands and goods, according to the effect of the said letters[1]. And that you will certify me what you shall find in that behalf with all expedition possible.

I am informed, that the diocese of Oxford is more replenished with such recusants, for the quantity thereof, than any other diocese of this realm. Thus fare you heartily well. From my house at Lambeth, this 18th of November, 1577.

[[1] The popish emissaries had, it seems, by this time, by their diligence, drawn over great numbers from going to church; and so had made a dangerous schism among the queen's subjects. It was seriously debated hereupon concerning the best course to stop this evil: and it was thought the easiest punishment, and withal the most likely way to reduce the offenders, and such as wholly absented from the church, to punish them in their purses, by the forfeiture of money for that neglect. Strype, Grind. p. 345.]

LETTER LXXXV.

TO LORD BURLEIGH.
May 24, 1578.
[Lansdown MS. 24. No. 14.]

AFTER my right hearty commendations to your good lordship. Whereas I am informed, that some (who have authority to take timber for her Majesty's provision) have appointed to take presently some timber in the woods of this see of Canterbury, standing near unto the city of Canterbury: for so much as there is but small store of timber in the said woods, and that not only three of the archbishop's own mansion houses, standing at and near unto Canterbury, and divers of farmers' houses and mills, are to be maintained therewith, but also that timber is necessarily to be brought from thence hither to Lambeth by water, for maintenance of this house, for that the woods of this see in these parts are so decayed that there is not therein convenient timber to make (your honour saved) as planchers for a stable: These are to desire your good lordship (if it may so seem good unto you) to give order either for the staying of that which is now so appointed to be taken, or otherwise that neither now nor hereafter, during your lordship's pleasure, none may be taken in the same woods, as may seem to your lordship most convenient. I have the rather been bold to make this suit unto your lordship, for that I am informed, that others in that part of Kent have such store that they can spare, and do sell: whereas, for mine own part, as I have ever been careful to preserve my timber, so I do not intend during my incumbency to make any sale of any timber that shall grow within any woods of this see. So taking my leave, I most heartily commend your good lordship to the grace of God. From Lambeth, this 24th of May, 1578.

Your lordship's in Christ,
EDM. CANTUAR.

To the Right Honourable my very good lord, the Lord Burleigh, Lord high Treasurer of England.

LETTER LXXXVI.

TO QUEEN ELIZABETH.

March 22, 1579.

[State Paper Office.]

It may please your most excellent Majesty to be advertised, that, whereas by your Highness' letters, dated the 20th day of February last past, I received commandment to make a true certificate of my doings, touching any spoil or waste by me made or committed, in felling and cutting down of timber trees upon the lands belonging to my see of Canterbury; these are in most honourable manner to signify unto your most excellent Majesty, that I have not, sithence my first entry into this see of Canterbury, sold any of the timber of the same see, no, not so much as one timber tree, neither have I caused any timber trees to be felled for any other purpose, (certain given trees hereafter mentioned only excepted,) but only for the necessary convenient reparations and buildings of the houses belonging to the said see, and for the making and repairing of bridges, water-sewers, and other necessary common uses, within the lands and liberties thereof, for the which I and my successors stand bound by law.

I confess that I have given to divers persons, upon reasonable considerations, some small timber trees of oak, that were felled in the woods called the Bleane, parcel of the possessions of the said see, situated in the county of Kent: but the number of the trees so given, during my four years of incumbency, hath not exceeded the number of twelve trees at the most. And as for my doings in this behalf in the bishoprics of London and York, during my incumbency in them, I was no spoiler, but a careful preserver of timber; as will be testified, I am sure (if the case so require) by a number that know my doings in those places. So with my continual and most hearty prayer unto God for the continuance of your Majesty's most prosperous and happy estate, I most humbly commend your Majesty to the grace and protection of the Almighty.

A.D. 1579.

Lambeth, 22° Martii, 1579.

Your Majesty's most humble subject
and daily orator,

To the Queen's most excellent majesty, my most gracious Sovereign Lady.

EDM. CANTUAR.

LETTER LXXXVII.

TO LORD BURLEIGH,
CHANCELLOR OF THE UNIVERSITY OF CAMBRIDGE.
June 30, 1580.
[Lansdown MS. 30. No. 52.]

AFTER my right hearty commendations to your good lordship. According to the request of your lordship's late letter[1], I have had before me this forenoon (being accompanied with my neighbour, Mr Dean of Westminster) Mr

[1 In the month of June his experience and wisdom was required and made use of in a controversy arisen in the university of Cambridge; where a contention arose between the vice-chancellor and doctors of the town on the one part, and the masters and heads of the colleges on the other, touching two graces lately propounded by the late vice-chancellor in favour of the doctors of the town and others. Wherewith the doctors being heads found themselves aggrieved, for that such graces should be propounded and proceeded in without their privity, as they pretended, against the late statutes and ordinances of her majesty. Hereupon the lord Burleigh, chancellor of that university, earnestly prayed our archbishop,—for that either party had sent up one, viz. for the vice-chancellor Dr Barrow, and for the heads of the colleges Dr Howland, master of St John's college, to open unto him as well the reasons of the one, as the griefs of the other, for the proceedings,—that he would do the said lord the pleasure and ease, at that present being busily occupied at court about great causes, as to hear both parties, and to examine the same; which he the rather desired his grace's travail in, for that he was sure the university and their statutes were better known unto his grace, than unto him. He left this business either to himself alone, or to call any other that had been of that university to assist him therein, as he should see cause. The archbishop accordingly took this matter into his hand, and the last day of June signified to him the sum of his thoughts concerning it. Strype, Grind. p. 371.]

A.D. 1580. Dr Howland, and Dr Barrow, and heard at some length what each party could say; and have thought good to send unto your lordship herein the substance of that which was uttered on both sides.

The controversy did stand in two principal points:

First, Whether these two late graces were disorderly and somewhat fraudulently obtained.

Secondly, Whether the very matter and substance of the graces were against the statutes.

In the first matter we did not dwell long, being a matter of circumstance. Yet thus much we perceived; that in the manner of proceeding for the obtaining the said graces, things were handled (though not directly against the words of the statute,) yet with some cunning and finesse, and not so sincerely as were to be wished in such cases, and with such circumstance.

About the second we stood most: wherein Dr Howland alleged the precise words of the statute, cap. 34. that the *pricking*, as they term it, of officers is by special privilege in the same statute reserved to the heads of houses, and by a latter interpretation from your lordship, to the heads or their deputies.

To that Mr Dr Barrow allegeth another statute, cap. 42. entituled *De Officio Cancellarii*, wherein is a branch, that the chancellor, or in his absence the vice-chancellor, may make new statutes, with this proviso, *Sic ut ea iis decretis nostris nihil detrahant aut officiant*[1]: "Which in this case," saith Dr Barrow, "this new statute, to adjoin the doctors to the heads of colleges, doth not," although Mr Dean and I are of contrary opinions, referring the determination to your lordship. The said Mr Barrow, for further defence, allegeth another statute, made by grace, as these two last were, concerning the scrutators: which office is now brought from free election appointed by the Queen's Majesty's statute, cap. 36. to go in course by combination, as the office of the proctors doth. To this Dr Howland answered, that he believed your lordship was made privy to the alteration of that statute for the scrutators; and added further, that if error were committed in that, it was no sufficient warrantize for other errors afterwards to be attempted; and especially

[1 So that they detract nothing from nor prejudice those our decrees.]

for these late errors in these two last graces. And thus much in substance was alleged on both parts for the former grace, to adjoin doctors to the heads for election of offices.

For the second grace, that heads of colleges, being divines, should be bound to preach in course as other younger men do : Dr Howland alleging, that by express words of her Majesty's statute, cap. 11. they are not bound further than their own free good-will shall move them; (the words be these, *Post tantum laboris susceptum, et tot pericula atque examina, nolumus plus laboris doctoribus imponere, quam ipsi volunt sua sponte suscipere*[2];) Dr Barrow, besides some glance at the usual commonplace, that heads ought to give good example, &c. alleged, that another of the Queen's statutes, which appointeth order only for sermons to be had on Sundays before noon, was altered by grace to sermons on Sundays and holy days, both forenoon and afternoon: which was answered to be no derogation to the Queen's statute, but contrariwise rather a more ample accomplishing of the same.

A little was said also by Dr Barrow of the interpretation of another statute, wherein is declared that it shall suffice to dispute twice against a Master of Art answering in divinity, where the words of the statute be, A man for his form to proceed in divinity should dispute twice against a bachelor in divinity. And yet was it thought by Dr Howland, that your lordship's consent was given to all the said interpretations and alterations. And surely for the time to come, I wish your lordship should give strait charge, that no alteration or interpretation of statute hereafter do pass by grace, before the same have been seen and allowed by your lordship.

Now, where your lordship is desirous to know mine opinion for quieting and ordering of this contention, I know your lordship of yourself can best do it; and I count the university happy, that it hath you for chancellor in these unquiet times. Your wisdom and authority may work more good with them than could be done otherwise. Notwithstanding I will most gladly impart mine opinion; which is this: I think it very requisite that these last graces should remain

[[2] After enduring so much labour, and so many trials and examinations, we are unwilling to impose more toil upon the doctors, than they, of their own accord, are willing to undertake.]

A.D. 1580. as dashed, and not put in execution. The example will do harm, if the Queen's statutes be thus tossed, and the plain meaning of them overthrown. So that some mild admonition from your lordship, joined with exhortation to concord and amity, I trust, will pacify the now vice-chancellor and the regents, &c. who have of long time repined at that statute for elections by the heads: although the altering of it (in mine opinion) would be occasion of many bitter contentions. And especially they will remain the better satisfied, if your lordship some way signify, that if the heads have any way abused their privileges, they will see it reformed for the time to come.

On the other side, (for the heads I mean,) I wish that your lordship should admonish and exhort them also to use their authority well and indifferently, to choose the best learned for their lectures; and for the vice-chancellor always to prick two fit men, and never hereafter to practise, that of the two nominated one should be an unfit man, and as it were a *stale*[1], to bring the office to the other, (which they did now in nominating Dr Hatcher, and taste of the fruits thereof,) which ministereth a just offence to the rest of the University.

I wish also that the heads which are divines should be exhorted to preach diligently without compulsion: which will satisfy in the other point.

And further, when the vice-chancellor sendeth for assistance in conferences in public matters, I would like well of it, if he sent also for the doctors of law and physic to join with the heads; it would be some contentation to them. And indeed so it was most usually (though not always) practised in my time.

This is my simple opinion, to the which Mr Dean also agreeth: referring notwithstanding the whole order to your lordship. I have warned Dr Howland and Dr Barrow to be with your lordship to-morrow morning. I make the more haste, because I wish things quieted before the commencement[2].

[1 Stale: a bait, a pretence, or stalking-horse. It properly means a decoy to catch birds.]

[2 Lord Burleigh wrote the following letter on the day after to the heads of houses. "I have received your letters by Dr Howland, master of St John's college. By which, and by his report, I have understood

I do greatly commend the sentences of humility and submission contained in the letters of the university to your lordship. God keep your lordship! From Lambeth, this last of June, 1580.

Your lordship's in Christ,

EDM. CANTUAR.

*To the Right Honourable my very
good lord, the Lord Burleigh,
Lord High Treasurer of England.*

many more particular things than presently I am at leisure to answer by writing. But considering the state of the controversies arisen, both for lack of good leisure, and doubting mine own understanding in such academical questions, I did commend the whole causes with all appendances to my lord the archbishop of Canterbury's good grace, to be by him considered at length, and to advertise to me his opinion: which he hath done at good length. And therein, after a further private weighing of the matters, I have at one instant time imparted my determination to both the messengers, Mr Dr Howland, and Mr Dr Barrow. And for a fuller satisfaction of the Vice-chancellor and the body of the university, I have at more length than well my leisure served me, for greater matters at this time concerning her majesty, written, or rather in haste scribbled, my letters. To which I doubt not, but Mr Vice-chancellor will make you, with the rest, acquainted. And therefore I omit to repeat the same unto you, praying you, as heads or fathers of great families, so to behave yourselves in temperance, as concord may rest in your families; and that for no particular interest in gain or preferment the public bands of charity be broken. But as you can teach us your scholars under your pupils, so in your own actions let it appear that every one of yourselves can forgive the errors of others. And though I do disannul both the graces, which are different in nature, yet for the latter tending to increase preaching, though by any new law you be not compelled, yet see that you be a law to yourselves; that of *non docendo* you keep not the name of *Doctores*. And so by haste I end. From the court at Norwich, primo Julii, 1580."
Strype, Grind. p. 376.]

LETTER LXXXVIII.

TO JOHN WHITGIFT[1], BISHOP OF WORCESTER.
Feb. 1582.

[Grind. Reg. Fo. 140.]

AFTER my very hearty commendations to your good lordship. Where, by order from the lords and others of the Queen's majesty's most honourable privy council, I sent to your lordship a commission to visit the dean and chapter of Litchfield, being then in hope that their lordships and I should be able, without your lordship's trouble, to order and compound the controversy between my lord of Coventry and Litchfield and Beacon and Babington, for the office of chancellor within that diocese: but now having travailed with my lord bishop to yield his conformity and consent, that Beacon and Babington together, according to a joint commission of his own granting, might quietly exercise the jurisdiction, until the right and validity of that patent might be tried by order of law, as my chancellor and Dr Hammond, after deliberate hearing of the cause, did also think reasonable, (as by the copy of their order herein inclosed may appear to your lordship,) and being no way able to win his lordship to suffer that order to take place, whereof the lords of the council and I like well, I am enforced to execute it by my own authority, which I could not so conveniently do any way, to void appeal and other impeachments, as by a visitation; the burden whereof, partly by direction of the lords of the council, I make bold to lay upon your lordship. Not meaning, notwithstanding, to trouble you and the rest to travel any further than to Litchfield itself; and there only, while you are in visiting of the cathedral church, to call

[1 The archbishop now wrote letters to bishop Whitgift, to direct him in the deciding a great debate between two civilians, Beacon and Babington, contending for the chancellorship of the diocese of Litchfield and Coventry; which controversy, it seems, came before the council, and they referred it to the archbishop. See Strype, Grind. 405.]

my lord bishop and those two competitors of the office before you, and by your lordship's good wisdom to compound the controversy quietly, if you can; and if your lordship cannot, then to take the pains to examine the matter; and to certify at your convenient opportunity in whom you shall think the fault to be, and to prorogue the visitation of the diocese until the last of June, and the other for the church, as your lordship shall think convenient.

And for your lordship's better information, I have sent you, sealed in a packet herewith, all such writings as were exhibited unto me by my lord bishop and both the competitors; to the end that your lordship, if the necessity of the case shall so require, may frame articles for the examination of all whom the controversy doth concern. I have likewise sent to your lordship a commission, in your lordship's name, to Beacon and Babington, to exercise the jurisdiction for the government of the dioceses, *pendente visitatione*, being conformable to the order; with a determination notwithstanding, that your lordship shall alter or revoke the same commission upon any cause, making me privy thereof by your lordship's letter.

And for that this only controversy is the cause of this visitation, I do mean that it shall be merely charitative, and not to burden the clergy of any procurations as yet; and withal not to trouble your lordship much longer about this matter there, than you shall be occasioned otherwise to tarry for the speeding of the visitation of the church: yet your lordship may direct these competitors to attend upon your lordship elsewhere, if you think good, and find occasion for the appeasing of the controversy, and which is so offensive in the opinion of the lords of the council and mine, and so scandalous to all parties whom it concerneth, and so prejudicial and hurtful to the quietness of the diocese, that I trust your lordship will take pains to end it: and if you cannot so do, yet until it may be otherwise done, to have care of the government of the diocese, in effect yours, during this commission. And thus laying many burdens upon your lordship, I commit the same to the grace and protection of the Almighty. From Lambeth, this —— day of February, 1582.

LETTERS AND DOCUMENTS

RELATING TO

ARCHBISHOP GRINDAL'S SEQUESTRATION AND RESIGNATION.

INTRODUCTORY REMARKS.

[The following extract from Strype, (Grindal, pp. 325—seq.) will put the reader in possession of the circumstances which gave rise to the following letters.]

A. D. 1576.
The queen's offence with him about prophecies.

I SHALL now proceed to relate a matter well-meant by the archbishop, and therefore wherein he took much pains; but it proved the cause of much trouble, sorrow, and affliction to him, as long as he was archbishop, laying him under the Queen's lasting displeasure. The matter was this: he well perceived the ignorance of the clergy, and the great need there was of more frequent preaching for the instruction of the people in the grounds and truth of religion. In order to which he encouraged a practice that was taken up in divers places of the nation, and particularly in Northamptonshire, and allowed by many bishops in their dioceses: the manner whereof was, that the ministers of such a division, at a set time, met together in some church belonging to a market or other large town; and there each in their order explained, according to their ability, some particular portion of scripture allotted them before. And after all of them had done, a moderator, who was one of the gravest and best learned among them, made his observations upon what the rest had said, and determined the true sense of the place. And all was to be despatched within such a space of time. And these were commonly called *exercises* or *prophesyings*. At these assemblies there were great confluxes of people to hear and learn. And by this means the ministers and curates were forced to read authors, and consult expositors and commentators, and to follow their studies, that they might speak to purpose when they were to appear in public: and hereby they considerably profited themselves in the knowledge of the scripture. But the inconvenience was, that at these meetings happened at length confusions and disturbances; some affecting to shew their parts, and to confute others that spake not so appositely perhaps as themselves. They also sometimes would broach heterodox opinions. And some that had been silenced from their preaching, for their incompliance with the established worship, would intrude themselves here, and vent themselves against the liturgy and hierarchy; some would speak against states or particular persons. The people also fell to arguing and disputing much upon religion: sometimes a layman would take upon him to speak; so that the exercises degenerated into factions, divisions, and censurings. Hence they began to be by some cried out against, and disliked.

The archbishop hereupon laboured to redress these mischiefs and irregularities, by setting down rules and orders for the more useful management of these exercises, which bore this title:

Orders for reformation of abuses about the learned exercises and conferences amongst the ministers of the church.

[Cotton. MS. Cleopatra F. II. p. 261.]

1. IMPRIMIS, The said exercises are to be used only in such churches, and at such times, as the bishop of the diocese shall under his hand and seal appoint.

2. ITEM, That in all such assemblies for the said conferences or exercises, either the archdeacon, if he be a divine, or else some one other grave learned graduate, at the least, to be appointed and allowed by the bishop as before, be present, and moderate the said exercises.

3. ITEM, That a catalogue of names be made and allowed of those that are judged meet to be speakers in course in the said exercises; which are known to be able to speak aptly, and to the profit and edifying of the hearers: and such parts of the scripture entreated of as the bishop shall appoint.

4. ITEM, That the rest of the ministers, not able to speak publicly with commendation, be assigned by the mode-

rators some task for the increase of their learning, to be comprised in writing, or otherwise, concerning the exposition of some part of scripture. And those tasks to be published privately before the ministers only, and not before the laity.

5. ITEM, *Ante omnia*, that no lay person be suffered to speak publicly in those assemblies.

6. ITEM, That no man speaking in the said exercises shall be suffered to glance openly or covertly against any state, or any person public or private. If he do, the moderators shall immediately interrupt him, and put him to silence; and notice to be made of the cause of interruption to the bishop; and the party interrupted not to be again admitted without the bishop's approbation, and the knowledging of his offence.

7. ITEM, That no man be suffered in the said exercises to make any invection against the laws, rites, policies, and discipline of the church of England established by public authority. If any attempt the contrary, he is immediately to be commanded to silence. And the moderator or moderators are therein to satisfy the auditory. And the speaker shall not be admitted to speak any more, till he, after public satisfaction made, shall obtain a new admission and approbation of the bishop.

8. ITEM, Forasmuch as divers ministers, deprived from their livings, and inhibited to preach, for not obeying the public orders and discipline of the church of England, have intruded themselves in sundry places to be speakers in the said exercises; and being excluded from pulpits, have in the said exercises usually made their invections against the orders, rites, and discipline of the church, which hath been the cause to move divers to a mislike of the said exercises, (being of themselves, if they be well used, very profitable for many respects,) every bishop is to take strict order in his diocese, that hereafter none be suffered to be speakers in the said exercises, which remain deprived or inhibited for the causes aforesaid, except they shall have before conformed themselves to order; neither any other which shall not, both by subscription and daily practice, conform himself to public orders and discipline of this church by law established.

EDM. CANTUAR.

All this pains did the archbishop take to rectify and take away the abuses of these religious exercises, rather than wholly to abolish them. However the Queen liked not of them, nor would have them continued; as seeing probably how very apt they were to be abused. Nor did she like that the laity should neglect their secular affairs by repairing to these meetings; which she thought also might fill their heads with notions, and so occasion dissensions and unquiet disputes, and it may be, seditions in the state. And the archbishop being at court, she particularly declared herself offended at the numbers of preachers, as well as at the exercises, and warned him to redress both: urging, that it was good for the church to have few preachers, and that three or four might suffice for a county; and that the reading of the homilies to the people was enough. In short, she required him to do these two things, viz. to abridge the number of preachers, and to put down the religious exercises. The speeches she used to him were somewhat sharp; and she was very resolute to have no more exercises of this sort, and cared not for any great increase of preachers; but that the licenses for preaching should be more sparingly granted out[1]; and she expected the archbishop should give especial orders for both.

A.D. 1576. The queen likes not of them.

This did not a little afflict the grave man. He thought the queen made some infringement upon his office, to whom the highest trust in the church of England, next to herself, was committed; and therefore, that she was somewhat too peremptory to require this to be done, without advising at all with him in a matter so directly respecting religion and the souls of her subjects: nor could he in conscience comply with her commands. Therefore, when he came home, he resolved to write at large his mind to her. And he had to back him two great men at the court, the lord Treasurer and the earl of Leicester: the latter whereof was not perhaps so much to be depended upon; but he delivered his letter to the queen, dated December 20, for which the archbishop thanked him.

The archbishop writes to the queen about them.

[1 See her letter to the Bishops, Appendix I.]

LETTER LXXXIX.

TO THE QUEEN,

CONCERNING SUPPRESSING THE PROPHECIES, AND RESTRAINING THE NUMBER OF PREACHERS.

Dec. 20, 1576.

[Lansdown MS. 23. No. 12.]

WITH most humble remembrance of my bounden duty to your Majesty: It may please the same to be advertised, that the speeches which it hath pleased you to deliver unto me, when I last attended on your Highness, concerning abridging the number of preachers, and the utter suppression of all learned exercises and conferences among the ministers of the church, allowed by their bishops and ordinaries, have exceedingly dismayed and discomforted me. Not so much for that the said speeches sounded very hardly against mine own person, being but one particular man, and not much to be accounted of; but most of all for that the same might both tend to the public harm of God's church, whereof your Highness ought to be *nutricia*, and also to the heavy burdening of your own conscience before God, if they should be put in strict execution. It was not your Majesty's pleasure then, the time not serving thereto, to hear me at any length concerning the said two matters then propounded: I thought it therefore my duty by writing to declare some part of my mind unto your Highness; beseeching the same with patience to read over this that I now send, written with mine own rude scribbling hand; which seemeth to be of more length than it is indeed: for I say with Ambrose, *Scribo manu mea, quod sola legas*[1].

MADAM,

First of all, I must and will, during my life, confess, that there is no earthly creature to whom I am so much bounden as to your Majesty; who, notwithstanding mine insufficiency, (which commendeth your grace the more,) hath bestowed upon me so many and so great benefits as I could never hope for, much less deserve. I do therefore, accord-

Esa. xlix. 33.
Queens shall be thy nursing mothers.

Ambrosius ad Valentinian. Imperator.

[1 I write with mine own hand, for you alone to read it.]

ing to my most bounden duty, with all thanksgiving, bear A.D. 1576.
towards your Majesty a most humble, faithful, and thankful
heart; and that knoweth He which knoweth all things.
Neither do I ever intend to offend your Majesty in any thing,
unless, in the cause of God or of his church, by necessity
of office, and burden of conscience, I shall thereunto be enforced: and in those cases, (which I trust in God shall never
be urged upon me,) if I should use dissembling or flattering
silence, I should very evil requite your Majesty's so many and
so great benefits; for in so doing, both you might fall into
peril towards God, and I myself into endless damnation.

The prophet Ezechiel termeth us, ministers of the church, Ezekiel [xxxiii.]
speculatores[2], and not *adulatores*[3]. If we see the sword coming
by reason of any offence towards God, we must of necessity
give warning, or else the blood of those that perish will be
required at our hands. I beseech your Majesty thus to think
of me, that I do not conceive any evil opinion of you, although I cannot assent to those two articles then propounded.
I do with the rest of all your good subjects acknowledge,
that we have received by your government many and most
excellent benefits, as, among others, freedom of conscience,
suppressing of idolatry, sincere preaching of the gospel, with
public peace and tranquillity. I am also persuaded, that even
in these matters, which you seem now to urge, your zeal
and meaning is to the best. The like hath happened to
many of the best princes that ever were: yet have they not
refused afterwards to be better informed out of God's word.
King David, so much commended in the scriptures, had no 2 Sam. xxiv.
evil meaning, when he commanded the people to be numbered:
he thought it good policy in so doing, to understand what
forces he had in store to employ against God's enemies, if
occasion so required. Yet afterward, (saith the scripture,)
his own heart stroke him; and God, by the prophet Gad,
reprehended him for his offence, and gave him for the same
choice of three very hard penances, that is to say, famine,
war, and pestilence. Good king Ezechias, of courtesy and 2 Kings xx.
good affection, shewed to the ambassadors of the king of
Babylon the treasures of the house of God and of his own
house; and yet the prophet Esay told him, that God was

[2 Watchmen.]   [3 Flatterers.]

378 DOCUMENTS RELATING TO THE ARCHBISHOP'S SEQUESTRATION.

A.D. 1576.

therewith displeased. The godly king Jehoshaphat, for making league with his neighbour king Achab, (of like good meaning, no doubt,) was likewise reprehended by Jehu the prophet in this form of words: *Impio præbes auxilium, et his qui oderunt Dominum amicitia jungeris*, &c.¹ Ambrose, writing to Theodosius the emperor, useth these words: *Novi pietatem tuam erga Deum, lenitatem in homines; obligatus sum beneficiis tuis²*. And yet, for all that, the same Ambrose doth not forbear in the same epistle earnestly to persuade the said emperor to revoke an ungodly edict, wherein he had commanded a godly bishop to re-edify a Jewish synagogue, pulled down by the Christian people.

2 Chron. xix.

Prima Pars. Concerning suppressing preachers.

And so, to come to the present case; I may very well use unto your Highness the words of Ambrose above written, *Novi pietatem tuam*, &c. But surely I cannot marvel enough, how this strange opinion should once enter into your mind, that it should be good for the church to have few preachers.

Expostulates with the queen for the number of preachers. Matt. ix.

Alas, Madam! is the scripture more plain in any one thing, than that the gospel of Christ should be plentifully preached; and that plenty of labourers should be sent into the Lord's harvest; which, being great and large, standeth in need, not of a few, but many workmen?

1 Kings v.

There was appointed to the building of Salomon's material temple an hundred and fifty thousand artificers and labourers, besides three thousand three hundred overseers: and shall we think that a few preachers may suffice to build and edify the spiritual temple of Christ, which is his church?

Matt. xxviii.

Christ, when he sendeth forth his apostles, saith unto them, *Ite, prædicate evangelium omni creaturæ³*. But all God's creatures cannot be instructed in the gospel, unless all possible means be used, to have multitude of preachers and teachers to preach unto them.

Colos. iii.
2 Tim. iv.

Sermo Christi inhabitet in vobis opulente⁴, saith St Paul to the Colossians; and to Timothy, *Prædica sermonem, insta*

[¹ Thou helpest the ungodly, and art joined in friendship with those who hate the Lord.]

[² I know thy piety towards God, thy kindness towards men; I am bounden by thy benefits, &c. S. Ambros. Epist. xxix. Basil. 1567. Tom. III. p. 109.]

[³ Go ye, preach the gospel to every creature. Mark xvi. 15.]

[⁴ Let the word of Christ dwell in you richly.]

tempestive, intempestive, argue, increpa, exhortare[5]. Which things cannot be done without often and much preaching. {A.D. 1576.}

To this agreeth the practice of Christ's apostles, *Qui constituebant per singulas ecclesias presbyteros*[6]. {Acts xiv.} St Paul likewise, writing to Titus, writeth thus, *Hujus rei gratia reliqui te in Creta, ut quæ desunt pergas corrigere, et constituas oppidatim presbyteros*[7]. {Ad Tit.} And afterwards describeth, how the said *presbyteri* were to be qualified; not such as we are sometimes compelled to admit by mere necessity, (unless we should leave a great number of churches utterly desolate,) but such indeed as were able to exhort *per sanam doctrinam, et contradicentes convincere*[8]. {Ibid.} And in this place I beseech your Majesty to note one thing necessary to be noted; which is this, If the Holy Ghost prescribe expressly that preachers should be placed *oppidatim*[9], how can it well be thought, that three or four preachers may suffice for a shire?

Public and continual preaching of God's word is the ordinary mean and instrument of the salvation of mankind. {1 Pet. ii. 2.} St Paul calleth it the *ministry of reconciliation* of man unto God. {2 Cor. v.} By preaching of God's word the glory of God is enlarged, faith is nourished, and charity increased. By it the ignorant is instructed, the negligent exhorted and incited, the stubborn rebuked, the weak conscience comforted, and to all those that sin of malicious wickedness the wrath of God is threatened. {Psal. xxx.} By preaching also due obedience to Christian princes and magistrates is planted in the hearts of subjects: for obedience proceedeth of conscience; conscience is grounded upon the word of God; the word of God worketh his effect by preaching. So as generally, where preaching wanteth, obedience faileth.

No prince ever had more lively experience hereof than your Majesty hath had in your time, and may have daily. {Preaching God's word makes loyal subjects.} If your Majesty come to the city of London never so often, {London.} what gratulation, what joy, what concourse of people is

[5 Preach the word, be instant in season, out of season, reprove, rebuke, exhort.]

[6 Who appointed elders in every church.]

[7 For this cause I left thee in Crete, that thou mayest go on to set in order what is wanting, and appoint elders throughout every town.]

[8 By sound doctrine, and to convince gainsayers.]

[9 In every town.]

A.D. 1576. there to be seen! Yea, what acclamations and prayers to God for your long life, and other manifest significations of inward and unfeigned love, joined with most humble and hearty obedience, are there to be heard! Whereof cometh this, Madam, but of the continual preaching of God's word in that city, whereby that people hath been plentifully instructed in their duty towards God and your Majesty? On the contrary, what bred the rebellion in the north? Was it not papistry, and ignorance of God's word, through want of often preaching? And in the time of that rebellion, were not all men, of all states, that made profession of the gospel, most ready to offer their lives for your defence? insomuch that one poor parish in Yorkshire, which by continual preaching had been better instructed than the rest, (Halifax I mean,) was ready to bring three or four thousand able men into the field to serve you against the said rebels. How can your Majesty have a more lively trial and experience of the contrary effects of much preaching, and of little or no preaching? The one working most faithful obedience, and the other most unnatural disobedience and rebellion.

Halifax.

But it is thought of some, that many are admitted to preach, and few be able to do it well. That unable preachers be removed is very requisite, if ability and sufficiency may be rightly weighed and judged: and therein I trust as much is, and shall be, done as can be; for both I, for mine own part, (let it be spoken without any ostentation,) am very careful in allowing such preachers only, as be able and sufficient to be preachers, both for their knowledge in the scriptures, and also for testimony of their good life and conversation. And besides that, I have given very great charge to the rest of my brethren, the bishops of this province, to do the like. We admit no man to the office, that either professeth papistry or puritanism. Generally, the graduates of the university are only admitted to be preachers, unless it be some few which have excellent gifts of knowledge in the scriptures, joined with good utterance and godly persuasion. I myself procured above forty learned preachers and graduates, within less than six years, to be placed within the diocese of York, besides those I found there; and there I have left

The archbishop careful what preachers be allowed.

them: the fruits of whose travail in preaching your Majesty A.D. 1576. is like to reap daily, by most assured, dutiful obedience of your subjects in those parts.

But, indeed, this age judgeth very hardly, and nothing indifferently of the ability of preachers of our time; judging few or none in their opinion to be able. Which hard judgment groweth upon divers evil dispositions of men. St Paul doth commend the preaching of Christ crucified, *absque* 1 Cor. i. *eminentia sermonis*[1]. But in our time many have so delicate ears, that no preaching can satisfy them, unless it be sauced with much finess[2] and exornation of speech: which the same apostle utterly condemneth, and giveth this reason, *Ne evacueter crux Christi*[3].

Some there be also, that are mislikers of the godly reformation in religion now established; wishing indeed that there were no preachers at all; and so by depraving the ministers impugn religion, *non aperto marte, sed cuniculis*[4]: much like to the popish bishops in your father's time, who would have had the English translation of the Bible called in, as evil translated; and the new translating thereof to have been committed to themselves; which they never intended to perform.

A number there is, (and that is exceeding great,) whereof some are altogether worldly-minded, and only bent covetously to gather worldly goods and possessions; serving mammon, and not God. And another great sum have given over themselves to all carnal, vain, dissolute, and lascivious life, *volup-* 2 Tim. iii. *tatis amatores, magis quam Dei: et qui semetipsos dediderunt* Eph. iv. *ad patrandum omnem immunditiam cum aviditate*[5]. And Psal. cxix. because the preaching of God's word, which to all Christian consciences is sweet and delectable, is to them, having *cau-* 1 Tim. iv. *teriatas conscientias*[6], bitter and grievous, (for, as St Ambrose saith, *Quomodo possunt verba Dei dulcia esse in faucibus tuis,*

[1 Without excellency of speech.]

[2 Rhetorical artifice.]

[3 Lest the cross of Christ be made of none effect.]

[4 Not by open opposition, but by secret undermining.]

[5 Lovers of pleasure more than of God, and who have given themselves over to commit all uncleanness with greediness.]

[6 Consciences seared.]

in quibus est amaritudo nequitiæ[1]?) therefore they wish also, that there were no preachers at all. But because they dare not directly condemn the office of preaching, so expressly commanded by God's word, (for that were open blasphemy,) they turn themselves altogether, and with the same meaning as the other do, to take exceptions against the persons of them that be admitted to preach.

But God forbid, Madam, that you should open your ears to any of these wicked persuasions, or any way go about to diminish the preaching of Christ's gospel: for that would ruinate all together at the length. *Quum defecerit prophetia, dissipabitur populus*[2], saith Salomon.

Now, where it is thought, that the reading of the godly homilies, set forth by public authority, may suffice, I continue of the same mind I was when I attended last upon your Majesty. The reading of homilies hath his commodity; but is nothing comparable to the office of preaching. The godly preacher is termed in the gospel *fidelis servus et prudens, qui novit famulitio Domini cibum demensum dare in tempore*[3]; who can apply his speech according to the diversity of times, places, and hearers, which cannot be done in homilies: exhortations, reprehensions, and persuasions, are uttered with more affection, to the moving of the hearers, in sermons than in homilies. Besides, homilies were devised by the godly bishops in your brother's time, only to supply necessity, for want of preachers; and are by the statute not to be preferred, but to give place to sermons, whensoever they may be had; and were never thought in themselves alone to contain sufficient instruction for the Church of England. For it was then found, as it is found now, that this Church of England hath been by appropriations, and that not without sacrilege, spoiled of the livings, which at the first were appointed to the office of preaching and teaching. Which appropriations were first annexed to abbeys; and after came to the crown; and now are dispersed to private men's possessions, without hope to

[1] How can the word of God be sweet in thy mouth, in which is the bitterness of sin? Serm. 13 in Psal. cxviii. Tom. IV. p. 695.]

[2] When prophesy shall fail, the people shall be scattered.]

[3] A faithful and wise servant, who knoweth how to give his Lord's family their apportioned food in season.]

reduce the same to the original institution. So as at this A.D. 1576. day, in mine opinion, where one church is able to yield sufficient living for a learned preacher, there are at the least seven churches unable to do the same: and in many parishes of your realm, where there be seven or eight hundred souls, (the more is the pity,) there are not eight pounds a year reserved for a minister. In such parishes it is not possible to place able preachers, for want of convenient stipend. If every flock might have a preaching pastor, which is rather to be wished than hoped for, then were reading of homilies altogether unnecessary. But to supply that want of preaching of God's word, which is the food of the soul, growing upon the necessities afore-mentioned, both in your brother's time, and in your time, certain godly homilies have been devised, that the people should not be altogether destitute of instruction: for it is an old and a true proverb, "better half a loaf than no bread."

Now for the second point, which is concerning the learned exercise and conference amongst the ministers of the church: I have consulted with divers of my brethren, the bishops, by letters; who think the same as I do, viz. a thing profitable to the church, and therefore expedient to be continued. And I trust your Majesty will think the like, when your Highness shall have been informed of the manner and order thereof; what authority it hath of the scriptures; what commodity it bringeth with it; and what incommodities will follow, if it be clean taken away. *Secunda Pars. Concerning the exercises.*

The authors of this exercise are the bishops of the diocese where the same is used; who both by the law of God, and by the canons and constitutions of the church now in force, have authority to appoint exercises to their inferior ministers, for increase of learning and knowledge in the scriptures, as to them seemeth most expedient: for that pertaineth *ad disciplinam clericalem*[4]. The times appointed for the assembly is once a month, or once in twelve or fifteen days, at the discretion of the ordinary. The time of the exercise is two hours: the place, the church of the town appointed for the assembly. The matter entreated of is as followeth. Some text of scripture, before appointed to be spoken of, is *An account of the exercises.*

[4 To the discipline of ministers.]

interpreted in this order: First, the occasion of the place is shewed. Secondly, the end. Thirdly, the proper sense of the place. Fourthly, the propriety of the words: and those that be learned in the tongues shewing the diversities of interpretations. Fifthly, where the like phrases are used in the scriptures. Sixthly, places in the scriptures, seeming to repugn, are reconciled. Seventhly, the arguments of the text are opened. Eighthly, it is also declared, what virtues and what vices are there touched; and to which of the commandments they pertain. Ninthly, how the text hath been wrested by the adversaries, if occasion so require. Tenthly, and last of all, what doctrine of faith or manners the text doth contain. The conclusion is, with the prayer for your Majesty and all estates, as is appointed by the Book of Common Prayer, and a psalm.

The orders of them.

These orders following are also observed in the said exercise. First, two or three of the gravest and best learned pastors are appointed of the bishop to moderate in every assembly. No man may speak, unless he be first allowed by the bishop, with this *proviso*, that no layman be suffered to speak at any time. No controversy of this present time and state shall be moved or dealt withal. If any attempt the contrary, he is put to silence by the moderator. None is suffered to glance openly or covertly at persons public or private; neither yet any one to confute another. If any man utter a wrong sense of the scripture, he is privately admonished thereof, and better instructed by the moderators, and other his fellow-ministers. If any man use immodest speech, or irreverent gesture or behaviour, or otherwise be suspected in life, he is likewise admonished, as before. If any wilfully do break these orders, he is presented to the bishop, to be by him corrected.

The ground of them.
1 Sam. xix.
1 Sam. x.
2 Kings ii.

The ground of this, or like exercise, is of great and ancient authority. For Samuel did practise such like exercises in his time, both at Naioth in Ramatha, and at Bethel. So did Elizæus the prophet, at Jericho. Which studious persons in those days were called *filii prophetarum*[1], that is to say, the disciples of the prophets, that being exercised in the study and knowledge of the scriptures, they might be able men to serve in God's church, as that time required.

[[1] The sons of the prophets.]

St Paul also doth make express mention, that the like in effect was used in the primitive church; and giveth rules for the order of the same; as namely, that two or three should speak, and the rest should keep silence. A. D. 1576.
1 Cor. xiv.

That exercise of the church in those days St Paul calleth *prophetiam*, and the speakers *prophetas*: terms very odious in our days to some, because they are not rightly understood. For indeed *prophetia*, in that and like places of St Paul, doth not, as it doth sometimes, signify *prediction* of things to come, which gift is not now ordinary in the church of God; but signifieth there, by the consent of the best ancient writers, the interpretation and exposition of the scriptures. And therefore doth St Paul attribute unto those that be called *prophetæ* in that chapter, *doctrinam ad ædificationem, exhortationem, et consolationem*². Called prophecies in scripture.

1 Cor. xiv.

This gift of expounding and interpreting the scriptures was, in St Paul's time, given to many by special miracle, without study: so was also, by like miracle, the gift to speak with strange tongues, which they had never learned. But now, miracles ceasing, men must attain to the knowledge of the Hebrew, Greek, and Latin tongues, &c. by travail and study, God giving the increase. So must men also attain by like means to the gift of expounding and interpreting the scriptures. And amongst other helps, nothing is so necessary as these above named exercises and conferences amongst the ministers of the church: which in effect are all one with the exercises of students in divinity in the universities; saving that the first is done in a tongue understood, to the more edifying of the unlearned hearers. Acts ii.

Acts x.

Howsoever report hath been made to your Majesty concerning these exercises, yet I and others of your bishops, whose names are noted in the margin hereof, as they have testified unto me by their letters, having found by experience, that these profits and commodities following have ensued of them: 1. The ministers of the church are more skilful and ready in the scriptures, and apter to teach their flocks. 2. It withdraweth them from idleness, wandering, gaming, &c. 3. Some, afore suspected in doctrine, are brought hereby to open confession of the truth. 4. Ignorant ministers are Cantuar.
London.
Winton.
Bathon.
Litchfield.
Glocestren.
Lincoln.
Cicestren.
Exon.
Menevensis, al. Davidis.

[² *Teaching unto edification, exhortation, and comfort.*]

A.D. 1576. driven to study, if not for conscience, yet for shame and fear
The benefit of these exercises. of discipline. 5. The opinion of laymen, touching the idleness of the clergy, is hereby removed. 6. Nothing by experience beateth down popery more than that ministers (as some of my brethren do certify) grow to such good knowledge, by means of these exercises, that where afore were not three able preachers, now are thirty, meet to preach at St Paul's Cross; and forty or fifty besides, able to instruct their own cures. So as it is found by experience the best means to increase knowledge in the simple, and to continue it in the learned. Only backward men in religion, and contemners of learning in the countries abroad, do fret against it; which in truth doth the more commend it. The dissolution of it would breed triumph to the adversaries, and great sorrow and grief unto the favourers of religion; contrary
Ezek. xiii. 18. to the counsel of Ezekiel, who saith, *Cor justi non est contristandum*[1]. And although some few have abused this good and necessary exercise, there is no reason that the malice of
Abuses of them. a few should prejudice all. Abuses may be reformed, and that which is good may remain. Neither is there any just cause of offence to be taken, if divers men make divers senses of one sentence of scripture; so that all the senses be good and agreeable to the analogy and proportion of faith: for otherwise we must needs condemn all the ancient fathers and doctors of the church, who most commonly expound one and the same text of the scripture diversely, and yet all to the good of the church. Therefore doth St Basil compare the scriptures to a well; out of the which the more a man draweth, the better and sweeter is the water.

Epilogus secundæ partis. I trust, when your Majesty hath considered and well weighed the premises, you will rest satisfied, and judge that no such inconveniences can grow of these exercises, as you have been informed, but rather the clean contrary. And for my own part, because I am very well assured, both by reasons and arguments taken out of the holy scriptures, and
He refuses to suppress these exercises. by experience, (the most certain seal of sure knowledge,) that the said exercises, for the interpretation and exposition of the scriptures, and for exhortation and comfort drawn out of the same, are both profitable to increase knowledge

[1 The heart of the righteous must not be made sad.]

among the ministers, and tendeth to the edifying of the hearers,—I am forced, with all humility, and yet plainly, to profess, that I cannot with safe conscience, and without the offence of the majesty of God, give my assent to the suppressing of the said exercises: much less can I send out any injunction for the utter and universal subversion of the same. I say with St Paul, "I have no power to destroy, but to only edify;" and with the same apostle, "I can do nothing against the truth, but for the truth." *A.D. 1576.*

2 Cor. x.
2 Cor. xiii.

If it be your Majesty's pleasure, for this or any other cause, to remove me out of this place, I will with all humility yield thereunto, and render again to your Majesty that I received of the same. I consider with myself, *Quod horrendum est incidere in manus Dei viventis*[2]. I consider also, *Quod qui facit contra conscientiam (divinis juribus nixam) ædificat ad gehennam*[3]. "And what should I win, if I gained" (I will not say a bishoprick, but) "the whole world, and lose mine own soul?" *O episcopus vere apostolicus!*

Heb. x.

Cyprian. O homo vere divinus!
Matt. xvi.

Bear with me, I beseech you, Madam, if I choose rather to offend your earthly majesty, than to offend the heavenly majesty of God. And now being sorry, that I have been so long and tedious to your Majesty, I will draw to an end, most humbly praying the same well to consider these two short petitions following. *His advice to the queen.*

The first is, that you would refer all these ecclesiastical matters which touch religion, or the doctrine and discipline of the church, unto the bishops and divines of your realm; according to the example of all godly Christian emperors and princes of all ages. For indeed they are things to be judged, (as an ancient father writeth,) *in ecclesia, seu synodo, non in palatio*[4]. When your Majesty hath questions of the laws of your realm, you do not decide the same in your court, but send them to your judges to be determined. Likewise for doubts in matters of doctrine or discipline of the church, the ordinary way is to refer the decision of the same to the bishops, and other head ministers of the church. *Prima petitio.*

[2 That it is a fearful thing to fall into the hands of the living God.]

[3 That he who acts against his conscience, (resting upon the laws of God,) builds for hell.]

[4 In the church, or a synod, not in a palace.]

Ambrose to Theodosius useth these words: *Si de causis pecuniariis comites tuos consulis, quanto magis in causa religionis sacerdotes Domini æquum est consulas*[1]? And likewise the same father to the good emperor Valentinianus: *Si conferendum de fide, sacerdotum debet esse ista collatio; sicut factum est sub Constantino augustæ memoriæ principe, qui nullas leges ante præmisit, sed liberum dedit judicium sacerdotibus*[2]. And the same father saith, that Constantius the emperor, son to the said Constantine the Great, began well, by reason he followed his father's steps at the first; but ended ill, because he took upon him *de fide intra palatium judicare*[3], (for so be the words of Ambrose,) and thereby fell into Arianism; a terrible example!

The said Ambrose, so much commended in all histories for a godly bishop, goeth yet farther, and writeth to the same emperor in this form: *Si docendus est episcopus a laico, quid sequetur? Laicus ergo disputet, et episcopus audiat; episcopus discat a laico. At certe, si vel scripturarum seriem divinarum vel vetera tempora retractemus, quis est qui abnuat, in causa fidei, in causa, inquam, fidei, episcopos solere de imperatoribus Christianis, non imperatores de episcopis judicare*[4]? Would God your Majesty would follow this ordinary course! You should procure to yourself much more quietness of mind, better please God, avoid many offences, and the church should be more quietly and peaceably governed, much to your comfort, and commodity of your realm.

The second petition I have to make to your Majesty is

[1 If in pecuniary matters you consult with your earls, how much more is it fit that you consult with the Lord's priests in the cause of religion? Basil. 1567. Tom. III. p. 108.]

[2 If we confer about faith, the conference ought to be left to the priests; as it was done under Constantine, a prince of most honourable memory; who set forth no laws, before he had left them to the free judgment of the priests. Tom. III. p. 123.]

[3 To judge of faith within the palace. Ibid.]

[4 If a bishop be to be taught by a layman, what will follow? Let the layman then dispute, and the bishop hear: let the bishop learn of the layman. But certainly, if we have recourse either to the order of the holy scriptures or to ancient times, who is there that can deny, that in the cause of faith, I say, in the cause of faith, bishops were wont to judge concerning Christian emperors, not emperors of bishops? P. 122.]

this: that, when you deal in matters of faith and religion, or A. D. 1576. matters that touch the church of Christ, which is his spouse, bought with so dear a price, you would not use to pronounce so resolutely and peremptorily, *quasi ex auctoritate*, as ye may do in civil and extern matters; but always remember, that in God's causes the will of God, and not the will of any earthly creature, is to take place. It is the antichristian voice of the pope, *Sic volo, sic jubeo; stet pro ratione voluntas*[5]. In God's matters all princes ought to bow their sceptres to the Son of God, and to ask counsel at his mouth, what they ought to do. David exhorteth all kings and rulers to *serve God with fear and trembling*. [Juvenal. Sat. vi. 223.] Psal. ii.

Remember, Madam, that you are a mortal creature. "Look not only (as was said to Theodosius[6]) upon the purple and princely array, wherewith ye are apparelled; but consider withal, what is that that is covered therewith. Is it not flesh and blood? Is it not dust and ashes? Is it not a corruptible body, which must return to his earth again, God knoweth how soon?" Must not you also one day appear *ante tremendum tribunal Crucifixi, ut recipias ibi, prout gesseris in corpore, sive bonum sive malum*[7]? Theodoret. Eccles. Hist. lib. v. cap. 18. 2 Cor. v.

And although ye are a mighty prince, yet remember that He which dwelleth in heaven is mightier. He is, as the Psalmist sayeth, *terribilis, et is qui aufert spiritum principum, terribilis super omnes reges terræ*[8]. Psal. lxxvi.

Wherefore I do beseech you, Madam, *in visceribus Christi*[9], when you deal in these religious causes, set the majesty of God before your eyes, laying all earthly majesty aside: determine with yourself to obey his voice, and with all humility

[5 So I will have it; so I command: let my will stand for a reason.]

[6 Χρὴ μέντοι εἰδέναι τὴν φύσιν, καὶ τὸ ταύτης θνητόν τε καὶ διαρρέον, καὶ τὸν πρόγονον χοῦν ἐξ οὗ γεγόναμεν, καὶ εἰς ὃν ἀπορρέομεν· καὶ μὴ τῷ ἄνθει τῆς ἁλουργίδος ἀποβουκολούμενον, ἀγνοεῖν τοῦ καλυπτομένου σώματος τὴν ἀσθένειαν. Theodoreti Eccles. Hist. Lib. v. c. 18. Paris. 1673, p. 220.]

[7 Before the fearful judgment-seat of the Crucified, to receive there according as you have done in the body, whether it be good or evil?]

[8 Terrible, and he who taketh away the spirit of princes, and is terrible above all the kings of the earth.]

[9 In the bowels of Christ.]

say unto him, *Non mea, sed tua voluntas fiat*[1]. God hath blessed you with great felicity in your reign, now many years; beware you do not impute the same to your own deserts or policy, but give God the glory. And as to instruments and means, impute your said felicity, first, to the goodness of the cause which ye have set forth, (I mean Christ's true religion;) and, secondly, to the sighs and groanings of the godly in their fervent prayer to God for you; which have hitherto, as it were, tied and bound the hands of God, that he could not pour out his plagues upon you and your people, most justly deserved.

<small>2 Chron. xxiv.</small>

Take heed, that ye never once think of declining from God, lest that be verified of you, which is written of Ozeas, [Joash,] who continued a prince of good and godly government for many years together; and afterwards, *cum roboratus esset*, (saith the text,) *elevatum est cor ejus in interitum suum, et neglexit Dominum*[2]. Ye have done many things well; but except ye persevere to the end, ye cannot be blessed. For if ye turn from God, then God will turn away his merciful countenance from you. And what remaineth then to be looked for, but only a terrible expectation of God's judgments, and an heaping up of wrath against the day of wrath?

<small>Heb. x. Rom. ii.</small>

But I trust in God, your Majesty will always humble yourself under his mighty hand, and go forward in the zealous setting forth of God's true religion, always yielding due obedience and reverence to the word of God, the only rule of faith and religion. And if ye so do, although God hath just cause many ways to be angry with you and us for our unfaithfulness, yet I doubt nothing, but that for his own name's sake, and for his own glory's sake, he will still hold his merciful hand over us, shield and protect us under the shadow of his wings, as he hath done hitherto.

I beseech God, our heavenly Father, plentifully to pour his principal Spirit upon you, and always to direct your heart in his holy fear. Amen.

[[1] Not mine, but thy will be done.]

[[2] When he was strengthened, his heart was lifted up to his destruction, and he regarded not the Lord.]

LETTER XC.

TO LORD BURLEIGH.
Dec. 16, 1576.
[Lansdown MS. 23. No. 9.]

I WROTE my opinion to her Majesty about eight days ago, touching the two matters wherewith her Highness shewed herself offended at my last being at court. My lord of Leicester delivered my said writing to her Majesty. I thank him therefor. But I cannot yet understand, whether her Highness have read it or no, much less whether she like or dislike of it. The writing was somewhat long, and could not be otherwise, if any proofs should be used. I pray your lordship, if you understand at any time any thing concerning the premises worthy the advertisement, to let me hear from you. God keep your lordship! Lambeth, 16 of December, 1576.

Your lordship's in Christ,
EDM. CANTUAR.

To the Right Honourable my very good lord, the Lord Burleigh, Lord Treasurer of England.

LETTER XCI.

TO LORD BURLEIGH.
Dec. 17, 1576.
[Lansdown MS. 23. No. 10.]

I THANK your good lordship, that you are so careful in this cause of the church. My lord of Leicester writeth to me in form, as you see. I pray your lordship, return me his letter. I see no reason why the people should be excluded, seeing St Paul giveth so great commendation to that 1 Cor. xiv. which was used in the primitive church; especially for the benefit that groweth thereby to the hearers. I have written thanks to my lord of Leicester. I pray your lordship, let

A.D. 1576. one of your servants deliver my letter. I pray your lordship, appoint when you come to take an evil[1] dinner with me, and let me know aforehand of your coming; not meaning your diet more sumptuous, but more wholesome. God keep your lordship! From Lambeth, 17°. Decembr. 1576.

Your lordship's in Christ,
EDM. CANTUAR.

*To the Right Honourable my very
good lord, the Lord Burleigh,
Lord Treasurer of England.*

LETTER XCII.

TO THE RIGHT HONOURABLE THE LORDS OF HER MAJESTY'S PRIVY COUNCIL IN THE STAR-CHAMBER[2].

Nov. 30, 1577.

[Cott. MSS. Cleop. F. 2, fo. 280.]

RIGHT honourable and my singular good lords: I cannot deny, but that I have been commanded both by the Queen's majesty herself, and also by divers of your honourable lordships in her name, to suppress all those exercises within my province, that are commonly called prophecies. But I do protest before God, the judge of all hearts, that I did not of any stubbornness or wilfulness refuse to accomplish the same, but only upon conscience; for that I found such kind of exercise set down in the holy scriptures, and the

[1 Plain.]

[2 Six months being now expired, and growing towards the latter end of November, the lord treasurer sent a private and kind message to the archbishop by Goodman, dean of Westminster, containing some account after what manner the Star-chamber would proceed in his business; and withal his lordship's directions to him, how he should demean himself in respect of the offence he gave the queen by the exercises. (See Appendix II.) But the archbishop thought not fit to comply so far as was advised; but still esteeming himself not to have done amiss, he would not ask pardon, which supposed a fault. Nor did he appear in person before the lords in the Star-chamber, but sent an humble writing to them the next day, viz. November the 30th, brought by Sir Walter Mildmay. Strype, pp. 348—350.]

use of the same to have continued in the primitive church: A.D. 1577. and was persuaded, that (the abuses being reformed, which I always offered myself ready to labour in) the said exercises might yet serve to the great profit of the church; and feared that the utter suppressing of them would breed offence. And therefore was a most humble suitor unto her Majesty, that I might not be made the chief instrument in suppressing the same: yet not prejudicing or condemning any, that in respect of policy, or otherwise, should be of contrary judgment, or being of authority should suppress them. For I know right well, that there be some things of that nature, wherein divers men may be of divers opinions, and abound in their own sense (being not repugnant to the analogy of faith) without any prejudice to their salvation, or any prejudice of either to other. Notwithstanding, howsoever others, being otherwise persuaded, might safely do it, yet I thought it not safe for me (being so persuaded in mind) to be the doer of that, whereof mine own heart and conscience would condemn me.

And whereas I have sustained the restraint of my liberty, and sequestration of my jurisdiction, now by the space of six months, I am so far from repining thereat, or thinking myself injuriously or hardly dealt withal therein at her Majesty's hands, that I do thankfully embrace, and frankly with all humility acknowledge, her princely, gracious, and rare clemency towards me: who, having authority and power to have used greater and sharper severity against me, and for good policy and example thinking it so expedient, hath notwithstanding dealt so mercifully, mildly, and gently with me.

But the greatest grief that ever I have had, or have, is the loss of her Majesty's favour, and the sustaining of the displeasure of so gracious a sovereign, by whom the church and realm of England hath been so long so happily governed; and by whom myself, privately and specially above other subjects, have received so many and so great benefits above all my deserving. For the recovery of whose gracious favour, I most humbly beseech your lordships to be means to her Majesty for me: the which obtained I shall esteem far above all worldly benefits whatsoever. And I protest here before God and your honours, that not only my dutiful and humble

A.D. 1577. obedience to her Majesty shall be such, as she shall have no cause to repent her of her gracious goodness and clemency shewed unto me; but also that by my most fervent, hearty, and daily prayer, as I have done hitherto, so I will continue, according to my bounden duty, to make most earnest suit unto Almighty God for the long preservation of her Majesty's most happy reign, to the unspeakable benefit of the church and realm of England[1].

EDM. CANTUAR.

30th November, 1577.

LETTER XCIII.

TO DR MATTHEW HUTTON, DEAN OF YORK.

Dec. 2, 1577.

[From the Lambeth MSS. No. 1138, 3.]

SALUTEM in Christo. This bringer can inform you something of my state, both for health of body and other my troubles. About six weeks ago, and so on farther till the

[1] Notwithstanding, the before specified submission of the archbishop would not take effect, neither would the declaration of these inconveniences prevail. Nor was he restored to his liberty, nor the exercise of his jurisdiction, as yet. Nor do I find that he ever after much enjoyed the queen's favour: insomuch that he was desirous to resign his archbishopric, perhaps upon the grief of the small countenance he had from her, as well as for the affliction of losing his sight; as we shall see hereafter.

In January following it came to that pass with the archbishop, that there was much talk of depriving him, since his submission and recantation was not thought sufficient, and considering the need there would be of an archbishop to act and preside in the church. This was very ill resented by the true protestants, and they were highly concerned at it; and urged, how much it would prove to the joy of papists, and their encouragement....But the archbishop's crime was not thought so big as to merit a deprivation; and the disgust it might give being considered, the thought of depriving him was laid aside; and it was determined to proceed more mildly, and that the archbishop should only still continue under his sequestration *ab officio*. Strype, Grind. p. 354.]

26th of November, I was put in assured hope of liberty, &c. A.D. 1577. About that time arose a sudden contrary tempest, which had brought me to have appeared in the Star-chamber², 29° Novembris last, if God had not laid me up two days before of my old disease, the stone. By that occasion my appearance was respited; and I now remain as a man in suspense, *inter spem metumque*³; but hope that God will in the end turn all to the best. I thank you for your manifold significations of your good will towards me and mine. I pray you be good to the bringer, in that you may lawfully commend [command] me, as you know. God keep you! 2. Dec. 1577.

    Yours in Christ,
      EDM. CANTUAR.
To my loving friend, Mr Dean of York.

LETTER XCIV.

TO DR MATTHEW HUTTON.
Feb. 18, 1579.
[Lambeth MSS. Ibid.]

SALUTEM in Christo. This bringer can inform you that I am, (thank be to God!) in reasonable good health. My case dependeth long, as you see, and some repulse of suit lately made hath been given; and yet, if a man may believe court promises, I was at no time so near an end of my troubles as this present. *Domini voluntas fiat*⁴. Keep this to yourself. I pray you, shew favour unto this stranger for perfecting of his long travels. Sir Peter is a good man and lendeth freely. The merchant always harpeth upon interest. He will engage all to Sir Peter or one of his deputies. Surely the thing will prove to undoubted benefit, both public and private. If I had remained with you, I would have helped him in this case, especially now when the matter is growing ripe, &c. How the world goeth here, ye shall hear by other men. I

[² See Appendix III. p. 408.]
[³ Between hope and fear.]
[⁴ The will of the Lord be done.]

would ye had a good errand to town, that I might see you. I thank you for my poor kinsfolk and servants. 18. Feb. 1578. [1579.]

God keep you,

EDM. CANTUAR. tuus.

To my loving friend, Mr Dean of York.

LETTER XCV.

TO THE LORDS AND OTHERS OF THE PRIVY COUNCIL.
March 30, 1580.

[Cotton MSS. Vespasian, F. 12, fo. 192.]

My duty to your honourable lordships humbly remembered. I must still crave pardon of your good lordships for my often troubling of you with my importune letters. The 24th of January last past (as divers times before), I made most humble petition to your good lordships to be means for me to her Majesty, for my liberty and restitution to her Majesty's favour. Occasion of sickness and other accidents have been the cause, that I have not so diligently and effectually prosecuted my said suit, as otherwise I would have done. Now, being restored to reasonable health, (I thank God for it,) I am bold to renew my said most humble suit, beseeching your good lordships to take some good opportunity to move her Majesty for me, to the effect aforesaid. Her Majesty's most gracious benefit herein, and your lordships' most honourable travail for obtaining the same, I shall always most dutifully and thankfully acknowledge, with my continual prayer to God for her Majesty and your good lordships, whom I beseech God always to have in his most blessed custody. From Lambeth, this 30th of March, 1580.

Your lordships' in Christ,

EDM. CANTUAR.

To the Right Honourable and my very good lords, the Lords and others of her Majesty's most Honourable Privy Council.

LETTER XCVI.

TO LORD BURLEIGH.
Jan. 30, 1583.
[Lansdown MS. 37. No, 17.]

MAY it please your good lordship to be advertised, that some hope of recovering my sight, as some other in like case have done; and also good hope of recovering her Majesty's gracious favour, which I had by divers good likelihoods conceived, which being obtained, I trusted to discharge the duty of a bishop as well as some other; the foundation also of a school in the north where I was born, for lack of a mortmain not yet finished; divers suits commenced to the overthrow of certain leases granted unto some my poor servants, being the only reward of their long service; wherein my little authority, as long as I remained archbishop, might somewhat help to the maintenance of their right; the multitude of my other servants not provided for; my opinion that her Majesty did not desire my resignation, which I had before in the time of my better health offered; and some other also, as unable to serve as I, had offered the like, and yet her Majesty, as I have been informed, would not admit the same: were the considerations which hitherto have stayed me from offering of the resignation of my place. But now understanding from your good lordship, and not long before by my lord bishop of Sarum[1], that her Majesty's pleasure is, that I should resign, and thereby enjoy her Majesty's favour, which I esteem above all other worldly things; having also a reasonable, or, as it was to me named, an honourable pension assigned, I will with all my heart prepare myself to satisfy her Majesty's pleasure therein: trusting yet, and humbly praying, that by your honourable lordship's good means her Majesty will graciously permit and tolerate me to continue in place till a little after Michaelmas next, when as the audit of this see is kept for the whole year, that I may see some end of the said suits, the finishing of my school, and the multitude of my poor servants provided for; mean-

[1 John Piers.]

ing in the mean time, both by my officers and myself, by God's grace to have a vigilant care for the good government and well ordering of my cure; in which time I shall be also more able to make a perfect account of all things, to the satisfaction of my successor. And after that time I will be most ready, with all humble thanks to her Majesty, to resign my place unto her Highness's disposition. Which favour if I may obtain by your lordship's good mediation, I shall think myself much bounden unto the same, and most bounden (as I continually do) to pray for her Majesty. And thus taking my leave, I commend your honourable lordship to the most blessed protection of Almighty God. From Lambeth this 30th of January, 1582. [1583.]

Your lordship's in Christ,

E. CANT.[1]

To the Right Honourable my very good lord, the Lord Burleigh, Lord Treasurer of England.

LETTER XCVII.

TO LORD BURLEIGH.
Feb. 9, 1583.
[Lansdown MS. 37. No. 18.]

I MOST humbly submit myself to her Majesty's order for my resignation to be made immediately after the Annuntiation next. And also with like humbleness I thank her Majesty, that of her gracious goodness she made mention (as I am informed) of an honourable portion to be assigned unto me for my sustentation in these few and evil days which I have yet to live. I thank your good lordship most heartily for your mediation and pains taken concerning the premises; praying the same to continue with honourable favour towards me, till this matter come to a perfect end. I am bold to acquaint your good lordship now in the beginning with two humble petitions, the which by your good advice I purpose

[[1] The signatures in the original MSS., from this date, give evident proof of the archbishop's blindness.]

to offer before the end of this suit. The first is, that her Majesty will be so good unto me as to grant me the house of Croydon, and some small grounds pertaining to the same, of no great value; forasmuch as I have not at this hour any house of my own to put my head in, after I be removed from this place. In all resignations of bishops, so far as I have heard or read, there hath been always one house, at the least, pertaining to the see assigned to the resigner, as partly may appear in a note inclosed herein[2]. Croydon house is no wholesome house, and that both my predecessor and I have found by experience. Notwithstanding, because of the nearness to London, whither I must often repair or send to have some help by physic, I know no house pertaining to the see so convenient for me, nor that may be better spared, for the short time of my life, of my successor.

The second petition is, that I be not called to trouble after my resignation for dilapidations, for which (as I am informed by the learned in the laws) I am by law, upon a resignation, excused. Notwithstanding (although I do not

---

[2] De resignatione facta per Nicolaum de Farnham Episcopum Dunel. Ex Mattheo Paris. [p. 759. Lond. 1640.]

Purificatione beatæ Mariæ imminente, episcopus Dunelmensis Nicolaus, sentiens se annosum, valetudinarium, et infirmum, etc. episcopatum suum Dunelmensem, obtenta tali a domino papa licentia, resignavit. Et datis ad hoc provisoribus, archiepiscopo Eboracensi, et Londinensi et Wigorniensi episcopis, assignata sunt ei tria maneria, viz. de Hoveden cum pertinentiis, Stoctuna, et Esingtuna. Recedens igitur a Dunelmo, accepta ibidem a fratribus licentia ad alterutrum dictorum maneriorum mansurus perrexit, ut in pace ibidem, sine querelarum vel causarum strepitu, exutus a sollicitudinibus mundanis, sibi jam expectanti donec ejus veniret immutatio, liberius orationi vacaret, etc.

Idem alio in loco. [p. 811.]

Adulatores quidam pessimi, cupientes placere Dunelmensi episcopo Waltero, petierunt a papa episcopatum vel redintegrari vel saltem minus damnificari: quibus papa: "Miramur super his. Nonne facta fuit distributio illa et partitio per magnam deliberationem et considerationem virorum peritorum, et consensum partium? Et res jam confirmata est per nos, et regem Angliæ, et per provisores." Et sic repulsi sunt accusatores cum probris.

Idem alio in loco.

Eodem tempore obiit magister Nicolaus de Fernham, quondam episcopus Dunelmensis, qui cesserat episcopatui, ut quietius et liberius fructus carperet contemplationis. Obiit autem apud Stoctunam, nobile suum manerium.

distrust the equity of my successor), yet because I have been so much troubled with suits for dilapidations, I am fearful; and therefore pray that I may have some good assistance, if the case shall so require. But of these two things I pray your lordship that I may be so bold as to inform your lordship hereafter more at length; praying the same also to further the said humble petitions, as opportunity may serve. God keep your good lordship! From Lambeth, this 9th of February, 1582. [1583.]

Yours in Christ,

E. CANT.

*To the Right Honourable my very
good lord, the Lord Burleigh,
Lord Treasurer of England.*

THE ARCHBISHOP'S SUBMISSION.

[I meet with a submission by him made without mention of the month or year; which being well taken of the queen might occasion the taking off his suspension: and therefore perhaps this may be the proper place for it. After which submission, the lords of the council signified to him the reason of the queen's displeasure that had been conceived against him. Upon which the archbishop made this following further confession and declaration of himself. Strype, Grind. p. 403.]

THAT being advertised of the cause of her Majesty's offence, as was set down by the lords of the council, and of her gracious inclination towards him upon his humble submission, doth confess that he is most heartily sorry that her Majesty hath been offended with him, as a matter more grievous to him than any worldly calamity. And though he refused to execute her Majesty's commandment, by reason of scruple of conscience, which moved him to think, that the exercises might have been in some points reformed, and so continued; and understanding that her Majesty therein did use the advice and allowance of certain bishops, his brethren, who by likelihood certified, that they in their own dioceses found the same more hurtful than profitable: in and for that he is persuaded that her Majesty had herein a sincere and godly meaning to the quietness of her people; and that also her commandment was not against positive law or constitution of the realm; he cannot but think and speak honourably and dutifully of her Majesty's doings, as of a godly prince, meaning well of the church and her people in this her Majesty's direction and commandment. And as he is most heartily sorry that he hath incurred her Majesty's grievous offence for not observing that her commandment; so doth he most humbly and lowly beseech her Highness not to impute the same to any obstinate intent, meaning to disobey her Majesty; but only that he was then moved in conscience to be an humble suitor to her Majesty to be spared from being the special instrument in suppressing the said exercises. And to the intent her Majesty may think that he meant no disobedience in any maintenance of them to continue contrary to her commandment, he doth pray her Majesty to be truly informed, how he himself did in his own bishopric, and other peculiar jurisdictions, suffer no such exercises to be used after the time of her Majesty's said commandment.

LETTER XCVIII.

TO LORD BURLEIGH.
Feb. 27, 1583.
[Lansdown MS. 37. No. 23.]

It may please your lordship to be advertised, that I have been loth of late to trouble your lordship with any suits, because I have been informed that you were very sickly; but trusting now that your lordship is in better case, and my time drawing on so fast, and also understanding by Doctor Aubrey that your lordship would have some notes of the value of this bishopric, I am bold to send the said Doctor Aubrey and my steward to inform your lordship of the state of the same; most instantly praying your good lordship to be a mean to her Majesty, both for proportioning my pension (wherein I doubt not her Majesty will have honourable consideration of my place, age, and infirmities) and

26

[GRINDAL.]

A.D. 1583. also to declare her Majesty's pleasure for order, how the same may be answered unto me for the short time that I have to live. And as your lordship hath been, next unto her Majesty, the principal procurer of all my preferments, which I will acknowledge whilst I live with all thanksgiving; so I beseech you in this doing to be a mean to bring me to some hope of quietness in a private life, now in the end of my days, being now by age, sickness, and infirmities not able to sustain the travails which appertain unto this great office. And by the grace of God I shall not fail at the time heretofore appointed to resign up my place in due form, for her Majesty's better satisfaction in that behalf. So I take my leave of your good lordship, commending the same to the grace and protection of Almighty God. From Lambeth, this 27th of February, 1582. [1583.]

Your lordship's in Christ,

E. CANT.

To the Right Honourable and my very good lord, the Lord Burleigh, Lord High Treasurer of England.

LETTER XCIX.

TO LORD BURLEIGH.
April 12, 1583.

[Lansdown MS. 38. No. 69.]

AFTER my right hearty commendations to your good lordship. Where, according to her Majesty's gracious pleasure, I am fully resolved to go through with the resignation of this place, as soon as it may please her Highness to appoint; I have sent Mr Dr Aubrey, my officer, to your good lordship, to understand your further good direction therein; heartily praying your good lordship, that it may please you to have favourable care of my pension, according to your continual wonted friendship towards me, and that my learned counsel, at your lordship's best opportunity and leisure, may have leave to attend upon your lordship, and use such short conference as your lordship may well spare, for the manner of the assurance thereof, which I wholly refer to your good lordship's wisdom and consideration. And so, having sent to your good lordship a draught of my resignation by the bearer, to whom I have committed by mouth to understand your lordship's pleasure in a point or two touching that matter, I heartily commit your good lordship to the grace and protection of the Almighty. From Lambeth, this 12th of April, 1583.

Your lordship's in Christ,

E. CANT.

*To the Right Honourable and my very
good lord, the Lord Burleigh,
Lord High Treasurer of England.*

THE ARCHBISHOP OF CANTERBURY'S PETITIONS.

To have the house at Croydon, which hath been seldom lien at by his last predecessors.

Item, To have the park at Croydon, wherein, at his entry to this see, Sir Francis Carew, knight, and one George Withers had several interests; for redemption whereof the said archbishop gave to them eighty-three pounds, six shillings, and eight-pence; and did mind to leave the same, after his death, clear to his successor.

Item, To have a close called Stubbs, containing twenty-three acres, lying near to the said house.

Item, To have eighteen acres of meadow, lying at Norbury, in Croydon.

LETTER C.

TO THE BISHOP OF LONDON[1],
CONCERNING A COLLECTION FOR ONE THOMAS BROWN.

[Grind. Reg. fo. 149.]

SALUTEM in Christo. I have received a letter directed to me from the lords of her Majesty's most honourable privy council, in the favour of one Thomas Brown, of Shrewsbury, the tenor whereof is as followeth. Now, whereas my said lords refer unto me the manner of collecting a benevolence for the relief of the said Brown, I cannot devise any better order than that which hath of late been used in cases not unlike, with exhortations to all our brethren the bishops of this province, both to contribute liberally for their own persons, and also to further a collection to be made of men's benevolence in every parish church of their several dioceses; and the sums so collected to be reserved in good sure order to the use of the said Brown, by such persons of trust as every several bishop shall think meet for that purpose. These are therefore, by virtue of my said lords' letters, to require your lordship to transmit a copy of the council's said letters inserted herein, as afore is specified, together with this my letter, to all our brethren the bishops of this province, as in such public cases heretofore hath been accustomed. So I end, commending your lordship to the grace of God. From Lambeth, this 7th of November, 1576.

Yours in Christ,

EDM. CANTUAR.

*To the Right Rev. Father in God,
my loving brother, the bishop
of London.*

[[1] The following letters are of an official nature, consisting of communications from archbishop Grindal to his suffragan bishops, or to the officers of his diocese, arising out of letters from the privy council. The first, relating to Thomas Brown, is given as one out of many instances of the burdens which the state, at this period, frequently threw upon the clergy. Similar letters are of frequent occurrence in the archiepiscopal registers at Lambeth. It has been thought desirable to place these documents by themselves, as forming a distinct class from the general correspondence of the archbishop.]

THE COUNCIL'S LETTER TO THE ARCHBISHOP.

AFTER our right hearty commendations to your good lordship. Being of late given to understand of the poor and miserable state of this bearer, Thomas Brown, whereunto he is fallen by no unthriftiness of his own, but only through the unfaithful dealing of his evil factors, in whom he reposed the trust of his whole trade; and further knowing how sound and honest the man is, as well in religion as conversation, what special service, not many years since, he did to the great benefit of this realm, by the discovery of such dangers and perils hanging over this state, as, if they had not in time been foreseen, might have burst out into some dangerous fire, to the disquieting of this realm: We therefore, greatly pitying his estate, have in consideration of the premises, and for that he is greatly charged with wife and children, thought it very necessary earnestly to desire your lordship so to recommend his case to the rest of your brethren the bishops, as by some liberal collection amongst you his decayed state may be repaired. In what order this benevolence amongst you may be gathered, we refer to your lordship's good consideration, which for some good respects we wish to be done with speed, in respect of his present necessity. And so not doubting but that so charitable an action shall have the best furtherance you may give it, we commend your lordship most heartily to God. From the court at Reading, the second of October, 1576.

Your lordship's very loving friends,

N. BACON, C. S.,   Wm. BURLEIGH.
A. WARWICK,   F. BEDFORD,
R. LEICESTER,   F. KNOLLYS,
JAMES CROFT,   FRA. WALSINGHAM.

LETTER CI.

TO THE BISHOP OF LONDON,
CONCERNING THE OBSERVATION OF EMBER-DAYS AND LENT[1].

Dec. 21, 1576.

[Grind. Reg. fo. 150.]

SALUTEM in Christo. I have received a letter directed to me from the lords of her Majesty's most honourable privy council; the tenor whereof is as followeth. These are therefore to require your lordship, not only to transmit a copy, as well of the council's said letters inserted herein, as is above specified, as also of these my letters to all our brethren the bishops of this province, as in such cases heretofore hath been used and accustomed; requiring them, and every of them, to accomplish the contents thereof accordingly, as to every of them appertaineth; but also that your lordship do likewise cause the same to be accomplished throughout your own diocese and jurisdiction, so far forth as in you shall lie. Thus I end, commending your lordship to the grace of God. From Lambeth, this one and twentieth of December, a thousand five hundred and seventy-six.

Yours in Christ,
EDM. CANTUAR.

To the Right Rev. Father in God,
  my loving brother, the bishop
  of London.

[[1] It was about this time, in the month of December, that the queen and her privy council signified to the archbishop her pleasure for the punctual observation of the Ember-days and season of Lent; at which times abstinence from flesh should be strictly observed by all: which he was commanded to signify to the rest of the bishops; the thing being so advantageous for the breeding of seafaring men, so necessary in these times of danger: which was the reason urged for the observation of it; and not upon any superstitious account, as some might imagine. And of this all ministers were commanded to instruct and excite their people in their sermons. Strype, Grind. p. 336.]

THE COUNCIL'S LETTER TO THE ARCHBISHOP.

Dec. 13, 1576.

[Grind. Reg. fo. 150.]

AFTER our right hearty commendations to your good lordship. The Queen's majesty, of late entering into some consideration, how that, notwithstanding sundry good statutes and laws made heretofore by common consent in parliament to the contrary, the observation of the embering and fish-days is not so duly looked unto as it ought to be, and as is requisite in policy for the maintenance of mariners, fishmen, and the navy of the realm, hath thought convenient for that cause, first in her Highness's own household, to give strait charge unto the officers for the observation of them: and it is ordered, that they shall be more carefully seen unto and continued than heretofore they have been. The like we have signified, by her Majesty's special appointment, to the lord mayor of the city of London, and other her Majesty's officers and loving subjects abroad; to the intent that by an unfeigned observation, in all places throughout the realm, of the said laws already provided and meet to be put in execution in this respect, the estate might take such benefit thereby, as was at the time of the making intended: which we can assure your lordship is the only cause why at this time the observation of them is so much urged. Howbeit for that it may be, that this her Majesty's good meaning may either be misconstrued by some, and depraved by others, as though any superstition (wherewith her Majesty, God be thanked! is not to be touched or suspected) were thereby intended; for the meeting with and answering such slanderous conceits, as may be spread and mistaken among her Highness's subjects, we have thought good to require your lordship to give order within your province, that the ministers and preachers, which are, or shall be, admitted to that function, be commanded, in their sermons and exhortations to the people, to instruct and teach them to be willing and obedient to conform themselves and their families to the observation of the said laws, as in duty they are bound; and further declare unto them, that the same is not required for any liking of popish ceremonies heretofore used, (which utterly are detested,) but only to maintain the mariners and navy in this land by setting men a fishing. Which thing is so necessary for the realm, especially in these dangerous times, as no means are to be omitted, whereby it may be thought the same may be according to the laws brought to pass, and perfected accordingly.

And for that the exhortations and doctrines of good and dutiful ministers may do much good in this matter, both to remove the scrupulousness and misconceits of some few, and also to induce the greater and common number to obey and observe the said laws, we have thought good to signify so much unto your lordship; that by the good assistance of you, and others under you, the matter might be furthered, and take such good success for the benefit of this realm as we desire; and so bid your good lordship right heartily well to fare. From Hampton court, the thirteenth of December, one thousand five hundred and seventy-six.

Your lordship's right assured loving friends,
W. BURLEIGH, A. WARWICK.
R. LEICESTER, F. KNOLLYS,
JAMES CROFT, FRA. WALSINGHAM.

LETTER CII.

TO DR AUBREY AND DR CLERK,

RESPECTING THE LIBEL, CALLED "THE GAPING GULPH [1]."

Oct. 8, 1579.

AFTER my hearty commendations. This present afternoon I received letters from the lords of her Majesty's most ho-

[1 In this year happened a matter that gave the queen high disgust. She was in treaty with the duke of Anjou about joining herself in marriage with him. This was a thing, which, however desirous the people were of seeing her married in hopes of issue, yet they could not endure to hear of; partly out of an innate hatred to the French, and partly out of a particular dislike of this person: of whom many reports went concerning his dissolute life and manners. But of all others, the Puritans made the most noise. And one of them, named Stubbs, a student in the law, and a man of parts, but very hot, wrote a most

nourable privy council, with a proclamation inclosed in the same, both which are sent unto you herewith. Forasmuch as I cannot conveniently repair to Lambeth before Tuesday next, I have thought good to will and require you, with all possible diligence and celerity, to see the contents of the said proclamation and letters duly executed; and that upon Saturday next, at the furthest, ye call before you all the pastors, preachers, and curates, remaining and abiding in those parishes of London which be of my peculiar jurisdiction, giving them in charge that they, and every of them, shall do their best endeavour to accomplish and perform the good orders and directions in the said letters and proclamation contained. And if ye shall find any untowardness or ill disposition in any of the said persons, so called before you, that then ye warn all such personally to appear before me at my first coming to Lambeth, whereof ye shall have notice in due time. And furthermore, I do will and require you, with all convenient expedition, to transmit a copy of my said lords' letters, inclosing therein also a printed copy of her Majesty's said proclamation, as well to mine officers for my diocese of Canterbury, as to all other mine officers exercising any peculiar jurisdiction under me elsewhere, giving unto them, and every of them, like charge, in her Majesty's name, to see the contents of the said proclamation and letters duly executed in their several circuits, as they and every of them will answer for the contrary. Given at Croydon, this 8th of October, 1579.

A. D. 1579.

Yours in Christ,

EDM. CANTUAR.

To my loving friends, Mr Dr Aubrey,
Mr Dr W. Clerk, now exercising the
jurisdiction of the see of Canterbury,
and to either of them.

violent book against the match, entitled "The Gaping Gulph." The queen saw how dishonourable these clamours were to herself, and how offensive they might prove to the French, with whom she saw it her interest to keep all fair. Therefore she speedily issued out a proclamation for seizing the book, the author, and printer. And withal, the lords of the council wrote a letter dated in October to this purpose to our archbishop, with the proclamation inclosed. Strype, Grind. p. 359.]

THE COUNCIL TO THE ARCHBISHOP, CONCERNING A LIBEL PRINTED AGAINST HER MARRIAGE WITH MONSIEUR, THE FRENCH KING'S BROTHER.

Oct. 5, 1579.

[Grind. Regist. fo. 184.]

AFTER our right hearty commendations to your good lordship. You shall understand, how of late hath been printed within the city of London a certain libel, intituled, *The Gaping Gulph*. Wherein the author, under pretence of misliking of some dealings treated of between her Majesty and the duke of Anjou, the French king's brother, in very deed seemeth to go about to draw her Majesty's subjects into some mistrust and doubt of her Highness's said actions; as though thereby some alteration were like to ensue, especially in religion, which her Highness hath heretofore established and maintained, and is fully determined, with the assistance of God's goodness and grace, to uphold and maintain during her life, yea, even with the hazard of her own person: whose constancy in that behalf cannot in reason be called in question, if with thankfulness it be thought on, how her Majesty hitherto, for the maintenance of the same, hath willingly sustained the malice of the great and mighty princes, her neighbours; as one that wholly dependeth on God's providence, with assurance, that so long as she shall continue a nurse to his church, she shall never lack his merciful assistance.

Notwithstanding, forasmuch as we know that divers of the said books have been seditiously cast abroad and dispersed in sundry places of this realm; and have good occasion to think that [the] same hath been done within your lordship's diocese; by the reading whereof her Majesty's good subjects, specially those of the clergy, may perhaps by overlight credit, upon vain suspicions and presumptions, be induced to think and speak otherwise of her Majesty's doings, than either they have cause to do, or it becometh dutiful and obedient subjects: her Majesty, for the removing of all such doubts as may be conceived in that behalf, and the better confirming of her faithful subjects in such a good opinion of her Highness, as both her doings and government over them (the like whereof never happened within this realm) A.D. 1579. have deserved, and appertaineth before God and man unto their duties, hath at this present caused a proclamation to be made, printed, and published, which we send your lordship herewith. Upon the receipt whereof, her Majesty's pleasure is, that, with as much speed as you conveniently may, you should assemble the special noted preachers, and other ecclesiastical persons of good calling within your diocese, and upon the reading of the said proclamation to signify unto them her Highness's constant and firm determination to maintain the state of religion without any alteration or change, in such sort as hitherto she hath done; and that as heretofore she could not, by any persuasion or practice of sundry adversaries, be brought to alter or change the same, so now much less her meaning is at this present, by any treaty with the said duke, to do the like; who hath heretofore shewed himself a friend to those of the religion, even with the hazard of his estate and life, (a thing notoriously known, though by the author of the libel it be otherwise untruly given out,) and doth deserve, in respect of the honour he did of late to her Majesty, in vouchsafing to come to see her in such a kind and confident manner, without respect of the peril he did expose himself [to] in the said voyage, both by the sea and by the land, to be honoured and esteemed of all those that truly love her Highness.

You shall also admonish them, that in their sermons and preachings they do not intermeddle with any such matters of estate, being in very deed not incident nor appertaining to their profession; but command them to contain themselves within the limits and bounds of their calling; which is to preach the gospel of Christ in all purity and singleness, without entangling and confounding themselves in secular matters, wherewith they ought to have nothing to do at all; but rather teach the people to be thankful towards Almighty God for the great benefits, both of liberty of conscience, peace, and wealth, which they have hitherto enjoyed by her Majesty's good means; and to beseech him to continue and increase his blessings over us, to the intent, in all humbleness and obedience, under her gracious government, we may lead a quiet and Christian life; rather than, by intermeddling in such matters impertinent to their calling, go about to give occasion of distrust or disquietness among the subjects of this realm. By which their unorderly dealings there cannot but grow great prejudice to the cause of religion: which may be perhap pretended, but in very deed is like by these means rather to be hindered than furthered.

And to such of the said preachers as dwell in remote places, and cannot be present at the said assembly, you shall signify so much by your letters. And in case any of them shall understand, that any persons whatsoever by the said books, or otherwise, shall have been seduced, and carried into any such doubt or mistrust of religion, or prejudice like to ensue in this realm; you shall charge them by all godly and Christian persuasions, to do their best endeavour to remove all such undutiful and unnecessary conceit; being far contrary to her Majesty's most gracious meaning. And in case they shall not be able so to prevail as were convenient, but shall understand that either some other persons shall otherwise deal in this matter, or that the people rest not therewith satisfied; and so shall think that some further order is necessary to be taken in that behalf; you shall charge them forthwith to give notice thereof unto you, the ordinary. And thereupon you, by your authority, shall call such persons before you, as in whom you shall find any cause to be reformed; and by your information, or otherwise, correct them in their error; so as no further inconvenience follow by such disordered behaviour.

And so requiring your lordship, that herein there may be no want of your diligence, as you tender her Majesty's service, and will answer to the contrary at your peril, we bid you right heartily farewell. From Greenwich, the 5th of October, 1579.

Your lordship's very loving friends,

THO. BROMLEY, *Canc.*	H. SIDNEY,
WILL. BURLEIGH,	F. WALSINGHAM,
HUNSDON,	THO. WILSON.
F. KNOLLYS,	

LETTER CIII.

THE ARCHBISHOP TO HIS OFFICERS,

CONCERNING SOME PREACHERS WHO REFUSED TO CELEBRATE THE COMMUNION [1].

Jan. 18, 1580.

[Grind. Reg. fo. 191.]

SALUTEM in Christo. Having received letters from the lords and others of her Majesty's most honourable privy council, the true copy whereof I send unto you herein inclosed; I have thought good, for the due accomplishment of the contents of the said letters, to will and require you, and either of you, that with all convenient speed, by inquisition and all other good means, ye take a view within my diocese of all such ecclesiastical persons, as are any way culpable in any the disorders expressed and mentioned in the said letters. And such as will not, upon your admonition, conform themselves to the due accomplishment of the contents of the said letters, but shall shew themselves obstinate and intractable, to certify their names unto me, to the intent that her Majesty be satisfied in that behalf accordingly. And thus I bid you well to fare.

From my house, at Lambeth, this 18th of January, 1579. [1580.]

[1 Many ministers now-a-days took livings, and would only preach to their congregations, but refused to administer the sacraments; because, I suppose, they did not like some things in the offices appointed by the Book of Common Prayer. But they provided others for that part of the ministerial office; a thing which gave much offence to the queen. This occasioned the lords of the privy council to write a letter in January to our archbishop. Strype, Grind. p. 363.]

THE COUNCIL TO THE ARCHBISHOP.

Jan. 17, 1580.

[Grind. Reg. fo. 191.]

AFTER our hearty commendations. Whereas her Majesty is credibly informed, that divers and sundry preachers in this realm do only apply themselves to the office of preaching; and upon some light conceit, to the dishonour of God, the breach of her Majesty's laws, the offence of good subjects, and the great contempt of the sacraments, which groweth thereby, do separate themselves from the executing of the one part of the office of a priest, which is as well to minister the said sacraments as to preach the gospel; and that by this occasion some are counted and termed *reading* and *ministering* ministers, and some preachers and no-sacrament ministers: therefore we are, in her Majesty's name, to require your lordship to take a view of all such within your diocese, as do so disjoin the one part of the function from the other, and do not at certain times in the year, as well minister the holy sacrament in their own person, in what place soever they receive any portion for preaching; and yourself by your ecclesiastical censures to compel them to execute both; and such as you shall find intractable, to send them up to us; and to certify us immediately upon your said view, how many you find of those recusants within your said diocese, that we may thereupon satisfy her Majesty in that behalf. And so we commit your grace to God.

From London, the 17th day of January, 1579. [1580.]

Your lordship's very loving friends,

THO. BROMLEY, *Canc.* T. SUSSEX,
CHR. HATTON,   W. BURLEIGH,
H. HUNSDON,   FR. WALSINGHAM,
E. LINCOLN,   JAM. CROFTE.
THO. WILSON,

LETTER CIV.

THE ARCHBISHOP TO HIS OFFICERS,
CONCERNING PRAYER ON ACCOUNT OF THE EARTHQUAKE[1].
April 30, 1580.
[Grind. Reg. fo. 199.]

AFTER our very hearty commendations. Whereas an order of prayer and other exercises, upon Wednesdays and Fridays, to turn God's wrath from us, threatened by the late terrible earthquake[2], to be used in all parish churches and households throughout the realm, is set forth, and by order given from her Majesty's most honourable privy council com-

[1] The beginning of this year, 1580, was thought fit (especially a terrible earthquake happening) to be set apart for devotion and prayer, repentance and alms. Therefore the archbishop was minded, that all his diocese should be exhorted and stirred up to these points of devotion, resorting publicly to the church, and at night each family privately to pray together. And Redman, his archdeacon, and Lawse, his commissary, had this letter and charge in order thereunto, for the peculiars in London, from his officer Dr Aubrey:

"After my hearty commendations premised. My lord his grace's pleasure is, that with all convenient speed you shall give order to every parson, vicar, and curate, of the peculiar jurisdiction of the deanery of the Arches in London, that they exhort their parishioners to resort devoutly to their churches upon Wednesdays and Fridays, to hear some short exhortations to repentance, either by preaching or homilies, with other service of the day. And that they do of their own accord, without constraint of law, spare those days one meal, converting the same, or some part thereof, to the relief of the poor, calling also their households together at night, to make hearty prayer to God, to shew mercy to us who have deserved his anger. And that with the Litany they join such psalms and prayers as they shall choose and devise, fit for that purpose. And thus I bid you heartily well to fare. London, April 12, 1580." Strype, Grind. p. 368.] (Grind. Reg. fo. 198.)

[2] The sixth day of April, at six of the clock in the evening, the air being clear and calm, England on this side York, and the Netherlands almost as high as Colen, in a moment (as it were) fell a trembling in such a manner, that in some places stones fell down from buildings, the bells in steeples struck against the clappers, and the very sea, which as then was very calm, was vehemently tost and moved to and fro. The night following, the ground in Kent trembled two or three times: and the like again on the first of May in the dead time of the night. Camden, Eliz. A.D. 1580. p. 297. Ed. Lond. 1515.]

A.D. 1580. manded to be executed, the copy of which book and order you shall receive herewith: these shall be to pray and require you, and either of you, to see the said order put in due execution throughout the whole diocese of Canterbury; and such as refuse obstinately to participate in the said exercises, to gather their names, that they may be known to her Majesty's said honourable privy council, to the intent further order may be taken with them according to their demerit. And thus we commit you to the tuition of the Almighty.

London, this last day of April, 1580.

To our very loving friends, Mr
William Redman, Archdeacon
of Canterbury, and Mr Doctor
Lawes, Commissary General
of the diocese of Canterbury,
and to either of them, give
these.

THE COUNCIL TO THE ARCHBISHOP.

April 23, 1580.

[Grind. Reg. fo. 199.]

AFTER our very hearty commendations to your lordship. Considering the state of this present time, wherein it hath pleased the Most Highest, for the amendment of all sorts of people, as well to visit the most part of this realm with the late terrible earthquake, as an extraordinary token of his wrath against them, and fatherly admonition to turn them from their offences, and contempt of his holy word, as also of his infinite goodness and mercy to deal more favourably with us therein, than he hath dealt with other nations in the like case; in that we (thanks be unto his majesty!) have received no great hurt thereby, in comparison of that they have had sundry times heretofore by the like occasion; whereby not only their houses and cities have been overthrown and destroyed, but also many thousands of people have pitifully perished.

And understanding that you have considered upon and appointed a good and convenient order of prayer, and other exercises to be used in all the parish churches of your diocese, upon Wednesdays and Fridays, for the turning of God his wrath from us, threatened by the said earthquake; with a goodly prayer for the like respect, to be used of householders with their families: we do not only commend and allow your good zeal therein, but also think the same very meet to be generally used in all other dioceses of this realm; requiring you to give order, that in every of the same the said wholesome and godly order of prayer may, for the respect aforesaid, be executed, followed, and obeyed, during such time as you think meet. And so we bid your lordship most heartily well to fare.

From the court, April 23, 1580.

Your lordship's loving friends,

T. BROMLEY, *Canc.*   T. SUSSEX,
W. BURLEIGH,   F. BEDFORD,
F. KNOLLYS,   F. WALSHINGHAM,
R. LEICESTER,   T. WILSON,
J. CROFTES,   W. MILDMAY.
C. HATTON,

LETTER CV.

THE ARCHBISHOP TO HIS OFFICERS, CONCERNING RECUSANTS[1].

June 21, 1580.

[Grind. Reg.]

SALUTEM in Christo. I have of late received letters from the lords and others of her Majesty's most honourable privy

[1 The state was awakened at this time by reports concerning a great many in the nation that formerly came to church, and were conformable to the laws of the realm in matters of religion, but now fell off, and forbore any more to resort to the public service. Whereat the queen admired, and was apt to lay the blame upon the bishops, to whom she had granted an ecclesiastical commission for the taking cognizance and punishment of such things. Wherefore the lords issued out their letters

council, the true tenor whereof ensueth. These are therefore, in her Majesty's name, to will and require you, with all convenient speed, to make diligent inquisition, throughout my whole diocese of Canterbury, of the contents of the council's said letters, and the articles inclosed: and that, upon such inquisition made, you will return unto me the names of all such as you shall find culpable therein. And further, that you will have due regard to the due execution of the council's said letters within the said diocese in all points, so far as the same do appertain to my charge; and namely touching the due examination of all schoolmasters teaching children, as well publicly as also in private houses, within the said diocese, and the displacing of all such as shall be found, or suspected to be, backward in religion now established by the laws of this realm, or that are thought to be secret hinderers thereof. Thus requiring you to have due regard and consideration of the premises, I bid you well to fare. Lambeth, 21mo. Junii. anno 1580[1].

THE ARCHBISHOP'S ARTICLES OF INQUIRY FOR RECUSANTS.

IMPRIMIS, Diligently to inquire what persons within your parish or charge, of what degree or calling soever they be, do absent themselves from their parish church upon pretence of conscience or religion; and how long they have so done.

2. ITEM, What persons have of late absented themselves

to the archbishop, for to have all such backsliders and neglecters of religion punished by such as attended the execution of the said commission. And that inquiry should be made concerning such as had been before convented, how they stood as to conformity. And if they were at liberty, and still remained obstinate, to be again taken up. That especial notice should be taken of such as had the education of children, that they should be chiefly looked unto; lest, if their principles were not sound, they might do much harm in their influence upon those that were under them. Strype, Grind. p. 377.]

[1 Letters of this tenor were written to the archdeacon of Canterbury, the commissary of the diocese, the bishop of London, and the other bishops of the province, and to the several deans of the peculiars. Grind. Reg.]

from their parish church upon contempt or pretence aforesaid, that heretofore resorted thereunto.

3. ITEM, What persons do you know within your parish that have been heretofore convented before the Queen's Majesty's high commissioners for causes ecclesiastical, for religion, and especially for not coming to church, that are at liberty, and yet have not conformed themselves.

4. ITEM, What schoolmasters are within your parish, and what their names are that teach publicly, or privately within any man's house, within your parish, of what state, calling, or condition soever he or they be, in whose house or houses any such schoolmaster or teacher is.

5. ITEM, Whether any such schoolmaster, or schoolmasters, is reported, known, or suspected to be backward in the religion now established by the laws of this realm, that are thought any way to be secret hinderers thereof.

THE COUNCIL TO THE ARCHBISHOP.

June 18, 1580.

AFTER our right hearty commendations. Whereas the Queen's Majesty hath been informed, that divers persons within the province of Canterbury, both of the common and better sort, who of late time have been conformable to the laws of this realm concerning religion, are now fallen away, and have withdrawn themselves from coming to church, to the evil example of others her Majesty's good subjects, and to the great offence of her Highness, who doth not a little marvel by what means this relapse should happen, having delivered sufficient authority unto your lordship, and others joined unto you, by virtue of her commission ecclesiastical, warranted by the laws of this realm, whereby you might at all times have repressed the insolency and corrected the disobediency of such as therein should have presumed to offend, if such care and vigilancy had been used within your charge as appertaineth:

Her Highness's pleasure therefore is, that for the present reforming and punishing of those that have, and do herein

A.D. 1580. disobey the laws, you give order to have them forthwith convented before such as do attend the execution of her Majesty's high commission, and proceeded withal according to the direction of the said high commission. And first, that consideration being had of such as have been heretofore convented before the high commissioners, in what terms they stand for their conformity; how many of them are at liberty; and in what sort; and how many do remain committed, and where. And such of them as shall be found at liberty, and do continue obstinate, to be returned to prison; and such further order to be taken with them and the rest, as is prescribed in the said commission.

Schoolmasters.
And forasmuch as a great part of the corruption in religion grown throughout the realm proceedeth of lewd schoolmasters, that teach and instruct children as well publicly as privately in men's houses, infecting each where the youth without regard had thereunto, (a matter of no small moment, and chiefly to be looked unto by every bishop within his diocese;) it is thought meet for redress thereof, that you cause all such schoolmasters as have charge of children, and do instruct them either in public schools or in private houses, to be by the bishop of the diocese, or such as he shall appoint, examined touching their religion: and if any shall be found corrupt and unworthy, to be displaced, and proceeded withal as other recusants; and fit and sound persons placed in their rooms.

And to the end her Majesty may understand what shall be from time to time done in the execution of the said commission, to give order, that certificate be made of the proceedings in the said commission unto us of her Majesty's privy council. Wherein not doubting but you will answer her Majesty's good expectation, according to the trust reposed in you, we bid your lordship heartily farewell.

From the court at Nonsuch, 18th of June, 1580.

LETTER CVI.

THE ARCHBISHOP TO THE BISHOP OF LONDON.
FOR NICHOLLS, A RECANTING JESUIT.
May 13, 1581.
[Grind. Reg. fo. 235.]

AFTER my hearty commendations to your lordship. I have of late received letters from the lords of her Majesty's most honourable council, on the behalf and in the favour of one John Nicholls, preacher[1], the tenor of which letters ensueth. I have thought good therefore, by virtue of the said letters, to pray and require your lordship, according to the old ancient order in such cases accustomed, to transmit to every of my brethren, the bishops of this province, a copy of these presents, with the rate taxed and appointed particularly to every of them; the whole sum among us all amounting to fifty pounds, yearly: nothing doubting but that your lordship, and all the rest of my brethren, will have due consideration of the request made by my lords, and of the reasons by their lordships alleged to move us thereunto; and the rather, for that this contribution is not like to be any long continuance. And forasmuch as appointing of the place and person, to whom the said contribution shall be paid to the use of the said Nicholls, is referred unto me; I have thought good to signify to your lordship and all the rest, that I have appointed my servant, Richard Frampton, to receive the said several contributions here at my house in Lambeth. And that Midsummer-day next shall be the first quarter-day for payment for us that dwell near London; and so from quarter to quarter, till the said Nicholls be provided: requiring the rest of our brethren that dwell far off to pay their rates half yearly; that is to say, at Michaelmas next, for one half year, and at the Annunciation following for another half year; or at the furthest, in the terms next following every of the said

[¹ For an account of this man see Wood's Athenæ Oxon. Shortly after his recantation of popery, he went abroad, and was taken up at Rouen. He then "recanted all that he formerly had uttered against them (the papists), protesting that what he had formerly divulged was either through vain-glory, envy, fear, or hopes of reward."—Athen. Oxon. I. col. 496. London, 1813.]

A.D. 1581. feasts, and so successively, so long as this contribution shall have continuance; heartily praying your lordship, and all the rest of my brethren, that the said days and times so appointed may be duly observed, so as my lords of the council shall have no cause to find us slack in so good a matter. So taking my leave, I commend your lordship to the grace of God.

May 13, 1581.

Your lordship's in Christ,

EDM. CANTUAR.

*To the Right Reverend Father in
God, my loving brother, the
Bishop of London.*

THE COUNCIL TO THE ARCHBISHOP.
May 10, 1581.
[Grind. Reg. fo. 234.]

AFTER our right hearty commendations to your lordship. Whereas among sundry Jesuits, seminary priests, and other mass-priests lately apprehended and committed to the Tower, one John Nicholls, by conference and by the grace of God Almighty, is now become reduced from that sink of error and false doctrine of the pope unto the true knowledge of the gospel of Christ, and hath not only made his recantation openly before sufficient audience in the Tower, but also, by books by him written and published, given forth unto the world good and apparent testimony of his faith and conformity; wherein we think it necessary to have him comforted and encouraged, to the end that by example thereof others, that do yet remain obstinate, may the rather be induced to follow the way by him begun unto them: and forasmuch as by his writings he appeareth to be well learned, and able to instruct in the church of God; it is intended that the next convenient living ecclesiastical that shall become void shall be conferred upon him. And in the meantime, for his reasonable maintenance, being now at liberty, and having no means to live, we have thought good to pray your lordship, notwithstanding your present sequestration, by virtue hereof, to deal with the rest of your brethren the bishops for a contribution to be had among you all, for some convenient portion of money, to be duly paid unto the said Nicholls quarterly, by some such person, and at such place, as by your lordship shall be appointed, so as his necessary wants for apparel, sustenance, and continuance of his studies, may be in that sort supplied, until he may be provided as is aforesaid. And herein, not doubting of your lordship's readiness and the rest, as a thing that you yourselves, in our opinions, would without our special motion devise and perform among you, we bid you right heartily farewell.

From Whitehall the 10th of May, 1581.

Your lordship's very loving friends,
T. BROMLEY, Chancellor,

W. GURNEY,	E. LINCOLN,
F. BEDFORD,	R. LEICESTER,
F. KNOLLYS,	J. CROFTE,
C. HATTON,	F. WALSINGHAM.

*To our very good lord, the Lord
Archbishop of Canterbury.*

LETTER CVII.

THE ARCHBISHOP TO HIS OFFICERS,
RESPECTING RECUSANTS[1].

May 30, 1581.

[Grind. Reg. fo. 237.]

SALUTEM in Christo. I have of late received letters from the lords and others of her Majesty's most honourable privy

[[1] The parliament having lately made a law for the better keeping the subjects under their obedience to the queen, and against such as refused to conform themselves in matters of religion, and especially in coming to church, the Queen's safety and the peace and good estate of the whole realm depending so much thereupon; the lords sent their letters to the archbishop to make an inquisition, what persons there were in his diocese that refused; and to procure learned and godly persons to have conference with them to reduce them; which if they refused, to return their names unto the *Custos Rotulorum*. This the archbishop communicated to his officers, and enjoined them to see to the performance. Strype, Grind. p. 392.]

A.D. 1581. council, the tenor whereof ensueth. These are therefore to will and require you, and either of you, to have due regard to see the said letters, with all convenient speed, duly executed throughout my whole diocese of Canterbury, according to the purport and tenor thereof. And hereof fail ye not, as you will answer to the contrary. And for your better instructions for inquiry to be made in this behalf, you shall receive certain articles herein inclosed. And so I commend you to the grace of God. From Lambeth this 30th of May, 1581.

To my loving friends, Mr W. Redman,
  Archdeacon of Canterbury, and Mr
  Doctor Lawse, my Commissary there,
  and to either of them, give these.

THE ARTICLES OF INQUIRY FOR RECUSANTS.

1. FIRST, You shall make inquiry, as well according to the former certificate heretofore made of recusants, as by other the best means you can, what persons above the age of sixteen years at this present do refuse to come to the church, and to conform themselves according to the statute made in the last session of parliament. When any such recusants are by inquisition known and found, you shall use conference with them, and every of them. And joining to you therein some learned and other godly disposed persons, you shall admonish, instruct, and persuade them to repair to the church, and there to behave themselves as by the said statute is required.

2. ITEM, If any such person, after warning so given, shall refuse so to do, then you shall take two witnesses thereof at the least, and cause the warning and refusal to be written; and the same being written, to be subscribed by the said witnesses, and by the parson, vicar, or curate, of that parish, where such recusant at the time of the refusal and warning shall happen to dwell.

3. ITEM, You shall send, or cause to be sent, the same writing, in good and plain form, to the *custos rotulorum* and justices of peace of that shire, where the persons recusants have their dwelling at the time of the warning and refusal,

at the next sessions; that the said obstinate persons may A.D. 1581. be there indicted and ordered, as by the said statute is appointed.

4. ITEM, You shall also inquire whether, since the end of the last parliament, any person or persons within my[1] [your] diocese have gone about, or practised, to move, withdraw, or persuade any her Majesty's subjects within your diocese or charge, from their natural obedience to her Majesty, or from the religion now by her Highness's authority established within her Majesty's dominions, to obey or to be reconciled to the usurped authority of the bishop of Rome, or to the Romish religion, or to promise any obedience to any pretended authority of the see of Rome, or of any other prince, state, or potentate.

5. ITEM, You shall inquire, whether any persons within your diocese, after the end of the said last session of parliament, have been willingly reconciled, absolved, or withdrawn, as aforesaid; or have promised any obedience to any such pretended authority, prince, state, or potentate, as is aforesaid.

6. ITEM, you shall inquire whether, since the said time, any person have said or sung mass within your diocese: and also, whether any person have since the said time willingly heard mass sung or said.

7. ITEM, You shall inquire, whether any schoolmaster of suspected religion, or that is not licensed to teach by the bishop or ordinary, doth teach in any public or private place within this diocese.

THE COUNCIL TO THE ARCHBISHOP.

May 28, 1581.

[Grind. Reg. fo. 236.]

AFTER our right hearty commendations unto your lordship. Whereas in the last session of parliament there was,

[[1] These articles of inquiry were addressed not only to the archbishop's own officers, but to all the bishops of his province. In the original MS. in the register, there is a confusion in the use of the pronouns, as in the text.]

A.D. 1581. upon good and advised deliberation by her Majesty, with the common consent of the whole realm, a certain act made for the retaining of such her Majesty's subjects in their due obedience as, abusing her Highness's former great goodness and lenity, refused to conform themselves in matters of religion, especially for coming to the church according to the law: forasmuch as the execution of the said statute was thought most needful for the assurance and safety of her Majesty's person and this realm, and the preventing of such mischiefs and inconveniences as otherwise might happen, if every one might be suffered to do what him listed; her Majesty, being very desirous to see all her subjects truly united in one consent and uniformity of religion, according to the laws of the realm, for the better service of Almighty God, and quietness of this realm, hath willed us to require your lordship forthwith, upon the receipt hereof, to make, or cause to be made, diligent search and inquiry, as well according to your former certificate of recusants, as by other the best means that you can, what persons there be within your diocese, which do at this present refuse to come to the church, and to conform themselves according to the said statute. And finding any such you shall do well, by conference with some learned and other godly disposed persons, to admonish them, and by instructions to persuade them to come to the church, and to behave themselves as by the said law is required.

And in case any shall refuse so to do, then to take, or cause to be taken, witnesses in writing, both of the warning so given unto them, and their refusal, under the hands of the parson, or curate, and some other honest persons, which we pray you in every shire within your diocese to prefer unto the *custos rotulorum* and to the justices of the peace at the next sessions; so as the said persons may be indicted and ordered, as by the same law is appointed.

And generally, we pray you to have a good regard to the execution of the rest of the branches of the said act touching reconcilers, sayers and hearers of mass, schoolmasters, and other like matters, appertaining to your pastoral duty and charge. So as there may be no remissness or negligence found in you, as you will answer the same before Almighty God and her Highness; who expecteth a good account at your

hands and your brethren's in these things. And so heartily A.D. 1581.
praying you that hereof there be no default, and from time
to time to advertise us of your proceedings, we bid your lordship right heartily farewell.

From Whitehall, the 28th of May, 1581.

Your lordship's very loving friends,

T. BROMLEY, *Canc.*	W. BURLEIGH,
E. LINCOLN,	T. SUSSEX,
F. BEDFORD,	R. LEICESTER,
F. KNOLLYS,	J. CROFT,
	F. WALSINGHAM.

To our very good lord, the Lord
Archbishop of Canterbury.

LETTER CVIII.

THE ARCHBISHOP TO HIS OFFICERS,
FOR CERTIFYING THE DWELLINGS OF RECUSANTS [1].

April 6, 1582.

[Grind. Reg. fo. 259.]

SALUTEM in Christo. I have of late received letters from the lords and others of her Majesty's most honourable privy council, the tenor whereof ensueth. These are therefore, by virtue and in accomplishment of their honours' commandment, to will and require you, and either of you, to have due consideration and regard to see the council's said letters duly and speedily executed throughout my whole diocese of Canterbury; and to use such care and diligence therein, as the tenor of the said letters importeth; and to return your certificate to me under your hand, and the hands of some of the justices

[1 Letters again came to the archbishop, in April, 1582, against recusants, who still required more looking after. And as their inconformity had been the last year certified by our archbishop and all the bishops, for their respective dioceses; so now it was required of them to certify the place of their residences, in order to their imprisonment in the King's Bench the next Easter, according to the late law. Strype, Grind. p. 399.]

of peace of the shire, according to the council's said letters, before the beginning of the next Easter term, whereby I may certify the council's commandment accordingly: and hereof fail you not, as you will answer to the contrary. And so I commend you to the grace of God.

From Lambeth, this 6th day of April, 1582.

To my loving friends Mr Redman, Archdeacon of Canterbury, and Mr Doctor Lake, my Commissary there, and to either of them, give these.

THE COUNCIL TO THE ARCHBISHOP.

April 1, 1582.

[Grind. Reg. fo. 259.]

AFTER our hearty commendations to your lordship. Whereas the Queen's Majesty is given to understand, that notwithstanding many favourable means, heretofore used for the reducing and retaining her Highness's subjects in their due obedience to the same, hath hitherto very little prevailed, but that divers remain still obstinate, refusing to come to the church, and conform themselves in matters of religion, according to her Majesty's [laws:] albeit we doubt not but that, according to our former letters, you have made true and perfect certificate of all such persons within your diocese unto the justices, &c. and that they have thereupon caused them to be proceeded with according to law; yet to the intent we may particularly understand how things have passed both in your diocese and elsewhere, we have, for certain good considerations, thought meet to require you, as we have done the like to the rest of the bishops, to cause in every parish within your diocese a diligent search and inquiry to be made of all such persons, as sith the end of the last session of parliament have forborne to come to the church, and having been thereof lawfully convicted, do nevertheless not conform themselves as they ought to do; and thereupon to cause a certificate to be made in writing subscribed with your hand, and the hands of some of the justices of peace of the shire, where every such offender

hath his residence; to the intent the same may be, according
to the meaning of the law, delivered over into the court,
commonly called the King's Bench, in the next Easter term.
Wherein we pray you to use all such expedition as you may,
and to address the said certificates unto us first in some convenient time, before or at the beginning of the said term;
to the intent that we may peruse and consider the same, as
cause shall require. And so, on her Majesty's behalf, willing
and charging you that hereof you make no defaults, we bid
you right heartily farewell.

From Greenwich, the 1st of April, 1582.

Your lordship's very loving friends,

T. BROMLEY, *Canc.*   E. LINCOLN,
T. SUSSEX,   H. HUNSDON,
F. KNOLLYS,   J. CROFT,
C. HATTON,   F. WALSINGHAM.

*To our very good lord, the Lord
Archbishop of Canterbury.*

LETTER CIX.

THE ARCHBISHOP TO THE BISHOPS,
FOR A COLLECTION IN BEHALF OF GENEVA[1].

Jan. 1583.

[Grind. Reg. fo. 275.]

SALUTEM in Christo. I have sent to you inclosed herein
a letter from my lords and others of her Majesty's most

[1 In the midst of these his concerns and afflictions, a matter came
before him, wherein he shewed his earnest care and charitable heart.
In the year 1581, the duke of Savoy, by the pope, and other popish
setters on, and by his own ambition accompanying, laboured to obtain
the city and dominion of Geneva, famous for its religion, and a great
nurse of pious men, and harbourer of exiles for religion; and which
had been taken, had it not been prevented by the seasonable aid of
some of their neighbours, the Helvetians. Their condition by this time
was reduced very low: and a gentleman was sent from them hither into
England, to obtain contribution for them in this their necessity. ......
Their cause was heartily espoused by the queen and her council.

A.D. 1583. honourable privy council, in the favour and for the relief of the city of Geneva; which city of late hath been sore distressed by wars, and brought to very low state, as more at large may appear by my said lords' letters. Wherein their lordships have laid down most godly and effectually many weighty reasons, drawn out of Christian charity and the word of God, sufficient to move and persuade all men to have pitiful and charitable consideration of the miserable state of that poor town, that hath been many years a safe refuge and haven for such as have been constrained, for profession of the truth, to fly from all places of the world. And although the same reasons and exhortations in their lordships' letters are so deeply and so fully delivered, that neither I can or need to add anything thereunto; yet considering that, under her Majesty and their lordships of her most honourable privy council, the immediate charge of the province doth appertain to me, and especially of the clergy, and that the consideration of this pitiful relief, tending to the defence of so notable and sincere a church, dangerously sought[1] and distressed by many mighty enemies, in truth common to all such as love and tender the maintenance of the gospel, doth more peculiarly and nearly touch and concern us of the state of the church:

And in January letters were written from the council to all the bishops, to promote a liberal charity upon this occasion through their several dioceses; shewing at large the present low and afflicted condition of Geneva. By the council's special order the gentleman, the agent, was also conducted by Piers, the queen's almoner, bishop of Salisbury, and Cary the dean of Windsor, to the archbishop, to whom he was particularly recommended by that state; that by his advice a course might be resolved upon, the fittest and most convenient to be taken. The council also advised him to request the bishop of London and the dean of St Paul's, to join with them and the other in this so needful a service for the church. ...... Upon this our archbishop in the said month of January, though it were in the midst of his troubles, wrote this large and effectual letter to all the bishops of his province; and likewise to his dean of Canterbury, his archdeacon, and Dr Lake, his commissary there: likewise to the deans of every cathedral church, and the guardians of the spiritualties in the sees vacant, viz. Ely, Bath and Wells, Chichester, and Oxford; exciting them to further the good work, and directing them in what method to proceed. See Strype, pp. 412—417. See also Queen Elizabeth's letter to the thirteen cantons, Zurich Letters, p. 333.]

[1 Attacked, as in the Latin *peto*.]

I think it my part and bounden duty to recommend the furtherance of so good a cause to your lordship, and to do as much as in me lieth to increase your care herein; and therefore most earnestly to pray and exhort your lordship, to employ all your travail and study towards the effectual and speedy execution of my said lords their honourable and godly meanings: so as, when returns shall be made to their honours and me of your proceedings in this cause, your godly faithfulness, diligence, and zeal therein, (besides the reward that you may assuredly look for at God's hand,) may also receive at their lordships' hands good testimony and commendation.

The particular means and manner of the accomplishment of this piece of good service to God and his church are to be referred to your lordship's own wisdom and direction, with remembrance of the caution well touched in their lordships' letters; that all things be done with as much secrecy and with as little discontentment as may stand with the nature of such a matter. In my opinion it shall not be inconvenient for your lordship, before you assemble the clergy, to call unto you the dean of the cathedral church, and some well inclined persons of the chapter of the same church, with some other of the better sort of the clergy in the diocese well affected, and imparting unto them the contents of the lords' letters, to consult and deliberate with them in what manner, and in what places and times, the rest of the clergy is to be assembled together for this purpose; and whether all in one day, as it were in a general synod; or one deanery at a time; which is in my opinion more convenient and easy. And in this conference it is fit that your lordship, with their advice, shall make in writing a catalogue of all such of the clergy, that are known of any sort to be of any ability and meet to contribute; and to call together all such, and to use unto them, by yourself, or by some other sufficient person to be appointed by you, such exhortation and persuasion, as shall seem to you agreeable to the matter and nature of the assembly, excluding all others from the place. And in this first conference you shall do well, with the advice of the dean and other, to make choice of two or four gentlemen of the laity of best calling and affection within the diocese, and to communicate to them of their lordships' said letters;

A.D. 1583, and to treat with them both for their own relief, and also to give their good advices, with whom of the laity it shall be fit to deal; and to entreat them to be contented to be used as instruments to further this good deed; and to receive themselves, or with you, the benevolence of such as shall be disposed. And to the end that your lordship may the better direct the course of this service for yourself and other of the clergy, I have made a schedule herein inclosed, what portions myself, and my very good lords and friends, the bishops of London and Sarum, and the deans of Paul's and Windsor, to whom it pleased the lords to commit the consideration of this cause, have severally given[1]; wishing that this rate and portion may be followed, as nigh as may be, by your good inducement and persuasion, according to the calling and ability of every man: heartily and earnestly praying and requiring your lordship not to fail to cause to be delivered to their lordships, before Easter next, a full certificate of this collection; sending therein inclosed one schedule or catalogue, containing the names of the clergy, with such sums noted upon his name, what every man shall give to this relief; and another, containing the names of them of the laity that shall contribute in like manner, together with the whole sum of money contained in both. Thus referring the rest to your further care and good consideration, I commit you to the grace and tuition of the Almighty.

From Lambeth the — day of January, anno dom. 1582. [1583.]

THE COUNCIL TO THE ARCHBISHOP.

Jan. 5, 1583.

[Grind. Reg. fo. 275.]

AFTER our hearty commendations to your lordship. This gentleman, the bearer hereof, being also especially directed unto your lordship, as we are informed, will acquaint you at large with the cause of his repair into this realm, and with the request which we think good to make in their be-

[1] The archbishop 100 mark, the bishop of London 50 mark, the bishop of Sarum 50 mark, the deans of St Paul's and Windsor 20 mark a-piece. Grind. Reg.]

half from whom he is sent; so that we shall not need to enter into any particular discourse thereof in these our letters. For the matter itself, it is of so great charity and compassion, as that we doubt not but that your lordship, upon the understanding thereof, will most readily take such good order for some convenient and speedy relief, as the necessity of the cause requireth. In which behalf, and for the furtherance of so good a purpose, we have prepared letters to be directed from ourselves to such of your lordship's brethren the bishops, as to your lordship shall be thought meet. Who we hope, (and the rather if you shall accompany this our general recommendation with your particular exhortatory letters,) will have that charitable regard that is to be had of the poor and needy; referring them, notwithstanding, to such further order and direction, for their manner of proceeding therein, as they shall receive from your lordship, which we wish may be done in most discreet and secret sort, as the cause may bear. For better accomplishment whereof we have also requested our very good lord the bishop of Sarum, and the dean of Windsor, to take the pains to repair to your lordship with this gentleman, that with their advice you may resolve upon such a course as is fittest and most convenient to be taken. And we think your lordship shall do well to request the bishop of London and the dean of Paul's, to join with you and the other in this so needful a service for the church. Wherein not doubting but you will have such a care as appertaineth, and thereof make us privy of your intent and proceedings, we bid your lordship right heartily farewell.

From the court at Windsor, the 5th of January, 1582. [1583.]

Your lordship's very loving friends,

T. BROMLEY, *Canc.*   W. BURLEIGH,
E. LINCOLN,   R. LEICESTER,
H. HUNSDON,   J. CROFT,
C. HATTON,   F. WALSINGHAM.

To our very good lord, the Lord Archbishop of Canterbury.

THE COUNCIL TO THE BISHOPS.

Jan. 1583.

[Grind. Reg. fo. 275.]

AFTER our hearty commendations unto your good lordship. Whereas through the manifold and dangerous practices intended by the pope, and certain other princes his confederates, the last year against the town of Geneva, (a matter publicly known,) the young duke of Savoy being made an instrument therein, (as by whose pretensions to some kind of an ancient title to that *seigniorie* their counsels might be best disguised,) the said duke having for certain months, with a good power, most straitly besieged it; and standing in great likelihood to have taken it, had not the Bernates and the cantons of Switzerland, confederates of that town, entered into the association for their defence: the said town of Geneva is now by this means brought into great extremity and need of relief, the most part of their revenues being, as we are credibly informed, well near wasted in maintaining of soldiers for their better defence: and the magistrates thereof, being forewarned sundry ways, that the fire is not altogether quenched, but that the next spring it is meant that some new attempt shall be made by force against them, have of late sent a gentleman with letters to her Majesty, to acquaint her Highness with this hard state they stand in; and for their better support to require a loan of some competent sum of money for their aid: forasmuch as the occasions her Majesty hath of employment of great sums of money are many and weighty, beside the chargeable war of Ireland, moved also by the pope and his adherents, by reason whereof her Highness hath not at this present such opportunity to relieve them as their necessity requireth, and as otherwise she would, if time might thereto serve:

We have therefore thought good, for the care we have of an action of so good importance, and as we persuade ourselves your lordship also hath, that that poor town may in some sort taste of the Christian charity that ought to be in us, to recommend their cause unto you, and heartily to pray you, (as in a matter that specially toucheth all of your quality, both in conscience and calling,) by way of Christian persuasion to move the wealthier sort of the clergy, and other godly affected within your diocese, to contribute some part of that blessing that God hath bestowed upon them towards the relief of that poor, afflicted town which in some part may seem to have deserved the fruits of Christian compassion, by former courtesies and favours shewed to sundry her Majesty's subjects, in the time of the late persecution in Queen Mary's time. Wherein, as they shall render charity for charity, and give good demonstration to the world, that in this their wealth and peace they are not careless of the affliction of Joseph, agreeable with the apostle's doctrine, *Memores estote afflictorum, quia fuistis afflicti*[1]; so shall you give us cause to think, that you have not only care, as in Christian compassion you are bound, to relieve the present distress of that poor town, which, through God's goodness, hath served in this latter age for a nursery unto God's church, but also to satisfy this our request; to the end we may continue that good opinion we have of your lordship's zeal in the maintenance and conservation of true religion, as apperteineth to one of your calling. And so praying your lordship, for your better direction in this collection, to follow such order as shall be prescribed unto you by our very good lord, the archbishop of Canterbury, to whom we have especially recommended the care hereof within his province, not doubting but he will carefully and circumspectly direct you how to advance this charitable relief, and that without any open occasion of grudge or offence, we bid your lordship right heartily farewell.

From the court at Windsor the — day of January, 1582. [1583.]

Your Lordship's very loving friends,

T. BROMLEY, *Canc.*	W. BURLEIGH,
E. LINCOLN,	R. LEICESTER,
H. HUNSDON,	J. CROFT,
C. HATTON,	F. WALSINGHAM.

[[1] Remember them that are afflicted, because ye have been afflicted. Heb. xiii. 3.]

MISCELLANEOUS PIECES.

I.

Episcopi Londinensis Animadversiones in Justi Velsii Normam[1].

[State Paper Office[2].]

In scripto Velsii, (scil. in Christiani hominis Norma,) hæc animadvertantur.

Fidei Confessionem exigit. Non edi ab ipso fidei confessionem, ut oportuit, si modo cupit satisfacere iis, qui resipiscentiæ fructus in eo desiderant; sed veluti normam præscribi ad quam omnium conscientias exigi vellet.

Nulla mentio fidei. Atqui in hac norma nulla fidei fit mentio, sine qua frustra de religione Christiana, frustra de regeneratione aut novo homine disceptatur.

Justificatio per fidem præteritur. De libero arbitrio. Astute ergo præterit vim et modum justificationis per fidem; item quid de viribus hominis ejusque arbitrio, quid de operibus sentiat.

Erravit in his. In iis vero ipsum perniciose errasse, multorum turbasse conscientias, et orthodoxæ doctrinæ contraria docuisse, certissimum est. Nec desunt in Anglia oculati testes, qui ipsum convincant.

Quæ vero nunc scripta dedit, tametsi multis sacræ scripturæ verbis intertexta sunt, tamen a pura scripturæ sententia veraque doctrina longe discedunt.

A.   Nam Christiani hominis definitio quam tradit, præterquam quod jejuna nec sufficiens est, absurditatem maximam et a fide nostra alienam continet. *Christianus*, inquit, *is est, qui quod Christus per se et natura est gratia redditur.* Ac subjungit, *Christus per se et natura est Deus in homine et homo*

B.   *Deus.* Quid hinc sequitur? Christianum esse Deum in homine et hominem Deum. Ac ne videar id ex meipso inferre, id postea aperte concludit.

[1] The "Christiani Hominis Norma" of Justus Velsius, which is the subject of these animadversions, will be found in Appendix IV.]

[2] There are in the State-paper office several documents relating to this work of Velsius, including his letter to queen Elizabeth, and also to Calvin. See bishop Grindal's letter to Cecil on the subject. Supra, p. 254.]

At non ita loquitur scriptura. Nam quæ proprie et unice competunt Christo, Capiti nostro, id membris tribui sine sacrilegio et blasphemia non potest. Nullus ergo Christianus Deus in homine aut homo Deus dici debet. CHRISTUS enim solus est *Immanuel*, solus Redemptor, solus μεσίτης, ἱκέτης, &c. Hanc dignitatem, hæc officia membris non dispertit: *Gloriam meam alteri non dabo*, dicit Dominus. Efficacia quidem et fructus eorum distribuuntur membris, quos percipiunt per fidem. Fiunt enim filii Dei, templa Dei, quia Spiritus Sanctus in ipsis habitat; sed non ideo Dii in hominibus aut homines Dii dici possunt.

Scriptura non ita loquitur.

Detegendus ergo est anguis, qui sub involucris scripturæ tanquam sub herba latet, et in lucem proferendus est. Nam quæ garrit de unione nostra cum Christo captiosa et fallacia sunt.

Præterea, cum initiatorem Christum vocat, multum de ejus majestate et virtute imminuit. Hoc enim solummodo ei tribuit, ut introducat, ac veluti elementa doceat; ut nos post talem initiationem nostris viribus ad perfectionem contendamus.

C. *Initiator Christus.*

Quod regenerationem facit duplicem, unam interni, alteram externi hominis, ex scriptura non didicit, quæ totum hominem renovari jubet. *Nisi quis renatus*, etc. Joan. iii. De externo homine sic loquitur Paulus, 2 Corinth. iv. *Licet is qui foris est homo noster corrumpatur, tamen is qui intus est renovatur de die in diem.* Eundem vero esse *externum* hominem, qui *vetus* dicitur, apparet ex aliis locis, ut Eph. iv. *Vos edocti estis deponere veterem hominem secundum pristinam conversationem, qui corrumpitur secundum desideria erroris. Renovamini autem spiritu mentis vestræ: et induite novum hominem, qui secundum Deum creatus est in justitia et sanctitate veritatis.*

D. *Duplex regeneratio.*

Quod interni hominis regenerationem Deos in hominibus constituere dicit in hoc seculo, alienum est a forma loquendi qua scriptura utitur. Nusquam enim dicit nos regeneratione fieri Deos, sive in hoc seculo sive in futuro. Sed hinc apparet, quorsum prius dixerat nos fieri id quod Christus est, et Christianos reddi Deos in hominibus. Vult enim statuere perfectionem, quam sibi ipse finxit esse in homine Christiano, et persuadere omnes Christianos esse Deos; id est, ab omni labe et

E. *Deos in hominibus.*

culpa immunes. Quæ arrogantia quam detestabilis et execranda sit, nemo pius non videt.

F. Christianum in futuro seculo Deum fore.

Non minus alienum atque impium est, quod dicit, Christianum in futuro seculo Deum fore; idque nullo colore aut ulla expositione tegi aut leniri potest. Nec enim dicit Christus, "Eritis Dii;" sed, eritis beati, benedicti, vivetis, vitam æternam possidebitis. Nec quisquam est qui plus expectare, aut sibi polliceri, possit aut debeat, quam quod Christus dixit Apostolis, Matth. xix. *Vos qui me sequuti estis, in regeneratione, cum sederit Filius hominis in sede majestatis suæ, sedebitis et vos super duodecim sedes, judicantes duodecim tribus Israel.* Unicuique ergo sufficere debet, si gloriæ Christi pro mensura sua particeps reddatur.

G. Regeneratio externa pro resurrectione.

Videtur autem externi hominis regenerationem accipere pro ultima resurrectione, in qua quid somniet nondum assequor.

Rejicit doctrinam fidei.

In eo vero se maxime prodit, cum testatur se nullam aliam normam Christianæ religionis agnoscere. Nec enim posset apertius rejicere doctrinam fidei et remissionis peccatorum. Atque hinc constat ipsum novum quoddam evangelium fabricare; nec dubito, quin alia monstra alat, quæ nondum ex iis quæ protulit detegi possunt.

EDM. LONDON.

Translation.

Bishop Grindal's Animadversions upon Justus Velsius' scheme of Christian religion, or his Rule whereby Christians should examine themselves[1].

In the writing of Velsius, i.e. in his "Christian man's Rule," the following things are to be noted:

[1 There was now, in January, 1563, and after, one Justus Velsius, of the Hague in Holland, appearing in London, and making some disturbance about religion. He was a learned man, but hot-headed and enthusiastical, and held peculiar opinions, and had some followers and admirers: and being very forward to discover himself, he drew up a certain summary of his religion under this title, *Christiani Hominis Norma*, &c. that is, "The rule of a Christian man, according to which every one ought continually to try himself." ...... The bishop of London was concerned with this man, both as he was of the Dutch congrega-

That he has set forth no confession of faith, as he ought to have done, if he wished to satisfy those who desire in him the fruits of repentance; but has prescribed a rule, according to which he would have the consciences of all to be tried.

But in this rule there is no mention of Faith, without which in vain he treats of Christian religion, in vain of Regeneration, or the New Man.

Accordingly he craftily passes by the power and mode of justification by faith; as also, what are his opinions of the powers of man, and free-will, and what concerning works.

But in these points it is most certain, that he has dangerously erred, disturbed the consciences of many, and taught contrary to orthodox doctrine. Nor are there wanting in England eye-witnesses who can convict him.

As to the writings which he has now put forth, although they are interwoven with many words of holy scripture, yet they are very far from the pure declaration of scripture, and from true doctrine.

For the definition which he gives of a Christian man, besides being jejune and insufficient, contains the greatest absurdity, and wholly foreign to our faith. "A Christian," he says, " is he, who by grace is made that which Christ is of himself and of his own nature." And he adds, " Christ is of himself, and of his own nature, God in man, and Man-God." What follows hence? That a Christian is God in man, and Man-God. And, that I may not seem to infer this of myself, he afterwards openly asserts it.

But scripture speaks not so. For those things which properly and exclusively belong to Christ our Head, cannot, without sacrilege and blasphemy, be attributed to the mem-

tion, and had made disturbance there, over which our bishop was superintendent; as also because his opinions came as far as the ears of the court: for he presumed in the month of March to write bold letters to the secretary, nay to the queen herself, superscribing, To the queen, *Ad proprias manus*, sending withal this his book to them; which he did also two months before to the bishop. And he avowed it to be by him conceived and writ from the enlightening of the Spirit of Christ. The bishop therefore thought very fit, and that upon the secretary's advice also, to write shortly some animadversions upon it. Strype, p. 135.]

bers. No Christian therefore ought to be called God in man, or Man-God. For Christ alone is Immanuel, alone Redeemer, alone Mediator, Intercessor, &c. This dignity, these offices, he doth not communicate to his members. "My glory will I not give to another," saith the Lord. To the members, indeed, are distributed the efficacy and fruits of them, which they receive by faith. For they are made sons of God, temples of God, because the Holy Spirit dwells within them; but they cannot therefore be called Gods in men, or Men-Gods.

[Isai. xlii. 8.]

The snake therefore, which lies concealed under the folds of scripture, as under grass, must be uncovered and brought out into the light. For what he idly talks about our union with Christ is captious and fallacious.

Moreover, when he styles Christ Initiator, he derogates much from his majesty and power. For this only he attributes to him, that he introduces us, and, as it were, teaches us the elements; and that after such initiation, we must in our own strength go on unto perfection.

Whereas he makes regeneration twofold, one of the inner, the other of the outward man, he has not learned this from scripture, which commands the whole man to be renewed. "Except a man be born again, &c." St John iii. 3. Of the outward man thus speaks St Paul, 2 Corinth. iv. 16. "Though our outward man perish, yet the inward man is renewed day by day." But that the outward man is the same as that which is called the old man, appears from other places; as Ephes. iv. 22-24. "That ye put off, concerning the former conversation, the old man, which is corrupt according to the deceitful lusts; and be renewed in the spirit of your mind; and that ye put on the new man which after God is created in righteousness and true holiness."

Whereas he says, that the regeneration of the inward man constitutes Gods in men in this world, it is quite different from the manner of speaking used in scripture. For it nowhere says, that by regeneration we become Gods, either in this world, or the next. But hence it appears, for what purpose he had before said, that we become that which Christ is, and that Christians are made Gods in men. For his design is to establish perfection, which he has feigned to be in a Christian, and to persuade us that all Christians are Gods, that is, free from all spot and fault: which arrogance how detestable and abominable it is, there is no pious man but sees.

Not less strange and impious is it, when he says, that a Christian shall be a God in the world to come; and this assertion can neither be glossed over nor modified by any pretence or exposition whatever. For Christ does not say, Ye shall be Gods, but, Ye shall be happy, blessed, Ye shall live, Ye shall have eternal life: nor can any one expect more, nor can he or ought he to promise himself more, than what Christ said to his apostles, Matth. xix. 28. "Ye who have followed me, in the regeneration, when the Son of man shall sit on the throne of his glory, ye also shall sit upon twelve thrones, judging the twelve tribes of Israel." Every man therefore ought to be satisfied, if he be made partaker of Christ's glory according to his measure.

But he seems to take the regeneration of the outward man for the final resurrection, his dreamings on which subject I do not comprehend.

But he chiefly betrays himself in declaring that he recognizes no other rule of Christian religion. For he could not more openly reject the doctrine of faith and remission of sins. And hence it is evident that he fabricates some new gospel; nor do I doubt but that he cherishes other monstrous doctrines, which cannot yet be detected from the statements which he has put forth.

II.

Brevis quædam formula revocationis Hadriano Hamstedio per reverendum Episcopum Londinensem oblata, ultima Julii, anno M.D.LXII.

[Ex Biblioth. Eccl. Londino-Belgic.]

Ego Hadrianus Hamstedius, propter assertiones quasdam meas, et dogmata verbo Dei repugnantia, dum hic in ecclesia Londino-Germanica ministrum agerem, decreto domini episcopi Londinensis ministerio depositus atque excommunicatus, nunc post sesquiannum vel circiter, rebus melius perpensis, et ad verbi Dei regulam examinatis, aliter sentio: et culpam meam ex animo agnosco, doleoque me tantas offensiones et scandala peperisse.

Hi sunt autem articuli, seu assertiones, in quibus me errasse fateor:

I. Primo, Quod scripto quodam meo contra verbum Dei asseruerim, atque his verbis usus fuerim, scil.

"Quod Jesus Christus ex mulieris semine natus sit, ac nostræ carnis particeps factus, id non fundamentum esse, sed ipsius fundamenti circumstantiam quandam, etiam pueri primis literis imbuti agnoscent. Itaque qui Christum ex mulieris semine natum esse negat, is non fundamentum negat, sed unam ex fundamenti circumstantiis negat."

II. Secundo, Quod Anabaptistas, Christum verum mulieris semen esse negantes, si modo nos non proscindant et condemnent, pro fratribus meis membrisque corporis Christi debilioribus, in scriptis quibusdam meis atque aliis disceptationibus agnoverim; et per consequens, salutem vitæ æternæ illis ascripserim.

III. Tertio, Quod negantes hujusmodi Christi ex virgine incarnationem asseruerim in Christo Domino unico fundamento fundatos esse; eorum hujusmodi errorem, lignum, stipulam, et fœnum, fundamento superædificata appellans; quo non obstante ipsi servandi veniant, tanquam per ignem: de quibus testatus sum me bene sperare, quemadmodum de omnibus aliis meis caris fratribus in Christo fundatis. Cum tamen Spiritus Sanctus per Joannem Apostolum manifeste affirmet, Negantes Christum in carne venisse (de ipsa carne loquens, quæ assumpta erat ex semine Abrahæ et ex semine Davidis) esse seductores, et antichristos, et Deum non habere.

1 Joan. iv. Joan. Epis. ii.

IV. Quarto, Etiam in hoc graviter me peccasse fateor, quod constanter asseruerim, negantes Christum esse verum mulieris semen non proinde necessario et consequenter negare eum esse nostrum Emanuelem, Mediatorem, Pontificem, Fratrem; neque propterea negare ipsum verum hominem esse, carnisve resurrectionem. Nam istam consequentiam negantes, Christum esse verum mulieris semen, eadem opera negare Christum esse nostrum Emanuelem, Mediatorem, etc. plane necessarium esse agnosco: et non minus quam illam, qua usus est divus Paulus prioris ad Corinthios decimo quinto, "Si resurrectio mortuorum non est, nec Christus quidem resurrexit. Quod si Christus non resurrexit, inanis est videlicet prædicatio nostra, inanis autem est et fides vestra."

1 Cor. xv.

V. Quinto, Quod aliquoties in meis concionibus, præter officium pii ministri, usus fuerim argumentis, persuasionibus, similitudinibus, et dicteriis, ad istas assertiones populo persuadendas: videlicet similitudine, Non referre cujus sit coloris vestis regia; et litigantes de carne Christi militibus de tunica Christi alea ludentibus comparando: ceterisque hujusmodi. Quæ omnia eo tendunt, ut hunc fundamentalem fidei nostræ articulum extenuarent, et negantibus salutis spem non præcluderent. Agnosco enim plurimum interesse, utrum Christus nostram carnem, an aliquam aliam cœlestem seu æthere"am assumpserit; cum non nisi in nostra carne judicio Dei satisfieri, et pro peccatis hostia Deo accepta offerri potuisset.

VI. Sexto, Agnosco etiam in hoc culpam meam, quod in concionibus meis affirmaverim, unicuique in ecclesia reformata liberum esse infantem suum sine baptismo ad aliquot annos reservare, neque ullius fratris conscientiam hac in re ad aliquod certum tempus astringi posse.

VII. Postremo, Quod horum præscriptorum errorum monitores utriusque ecclesiæ ministros contempserim; atque ipsum adeo reverendum episcopum Londinensem, utriusque peregrinorum ecclesiæ superintendentem; imo potius, contemptis omnibus admonitionibus, ad jus provocarim; quo tamen convictus, legitimis et fide dignis testimoniis, culpam agnoscere renuerim: quodque prædictos omnes ecclesiarum ministros, et alios monitores accusarim, tam dictis quam scriptis et literis, Londini et in partibus ultramarinis, quasi non ordine, juste, et debite ejectus et excommunicatus fuerim. Agnosco enim me optimo jure hoc promeruisse, atque ordine a dicto episcopo mecum fuisse actum.

Cui dictus Hadrianus subscribere recusat.

Translation[1].

A short form of revocation offered to Hadrian Hamsted by the reverend Bishop of London, 31 July, 1562.

I, Hadrian Hamstead, by reason of certain assertions and doctrines of mine, contrary to the word of God, while I acted here as minister in the Dutch church, London, being deposed and excommunicate from my ministry by the decree of the bishop of London; now after a year and half, or thereabouts,

[[1] This translation, with the exception of a few corrections, is by Strype.]

weighing things better, and examining them by the rule of God's word, do think otherwise, and from my heart acknowledge my fault, and am sorry that I have given so great offences and scandals.

And these are the articles or assertions, in which I confess that I have erred:

I. First, That in a certain writing of mine I have asserted, contrary to the word of God, and used these words, viz. "That the doctrine, that Jesus Christ was born of the seed of the woman, and made partaker of our nature, is not a foundation, but a certain circumstance of the foundation, even boys, that begin first to learn their letters, will acknowledge: therefore, he that denieth Christ to be born of the seed of the woman, he doth not deny a foundation, but one of the circumstances of the foundation."

II. Secondly, That I have, in some of my writings and discourses, acknowledged for my brethren, and weaker members of the body of Christ, the anabaptists, denying Christ to be the true seed of the woman, provided they do not accuse and condemn us; and by consequence have ascribed to them the salvation of eternal life.

III. Thirdly, That I have asserted, that those who deny such incarnation of Christ by the virgin are founded in Christ the Lord, the only foundation; calling such their errors wood, stubble, hay, built upon the foundation, notwithstanding which they come to be saved as through fire: of whom I testified, that I hoped well, as of all other my dear brethren founded in Christ. Whereas the Holy Ghost by the apostle John affirmeth, that those that deny Christ to have come in the flesh, (speaking of that flesh which was assumed of the seed of Abraham and of the seed of David,) are seducers, and antichrists, and have not God.

<small>1 John iv. and Epist. ii.</small>

IV. Fourthly, Also in this, I confess, I have greatly erred, that I have constantly asserted, that those that deny Christ to be the true seed of the woman do not from thence, necessarily and by consequence, deny him to be our Immanuel, Mediator, Priest, Brother; nor therefore deny him to be true man, nor his resurrection from the dead. For I acknowledge it to be plainly necessary, that those who deny the consequence, that Christ is the true seed of the woman, do by the same act deny Christ to be our Immanuel, Mediator, &c. and not less than that inference which St Paul draws: 1 Cor. xv., "If there be no resurrection of the dead, neither is Christ risen; and if Christ be not risen, our preaching is vain, and your faith is vain."

V. Fifthly, That sometimes in my sermons, straying from the duty of a pious minister, I have used arguments, persuasions, similitudes, and jests, to convince the people of these assertions: for instance, by the similitude, It is no matter what colour the king's robe is of; and by comparing those that contend concerning the flesh of Christ to the soldiers that cast dice upon Christ's garment; and others of the like nature: all which tend to this, to extenuate this fundamental article of our faith, and not to shut out the hope of salvation from them that deny it. For I acknowledge, that it is of great concern, whether Christ took our flesh, or it were some other celestial or ethereal matter; since he could not, except in our flesh, satisfy the justice of God, and be a sacrifice acceptable to God for our sins.

VI. Sixthly, I acknowledge also my fault, in that in my sermons I have affirmed, that it is free to every one in the reformed church to reserve his child for some years without baptism: nor that the conscience of any brother can be restricted in this matter to any certain time.

Lastly, that I have contemned the ministers of both churches, admonishing me of these errors above written, and even the reverend the bishop of London himself, superintendent of both the churches of the strangers. Yea rather, contemning all admonition, I appealed to the law; whereby, being convicted by lawful and trustworthy testimonies, I notwithstanding refused to acknowledge my fault. And that I accused all the foresaid ministers of the churches, and others that admonished me, as well by word as in writing and letters, in London and in parts beyond sea, as though I were not orderly, justly, and lawfully ejected and excommunicated. For I acknowledge I have very justly deserved this, and that the said bishop of London hath dealt orderly with me.

To this form of revocation the said Hadrian refuses to subscribe.

III.

ACCOUNT OF THE COURT OF FACULTIES[1].

[Cleopatra, F. 2, fo. 188.]

Archiepiscopus Cantuar. habet in curia facultatum,
Commissarium, Wm. Drury, LL.D.
Registrarium, Wm. Park, Generosum,

In qua curia aliquot dispensationes emanant juxta taxationes approbatas inde factas vigore actus parliamenti, in qua taxatione regia Majestas habet dimidiam partem totius, dominus cancellarius cum suo registrario, archiepiscopus Cantuar. cum suo commissario et registrario habet alteram dimidiam.

$$\text{Exempli causa} \atop \text{Taxatio § ix}^{li}\left\{\begin{array}{ll}\text{Dna Regina}\ldots\ldots\ \S\text{iiij}^{li} & \text{x}^s \\ \text{D. Cancellarius}\ldots\ldots & \text{xx}^s \\ \text{Registrarius}\ldots\ldots & \text{x}^s \\ \text{Archiepiscopus}\ldots\ldots & \text{xl}^s \\ \text{Commissarius}\ldots\ldots & \text{x}^s \\ \text{Registrarius}\ldots\ldots & \text{x}^s\end{array}\right.\left.\begin{array}{l}\bigg\}\ \text{vj}^{li}.\\ \\ \bigg\}\ \text{iij}^{li}.\end{array}\right\}\ \text{ix}^{li}.$$

Observationes in hac curia sunt:

a. Primo. Pluralitates beneficiorum &c., dantur parsonis tantum qualificatis per statuta regia, cum limitatione triginta miliarium inter se invicem distantium, nisi aliqua probabilis causa aliud suadeat.

b. Dispensationes pro minore (ut vocant, hoc est, cum ætas eorum non sinit eos ordinari) non dantur nisi iis qui ad minimum attigerunt annum sexdecimum, et iis qui resident studentes in academiis, &c.

c. Hujusmodi dispensationes, cum dispensationibus de non residendo, non conceduntur nisi ad preces et approba-

---

[1] The Queen and council, having taken notice of some abuses in his Court of Faculties, required him, as it seems, to give some account of matters transacted in it. In the answer the archbishop sent, he shewed himself very indifferent for it; and if the Queen and council so pleased, they might dissolve it for him: but he vindicated himself in the faculties that had passed thence by his allowance, and he caused a scheme to be drawn out that gave a particular account of it, in Latin. Strype, Grind. p. 324.]

tionem episcoporum ordinariorum, et per literas suas privatas, et his conditionibus, ut ipsi ordinarii assignent salaria curatis in hujusmodi ecclesiis servientibus juxta arbitrium eorundem, habita consideratione qualitatis et quantitatis curæ illius ecclesiæ, etc.

d. Dispensationes de comedendo carnes etc. raro conceduntur, et hoc ad testimonium medicorum. Ut plurimum in his archiepiscopus remittit portionem taxationis suæ.

e. In omnibus hujusmodi dispensationibus archiepiscopus plures repellit quam admittit; et non ille contradicet, si tota hæc curia interciderit, si ita visum fuerit Dominæ Reginæ et suis consiliariis, et si possint ita placari qui cum hac curia offenduntur.

f. Licentia solemnizandi matrimonium absque bannis, vel in tempore prohibito etc., non conceditur nisi iis qui cum fide-jussoribus obligantur in centum libris, nullum esse impedimentum, nec ullum præcontractum alterutrius, nec ullam litem motam esse, quæ pendeat de hujusmodi contractu.

g. Literæ dimissoriæ (hoc est, ne quis ordines accipiat in alia diocesi quam ubi natus est) raro dantur, et nisi cum istis conditionibus, viz. quod sit habilis ætate, moribus, natalibus, et scientia, et Latino sermone mediocriter eruditus, et in litteris sacris versatus, nec in artibus servilibus fuerit educatus; super quibus ordinantis conscientia in istis literis distincte oneratur.

Translation.

The Archbishop's Account of his Court of Faculties, made to the Queen and Council.

The archbishop of Canterbury hath in his Court of Faculties a { Commissary, Wm Drury, LL.D.
Registrar, Wm Park, Gent.

In which court certain dispensations are granted according to approved charges, made by virtue of an act of parliament; in which charge the Queen's Majesty hath one half of the whole, the lord chancellor with his registrar, the archbishop of Canterbury with his commissary and registrar, hath the other half.

For example, charge ix £.
The Queen	£iv	x^s	
The Lord Chancellor		xx^s	vi £.
The Registrar		x^s	
The Archbishop		xl^s	
The Commissary		x^s	iii £.
The Registrar		x^s	

Total: ix £.

The observations made upon this court are these:

1. First. Pluralities of benefices, &c. are granted only to parsons qualified by royal statutes, with the limitation of the distance of thirty miles between them; unless some sufficient cause determine otherwise.

2. Dispensations for a minor (as he is termed, that is, for one whose age forbids ordination) are not granted to any but to those who, at the least, are sixteen years old, and are resident students in the universities.

3. Dispensations of this sort, together with dispensations for non-residence, are not granted except upon the petition and approbation of the ordinary bishops, and by their private letters; and upon these conditions, that the ordinaries themselves assign salaries to the curates, who serve such churches, according to their discretion, consideration being had of the quality and quantity of the cure of that church.

4. Dispensations for eating flesh, &c. are rarely granted, and this upon testimonial of physicians. The archbishop for the most part remits his portion of his fee.

5. In all dispensations of this sort, the archbishop rejects more than he allows; nor will he say nay, if this whole court be abolished, if so it should please the Queen and her council, and if they who are offended with this court could so be pacified[1].

[[1] Archbishop Parker expressed the same feeling, A.D. 1570. "Our archbishop (says Strype) had much trouble with the Court of Faculties at divers times, having been put upon granting dispensations which himself liked not of; insomuch as he had a long time offered in convocation to his brethren to procure the despatchment of that *offensive* court, as he called it. And the same he signified unto the secretary and the privy council: for he had, he said, more grief thereby than gain, wishing it were wholly suppressed, as reason and statute would bear withal; or else committed to some others that could do it, to use his own modest words, with better discretion. It nettled him also, that divers in their open sermons, and others in their private letters, accused the management of this court. And therefore he wished it were committed to some

6. Licence for solemnizing matrimony without banns, or in time prohibited, &c., is not granted excepting to those who are bound in sureties of £100., that there is no impediment, nor any pre-contract on either side, nor any suit stirred, which depends upon such contract.

7. Letters dimissory (that is, [a dispensation of the rule,] that no one should receive orders in another diocese than where he was born) are seldom given, and not without these conditions, viz. that the candidate be fit, for his age, manners, birth, and knowledge, and be moderately learned in the Latin language, and skilled in holy scripture, and not brought up in servile trades; upon which points the conscience of the ordaining bishop is strictly charged in those letters.

DISPENSATIONS GRANTED BY THE COURT OF FACULTIES.

I. *Dispensations left to the consideration of the Lords of the Council*[2].

1. A *commendam*. It is to be considered, whether this kind of dipensation may have continuance, being used in this case only, where certain of the smallest bishoprics want sufficiency for maintenance of the bishops; and therefore have need of some supply.

2. A *plurality*. It is also to be considered, whether this dispensation may have continuance; so as only learned men, being bachelors of divinity, or preachers lawfully allowed, may enjoy the same; the distance between the benefices not exceeding twenty miles: with a proviso also, that the party dispensed withal preach at the benefice, whereupon he com-

others that could do it with better discretion, and, as he said, he was sure there were many; for so several have professed, said he, in their sermons and letters." Parker, II. p. 12.]

[2 The Court of Faculties had been often complained of, and the former diligent archbishop Parker had laboured a reformation therein. As for the dispensations that issued out of that court, the present archbishop set them in two ranks: first, such as in his judgment were utterly to be abolished; and secondly, such as he was willing to leave to the consideration of the lords of the council, whether to abolish or retain them. Concerning both which, in the month of April, he wrote a very discreet paper, (and that, as appears, by order from above,) to be presented to the lords of the council. Strype, Grind. p. 300. See also Strype, Parker, II. p. 15.]

[GRINDAL.]

monly dwelleth not, thirteen sermons every year, according to the Queen's injunctions; and also keep hospitality there eight weeks in every year at the least.

3. *Legitimation.* This kind of dispensation, which is the enabling of men base-born to take ecclesiastical orders and promotions, seemeth not convenient to be used, but where there is good proof of great towardness in learning, and of godly disposition in the party so dispensed withal: for that bastards seldom prove profitable members of God's church. Which is likewise to be considered of in the said case.

4. *Non-residence.* To be considered, whether this dispensation may be granted for some short time only, for recovery of health, or such like urgent cause, and not during life, or for any long time; as it hath been heretofore used.

5. *License to eat flesh.* Whether this dispensation be to be continued for some persons.

6. *Creation of Notaries.* Whether this faculty be to be retained still in actuaries and scribes.

7. *De non promovendo.* Whether in case of the prince's service this dispensation may be granted to a doctor of the civil law, to enjoy some kind of ecclesiastical promotion, notwithstanding he be not within orders.

II. *Dispensations to be utterly abolished.*

1. Trialities, and faculties for more benefices, or for so many as the parties could get.

2. Dispensation for children and young men under age to take ecclesiastical promotions.

3. Dispensations, called by the name of *perinde valere*, making grants good which by law were void, and a right grown to some other person.

4. Dispensations to take all orders of the ministry at one time.

5. Dispensations to take orders out of their own diocese at any other bishop's hands.

6. Licences to marry without banns asking, and out of the parish-church of any of the parties[1].

[[1] These propositions of the archbishop concerning his faculties were allowed and approved of by the Queen's council, according to his judgment about them. Strype, Grind. p. 302.]

IV.

THE ARCHBISHOP'S OPINIONS AND DIRECTIONS CONCERNING ECCLESIASTICAL DISCIPLINE.

An Argument propounded in the Convocation concerning reforming the ordinary use of Excommunication[2].

[Petyt MSS.]

EXCOMMUNICATION by the law was never used, nor could be used, as a punishment of any crime, saving of notorious heresy, usury, symony, piracy, conspiracy against the person of the prince, of his estate, dignity, and crown, perturbers of the common peace and quietness of the church or realm, wilful murderers, sacrilegers, perjurers, and incorrigible and notorious committers of incest and adultery, false witnesses and suborners thereof, violent layers of hands

[[2] Whereas the censure of excommunication, as executed by lay persons in ecclesiastical courts, was much disliked by the archbishop and the other bishops, and especially being used upon such slight occasions sometimes, (a thing which made the church so clamoured against;) therefore the upper house had earnestly recommended the consideration of this matter to the lower house; and they gave their judgment as follows: "That excommunication might not be taken away wholly from ecclesiastical judges, having been always used to be inflicted by them; and the alteration of that punishment being accompanied with so many difficulties, to the interrupting almost of all ecclesiastical jurisdiction, unless many other matters of bodily punishment were granted in the room of it; which they thought in these days would be more offensive. And they desired that certain honest persons, skilled in the law ecclesiastical, might open to them the inconveniences that would ensue; and how hardly this point would abide alteration."

But about the reformation of the abuse of this church-censure there was much agitation in this synod. And one there was (who I am apt to believe was our archbishop, or some one of his officers) drew up a writing, shewing an expedient for keeping up the authority of the spiritual courts, against such as contemned and disobeyed them; whereby they incurred the crime of contumacy, commonly punished by excommunication: in the room whereof he propounded, that that censure should be wholly abolished; but the consequence of it after forty days (viz. imprisonment) should remain in force: and that instead of the writ *de excommunicato capiendo*, should be a writ *de contemptore jurisdictionis ecclesiasticæ capiendo.* Strype, Grind. p. 385.]

upon ecclesiastical persons, demanders of more cured benefices than one without authority; and such other great and horrible crimes, which were called *sententiæ canonum*. Wherein, beside the particular penances that bishops and their officers did impose, it was for more terror provided by ancient canons, that there should be a general open denunciation of this excommunication in every cathedral and parish church twice in the year.

For other light faults there was no excommunication permitted or used as a punishment, other than for manifest and wilful contumacy or disobedience in not appearing, when persons were called and summoned for a cause ecclesiastical; or when any sentence or decree of the bishop or his officer, being deliberately made, was wilfully disobeyed, or not performed.

Such wilful contumacy and disobedience to authority is in the law accounted so great, that it was called a contempt of that *Quod est in jurisdictione extremum;* that is to say, if the judge cannot have appearance of the parties, or execution of the judgments, he is at the wall, and can go no farther.

Of very ancient time this was their manner of proceeding in this realm, and the only means of reducing obstinate persons to the obedience of the law. It may appear by the ancient statute or act of parliament in the ninth year of Edward II, that it was the old custom and usage of the realm long before that time. The words are these, *Si aliqui, &c. propter suam contumaciam manifestam excommunicentur, ac post* 40 *dies pro eorum captione scribatur, pretendunt se privilegiatos, et sic denegatur breve regium pro captione corporum, responsio regis nunquam fuit negatum* [*negata*], *nec negabitur in futurum.*

It is to be considered, whether this manifest contumacy, and wilful disobedience to the magistrate and authority, be not as well punishable, when the original cause or matter is light, as weighty. The difference whereof doth nothing alter the matter of the disobedience. If for such disobedience it seemeth that it is either unlawful or offensive to use excommunication, there is great consideration and wariness to be used in devising some other means and remedy instead thereof, to procure obedience and execution in causes ecclesiastical; and that the judge ecclesiastical may have those means laid down with such caution, that thereby, upon pretence and colour of the reformation of this, all jurisdiction ecclesiastical be not utterly overthrown.

The means that were thought fit to be used instead of excommunication by archbishop Cranmer, Peter Martyr, Bucer, Mr Haddon, and others that did assemble for that purpose at that time, were imprisonment or mulct pecuniary; and besides, in persons ecclesiastical, sequestrations of their livings, and suspensions from the execution of their offices. But these means will be as commonly offensive, in some respects, as the excommunication is now; and will be so hardly executed, that all the excommunications of the law ecclesiastical will be made frustrate.

And therefore, if the course that hath so long continued cannot hold, but must needs be altered, I would wish it to be done by some other means; whererein we should not need to deal with any body, but as we were wont to do ordinarily, in effect as followeth, viz.

Where now for not appearing, or for not satisfying any sentence, decree, or order, the ecclesiastical judge doth pronounce the party *contumacem*, and, *in pœnam contumaciæ*, excommunicates him, he shall pronounce him *contumacem*, and, *in pœnam contumaciæ*, pronounce him *ecclesiasticæ jurisdictionis contemptorem;* and so denounce him. And if he shall continue forty days in not appearing, or in not satisfying, he shall signify the contempt *jurisdictionis ecclesiasticæ* to the prince, in the chancery, as he was wont to signify *contemptum censuræ ad claviam*, [to the chancellor,] without any more change. And as the writs that were sent were wont to be, *de excommunicato capiendo et relaxando;* so they may be, *de contemptore jurisdictionis ecclesiasticæ capiendo vel relaxando*.

Then there may be general words, that such a contemner, so pronounced and denounced in all respects, (saving for coming to the church, receiving of sacraments, and keeping company with others,) shall in all respects, and to all purposes, be as incapable, and shall sustain all such other penalties, as a person excommunicate did sustain before the making of this law.

In all heinous, great, horrible crimes, excommunications may be used by the archbishops and bishops in their own persons, with such assistance as shall be thought meet, as it was wont to be in the primitive church.

In this our realm, of very ancient time, it hath been truly observed from time to time, that there was never alteration made of any law ecclesiastical, although it had appearance to benefit the state of the clergy, but that it turned ever to some notable prejudice.

Propositions to be considered of for the reforming of Excommunication[1].

First, To name those crimes which are termed *graviora*, i. e. more grievous, for which excommunication was only to be inflicted.

Secondly, In greater crimes, if the party appear not after the third citation, (every one containing the crimes laid to his charge,) then to be excommunicated.

So in lesser crimes, or in causes between party and party, if he that is cited do not appear upon the first citation, then *facta fide* of the serving of it, he may be pronounced *contumax*. If upon the second citation he continue his obstinacy, then *facta fide*, he may be fined. And thirdly, if that will not avail, then he may be suspended *ab ingressu ecclesiæ*, if a layman; or *a beneficio*, if he be a clerk. Fourthly, and if all the premises will not bring him in, then the bishop may have authority to send his warrant to the sheriff, or some justice of the peace, for the attaching of the party, and committing him to prison, until he enter bond with sufficient sureties to appear, and pay the charges past.

[1 The handling of this weighty subject of excommunication, which had been so abused hitherto, (though upon it the discipline of the church did so much depend,) was owing in a great measure to our archbishop, who earnestly recommended the consideration and reformation of it to this synod. To that which was already moved concerning this matter, I shall mention another paper put in, to be considered of the same argument: the substance whereof was, that excommunication should be used only in greater crimes; and that in less, suspension and imprisonment, together with the manner how either should be inflicted. Strype, Grind. p. 386.]

Secondly, If, any sentence given, the party appear not at the time appointed, *quum sententia debeat executioni mandari*, then to be suspended. And if he continue so by the space of a month, then to be imprisoned, either by the bishop himself, or by his warrant, as before, till he conform himself to the said sentence.

The Archbishop's direction for Penance[2].

[Petyt MSS. 38, fo. 165.]

First, I wish at every public penance a sermon, if it be possible, be had.

Secondly, In the same sermon the grievousness of the offence is to be opened; the party to be exhorted to unfeigned repentance, with assurance of God's mercy, if they so do; and doubling of their damnation, if they remain either obstinate, or feign repentance where none is, and so lying to the Holy Ghost.

Thirdly, Where no sermon is, there let a homily be read, meet for the purpose.

Fourthly, Let the offender be set directly over against the pulpit during the sermon or homily, and there stand bareheaded with the sheet, or other accustomed note of difference; and that upon some board raised a foot and a half, at least, above the church floor; that they may be *in loco editiore, et eminentiores omni populo*[3].

Fifthly, ITEM, It is very requisite that the preacher, in some place of his sermon, or the curate after the end of the homily, remaining still in the pulpit, should publicly interrogate the offenders, whether they do confess their fault,

[[2] But besides these cares about the due and regular execution of this highest censure of the church, another business lay also before this convocation, namely penance for open sins, another great and necessary part of ecclesiastical discipline. This also needed reformation. And herein the archbishop contributed his pains: that it might not be performed only as a matter of form, but produce a good effect, to bring the sinner to amendment, and to serve as a seasonable warning and example to all. Therefore did he himself devise a form of penance to be for the future observed; and laid it before the synod. Strype, Grind. p. 387.]

[[3] In a higher place, and above all the people.]

and whether they do truly repent; and that the said offenders or penitents should answer directly every one after another; (if they be many,) much like to this short form following, *mutatis mutandis.*

Preacher. Dost thou not here before God, and this congregation assembled in his name, confess that thou didst commit such an offence, viz. fornication, adultery, incest, &c.?

Penitent. I do confess it before God and this congregation.

Preacher. Dost thou not also confess, that in so doing thou hast not only grievously offended against the majesty of God, in breaking his commandment, and so deserved everlasting damnation, but also hast offended the church of God by thy wicked example?

Penitent. All this I confess unfeignedly.

Preacher. Art thou truly and heartily sorrowful for this thine offence?

Penitent. I am from the bottom of my heart.

Preacher. Dost thou ask God and this congregation heartily forgiveness for thy sin and offence; and dost thou faithfully promise from henceforth to live a godly and christian life, and never to commit the like offence again?

Penitent. I do ask God and this congregation heartily forgiveness for my sin and offence; and do faithfully promise from henceforth to live a godly and christian life, and never to commit the like offence again.

This done, the preacher or minister may briefly speak what they think meet for the time, place, and person; desiring in the end the congregation present to pray to God for the penitent, &c. and the rather, if they see any good signs of repentance in the said penitent.

Provided always, that order be given by the ordinaries, when they assign penances, that if the penitents do shew themselves irreverent or impenitent at their penances, that then their punishments be reiterated; and be removed from the church to the market-place: that though themselves may thereby seem incorrigible, yet their public shame may be a terror to others.

If the ordinary see cause to commute the wearing of the sheet only, (for other commutation I wish none,) then appoint a good portion of money to be delivered, immediately after the penance done in form aforesaid, by the penitent himself to the collectors for the poor; with this *proviso*, that if he shew not good signs of repentance, he is to be put again to his penance with the sheet: and then no money at no time to be taken of him.

ARCHBISHOP GRINDAL'S
LAST WILL AND TESTAMENT.

[State Paper Office.]

IN the name of God, *Amen*. The 8th day of May, in the year of our Lord 1583, and in the 25th year of the reign of our sovereign lady Elizabeth, by the grace of God, of England, France, and Ireland, Queen, Defender of the Faith, &c. I Edmund Grindal, Archbishop of Canterbury, being whole in mind and of perfect remembrance, do make this my last will and testament, in manner and form following, revoking all other wills whatsoever heretofore by me made, except one bearing date the 12th day of April, 1583, concerning a certain portion of tithes in the parish of Ashwell, within the county of Hertford, given to the master, fellows, and scholars of Pembroke Hall in Cambridge.

First, I bequeath my soul into the hands of my heavenly Father, humbly beseeching him to receive the same into his gracious mercies for his Christ's sake: and my body I will to be buried in the choir of the parish church of Croydon, without any solemn hearse or funeral pomp. Notwithstanding, my meaning is, that if it please God to call me out of this transitory life, during the time that I shall remain in the possession of the archbishoprick of Canterbury, that the heralds shall be reasonably compounded withal, and satisfied for their accustomed fees in such cases.

And as concerning my worldly goods, wherewith the Lord hath blessed me, my will is, that they shall be bestowed by my executors as followeth:

First, having nothing worthy to be presented to her Majesty, I humbly beseech the same to accept at my hands the New Testament of Jesus Christ in Greek, of Stephanus his impression, as an argument of my dutiful and loving heart towards her Highness, whom I pray Almighty God long to prosper and preserve to the benefit of his church. *Item*, I will and bequeath to my next successor, that shall be in the archbishoprick of Canterbury, the pictures of archbishop Warham and Erasmus, and all such instruments of music, and other implements, as were bequeathed and left unto me by my predecessor that last was. *Item*, I give and bequeath to the right honourable the lord Burleigh, lord high treasurer of England, that my standing cup which her Majesty gave unto me at new-year last before the date hereof; and I make him supervisor of this my testament, desiring his honour to take that burden upon him. *Item*, I give unto the reverend father in God, the bishop of Worcester, that now is, my gold ring with a sapphire; and to my honourable good friend Sir Francis Walsingham, principal secretary to her Majesty, my best standing cup which I brought from York, praying his honour to be good and favourable towards the accomplishing of this my testament. *Item*, I give unto my faithful friend Mr Nowel, dean of Paul's, my ambling gelding, called Grey Olephant. *Item*, I give and bequeath to the petty canons and other inferior officers belonging to the church of Christ's Church Canterbury, to be divided amongst them by the advice of the dean of Canterbury for the time being, ten pounds. *Item*, I give and bequeath to the master and fellows of Pembroke Hall in Cambridge, one standing cup double gilt, which her Majesty gave unto me the first year after I was archbishop of Canterbury; and these books following, viz. an Hebrew Bible in *decimo sexto*, noted with Mr Dr Watts' hand; Chrysostom in Greek upon St Paul's Epistles; Pagnine's Thesaurus; Eusebius in Greek, and the Ecclesiastical History of Eusebius and others, of Christopherson's translation. *Item*, I give to the provost and fellows of Queen's College in Oxford one nest of bowls, brought from York, with a cover, viz. the newest three of the nine, and forty pounds which they do owe unto me; also, all such books as I have assigned unto them, to be kept in their library, contained in a catalogue subscribed with my hand, and ten pounds towards the clasping, bossing, and chaining of the same. *Item*, I give and bequeath to the mayor and citizens of Canterbury one hundred pounds, to be kept in a stock for ever, to the use of the poor of that city, upon condition that they enter into sufficient bond unto my executors, as well that the said stock of one hundred pounds shall not be diminished, as also that it shall be yearly employed upon wool, flax, tow, hemp, and other stuff, whereby the poor people of the said city may be set on work. *Item*, I give to the poor of Lambeth ten pounds; and to the poor of Croydon other ten pounds; and to the poor of the town and lower part of the parish of St Bees aforesaid, thirteen pounds, six shillings and eight pence. And I give to the use of the parish church of St Bees my communion-cup, with the cover double gilt, and my fairest English Bible, of the translation appointed to be read in the church. *Item*, I give to every household servant that I shall have at the time of my death, which is not better provided for in this my testament, one half year's wages. And I will, that my said household servants shall be kept together by the space of one month after my decease, and have their ordinary diet during the said time, to be provided by mine executors, without admitting any stranger thereunto. *Item*, I give unto Mr Dr Gibson one of my lesser standing cups double gilt, with a cover. *Item*, I will and bequeath to William Woodhall, my nephew, two nests of gilt bowls, viz. the greater and the less, and the bed wherein I use to lie in Lambeth; two pillows, and two pair of fine sheets, a pair of my best fustain blankets, my tapestry coverlid wrought with green leaves, a livery bed, and two pair of sheets, and other furniture meet for the same, my signet of gold, my great nut, my best salt, double gilt; all the silk in my wardrobe that shall not be made into apparel at the time of death; one dozen of silver spoons parcel gilt; one garnish of vessel, and two of my best geldings that are not given by name in this my testament; and my black stray nag, called Nix. And I do further forgive him all such debts as he oweth unto me upon specialties. *Item*, I give and bequeath unto Mr Wilson, my chaplain, all such books as I have assigned unto him, contained in a schedule subscribed with my hand. And I will, that my executors shall assign unto him the advowson of the parsonage of Wonston, in the diocese of Winchester, if it fall void in his lifetime. But if it shall fall void after the death of the said Mr Wilson, then I will, that my executors shall assign the same to my chaplain, Mr Robinson, now provost of Queen's College in Oxon, unless he shall before have received some one of the advowsons hereafter specified: and I do forgive unto the said Mr Wilson all such debts as he oweth me upon specialties. Also I will, that my executors shall assign unto the said Mr Robinson the advowson of the dignity and prebend in the church of Litchfield, or the advowson of certain dignities and prebends in the church of St David's, as soon as either of them shall fall void, at the election and choice of the said Mr Robinson, unless he shall before have received the advowson of Wonston aforesaid. But if the said dignities and prebends, or either of them, shall not fall void in the lifetime of the said Mr Robinson; or if they shall fall void after that he hath received the advowson of Wonston aforesaid, then I will, that my executors shall assign one of the said advowsons unto my chaplain, Mr John Chambers, so soon as either of the said dignities and prebends shall fall void, at the election and choice of the said Mr Chambers. *Item*, I will, that my advowson of the dignity of the church of Paul's shall be bestowed upon some learned man, at the discretion of my executors, or the longest liver of them.

Item, I give and bequeath unto my nieces, Mabel, Anne, Barbara, and Frances, the daughters of Robert Grindal, my brother lately deceased, to every of them fifty pounds. And to my nieces, Dorothy, Katharine, Elizabeth, and Isabel, the daughters of Elizabeth Woodhal, my sister late deceased, to every of them fifty pounds; to be divided amongst them at the discretion of William Woodhal their uncle. *Item*, I give to my niece Woodhal one bowl double gilt, without a cover; and to my niece Isabel Wilson one other bowl double gilt, without a cover; and to Edmund Woodhal my god-son one of my little standing cups, with a cover, double gilt. *Item*, I will and bequeath to my niece Frances Young, widow, one dozen of silver spoons parcel gilt, a garnish of vessel, my little nut, and my can or tankard, double gilt. *Item*, I give unto John Scott, Esq. now steward of my household, my gelding called Old Marshall; and my servant William Henmarsh, gent. a ring, price twenty shillings; and to Robert Sandwich of Stillington, a ring, price thirty shillings. *Item*, I give to Robert Estwick, my gentleman usher, ten pounds for his fee at my burial: and to my servant Peter Palmer, gent. ten pounds. And to Thomas Nicolson, usher of my hall, five pounds. And to my servant William Grindal, ten pounds. And to my servants William Henley and Richard Matthew, to each of them one year's wages, and three pounds six shillings and eight pence. And to my servant John Acklam six pounds thirteen shillings and four pence. And to my servant William Hales five pounds. Unless they be otherwise considered by me to the value thereof before my death. *Item*, I give to William Tubman my servant, ten pounds, and such books as are assigned unto him, contained in a schedule subscribed with my hand, and the advowson of the parsonage of Newington in Surrey, if it shall fall void in his lifetime. *Item*, I give to my servant Reginald Gledal a good nag, at the discretion of my executors, and forty shillings. *Item*, I give unto my servant John Sharpe, now clerk of my kitchen, twenty pounds. *Item*, I give unto Richard Ratcliff, gent. my comptroller, thirty pounds, which he oweth me. And to Richard Frampton, gent. my secretary, ten pounds, out of his debt which he oweth me. *Item*, I give to Richard Somerdine, late yeoman of my horse, forty pounds, to be deducted out of his debt which he oweth unto me, upon specialty for his lease of Rippon. *Item*, I give unto my loving friend Mr Thomas Eaton, and to his wife, to either of them, a ring, price twenty shillings; and I do forgive him fifty pounds which he oweth unto me. *Item*, I give to Mr William Strickland eight pounds. To Mr Atherton seven pounds. To Mr John Shutt ten pounds. To Mr Warefeld of London, ten pounds. To Barston and Ponder, eleven pounds: and to Saltmarsh forty shillings, of those debts which they and every of them do owe unto me. *Item*, I give and bequeath to John Browne, fellow of Pembroke Hall in Cambridge, ten pounds, and all such books as are assigned unto him in a schedule subscribed with my hand; and my morning gown and hood given to me at the burial of the late bishop of Ely; and also a bed, with two pair of sheets, and other furniture to the same, if he receive not the same bed and furniture before my death. *Item*, I give Mr Redman, archdeacon of Canterbury, my white hobby called York.

Item, I do ordain and constitute William Redman, archdeacon of Canterbury, John Scott, esq. now steward of my house, and William Woodhal my nephew, executors of this my last will and testament. And I give to every of them that shall take upon them the execution of this my testament fifty pounds: and to every one of them that shall refuse the same I give ten pounds, to the intent they be favourers and furtherers of the execution thereof. The residue of all my goods and chattels, my debts and legacies being paid, and all other manner of charges being borne and fully satisfied, I will shall be bestowed upon the poorest of my kinsfolk and servants, and upon poor scholars, and other godly uses, at the discretion of my executors. In witness whereof I have set my hand and seal hereunto, in the presence of the witnesses underwritten.

E. CANT.

JOHN. WALKERUS, *Archidiac. Essexiæ.*
Per me JOHAN. INCENT, *Notar. Public.*
Per me THOMAM REDMAN, *Notar. Public.*
WILL. ARCHBOLD.
JOSUA GILPIN.
WILLIAM KIRTON.

APPENDIX.

		PAGE
I.	The Queen's Letter to the Bishops	467
II.	Lord Burleigh's Message to the Archbishop	469
III.	Speech to the Archbishop in Council	471
IV.	Christiani Hominis Norma, auctore Justo Velsio	474
V.	A Form of Meditation	477

APPENDIX I.

FROM THE QUEEN'S MAJESTY,
SENT TO THE BISHOPS FOR THE PURPOSE OF SUPPRESSING THE EXERCISE CALLED PROPHESYING, AND ANY OTHER RITES AND CEREMONIES BUT WHAT ARE PRESCRIBED BY THE LAWS[1].

May 8, 1577.

[Cotton MS., Cleopatra, F. 2, fo. 287.]

RIGHT reverend father in God, we greet you well. We hear, to our great grief, that in sundry parts of our realm there are no small numbers of persons presuming to be teachers and preachers of the church, (though neither lawfully thereunto called, nor yet fit for the same,) which, contrary to our laws established for the public divine service of Almighty God, and the administration of his holy sacraments, within this church of England, do daily devise, imagine, propound, and put in execution, sundry new rites and forms in the church, as well by their preaching, readings, and ministering the sacraments, as well by procuring unlawful assemblies of a great number of our people out of their ordinary parishes, and from place far distant, and that also of some of good calling, (though therein not well advised,) to be hearers of their disputations, and new devised opinions, upon points of divinity, far and unmeet of unlearned people: which manner of invasions they in some places term *prophesyings*, and in some other places *exercises*. By which manner of assemblies great numbers of our people, especially the vulgar sort, meet to be otherwise occupied with honest labour for their living, are brought to idleness, and seduced; and in manner schismatically divided among themselves into variety of dangerous opinions, not only in towns and parishes, but even in some families, and manifestly thereby encouraged to the violation of our laws, and to the breach of common order, and finally to the offence of all our quiet subjects, that desire to serve God according to the uniform orders established in the church: whereof the sequel cannot be but over dangerous to be suffered.

[1 See p. 375.]

A. D. 1577. Wherefore, considering it should be the duty of the bishops, being the principal ordinary officers in the church of God, as you are one, to see this [these] dishonours against the honour of God and the quietness of the church reformed; and that we see that by the increase of these through sufferance great danger may ensue, even to the decay of the Christian faith, whereof we are by God appointed the defender; besides the other inconveniences, to the disturbance of our peaceable government: We therefore, according to [the] authority we have, do charge and command you, as the bishop of that diocese, with all manner of diligence, to take order through your diocese, as well in places exempt as otherwise, that no manner of public and divine service, nor other form of administration of the holy sacraments, nor any other rites and ceremonies be in any sort used in the church, but directly according to the orders established by our laws. Neither that any manner of person be suffered within your diocese to preach, teach, read, or anywise exercise any function in the church, but such as shall be lawfully approved and licensed, as persons able for their knowledge, and conformable to the ministry in the rites and ceremonies of the church of England. And where there shall not be sufficient able persons for learning in any cures, to preach or instruct their cures, as were requisite, there shall you limit the curates to read the public homilies, according to the injunctions heretofore by us given for like causes.

And furthermore, considering for the great abuses that have been in sundry places of our realm, by reason of our foresaid assemblies, called exercises, and for that the same are not, nor have not been appointed nor warranted by us, or by our laws; We will and straitly charge you, that you do cause the same forthwith to cease, and not to be used: but if any shall attempt, or continue, or renew the same, we will you not only to commit them unto prison, as maintainers of disorders, but also to advertise us, or our council, of the names and qualities of them, and of their maintainers and abettors; that thereupon, for better example, their punishment may be more sharp for their reformation.

And in these things we charge you to be so careful and vigilant, as by your negligence, if we should hear of any person attempting to offend in the premises without your correction or information to us, we be not forced to make some example in reformation of you according to your deserts.

Given under our signet at our manor of Greenwich, the 7th of May 1577.

APPENDIX II.

THE LORD TREASURER'S MESSAGE TO THE ARCHBISHOP CONCERNING MAKING HIS SUBMISSION[1].

November, 1577.

It is meant, that declaration shall be made of the Queen's majesty's doings in directing the exercises to cease, with the causes thereof: and namely, upon sundry informations from the bishops and judges of the realm, of the inconvenience of the continuance. And so her actions shall be justified by the council.

Secondly, It shall be declared, how her Majesty did direct the archbishop to notify her order for the cessation of the said exercises to all the bishops of the realm; and how he refused so to do: whereby he did shew himself disobedient to her Majesty and her supreme authority ecclesiastical. And for that purpose her Majesty could do no less than to restrain him, as she hath done. And that her Majesty findeth it expedient to have the world understand her actions in this matter; and also to have the archbishop's misdemeanors declared; and to call him to answer to the same. Therefore he is to answer hereunto in that open place.

And where he hath many times since by humble writings submitted himself to her Majesty's mercy, and hath shewed himself sorrowful for the offending of her Majesty, desiring forgiveness thereof, and promising hereafter due obedience in all his ministry and charge; her Majesty, notwithstanding such private submission, findeth it expedient to have his submission and acknowledgment of his fault made in places public. And therefore he is there to make answer to these things.

In these things percase[2] some enlargements shall be, both

[1 See p. 392, note 2.]   [2 percase: perhaps.]

to set forth her Majesty's doings justifiably, and his refusal to obey reprehensively. But in these two parts will, I think, consist the whole.

It is meet for the archbishop to these things to answer, as may content her Majesty, for so many needful respects as is hard in few words to recite; as well for God's cause and his religion, as for the satisfaction of her Majesty, and pacifying her displeasure.

And therefore it were good for the archbishop, by way of answer to the first, to allow of the Queen's majesty's proceeding, grounded upon such causes, as to him it doth now appear did move her Majesty thereto: and herein to use good speeches of her Majesty, as a prince that in all her public doings hath shewed her wisdom, in doing nothing without good cause to move her thereto; and therefore they were to be greatly condemned, that would in any wise seek to find fault with her Majesty. And in this point the archbishop should do well to use the more large speech, as in good reason he may do without offence of his conscience.

To the second, concerning his offence to her Majesty, if he forbear the particular recital of his fault with the circumstances, he may, with the better estimation and less burden to his conscience, use a more general speech to acknowledge his fault, and to cry pardon. For which purpose his grace may say, that he is very sorry that he hath in this sort offended her Majesty, as he is charged; and that he requireth her Majesty to pardon him, and not to interpret his doing to have been with any meaning to offend her Majesty. But considering he now seeth upon what considerations her Majesty did proceed, he is very sorry that he hath herein offended her Majesty. And to conclude with all humble request of pardon, and firm promise of obedience to her Majesty, as far forth as in all duty he is bound.

If the archbishop would consider hereof, and set down in writing his answer, or the sum thereof, that it might be seen aforehand, it is thought that thereby some good might follow. And herein he is to be admonished to frame himself as far forth as by any good means he may, to seek to satisfy her Majesty.

APPENDIX III.

A SPEECH USED TO EDMUND GRINDAL, THE ARCHBISHOP OF CANTERBURY, IN COUNCIL, BEING IN HER MAJESTY'S DISPLEASURE[1].

[Ex Harleian MS. 5176, fo. 107.]

My Lord,—The cause of your calling hither at this time, by her Majesty's commandment, groweth upon three points. The first, to publish to this assembly in your presence her Majesty's proceeding with you, touching the removing of certain exercises and prophesyings, used as well by lay and unlearned people, as by other. The second is, to open your offences in not following those proceedings, according to her Majesty's commandment and direction. And the third and last is, to receive your answer.

For the first, her Majesty being given to understand, well nigh from all the parts of the realm, of the great divisions and sects that had grown, and were like to increase, by reason of these exercises, amongst her good and loving subjects in the cause of religion, and that so far forth, that if they had not been made in time, it was like that religion, which of his own nature should be uniform, would against his nature have proved milliform, yea, in continuance nulliform, specially in rites and ceremonies, and sometime also in matters of doctrine. And here it is to be noted, that these great inconveniences and disorders, grown by reason of these exercises amongst her people, came not to her Majesty's understanding by particular advertisements from private persons, but from sundry of the bishops, and sundry also of her justices of circuits within her realm, who by their several letters did not only pity the case, but also wished that by her Majesty's good and gracious help, some order might be had in this matter. Whereupon her Highness, calling to mind how she is supreme head in this realm in ecclesiastical causes, whereby the looking to this doth pertain to her

[1 It does not appear when, or by whom, this speech was delivered. Compare Letter XCIII. p. 395.]

A.D. 1577. princely charge and dignity, thought it good to call you as her principal minister in those causes, and to make you acquainted with the said great disorders, whereof she was informed, and thereupon to will and command you to take order for the putting down of those exercises, as the causes whereupon these inconveniences and divisions were grown, and were like to increase, greatly to the trouble of her Majesty, and to the peril of the common quiet of the realm; which commandment of her Majesty you did not perform and execute, whereby you did incur into the offence of disobedience. And yet, this notwithstanding, her Majesty afterward, of a greater grace and favour, caused certain of my lords of the privy council to call you before them, the rather by their good persuasions and means to move you to see her Majesty's pleasure and commandment to be put in execution. And albeit that were done also to the best of their understandings, as well by declaring to you that these matters of exercises, wherein the lay people should be parties, were but only newly begun, and therefore the less to be stood to by you, and also for that (as it was said) in many reformed churches they were not in use, where religion doth very well proceed and prosper; yea, in sundry parts of this realm never in use, and in sundry parts of this realm, where they were in use, decayed of themselves; that therefore you were the rather to condescend to perform this her Majesty's commandment, and specially because (as it was affirmed) public preaching and reading was permitted, which might serve sufficiently, as it hath done, and I trust shall, for the instruction of the people, with sundry other persuasions, that I do not now remember. And yet thereby you were nothing moved to perform that was committed to your charge; whereby you committed a second offence of disobedience, greater than the first. And thus it appeareth, that albeit her Majesty hath used all the good ways and means that pertaineth to her Highness to do, in bringing you to perform that her Majesty's commandments, for the taking away of these exercises, which by her said advertisements she found to be the original causes of the new innovations and divisions that happened; yet by no means you would be brought to remove and put down the same, according as her Majesty had commanded, and according to the advice given you by her council, as is aforesaid; wherein it must be concluded that you have very greatly offended her Majesty. And thus having declared to you how honourably and how graciously her Majesty hath dealt with you in these matters, and how disobediently and wilfully you have withstood her Majesty's orders and commandment in this behalf, I am to leave the rest to be said and declared by my lords here present. For it may be, and is very likely, that I have forgotten some things meet to be remembered. Marry, withal it is not amiss to let you understand, that the cause why you have been no sooner called, hath been partly by reason of your own infirmity, partly her Majesty's greater business, partly the adjournment of the term, and sometime the absence of councillors. So as I have now no more to say unto you, but to require you to hear what the rest of my lords and councillors shall think meet further to declare; and that done, to understand your answer[1].

[1] In the convocation, which met at St Paul's, on the 17th of January, 1581, "some of the members were strongly affected with the disgrace of Grindal's sequestration. These men, out of a generous zeal for their metropolitan, moved against entering upon any business, or so much as granting a subsidy, till the embargo was taken off, and the archbishop restored. But the majority were too cautious to be governed by this suggestion. However, Fuller reports, they came to a unanimous resolution for petitioning the Queen for Grindal's restitution. The address was drawn up in Latin by Toby Mathews, dean of Christ-church. That such an address was presented to the Queen, needs not to be questioned; but that it was passed as an act of convocation, is more than appears by the extracts from the journal."—Collier's Eccl. Hist., vol. vi., p. 612.

The address, above alluded to, may be seen in Fuller's Church Hist. Book ix. Sect. 4. p. 119.

There is also another letter, addressed to the Queen by the bishops of the province of Canterbury, entitled, *Episcoporum Epistola ad reginam Elizabetham pro restauratione Archiepiscopi Cant. Edm. Grindal;* in which they earnestly implore her Majesty to restore the archbishop to the full exercise of his authority. This letter may be read in Cardwell's Doc. Ann., vol. i., p. 386.]

APPENDIX IV.

Christiani Hominis Norma, ad quam se explorare perpetuo quivis debet, auctore Justo Velsio.

[State Paper Office.]

A 1. Quisnam est Christianus? Qui quod Christus per se et natura extitit et est, id participatione atque gratia est redditus et reddendus.

B 2. Quidnam per se et natura extitit Christus, et est? Primum, Deus in homine, deinde et homo Deus.

3. Quare Christum Deum in homine extitisse dicis? Quia dum Verbum caro factum est, et habitavit in nobis, Deum ad nos cœlitus deduxit, nostræque passibili naturæ conjunxit et univit, ut nobis in terra tanquam advenis quibusdam con-

C stitutis, ad cœlestem patriam, unde primi hominis inobedientia excidimus, reditus et itineris initiator esset et dux, perfecta sua ad mortem usque crucis obedientia; per quam peccato mortuus est semel.

4. Quomodo peccato mortuum Christum dicis, cum in peccato nunquam vixerit? *Peccatum enim non fecit, nec inventus est dolus in ore suo.* Quia etsi ipse in peccato nunquam vixerit, corpore, anima, et spiritu ab omni injustitiæ contagione immunis; tamen nostra peccata in carne sua pertulit, dum et a peccato inflictum passibilitatis et mortalitatis vulnus in se recepit, et pœnam peccati pro nobis ἀντίλυτρον redditus sustinuit, seseque pro eo hostiam immaculatam per Spiritum æternum Deo Patri exhibuit et obtulit.

5. Quare eundem hominem Deum esse asseris? Quia dum ab elementis hujus mundi mortuus est, et moriendo omnem corruptibilitatem et mortalitatem exuit, gloriosa sua resurrectione, carne Verbum facta et habitante in Deo, hominem ad Deum evexit, ipsiusque impassibili naturæ conjunxit et univit.

D
E F 6. Quomodo utrumque id homo participatione et gratia reddi potest? Per duplicem regenerationem, interni alteram, alteram externi hominis: quarum illa nos Deos in hominibus in hoc seculo constituit, hæc homines-deos in futuro efficit.

7. Quænam est interni hominis regeneratio? Qua ex aqua et Spiritu renascimur.

8. Quidnam est ex aqua nasci? Secundum internum hominem peccato mori, et corruptionis mortisque metus servitute liberari, exuendo corpore peccatorum carnis per non manufactam circumcisionem Christi, et veteri homine cum actibus suis deponendo; atque in aqua baptismatis, tanquam in mari rubro, submergendo, et cum Christo consepeliendo in mortem, ut deinceps actuosus non sit.

9. Quidnam est ex Spiritu nasci? Secundum eundem internum hominem justitiæ reviviscere, et in spem omnimodæ incorruptibilitatis et immortalitatis erigi, per vim resurrectionis Christi, et renovationem Spiritus Sancti in mentem nostram copiose effundendi; ut induto novo homine, qui secundum Deum conditus est in justitia et sanctitate veritatis, tum in novitate vitæ ambulemus, membra nostra accommodantes arma justitiæ Deo, tum externum hominem continenter supplantantes, et in servitutem redigentes, mortificationem Jesu in corpore nostro perpetuo circumferamus, quo et vita Jesu in corpore nostro, per externi hominis fiendam regenerationem, manifestetur.

10. Quænam est externi hominis regeneratio? Ejus ad incorruptibilitatis et immortalitatis consortium a mortuis in novissimo die resuscitatio; quando erit et Deus, perfecta obedientia omnibus ipsi jam subditis, omnia in omnibus. Ad quam nemo perventurum se tum speret, qui non hic in interno homine vere renatus, mortem primam, id est, animi et interni hominis devicerit. Nam hic solus, eam qui devicerit, nec a morte secunda et corporis, quæ ipsi ad vitam est transitus, nec ab æterna illa cum corporis tum animi, qua æternis suppliciis utrumque addicetur, quicquam, utpote nihil juris in ipsum obtinente, lædetur; reliquis omnibus nunquam finiendos intolerabiles cruciatus perpessuris.

> Hanc ego, nec aliam ullam Christiani hominis normam novi, quæ tuta certe sit et fidelis: ad quam me meaque jugiter examino: quod et cuivis, qui seipsum decipere nolit, faciendum censeo. Atque ad hanc dum ex hominis Christiani vero affectu et caritate alios quoque revocare conor, id mihi Psalmistæ usu venire experior, *Et posuerunt adversum me mala pro bonis, et odium pro dilectione mea.* Quid igitur ipsis (proh dolor!) expectandum sit, ex eodem illo discant psalmo, cujus initium, *Deus laudem*

meam ne tacueris; quia os peccatoris et os dolosi super me apertum est. Vos autem mihi in Christo dilectos sedulo moneo et hortor, ut hanc normam a mentis vestræ oculis nunquam amoveatis, sed omnem vestram vitam ad eam perpetuo exploretis ac dirigatis. Nam sic tantummodo servari hoc pessimo tempore poteritis.

Vestræ omniumque salutis amantissimus,

JUSTUS VELSIUS, HAGANUS.

APPENDIX V.

A Forme

of Meditation, very meete to be daylye used of house holders in their houses, in this daungerous and contagious time.

Set forth accordyng to the order in the Quenes majesties Injunction.

℃ Imprinted at London withoute Aldersgate, in little Britaine strete, by Alexander Lacy.

A FORM OF MEDITATION[1].

The master, kneeling with his family in some convenient place of his house, perfumed before with frankincense, or some other wholesome thing, as juniper, rosemary, rose-water, and vinegar, shall with fervent heart say, or cause to be said, this that followeth. The servants and family to every petition shall say: Amen.

MEDITATION.

<small>Deut. xxviii.
Lev. xxvi.</small>　WE read in thy holy word, O Lord, what blessings thou hast of thy mercy promised to them that live obediently, according to thy blessed will and commandments: we read also the curses that thy justice hath pronounced against such as despise thy word, or negligently pass not to live thereafter.

And among the rest of thy heavy curses, thou threatenest by name the plague and the pestilence, with other noisome and most painful diseases, to such as, forsaking thee, worship strange gods, and follow their own vain fantasies, instead of thy sacred ordinances.

We find also, how extremely thine own people, the Jews, have often felt the performance of these thy bitter threatenings, and that for sundry and divers offences.

<small>Num. xi.</small>　Because they loathed manna, and were not contented with thy miraculous provision, but would have quails, and other dainty victuals, to content their luxurious appetites,

---

[1 In a letter to Sir W. Cecil, dated Aug. 21, 1563, (see Letters, p. 264.) Grindal observes, "There was committed also to the print a short Meditation, to be used in private houses, which I suppose is abroad." The above Form is without a date, but there seems to be a strong probability that it is the Meditation alluded to by the bishop. It is taken from a printed copy contained in a volume of Forms of Prayer put forth by authority in the reign of Elizabeth, among archbishop Harsnett's collection in the library in Colchester Castle. Lacy seems to have been a contemporary printer of popular books and ballads, including some religious publications: this may probably account for a work, intended to be sold from house to house, being placed in his hands, rather than in Jugg's.

thou slewest so many with a sudden and mighty plague, that the place of their burial was named thereof, and called *the graves of lust*[2].

Also, for murmuring against the ministers of thy word, Moses and Aaron, thou destroyedst with a sudden plague fourteen thousand and more, besides those traitors, whom the earth swallowed for their rebellion: and had not Aaron entreated for them, and gone between the quick and the dead, thou wouldest have consumed them all, as thou wast minded to have done before, when they despised the plentiful land which thou hadst promised them, had not Moses stayed thy wrath, when thou saidst, "I will strike them with the pestilence, and utterly destroy them." Num. xvi. Num. xiv.

Further, when they had lost thine ark through their own sins, and the sins of their priests, the keepers thereof, after that the Philistines were forced, through thy plaguing hand, religiously to send it home again, thou struckest with the plague fifty thousand of the Bethsamites, thy people, for rashly presuming to look into the same, not having the warrant so to do. 1 Sam. iv. v. vi. vii.

In the time of king David thou destroyedst three-score and ten thousand of thy people in three days, with the wasting plague of pestilence; moved thereto by the transgression of David, whom, for the sins of his people, thou sufferedst to be tempted and subdued with a vain curiosity to number the people. 2 Sam. xxiv.

Also, shortly after the death of that immaculate Lamb our Saviour, thou sufferedst the plague to reign among the members of his body (the church of the Corinthians), for not worthily preparing themselves, and for misusing the sacrament of the body and blood of our Saviour Jesus Christ; and many died therefore, as thy holy apostle St Paul hath taught us. 1 Cor. xi.

Since which time, O Lord, as the monuments of thy church and other chronicles do declare, thou hast from time to time so plagued with pestilence, not only cities, but also whole countries, for these and other like causes, that we may justly look for the coming of our Saviour; so many and so horrible pestilences have been amongst us already.

[[2] Kibroth-hattaavah. Numb. xi. 34.]

All which causes, O Lord, for the which thou hast so afflicted thy people, are through the malice of Satan, and our wilful consenting unto him, grown so ripe in us, that, were it not for the exceeding greatness of thy mercy and compassion, we should all presently perish, and that worthily; so horrible and outrageous are our iniquities.

For we loathe not only the plentiful provision of wholesome victuals and apparel, which thou hast given us for our bodies, more abundantly than to many nations; travailing by all means to get wherewith to pamper our flesh, with wines, spices, silks, and other vain, costly, delighting things; but the precious manna of our souls, thy holy word and sacraments, we cannot away with; we are so full that we are glutted therewith.

We so little esteem the heavenly kingdom, which our Saviour hath so dearly prepared and kindly promised to us, that we abhor it, and are ready to stone those few that commend it, and exhort us for our own good to travel thitherward; better liking and crediting those false prophets, the Epicures and Papists, who with their lies discourage us therefrom.

What murmuring and grudging make we against the ministers of thy sword and word, which thou, of thy especial goodness, hast in mercy given us! How despise we our bishops and preachers, and other ministers of thy holy sacraments, whom thou hast commanded us to reverence and honour!

Did not we through our wicked lives wretchedly leese[1] the Ark of thy holy word, and the true ministration of thy sacraments, not many years ago, which the popish Philistines took from us? And now, when thou, through thy plagues laid upon them, hast miraculously sent it us again; see how bold we be, with the Bethsamites, unreverently to receive it.

[1 Sam. vi. 19.]

For many make of it a gazing-stock to serve their eyes and tongues, rather than a law to obey and follow in their lives. Yea, the knowledge of thy truth, goodness, and mercy, breedeth in many of us a careless security, and a contempt of thy holy ordinances. For we presume upon thy mercy and promises, not regarding the conditions, nor any of thy

[1 Lose.]

commandments, which in our baptism we vowed to observe. Yea, we make thy gospel a cloak of our covetousness, under colour whereof we seek our own lucre, and hide all our wicked and filthy practices.

If the Corinthians deserved to be plagued for abusing thy holy sacrament, how much more are we worthy of thy fierce wrath, that not only abuse it, but also abhor and contemn it, because it is ministered as it ought! For thou knowest, O Lord, what a sort there are, which, bewitched with the devil and the pope's doctrine, do utterly abhor Christ's holy Communion, and, saving for fear of the law, would never come at it. In what sort these receive, and how they be prepared, is not unknown unto thee. How rashly also, and unadvisedly, and unprepared the common multitude do frequent it, partly appeareth in that many of them never forgive old offences, nor reconcile themselves, nor in any thing do amend their old sins and vices.

Seeing then that we, Lord, the common sort and multitude, do thus abound in all kind of wickedness, how can it be, but that thou of thy justice must suffer our magistrates to offend also in somewhat, to the end thou mayest justly take vengeance on our sins?

For these manifold heaps of sins and wickednesses, O Lord, thou hast justly at this present sent this dangerous pestilence among us, as thou hast often and long time threatened by the mouths of thy faithful preachers, who continually have called upon us to stay thy wrath by earnest repentance and amendment of life. But we have alway been deafer and deafer: the delight in our sins not only stopped our ears, but also hardened our hearts against their hearty and friendly admonitions. And in that we now, O Lord, do begin to feel and acknowledge our sins, it cometh more of thy rigour in plaguing us, than of any good inclination of ourselves. Mollify therefore, O Lord, our flinty hearts with the suppling moisture of thy Holy Spirit: make us to reverence thee, as children, for love of thy mercies, and not to dread thee, like slaves, for fear of thy punishment. *Amen.*

O DEAR FATHER, reclaim us thy lost children; O merciful Saviour, pity us thy putrified members: O Holy Ghost, repair us thy decayed temples: O holy, blessed, and glorious Trinity, have mercy upon us miserable sinners. *Amen.*

[GRINDAL.]

GRANT US, O LORD, such true repentance, as may, through the blood of our Saviour, blot out the stains of our heinous iniquities. Forgive us our sins, O Lord, forgive us our sins, for thine infinite mercy's sake. *Amen.*

FORGIVE us our blasphemies, idolatries, and perjuries; forget our vain and outrageous oaths. As thou hast, by thy rigour and plagues, forced us to acknowledge thee to be our just and righteous Lord, so let us, through thy mercy and forgiveness, feel thee to be our mild and loving Father; and give us grace for ever hereafter to reverence this thy glorious name. *Amen.*

TAKE from us, O God, the care of worldly vanities; make us contented with necessaries. Pluck away our hearts from delighting in honours, treasures, and pleasures of this life; and engender in us a desire to be with thee in thy eternal kingdom. Give us, O Lord, such taste and feeling of thy unspeakable joys in heaven, that we may alway long therefore, saying with thine elect, "Hasten thy kingdom, O Lord, take us to thee." *Amen.*

MAKE us, O Lord, obedient to thy will, revealed in thy holy word; make us diligent to walk in thy commandments; forgive us our contempt and murmuring against the magistrates and ministers, which thou hast in thy mercy appointed; make us obedient unto their godly laws and doctrine. Save and preserve, O Lord, thine anointed, our Queen Elizabeth, that she in thy grace and fear may long reign among us. Give peace to all Christian nations. Move us by thy Spirit to love one another, as the members of one body, that we may all do thy will here in earth, as it is in heaven. *Amen.*

DIG out of us, O Lord, the venomous roots of covetousness and concupiscence; or else so repress them with thy grace, that we may be contented with thy provision of necessaries, and not to labour, as we do, with all toil, sleight, guile, wrong, and oppression, to pamper ourselves with vain superfluities. Feed our souls, O Lord, daily with the true manna of thy heavenly word, and with the grace of thy holy sacraments. Give us grace continually to read, hear, and meditate thy purposes, judgments, promises, and precepts, not to the end we may curiously argue thereof, or arrogantly presume thereupon, but to frame our lives according to thy will;

that by keeping the covenants we may be sure of the promises; and so make our election and vocation certain, through our constant faith, and virtuous and godly living. *Amen.*

CONFORM us, O Lord, to the image of our Saviour: so burn our hearts with the flames of love, that no envy, hatred, or malice, do remain in us, but that we may gladly forgive whatsoever wrong is, or shall be, either maliciously or ignorantly, done or said against us. And here, Lord, in thy presence (thy majesty is every where), we forgive whatsoever hath been by any man practised against us, beseeching thee of thy goodness likewise to forgive it. And further, for thy mercy's sake, and for our Saviour Jesus Christ's sake, we beseech thee, O dear Father, to forgive us those horrible and damnable sins, which we have committed against thy majesty, for which thou hast now justly brought this pestilence and plague upon us. Let the ceasing thereof, we beseech thee, certify us of thy mercy and remission. *Amen.*

WE KNOW, O Lord, the weakness of ourselves, and how ready we are to fall from thee: suffer not therefore Satan to shew his power and malice upon us; for we are not able to withstand his assaults. Arm us, O Lord, alway with thy grace, and assist us with thy Holy Spirit in all kinds of temptation. *Amen.*

DELIVER us, O dear Father, from all evils, both bodily and ghostly. Deliver, O Lord, from trouble of conscience all that are snarled[1] in their sins. Deliver, O Lord, from all fear of persecution and tyranny our brethren, that are under the cross for profession of thy word. Deliver, O merciful Father, those that, for our sins and offences, are already tormented with the rage of pestilence. Recover those, O Lord, that are already stricken, and save the rest (of this my household) from this grievous infection. *Amen.*

GRANT this, O dear Father, for our Saviour Jesus Christ's sake, to whom with Thee, and the Holy Ghost, be all honour and glory, world without end. *Amen.*

¶ *End with the Lord's Prayer.*

[1 snarled: entangled.]

¶ *A Prayer to God to cease the Plague.*

O LORD GOD, which, for our innumerable sins, dost here fatherly correct us, to the end we should not feel the rigour of thy severe judgment in eternal condemnation, we humbly submit ourselves unto thy grace and pity, beseeching thee, for our Lord Jesus Christ's sake, that although we have justly deserved this plague now laid upon us, yet it may please thee, in the multitude of thy mercies, to withdraw thy rod from us. Grant us, O Lord, true repentance of our sins, which (as it did in that good king Ezekias), may deliver us from the plague laid upon us, and cause those that be sick to recover. Or if thou have determined to take a number of us out of the miseries of this present world, give us the comfort of thy Holy Spirit, that may make us glad and willing to come unto thee. Give us grace, O Lord, so to prepare ourselves, that we may be ready, with the wise virgins, to enter into life with our Saviour Christ, whensoever it shall please thee to call us. Grant us this, O dear Father, for Jesus Christ's sake, our only Mediator and Advocate; to whom with Thee, and the Holy Ghost, be all honour and glory, world without end. *Amen.*

INDEX OF MATTERS, &c.

A.

Accounts, injunction respecting those of the church of York, 152.

Admonition, to be read by ministers to their people, respecting infection, 271.

"Admonition to Parliament," Thos. Cartwright the principal author, 348.

Adulterers, names of, to be presented to the ordinary, 143.

Advowsons, article to be inquired respecting those in the province of Canterbury, 179; archbishop Grindal's dislike to the granting of, especially by ecclesiastical persons, 329.

Æschylus, death of, 8.

Affinity, Table of, to be affixed in the parish church, 126; to be read at least twice a year, *ibid*.

Agues, their prevalence in Yorkshire, 325.

Albs to be destroyed, 135, 159.

Alexander, pope, sets his foot on the neck of the emperor Frederic Barbarossa, 21, but this event called in question by the greatest part of modern authors, 21, *n*. 5.

Allen, cardinal, various tracts written by him in furtherance of the Spanish invasion, 169.

Altar, an, though made but of lime and stone, called by Jacob, "The mighty God of Israel," 41.

Altar-cloths, not to be used, 155.

Altars, to be taken down by the churchwardens, 134; article concerning, in the province of Canterbury, 158.

Altar-stones to be broken, defaced, and bestowed to some common use, 134.

Amalekites conquered by Moses, 41.

Ambrose, St, highly commends Valentinian and Theodosius, 11; his commendation of the emperor Gratian, 18; why he commends Theodosius, 25; his remark where we ought to seek the Lord, 54; declareth the meaning of St Paul's words, "Whoso eateth of this bread, &c.," 55; words of, that he taketh the sacrament unworthily that taketh i otherwise than Christ ordained it, 57; saith, because we are delivered by the Lord's death, in the remembrance of the same by eating and drinking we signify the body and blood which were offered up for us, 65; saith, such is the force and strength of the word, that the bread and wine remain the same as they were, and yet are changed into another thing, 69; calleth the sacrament, *typum Corporis Christi*, 69; words of, to Theodosius, 388; and to Valentinian, that the conference about faith ought to be left to the priests, 388.

Anabaptists, seize the city of Münster, and commit atrocities which, as Mosheim observes, would surpass all credibility, were they not attested in a manner that excludes every degree of doubt and uncertainty, 256, *n*. 1.

Ananias and Sapphira, death of, 8.

Anne of Hungary, p. 14.

Antiphoners, to be utterly abolished, 135.

Antoine de Bourbon, king of Navarre, the second Julian, death of, 253.

Apprentices, article respecting the instruction of, 161.

Archdeacons, article to be inquired respecting their residence, &c., 179; to appoint portions of the New Testament to the clergy to be conned without book, 184.

Arians, whence their heresy sprung, 41.

Articles, to be put in execution within the archdeaconry of York, 154; to be inquired of within the province of Canterbury, 156; to be inquired of in all cathedrals and collegiate churches, 178; of convocation touching the clergy of the province of Canterbury, 184.

Articles of Religion, when to be openly read in church, 128.

Articles of the Faith, when to be recited, 161.

Articles and Discipline, book of, (Liber quorundam canonum,) archbishop Grindal's opinion of, 327.

Athanasius, St, his funeral sermon written by Gregory Nazianzen, 10; on these words, "Whosoever shall speak a word against the Son of Man," saith, the words that Christ here speaketh, be not carnal, but spiritual. For what body might have sufficed for all that should eat, to be a nourishment of the whole world. But therefore he maketh mention of the ascension of the Son of man into heaven, to the intent to pluck them away from that corporal cogitation, 67, 8.

Augustine, St, saying of, respecting the last day of our life, 5; saying of, that he cannot die evil, that hath lived well, and hardly can he die well, that hath lived evil, 30; declareth that Christ's body is placed in one room, 52; saith, the sacrament is an outward token of love and charity, 55; sharply rebuketh them that think to eat Christ with their mouth, 44; his words to the Capernaites, which took Christ grossly in the sacrament, 44; remark respecting the unfaithful receiving not the body of Christ, 58; giveth a good cause why the sacrament, although it be not the body of Christ, is notwithstanding called the body of Christ, 61; saith, a figurative speech is not to be taken after the letter, 63; teacheth, to know the plain sense from a figure, 63; says, Christ doubted not to say, This is my body, when he gave but a sign of his body, and received Judas to the supper, in which he commanded and delivered a figure of his body and blood unto his disciples, 65; saith, in those carnal oblations the flesh of Christ was figured which he should offer for our sins, and the blood which he should bestow for us: but in this sacrifice, the sacrament, is the giving of thanks and memorial of the flesh of Christ which he hath offered for us, and of the blood which he hath shed for us. In that sacrifice, therefore, is signified figuratively what should be given for us; in this sacrifice what is given to us is evidently declared. In those sacrifices the Son of God was before preached to be slain; in this sacrifice he is shewed to be slain already for the wicked, 68; saith, no man ought in any wise to doubt but that every faithful man is then partaker of the body and blood of the Lord, when in baptism he is made a member of Christ. For he shall not be deprived of the participation and benefit of that sacrament when he findeth in himself that thing which the sacrament doth signify, 69; declareth that the sacrament must needs be a figure and a remembrance of the body of Christ; for otherwise it seemeth to be more horrible to eat man's flesh, than to kill a man; and more horrible to drink man's blood, than to shed it, 70; on psalm xcviii, saith, Ye shall not eat this body which you see, and drink that blood which they shall shed that shall crucify me. I commend unto you a sacrament, 70; seeketh no starting holes, nor yet any indirect shifts to obscure the truth, 197; saith, places that be dark, are to be expounded by other that be light, 197; saith, to eat Christ's body is a figurative speech, 198.

Augustus, emperor, saying of, 17.

Auricular confession in Lent or at any other time, not to be made, 140.

Aylmer, Mr, archdeacon of Lincoln, afterwards bishop of London, a fit person to answer the Latin book of Discipline, 353.

B.

Baker, Dr. Philip, provost of King's College, Cambridge, misdemeanors objected against him, 308; deprived by the Queen's commissioners, *ibid.*

Baldwin, Dr. Francis, professor of civil law, and reader at Heidelberg, his fitness to attend the conference at Poissy between the papists and French protestants, 245.

Bangor, cathedral church of, injunction given to the dean and chapter, 183.
Banns of marriage, injunctions respecting, 126.
Baptism, private, article of convocation respecting, 188.
Baptism, sacrament of, article respecting, 161; Glin affirms that it doth not consist in the word "I," or in the word "thee," or in the words "in the name, &c.," but in all the words spoken in order, 196.
Baptism, water of, is, after a certain manner, the blood of Christ, 62.
Barbarossa, Frederic, emperor, kisses the foot of pope Alexander, 21.
Bartlett, a reader of a divinity lecture in St Giles' Parish without Cripplegate, though suspended by the bishop, took upon him to read again without licence, 288.
Barton (George), parson of Abchurch, an infamous clergyman, deprived by Bishop Grindal, 266.
Basilides, espouser of the heresy of the Gnostics, 59, n. 5.
Basilius Magnus, his funeral sermon, written by Gregory Nazianzen, 10; calleth the sacrament antitypum corporis Christi, 69.
Bate-maker, maker of discords, article respecting, 181.
Bawds, names of, to be presented to the ordinary, 143.
Beads, injunction respecting the not wearing of, 140.
Beddern, a house so called in York, injunction respecting, 148.
Bede, quotation from respecting the bread and wine in the Lord's supper, 47; on the words of Christ, "Now a little while you shall see me," 54.
Bedell, challenged of false doctrine, 204.
Bella Domini, what called in the scriptures, 13.
Bells, ringing and tolling, injunction respecting, 136; article to be inquired of respecting, 160.
Berny, or Verny, hired by the Spanish ambassador's secretary to murder lord Burleigh, 332, n. 1.
Bertramus, or Ratramnus, his book, written at the request of Charles the Bald, not of Charlemagne, 73, n. 4.
Best, John, bishop of Carlisle, recommendation of him to sir Wm. Cecil, 268, and see n. 2.; complains of want of preachers in his diocese, 285.
Bing, Dr, recommended as visitor for St John's College, Cambridge, 359.
Blasphemers, names of to be presented to the ordinary, 143.
Bonham, Wm., preacher, promise made by him, 318.
Bonner, Edmund, late bishop of London, death of, 307.
Borgest, the Spanish ambassador's secretary, hires two desperate men to murder lord Burleigh, 332, n. 1.
Boweland, Thomas, a Londoner, examined before the ecclesiastical commissioners, 201.
Bowls, game of, injunction respecting, 138.
Brazen serpent, a token, 42.
Breaking of bread, what meant by, 42.
Breathing over the sacramental bread and wine, article respecting, 159.
Bristow, a popish author, 169.
Brown, Thomas, of Shrewsbury, archbishop Grindal's letter to the bishop of London respecting a collection to be made for him, 404.
Broxbourn parsonage, statement of archbishop Grindal, respecting, 332.
Burleigh, lord, *see* Cecil.
Bullinger (Henry), quotation from, respecting wearing of ecclesiastical garments, 207; references to bishop Grindal's letters to him, 290; writes a book against the bull of pope Pius the Fifth, deposing queen Elizabeth, 328.
Burning candles, what signified by the expression, 6.
Bursars, in cathedral churches, article to be inquired respecting, 180.

C.

Calvin, quotation from, on justification, 255, n.
Candlemas Day, why so called, 140, n. 1.

Candles, not to be burnt superstitiously in the church, on Candlemas Day, 140.
Candlesticks to be destroyed in the province of York, 135; article respecting same in the province of Canterbury, 159.
Capernaites, how they took Christ in the sacrament, 44.
Cards, playing at, injunction respecting, 138.
Carmichel, warden of Liddisdale, in Scotland, taken prisoner, sent into England, kept at York, and then sent home with honour and certain presents, 355, n. 4.
Cartwright, Thomas, not to be permitted to read again in the University, 305; reader of Lady Margaret's divinity lecture, account of him, 323, n. 3, 4.
Catechism, the children and servants to be taught, 124, 137; Nowel's Catechism, injunction respecting, 142, 152; article respecting, 162, 188.
Cathedrals and collegiate churches, articles to be inquired of respecting, 178.
Cecil, sir William; 11th mourner at the funeral of the emperor Ferdinand, 33; sends a letter to Grindal to consult concerning a fast for the judgment of the plague, 79; letters of Grindal to, see table of contents; created baron Burleigh, and made lord high treasurer, 329; recommended as visitor for St John's College, Cambridge, 359.
Censers, to be destroyed, 135, 159.
Cerdon, an espouser of the heresy of the Gnostics, 59, n. 5.
Chancellor, of the cathedral of Canterbury, article to be inquired respecting, 178.
Chancels, or choirs of churches and chapels, to be repaired and maintained in good estate, 131.
Chapter, meeting annually of the dean and chapter of York, 151.
Charles the Bald, the book of Bertramus, or Ratramnus, written at the request of, 73.
Chatillon, cardinal, Odet de Coligni, brother of the admiral of France, his arrival in England, 299, n. 3.
Cheke, Sir John, one of K. Edward's visitors at the disputation held at Cambridge, 1549, 194.
Chest, for the alms of the poor, with three locks and keys to be provided by the churchwardens of York, 134; article respecting, in the province of Canterbury, 158.
Children, injunctions to the clergy respecting their instruction, 124.
Choristers of the church of York, injunction respecting, 152.
Chrism, article respecting the use of, in the ministration of the sacrament of baptism, 160.
Chrismatories, to be destroyed, 135, 159.
Christ, dialogue respecting his words "This is my body," 39; sense of them expounded, 40; ordained not his body, but a sacrament of his body, 43; is no food for the body, but the soul, 44; how his body is taken by faith, 46; his body spiritual meat, 47; his body imprisoned by the papists in a box, and afterward burned when it is mouldy, 50; his body spiritual in the sacrament, say the papists, 50; must be received with faith, says Gregory, 58; took bread and made it his body, saying, "This is my body," that is to say, a figure of my body, 65; doubted not to say, This is my body, when he gave but a sign of his body, 65; received Judas to the supper, in which he commended and delivered a figure of his body and blood unto his disciples, 65; said twice, "I will not drink of the fruit of the vine," 196; "to eat his body," saith Augustine, a figurative speech, 198.
Christ Church, Oxford, book of injunctions to be observed there till their book of statutes is finished, 282.
Chrysostom, St, quotation from, 26; saith, all mysteries must be considered with inward eyes; that is to say, spiritually, 62, 64; saith, when they object unto us, and ask, How know you that Christ was offered up? then, alleging these things, we stop their mouths. For if Christ died not, then

whose sign or token is this sacrifice? 65; preferreth a poor man before the sacrament, and calleth him the body of Christ, rather than the other, 66; says, if it be so perilous a matter to translate these sanctified vessels into private uses, in the which is not the true body of Christ, but a mystery of the body of Christ is contained, how much more then these vessels of our body? 67; saith, after the bread is sanctified, it is called bread no more, although the nature of bread still remains, 72; manuscript of some of his homilies taken to bishop Grindal, 291.

Churches, injunction respecting, 134, 5.

Churchwardens, to provide pulpit at the charges of the parish, 132; how to be chosen, 133; their duties, ibid.

Churchyards, to be well fenced, &c., 135.

Cicero, quoted, 4.

Circumcision, called the covenant, whereas it was but a token of the covenant, 41.

Clergy, injunctions for, 123.

Coffer, with two locks and keys to be provided by the churchwardens, 134; for the keeping of the register book, in the province of Canterbury, 158.

Coligni, Odet de, *see* Châtillon, cardinal.

Commination, form of, when to be read, 127; article respecting, within the province of Canterbury, 158.

Commissaries, article to be inquired respecting, 178.

Common Prayer, book of, to be provided by the churchwardens, 133; article concerning, in the province of Canterbury, 157.

Common Prayer, form of, during the plague, 84, sqq.

Communion, to whom not to be administered, 125; to be received thrice a year, at the least, by all men and women of fourteen years and upwards, 137; injunction to the dean and chapter of York respecting the ministration of, 148; injunction respecting, in the cathedral church of Bangor, 184.

Communion-bread, how to be delivered to the people, 124; communion bread and wine to be provided by the churchwardens, 134; article respecting, in the province of Canterbury, 158.

Communion-cup of silver, and cover of silver for the same, to be provided by the churchwardens of York, 133; article respecting, in the province of Canterbury, 158.

Concealments; letter of archbishop Grindal to lord Burleigh, complaining of injuries offered to the clergy by those who were sent down upon concealments, 343.

Conducts, conducti; hired chaplains, article respecting, 181.

Confession, if discreetly used, a laudable custom, 57; auricular not to be used in Lent or at any other time, 140.

Contentious persons, names of, to be presented to the ordinary, 143.

Convocation, articles agreed upon at one held at Westminster, in the year 1575, 185.

Cope, article respecting the wearing of, 159.

Corpus Christi day and Corpus Christi masses, when they ensued, 73.

Corranus, a Spaniard, account of him, and his contest with one Hieronymus, 309, *n.* 3; preferred to be reader of divinity at the Temple, 312, *n.*; bishop Grindal's judgment on him, 313, 14.

Cosmus, a servant to the Dutch ambassador, fasts five or six days by Velsius's persuasion, that after his abstinence he might receive illuminations à cœlo, 255; but in the end fell mad, *ibid.*; Grindal's advice respecting, *ibid.*

Counterfeit ministers, names of to be certified to the bishops, 186.

Coverdale, Miles, his letter to Cecil upon his appointment by bishop Grindal to St Magnus, London, 284, *n.* 1.

Cross-week, or gang-days, what so called, 141.

Crosses to be destroyed, 135, 159.

Crossing, article respecting, 159.

Cup, " is the new Testament," saith Paul, and yet is not the cup indeed the very new Testament, 41.

Curate, not to serve any one cure, without letters testimonial of the ordinary of the place whence he came, 128.

Cures, no minister or priest to serve two, without special licence under the ordinary's seal, 128.

Cyprian, St, his funeral sermon written by Gregory Nazianzen, 10; saith, in taking the sacrament, we sharpen not our tooth, nor prepare our belly, 46; but the treatise De Cœna Domini, whence this is taken, attributed to him on doubtful authority, 46, *n.* 1.; passage of explained, 198.

D.

Dacres, Leonard, younger son of William Lord Dacres, raises a rebellion, 1569, 322.

Dacres, William, son of Richard Dacres, of Carlisle, married to Anne Grindal, niece of bishop Grindal, 322.

Damasus, bishop, quotation from, respecting the body of Christ, 53.

Darly, Henry lord, sixth mourner at the funeral of the emperor Ferdinand, 32.

David, king, wonderfully exercised in worldly troubles, 105; confesseth that God was ever his helper and deliverer, when he called upon him, 105.

" Day's minds," what they were, 136.

Dead, prayer for, lacks all authority and example of the canonical scriptures, 24; and although in Chrysostom and St Ambrose there is mention of it, yet it is in a far other meaning with them than the schoolmen and others have collected and gathered of them, 24, 5.

Deans, article to be inquired respecting their residence, &c., 179.

Death, inevitable necessity of, 6; uncertainty of, 7; examples of the latter, *ibid.*; all subject to, 10.

De Profundis, an antiphone in the office for the dead, injunction respecting, 140.

Devotions, oblations devoted to charitable or pious purposes, 163.

Dilapidation of the goods, &c., of the church of Canterbury, article respecting, 178.

Disputation, second one holden at Cambridge, in the presence of king Edward's visitors, respecting transubstantiation, 195, sqq.

Disturbers of divine service, names of, to be presented to the ordinary, 144.

Divine service, all persons not attending every Sunday, to be presented to the ordinary, &c., 129; disturbers of, their names to be presented to the ordinary, 144; article respecting to be inquired into, 180.

Docetæ, or Gnostics, *see* Gnostics.

Doctors, how they call the sacrament the body of Christ, and why, 63; words of against the pope's doctrine, 63.

Doctrine, erroneous or seditious, inquiry to be made respecting, 181.

Dorman (Thomas), Jewel's Apology attacked by, 169.

Dorrell, Mr, bishop Grindal's opinion as to his being primate of Armagh, 292.

Doubts, respecting private baptism, to be resolved by the bishop of the diocese, 188.

Drinking of the cup, what meant by, 42.

Drunkards, names of to be presented to the ordinary, 143.

Druthmarus, Christianus, a monk of Corbey, says, Wine maketh glad the heart and increaseth blood, and therefore the blood of Christ is not unaptly signified thereby, 66.

Dudley, lord Robert, earl of Leicester, letter of bishop Grindal to, respecting Sebastian Westcote, 261.

E.

Earl, Mr, minister of St Mildred's, Bread-street, letter to him, enjoining him not to suffer any unlicensed preacher to use his pulpit, 293.

Earthquake, letter of archbishop Grindal to his officers concerning prayer on account of the earthquake, 415.

Ecclesiastical discipline, archbishop Grindal's opinions and directions concerning, 451.

Elizabeth, queen, persuaded by archbishop Parker, Grindal, and Cox, to marry, 19, *n.*; offended with archbishop Grindal in the matter of exercises or prophesyings, 372; letter of, to the bishops for the purpose of suppressing the exercise called prophesying, &c., 467.

Ember days and lent, letter of archbishop Grindal to the bishop of London respecting, 406.

Erasmus, his paraphrases in English upon the gospels to be set up in some convenient place, in every church and chapel, by the churchwardens, 134, 157.

Eucharist, conference at Marpurg respecting, 251, *n.*

Excommunication, argument propounded in the convocation concerning the ordinary use of, 451.

Exercises, orders for reformation of abuses about, 373; account of them, 383; orders of them, 384; ground of them, *ibid.*; called prophecies in scripture, 385; benefit of them, 386; abuses of them, 385.

F.

Faculties, court of, account of the, 446.

Family of Love, Henry Nicolas of Holland, founder of, 360, *n.* 1.

Fasting-days, injunction respecting observance of, 128; article respecting those abrogated, 160.

Fat images to be destroyed, 135.

Favourers of the Romish or foreign power, names of to be presented to the ordinary, 144.

Fecknam, John, late abbot of Westminster, under the care of Dr Goodman, dean of Westminster, 282.

Ferdinand, emperor, sermon at the funeral solemnity of, 3; commendation of him, 11; gifts of his mind, and his godly virtues, 12; his wars against infidels, 13; valiantly defends Vienna against the Turk, 15; compared with David and Solomon, 17; crowned emperor without a mass, 20; request made by him to the Tridentine Council, that liberty may be granted to have the communion administered in both kinds, 22.

Fermer, meaning of the word, 161.

Figurative speeches, most common in scripture, 42.

Fitzherbert, Sir Thomas, his case alluded to, 274.

Fornicators, names of to be presented to the ordinary, 143.

Forster, Sir John, warden of the Middle March, taken prisoner and carried into Scotland, 355, *n.* 4.

Foxe, John, letters to, from bishop Grindal, 219, 221, 224, 228, 232, 237; his letter to Grindal, 230.

Frankfort, letter of bishop Grindal to the magistrates of, in behalf of the congregation of Dutch protestants there, 247.

Fratries, or refectories, description of them, 272, *n.*

Froschover, fittest man to commit the business of printing Cranmer's controversy with Gardiner on the eucharist, 221.

G.

Gang-days, what so called, 141, 168.

"Gaping Gulph, the," a book written by John Stubbs, against the marriage of queen Elizabeth to the duke of Anjou, 408, *n.*

Garments, article to be inquired respecting those of the deans, &c., 179.

Gelasius saith, in the eucharist the substance of the bread and nature of the wine cease not to be. For the image and similitude of the body and blood of the Lord is celebrated in the action of the mysteries, 66.

Geneva, letter of archbishop Grindal to the bishops for a collection in behalf of, 429.

Geneva, church of, communicate with wafer cakes, 208.

Gibson, prebendary of Botevant, enjoined to view the statutes relating to the church of York, 151.

Girding of the loins, what signified by the expression, 6.

Glin, one of the Romish disputants at

the disputation held at Cambridge, 1549, 194.

Goodman, Christopher, remarks on a tract of his, printed at Geneva, 327.

Grammar-schools, article to be inquired respecting, in cathedral churches, 180.

Gnostics, or Docetæ, their origin, 59; why so called, 59, *n*. 5; founder of, *ibid.*

Goad, Roger, made provost of King's College, Cambridge, in the room of Dr Philip Baker, deprived, 308, *n.*; recommended as visitor for St John's College, Cambridge, 359.

Godfathers, injunctions respecting, 126.

Godmothers, injunctions respecting, 126.

Goodman, Dr Gabriel, dean of Westminster, one of the ecclesiastical commissioners, June 20, 1567, 201.

Goodrich, Thomas, bishop of Ely, one of K. Edward's visitors, at the disputation held at Cambridge, 1549, 194.

Gorgonia, sister of Gregory Nazianzen, miraculous cure of, by application to the reserved sacramental elements, 48, *n.*

Goths, why sent against the Christians, 98.

Grailes, book of, to be abolished, 135.

Grants by the chapter-seal, article to be inquired respecting in the province of Canterbury, 179.

Gratian, emperor, commended by St. Ambrose, 18.

Gregory Nazianzen, why called Theologus, 10; writes the funeral sermons of Basilius Magnus, and others, *ibid.*

Gregory, St, what he calls Christ's body, 46; says that Christ's body must be received by faith, 58.

Grindal, Edmund, birth of; narrow escape from an accident; sent to Magdalene College, Cambridge, and removed to Christ's College and Pembroke Hall, of which last he became fellow, president, and master; took the degrees of B.A. and M.A.; admitted to a fellowship; ordained by Bird, bishop of Winchester; served the office of senior proctor, i.; selected as one of the disputants against transubstantiation; appointed lady Margaret's preacher, and also president of his college; appointed chaplain to bishop Ridley; engaged in two private conferences on the eucharistic controversy, ii.; appointed chaplain to king Edward VI., and obtains a prebend in Westminster, iii.; on the death of king Edward, goes to Strasburgh and other places abroad, and assists Foxe in his Acts and Monuments, *ib.*; deputed to visit Frankfort, in the hope of allaying the dissensions amongst the English exiles there, iv.; on the death of queen Mary, returns to England, *ib.*; assists at the revision of the Book of Common Prayer, and at a conference held at Westminster, between eight divines on the Romish and eight on the Protestant side, v.; one of the commissioners for the royal visitation in the north of England, *ib.*; consecrated bishop of London, vi.; holds his primary visitation, and is engaged in a synod held at St Paul's for the purpose of establishing an uniformity in worship, vii.; draws up a form of prayer and fasting, in consequence of the plague, *ib.*; proceeds to the degree of doctor in divinity; preaches a sermon at the funeral solemnity of the emperor Ferdinand VII., and is engaged on the bishops' bible, viii.; nominated archbishop of York, *ib.*; and archbishop of Canterbury, x.; falls under the queen's displeasure in regard to the exercises called prophesyings, xi.; writes to the queen in defence of them, xii.; is confined to his house, and sequestered for six months, xiii.; restored to a certain extent to the exercise of his ecclesiastical jurisdiction, xv.; afflicted with blindness, *ib.*; death, and character, *ib.*; burial, *ib.*; inscriptions on his tomb, xvi.; bishop Tanner's account of him, xvii., *n.* 3; list of his remains, xviii. sq.; letter to Mr Mullins, archdeacon of London, respecting the plague, 78; his form of common prayer, 84; order for the general fast, 93; thanksgiving for the abatement of the plague, 111; short form of thanksgiving for the ceasing of the plague, 115; injunctions and articles of inquiry given at various times, 121; argues against transubstantiation, 193; saith, that the sacrament remaineth bread and wine after the consecration, 196; letters of, to different persons, 238; contention in the university of Cambridge, between the vice-chancellor and doctors, and the masters and heads of colleges, referred to him, 365, *n.*; letter to the queen about prophesyings and exercises, 384; his submission, 400; will, 458.

Guest, one of the disputants at the second disputation held at Cambridge, 1549, 194.

H.

Hamsted, Hadrian, apologist for some anabaptists, cited before the bishop of London, and openly censured, *n.* 243; revocation offered to him by the bishop of London, 441.

Hand-bells to be destroyed, 135, 159.

Hanun, king of the Ammonites, a princely embassage sent to him by David, to comfort him upon the death of his father, 29.

Harding (Thomas), bishop Jewel's Apology attacked by, 169.

Hare, Michael, a popish guest, sent to bishop Grindal by the council, 319.

Hawford, Dr, recommended as visitor for St John's College, Cambridge, 359.

Hawkins, Robert, a Londoner, examined before the ecclesiastical commissioners, 201.

Hearers, or sayers of mass, names of, to be presented to the ordinary, 144.

Henry VII. (not VI.), emperor, said by some authors to have been poisoned by a Dominican named Bernard Politian, in administering the eucharist, 60, *n.* 3.

Herbert, Henry, lord, fifth mourner at the funeral of the emperor Ferdinand, 32.

Herod Agrippa, death of, 8.

Hildebrand, pope Gregory VII., procured the deposing and death of the emperor Henry IV., 21.

Histriones, or common players, suggestion of bishop Grindal, that they should be prohibited for one whole year, 269.

"Hoc est corpus meum," expounded, 40.

Holydays, injunction respecting observance of, 128.

Holy-water-stocks to be destroyed, 135, 159.

Homilies, to be read in order on Wednesdays, 85; injunctions respecting, 127; two tomes of to be placed in parish churches and chapels, 157; article respecting the reading of, 161.

Horace, quotation from, 7.

Howard, sir George, master of the armoury, at the funeral of the emperor Ferdinand, 33.

Huns, why sent against the christians, 89.

Hunsdon, Henry, lord, eighth mourner at the funeral of the emperor Ferdinand, 32.

Huntington, Henry, earl of, third mourner at the funeral of the emperor Ferdinand, 32.

Hutton, Dr, dean of York, enjoined to examine the statutes relating to the church of York, 151.

Hysteron proteron, figure of, 197.

I.

Images, to be destroyed, 159.

Incestuous persons, names of, to be presented to the ordinary, 143.

Indulgences, how used by some, 29.

Infection, remedy against, suggested by bishop Grindal, 268.

Injunctions by Edmund, archbishop of York, as well to the clergy as to the laity, 122; to be read every half year, 129; of queen Elizabeth, to be read once every quarter of a year, 129; for the laity, 132; injunctions to the dean and chapter of York, 145; to the dean and chapter of the cathedral church of Bangor, 183.

Inquisition for forged or counterfeit letters of orders, to be made in every diocese, 186.

Inquisition, set on foot in London, into the order and conformity of the ministers there, 348.

Irenæus, quotation from, respecting the sacrament, 47; witnesseth, that in the sacrament remaineth bread and wine, by these words, "as the earthly bread, receiving the vocation of God, is now no common bread, but the eucharist, consisting of two things, the one earthly and the other heavenly," 66.

Ireland, James, a Londoner, examined before the ecclesiastical commissioners, 201.

Ismael, and his mother, mercifully relieved, 106.

Ithel, Dr, recommended as a visitor for St John's College, Cambridge, 359.

J.

Jehoiakim, rebuked by the prophet Jeremiah, 28.

Jeremiah, the prophet, king Jehoiakim rebuked by, 28.

Jerome, St, permitteth the books of Maccabees to be read; but because they be not of the canon of the scriptures, they be not sufficient of themselves to establish any doctrines in the church of God, 23; remark on the word Jehovah, 41; proveth, that the body of Christ must needs be contained in some place, and calleth it a foolish thing to seek for him in a narrow place, or in a corner, which is the light of all the world, 54.

Jewel, bishop, his Apology attacked by Harding and others, 169.

Jews, ever most stubborn against God, yet, in their distress calling upon the Lord, were relieved, 106.

Joannes Zapolia, 14.

Johnson, a leading man among the puritans, allowed to hold church preferment, 348.

Jonas, by prayer delivered out of the belly of hell, 106.

Josiah, king, commended by the prophet Jeremiah, 28.

Judas Machabæus, not to be followed in offering a sacrifice for the dead, 24.

Jurisdictions, injunction respecting those belonging to the prebendaries of the cathedral church of York, 150.

K.

Keepers of secret conventicles, preachings, or lectures, names of, to be presented to the ordinary, 144.

Kneeling to the sacrament, forbidden in old councils, 47.

Knolles, sir Francis, tenth mourner at the funeral of the emperor Ferdinand, 32.

L.

Laity, injunctions for, 132.

Lakin, Dr, prebendary of Wistow, enjoined to view the statutes relating to the church of York, 151.

Lamb, the, named the passover; and yet eaten in remembrance only of the passover, 41.

Langdale, one of the Romish disputants at the disputation held at Cambridge, 1549, 194.

Lasco, John à, first minister of the foreigners' church at Austin Friars, London, 254, n. 2.

Leach, a Scotchman, recommendation of him to sir Wm. Cecil by bishop Grindal, 275.

Legendaries, books of, to be abolished, 135, 159.

Leslie, John, bishop of Ross, queen Mary's agent in England, account of him, 315, n. 2.

Letters dimissory, article respecting, 186.

Letters, or hinderers of true religion, names of to be presented to the ordinary, 144.

Lever, Thomas, connived at in his non-conformity as to habits, 205; archbishop Grindal's commendation of his suit for Sherborn Hospital, 351.

Lewis the Young, slain in battle, 14.

Licences for preaching, bearing date before the 8th of February, 1575-6, to be void, 187.

Life, inconveniences attending the hope of a long life, 4; a vapour, a shadow, &c., 109.

Lily's Grammar, originally written for St Paul's school, article respecting the teaching of, 173.

Lœne, Peter de, minister of the Dutch church, London, letter of bishop Grindal to, 242.

Londoners: examination of certain Londoners before the ecclesiastical commissioners, 201.

Lord's supper, disputation at Cambridge respecting, 193; *see* also Sacrament, *infrà*.

Lowth, a puritan, archbishop Grindal's account of him, and hope that his pardon will be staid, 353.

Lucian, death of, 8.

Lumley, John lord, seventh mourner at the funeral of the emperor Ferdinand, 32.

Luther, Martin, one of the principal champions at the conference at Marpurg, 251, *n*.

Lynley, Mr, prebendary of Husthwaite, enjoined to examine the statutes of the church of York, 151.

M.

Maccabees, books of, permitted to be read, but because they are not of the canon of scripture, they are not, saith St Jerome, sufficient of themselves to establish any doctrine in the church of God, 23.

Madew, Dr, protestant disputant at the disputation held at Cambridge, 1539, 194.

Magistrates, reverence and honour to be paid to their authority, 28.

Mahomet, the deceiver of the world, 98.

Maintainers of sectaries, names of, to be presented to the ordinary, 144.

Malicious persons, names of, to be presented to the ordinary, 143.

Malta, besieged by the Turks, 287.

Manasses, mercy shewn to, on his repenting, 106.

Mandate of archbishop Grindal, respecting the publication of the articles agreed upon in the convocation of 1575, 190.

Manichees, espousers of the heresy of the Gnostics, 59, *n*. 5.

Mansion-houses of parsons, &c., to be kept in good repair, 131; not to be let to any lay person, 146.

Manuals, books of, to be abolished, 135, 159.

Marcion, an espouser of the heresy of the Gnostics, 59, *n*. 5; taught that the creatures of God, as flesh, bread, &c., were naught and uncleanly, 69.

Marcus, an espouser of the heresy of the Gnostics, 59, *n*. 5.

Marpurg, conference at, 251, *n*.

Marriage, article of convocation touching, 189.

Marshall, John, a Popish writer, 169. (See *Corrigenda*, p. xx.)

Martin, a German, servant to bishop Grindal, recommended by the bishop to Utenhovius, 286.

Martyr, Peter, commendation of him by bishop Grindal, 245.

Mass, names of hearers or sayers of, to be presented to the ordinary, 143; mass forbidden in scripture, 211.

Mass-books to be abolished, 135.

Mather, hired by the Spanish ambassador's secretary to murder lord Burleigh and the queen, 332, *n*. 1.

Matrimony, breach of, accounted a thing unworthy of reprehension in Grindal's days, 17; injunction respecting the solemnization of, 132; article respecting the solemnizing of, 161.

Maundy, meaning of the word, 51.

Maximilian, prince, crowned king of the Romans, 19.

May, Dr, one of king Edward's visitors at the disputation held at Cambridge, 1549, 194.

Melancthon, Philip, saith, "when the opinion of holiness, of merit, or necessity, is put unto things indifferent, then they darken the light of the gospel, and ought by all means to be taken away," 210; one of the principal champions at the conference at Marpurg, 251, *n*.

Melchizedek, allusion to, 41.

Memories, what so called, 136, *n*. 2.

Midwives, article to be inquired respecting, 174.

Milerus, an Irish priest, committed to the custody of bishop Grindal, 307.

Misrule, lords of, injunction respecting, 141; account of them, 175.

Month-minds, not to be observed, 136.

Morecroft, Richard, a Londoner, examined before the ecclesiastical commissioners, 201.

Mosheim, quotation from, p. 21.
Muniment, &c., of the church of York, not to be taken out of the treasury, &c., unless under certain conditions, 152.

N.

Nabal, death of, 8.
Nabuchodonosor, example of, 8; mercy shewn to him, on his turning to the Lord in his trouble, 106.
Nahash, father of Hanun, king of the Ammonites, 29.
Nevyl, archbishop, sumptuous feast given by, 328.
Newhaven (Havre de Grace), surrendered to the French, 260, n. 1.
Nicholas II., pope, confirmed the opinion of the changing of bread in the sacrament, and would have made an article of the faith, and placed it in the credo, 73.
Nicholls, John, a recanting Jesuit, letter of archbishop Grindal for him, 421.
Nicolas, Henry, of Holland, founder of the family of love, 360, n. 1.
Nixson, William, a Londoner, examined before the ecclesiastical commissioners, 201.
Nowel, dean, composes a prayer for the deliverance from the plague of 1563, 79; homily composed by, on occasion of the plague, 96; his catechism approved by the convocation of 1562, but not printed until 1570, injunction respecting, 142.

O.

Oath to be administered to churchwardens and sworn men, 177.
Œcolampadius, a champion at the conference at Marpurg, respecting the eucharist, 251, n.
Oil, article respecting the use of in the ministration of the sacrament of baptism, 160.
Origen, saith, they are not to be heard which shew Christ in houses, 54; saith, if ye follow, after the letter, that which is written, Unless ye shall eat the flesh of the son of man, there shall be no life in you; this letter killeth, 63; expounding the words, " This is my body," saith, the bread which Christ confesseth to be his body, is a nutritive word of our souls, 68; speaking of the drinking of Christ's blood, saith, We do not desire the blood of the flesh, but the blood of the word, 69; on Matt. xv. saith, in this bread, that thing which is material passeth through man's body; but that which is made by the word of God by means of faith doth profit; these things we have spoken of the mystical bread, 70.
Ornaments for churches, article to be inquired respecting, 181.
Osculatorium, what so called, 135, n. 11.
Osiander, Andrew, a German divine, account of him and his system, 252, n. 3.
Ovid, quotation from, n. 13.

P.

Paget, sir William, one of king Edward's visitors at the disputation held at Cambridge, 1549, n. 194.
Palmer, Mr, chancellor of the church of York, enjoined to view the statutes of the said church, 151.
Papists, doctrine of, commonly standeth upon false reports, 40; proceedings in the ecclesiastical commission respecting them, 350.
Parish clerk, injunction concerning the appointment of, and his duties, 142, 168.
Parishioners, to be exhorted to contribute to the relief of the poor, 128; to be exhorted to obedience towards their prince, and all in authority, and to charity and mutual love among themselves, 130.
Parker, archbishop, letters of Grindal to, 252, 267; death of, 356, n. 3.
Parker, one of the disputants at the third disputation held at Cambridge, 1549, 194.
Pascal, II., pope, encourages the unnatural rebellion of a son against his father, 21, n. 4.

Passover-lamb, in memory of the great benefit of God, when he destroyed the Egyptians, 42.

Patents, article to be inquired respecting those granted by the seal in the province of Canterbury, 179.

Paul IV., pope, would not admit the validity of the renunciation of Charles, or the election of his brother, because in neither case had the consent of the holy see been obtained, 20, n. 2.

Paxes, to be destroyed, 135, 159.

Pead, Eleanor, extract from the oath taken by her before being licensed to be a midwife, 174.

Pedlers, or others, injunction respecting, 138.

Penance, commutation of, article of convocation touching, 189; archbishop Grindal's direction for, 455.

Penny, Dr, suffered to enjoy a good prebend in St Paul's, though he had become a lay man and a physician, 348.

Perambulation of the parish, what psalms to be said at, 141.

Perne, one of the disputants at the disputation held at Cambridge, 1549, 194.

Phanons, to be destroyed, 135, 159.

Philip, Landgrave of Hesse, invites to a conference concerning the eucharist at Marpurg, Luther, Zuingle, and others, 251, n.

Pilkington, one of the disputants at the disputation held at Cambridge, 1549, 194.

Pius V., pope, bull of, deposing queen Elizabeth, remark on, 328.

Pixes, to be destroyed, 135, 159.

Plague, the, of 1563, occasional services for, 75, sqq.; first got in among the English army, at Newhaven, near Boulogne, 77; notification to be given respecting, to the curates of London, 78; dean Nowell requested to make a homily meet for the time, 79.

Pliny, quotation from, 7.

Politian, Bernard, said to have poisoned the emperor Henry VII., in administering the eucharist, 60, n. 3.

Pollard, one of the disputants at the third disputation held at Cambridge, 1549, 194.

Poor, parishioners to be exhorted to contribute to the relief of, 129; collections to be made for, at Midsummer, 140.

Portesse, meaning of the word, 9; portesses to be abolished, 135, 213.

Prayer for the dead, article respecting, 160.

Preachers of corrupt or popish doctrines, names of, to be presented to the ordinary, 144.

Preaching God's word, makes loyal subjects, 379.

Prebendaries, four to be annually appointed to survey the fabric of the church of York, 150; article to be inquired respecting their residence, 179; injunction respecting sermons to be preached by, in the cathedral church of Bangor, 183.

Precentor of the church of York, injunction to, respecting the choristers, 152.

Pricking of officers in the university of Cambridge, to whom reserved, 366.

Processionals, books of, to be destroyed, 135.

Proctor, to be appointed by those who have dignities or prebends within the cathedral church of York, 151.

Prophesyings, queen Elizabeth's displeasure with archbishop Grindal respecting, 372; orders for reformation of abuses about, 373; queen Elizabeth's letter sent to the bishops for the purpose of suppressing them, 467.

Prosperus, quotation from, 59.

Protestant succession, a matter of deep anxiety to the bishops of the reformed church, 19.

Pulpit, injunction respecting the erection of, in churches, &c., 132; form of, to be referred to the archdeacon or his official, 132; to be provided by the churchwardens, 132; injunction respecting, to the archdeacons, 155.

Purgatory, and praying for the dead, doctrine of, maintained principally by feigned apparitions, &c., contrary to the scriptures, 24; article respecting, 160.

32

Q.

Quarter sermons, injunction respecting, in the cathedral church of Bangor, 183.

Querele, meaning of the word, 289.

R.

Rabanus, Maurus, abbot of Fulda, and afterward archbishop of Mentz, says, because bread strengtheneth the body, therefore it is aptly called Christ's body; and likewise the wine, because it increaseth blood in the flesh, it doth resemble the blood of Christ, 65, 66.

Railers, names of, to be presented to the ordinary, 143.

Ratramnus, *see* Bertramus.

Receivers of vagabond popish priests, &c., names of, to be presented to the ordinary, 144.

Receivers in cathedral churches, article to be inquired respecting, 180.

"Receiving unworthily," place of St Paul expounded, 56.

Recusants, popish, employ themselves in writing very dangerous and seditious books against queen Elizabeth and her government, 169.

Recusants, letter of archbishop Grindal to his officers respecting, 417, 423; articles of inquiry for, 418, 424; letter for certifying the dwellings of, 427.

Recusants, at Oxford, letter of archbishop Grindal respecting, 362.

Register book, to be kept in a coffer, with two locks and keys, and provided by the churchwardens, 134.

Registers of weddings, &c., injunction respecting, 128.

Reuben, his saying respecting his brother Joseph, 41.

Ribalds, names of, to be presented to the ordinary, 143.

Ridley, Nicholas, one of K. Edward's visitors at the disputation held at Cambridge, 1549, 194; his judgment of popish apparel, 211, *n*. 1.

Robertson's Charles the Fifth, quotations from, 15.

Rogers, sir Edward, knight, ninth mourner at the funeral of the emperor Ferdinand, 32.

Rood-loft, what it was, 154,

Rood-lofts to be taken down and altered, 134; injunction respecting, 154; order of the ecclesiastical commissioners for the removal, 154, *n*. 2.

Rookby, Dr, precentor of the church of York, enjoined to review the statutes of the said church, 151.

Rothman, Bernard, an ecclesiastic of Münster, introduces the reformation into that city, but afterwards is infected with the enthusiasm of the Anabaptists, 256.

Rouen, taken and sacked by the duke of Guise, 253, *n*.

Rush-bearings, injunction respecting, 142.

S.

Sackville, sir Richard, twelfth mourner at the funeral of the emperor Ferdinand, 33.

Sacrament, how defined by St Augustine, 43; kneeling to, forbidden in old councils, 47; carried home in napkins, *ibid.*; sent to sick persons by a child, 48; pope Honorius the third, first author of worshipping, 48; apostles and old doctors make no miracle nor marvel at, 49; not the real body of Christ, and why, 55, 67.

Sacring-bells, to be destroyed, 135, 159.

St John's College, Cambridge, bishop Grindal, letter to on behalf of, 358.

St Paul's cathedral, set on fire by lightning, 246, *n*.; queen Elizabeth much affected at the misfortune, and resolves to have the damage speedily repaired, *ibid.*

Sales, article to be inquired respecting those confirmed by the chapter-seal of the cathedral church of Canterbury, 179.

Salomon, interpretation of the name, 17.

Sampson, Thomas, connived at in his nonconformity as to habits, 205; as dean of Christ Church, Oxford, sends to bishop Grindal a copy of certain injunctions delivered him by the lord keeper, 282.

Saracens, why sent against the christians, 98.

Saturninus, an espouser of the heresy of the Gnostics, 59, *n.* 5.
Saunders, bishop Jewel's Apology attacked by, 169.
Savoy Hospital, Strand, account of it, 302, *n.* 1; letter of archbishop Grindal respecting, 349.
Scholars of grammar-school of Bangor, injunction respecting, 184.
Schoolmaster injunction respecting, 142; of grammar-school of Bangor, injunction respecting, 184.
Scolders, names of, to be presented to the ordinary, 143.
Scot, Mr, recommended by bishop Grindal to be one of the prebendaries of Carlisle, 285.
Scotus, Johannes, condemned for a heretic, 200 years after his death, 74.
Scripture, not to be taken always as the letter soundeth, 40.
Sedgwick, one of the Romish disputants at the disputation held at Cambridge, 1549, 194.
Serapion, an aged christian, sacrament sent to him, 48.
Sermons, injunction respecting, 128; article respecting quarterly and monthly, 160.
Servants, injunctions to the clergy respecting their instruction, 124; article respecting, 161.
Sherborn Hospital, near Durham, founded by Pudsey, bishop of Durham, for sixty-five poor lepers, 352.
Sheriffs, archbishop Grindal's remark respecting, 345.
Shrift, meaning of the word, 140, *n.* 2; injunction respecting, 140.
Simon Magus, founder of the Gnostics or Docetæ, 59, *n.* 5.
Simony, article to be inquired of in cathedral churches, 181.
Slanderers of their neighbours, names of to be presented to the ordinary, 143.
Smith, John, a Londoner, examined before the ecclesiastical commissioners, 201.
Smith, sir Thomas, one of king Edward's visitors at the disputation held at Cambridge, 1549, 194.
Somerset, protector, pulls down many churches and religious fabrics for the building of Somerset House, 29.

Somerset House, many churches, &c. pulled down for the building of it, 29.
Southworth, sir John, a Lancashire knight, account of him, 305.
Sowers of discord, names of to be presented to the ordinary, 143.
Spattle, article respecting the use of in the ministration of the sacrament of baptism, 160.
Spencer, Dr, parson of Hadley, commended by bishop Grindal to sir W. Cecil, 292.
Stanley, sir Rowland, desiring to be sheriff of Cheshire, archbishop Grindal writes a letter to lord Burleigh respecting his unfitness, 345.
Stapleton, bishop Jewel's Apology attacked by, 169.
Statutes of the church of York, injunction respecting, 150.
Steeples, to be diligently and well repaired with lead, &c. 134.
Stewards, article to be inquired respecting, in cathedral churches, 180.
Stoles to be abolished, 135, 159.
Strange, Henry lord, fourth mourner at the funeral of the emperor Ferdinand, 32.
Strangers, articles of inquiry for, 296; bishop Grindal's remembrance concerning, 297; queen's proclamation against, *ibid.*
Strype, John, quotation from, 29, *n.* 2.
Stubbs, John, writes a violent book, called the Discovery of a Gaping Gulph, against the proposed marriage of queen Elizabeth to the duke of Anjou, 408, *n.*
Suetonius, quotation from, 17.
Summer lords or ladies, injunction respecting, 141.
Sumners, summoners, article to be inquired respecting paying for their offices, 176.
Surplice, directions respecting, 124, 155.
Survey to be made of lands and revenues of the church of York, 149.
Sussex, Thomas earl of, second mourner at the funeral of the emperor Ferdinand, 32.
Swearers, names of, to be presented to the ordinary, 143.

T.

Table of affinity, to be affixed in the parish church, 126.

Table, for the holy communion, to be provided by the churchwardens, 133.

Table for sermons, to be had in the cathedral of York, to be provided by the dean and chapter of York, 147.

Tables, game of, injunction respecting, 138.

Tapers, article respecting the use of, in the ministration of the sacrament of baptism, 160.

Ten commandments, table of to be provided by the churchwardens, 133; article respecting, within the province of Canterbury, 157, 161.

Tertullian saith, the emperor is greater than all men, and yet less than God alone, 12; writeth, that women were suffered to take the sacrament home, and to lap it up in their chests, 47, 8; how he understood the saying of Christ, "This is my body," 65; writing against Marcion, who taught that the creatures of God, as flesh, bread, &c. were naught and uncleanly, saith, God hath not cast away his creature, but by it he hath represented his body, 69; saith, Jesus hath another body than bread; for bread was not given for us, but the very true body of Christ was given upon the cross; which body was exhibited in the supper under the figure of bread, 71; saith, Christ took bread and made it his body, saying, "This is my body," &c. 198.

Tetragrammaton, what so called, 41.

Thanksgiving for the abatement of the plague, 111; for the ceasing of, 116.

Theodoret avoweth that there is no turning or altering of the bread in the sacrament, 71.

Theodosius, emperor, commended by St Ambrose, 11.

Thickpenny, David, curate of Brighthelmstone, suspended for irregularities, 359; his case referred to archbishop Grindal, 359, *n.* 3; the archbishop's resolution concerning him, *ibid.*

"This is my body," fruitful dialogue on these words of Christ, 39; sense of expounded, 40.

Throckmorton, sir Nicholas, thirteenth mourner at the funeral of the emperor Ferdinand, 33; queen's ambassador in France, put under restraint, 260, *n.* 2.

Thuanus, quotations from, 14, 16, 19, 21, 23.

Thurland, master of the Savoy hospital, abuses his trust, 302, *n.*; archbishop Grindal's letter to lord Burleigh respecting him, 349.

Transubstantiation, reasoning against, 59; a new invention, 72.

Treasurers, article to be inquired respecting in cathedral churches, 180.

Trent, council of, evades the question respecting the administration of the sacrament in both kinds, by referring it entirely to the decision of the pope, 22, *n.* 2.

Trentals, what they were, 30.

Tunicles, to be abolished, 135, 159.

Turks, why sent against the christians, 98.

U.

Unmarried woman, with child out of lawful matrimony, not to be churched, except on Sunday or some holy-day, except she do penance, &c. 127.

Uncharitable persons, names of to be presented to the ordinary, 143.

Usher of grammar-school at Bangor, injunction respecting, 184.

Usurers, injunction respecting, 143.

Utenhov, John, minister of the Dutch church, London, letter of bishop Grindal to, 243.

Uzziah, king, case of alluded to, 271.

V.

Valentinian, emperor, commended by St Ambrose, 11.

Valentinus, espouser of the heresy of the Gnostics, 59, *n.* 5.

Valerius Maximus, quotation from, 7.

Vandals, why sent against the christians, 98.

Vavasor, one of the disputants at the third disputation held at Cambridge, 1549, 194; account of him, and of his committal to prison at Hull, 351.

Velsius, Justus, a sectary from the Hague, account of him, 254; bishop Grindal's animadversions on his "Christiani Hominis Norma," 436; account of him, 438, n. 1.

Vergers, injunction to those of the cathedral church of York, 152.

Vestments, article respecting, within the province of Canterbury, 158.

Vicars choral, and other inferior ministers to be daily present in the cathedral of York, and to give diligent care to the hearing of the divinity lecture, and to be examined by the chancellor, 147.

Vice, the, of the old moralities, a buffoon or fool fantastically dressed, 211, n. 2.

Victor III., bishop of Rome, poisoned, 60.

Vidame, Monsieur, a great nobleman of France, Strype's description of him, 305.

Vienna, defended by the emperor Ferdinand against the Turk, 15.

W.

Wake, the, or feast of dedication, in honour of the patron saint, why called rush-bearing, 142.

Walker, Thomas, parson of Shadwell, Essex, his suit for non-residence recommended to archbishop Parker by bishop Grindal, 294.

Watson, late bishop of Lincoln, transferred by order of council from Grindal's house to the care of Dr Cox, bishop of Ely, 281.

Watts, Dr, recommended as visitor for St John's College, Cambridge, 359.

Watts, master, chaplain to bishop Grindal, one of the ecclesiastical commissioners, 201.

Webster, Mr, contest between him, Mr Woodroff, and archbishop Grindal, respecting a prebend in York cathedral, 329, n.; the archbishop's opinion of his case, 329.

Wendelin, a printer at Strasburgh, Grindal's opinion of him, 221.

Wendy, Dr, one of K. Edward's visitors at the disputation held at Cambridge, 1549, 194.

Westcote, Sebastian, letter of bishop Grindal to lord Robert Dudley, respecting him, 262.

White, William, a Londoner, examined before the ecclesiastical commissioners, 201.

Whitgift, Dr, recommended as visitor for St John's College, Cambridge, 359; letter to him from archbishop Grindal, respecting the debate between Becon and Babington, for the chancellorship of the diocese of Litchfield and Coventry, 370.

Whittingham, dean of Durham, an opposer of the communion book in the days of queen Mary, and writer of a preface to the book of Goodman, against the lawfulness of women's government, 327, n. 2.

Wiburn, Perceval, a leading man among the puritans, allowed to hold church preferment, 348.

Wicked, the, receive not the body of Christ, 55.

Wickham, Mr, recommended by archbishop Grindal to be master of the Savoy, 349.

Winchester, William, marquess of, chief mourner at the funeral of the emperor Ferdinand, 32.

Wing, Gotfred, bishop Grindal's commendation of him, 250.

Wolton, John, a preacher, dispensation for him requested by bishop Grindal, 299.

Wood, a Scotchman, declared by bishop Grindal to be a factious fellow, 291.

Woodroff, Mr, archbishop Grindal's opinion of his presentation to a prebend of York cathedral, 330.

Y.

Year's minds, what they were, 136.

Young, one of the Romish disputants at the disputation held at Cambridge, 1549, 194.

Z.

Zanchy, Hierom, letter of Grindal to, 276, sqq.; account of him, 277, n. 2; fragment of an epistle to him, 333, sqq.

Zuingle, opposed by Melancthon at the conference at Marpurg, respecting the eucharist, 251, n.

INDEX

OF

TEXTS OF SCRIPTURE

CITED, ILLUSTRATED, OR EXPLAINED.

OLD TESTAMENT.

	PAGE		PAGE
Gen. ii. 24	41	2 Chron. xx. 9	104
v. 27	10	xxiv.	390
xii.	96	xxvi.	271
xvii. 13	41	xxviii.	100
xxi.	106	xxxiii.	106
xxxiii. 20	41, 42	xxxiv.	83
xxxvii. 27	41	Neh. ix.	106
l.	28	Job v.	96
Exod. xvii. 15	41	v. 17	101
xx. 10	215	v. 18	86
Levit. xiii.	271	vii.	109
xxvi.	83, 97, 100, 478	viii. 9	7
xxvi.	40, 100	xiii.	109
Num. xi.	478	xxvii. 6	117
xiv.	479	xxxiii. 19	117
xvi. 12	479	xxxiv.	120
xxi. 14	13	xxxvi.	96
Deut. iv.	107	xxxvi. 11	101
iv. 30, 31	102	xl. 17	117
vii.	205	xlvii. 6, 7	117
viii.	100	Psal. i.	93
xvii.	207	ii.	93, 389
xxviii.	83, 97, 478	iii.	93
xxx. 1, sqq.	102	iv.	93, 105
xxxii.	110	v.	93
Josh. xxii.	27	vi. 1	86
1 Sam. iv. v. vi. vii.	479	vi.	93
vi. 19	480	vii.	96
x.	384	xii.	96
xix.	384	xiii.	93
xxv. 38	13	xiii. 6	112
xxxi.	7	xv.	93
2 Sam. x. 2	29	xviii.	105
xxii.	105	xxii. 4	86
xxiv.	377, 479	xxv.	93
xxiv. 15	105	xxv. 7	86
1 Kings i. 48	18	xxvi.	93
ii. 2	7	xxx.	93, 379
v	378	xxx. 1, 2	112
viii. 27	49	xxx. 5	112
viii. 44	103	xxx. 11	113
xii.	206	xxxi.	105
2 Kings ii.	384	xxxii.	93
xx.	377	xxxiii.	198
xxiv.	83	xxxiv.	105
2 Chron. vi.	103	xlvi.	93
xix.	378	l. 15	103, 116
xx. 3	93	li.	93

	PAGE		PAGE
Psal. li. 3	86	Psal. cxlv.	107, 120
lvii. 10	117	cxlv. 1, 2, 21	117
lxii. 1	116	cxlv. 19	108
lxvii.	93	cxlvi.	120
lxviii.	112	cxlvii.	93, 120
lxxi. 22	117	cxlvii. 1	111
lxxii. 18, 19	117	cxlviii	120
lxxvi.	389	Prov. i.	100
lxxvi. 15	112, 117	iii. 11	101
lxxvii.	105	xxix.	100
lxxix.	93	Eccles. ii.	107
lxxix. 9	87	ii. 16	6
lxxxi. 7	105	Isai. i.	83
lxxxiv.	93	ii.	206
lxxxv. 1	116	iii.	206
lxxxv. 2, 3	112	iv.	206
lxxxv. 3	116	v.	98
lxxxvi.	105	xxvi.	96, 101
lxxxvi. 5	103	xxx.	100
lxxxvi. 13	112	xlix. 33	376
xc. 13, 14, 15	113	lviii.	107, 109
xc. 16, 17	113	lxiv. 6	86
xci.	93	lxv. 1	245
xci. 4	17	lxvi. 1	49
xci. 6, 10, sqq.	103	Jerem. ii.	100
xcii. 1, 2	111	v.	100
xcii. 4	112	xiv.	105
xciv. 17	116	xiv. 7	92
xciv. 18, 19	116	xvi.	105
xcv.	120	xviii.	83
xcv. 6	85	xx. 5	98
xcv. 7	85	xxii.	28
xcvi.	120	xxii. 18, 19	28
xcviii. 1	117	xxix.	107
c.	120	xxix. 12, sqq.	104
cii.	93	xxx.	96
ciii.	93, 112, 120, 141, 168	xxxi. 18	104
ciii. 9—14	112	Ezek. xviii. 21, sqq.	104
civ.	141, 168	xix	83
cv. 1	111	xxiv.	100
cvi. 1	117	xiii. 18	386
cvii.	93, 120	xxxiii.	377
cvii. 6, 13, 19, 43	106	Dan. iv.	106, 109
cviii. 4	117	iv. 39	8
cxiv. 18	103	ix. 19	86
cxvi.	105, 120	Hosea vi. 1	85, 86
cxvi. 5	112	vi. 6	101
cxviii.	100, 105, 120	Joel ii	83
cxix.	96, 381	ii. 12	105
cxix. 105	23	Jonah ii.	83
cxxiii.	93	ii. 1, sqq.	106
cxxviii. 6	18	ii. 2	86
cxxx.	93	iii.	83
cxxxii. 14	9	iii. 5	93
cxxxviii.	105, 212	iii. 8, 9	86
cxlii.	105	Zephaniah iii	100
cxliii.	93	Haggai ii	100
cxliv.	105		

APOCRYPHA.

	PAGE		PAGE
2 Esdras ix.	83	Ecclus. iii. 26	271
Tob. iii.	96, 101	xlviii.	106
Judith viii.	100	2 Mac. xii.	23
Wisd. vi.	18	xiv.	24
xvi.	110		

NEW TESTAMENT.

Reference	PAGE
Matt. iii.	83
v. 6	45
vi.	83
vii.	83
ix.	378
xi. 28	105
xv. 17	45
xviii.	215
xx.	30
xxiv.	83
xxiv. 2.	98
xxiv. 27	4
xxiv. 44	3, 65
xxv.	83, 352
xxvi.	196
xxvi. 26	39, 40
xxviii.	378
xxviii. 20	208
Mark xiii. 2	98
Luke i. 74, 75	107
xii. 10	67
xii. 18	8
xii. 48	18
xiii.	83
xv.	106
xvi. 15	212
xix. 7	212
xxi. 35	4, 7
xxiii.	30
John vi. 35	41, 46
vi. 63	44
x. 30	41
xiv. 1	49
xiv. 28	41
xvi. 7	49
xvi. 16	54
xviii.	110
Acts ii.	83, 385
iii. 19	85
iii. 21	49
iv. 32	41
v. 5, 10	8
vii. 48	49
vii. 56	49
x.	385
xii. 23	8
xiv.	379
Rom. ii.	83, 390
v. 3, sqq.	109
vi.	83
vi. 3	41
viii. 38, 39	102
x. 12	106
x. 20	245
x. 21	245
xii.	83
Rom. xiii.	83
xiv.	110
xvi. 17	214
1 Cor. i.	381
v. 5	263
x. 4	41
x. 17	41
xi.	479
xi. 25	41
xi. 32	102, 107
xiv.	385
xvi. 9	304
2 Cor. i.	109
i. 3	105
iv.	109
v.	379, 389
v. 10	4
vi. 14, 15	213
x.	212, 387
xiii.	387
Gal. iii. 27	41
v.	83
Eph. iv	83, 381
v.	83
Phil. i. 18	330
i. 23	49
Col. iii.	378
1 Thes. iv. 16	4
2 Thes. iii. 18	245
1 Tim. ii.	83
iv.	381
2 Tim. iii.	381
iv.	378
Titus i.	30
i. 5	379
i. 9	379
Heb. vii. 3	41
ix. 27	6
x.	387, 390
xii. 5	102
xiii. 3	435
James i	109
i. 17	19
iv.	109
iv. 14	7
v. 4	302
1 Pet. i. 19	5
ii. 2	379
iv. 4	17
iv. 5	17
iv. 7	6
2 Pet. iii.	96
Rev. ii.	83
iii. 19	102
xiv. 13	29

THE

SECOND ANNUAL REPORT

[FOR THE YEAR 1842]

OF

The Parker Society,

For the Publication of the Works of the Fathers and Early
Writers of the Reformed English Church.

PROCEEDINGS

AT THE SECOND ANNUAL MEETING OF

The Parker Society,

HELD AT

THE FREEMASONS' TAVERN,

GREAT QUEEN STREET, LINCOLN'S INN FIELDS, LONDON,
ON TUESDAY, THE 30th OF MAY, 1843.

THE RIGHT HONOURABLE LORD ASHLEY, M.P.,
President,

IN THE CHAIR.

COLLECTS suitable to the occasion were read by the Rev. M. M. PRESTON, Vicar of Cheshunt.

The Honorary LIBRARIAN read the Report of the Council; and it was

RESOLVED,

That the Report which has been read be received and adopted, and printed for the use of the Members, and that the thanks of the Society be given to the Council and Honorary Officers for their services during the past year.

The SECRETARY for general business then read the general statement of the Receipts and Expenditure for the past year to the present time, as examined and approved by the Auditors, when

IT WAS RESOLVED,

That the Statement be received, and when finally closed, and reported upon by the Auditors, be printed and sent to the Members, and that the thanks of the Society be given to the Auditors for their services.

Thanks were voted to the Local Correspondents of the Society, and other persons who had co-operated with the Council in promoting its objects.

The CHAIRMAN then having directed the attention of the Meeting to the Law respecting the election of a President, Treasurer, Honorary Librarian, and Council for the year ensuing, the SECRETARY read the List of persons proposed for those offices, and

The Right Honourable LORD ASHLEY, M.P., was elected *President*.
Sir WALTER R. FARQUHAR, Bart., was elected *Treasurer*.
GEORGE STOKES, Esq., was elected *Honorary Librarian*.

Rev. R. G. BAKER.—Rev. C. BENSON, Master of the Temple.—Rev. E. BICKERSTETH.—JOHN BRIDGES, Esq.—JOHN BRUCE, Esq.—Rev. GUY BRYAN.—Rev. RICHARD BURGESS.—Hon. WILLIAM COWPER.—Rev. W. H. COX, Vice Principal of St Mary Hall, in the University of Oxford.—Rev. J. W. CUNNINGHAM.—Rev. THOMAS DALE, Canon of St Paul's.—Rev. Dr DEALTRY, Chancellor of Winchester.—Rev. JOHN HARDING.—Rev. EDWARD HOARE.—Rev. T. H. HORNE, Canon of St Paul's.—JOSEPH HOARE, Esq.—Hon. ARTHUR KINNAIRD.—Rev. Dr MORTIMER, Head Master of the City of London School.—Hon. and Rev. B. W. NOEL.—HENRY POWNALL, Esq.—Rev. JOSIAH PRATT, Jun.—Rev. M. M. PRESTON.—Rev. DANIEL WILSON, and the Rev. JAMES SCHOLEFIELD, Regius Professor of Greek in the University of Cambridge,—were elected as the *Council*, with power to fill up all vacancies during the year; and

The Rev. R. HANKINSON and FRANCIS LOWE, Esq., were elected *Auditors* for the year ensuing.

It was then

RESOLVED,

That the sincere thanks of the Society and of this Meeting are due to Lord ASHLEY for his very important services to the Society as its President, and for his kindly presiding at this Meeting, but especially for the deep interest he has always shewn for the Parker Society, and his anxiety to promote its operations.

Lord ASHLEY in acknowledging the vote of thanks expressed his deep conviction of the great value of the Parker Society, his cordial approval of its proceedings, and his earnest desire to support an institution which he considered to be among those of the greatest importance at the present day.

THE

SECOND ANNUAL REPORT

OF

The Parker Society,

INSTITUTED A.D. 1840,

FOR THE PUBLICATION OF

THE WORKS OF THE FATHERS AND EARLY WRITERS OF THE REFORMED ENGLISH CHURCH.

PRESENTED TO THE GENERAL MEETING, MAY THE 30TH, 1843.

" He (*Archbishop Parker*) was a great collector of ancient and modern writings, and took especial care of the safe preservation of them for all succeeding times; as foreseeing undoubtedly what use might be made of them by posterity : that, by having recourse to such originals and precedents, the true knowledge of things might the better appear."
"As he was a great patron and promoter of good learning, so he took care of giving encouragement to printing—a great instrument of the increase thereof."
Strype's Life of Archbishop Parker.

THE Council of the PARKER SOCIETY present the Second Annual Report, detailing their proceedings since the last General Meeting on the 31st of May, 1842.

The Members are referred to the Cash Account for particulars of the Receipt and Expenditure: it will be seen that the receipts for the present year are largely increased by the amount received for the reprints of the publications of 1841. This is stated separately; but the expenses of the office, and other charges arising out of the reprints, could not be apportioned, and the whole of the pecuniary transactions for the past year are, therefore, exhibited in one account.

The number of Subscribers for 1842 so far exceeded 6,000, that the Council were obliged to provide 7,000 copies of the books to be printed with the subscription of that year; and it appearing in November last, when the list had been corrected and revised, that there would be a few surplus copies, the subscription for them was fixed at £1 12s., the same as the reprint, in justice to those who had previously become members. The applications for these copies exceed the number thus to be disposed of; but a list of the applicants is kept, and if any copies can be obtained, they will be apprised when the delivery of the books for the year is finally completed.

The Council have next to report respecting the reprint of the volumes for 1841, which was undertaken at the request of a large number of applicants who had not been aware of the formation of the Society. When these reprints were begun, it was found impossible correctly to ascertain all the names that had been forwarded, so that the Council deemed it requisite to provide a sufficiency of copies to supply the whole of the new Members. They have the pleasure to state that this course has been satisfactory to the Subscribers, and advantageous to the Institution; more than 2,200 sets have been already paid for. The final result cannot be correctly ascertained at present; the few remaining copies will be issued only to Members.

Much additional trouble and responsibility have been occasioned by these reprints, with some unavoidable delay in the proceedings of the year, and the Council do not hesitate to express their opinion that no reprint should be undertaken in future.

The books printed for 1842 are—the Examinations and Writings of Archdeacon Philpot; the Zurich Letters; Christian Prayers and Holy Meditations, collected by Henry Bull; Remains of Archbishop Grindal; and the early Writings of Rev. Thomas Becon, Prebendary of Canterbury, and Chaplain to Archbishop Cranmer. The quantity of letter-press thus given is fully equal to 2,700 pages of demy octavo, being a considerable increase on the quantity returned for the subscription in the first year; and as the Works of Becon are printed in a larger form, the whole quantity is quite equal to six volumes of the usual size. The volumes of Becon and Grindal are finished at the press, and will be ready for delivery some time in June.

The arrangement adopted for Becon's Works was concluded upon by the Council after careful consideration at several successive meetings: by pursuing the same plan with a few other authors, the proceedings of the Society will be expedited some years, and a saving of several thousand pounds will be effected, while the books are more conformed to their original size.

Many of the Subscribers have applied for information as to what are the works which the Parker Society intend to print. The List appended to this report may be considered as approximating to what it is hoped may be the result.

It will be observed that no translations of Foreign Reformers, excepting the Decades of Bullinger, are included in this list. Such works are within the plan of the Parker Society, as stated in its laws; and many of its Members have urged that the printing of them should be commenced, with an additional subscription if necessary. But the Council felt that the English Reformers require primary and almost exclusive attention for many years, and that to undertake the management of an additional contribution would lead to serious difficulties: they therefore recommended those who felt interested in the immediate progress of this important design, to institute separate proceedings; and the Council understand that two efforts for the purpose will be made—one for the Translation of the Writings of Calvin, which are sufficient to require the subscriptions of some years; and a second for select portions of the

Works of the other Foreign Reformers. These arrangements will bring before the public a valuable class of writings, closely connected with our own Reformers, more speedily and effectually than could otherwise be effected, and will leave the Council of the Parker Society at liberty to consider whether such authors as Bishop Bilson, Bishop Babington, Hooker, Perkins, Rogers, and some others who wrote and printed a great part of their works in the reign of Queen Elizabeth, may not in future years be advantageously added to the present list.

It is requisite to give this information to the members; but it is desirable, at the same time, to refer to a notice circulated some months ago, that the operations of the Parker Society are not to be identified, but are entirely unconnected, with the publications either of individuals or of any other publishing society.

The Council have been unremitting in their endeavours to place a number of volumes in the hands of competent editors, but regret that previous engagements, and the pressure of other duties, prevent many whose aid they expected, from engaging in this undertaking. Under the uncertainties which always must attend editorial arrangements, they think it best only to announce that the volumes most advanced, and which they expect to deliver for the subscription of 1843, are—

The Liturgies and other Documents of the Reign of Edward VI.—The Catechism of Thomas Becon.—Fulke's Defence of the Translations of the Scriptures.—The Early Works of Bishop Hooper.

Also part of the Works of Archbishop Cranmer are to be included in the books for 1843.

The Council hope to deliver the volumes for 1843 earlier than in the two preceding years, and have made arrangements accordingly; but the many circumstances which unavoidably delay books while at press, render it necessary to withhold any pledge, beyond an assurance that no efforts will be wanting to expedite the work. What has been already effected has been done with less delay than in any other recent undertaking of similar labour.

Some of the books most advanced in editorial preparation are, the Sermons and other Writings of Bishop Latimer, and another volume of Letters from the Archives of Zurich. Amongst those which the Council are most anxious to forward are the Writings of Archbishop Whitgift and Bishop Jewell: arrangements to expedite these have been made; but in a work so extensive, so varied, and involving so many and such peculiar difficulties, it is impossible to hasten particular books, or to decide positively upon the course of publication.

The number of subscriptions paid for 1843 appears to be rather more than last year. By seeking greater publicity the Subscription List might have been increased; but the number of SEVEN THOUSAND is so far beyond the demand which any one anticipated for these books, that it must be deemed a very gratifying result. With much pleasure the Council state that the subscription for the present year requires 7,500 copies of the publications. If any books are at liberty by the death or discontinuance of members not yet reported to the Office, these sets will be allotted to applicants according to their order; but for any so allotted after 1st July, and for any of the old members who do not pay their subscriptions before that time, an addition or fine of five shillings will be required.

To prevent disappointment, it is desirable to state that these surplus copies cannot be numerous; they only arise from the uncertainties unavoidable among so many names, and the necessity for printing a number requisite to secure the due supply of all who appear to be subscribers.

No change in the officers of the Society has been found necessary, and exertions have been made to bring the business details more and more into systematic order. Most of the difficulties arising from a new and wholly untried plan of such magnitude have been overcome: another year will allow the adoption of further improvements, especially as the office will be relieved from any more reprints.

The Council thank the Members for the kindness with which they have assisted in correcting errors and mistakes as to names and residences; they trust these will not be found numerous, but they cannot be wholly avoided in an establishment having what may be termed seven thousand customers, and, in one instance, more than seventy of the same surname. All who subscribe should take care that their names and full addresses be accurately sent in the first instance; and changes in their residences, or of the places to which their books are to be forwarded, should be regularly communicated to the office. Almost every case of inaccuracy has arisen from want of precision in stating the name, and directing the mode of the delivery of the books.

The Council again thank the many kind friends who have assisted in delivering the books and collecting the subscriptions in their respective neighbourhoods, with much trouble to themselves. They hope for the continuance of their valuable aid, and also in procuring additional support from year to year, to supply the places of those whose names are removed by death or the changing circumstances of life. Here the great value of having every volume complete in itself is felt; for, in any year, any person can join the Society without being obliged to purchase the preceding volumes; while the large number issued renders it certain that if the earlier volumes are desired, they may be obtained with a little research. The subscriber of each single pound is assured of a very ample return for his outlay, even if he does not proceed farther; while a complete set, for the cost of fifteen or sixteen pounds in as many years, will place the regular subscriber in possession of books which he could not now procure for two hundred pounds. And these volumes, it must ever be distinctly remembered, shew the doctrines and principles held and taught by Cranmer, Ridley, Parker, Whitgift, with their learned and venerable coadjutors, rendering them accessible to every member of the Church of England. The support given to this plan proves that it is regarded as a NATIONAL effort, calculated largely to benefit this PROTESTANT land.

The Parker Society, and other kindred efforts, shew that the advantages of the noble art of PRINTING are not yet fully developed;

and the words of the venerable and indefatigable Foxe may be applied: "By reason whereof, as printing of books ministered matter of reading, so reading brought learning, learning shewed light, by the brightness whereof blind ignorance is suppressed, error detected, and God's glory with truth of his word advanced."

May this simple setting forth of the doctrines and principles of the Fathers and early Writers of the Reformed English Church be largely beneficial to that Church in the present day! Let all unite in the aspiration of the Martyrologist—"The God of peace, who hath power both of land and sea, reach forth his merciful hand to help them that sink, to keep up them that stand, to still those waves and surging seas of discord and contention amongst us; that we, professing one Christ, may, in one unity of doctrine, gather ourselves into one ark of the true Church together, where we continuing stedfast in faith, may at the last be conducted to the joyful port of our desired landing-place by his heavenly grace. To whom, both in heaven and earth, be all power and glory, with his Father and the Holy Spirit, for ever. AMEN."

A LIST OF THE WORKS PUBLISHED, AND PROPOSED TO BE PUBLISHED, BY THE PARKER SOCIETY.

IN ROYAL OCTAVO.—BECON.—CRANMER.—JEWELL.—WHITGIFT.—TINDAL, FRITH, & BARNS.—BULLINGER'S DECADES.—ALLEY.—WHITTAKER.

IN DEMY OCTAVO.—RIDLEY.—PILKINGTON.—PHILPOT.—FULKE.—NOWELL.—COVERDALE.—PARKER.—BALE.—RAINOLDS.—SANDYS.—HUTCHINSON.—GRINDAL.—HOOPER.—LATIMER.—BRADFORD.—FOXE.—TAVERNER.—And some others.—ROYAL AUTHORS.—DOCUMENTS OF THE REIGN OF EDWARD VI.—DOCUMENTS RELATIVE TO THE REIGN OF QUEEN MARY.—DOCUMENTS OF THE REIGN OF QUEEN ELIZABETH.—ZURICH LETTERS (two series).—LETTERS AND DOCUMENTS FROM ARCHBISHOP PARKER'S MSS. IN C.C.C.C.—OCCASIONAL SERVICES OF QUEEN ELIZABETH'S REIGN.—THE HOMILIES.—SOME VOLUMES OF SERMONS PREACHED BEFORE KING EDWARD VI. AND QUEEN ELIZABETH, AT PAUL'S CROSS, IN THE UNIVERSITIES, AND ON VARIOUS OCCASIONS.—SEVERAL VOLUMES OF TRACTS AND SMALL PIECES.—VARIOUS LETTERS AND DOCUMENTS.—THE REFORMATIO LEGUM ECCLESIASTICARUM.—QUEEN ELIZABETH'S PRAYER BOOK.—DEVOTIONAL POETRY OF THE SIXTEENTH CENTURY.—CHRISTIAN MEDITATIONS AND PRAYERS, AND SOME OTHER DEVOTIONAL MANUALS.

It is calculated that the works above stated may be included in about 18 or 20 volumes royal octavo, and 50 volumes demy, and the whole may be completed in sixteen years from the commencement. A few pieces of peculiar interest may probably be printed as fac-similes, and these will be the size of the originals. It is not possible to state the order in which the volumes will appear, but each will be complete in itself, and the whole series (fully equal to a hundred volumes demy octavo), when completed, will have cost the original subscribers only about sixteen pounds, paid in as many years, and in proportion for parts of the series.

LAWS OF THE PARKER SOCIETY.

I.—That the Society shall be called THE PARKER SOCIETY, and that its objects shall be—first, the reprinting, without abridgment, alteration, or omission, of the best Works of the Fathers and early Writers of the Reformed English Church, published in the period between the accession of King Edward VI. and the death of Queen Elizabeth; secondly, the printing of such remains of other Writers of the Sixteenth Century as may appear desirable (including, under both classes, some of the early English Translations of the Foreign Reformers); and thirdly, the printing of some manuscripts of the same authors, hitherto unpublished.

II.—That the Society shall consist of such a number of members, being subscribers of at least One Pound each annually, as the Council may determine; the subscription to be considered due on the First day of January in each year, in advance, and to be paid on or before such a day as the Council may fix; sufficient notice being given of the day appointed.

III.—That the management of the Society shall be vested in a President, a Treasurer, an Honorary Librarian, and a Council of twenty-four other subscribers, being members of the Established Church, and of whom not less than sixteen shall be Clergymen. The Council and Officers to be elected annually by the subscribers, at a General Meeting to be held in the month of May; and no persons shall then be proposed who are not already members of the Council, or Officers, unless their names shall have been transmitted to the Secretaries on or before the 15th of April in the current year, by nominations in writing, signed by at least five subscribers. And that there be two Secretaries appointed by the Council; also, that the Council have power to fill all vacancies during the year.

IV.—That the accounts of the receipt and expenditure of the Society shall be examined every year, previously to the General Meeting, by four Auditors, two of them selected from the Council, and two appointed by the preceding General Meeting.

V.—That the funds shall be expended in payment of the expenses incurred in producing the works published by the Society, so that every member not in arrear of his annual subscription shall receive a copy of every work published by the Society during the year, for each sum of One Pound subscribed, without any charge for the same; and that the number of copies printed in each year shall be limited to the quantity required for the number actually subscribed for.

VI.—That every member of the Society who shall intimate to the Council a desire to withdraw, or who shall not pay the subscription by the time appointed, shall thereupon cease to be a member of the Society; and no member shall at any time incur any liability beyond the annual subscription.

VII.—That, after the commencement of the proceedings, no rule shall be made or altered excepting at a General Meeting, and after notice of the same has been communicated to the members by circulars, or by advertisement in two London daily newspapers, at least fourteen days before the General Meeting.

VIII.—Donations and Legacies will be thankfully received; the amount of which shall be expended by the Council in supplying copies of the publications to clerical, or other public libraries, destitute of funds to purchase the same, and for such other purposes, connected with the objects of the Society, as the Council may determine.

REPORT OF THE AUDITORS.

30th May, 1843.

THE Auditors of the Parker Society, having examined the Accounts for the year 1842, with the general statement of the Receipts and Expenditure, and the vouchers for the same,

REPORT, That the Accounts appear to be correct and satisfactory, and there is now a balance of cash, at Messrs HERRIES, FARQUHAR and Co.'s, and in the Office, amounting to £645. 12s. 5d., with Exchequer Bills for £1500; and that there are amounts due, to be paid for the year 1842, estimated to amount to £2125, the Accounts for which are expected in a few days from the University of Cambridge, and the Binders, for the volumes now just completed.

HENRY POWNALL.
R. HANKINSON.
JOSEPH HOARE.

FURTHER REPORT OF THE AUDITORS.

The Office of the Parker Society,
33, Southampton Street, Strand, London, 15th June, 1843.

The Auditors of the Parker Society, having examined the remaining Accounts of the Society, referred to in their Report of May the 30th, find the same to be correct and satisfactory; and now further report that the following is a correct Abstract of the Receipts and Expenditure of the Society for the year 1842, to the present time, leaving a balance of £170. 6s. 1d. in the hands of the Treasurer.

They also Report, that the Balance of the year 1841 as stated in the last Report, with the sum of £14. subsequently received, on account of that year, has been invested in the names of Trustees in the 3 per cent. Consolidated Annuities, being £129. 8s. 2d. Stock. Also that a temporary investment of £1552. 7s. 10d. Stock, 3 per cent. Consolidated Annuities, has been made from the proceeds of the reprints as stated in the Cash Account.

HENRY POWNALL.
R. HANKINSON.
JOSEPH HOARE.

AN ABSTRACT OF THE RECEIPTS AND OF THE EXPENDITURE OF THE PARKER SOCIETY, FOR THE YEAR 1842.

Received.	£.	s.	d.	£.	s.	d.
To Amount received for the Subscription of Members for the year 1842, to the present	6899	1	3			
To Ditto on account of the reprint of the four volumes of the year 1841	3760	12	0			
				10,659	13	3
From the Exchequer Bill Account for the year 1842, being on account of the amount received for Interest and increased Premium on the temporary investment				126	12	5
Total of Receipts for the year				£.10,786	5	8

Paid.	£.	s.	d.	£.	s.	d.
By Amount paid on account of Printing and Paper of the Books published by the Society for the year 1842, and for the reprints of the four volumes for 1841				5211	16	11
Paid on account of Binding and delivering ditto				1975	18	6
Editorial Expenses				647	8	6
Insurance from Fire				6	16	1
Books purchased and Transcripts				90	8	6
Printing Plans of the Society, Reports, Circulars, and Advertisements				154	10	8
Rent of Office, Salary of Secretary for General Business, Assistant Secretary, and Wages of Clerks and Porters				633	4	2
Furniture and Fittings for the Office and Store Rooms				43	18	1
Stationery and Account Books				47	12	9
Incidentals, including Postages, Carriage of Parcels, Coals, and various expenses				304	5	5
Total of Expenditure for the year				9115	19	7
Temporary Investment of £1552. 7s. 10d. Stock in the 3 per cent. Consolidated Annuities, from the proceeds of the Reprints of 1841				1500	0	0
Balance, Cash in the Treasurer's hands				170	6	1
Total				£.10,786	5	8

Henry Pownall,
R. Hankinson, } *Auditors.*
Joseph Hoare.

LIST OF THE MEMBERS.

THE FOLLOWING NAMES, WITH OTHERS, IN THE WHOLE

SEVEN THOUSAND,

ARE IN THE LIST OF SUBSCRIBERS TO

The Parker Society.

HER MOST GRACIOUS MAJESTY ADELAIDE, QUEEN DOWAGER.
HIS ROYAL HIGHNESS THE PRINCE ALBERT.
HIS MAJESTY THE KING OF PRUSSIA.
HIS (LATE) ROYAL HIGHNESS THE DUKE OF SUSSEX.
HER ROYAL HIGHNESS THE DUCHESS OF KENT.

HIS GRACE THE DUKE OF DEVONSHIRE.
HIS GRACE THE DUKE OF MANCHESTER.
HIS GRACE THE DUKE OF SUTHERLAND.
THE MOST HONOURABLE THE MARQUESS OF BUTE.
THE MOST HONOURABLE THE MARQUESS OF CHOLMONDELEY.
THE MOST HONOURABLE THE MARQUESS OF CONYNGHAM.
THE MOST HONOURABLE THE MARQUESS OF DOWNSHIRE.
THE MOST HONOURABLE THE MARQUESS OF NORTHAMPTON.
THE MOST HONOURABLE THE MARQUESS OF ORMONDE.
THE MOST HONOURABLE THE MARQUESS OF SALISBURY.
HIS EXCELLENCY THE RIGHT HONOURABLE EARL DE GREY, LORD LIEUTENANT OF IRELAND.
THE RIGHT HONOURABLE THE EARL OF CHICHESTER.
THE RIGHT HONOURABLE THE EARL OF CLANCARTY.
THE RIGHT HONOURABLE THE EARL OF DALHOUSIE.
THE RIGHT HONOURABLE THE EARL OF GALLOWAY.
THE RIGHT HONOURABLE THE EARL HOWE.
THE RIGHT HONOURABLE THE EARL JERMYN.
THE RIGHT HONOURABLE THE EARL OF MOUNTNORRIS.
THE RIGHT HONOURABLE THE EARL NELSON.
THE RIGHT HONOURABLE THE EARL OF ROSSE.
THE RIGHT HONOURABLE THE EARL SPENCER.
THE RIGHT HONOURABLE THE EARL OF WICKLOW.
THE RIGHT HONOURABLE LORD VISCOUNT ADARE.
THE RIGHT HONOURABLE LORD VISCOUNT ALFORD.
THE RIGHT HONOURABLE LORD VISCOUNT ARBUTHNOT.
THE RIGHT HONOURABLE LORD VISCOUNT CAMPDEN.
THE RIGHT HONOURABLE LORD VISCOUNT DE VESCI.
THE RIGHT HONOURABLE LORD VISCOUNT HILL.
THE RIGHT HONOURABLE LORD VISCOUNT LORTON.
THE RIGHT HONOURABLE AND RIGHT REVEREND THE LORD BISHOP OF LONDON.
THE RIGHT REVEREND THE LORD BISHOP OF DURHAM.
THE RIGHT REVEREND THE LORD BISHOP OF WINCHESTER.
THE RIGHT REVEREND THE LORD BISHOP OF CHESTER.
THE RIGHT REVEREND THE LORD BISHOP OF CHICHESTER.
THE RIGHT REVEREND THE LORD BISHOP OF HEREFORD.
THE RIGHT REVEREND THE LORD BISHOP OF LICHFIELD.
THE RIGHT REVEREND THE LORD BISHOP OF LINCOLN.
THE RIGHT REVEREND THE LORD BISHOP OF LLANDAFF.
THE RIGHT REVEREND THE LORD BISHOP OF PETERBOROUGH.
THE RIGHT REVEREND THE LORD BISHOP OF RIPON.
THE RIGHT REVEREND THE LORD BISHOP OF ROCHESTER.
THE RIGHT REVEREND THE LORD BISHOP OF WORCESTER.
THE RIGHT REVEREND THE LORD BISHOP OF SODOR AND MANN.
THE RIGHT HONOURABLE AND RIGHT REVEREND THE LORD BISHOP OF CLOGHER.
THE RIGHT HONOURABLE AND RIGHT REVEREND THE LORD BISHOP OF MEATH.
THE HONOURABLE AND RIGHT REVEREND THE LORD BISHOP OF KILLALOE AND CLONFERT.

LIST OF THE MEMBERS.

The Right Reverend the LORD BISHOP OF DOWN AND CONNOR.
The Right Reverend the LORD BISHOP OF OSSORY AND FERNS.
The Right Reverend the LORD BISHOP OF CASHEL AND WATERFORD.
The Right Reverend the LORD BISHOP OF CALCUTTA.
The Right Reverend the LORD BISHOP OF TORONTO.
The Right Reverend the LORD BISHOP OF GUIANA.
The Right Reverend the BISHOP OF MORAY, ROSS, AND ARGYLE.
The Right Reverend the BISHOP OF OHIO.
The Right Reverend the BISHOP OF NEW JERSEY.
The Right Reverend the BISHOP OF SOUTH CAROLINA.
The Right Reverend the BISHOP OF VIRGINIA.
The Right Reverend the BISHOP OF GEORGIA.
The Right Reverend the BISHOP OF DELAWARE.
The Right Honourable and Reverend LORD ASTON.
The Right Honourable LORD ASHLEY (President).
The Right Honourable LORD BOLTON.
The Right Honourable LORD CALTHORPE.
The Right Honourable LORD FARNHAM.
The Right Honourable LORD LYTTLETON.
The Right Honourable LORD RAYLEIGH.
The Right Honourable LORD TEIGNMOUTH.
The Right Honourable and Reverend LORD ARTHUR HERVEY.
The Right Honourable and Reverend LORD WRIOTHESLEY RUSSELL.
The Right Honourable and Reverend LORD JOHN THYNNE.
The Right Honourable and Reverend LORD CHARLES THYNNE.
The Right Honourable LORD GEORGE A. HILL.
LORD HENRY CHOLMONDELEY, LORD LINDSAY, &c. &c.

Her Grace the DUCHESS OF ARGYLE.
The Right Honourable the COUNTESS OF ANNESLEY.
The Right Honourable VISCOUNTESS VALENTIA.
The Right Honourable LADY WARD, &c. &c.

The Right Honourable the LORD CHIEF JUSTICE OF IRELAND.
The Right Honourable the LORD JUSTICE CLERK, SCOTLAND.
The Right Honourable Mr. JUSTICE ERSKINE.
The Honourable Mr. JUSTICE JACKSON.
The Chevalier BUNSEN.
The Right Honourable HENRY GOULBURN, Chancellor of the Exchequer, M.P. for the University of Cambridge.
The Right Honourable W. E. GLADSTONE, M.P. Vice-President of the Board of Trade, and Master of the Mint.
The Very Reverend the DEAN OF CHESTER.
The Very Reverend the DEAN OF DURHAM.
The Very Reverend the DEAN OF GLOUCESTER.
The Very Reverend the DEAN OF MANCHESTER.
The Very Reverend the DEAN OF NORWICH.
The Very Reverend the DEAN OF SALISBURY.
The Very Reverend the DEAN OF WESTMINSTER.
The Very Reverend the DEAN OF WINCHESTER.
The Very Reverend the DEAN OF WINDSOR.
The Very Reverend the DEAN OF WOLVERHAMPTON.
The DEAN AND CHAPTER OF LICHFIELD.
The DEAN AND CHAPTER OF WORCESTER.
The Very Reverend the DEAN OF CLOGHER.
The Very Reverend the DEAN OF CLOYNE.
The Very Reverend the DEAN OF CONNOR.
The Very Reverend the DEAN OF CORK.
The Very Reverend the DEAN OF DERRY.
The Very Reverend the DEAN OF CASHEL.
The Very Reverend the DEAN OF EMLY.
The Very Reverend the DEAN OF OSSORY.
The Very Reverend the DEAN OF KILDARE.
The Very Reverend the DEAN OF KILMACDUAGH.
The Very Reverend the DEAN OF JERSEY.
The Honourable and Worshipful T. W. LAW, Chancellor of Bath and Wells.
The Worshipful Dr. DEALTRY, Chancellor of Winchester.
The Worshipful H. RAIKES, Chancellor of Chester.
The Worshipful E. T. M. PHILLIPS, Chancellor of Gloucester.
The Worshipful F. R. SANDYS, Chancellor of Ossory.
The Venerable Archdeacon BATHER.
The Venerable Archdeacon BERNERS.

LIST OF THE MEMBERS.

The Venerable Archdeacon BEVAN.
The Venerable Archdeacon BROWNE.
The Venerable Archdeacon HARE.
The Venerable Archdeacon HODSON.
The Venerable Archdeacon HOARE.
The Venerable Archdeacon LAW.
The Venerable Archdeacon LONSDALE.
The Venerable Archdeacon LYALL.
The Venerable Archdeacon MAC DONALD.
The Venerable Archdeacon PHILPOT.
The Venerable Archdeacon SHIRLEY.
The Venerable Archdeacon SPOONER.
The Venerable Archdeacon THORP, Warden of the University of Durham.
The Venerable Archdeacon S. WILBERFORCE.
The Venerable Archdeacon R. J. WILBERFORCE.
The Venerable Archdeacon BERESFORD.
The Venerable Archdeacon CREERY.
The Venerable Archdeacon DIGBY.
The Venerable Archdeacon MANT.
The Venerable Archdeacon MANSELL.
The Venerable Archdeacon OLDFIELD.
The Venerable Archdeacon POWER.
The Venerable Archdeacon STOPFORD.
The Venerable Archdeacon STUART.
The Venerable Archdeacon VERSCHOYLE.
The Venerable Archdeacon ST. GEORGE.
The Reverend W. WHEWELL, Master of Trinity College, Vice-Chancellor of the University of Cambridge.
The Reverend Dr. GRAHAM, Master of Christ's College, Cambridge.
The Reverend Dr. ARCHDALL, Master of Emmanuel College, Cambridge.
The Reverend Dr. WORDSWORTH, late Master of Trinity College, Cambridge.
The Reverend Dr. TATHAM, Master of St. John's College, Cambridge.
The Reverend Dr. PLUMPTRE, Master of University College, Oxford.
The Reverend Dr. FOX, Provost of Queen's College, Oxford.
The Reverend Dr. SYMONS, Warden of Wadham College, Oxford.
The Reverend Dr. THACKERAY, Provost of King's College, Cambridge.
The Reverend Dr. AINSLIE, Master of Pembroke Hall, Cambridge.
The Reverend Dr. FRENCH, Master of Jesus College, Cambridge.
JOSHUA KING, Esq., D.C.L., President of Queens' College, Cambridge.
The Reverend Dr. PROCTER, Master of Catharine Hall, Cambridge.
The Reverend Dr. WEBB, Master of Clare Hall, Cambridge.
The Reverend ROBERT PHELPS, Master of Sidney Sussex College, Cambridge.
The Reverend Dr. HAMPDEN, Principal of St. Mary Hall, and Regius Professor of Divinity, Oxford.
The Reverend Dr. CRAMER, Principal of New-Inn Hall, Oxford.
The Reverend E. CARDWELL, Principal of St. Alban's Hall, Oxford.
The Provost and Fellows of Worcester College, Oxford.
The Reverend Dr. SADLEIR, Provost of Trinity College, Dublin.
The Very Reverend Dr. LEE, Principal of the University of Edinburgh.
The Reverend R. P. BUDDICOM, Principal of St. Bees College.
The Venerable J. LONSDALE, Principal of King's College, London.
The Reverend Dr. WILLIAMSON, Head Master of Westminster School.
The Reverend Dr. WORDSWORTH, Head Master of Harrow School.
The Reverend A. C. TAIT, Head Master of Rugby School.
The Royal Library, Berlin.
The Library of Cashel.
The Library of Edinburgh University.
The Library of Trinity College, Dublin.
The Library of King's College, Cambridge.
The Library of Queens' College, Cambridge.
The Library of Wadham College, Oxford.
The Library of Pembroke College, Cambridge.
The Library of Gonville and Caius College, Cambridge.
The Library of St. Bees College.
The Advocates' Library, Edinburgh.
The Library of Writers to the Signet, Edinburgh.
The London Institution.
The London Library, &c. &c. &c.

THE COUNCIL AND OFFICERS FOR 1843-4.

President.
THE RIGHT HONOURABLE LORD ASHLEY, M.P.

Treasurer.
SIR WALTER R. FARQUHAR, BART.

Council.

REV. R. G. BAKER.—REV. C. BENSON, Master of the Temple.—REV. E. BICKERSTETH.—JOHN BRIDGES, ESQ.—JOHN BRUCE, ESQ.—REV. GUY BRYAN.—REV. RICHARD BURGESS.—HON. WILLIAM COWPER.—REV. W. H. COX, Vice-Principal of St Mary Hall, Oxford.—REV. J. W. CUNNINGHAM.—REV. THOMAS DALE, Canon of St Paul's.—REV. DR DEALTRY, Chancellor of Winchester.—REV. JOHN HARDING.—REV. EDWARD HOARE.—JOSEPH HOARE, ESQ.—REV. T. H. HORNE, Canon of St Paul's.—HON. ARTHUR KINNAIRD.—REV. DR MORTIMER, Head Master of the City of London School.—HON. AND REV. B. W. NOEL.—HENRY POWNALL, ESQ.—REV. JOSIAH PRATT, JUN.—REV. M. M. PRESTON.—REV. DANIEL WILSON.

Honorary Librarian.
GEORGE STOKES, ESQ., Colchester.

Editorial Secretary.
REV. JAMES SCHOLEFIELD, Regius Professor of Greek in the University of Cambridge.

Secretary for General Business.
WILLIAM THOMAS, ESQ., at the Office of the Society, 33, Southampton Street, Strand, London.

Auditors.
REV. R. HANKINSON, and FRANCIS LOWE, ESQ.

Bankers.
MESSRS HERRIES, FARQUHAR, & Co., No. 16, St James's Street.

REGULATIONS FOR DELIVERY OF THE BOOKS PUBLISHED BY THE SOCIETY.

I. They will be delivered, free of expense, at the Office, or within three miles of the General Post Office, London.

II. They will be sent to any place in England beyond the distance of three miles from the General Post Office, by any conveyance a Member may point out. In this case the parcels will be booked at the expense of the Society, but the carriage must be paid by the Members to whom they are sent.

III. They will be delivered, free of expense, at any place in London which a Member, resident in the country, may name.

IV. They may remain at the Office of the Society until the Members apply for them, but, in that case, the Society will not be responsible for any damage which may happen from fire, or other accident.

V. They will be sent to any of the Correspondents, or Agents of the Society, each Member paying the Correspondent, or Agent, a share of the carriage of the parcel in which the books were included. Arrangements are made for the delivery on this plan, in many of the cities and large towns where a sufficient number of members reside; *and it will be esteemed a favour if gentlemen who are willing to further the objects of the Parker Society, by taking charge of the books for the Members in their respective neighbourhoods, will write to the Office on the subject.*

VI. They will be delivered in Edinburgh and Dublin as in London, and forwarded from thence to Members in other parts of Scotland and Ireland, in the same manner as is mentioned above with respect to England.

THE OFFICE OF THE PARKER SOCIETY, 33, SOUTHAMPTON STREET, STRAND, LONDON.

www.ingramcontent.com/pod-product-compliance
Lightning Source LLC
Chambersburg PA
CBHW071219290426
44108CB00013B/1220